EAGLE IN FLAMES

EAGLE IN FLAMES

THE FALL OF THE LUFTWAFFE

E. R. Hooton

ARMS AND
ARMOUR

ARMS & ARMOUR PRESS
An imprint of the Cassell Group
Wellington House, 125 Strand, London WC2R 0BB

Distributed in the USA by Sterling Publishing Co. Inc.,
387 Park Avenue South, New York, NY 10016-8810

British Library Cataloguing-in-Publication data:
A catalogue record for this book is available from the
British Library.

ISBN 1 85409 343 6

Edited and designed by Roger Chesneau/DAG
Publications Ltd

Printed and bound in Great Britain by
MPG Books Ltd, Bodmin, Cornwall

Contents

Preface

In July 1940 the *Luftwaffe* was at the peak of its powers and dominated European skies, yet four short years later it was incapable of protecting Germany from the Allied bomber fleets. This book describes the events which shaped this tremendous swing in fortune (Alfred Price's *The Last Year of the Luftwaffe* concludes the story).

At first sight the reader may wonder why this tale should be repeated, for the pitcher seems to have been 'oft to the well'. Yet while every aspect of the Third Reich appears to have been dissected and analysed since its fall, the *Luftwaffe* remains very much wrapped in mystery. Most accounts are chronicles rather than history, for there appears to be a consensus that the destruction of most *Luftwaffe* documents at the end of the Second World War has ruined all attempts to examine its progress in detail. Yet works by Ulf Balke, Wolfgang Dierich, Werner Gerbig, Manfred Griehl, Karl Gundelach, Gerhard Hümmelchen, Martin Middlebrook, Richard Muller, Sönke Neitzel, Alfred Price, Hans Ring and Christopher Shores have clearly established that this is a myth. Sufficient documents, biographies/autobiographies, and monographs exist to permit an evaluation of the *Luftwaffe*, and in this context this book must be regarded as a pathfinding exercise.

My intention, as with my earlier book *Phoenix Triumphant*, which covers the period from 1918 to 1940, is to clear away the undergrowth of mythology and to attempt a re-evaluation of the *Luftwaffe*'s development and effectiveness in order to challenge many of the comfortable assumptions with regard to the Battle of Britain, the Blitz (which had a crucial, if largely ignored, influence upon Bomber Command's much-criticised area bombing policy) and the battle for the sea lanes. Such a re-evaluation, for example of the British victory during the Battle of Britain, shows that it was a psychological rather than a physical one, due to the curious half-heartedness displayed by a *Luftwaffe* High Command increasingly preoccupied with preparations for other theatres. The air campaigns in the Mediterranean and the Eastern theatres became interdependent during crucial periods— for example, the Battle of Moscow, the Malta campaign and especially Operation 'Torch' and the Russian counter-offensive at Stalingrad, the last event even having a malign influence upon the Battle of the Atlantic.

I have also attempted a clearer evaluation of *Luftwaffe* doctrine using German, rather than contemporary Anglo-American, definitions. Most accounts attempt to define German air power in the over-simplified terms 'tactical' and 'strategic', but for a century before the Second World War Teutonic military thought had conceived a third term, 'operational' (*Operativ*). This applied to military activity at *Armee* and *Heeresgruppe* level, with German military thought restricting 'tactical' operations to activities carried out by *Armee Korps* and *Divisionen*. Because *Armee* and *Heeresgruppe* operations were designed to envelop the enemy, the *Luftwaffe*'s role, after neutralising enemy air power and establishing air superiority, was to interdict communications and to strike both headquarters and supply dumps, facilitating such an envelopment. The bombing of enemy industry was a feature of 'operational' activity, but, unlike strategic bombing, whose purpose was to defeat the enemy by destroying his industry, it was intended merely to disrupt the flow of war material at a crucial period. However, it is clear that from 1942 the 'operational' role was fading under Army pressure in favour of 'tactical', or close air support, operations, partly because the *Luftwaffe* was a victim of its own success in crushing the Soviet Air Force in June 1941. It is also clear that by 1943 the much-criticised chief of staff Jeschonnek was re-evaluating the *Luftwaffe*'s role, seeking to return to 'operational' warfare and examining the potential of strategic bombing, while his successors maintained and expanded this activity within the contracting limits of German strength. Unfortunately, by the time the *Luftwaffe* possessed a true strategic bombing force and doctrine it was incapable of executing such a policy and was restricted to the 'operational' role.

By then the Reich itself was under growing aerial threat, and in studying this I have followed the example of Williamson Murray in exploiting statistics to conduct a more rigorous study of German air defence than has been done previously. Such an evaluation in the past has been hindered by the empirical nature of British and American statistics. In assessing the effectiveness of the defence I have adapted those statistics in several ways, of which the most important is a division into 'strategic' (against the Reich) and 'operational' (against western Europe or Italy/southern France) sections, while in Bomber Command's case I have eliminated special duty flights and non-Reich bomber operations to produce a clearer picture of the threat from the German perspective. What is striking is the scale of casualties inflicted by a *Luftwaffe* supposedly weak in defence, for when losses are compared with the number of sorties it becomes evident that casualty rates were heavier than generally appreciated, except perhaps by the crews themselves. The only benchmark of which I am aware is that the RAF reckoned that loss rates of 4.8% (for bombers) and about 10% (for fighters) disrupted squadron effectiveness, and I have judged that this would apply on a larger scale. One intriguing result of the analysis is the discovery that the long-range fighter support in itself had only a limited effect upon Eighth Air Force loss rates until May 1944, and the subsequent sharp decline reflects the impact of the American fighter offensive upon the *Jagd*- and *Zerstörergruppen* which inflicted appalling casualties during the winter and spring of 1944. I have also attempted to indicate the similarities of approach by both sides during the Battle of Britain in 1940 and the Battle of Germany in 1943–44 in relation to defence and the question of fighter support for the bombers.

German statistics also produce some surprises. The impression given by most accounts is that with the collapse of the tightly controlled *Himmelbett* night fighter system the Germans quickly adapted the more flexible *Zahme Sau* system. Yet an analysis of *Jagdkorps I* statistics shows that *Wilde Sau* dominated German night fighting into the winter of 1943/44 and would indicate that *Zahme Sau* did not really take effect until early 1944, when new airborne radars became more widely available. The real surprise, however, is to observe how the Germans learned from their defeat in English skies to create in western Europe a defensive system which held the Allies at bay until the latter half of 1943, even when desperately short of fighters. Yet military operations are more than mere statistics, and the ills of the *Luftwaffe* owed much to its internecine struggles which, at the most senior levels, had a malign influence upon its development, noticeably in attempts to cut Allied sea lanes and also in blunting the edge of the sword, especially in the Mediterranean theatre. Sometimes there were tragic and unforeseen effects from apparently unrelated incidents: Rudolf Hess's defection, for example, indirectly led to the deaths of three of the *Luftwaffe*'s leading officers. Where possible I have, as in my previous book, produced thumbnail sketches of the leading personalities, although I have generally concentrated upon new characters, leaving the reader to discover the older ones in *Phoenix Triumphant*.

On the contentious matter of casualties I have relied wherever possible upon post-war research, including recently declassified Russian statistics published by Glantz and House. I would point out that, unlike German figures, they do not always include aircraft damaged beyond economic repair. I make no attempt to evaluate claims by *Luftwaffe* aircrew, which may be regarded as being as accurate as those made by Allied aircrew. Like them, *Luftwaffe* fighter pilots faced stringent requirements before being credited with victories, and I am content to accept these figures. Figures for *Luftwaffe* losses are, of course, based upon *Generalquartiermeister 6. Abteilung* records, which provide the most detailed accounts for aircraft and personnel casualties. However, they are neither infallible nor always comprehensive: some units were extremely slothful in providing details, while records after February 1944 no longer exist. (For further details the reader is referred to Francis Mason's exhaustively researched book *The Battle of Britain*, pp. 96, 97, 104.) The *Luftwaffe* assessed aircraft damage in percentage terms, with 100% representing total loss while 60% was damage beyond economic repair but with substantial elements of the aircraft capable of cannibalisation. In the following pages aircraft 'lost' are generally those which suffered 60% or more damage, those 'severely damaged' having suffered 40–60% damage and requiring repair at maintainance facilities, the remainder being 'damaged'. However, the *General-quartiermeister* returns are not always accurate, for, although units were supposed to register all losses and damage through *Fliegerkorps* quartermaster staffs, many were slow to do so until they realised that it compromised their chances of receiving replacements in men and machines. It appears that some *Fliegerkorps*, who had learned during the western campaigns of 1940 to circumvent official channels, continued to exploit the 'old boys' network' well into the Battle of Britain and in some cases long afterwards, although this practice was gradually eliminated. Certainly consolidated returns became the norm from 26 July 1940, and some units adopted a weekly return. Even then some units were very casual, especially *KG 40*, *KGr 100*, the *Küstfliegergruppen* and some second-line formations.

This book is predominantly about the airmen and their ground crews or 'black men', and as I have had to paint in broad brush strokes I have largely left in the background the *Luftwaffehelferinnen*, who appear to await their own history, as well as both the signallers and *Flak* personnel, who are well catered for in print. I leave others to tell the personal stories of the men and women who served in the *Luftwaffe*, but occasionally I have included a tale to illustrate or underline a particular point. While the fighters and strike forces dominate the story, I have tried to include most aspects of the air war, including the activities of the reconnaissance and transport forces, special duty operations and even electronic warfare. I hope this will provide a springboard for others to explore these and other subjects in greater detail, and provide new perspectives not only of German air operations but also of Allied ones.

Much of what the reader will discover comes from a jungle of archives, American, British and German, which are largely unexplored and which I have supplemented with service and formation histories as well as memoirs and biographies. I would like to thank the personnel of the Public Record Office and Imperial War Museum in Britain, the *Bundesarchiv*'s *Militärarchiv* in Freiburg (although I hope the oversight in failing to provide a complete index of *Luftwaffe* documents in the central research room will be quickly recitified), the US National Archives, the Smithsonian Institute and the *Service Historique de l'Armée de l'Air* in Vincennes, as well as the staff of Langley Library. One of the pleasures of a preface is the opportunity it provides to thank the individuals who have helped make this book possible, even when they may not always agree with the author. I would especially like to thank my good friend Alex Vanags-Baginskis, not only for translating material but also for providing me with literature, advice and the means of illustrating this book. Alfred Price most generously allowed me access to material and provided some timely advice, my more distinguished namesake Ted Hooton also provided valuable assistance and specialist advice, while Will Fowler played a key role in providing illustrations in the middle of urgent work. Others whom I would like to thank are Gus Brittain (Royal Navy Submarine Museum), R. T. Carter,

Major-General Joseph L. Dickman (US Air Force History Support Office), Pearlie M. Draughn (Research Librarian, US Air Force Association), Chris Ellis, Ben Franklin (Executive Director of the Fifteenth Air Force Association), Norman Friedman, Captain Jim Gates (US Air Force History Support Office), Dr Eric Grove, Mike Gething, Manfred Griehl, Dave List, Lieutenant-Colonel Michael J. Nisos (US Air Force History Support Office), Simon Parry, F. Pirie, Sten Stenersen, Martin Streetly and Barry Wheeler. The views expressed, however, are of course my own.

In addition, I would like to thank my wife Linda for her support over a long and trying period and also Roger Chesneau, who, as with *Phoenix Triumphant*, has produced this book and helped me to overcome the most glaring omissions of fact and aberrations of style in the original draft. Above all I would express my gratitude to Rod Dymott of Arms & Armour Press for his faith in this project and for his great kindness at a difficult time.

E. R. Hooton
Langley, Berkshire

CHAPTER ONE

Bomben auf England

July 1940–June 1941

It was July 1940, and the war was almost over, with the swastika waving over every town west of the Rhine except in Great Britain, whose fall was only a matter of time.

The time was obviously soon, and on 27 June *'Robinson'* (the codename for *ObdL*) ordered a systematic reconnaissance of British airfields to update target and intelligence files.[1] With awful symbolism 1 July saw two Do 215B-1s of *AufKlGr ObdL*, piloted by *Oberleutnant* Rothenberg and *Leutnant* Vockel, become the *Luftwaffe*'s first losses in the Battle of Britain, and during the next five weeks the *Aufklärungsgruppen* lost 26 aircraft. Another 23 bombers on reconnaissance missions fell to enemy action, the most distinguished victim being *Oberst* Georgi, *Kommodore* of *KG 27*; indeed, *KG 77* lost six aircraft on 1 July and within two days was withdrawn for conversion to Ju 88s.[2] These heavy losses reflected the weakness of relying upon lightly armed bombers flying at medium altitude for photographic reconnaissance and the ability of British radar, sometimes cued by the COMINT Y-Service, both to detect them and to help guide fighters to within 500m of their targets. Fighter escort, even in *Gruppe* strength, offered no guarantee of immunity, and the solution proved to be fast aircraft usually flying at high altitude—such as the Spitfire Type C used by the British Photographic Development Unit to fly 841 sorties between July and December with the loss of only 10 aircraft, a rate of 1.18%.[3]

Cloud and rain restricted daylight offensive operations over Britain until early August, but *Luftflotten 2* and *3* (under *Generalfeldmarschälle* Albert Kesselring and Hugo Sperrle respectively) were also catching their breath after racing through western Europe and losing 28% of their initial aircraft strength with more than 3,000 aircrew dead or missing and nearly 1,400 wounded.[4] Only 11 *Kampfgruppen* with 500 serviceable aircraft were available, but the eagles required new nests, while fuel and bombs were inadequate for a sustained campaign. Captured bases such as Antwerp-Deurne, which were occupied by twin-engine units, often required repair or were some distance from the Channel, leaving single-engine units to operate from converted fields which required utilities such as power and water.[5] Guernsey's airfield was the only one on British soil used by the *Luftwaffe* and was occupied by a *Staffel* of *Major* Günther, *Freiherr* von Maltzahn's *II./JG 53* and elements of *JG 27*. Re-grouping consumed much time and energy during July, while, as the signal network was turned 180 degrees along an east–west axis, supplies were assembled, but only after the Army rebuilt bridges often destroyed by the *Luftwaffe*. Time had also to be found to fight what *General der Flieger* Wolfram von Richthofen described as 'The Paper War', but there was also opportunity for relaxation (Richthofen enjoyed golf and strolling through the woods) or enjoying loot such as the American Hudson car with automatic transmission which he had acquired.[6]

The *Luftflotten* extended their areas of responsibility westwards from the mouth of the Seine, across the Channel roughly from Bognor Regis through Oxford and Birmingham. Kesselring, whose Brussels headquarters included *Generalleutnant* Rudolf Wenniger, the former Air Attaché to London, occupied bases north of the Seine, while Sperrle, with headquarters in the Paris suburbs, was south of the river.[7] Their command posts were at Cap Blanc Nez and Deauville respectively, and their forces were little changed after the June campaigns, although *Fliegerkorps II* and *IV* were exchanged because the latter's anti-shipping specialisation could best be exploited from bases in western France. Despite the problems there was great *Luftwaffe* activity and the Channel became a glacis over which aircraft swirled in ever-more intensive combat (see Tables 1 and 2). Night attacks upon British industry began early in June and by the end of the month were focusing upon aircraft factories and airfields. Although unready for a daylight campaign against land targets, *ObdL* recognised the importance of controlling the Channel before

---

Table 1. Estimated *Luftwaffe* Sortie Levels and Losses during the Battle of Britain

Week	Bomber and Dive-Bomber			Fighter	
	Total	Day	Night		
Jul 1–7	360	275 (18/2)	75 (–)	750 (3/9)	
Jul 8–14	500	400 (31/3)	100 (–)	1,100 (26/2)	
Jul 15–21	370	275 (12/5)	100 (1/–)	800 (9/3)	
Jul 22–Aug 4	325	200 (22/7)	125 (2/1)	700 (4/6)	
Aug 5–11	750	575 (26/10)	175 (1/–)	1,950 (40/5)	
Aug 12–18	2,150	1,650 (134/9)	500 (1/1)	3,825 (150/7)	
Aug 19-25	1,175	750 (44/2)	425 (2/3)	1,975 (41/5)	
Aug 26-Sept 1	1,925	875 (58/20)	1,050 (3/1)	4,700 (105/6)	
Sept 2–8	2,025	1,225 (28/17)	800 (7/1)	4,050 (121/8)	
Sept 9–15	1,775	975 (64/16)	800 (–)	1,875 (54/7)	
Sept 16–22	1,900	750 (22/12)	1,150 (7/1)	1,200 (14/7)	
Sept 23–29	2,075	1,175 (18/15)	900 (5/–)	1,325 (64/5)	
Sept 30–Oct 6	1,025	575 (30/16)	950 (7/–)	1,250 (44/8)	

Notes: Losses (in parentheses) are 60% damage and over for front-line units. The first figure is to enemy action and the second accidents. Bombers includes *Stukas* and fighters includes *Zerstörer* and *Jabo*.

Sources: *Luftkrieg gegen England—Gefechtskalender* (USNA Microfilm T321, Roll 176, fr.437ff); *Vorstudie zur Luftkriegsgeschichte, Heft 10* (USNA Microfilm T971, Roll 4, fr.606ff); *Luftflotte 3 Lagebericht* from 5 August (USNA Microfilm T321, Roll 88, fr.1ff); and Mason.

Table 2. Fighter Command Defensive Sorties

Week	Total (Losses)				Estimated (Losses)		
	Day		Night		10 Gp		11/12 Gp
Jul 1–7	2,357	(8/8)	61	(–)	550	(–/1)	1,225 (8/5)
Jul 8–14	3,900	(25/10)	127	(1)	530	(5/–)	3,110 (20/9)
Jul 15–21	3,468	(20/5)	142	(5)	420	(5/–)	2,780 (15/2)
Jul 22–28	4,154	(15/12)	95	(3)	545	(1/4)	3,390 (13/8)
Jul 29–Aug 4	3,653	(6/–)	181	(6)	320	(–)	2,830 (6/5)
Aug 5–11	3,256	(52/6)	191	(4)	640	(12/1)	2,265 (40/3)
Aug 12–18	4,730	(124/4)	186	(1)	900	(20/1)	3,365 (103/4)
Aug 19–25	3,833	(47/1)	224	(2)	890	(12/–)	2,550 (35/1)
Aug 26–Sept 1	5,005	(129/4)	197	(1)	775	(3/1)	3,930 (126/2)
Sep 2–8	4,911	(138/8)	225	(3)	590	(7/1)	4,025 (131/4)
Sep 9–15	3,389	(93/4)	296	(3)	420	(8/–)	2,630 (85/4)
Sep 16–22	3,635	(26/5)	268	(1)	285	(–/2)	2,920 (26/3)
Sep 23–29	4,825	(80/9)	310	(3)	745	(18/3)	3,710 (62/4)
Sep 30–Oct 6	1,782	(29/6)	245	(2)	695	(11/–)	760 (18/6)

Notes: Estimated Group sorties totals are for single-engine fighters during the day, with No 10 Group (formed 10 July) figures including No 11 Group squadrons transferred within it before formation. Casualties are all Category 3. Night fighter losses are to all causes. Loss figures are enemy action/accident.

Sources: Air Historical Branch Narrative, Battle of Britain Apps 4, 7, 15, 23; Fighter Command Air Staff Diary (PRO Air 24/526); RAF Fight Command Summary of Sorties (PRO Air 16/1037); Nos 10 Group (PRO Air 25/182) and 13 Group (PRO Air 25/232) Operational Record Books; and various squadron operational records.

an invasion of Britain and concentrated upon this attainable objective. Richthofen and his ever-mobile *Fliegerkorps VIII* were in the vanguard, covering the western and central Channel, while *General der Flieger* Bruno Loerzer's *Fliegerkorps II* brooded over the Strait of Dover, Loerzer subcontracting the task to *Oberst* Johannes Fink, *Kommodore* of *KG 2*, who was appointed *Kanalkampfführer* on 2 July.[8]

During the first five weeks of the battle some 70% of all daylight strike sorties (including *Jagdbomber-Jabo.*sorties) were against shipping, naval bases and ports, *Generaloberst* Ulrich Grauert's *Fliegerkorps I* striking Dover between 20 and 27 July to drive Royal Navy destroyers north of the Thames Estuary (for details of the campaign see Chapter 2). Land targets were subject to *Störangriffe* (harassing attacks) by individual aircraft or small formations; for example, four Do 17s, apparently from *KüFlGr 606*, struck the Rolls-Royce works in Glasgow from Brittany on 18 July.[9] While the British response to missions over the Channel was vigorous, and disturbingly prompt, the strong and vigilant escorts shielded the strike formations, whose loss rate was 2–3per cent, or half the 63 lost in this period. The Hurricanes and Spitfires proved equal to the Bf 109E and superior to the Bf 110, which, even in the hands of *ZG 26* veterans under the one-legged 'Old Eagle' *Oberstleutnant* Joachim-Friedrich Huth, had to adopt a defensive circle. However, it was *JG 51* under another 'Old Eagle', *Oberst* Theo 'Uncle Theo'

Osterkamp, which suffered half of the fighter losses. Since September 1939 Osterkamp had added six victories to the 32 he achieved in the Great War, a feat emulated by *ZG 2*'s *Kommodore Oberstleutnant* Friedrich Vollbracht, but on 27 July he was relieved by the young ace *Major* Werner 'Daddy'(*Vati*) Mölders to become *JaFü 1*. The next day Mölders was injured by the South African ace Squadron Leader Adolphus 'Sailor' Malan, and 'Uncle Theo' hastily returned until Mölders recovered from his wounds.

From 4 July Fighter Command also faced threats inland as *Jagdgeschwader* organised sweeps (*Freie Jagd*) of *Gruppe* strength which accounted for 28% of its losses during the first five weeks, their greatest success coming on 19 July when *II./JG 2* 'bounced' nine Defiants of No 141 Squadron whose two survivors were saved by the timely intervention of Hurricanes. Total losses to 4 August were 46 fighters, but it was pilot casualties which most concerned Air Chief Marshal Sir Hugh Dowding and ultimately made forward defence unsustainable. On 19 August he restricted interceptions to targets inland or within gliding distance of the coast because 'During the next two or three weeks we cannot afford to lose pilots through forced landings at sea.' Astonishingly, until late August the British had no air–sea rescue organisation, a deficiency overcome through the initiative of Air Marshal Arthur Harris, although an *ad hoc* organisation was created by Air Vice-Marshal Keith Park (commander of No 11 Group) and the Royal Navy in Dover a few weeks earlier.[10] *Luftwaffe* aircrew who fell in the Channel, which they called the 'Foul Water Sewer' (*Scheisskanal*), had a better chance of rescue, for at the start of the war the *Seenotdienst* (Sea Rescue Service) was established with *Seenotflugkommandos* using obsolete He 59 floatplanes and Do 18 Wal and Do 24 flying boats assisted by fast motor launches, all under a *Seenotbereich*. The 30–40 unarmed aircraft, painted white and with both civil and Red Cross markings, carried inflatable rubber boats, blankets and medicines to recover survivors and to provide first aid. Dowding, however, was determined to deprive the *Luftwaffe* of combatants and authorised attacks on the rescue aircraft, and on 1 July No 72 Squadron shot down *Leutnant* Hans-Joachim Fehske's He 59 of *Seenotflugkdo 3* near a convoy off Tyneside, Fehske bitterly protesting after rescue about the destruction of an aircraft on a mercy mission.[11] Further attacks forced the *Seenotdienst* to arm its aircraft, and on 20 July a *Seenotflugkdo 1* gunner shot down a Hurricane of No 43 Squadron. Neither enemy action nor the elements prevented the *Seenotdienst* operating, and during the Battle of Britain (1 July to 6 October) it rescued more than 100 men (some of them British) at the cost of 22 aircraft and 49 casualties.[12]

Meanwhile the *Luftwaffe* prepared for the main contest with extraordinary lethargy, due partly to a shortage of qualified staff officers (a perennial *Wehrmacht* problem) but largely because the German High Command believed that the British would soon sue for peace. True, on 30 June Göring had demanded a carefully coordinated assault, before which attacks upon mainland Britain would be confined to industrial and aircraft industry targets with weak defences, but only after 'the most thorough study of the target and its surrounding area'. He added: 'It is also stressed that every effort should be made to avoid unnecessary loss of life among the civilian population.' Once regrouping was complete, the *Luftwaffe*'s main blow, as usual, would fall upon the RAF infrastructure (industrial and logistical) with separate, but complementary, assaults upon British ports to help blockade the island nation.[13] The following day Hitler met Dino Alfieri, the Italian Ambassador to Berlin, and informed him of Germany's intention to conduct an air offensive against Britain which would be 'bloody' and a 'horror'.[14] On 11 July *ObdL* demanded intensified operations focusing upon the destruction of the RAF and its infrastructure, but formidable problems were anticipated. That day *Generalmajor* Otto Stapf (the Army liaison officer at *ObdL*) informed *Generaloberst* Franz Halder (the Army Chief of Staff) that '*Robinson*' estimated that it would take two to four weeks to neutralise the Royal Air Force, yet *OKW* stated that air supremacy was essential to compensate for German naval weakness in the event of an invasion.[15]

Hitler informed Navy commander *Grossadmiral* Erich Raeder that the invasion would be only a matter of last resort rather than a full amphibious assault, while *OKW* Director of Operations *Generaloberst* Alfred Jodl remarked on 30 June that it was regarded as a *coup de grâce* against limited resistance after the *Luftwaffe* had reduced the British defences. Two days later Jodl's master, *Generalfeldmarschall* Wilhelm Keitel, demanded from all the services detailed plans for the invasion, and there was a rapid response from both the Navy and Army commanders, Raeder and *Generaloberst* Walther von Brauchitsch. But Göring stubbornly boycotted tri-service conferences, refusing to share the glory with the conservative Army while his relations with the Navy were strained, and he was aped by his subordinates throughout the Battle of Britain. A *Luftwaffe* liaison officer was appointed to *Heeresgruppe A* (which was to carry out the invasion) only after the invasion was postponed, while as late as 11 November Kesselring rejected Army plans for a tri-service base to organise post-landing operations and insisted that all air units would remain under *Luftwaffe* command. Göring even ignored summonses by Hitler, and no *Luftwaffe* representative was present on 31 July when the *Führer* reviewed preparations for the invasion following the publication a fortnight earlier of *OKW* Directive 16 for *Unternehmen 'Seelöwe'* (Sealion). This demanded 'the closest liaison' between individual *Luftwaffe* units and the Army's invasion forces, although there was no such instruction for naval operations, where the *Luftwaffe* was merely to engage any British warships approaching the bridgeheads. The prime requirement for a landing, to be made east of the Isle of Wight, was the neutralisation of the RAF; other *Luftwaffe* tasks were the destruction of coast defences and the disruption of enemy reserves *en route* to the coast. The roles of the airborne forces (*Fliegerdivision 7* and *22. Luftlande Infanterie Division*) were not defined, and the directive suggested that they might remain in reserve, yet this issue led to a row when the *Luftwaffe*'s Director of Operations (*Chef des Führungsstab*), *Generalmajor* Otto Hoffman von Waldau, finally met his Army opposite number (*Generalmajor* Hans von Greiffenberg) on 21 August. The Army wished to use *Generalmajor* Richard Putzier's *Fliegerdivision 7*, which had been mauled in the Netherlands, but the *Luftwaffe* wished to refit and rebuild it for only *FJR 2* was fully operational and it had been despatched to Romania, returning to Germany in early September.[16]

ObdL waited until 5 September to define *Luftwaffe* assignments for '*Seelöwe*', with *Fliegerkorps VIII* supporting *Generaloberst* Ernst Busch's *16. Armee* on the right flank while Grauert's *Fliegerkorps I* (reinforced with some *Stukas*) aided *Generaloberst* Adolf Strauss's *9. Armee* on the left. The other *Fliegerkorps* would interdict communications between London and the sea while *Fliegerdivision 9* laid minefields to protect the invasion force's flanks. The previous day *OKW* complained to Hitler about *Luftwaffe* obstructionism, and only hours before A-Day did Göring and Putzier endorse Busch's plans for paratroops to be dropped at Dover and Folkestone despite opposition from both *OKH* and Kesselring, the latter waiting until 19 September to discuss air support with Busch.[17] The *Luftwaffe*'s failure to define its relationship to '*Seelöwe*' remained the perennial problem undermining the strategic foundation (in contrast to *Fall 'Gelb'*), yet it was not addressed even when '*Robinson*' moved to Beauvais (some 90km north-east of Paris). The first high-level conference on the forthcoming campaign, *Unternehmen 'Adler'* (Eagle), was at Carinhall on 18 July, yet Göring and his *Luftflotten* commanders discussed only peripheral matters while the *Luftwaffe* Chief of Staff, *General der Flieger* Hans Jeschonnek, attended Hitler's Berlin conference to discuss the strategy against Britain, during which Hitler openly mused about Stalin's unfriendliness and added, 'Thoughtful preparations must be made.' Within hours planning for the invasion of the Soviet Union began as a fall-back strategy in the event of the failure, or abandonment, of '*Seelöwe*'.[18]

Dynamic planning became vital from the following night after a great rally at the Kroll Opera House in Berlin, where Hitler liberally dispensed promotions before warning the British that their air raids would earn terrible retribution which would bring 'unending suffering and misery'. He also offered peace terms, which the British Foreign Secretary, Lord Halifax, dismissed as 'a summons to capitulate' on 22 July.[19] Nine days later a conference on '*Seelöwe*' set A-Day for 15 September and also adopted *OKW* Directive 17 'On the conduct of air and sea warfare against England', which demanded the subjugation of the RAF from 5 August, though 'after achieving temporary or local air superiority' attacks were to be switched against ports, the southern ports being attacked 'on the smallest possible scale, in view of our own forthcoming operations'. There was a proviso that the *Luftwaffe* would support naval forces or *'Seelöwe'* at short notice and, as usual, Hitler added, 'I reserve the right to decide on terror attacks as measures of reprisal.'

The *Luftwaffe*'s absence from this conference proved unfortunate, for it led Hitler to kick Göring's ample backside. Although the 'Fat Man' had urged his *Luftflotten* commanders on 18 July to be ready within a few days, preparations for *'Adler'* had proceeded at a slothful pace, with sharp disputes as to the best means of neutralising the RAF, and an outline plan appeared only during the last week of July. In *Luftflotte 2*, Grauert proposed mixed fighter/bomber formations to entangle enemy fighters which would then be swamped by *Jagdgruppen*, while Loerzer suggested making London the anvil upon which the *Jagd-* and *Zerstörergruppen* would hammer Fighter Command. *ObdL* received comments only on 31 July when *OKW*'s liaison officer, *General* Sigismund, *Freiherr* von Falkenstein, informed his masters that Göring remained undecided in an undefined dispute between Kesselring and Sperrle. The toady Jodl passed this comment to a Hitler still fuming at the *Luftwaffe*'s absence from the *'Seelöwe'* plans review, and on 1 August his wrath was teleprinted to *'Robinson'*: 'The *Führer* has ordered that preparations for the *Luftwaffe*'s great attack against England should be completed immediately and with great despatch so that it may commence within 12 hours of the *Führer* issuing the orders.'

A chastened Göring hastily called a conference for the following day at The Hague in the garden of the *Wehrmachtsbefehlshaber in der Niederlande,* former naval air ace *General der Flieger* Friedrich Christiansen.[20] It decided to strike Fighter Command, then feint at London in a three-phase, 13-day campaign starting with attacks on bases within a 100–150km arc south and east of the metropolis, concluding with attacks in a 50km arc, while simultaneously there would be a 24-hour offensive against the British aircraft industry. Kesselring and Sperrle reluctantly accepted this policy for they wanted first to destroy the British infrastructure with a night bombing campaign before the day offensive began, but the primary night operations would be conducted by *General der Flieger* Robert, *Ritter* von Greim's *Fliegerkorps V* against bomber bases in eastern England and by *Fliegerdivision 9*'s minelayers.

A feature of the conference was criticism of the Intelligence Branch (*Ic*) under the convivial, lizard-eyed *Oberst* Josef *'Beppo'* (Boy) Schmid, whose reports reflected his sources' prejudices, his inflexibility, an inability to analyse and a reluctance to present unwelcome news. His updated file on British air power, *Studie 'Blau'*, of 16 July exploited combat experience and prisoner-of-war interrogations yet neglected *Armée de l'Air* sources smarting from a sense of betrayal by their former allies and whose files possessed a treasure trove of data.[21] Schmid's study ignored radar but accurately estimated enemy strength at 900 fighters and 1,150 bombers while paying only cursory attention to the British air defence organisation. Contradicting Göring's comments on the enemy's 'well-developed defence forces' only a fortnight earlier, Schmid concluded: 'The *Luftwaffe* is in a position to go over to decisive daylight operations owing to the inadequate air defences of the island.' He grossly underestimated production, while his conclusion that Fighter Command could be rapidly whittled away because of its elderly leaders and inadequate supplies was wishful thinking.[22] Dowding's strength was actually growing and in mid-July he had more than 1,000 fighters, of which 700–750 were available for operations (not the 675 estimated by Schmid), with 333 ready for immediate issue by maintenance units. While British fighter production declined from 1,110 in July (432 Hurricanes and Spitfires) to 908 in September (408), Dowding increased squadron establishments from 16 to 20 aircraft.[23] *'Adler'*'s wings were also clipped by inadequate analysis, for, like accountants, who know the cost of everything and the value of nothing, Schmid's subordinates diluted the attack by repeating their mistake of May 1940 and failing to determine the type of bases to be struck, with the result that bombs were wasted upon bomber, Fleet Air Arm and even training airfields. Even where bases were located there was no consensus as to their most vulnerable points, while the factories producing Hurricanes and Spitfires were struck at random.

Although this was unknown to the combat units, there was disquiet over Schmid's estimates of enemy strength, fuelled by *Generalmajor* Wolfgang Martini's signal service and its COMINT element, the *Funkhorchdienst*.[24] Osterkamp, who monitored British radio traffic with the assistance of *Sonderführer* Horst Barth and noted fighter markings, concluded that the 'Tommies' had 500–700 fighters in the south, but Göring stubbornly backed Schmid's report and assured everyone that there were only 400–500, too few to dent the bomber formations.[25] However, when he sought to garner support he was told that there were only 700 bombers serviceable (the true figure was about 1,000) and muttered, 'Is this my *Luftwaffe*?' Martini quickly recognised that German aircraft were being detected by radar, with squadrons scrambled (*Alarmstart* in German terms) and directed by sector control headquarters whose locations, and those of the radar stations, he plotted. On his evidence Schmid reluctantly revised his estimates on 7 August, but his prejudices led him to conclude that ground control was extremely rigid and unable to mass strong fighter forces quickly. Park's No 11 Group was vulnerable because his squadrons rarely received more than 15 minutes' notice, and it took them 13 minutes to reach bomber formations, whose escorts could pounce at any time. During August, as his neighbour Air Vice-Marshal Trafford Leigh-Mallory of No 12 Group airily advocated attacks by massed squadrons or 'Big Wings', Park's squadrons had to intercept piecemeal, but when he was able to pair them in September and receive 'Big Wing' support the system could meet the strongest attack. Meanwhile, at Martini's insistence, experienced *Stuka* and *Jabo* crews were assigned to destroy British radar installations and 'blind' Park.

20

A further complication when planning '*Adler*' was the restrictions on strike force size imposed by the limited range of the Bf 109E or 'Emil'.[26] The early clashes demonstrated the vulnerability of *Zerstörergruppen* in dogfights with the nimble Hurricanes and Spitfires, yet the heavy fighters failed to exploit altitude for high-speed swoops which proved so effective for the P-38 Lightnings later in the Pacific. Attacks upon mainland targets had demonstrated the need for a 2:1 fighter:bomber ratio, but the *Luftwaffe* had only 975 'Emils' and some had to defend *Luftflotten* bases or the Reich. Only 600–700 were available for offensive operations, which confined the strike force during the coming weeks to a daily average of 250–300 bombers out of a force of more than 1,700.[27] The 'Emils'' combat radius was about 300km, with an endurance of 90 minutes (including 60 minutes for the round trip to England), and, even when not restricted by *ObdL*'s order of 3 August demanding tight escort for the bombers, operations were confined to England south of the Thames. A limited number of moulded-plywood drop tanks of 300-litre capacity were available to double the 'Emils'' range, but they tended to leak and may also have been unpopular because they reduced manoeuvrability. Pilots had not only to watch for the enemy but also to keep an anxious eye on the fuel warning light which flickered when capacity was only 25%, and many were no doubt glad that they had emptied their bladders behind their fighter's tail before take-off.

Ignoring the *Führer*'s deadline, another Carinhall conference set '*Adler*' for 10 August, only for the weather to force a three-day postponement during which the *Luftwaffe* continued to strike shipping. Meanwhile the 'Weather Frogs' (meteorologists) eagerly awaited the *Wekusta*'s two-to-seven *Zenit* (Zenith) flights a day, each lasting up to nine hours.[28] Ignored by Fighter Command until the end of the year, the *Wekusta* learned to fly the outward leg below the radar horizon and climb for the return journey to avoid interception by long-range fighters. '*Adler*' actually opened on 11 August, as Göring assured an increasingly restive Hitler that he would begin the offensive when he could be certain of three days' good weather. The following day the axe swung against the sinews of the British defensive system, its radar stations and fighter bases, spearheaded by the *Stukas* and *Jabos* of *Erprobungsgruppe 210* under Swiss-born *Condor Legion* veteran *Hauptmann* Walter Rubensdörffer.[29] From the afternoon of 13 August '*Adler*' was in full swing and 2,500 sorties were flown during the next three days, only to be compromised by slovenly staff work as the strike force suffered a 7% loss rate. On 15 August ('Black Thursday'), while Göring met *Luftflotten* and *Fliegerkorps* commanders at Carinhall, this soared to 10% when *Luftflotte 5*'s *Generaloberst* Hans-Jurgen Stumpff despatched 134 aircraft (a third of them *Zerstörer*) against targets in north-eastern England. His airmen anticipated weak resistance but encountered 60 fighters, which shot down 23 aircraft (17%) to end Stumpff's day campaign.[30] Three of the five *Kommandeure* lost in this period were flying the Bf 110, and these included the dashing Rubensdörffer, whose *Stabskette* was wiped out on 15 August.[31] The ill-armed *Stukas* also suffered severely, and one *StG 2 Staffel* lost seven out of nine aircraft, leading Göring at Carinhall to demand that three *Jagdgruppen* escort each *Stukagruppe*. The 'Fat Man' criticised attacks upon secondary targets, singling out a *Stuka* attack upon the Varne lightship the previous day, and questioned the value of attacks upon the radar stations, all of which latter appeared to remain operational (Martini failed to notice that Ventnor on the Isle of Wight was off line until 23 August). He demanded that the *Luftflotten* concentrate upon the RAF and its infrastructure, making more efficient use of the *Zerstörer* for deep-penetration missions.

While plans were revised, the *Kampfgruppen* continued droning across the Channel, often running the gauntlet from around the prominent headland of Dungeness, which crews christened *'Dünschiss'* (a descriptive word for diarrhoea). To pre-empt interception, low-level raids—usually undertaken by Do 17s, whose mid-wing design made it easier for crews to judge altitude—complemented medium-altitude bombing and worried Park throughout the battle. Success was not always assured, and poor coordination at Kenley on 18 August exposed *Hauptmann* Roth's *9./KG 76* to the full wrath of the defences: it lost four out of nine bombers, including Roth's. One damaged bomber reached safety thanks to the prompt action of the observer, *Feldwebel* Wilhelm-Friedrich Illg, who took over from the mortally wounded pilot and succeeded in landing the aircraft.[32] The same day ended *Stuka* daylight operations over England when four fighter squadrons slaughtered *Major* Clemens, *Graf* von Schönborn's *StG 77* during an attack upon Poling radar station, with 16 *Stukas* lost and two damaged beyond repair (21% of the force) in what Seidemann justly described as 'a black day'. Such was the intensity of combat during this period that both fighter forces appear to have suffered loss rates of about 3.5% during the week 12–18 August compared with about 2% for the preceding and succeeding weeks, while the *Luftwaffe* strike force's overall loss rate doubled to a peak of 8% compared with the preceding week.[33]

Yet German fortunes began to change from 20 August, beginning with another conference at Carinhall, where Göring announced, 'We have reached the decisive period of the air war against England.' The *Stuka* force was now to be committed only in the most favourable circumstances, effectively reducing the strike force by nearly one-fifth. While strengthening bomber escorts, Göring also encouraged the *Jagdgeschwader* to conduct sweeps while *Zerstörergruppen* sweeps would help the 'Emils' break off combat. There was no change in priorities, although Göring commented, 'There can no longer be any restriction on the choice of targets' but reserved authority for attacks upon either London or Liverpool. The bright spots were the rapid replacement of losses, while bomber serviceability was maintained at 70%, although for 'Emils' it declined from 95 to 85%. By contrast, the RAF appeared to be haemorrhaging: Schmid calculated that since 1 July it had lost 823 aircraft (77 on the ground), including 574 fighters, and, optimistically, he concluded that the enemy was left with only 300 Spitfires and Hurricanes. However, in the 10 days to 19 August 172 officers were lost or severely wounded, including *Obersten Dr* Johann Fisser and Alois Stoeckl, *Kommodoren* respectively of *KG 51* and *KG 55*, *Oberst* Frank (*LuftgauVIII* Chief of Staff), seven *Kommandeure* and 13 *Kapitäne*.[34] 'Robinson' now limited crews to no more than one commissioned officer, although exceptions were made for photo and maritime reconnaissance units.[35]

Luftwaffe staff work improved noticeably, with dynamic officers replacing the inefficient and the 'Old Eagles'. The Great War bombing *Experte Generaloberst* Alfred *'Bombenkeller'* Keller was replaced in *Fliegerkorps IV* on 20 August by *Generalleutnant* Curt Pflugbeil, the 'Old Eagle' and Lipetsk veteran. He had formerly commanded *Luftgau Belgien-Nord Frankreich* and was eight years younger than Keller, who relieved *General der Flieger* WilhelmWimmer of the eastern *Luftflotte 1*,Wimmer replacing Pflugbeil. Most changes took place within the *Jagdgeschwader*. Mölders returned to *JG 51*, while in *JG 26 Major* Adolf Galland (aged 28) became *Kommodore* on 22 August and a few days later another Condor Legion veteran, *Major* Johannes ('Hannes') Trautloft, took over *JG 54*. Their task was eased by Dowding's decision to fight over land after losing some 120 pilots dead or severely wounded in the previous nine days. The inexperience of their replacements was aggravated by rigid formations and tactics, which the *Experten* ruthlessly exploited.[36]

'Adler' continued intermittently during breaks in the weather but then faded away as the *Luftwaffe* decided to strike closer to London, partly because reconnaissance indicated that the bulk of Fighter Command had withdrawn to the capital's environs; indeed, many fighter bases were close to Tube stations. Although bombs struck legitimate targets in the southern suburbs on 16 August, Hitler's ban upon attacking London continued. For several days cloud and occasional rain restricted operations to hit-and-run raids, giving staffs time to analyse the defensive system and plan a more effective attack. Loerzer was straining on the leash and on 24 August clear skies allowed him to spearhead an assault which immediately forced Dowding to abandon his most exposed base at Manston (just outside Ramsgate). On succeeding days the *Kampfgruppen* systematically wrecked fighter bases pin-pointed by Martini, who considered jamming radars but lacked equipment until mid-September, although the *Funkhorchdienst* did exploit its knowledge of squadron codes and several times sent spoof messages which caused Polish pilots of No 303 Squadron to return prematurely to base.[37]

More fighters were available as the fighter force in the West was reorganised on 22 August. Until then they were under 'Old Eagles' *Obersten* Karl-Bertram von Döring (*JaFü 2*) and Werner Junck (*JaFü 3*). Döring, aged 50, had scored 11 victories while serving with *JG 1* in the Great War while Junck had five before becoming Heinkel's chief test pilot after Lipetsk training. Junck joined his friend Udet in the *Luftwaffe* and was responsible for development and testing, later playing a key role in the fatal reorganisation of the *Generalluftzeugmeister* which actually compromised development. He accompanied Udet on visits to the French and Royal Air Forces in the mid-1930s and until 4 June had been *Inspekteur der Jagdflieger*.[38] *Luftflotte 2* now had 18 *Jagdgruppen*, as it assumed greater responsibility for daylight operations, and with Kesselring expecting more from Sperrle these were now divided between Döring and Osterkamp (*JaFü 1*). Sperrle's *Jagdgruppen* could barely reach the British coast, forcing his *Kampfgruppen* increasingly into night operations, the last major daylight mission for three weeks being an afternoon raid on Portsmouth by *Major* Hans Korte's *KG 55* on 26 August. For night operations Sperrle received the specialist *KGr 100* on 17 August as night bombing sorties (including those by *Fliegerdivision 9*) doubled during the last week in August with heavy raids upon western ports, especially Merseyside. Seven *Jagd/Zerstörergruppen* were transferred to Kesselring (Sperrle acquired a *Zerstörergruppe* from *Luftflotte 5*), who also received *FliegerkorpsVIII* in the Pas de Calais area on 29 August to support the anticipated landing as well as *KG 26* from Stumpff.

The last week in August and the first in September saw the *Luftwaffe* reach a peak of activity, with some 10,800 sorties and an overall loss rate of about 2.8%. Bomber losses, at about 6.5% during the last week of August, dropped to 2.25% the following week through the escorts' efforts, allowing Kesselring's *Kampfgruppen* to devastate No 11 Group. By the end of August, of seven sector stations only Northolt (north of London) was undamaged and Park feared that his defences might buckle under the pressure of continual attacks. Dowding's overall loss rate in the south averaged 3.45% of sorties, but Nos 11 and 12 Groups bore the brunt with an average 4% rate which may have been higher. The escorts paid dearly with 230 lost, more than a quarter of them Bf 110s; this was an average rate of 2.6%, although fears of a temporary shortage of 'Emils' led to plans for re-equipping the home defence *JG 77* with French Bloch MB.152s.[39] Yet by 29 August Döring and Osterkamp were correctly reporting that the 'Tommies' were deliberately avoiding *Luftwaffe* fighter sweeps and conserving their strength for the *Kampfgruppen*. For two days from 30 August Park's radar screen vanished, following a failure of the electricity supply which ripped open a 130km gap that Kesselring sought to exploit by attacking most of the radar stations. Fighter Command was now suffering its heaviest losses, while *ObdL* claimed that it had been crippled, losing 10% of its infrastructure, permitting heavier attacks upon industrial towns and ports. On 30 August Halder commented in his diary: 'Whether or not England will then continue to fight is an open question.' Four days later *ObdL* claimed that, at a cost of 467 German aircraft, the RAF had lost 1,115 since 8 August while 18 airfields had been destroyed and 26 damaged.

Yet the strain was beginning to tell, and almost every day wreaths occupied some seats in each mess. Within the *Jagdgruppen* the general attitude of 'Devil take the hindmost' and the glory-seeking habits of some *Experten* rankled those who lacked luck or capability, while Göring's occasional hysterical accusations against fighter pilots further depressed morale. Combat fatigue was growing and ultimately contributed to the death of the leading *Experte Major* Helmut Wick (56 victories) on 28 November. The psychological and physical effects of combat fatigue earned it the nickname *'Kanalkrankheit'* ('Channel Sickness') and on rare occasions led to incidents such as that involving the *Feldwebel* pilot who promptly baled out of a *KG 26* bomber damaged by fighters on 11 September, leaving the observer, *Leutnant* F. Zimmerman, to take control and make a forced landing at Dieppe. Such incidents were rare, but numerous problems with the Ju 88, including mid-air fires, meant that by mid-October only five of 26 crews in one of Loerzer's *Gruppen* were ready to continue operations.[40] The 'black men', too, were nearing exhaustion: on 2 September a *JG 3* 'Emil' crashed at Le Portel, 'possibly the result of faulty servicing', and more were to follow in succeeding weeks.

Consequently *ObdL* was uneasy when it reviewed the situation on 28 August for, as Hitler knew, air superiority would not be attained for at least a fortnight. While considerable damage had been inflicted, estimates of fighter strength increased to 600 (420 in the south-east) with perhaps 100 in the factories. But *'Seelöwe'*s time was running out: shipping was already being assembled for the mid-September deadline. British fighters were avoiding combat and *ObdL* desperately sought new anvils upon which to smash Dowding's squadrons. The obvious solution, striking central London, was banned by *Führer* edict and the only alternative Waldau could produce was the aircraft industry, leading the *Luftflotten* to receive a list of another 30 industrial targets on 1 September although this meant diluting the main offensive against air bases. Until the target files were updated, Fighter Command bore the brunt, but the new policy lasted only another two days before being overtaken by events.

On the night of 24/25 August bombers scheduled to strike targets at the mouth of the Thames accidentally struck central London, leading to a retaliatory attack upon Berlin the following night and three more during the month. On the first night municipal farms were hit and wags said, 'Now they are trying to starve us out.' The laughter ceased four nights later when 10 died in the city centre, an American journalist observing that 'The Berliners are stunned . . . For the first time the war has been brought home to them.'[41] The Nazi leadership feared rioting if further bombing took place, and on 30 August Hitler authorised a strong reprisal against London with the proviso that it would not to be a *Terrorangriff* (terror attack) on residential areas. This was the *Luftwaffe*'s opportunity to bring Fighter Command to decisive battle, and plans were hammered out at a conference in The Hague on 3 September when Schmid, having claimed that only 100

British fighters were serviceable by the end of August, now hedged his bets by suggesting that a recent respite had allowed a recovery to 350 (on 23 August it was actually 672). Considerable scepticism was expressed, especially by Sperrle, who believed that the enemy had 1,000 aircraft, but the ever-optimistic Kesselring considered that the RAF was finished. Although aware that Fighter Command was receiving bomber pilots, Schmid did not recognise the implication that the RAF was desperately short of fighter pilots.[42] In accordance with Directive 17 the target was the city docks, and Hitler heralded the attack in a surprise appearance at the Berlin Sportpalast to open the *'Winterhilfe'* (Winter Help) campaign. In an atmosphere foreshadowing a 1960s pop concert, he told his largely female audience: 'When [the British] declare they will attack our cities in great strength, then we will erase their cities.'

Göring went to Cap Gris Nez on 7 September to watch his squadrons roar overhead in the late afternoon, 348 bombers and 617 fighters covering 2,000 square kilometres of space. Failing to anticipate an attack upon London, Park reacted late, and, despite the efforts of 21 fighter squadrons, bombs fell on London as the *Jagdgruppen* 'bounced' Leigh-Mallory's famous 'Duxford Wing', shooting down five fighters. Only eight bombers (2.29%) were lost, and miniature firestorms were created to act as beacons for 247 night bombers. The success of the mission, which did great damage (107,400grt of shipping alone required repair) and inflicted some 1,600 civilian casualties, owed much to the escorts, which destroyed 29 fighters (93 were claimed) and lost 20 (3.24%), more than one-third of them Bf 110s. Yet the *Kampfgeschwader Kommodore* demanded tighter and stronger escorts and the *Jagdgeschwader* were now ordered to break off combat with enemy fighters if the bombers were threatened. The fighter leaders wanted to loosen the chains and return to the effective high-altitude freelance patrols of the previous weeks, arguing that, covering the *Kampfgruppen* at 6,400–7,000m (21–23,000ft), the fighters' 'weaving' increased petrol consumption while preventing continual cover, thus adding to bomber crews' fears. Göring, the former fighter pilot, was deaf to their arguments and tied them tighter to the bombers, leaving the initiative to Fighter Command, so morale in both fighter and bomber units plummeted.

A deterioration in the weather prevented a follow-up attack until 11 September, although night bombing continued upon airfields and aircraft factories. On 9 September *ObdL* confirmed that London would be the primary target both day and night, adding, 'The destruction raids upon London will be accompanied, wherever possible, by raids upon armament areas and harbour facilities throughout England as before.' Neither the raid on 11 September nor another three days later was as strong as the 7 September mission, although the second one was supported by a radar-jamming campaign which degraded sensor performance without blinding the network. On these two days the British lost 43 fighters and the *Luftwaffe* only 14. Optimistic reconnaissance reports and advice from friendly military attachés encouraged Göring to believe that improving weather would enable a knock-out blow to be delivered, and his optimism was evidently conveyed to Hitler. Yet on 14 September, when Hitler examined the prospects for *'Seelöwe'* (with Jeschonnek deputising for Göring), he was critical of the *Luftwaffe*'s failure to destroy Fighter Command and noted: 'Our own air victory reports fail to give an entirely reliable picture.' Jeschonnek, believing that the British were on the verge of collapse, requested permission for a terror attack but Hitler authorised only the bombing of industrial, communications and public utility targets.[43]

The decisive moment came on 15 September when, with autumnal storms imminent, the *Luftwaffe* threw its Sunday Punch against London. Anticipating this, Dowding replaced Park's exhausted squadrons with fresh ones, which received the added bonus of a day's rest and time to provide 'green' pilots with a few precious hours of training. Park also decided to pair his fighter squadrons before interception and could count upon his neighbours for support. *ObdL* prepared a double attack on London by Kesselring, the first targeting railways and the second the docks. The first thrust, by 25 Dorniers of *KG 76*, supported by 21 *Jabos* of *II. (Sch)/LG 2* and 150 fighters, reached the target around noon, but many of the escorts were dispersed by 145kph (90mph) headwinds and the remaining formations encountered more than 190 defenders, who shot down six bombers and nine fighters. The main blow came that afternoon with 114 bombers and some 500 fighters and encountered some 325 fighters, including Bader's 'Big Wing'. The *Kampfgruppen* suffered 18% losses (21 aircraft), and while the escorts destroyed 15 fighters they themselves lost 23 and the defenders retained control of England's skies. Although Dowding's losses, at about 3.7% (4% for Nos 11 and 12 Groups), were higher than those of the escorts (2.88%), the *Kampfgruppen* loss rate nearly tripled to 6.5% compared with the previous week. In the concluding three weeks of the battle the *Luftwaffe* fighter loss rate exceeded that of Fighter Command by some 3:1 while the *Kampfgruppen* loss rate was 3.22%.[44]

Publicly Göring remained optimistic and, meeting *Luftflotten* and *Fliegerkorps* commanders at Boulogne the next day, claimed that 'four or five more days' of heavy losses would finish off the defenders. To achieve this objective, large attacks were to be launched on good-weather days while on others individual *Kampfgruppen* with tight escort would entice the enemy to combat or there would be harassing attacks by individual aircraft. When Döring commented the British were using large fighter formations, Göring argued that this assisted German strategy, although he still demanded that the invasion harbours be defended. London continued to be Kesselring's primary target, while Sperrle, who would assist him at night, focused upon Southampton and the western ports. Special crews were ordered to maintain pressure upon the aircraft industry, while *Fliegerdivision 9* was to experiment with dropping mines on London. Göring clearly continued to hope that the *Luftwaffe* alone would bring the British to their knees, but he recognised that it might be a long task and permission to prepare winter quarters was given.[45] In fact, the next day (17 September) Hitler postponed *'Seelöwe'* indefinitely, for he did not wish to gamble away Germany's hard-won international prestige by attempting so hazardous a venture until the *Luftwaffe* had crushed enemy resistance.[46]

Meanwhile Bomber Command had defiantly harassed both the *Luftwaffe* and preparations for *'Seelöwe'* throughout August and September, forcing part of the *Jagd-* and *Zerstörergruppen* to be retained for defensive operations (see Table 3). Most attacks were at night because Fighter Command had few aircraft to spare as escorts and British bombers remained extremely vulnerable in daylight, as *JG 77* and *III./ZG 76* demonstrated off Stavanger on 9 July when they shot down seven of a dozen Blenheims. Indeed, missions were usually abandoned if the skies were too clear.[47] Yet during early August daylight attacks exploiting cloud caught *II./JG 27* and *4./JG 54* on the ground, destroying a total of five fighters, with salt rubbed in *JG 27*'s wound when the bombers' gunners shot down another.[48] Despite the short summer nights, Bomber Command (augmented by Coastal Command) had considerable success, notably at Dunkirk and Ostend, the Naval Staff describing the damage as 'unacceptable'. By 21 September 12% of the steamers and 11% of the landing craft had been sunk or damaged, and while this could not prevent a landing it reduced the shipping reserve and provided an ominous hint of what the landing might expect.[49] On 10/11 September there was a bonus when 10 Heinkels of *KG 4* were destroyed at Eindhoven. where another had earlier been lost returning from a mission.

Unable to defeat the enemy conventionally, Kesselring used a combination of high-altitude sweeps by pairs of *Jagdgruppen* and coat-trailing missions by individual *Kampfgruppen*, supported by up to 300 fighters. The latter missions were spearheaded by *KG 77*, which lost nine bombers on its début on 17 September, including that of the *Kommandeur* of *III./KG 77*, *Major* Maxim Kless, despite an

---

Table 3. Bomber Command Operations over Western Europe (excluding the Reich), 1 July–31 October 1940

Month	Sorties		Failed to Return	
	Day	Night	Day	Night
Jul 1940	302	144	9	6
Aug 1940	283	352	18	13
Sep 1940	88	1,862	6	17
Oct 1940	82	455	2	3
Total	755	2,813	35	39

Sources: Based upon Middlebrook and Everitt; Day Bombing Raid Sheets (PRO Air 14/3361, 3362); and Night Bombing Raid Sheets (PRO Air 14/2666–72).

escort of 100 fighters. Ten days later it suffered nearly 22% casualties attacking London with fighter-bomber and fighter sweep support. On 25 September *Luftflotte 3* resumed major daylight attacks upon aircraft factories, inflicting heavy damage in Bristol and Southampton, but on 27 September *EprGr 210* suffered 21% casualties, including the *Kommandeur, Hauptmann* Martin Lutz, while returning to Bristol. Undaunted, the Germans attempted another double blow on 30 September against London and the Westland factory at Yeovil, with similarly disastrous results, although during the latter mission the *Zerstörergruppen* for once bested the British.[50] The *Luftwaffe* vainly rang the tactical changes, usually using *LG 1* and *KG 77*, to provide a viable daylight strike threat, and on 1 October No 10 Group pilots had the unique experience of encountering two of *KG 40*'s four-engine Fw 200 Condors on a bombing mission. The strain cut serviceability by the end of September to 68% for fighters and 52% for bombers, while by 7 October overall strength had dropped to 800 bombers (from 1,100) and 600 fighters (950).

To maintain daylight momentum, Kesselring ordered each *Jagdgeschwader* to fit bomb racks on one *Gruppe*'s aircraft for high-altitude (5,200m; 17,000ft) flight and to assemble 200 *Jabos* within a fortnight, but during their first major mission against south London on 5 October *EprGr 210* suffered 22% losses in a disastrous diversionary attack. Among the casualties was the acting *Kommandeur, Oberleutnant* Werner Weimann. Undaunted, the *Jabos*, rather than the *Kampfgruppen*, increasingly bore the brunt of daylight missions, especially as deteriorating weather during early October gave the *Kampfgruppen* the excuse to abandon large-scale daylight missions, effectively ending the Battle of Britain.[51] On 7 October Waldau visited Halder and sheepishly confessed that the *Luftwaffe* had underestimated enemy fighters by 100%, adding that by the spring of 1941 its strength would need to increase 400% to force the British to surrender. Halder was indifferent, for Hitler now intended striking Russia, although on hearing the news Waldau warned, 'A two-front war cannot be sustained.' Yet the troop trains still rolled eastwards, and by the end of October *OKH* headquarters moved to Zossen near Berlin. At the beginning of December Hitler informed Army leaders that they could ignore 'Seelöwe' (which was not formally cancelled until 2 March 1942), although in January 1941 he, Göring and the newly recovered Student discussed the possibility of an airborne assault upon Eire.[52]

The defeat was a bruising blow to *Luftwaffe* prestige, yet no blame could be placed upon either the aircrew or the 'black men', who had given their all. The 14-week daylight campaign had seen some 1,200 aircraft lost to enemy action and 2,800 men killed or missing in combat missions (another 340 were wounded). Some 750 of the missing were taken prisoner, to be joined over the next eight months by another 500 of their countrymen. Wearing distinctive uniforms and neither trained nor equipped for escape and evasion, most tamely surrendered to the first figure of authority they encountered because they anticipated an early

British surrender. An exception was *Feldwebel* Josef Markl, a *KG 55* observer shot down on the night of 29/30 July, who stayed on the run for nine days before thirst and hunger forced him to surrender to a chauffeur-driven Rolls-Royce![53] The sea was the ultimate gaoler, although the resourceful *Feldwebel* Walter Guttmann (*KG 30*) and his crew, after crash-landing in Norfolk, carried a rubber dinghy and were well on their way to the coast when their luck ran out.

Generally, captured airmen were treated correctly, although there were occasional tragic incidents due to misunderstandings, while one Bf 109 pilot trapped in a burning plane was mercifully shot. However, the strains of imminent invasion and heavy bombing led even the normally imperturbable British to atrocity. On 16 August two parachuting airmen were shot at, and one killed, by soldiers and the Home Guard militia who discovered only afterwards that they were British.[54] The Home Guard, sometimes with only a veneer of military discipline, are known to have attacked some airmen, such as *Oberleutnant* J. Loidolt (*JG 3*) on 31 August 1940 and *Oberleutnant* W. von Sieber (*KG 53*) on the night of 10/11 May 1941, while bombing goaded some civilians into ignoring the Geneva Convention. On 15 September the badly wounded *Oberleutnant* Robert Zehbe (*KG 76*) was savagely beaten by a mob when he landed near the Oval cricket ground and died of his injuries, while seven months later, on the night of 9/10 April 1941, a member of *Unteroffizier* Rudolf Müller's crew (*KG 27*) was badly beaten by a Birmingham mob and was saved only by the arrival of soldiers.

These incidents were the exception rather than the rule, although capture was humiliating.[55] Both of Zehbe's crewmates, for example, were taken prisoner, and the other side of the coin was demonstrated on 23 September when a severely wounded *Unteroffizier* Dilthey (*JG 2*) was shot down off Folkestone. He would undoubtedly have drowned had not a British soldier swum out to support him until both men were rescued by a fishing boat. Typical was the treatment to the *Kapitän* of 2./*JG 51*, *Oberleutnant* Viktor Mölders, brother of the famous ace, who was shot down on 7 October and given a cup of tea by his farmer captor. The only ill-treatment Mölders received was a 'kick' from the farmer's dog.[56] The first German airmen to fall into British hands were liable to end up in the Tower of London, where there was a reception and interrogation centre, but early in 1940 this moved to Trent Park, north London. Interrogators were sent to interview prisoners as soon as possible after capture, the first interview often taking place in a police station. Those believed to have valuable information were then sent to Trent Park, where skilled interrogators, after receiving nothing more than a prisoner's name, rank and serial number, made crude threats then placed him in solitary confinement. If this did not loosen the tongue, the prisoner would be placed in cells with other airmen (and sometimes an *emigré* stooge), where hidden microphones both inside and outside the cell would often pick up valuable information. This would help later interrogators, who displayed an intimate knowledge of the prisoner, his comrades and unit, even to the point of knowing the names of pets and when officers were last on leave. Consequently *Oberleutnant* Franz vonWerra, adjutant of *II./JG 3*, was embarrassed to learn that an air battle he had graphically described on the radio had been grossly exaggerated, although, like many of his comrades, he revealed nothing more.[57]

Werra was to be the only *Luftwaffe* man to make a 'home run'. Like many German prisoners he was transferred to Canada, but he escaped from the train and reached the neutral United States, from where he travelled through Russia to freedom.[58] His transfer to Canada followed an earlier escape attempt in which he almost flew away in a brand new Hurricane. Escapers *Oberleutnant* HarryWappler (*KG 27*) and *Leutnant* Heinz Schnabel (*KG 1*) had better luck in November 1941, stealing from a British airfield a Miles Magister trainer which they flew eastwards, only for it to run out of fuel and crash-land in Norfolk.[59] The only other German airmen to reach home before the war's end had severe medical conditions and were exchanged through the Red Cross, but *Oberfeldwebel* Günther Struck (*JG 52*) exploited this loophole by feigning mental illness to return in the summer of 1944, ending the war as a test pilot for Messerschmitt.

Having failed in its traditional, 'operational' role, the *Luftwaffe* exploited the autumn's lengthening nights to enter the unknown territory of strategic bombing, attacking industrial cities and ports to destroy war production and tighten the blockade. The perennial problems of spares meant that only some 700 bombers were available; indeed, throughout the Blitz serviceability remained at about 50%, and while the loss rate remained one-third that of daylight operations, this was offset by a higher accident rate, due partly to delays in extending instrument-landing facilities. While few *Kampfgruppen* were specifically trained for bad weather/ night operations, Milch's foresight meant that bombers had navigational aids, backed by a network of radio beacons, and crews were confident in using them, although replacement crews were of a lower quality due to the rush to maintain front-line strength. Navigation aids were augmented by the *Knickebein* radio-beam bombing support system, whose signals could be picked up by every bombers' Lorenz blind-approach receiver within a 290km radius of the nearest 30–33MHz transmitter for accurate attacks. For precision bombing there were the specialised 65–75MHz *X-Verfahren* (X-Procedure), with the same range as *Knickebein* but multi-target capability, and the more accurate *Y-Verfahren*, which could be used within a 195km radius of a transmitter and could be 'plugged into' the auto-pilot.[60] These were used by the specialist *KGr 100* with 'Three-Master' He 111H-3xs using 'X' while *II./KG 26* re-equipped with He 111H-5ys to use 'Y'. However, all the systems were under threat as the British introduced counter-measures, beginning in July with masking beacons ('meacons') to re-transmit radio naviga-tion signals, while from September onwards 'Asprin' jammers began to compro-mise *Knickebein* performance, so much so that by winter it ceased to be an asset.[61]

One reason for low casualties was the weak defences, with AA guns one-third below establishment, and with only 2,631 weapons even in May 1941 the British had to rob Peter to pay Paul. Dowding always intended to rely upon radar-equipped fighters, although the cumbersome nature of the temperamental AI (Airborne Interception) Mk III set meant that it could be carried only by the inadequate Blenheim IF pending the arrival of the formidable Beaufighter. But on the night of 23/24 July Flying Officer Glynn Ashfield and Sergeant Reginald Leyland, in a Fighter Interception Unit Blenheim, were guided to a *2./KG 3* Do 17 by Tangmere sector operations control and *Leutnant* Kahlfuss's crew had the melancholy distinction of being the first shot down by this combination. Technical resources remained limited and Dowding gave priority to the day battle, so the night offensive found Fighter Command woefully unprepared. There was a desperate response with obsolete Defiants, single-seat Hurricanes and former French Douglas DB-7 (Havoc) bombers pressed into service together with Bomber Command Hampdens, while flying searchlight teams and aerial minelaying were all tried with little effect. Of greater potential importance was the combination of gunlaying (GL) radars and searchlights with fighter direction from existing sector operational control rooms to produce the beginnings of a dedicated Ground Controlled Interception (GCI) system under Group control.

Whitehall's disquiet at Fighter Command's failure led to Dowding's replacement on 25 November by Air Marshal Sholto Douglas.[62] Douglas vigorously reorganised the defences, dispersing his few GL sets to create a 'carpet' of them in the southern counties as well as forming more night fighter squadrons, although even in February there were only seven, with 87 pilots—half the establishment. The GL 'carpet' was augmented by six GCI sets controlling radar-equipped night fighters, and by the height of the Blitz the defences were on the verge of success. The numbers of contacts and combats involving radar-equipped night fighters rose steadily during 1941, from 44 and two in January (84 sorties) to 204 and 74 in May (643 sorties), but even in May the majority (67%) of night fighter sorties were visual ('cat's-eye') missions. Curiously, while only 43% of contacts in May were by visual interception, they accounted for 61% of combats.[63] Yet, when compared with daylight operations, there was a sharp decline in *Luftwaffe* casualties, the overall loss rate was about 1% per month and vigilant crews usually saw the night fighters first and evaded them.

The night campaign had opened on 2/3 June 1940 with harassing attacks against ports, aircraft factories and airfields, excluding the London area, although on 15 July a *Störflug* (harassing sortie) was reported over the city. These were in retaliation for the bombing of the Ruhr but also implemented *OKW* Directive 13, with priority after 22 June given to the RAF's infrastructure. The loads were usually 50–250kg high-explosive bombs, occasionally supplemented by 500kg ordnance, with the first recorded use of incendiaries on 8/9 July against Newcastle-upon-

Table 4. The Blitz: Estimated *Luftwaffe* Bomber Sorties

Month	Day (Losses)		Night (Losses)		Sorties Luftfl 2	Luftfl 3	Attacks Major	Heavy
Oct 1940	2,300	(79)	5,900	(23)	2,400	3,500	25	4
Nov 1940	925	(65)	6,125	(48)	1,600	4,525	23	2
Dec 1940	650	(24)	3,450	(44)	700	2,750	11	5
Jan 1941	675	(7)	2,050	(22)	450	1,600	7	6
Feb 1941	500	(9)	1,450	(18)	475	975	–	2
Mar 1941	800	(8)	4,275	(46)	1,625	2,650	12	3
Apr 1941	800	(9)	5,250	(58)	1,500	3,750	16	5
May 1941	200 (1-15)	(3)	3,800	(55)	1,300	2,500	11	3
Total	6,850	(204)	32,300	(314)	10,050	22,250	105	30

Notes: Figures exclude minelaying operations and attacks by 'light bombers'.
Sources: *Luftkrieg gegen England—Gefechtskalender* (USNA Microfilm T 321, Roll 176, fr.437ff); *Vorstudie zur Luftkriegsgeschichte, Heft 10* (USNA T971, Roll 4, fr.606ff); *Luftflotte 3 Lagebericht* from 5 August (USNA T321, Roll 88, fr.1ff); and *Einsatz gegen England* (IWM, AHB 6, Tin 29).

Tyne. From the night of 12/13 July the scale increased and AA concentrations were avoided; indeed, on the night of 25/26 July *KG 76* flew via Land's End to approach Southampton from the north (see Table 4 for night operations). These missions were integrated with *'Adler'* and spearheaded by the precision bombing specialists of *Hauptmann* Kurd Aschenbrenner's *KGr 100*, whose first mission was on 13/14 August, but, pending completion of a chain of seven *X-Verfahren* transmitters, the *Gruppe* flew 144 *Knickebein* sorties during the month.

A four-night campaign against Merseyside (whose *Luftwaffe* code-name was *'Speisekammer'*, or Larder) from 28/29 August marked a change in strategy. Göring ordered Sperrle to plan this offensive at the 19 August conference, and the decline in *Luftflotte 3*'s daylight operations allowed the monocled general to despatch 629 sorties. These inflicted considerable damage upon the dock area with more than 450 tonnes of bombs (largely high-explosive), as well as hitting the battleship *Prince of Wales* under construction across the Mersey.[64] Within a week London received another 350 tonnes (including 15 tonnes of incendiaries) as the offensive struck the capital's centre and docks—operations code-named *'Loge'* (Theatre Box) and *'Seeschlange'* (Sea Snake) respectively—at 3,700m (12,000ft), the limits of British searchlight effectiveness. These targets were then struck every night until 13/14 November, the campaign involving 11,117 sorties (15,500 tonnes of bombs), severely damaging the docks and disrupting rail traffic both by destroying facilities and littering them with unexploded bombs which delayed movements. On 18 October Göring informed his airmen that they had 'reduced the British plutocracy to fear and terror', but, anticipating the campaign, the British had appointed special commissioners rapidly to restore communications.

Two days later *ObdL* issued new guidelines, with Sperrle carrying the burden of night operations. He was to despatch 250 sorties a night, including 100 against the Midlands and Merseyside as well as western harbours. Kesselring was to strike eastern harbours and despatch up to 50 sorties a night against London, assisted by the newly arrived Italian *CAI*, and also harass eastern ports during the day. Although *Fliegerkorps IX* (upgraded from *Fliegerdivision 9* on 16 October) was to concentrate upon mining operations, it also participated in the bombing campaign both conventionally, with the area between the Humber and the Wash as its bailiwick, and by dropping mines over land targets.[65] *KG 4* began the latter operations over London on 17/18 September, and by 19/20 April *Fliegerkorps IX* had dropped 3,984 mines on land, representing more than one-third of the total despatched in the previous 12 months.[66] The mines' ability to level whole streets made them much feared, but several fell into British hands, allowing countermeasures to be developed and adversely affecting the German anti-shipping campaign.

The profligate use of mines and incendiaries indicated a trend towards area attack dictated by tactical expediency rather than policy. While *Kampfgruppen* were allocated specific military targets, the difficulties of locating them in the gloom and industrial haze meant that they needed to be illuminated 'without regard of the civil population', as the Condor Legion was once informed.[67] From October *KGr 100* became the *Beleuchtergruppe* or *Anzündergruppe* (Firelighter or Fireraiser Group) as it used incendiaries and small high-explosive bombs to set ablaze property in the target's vicinity. The concept was steadily expanded into a tactic dubbed *'Feuerleitung'* (Blaze Control) with the creation of *Brandbombfelde* (Incendiary Fields) to mark targets, with follow-up illumination at intervals of two to five minutes from *III./KG 26* and *II./KG 55*, the latter specialising in dropping LC 50 parachute flares (previously used for route marking) as well as very heavy bombs delivered by experienced crews. Initially the SC 1000 'Hermann', SC 1400 and SC 1800 'Satan' were used to level whole streets and blocks, and just before Christmas they were joined by the monster SC 2500 'Max'.

The British monitored the offensive closely and noted that some 20% of high-explosive bombs failed to explode, but they were more interested in learning lessons which they would later apply in Germany. Three months after the Blitz finished a British air staff study concluded that the effect of bombing was in proportion to the weight of bombs per square mile of the town but that all towns recovered at approximately 2–3% of activity per day, measured by a variety of indicators.[68] Curiously, this study concluded that high-explosive bombs were more effective than incendiaries, although reluctantly admitting that 'the speed of recovery seems to be slightly slower after fire damage'.[69] Civilian agencies came to a different conclusion, and in December the Ministry of Home Security commented that, in Sheffield, 'For every ton of steel destroyed in factories by high explosives,

10 tons had been destroyed by fire.[70] Officially terror attacks (missions against residential areas) were banned, but this was a moot point when the *Luftwaffe*'s combination of big missions and Blaze Control tactics sought residential property for kindling, while the scale of attacks preventing fires from being contained.[71] The British also noted that the devastation of city centres and loss of offices, workshops, utilities and transport led to a decline in regional production, and all of this analysis helped to shape Bomber Command's area attack operations under Harris from 1942, although the first such venture on Mannheim on 16/17 December 1940 proved a fiasco. Yet the Blitz is largely ignored by historians, who have levelled whole forests examining every facet of the air offensive against Germany.[72]

As the night offensive gathered strength, the compromising of *Knickebein* forced the *Luftwaffe* to exploit moonlight and on 9 October both *Luftflotten* were ordered to prepare for large raids on London during the mid-month full-moon period, although they also found time to attacks ports, especially Merseyside. On 7 November *'Robinson'* issued a new directive, and while London remained the primary target (half the bomb loads were to consist of incendiaries), the Midlands were now given high priority, with offensives scheduled against Birmingham, Coventry and Wolverhampton under the code-names *'Regenschirm'* (Rainstorm), *'Mondscheinserenade'* (Moonlight Sonata) and *'Einheitspreis'* (Unit Price); the preparations were to be complete by 9 November.[73] *Unternehmen 'Einheitspreis'* was to start the offensive and see the operational début of the *X-Verfahren*, but the discovery of strengthened AA defences made an alternative target necessary. When Hitler, angry that an attack on Munich had spoiled celebrations of the Beerhall *Putsch*, demanded retaliation *ObdL* executed *'Mondscheinserenade'* against Coventry or target *'Korn'* (Corn). On 14/15 November 449 aircraft from *Luftflotten 2* and *3* were despatched with 530 tonnes of high explosive and incendiaries which turned the city into an inferno that could be seen by follow-up crews on the other side of the Channel—yet 18% of crews despatched failed to reach their target! The city centre was devastated; 21 factories were severely damaged, while the loss of utilities stopped work at nine others, disrupting industry for several months. The following day's *OKW* communiqué observed: 'After this large-scale attack . . . the English invented a new word, "to coventrate"', which rubbed salt in British wounds and stimulated demands for revenge. Despite 125 night fighter sorties, the only aircraft lost was to AA fire, yet *ObdL* made only a token follow-up attack because (like Bomber Command later) it greatly underestimated the defenders' capability for recovery.[74]

Hours before *'Mondscheinserenade'* Göring gave Milch command of the *Luftwaffe* and went on leave, returning to duty only in late January. Occasionally he would dictate orders to his deputy, once through his nurse, but Milch was generally able to indulge his desire for operational command unrestricted since Jeschonnek promptly followed Göring's example rather than serve under his enemy. Heavy attacks on other cities were rarely on the scale of Coventry, but when Southampton was struck on 17/18 November morale was briefly shaken, partly because key civic leaders joined the thousands who 'trekked' out of the city even before the raid.[75] Apart from a verbal Christmas truce brokered by Washington at German instigation, the campaign rolled into December with the bombers now flying in streams, or *Krokodile* (Crocodiles), and as *Y-Verfahren* was introduced more than 2,800 tonnes of bombs were dropped. Follow-up raids were launched on Sundays when week-end breaks weakened civil defence, the most successful being an attack on 29/30 December when unexpected high winds blew incendiaries into the publishing area to create the 'Second Great Fire of London'.[76]

Low cloud, freezing temperatures and snow brought some relief to Britain's battered cities during January and February 1941, when the total effort barely equalled the December figure, despite the use of *Stukas* from 15/16 January. The offensive reached its nadir in February partly due to waterlogged airfields and the withdrawal of some 18 *Kampfgruppen* for rest and re-equipment.[77] On 1 February a new *ObdL* directive assigned priority to harbours, anticipating by five days *OKW* Directive 23, 'Directions for operations against the British war economy', which replaced Directive 17. Bad weather meant that most targets escaped the bombing, but the lull was exploited both to service aircraft and to improve electronic counter-measures. In September the British had introduced 'Bromide' jammers for *X-Verfahren* and in February 1941 the 'Domino' jammer for *Y-Verfahren*; 'meaconing' remained effective, with one confused crew (possibly *Leutnant* Hans Thurner's of *KG 55*) on 14/15 February landing in rapid succession at three RAF airfields before escaping across the Channel.[78] To confuse the British, Martini arranged for beams to be directed over false targets then realigned at the last moment, while from 9/10 March rapid frequency changes were made during attacks. Security was strengthened by extending radio silence until after the first wave of attackers had dropped their bombs. Due to the general lack of confidence in electronic systems, the Germans confined major attacks on inland targets to moonlit nights until April and concentrated upon ports, where the beams could be used with minimum disturbance.

Improved weather in March and the return of *Kampfgruppen* saw a surge in activity, often against ports. Some targets were struck several nights in succession, beginning with Cardiff from 1/2 March.[79] These attacks often caused temporary drops in local morale, demonstrated by an increase in 'trekking', but the sudden crisis in the Balkans at the end of March meant the despatch southward of seven *Kampfgruppen* just as bad weather closed down the airfields. More frequencies gave the *X-Verfahren* greater tactical flexibility, with transmitters switched on as the bombers began their run in, but the *Y-Verfahren* was disrupted by selective jamming and during the first half of the month only 18 out of 89 sorties received bomb-release signals. An unusual feature was the despatch of some 50 'light bomb-ers' (nicknamed *'Leichte Kesselringe'*, or 'Light Kesselrings'), including *Jabos* and *Stukas*, which became a feature of the latter stages of the Blitz, with some 75 sorties in April and 100 in May, when two *Jabos* were lost.

After an unpromising beginning because of bad weather, April saw the offen-sive reach a new peak, with some 75% of sorties by Sperrle's *Gruppen*. The British had only three nights' respite—the Midlands bore the brunt—while twice (once to mark Hitler's birthday) more than 1,000 tonnes of bombs fell on London. In mid-April attacks were extended to Belfast (where firemen from neutral Eire helped fight the conflagration), and here, as well as Glasgow and Plymouth, morale was severely affected. The *Y-Verfahren* was becoming unreliable owing to counter-meas-ures, and only twice during the month did *KG 26* hear the bomb release signal, but interference with the *X-Verfahren* proved little more than a nuisance. The Bal-kans crisis required the despatch of more *Kampfgruppen*, and the loss of so many aircraft forced the *Luftwaffe* to demand from crews two or three sorties a night, using forward airfields to refuel and re-arm. The bombers were noisy and cold and they vibrated horribly, but tension and exhaustion drained the crews and killed many. En route to Portsmouth on his 50th mission (28/29 April), Peter Stahl (*KG 30*) fell asleep at the controls of his Ju 88 and awoke to discover the entire crew snoring at their stations. He roused them, ensured they took oxygen and Dextro-Energen tablets, then completed the mission.[80]

The pace became more frantic in May because most *Kampfgruppen* were sched-uled to move eastward for *'Barbarossa'*, but such was the scale that Herbert Morrison, the Minister of Home Security, warned that provincial morale might collapse under the sustained bombing; indeed, in Liverpool—where 39,126grt of shipping was sunk and 111,601grt was damaged, half the unloading berths were unavailable and the tonnage unloaded fell by 75%—there were brief public ex-pressions of defeatism.[81] Other ports were struck, and in Hull a third of the popu-lation became 'trekkers'. The campaign reached a crescendo in mid-May when London suffered the biggest attack of the Blitz (571 sorties and 800 tonnes of bombs) on 10/11 May; this caused more than 2,000 fires, with severe effects upon morale. An unusual feature of the night of 11/12 May was the despatch of 63 fighters with the bomber force, reflecting the *Luftwaffe*'s concern over the growing effectiveness of the defences since early April, but by the end of May the whole of *Luftflotte 2* had been withdrawn, leaving Sperrle with a token force to maintain an illusion of strategic bombing.

The proximity of bases during the Blitz compensated for the absence of heavy bombers, allowing the *Luftwaffe* to drop some 45,000 tonnes of bombs, bruising industry, disrupting transport, reducing food supplies and shaking morale, while the sinking of some 58,000grt of shipping and damaging of 450,000grt helped tighten the blockade. Though suffering at a regional level, British national production increased during most of the Blitz, but during April there were falls of 25% in rifle, 4.6% in filled-shell and 4.5% in small-arms ammunition production, although the RAF study considered that this might have been due to the Easter holidays.[82] The same study noted that cities generally took 10–15 days to recover, and slightly longer for Belfast and Liverpool in May, while the April attacks on Birmingham affected production for three months; sustained bombing exhausted the population, who required up to three weeks to recover.[83] The British official history of war production notes that the greatest contribution of the Blitz to the German war effort lay in disrupting the manufacture of parts (for example, engine magnetos), and the bombing, combined with the need to disperse the aircraft industry further, dashed hopes of manufacturing more than 2,500 aircraft a month.[84] More might have been achieved had *ObdL* sought a weak spot, but there were no 'oil' or 'transportation' plans; instead, cities were selected for attack and targets were then assigned from folders.[85] Disputes focused upon tactics rather than strategy, the best way to use electronic systems and which targets to strike, leading *Luftflotte 2* Operations Officer *Major* Viktor von Lossberg to leave following bitter arguments with Göring and Kesselring.[86] With the need for follow-up operations appreciated far too late, the campaign had an air of improvisation which helped provide the British civilian population with some respite and gave damaged industry time either to recover or to disperse.

NOTES TO CHAPTER 1

1. The *Luftwaffe* supreme command was referred to as *Oberbefehlshaber der Luftwaffe* or *ObdL* until 11 April 1944, when *ObdL* and the *Reichsminister der Luftfahrt* were merged and renamed *Oberkommando der Luftwaffe* or *OKL*.
2. The *Geschwader* remained nominally under *Oberst* Wolf von Stutterheim, although he had been injured in action and hospitalised on 15 June. He was relieved on 1 August but succumbed to his injuries in Berlin on 3 December and was posthumously promoted to *Generalmajor*.
3. Mason, p.108. Mason, with Wood and Dempster, has the detailed accounts of the Battle of Britain.
4. For convenience, all ranks shown in this chapter are those of 19 July, before which both Kesselring and Sperrle were *Generale der Flieger*.
5. For Antwerp-Deurne see van Ishoven pp.75–88.
6. Diary, BA MA N671/6.
7. Officially Wenniger's Christian name was Rudolf, but actually it was Ralph. See Hildebrand.
8. For part of July Richthofen was in Biarritz assisting Germany's diplomatic effort to persuade Spain's leader, General Franco, to enter the war and operations were directed by his Chief of Staff, *Oberstleutnant* Hans Seidemann. The latter was no stranger to British skies, having won the London to Isle of Man air race in May 1937.
9. Mason, p.138/n.50. *Störangriffe* were raids in which less than 50 tonnes of bombs were dropped.

10. Ibid., p.513.

11. Battle of Britain—Dowding Despatches, para.156 (PRO Air 8/863). With the same remorseless logic, Dowding also observed that, to deprive the RAF of pilots, the Germans were perfectly entitled to shoot parachuting British airmen. Paras 159, 160; Mason, p.101.

12. Mention should be made of *Oberleutnant* Helmut von Claer of *KG 51*, whose bomber crashed into the Channel after being damaged over London on 18 October. There was no time to launch a dinghy and the crew depended upon their lifejackets. The junior member of his crew was married with two children, and to help him swim to safety Claer handed him his lifejacket and perished with three other crew members. Dierich, *KG 51*, p.122.

13. For the full text see Wood and Dempster, pp.225–6.

14. Taylor, pp.52–3.

15. Ibid., pp.125, 127, 339/n.45.

16. On 2 September a Ju 52 of *1./KGzbV 172* crashed at Pritzwalk during a training drop, killing all three crew members and seven paratroops.

17. For *'Seelöwe'* planning see Taylor, pp.199–291, and pp.236–8 for airborne plans.

18. Ibid., pp.68, 72–5.

19. Ibid., pp.61–2.

20. A vivid personal account of this conference is in Osterkamp, pp.324–7.

21. See SHAA 1D37 for details of a No 13 Group mission on 22 February 1940 from the French liaison staff.

22. The full report is in Mason, App. H; and Wood and Dempster, pp.110–14.

23. Mason, App. E; and Wood and Dempster, Apps 5 and 6.

24. Martini was not directly answerable to Jeschonnek and did not always keep Schmid fully informed. Boog, in Probert and Cox, p.22.

25. Baker, p.174/n.1.

26. Although the Bf 109E-3 is regarded as the backbone of the *Jagdgruppen* during the Battle of Britain, research by the author's more distinguished namesake, Mr Ted Hooton, who analysed fighter casualties, indicates that the Bf 109E-4 and Bf 109E-1 bore the brunt of the battle, many E-3s being upgraded to E-4. The percentages of Bf 109 casualties are as follows:

Sub-Type	Jul	Aug	Sept	Oct
Bf 109E-1	44	40	38	36
Bf 109E-3	30	8	1	2
Bf 109E-4	20	52	61	62

The author would like to express his gratitude to Mr Hooton for this information.

27. The point appears first to have been raised by Alfred Price, *Blitz on Britain*, p.73.

28. In August there were 127 *Zenit* sorties compared with 80 in July. Meteorological information was also provided by ordinary reconnaissance aircraft and the Fw 200 Condors. WT Intelligence Summaries 25 June–31 August 1940 (PRO Air 22/478); and Analysis of Raids on the United Kingdom (PRO Air 2/7173).

29. The *Gruppe* was created from *1./ZG 1, 3./StG 77* and *4. (J)/TrGr 186* at the beginning of July, with the first two *Staffeln* operating Bf 110Ds and the last flying Bf 109Es.

30. The 16 August situation report (referring to the previous day's operations) assessed British fighter strength at 430 aircraft, with 30 'first class' fighters in 'northern' and 70 in 'central' Britain. Situation reports 16 July–18 November 1940 (IWM Ger/Misc/MCR/19 [3]). For details of the operation see Mason, pp.199–203.

31. He was awarded a posthumous *Ritterkreuz*. The others lost in Bf 110s were *Major* Ott of *I./ZG 2* and *Hauptmann* Restemeyer of *I./ZG 76*.

32. Illg was awarded a *Ritterkreuz* but was taken prisoner on 1 September. Ishoven's claim (pp.63–6) that Illg was a war correspondent appears to be wrong, but many German newspaper and radio reporters flew combat missions during the Battle of Britain, during which several were killed (op. cit., pp.35–6). Ishoven has the best personal accounts of the Battle of Britain from the *Luftwaffe* viewpoint.

33. The absence of authoritive figures, especially for Nos 11 and 12 Groups, means that these assessments are based upon estimated sortie levels. The RAF Air Historical Branch narrative lists total daylight defensive sorties from 10 July and it has not proved possible to find the originals for a breakdown. As only part of No 12 Group was involved in the battle, a deduction of 20% has usually been made from the combined sortie figures.

34. Fisser was lost during an attack upon Portsmouth on 12 August, when *KG 51* lost 11 aircraft. Also lost during this mission was *Leutnant* Paul Seidel, whose *Kette* accidentally bombed Freiburg on 10 May.

35. *Volksbesatzungen* (People's Crews) were those without officers. Kiehl, p.136.

36. Some RAF replacement pilots were killed within hours of joining their squadrons.

37. Mason, pp.284–5, 311.

38. See Hooton, pp.12, 153; and Ishoven, pp.147, 159, 338, 351, 365.

39. Aders and Held, *JG 51*, p.65.

40. See the comments of *Flieger* Robert Götz of *KG 55* in Ramsey, Vol. II, p.92; Irving, *Milch*, p.108; Scutts, p.44; and Steinhilper, pp.286, 299, 304, 306.

41. Middlebrook and Everitt, p.77; and Taylor, p.156, quoting William L. Shirer, *Berlin Diary, 1941*, pp.486, 490, 492–4.

42. From 24 August to 6 September Fighter Command lost 103 pilots killed and 128 wounded, or some 23% of its establishment. During August it received 250 replacements. Price, *Blitz on Britain*, p.73.

43. Taylor, pp.162–3.

44. This paragraph greatly benefits from Dr Alfred Price's exhaustively researched book *Battle of Britain Day*.

45. Ibid., pp.166–8.

46. For the contemporary views of Kesselring's Chief of Staff, *Generalleutnant* Wilhelm Speidel, expressed to *Generalmajor* Walter Warlimont, see the *OKW* War Diary entry for 23 September; and Taylor, pp.169–70, 285–6.

47. Day Bomber Raid Sheets, June–December 1940, PRO Air 14/3361.

48. Mason, pp.164, 169.

49. Taylor, pp.275–7.

50. Mason, pp.336–7, 342–5; and Sarkar, *Angriff Westland*.

51. For a comment on the failure to examine the Battle of Britain from the German viewpoint see Taylor, pp.79, 82. For the reasons for the German failure see BAM, pp.86–91.

52. Taylor, pp.281–2.

53. For details see Andy Saunders, *Josef Markl's Escapade*.

54. The survivor was Flight Lieutenant James Nicolson, who became the only member of Fighter Command to receive a Victoria Cross. See Mason, pp.213–14.

55. While hosting a pre-war visit by an RAF fighter pilot, a member of *JG 2* boasted of the Bf 109's superiority over the Hurricane. During the Battle of Britain he met his former guest in the RAF mess, having been shot down by a Hurricane!

56. Most of the stories are from Ramsey, Vol. II, supplemented by Foreman, *1941*.

57. For the processing of *Luftwaffe* prisoners see Ramsey, Vol. I, pp.114–15. See also Kiehl, pp.122–3.

58. He was killed in a flying accident a few months after reaching home.

59. For Wappler and Schnabel see Ramsey, Vol. I, p.92.

60. The *Verfahren* used *X*- and *Y-Gerät* (Equipment), sometimes called Plendl Equipment after their inventor *Dr* Hans Plendl. *Knickebein* (Knock-Knee) was a mythical raven. For descriptions of the German electronic bombing aids see Price, *Instruments of Darkness* (hereafter Price, *Instruments*), pp.20–3, and *Blitz on Britain*, pp.90–1; and Wakefield's article.

61. For the electronic war see Price, *Instruments*, pp.31–51, and Cockburn's article with Wakefield's. For further details and information on navigation systems see Hinsley, App. 11.

62. Soon afterwards Air Vice-Marshal Sir Leslie Gossage, who had been the British Air Attaché in Berlin during the early 1930s, took over Balloon Command.

63. Delve, p.90, Table 2.

64. This mission saw the night bombing début of the Condor, which flew a total of 25 sorties against Merseyside and Clydeside to 28/29 November according to Erhardt and Benoit. See also Argyle's article 'The Liverpool Blitz'.

65. IWM, AHB 6/29, fr.2839–2876.

66. Neitzel, p.110/n.281, quoting BA MA WF-04/34954.

67. Hooton, p.132.

68. The Blitz, AI 9 (Air Liaison) report of 14 August 1941 (PRO Air 40/288).

69. Ibid.

70. Quoted from Weekly Security Appreciation by Ray, p.180/n.80.

71. On 11 November the British overheard a *KG 1* prisoner talking about plans for future missions and stating that the targets would be workers' homes. Clayton, p.79, quoting PRO Air 20/2419.

72. Ray has one of the few overviews of the Blitz. Ramsey, Vol. II, is packed with information and incident.

73. The text of the directive is in Balcke, *KG 2*, p.194.

74. For Coventry see Ray, pp.150–8; Balke, *KG 2*, pp.195–7, and *KG 100*, pp.60–1; and Ishoven pp.113–16.

75. See Ramsey, Vol. II, pp.280–1, qualified by Ray, pp.162–4.

76. In January 1915 *Konteradmiral* Paul Behncke, Deputy Chief of the Naval Staff, proposed an area attack in this very area to burn out the heart of London. Fortunately for the British, this was beyond the capabilities of the airship services. Douglas H. Robinson, *Zeppelin in Combat*, G. T. Foulis & Co., London, 1962, pp.66–7.

77. *KG 2* began receiving Do 217 twin-engine 'heavy' bombers during March.

78. Foreman, *1941*, p.140.

79. A major raid was defined by the *Luftwaffe* as a mission in which more than 100 tonnes of bombs was dropped on a single target. A heavy attack was one in which 50–99 tonnes was dropped.

80. Stahl, pp.164–5. For descriptions of night operations see Ishhoven, pp.93–6, 111–12, as well as Hermann and Stahl. For a description of a follow-up reconnaissance mission see Ishoven, pp.117–18.

81. Ramsey, Vol. II, p.582.

82. PRO Air 40/288, ibid.

83. Ibid.

84. Poston, pp.124, 164–5, Table 22.

85. See Balke, *KG 2*, pp.195–6.

86. He became *Kommandeur* of *III./KG 26* and later an expert in night fighting, influencing the development of *Zahme Sau*.

CHAPTER TWO

The Cracked Cutlass

The Battle for the Sea Lanes, 1940–1944

Blockade was Germany's only strategic option after the failure of strategic bombing, but this required effective air support to compensate for the Reich's weak navy, whose leader had twice signed away his aviation heritage for a mess of potage.[1]

Raeder had little interest in aviation, and to assure funds for his nascent battle fleet he agreed in 1932 to abandon landplane development and to merge naval and military aviation, leaving himself with only seaplanes.[2] The agreement was signed as landplane performance significantly improved, but Raeder was slow to see the implications and when he realised he had deprived himself of a modern strike force he attempted to reverse the decision. However, his requests broke upon the breakwater of Göring's stubborn determination to control all aviation, reinforced by a strong streak of personal antipathy between the two men. Raeder regarded the 'Fat Man' as a posturing buffoon, while Göring saw in the admiral all the bourgeois features which the Nazis were pledged to remove from German society and his contempt for the Navy was barely concealed. In return for a pledge of support to expand the battle fleet (Plan Z), Raeder struck his colours on 27 January 1939, leaving himself with a *Seeluftstritkräfte* of a few hundred seaplanes to provide tactical air support under the *Führer der Seeluftstreitkräfte (FdL)* led by the naval 'Old Eagle' *Generalmajor* Hermann Bruch.

Victory in the West gave both the *Luftwaffe* and *Admiral* Karl Dönitz's U-boats bases from which to prosecute the maritime war more effectively, and in the aftermath of victory the *Kampf-* and *Stukagruppen* harassed shipping in British Home Waters (including the Western Approaches, 465km west of the British Isles). The bombers flew lone or *Kette*-strength armed reconnaissance missions against targets of opportunity, and *Oberst* Alfred Bülowius's *LG 1* distinguished itself by claiming nine ships sunk or damaged during the first half of July. These attacks merged with preparations for *'Seelöwe'*, for which the Channel's closure was an essential prerequisite, but the British Admiralty's desire to avoid congestion in western ports by running convoys to the eastern ones along the south coast meant that this 'operational' requirement accidentally merged into the 'strategic' anti-shipping campaign that opened on 4 July when 33 *Stukas* of Richthofen's *III./StG 51* attacked convoy OA.178 in Portland. Richthofen was responsible for the western Channel, while the Strait of Dover was the responsibility of the *Kanalkampf-führer*, established the previous day under *Oberst* Johannes Fink, the lugubrious

Table 5. Merchant Ship Losses due to the *Luftwaffe*, July 1940–December 1941

Month	Home Waters		Atlantic		Mediterranean	
Jul 1940	25	(50,528grt)	–		–	
Aug 1940	10	(50,151grt)	–		–	
Sept 1940	6	(22,856grt)	4	(24,819grt)	–	
Oct 1940	1	(840grt)	6	(35,485grt)	–	
Nov 1940	11	(33,453grt)	7	(32,945grt)	–	
Dec 1940	1	(6,941grt)	3	(6,104grt)	–	
Total	**54**	**(164,769grt)**	**19**	**(76,078grt)**	–	
Jan 1941	2	(12,466grt)	16	(65,370grt)	–	
Feb 1941	3	(8,495grt)	19	(79,074grt)	–	
Mar 1941	20	(64,908grt)	6	(27,280grt)	–	
Apr 1941	14	(28,877grt)	11	(46,630grt)	28	(112,537grt)
May 1941	10	(22,173grt)	2	(15,301grt)	8	(39,475grt)
Jun 1941	16	(48,775grt)	5	(7,923grt)	1	(4,352grt)
Total	**65**	**(185,694grt)**	**67**	**(241,578grt)**	**37**	**(156,364grt)**
Jul 1941	5	(5,378grt)	1	(1,174grt)	–	
Aug 1941	2	(6,662grt)	2	(7,189grt)	2	(5,869grt)
Sept 1941	7	(20,246grt)	2	(2,323grt)	1	(5,781grt)
Oct 1941	6	(18,168grt)	1	(2,473grt)	2	(8,861grt)
Nov 1941	5	(10,262grt)	–		–	
Dec 1941	1	(570grt)	–		–	
Total	**26**	**(61,286grt)**	**6**	**(13,159grt)**	**5**	**(20,511grt)**

Notes: Home Waters are defined as those within 40 miles (64km) of a fighter base. Fishing boat losses in 1940 were seven (1,513grt) and in 1941 37 (5,588grt). The October 1940 figure includes two ships (46,550grt) shared with U-boats and counted as half-kills.
Sources: British and Foreign Merchant Ships lost or damaged by enemy action during the Second World War (PRO Adm 186/804); The RAF in Maritime War, Vol. II, App. 17 (PRO Air 41/47).

Kommodore of *KG 2*, whose headquarters were in an old bus parked beside the memorial to Louis Blériot's first trans-Channel flight.[3] He had his own *Holzhammer* (Mallet) *Geschwader*, supported by two *Stukagruppen (II./StG 1* and *IV./LG 1)* and shielded by Osterkamp's *JG 51*, but could call on other units, including Rubens-dörffer's *Jabos*. Between 1 July and 9 August, aided by a naval *Freya (FuMG 80)* surface search radar covering the Strait of Dover, the combined strike forces flew some 1,300 anti-shipping sorties (representing 67% of the total strike effort against Britain from 1 July to early August), while more were flown by Bruch's airmen. Overseas convoys quickly ceased using the Channel, but coastal traffic ran the gauntlet until CW.9 was struck by Richthofen's *Stukas* on 8 August. Half the ships were hit and three (3,581grt) sunk, although the pilots claimed to have sunk 48,500grt (see Table 5 for losses).

Although Fighter Command was committing up to 80% of its patrols over the sea, this was the twenty-sixth convoy to be savaged, for combat air patrols over the ships were weak, rarely more than a dozen aircraft, and operated on the periphery of the radar screen with no radio link to their charges. The bombers' escorts usually kept them at arm's length, and the *Luftwaffe* loss rate on these missions was 4%, with the result that on 11 August sailings along the Channel were temporarily suspended.[4]

Yet *ObdL's* goal was air superiority over England, and with *'Adler'* there was a dramatic drop in *Kampfgruppen* anti-shipping sorties (see Table 6). The *Luftwaffe's* dedicated anti-shipping command, *Generalleutnant* Hans Geisler's *Fliegerkorps X* in Norway and Denmark, harassed shipping off the Scottish and Tyneside coasts, with Geisler's Chief of Staff, 38-year-old *Major* Martin Harlinghausen, setting a personal example, but Geisler lost several *Kampfgruppen* to Kesselring. The subordination of the campaign was clearly indicated by *OKW* Directive 17 of 1 August 1940 on 'The conduct of air and sea warfare against England'. This stated that 'air attacks upon enemy warships and merchant ships may be reduced except where some particularly favourable target happens to present itself, where such attacks would lend additional effectiveness [to continuing the air war against ports] or where such attacks are necessary for the training of aircrew for further operations'. Although ships in harbour seemed like fish in a barrel between July 1940 and July 1941, only 20 (71,566grt) were sunk. However, 148 (693,446grt) were damaged; indeed, the *Luftwaffe* may have been responsible for up to a third of enemy shipping damaged and immobilised and awaiting repair early in 1941 (see Table 7).

The *ObdL* Directive of 20 October ordered Sperrle to use his *Stukas* (reinforced by *KGr 606* and *806*) against shipping in the Channel 'which has appeared again during the last few days', while Fw 200 Condors were to be used in the

---

Table 6, The *Luftwaffe* Campaign against Shipping: *Kampfgruppen* Sorties, August 1940–June 1941

Month	Anti-ship	Bombs (t)	Minelaying	Mines
Aug 1940	239	113	246	328
Sept 1940	90	42	279	669
Oct 1940	60	135	610	562
Nov 1940	23	18	605	1,215
Dec 1940	8	6	192	557
Jan 1941	22	23	58	144
Feb 1941	163	71	207	376
Mar 1941	139	122	234	410
Apr 1941	263	285	212	433
May 1941	211	181	222	363
Jun 1941	312	103	371	647
Total	1,530	1,099	3,236	5,704

Notes: *Luftkrieg Gegen England-Gefechtskalender* (USNA T321, Roll 176). These figures appear to be only *Kampfgruppen* missions, excluding *KG 40*. The May 1941 figure excludes 158 sorties in support of the battleship *Bismarck*.

Table 7. Ships damaged by the *Luftwaffe* off Western Europe, July 1940–March 1944

Year	No of Ships	grt
1940	127	509,071
1941	164	548,488
1942	21	89,354
1943	19	106,373
1944	1	7,130

Notes: Fishing boat casualties were 19 (3,675grt) in 1940, 21 (3965grt) in 1941 and 4 (814grt) in 1943/44.
Source: British and Foreign Merchant Ships lost or damaged by enemy action during the Second World War (PRO Adm 186/804).

northern Irish Sea. The *Stukas* struck shipping in the mouth of the Thames during October and November, flying about 100 sorties, but were quickly neutralised by a dynamic defence, and in December Richthofen was transferred to Romania. The *Stukas* briefly revived the anti-shipping campaign and their departure left it in the doldrums, with much of the success here, and later, reflecting the weak fighter shield and the merchantmen's poor AA armament, so the effect of the relatively small numbers of aircraft committed 'was out of all proportion to the size of the force employed'.[5] Using tactics devised by Harlinghausen, the bombers approached at low level on the beam and released bombs to strike below the waterline. Lightships were also attacked, together with fishing boats, which the *Luftwaffe* regarded as legitimate targets—in contrast to Coastal Command, which sanctioned attacks only if the vessels fired on British aircraft.[6]

The *Kampfgruppen* returned in force to British coastal waters during February, initially to familiarise crews with daylight operations, which had declined sharply since October. However, on 6 February *OKW* published 'Directions for operations against the British war economy' (Directive 23), which belatedly recognised the validity of the Navy's argument that the merchant fleet was Britain's Achilles' heel. There was even a rare hint of *Führer* fallibility, for it began: 'Contrary to our former view, the greatest effect of our operations against the British war economy has been the heavy losses in merchant shipping inflicted by sea and air operations.' A stronger U-boat campaign was expected to lead to the collapse of British resistance, but Hitler warned that 'we are unable to maintain the scale of our air attacks as the demands of other theatres compel us to withdraw increasingly large air forces from operations against the British Isles'. The *Luftwaffe* was to concentrate upon ports as well as shipping, with priority given to the latter, while there was also to be an increase in the minelaying effort. There was an upsurge in activity, aided by improving weather, with nearly 1,100 sorties by the western *Kampfgruppen* and Stumpff until the withdrawal of units during the spring (as Directive 23 had warned) brought much needed relief to the British.

The relief may have been shared by the *Luftwaffe*, for, as convoys received stronger fighter protection, improved communications with the growing number of escort vessels and increased AA armament, the *Kampfgruppen* were increasingly forced to operate at dusk and dawn, using the sun to outline their targets. In the first quarter of 1941 some 60% of ships were sunk in daylight, but in the following quarter this dropped to 24% and the fate of *Oberleutnant* Hatto Kuhn's crew (*2./KG 26*) on 1 March 1941 showed why. While attacking convoy WN.91 off the Moray Firth his He 111 was hit by AA fire which set ablaze one engine and forced him to ditch off the Head of Garness. Kuhn, who was born in New Guinea and was an Olympic-standard pentathlon athlete, and his crew scrambled into a dinghy then paddled towards the Scottish coast, landing east of Banff. They surrendered to the Coast Guard and were then taken into custody by the Chief Constable of Banffshire, Mr George I. Strath! In the 1950s Kuhn joined the *Bundesluftwaffe*, retiring as an *Oberstleutnant*, and in 1977 he returned to Scotland with his son and was photographed with Strath.[7]

The *Luftwaffe* effort extended into the North and Central Atlantic, but support for the U-boats was more by accident than design. Dönitz had foreseen the need for very long-range reconnaissance aircraft and exercises during May 1938 had demonstrated the feasibility of such support. The elegant four-engine Do 26 flying boat was selected. In October 1939 a *Transozeanstaffel* was activated to operate it, but the unit lost most of its aircraft flying transport missions as *KGrzbV 108* during '*Weserübung*', and when the survivors resumed their original role from Brest on 16 August the force proved inadequate. At the end of January 1941 the *Staffel* was disbanded and, after a brief attachment to *I./KG 40*, the Do 26s returned to Germany in March.[8] The *Luftwaffe* intended using the He 177 Greif (Griffon) four-engine bomber for long-range maritime operations, but problems with this aircraft spurred the development of the stop-gap Fw 200 Condor, which entered service with *I./KG 40* in October 1939.

After participating in '*Weserübung*' the Condors were transferred to Brest in July 1940 and flew a dozen minelaying sorties under *Fliegerkorps IV*, but a 16.6% loss rate led *Major* Edgar Peterson (the *Kommandeur*) to telephone a protest to Jeschonnek at the end of the month and the *Gruppe* was then assigned the long-range armed reconnaissance role.[9] The first sorties from Bordeaux-Mérignac were flown on 8 August, flights being extended to Aalborg in Denmark three days later in a 3,500km journey lasting up to 13½ hours as far west as 20°W (600km from the British Isles), carrying six or eight 250kg bombs. The return trip was made the following morning, but, to avoid exhaustion, Peterson restricted crews to three sorties a fortnight. There were rarely more than two a day and their reports proved of little value to Dönitz, having passed first through *Fliegerkorps IV* and the naval command in France, *Marine Gruppe West*.[10] Despite its relatively low speed, the Condor proved to be a potent weapon, especially against unarmed independents (representing 14% of all transatlantic trade at this time) or stragglers. The first success was the sinking of the SS *Goathland* on 25 August in the Western Approaches, but within a month emboldened Condor pilots struck convoys, beginning with OA.218. They would approach at 200–400m (660–1,300ft), then make a shallow dive attack with bombs and automatic weapons to as low as 150m (500ft), the SS *Svien Jarl* being hit 256 times by 20mm cannon fire. The highlight came on 26 October when *Oberleutnant* Bernhard Jope set ablaze the liner *Empress of Britain*, which was later finished off by a U-boat.[11] Jope (who became the last *Kommodore* of *KG 100* in September 1943) and others such as *Leutnant* (later *Oberleutnant*) Hans Buchholz, who claimed 20 ships (200,000grt), and *Hauptmann* Verlohr (*Kapitän* of *1./KG 40*), who sank two ships (10,857grt) on 16 January 1941, became aces during these missions. By the end of the year the Condors had sunk 15 ships (74,543grt), which represented 37% of the total tonnage sunk by air attack and led Churchill to call them the 'Scourge of the Atlantic'.[12]

The operations were mostly with the delicate early production Condors, whose backs were sometimes snapped through the weight of bombs, and it was not until November 1940 that the main production version, the Fw 200C-3, with a stronger structure, became available. As they entered service Raeder secured a brief victory in his campaign for closer cooperation between the U-boats and Condors, for which he received some sympathy from Jeschonnek, who had two brothers in the Navy.[13] During the 'Fat Man''s prolonged leave, Hitler succumbed to naval pressure and on 6 January gave Dönitz operational control of *I./KG 40*, but this stimulated the furious Göring into some dextrous political manipulation. A month after Hitler's decision, Göring requested the *Gruppe*'s return in exchange for an air command in the Atlantic and, despite Raeder's objections, the *Führer* agreed on 28 February, also ordering the creation of what became *Fliegerführer Atlantik*. Not only had the 'Fat Man' thwarted Navy ambitions but he had also cunningly clipped Bruch's wings by confining *FdL* to the North Sea, the Atlantic being divided between the new command and Stumpff's *Luftflotte 5*.[14]

Harlinghausen, the *Luftwaffe*'s leading anti-shipping specialist and a former naval officer, was appointed *FlFü Atlantik* with added responsibilities for Fleet support, meteorological missions and even coastal protection, although he had barely 100 aircraft, including Ar 196 floatplanes![15] Dönitz wanted the Condors to detect and to shadow convoys supplementing his COMINT organisation, the *B-Dienst*, and Harlinghausen agreed to this symbiotic relationship, which might lead to coordinated assaults upon the convoys. Hopes were high after *U37* discovered HG.53, allowing *KG 40* to sink five ships (9,201grt), although 29,000grt was claimed, while at the end of the month a wolfpack savaged OB.288, which was discovered by Condors.[16] Chill reality swiftly overcame the warm glow of anticipation, for inadequate maritime navigation training, exacerbated by out-of-date meteorological data, created errors in location reports of up to 450km, while 19%

of all reports gave errors in course up to 90°.[17] For their part, U-boats were often unable to take sun or star sightings to provide accurate fixes, and, even when convoys were located, the submarines rarely homed in bombers because their short-range radio transmitters were too weak (although loud enough to alert the vengeful British). Harlinghausen was irritated when his aircraft transmitted accurate locations and the U-boats failed to respond, but only when he complained to Dönitz did the embarrassed admiral inform him that none was within striking distance, although the *Luftwaffe* had not been informed. By the end of March Dönitz bowed to the inevitable and abandoned plans for close cooperation in favour of a more flexible arrangement, his War Diary cynically noting that enemy radio signals of air attacks would help his *B-Dienst* to locate the convoys.

During the first quarter of 1941 the Condors continued to prowl the Western Approaches and sank 171,000grt, the majority of the victims lone ships, although in a sustained attack upon OB.290 on 26 February *KG 40* claimed nine vessels (49,865grt). However, with rarely more than six operational aircraft, this was an exception.[18] At first Condor casualties were light, but the Golden Age was coming to an end for the British were strengthening AA armament; indeed, on 21 May 1941 Buchholz was killed when he had the misfortune to encounter the well-armed and alert SS *Umgeni*.[19] Fulmar and Hurricane fighters carried by catapult aircraft merchant (CAM) ships were also encountered, while work had started on the first auxiliary aircraft carrier, HMS *Audacity*. Peterson's base was bombed, with little success, while serious thought was given to ambushing the airmen on the road to the airfield.[20]

By May 1941 *KG 40* had a base at Oslo-Gardersmoen in Norway, with a staging base at Stavanger, and the *Geschwader* could fly three sorties daily to, and from, Bordeaux, yet its inadequacy as a long-range strike force was vividly demonstrated almost immediately. On 24 May the battleship *Bismarck* and cruiser *Prinz Eugen* fought their way into the North Atlantic, sinking the pride of the Royal Navy, the battlecruiser *Hood*.[21] The two ships separated, but almost immediately *Bismarck* was damaged by carrier-borne aircraft and the following day, as she sailed towards the sanctuary of a French base, Göring ordered Stumpff and Harlinghausen to shield her. Harlinghausen was reinforced with five *Kampfgruppen* as air reconnaissance discovered the British Home Fleet closing on *Bismarck*, which was trapped on 27 May some 370km beyond the effective range of the Ju 88 and He 111 bombers. In the next two days 158 sorties were flown, near-missing a cruiser, sinking the destroyer *Mashona* and severely damaging her sister ship *Maori*, but by then *Bismarck* and most of her crew had perished, including the aviation team for her four Ar 196s.[22]

The Condor was adequate only against unarmed merchantmen, but Harlinghausen could look forward with confidence to the summer, when sufficient Condors were assembled to create *IV.(Erg)/KG 40*. But in June 1941 the enemy's growing ASW strength forced Dönitz to operate west of 20°W, beyond the range of the Condors, which now interdicted the sea lanes between Great Britain and Gibraltar, the aircraft being concentrated at Bordeaux from the end of July. Dönitz's decision, coming when it did, irritated Harlinghausen, and relations between the two men appear to have briefly cooled. They recovered, partly because, as ships became more effective in protecting themselves, the Condors had to revert to the reconnaissance role, attacking only when there was cloud cover. With Gibraltar traffic easier to monitor, the Condors flew *Fächer* (Fan) search patterns between 45°N and 34°S and out to 19°W (sometimes 25°W) and found prey for the wolfpacks, which savaged OG.69, OG.71, HG.73 and HG.75 between July and October 1941 to achieve 45% of their total success in tonnage terms.

The attack on OG.76, in September 1941, saw four U-boats lost, partly because of the presence of the carrier *Audacity*, whose fighters shot down two Condors. The Condors became more cautious and their success rate declined during the second half of 1941: losses rose to 13 aircraft, 10 to enemy action, as resistance increased. A captured Condor airman related how, after AA fire had smashed the radio and holed a petrol tank, his pilot was forced to fly across neutral Eire at 1,800m (6,000ft), only to find dense cloud over Brest airfield, which he circled for 20 minutes before crash-landing because of a punctured tyre.[23] With production low, crews were ordered to return to base if even slight damage was suffered, while new aircraft were collected immediately they had been accepted at the factory. To add a new iron to the fire, Harlinghausen sent a few Condor crews on a torpedo-bomber course during the summer of 1941. The first unsuccessful attack took place on 30 December 1941, a ship escaping three 'eels' from a single bomber before the need to assign a Condor *Staffel* as transports in the Mediterranean provided a face-saving means of abandoning this bizarre experiment.[24] The Condor was no stranger to the Mediterranean, for in August six had been sent to assist the maritime war in this theatre with nine He 111 torpedo-bombers as *Kommando Peterson*. The unit arrived in Athens on 26 August to interdict traffic in the Gulf of Suez, but Peterson barely had time to unpack before he was appointed Director of Research with special responsibility for the He 177 and replaced by *Oberst Dr* Georg Paswewaldt, later *Kommodore* of *KG 40*.[25]

Pearl Harbor was the decisive blow to cooperation between the U-boats and the *Luftwaffe*, for it encouraged Hitler's declaration of war upon the United States, although there was a swansong against HG.76 from 14 December during which *Audacity* was sunk by a U-boat after her fighters had despatched another Condor. But in January 1942 Dönitz began a six-month offensive in the Western Atlantic and Caribbean, *Unternehmen 'Paukenschlag'* (Drum Roll), to which he committed most of his boats. Between 1 August 1940 and 31 December 1941 the Condors had 41 contacts with convoys, of which 18 were exploited by U-boats that sank 48 merchantmen (129,771grt), two destroyers, a corvette and *Audacity*.[26]

Harlinghausen was in hospital when HG.76 was attacked, having become well aware of the strength of the defences. In addition to directing operations in the Atlantic, he had agreed with *General der Flieger* Joachim Coeler that their mutual shortage of resources meant dividing British coastal waters between them, with *Fliegerkorps IX* responsible for eastern waters, although little was achieved (see Table 8). Harlinghausen always sought personal experience of front-line conditions, and during a mission over the Irish Sea in November his bomber was crippled by AA fire from his intended victim.[27] He managed to ditch in French waters, from where he was rescued by fishermen, but spent several months in hospital and was formally replaced on 5 January by *Generalleutnant* Ulrich Kessler, a former Deputy Air Attaché in London, who arrived from a training command but had briefly been Geisler's Chief of Staff during May and June 1940.

Had Göring's character been as generous as his girth, the Navy might have met its aspirations in the anti-shipping campaign. However, it sought control through Bruch, who was under the Naval Staff (*Seekriegsleitung*, or *SKL*) operationally and under *ObdL* administratively. Most of his aircraft were seaplanes, whose crews faced danger not only from enemy fighters but also from mechanical failure and the ever-present prospect of a miserable death from drowning or exposure drifting in open rubber dinghies on the unfriendly sea. The *Seenotdienst* could operate only around the Channel, and captivity awaited those who ditched close to British shores elsewhere. *Leutnant zur See* Günther Schröder's crew, for example, whose minelaying He 115 of *KüFlGr 106* force-landed with engine failure 55km off Whitby on 1 July, spent 28 hours in the water before being captured.[28]

Not until November 1940 did Bruch receive an adequate seaplane, but the new Bv 138 three-engine flying boat had to be withdrawn from service after 25 days because the central engine proved temperamental, with seven aircraft lost in accidents. The problems were overcome and it returned to service in mid-1941, proving to be an extremely reliable and robust design (one aircraft fought off Sea

Table 8. *Luftflotte 3* Campaign against Shipping, July–December 1941

Month	Anti-Shipping		Minelaying	Total
	Day	Night		
Jul 1941	171	290	123	584
Aug 1941	227	261	111	599
Sept 1941	133	259	319	711
Oct 1941	126	249	293	668
Nov 1941	207	259	345	811
Dec 1941	99	157	385	641
Total	963	1,475	1,576	4,014

Source: *Luftkrieg Gegen England-Gefechtskalender* (USNA T321, Roll 176). The figures may exclude *KG 40* armed reconnaissance operations.

Hurricanes in a 90-minute battle off Norway), while its 700km radius made it a useful reconnaissance tool. Even as it re-entered service Bruch was under intense pressure as Göring slowly eroded his powers; the establishment of *FlFü Atlantik* was the excuse to detach two *Küstfliegergruppen* to *Luftflotten 3* and *5*, leaving *FdL* with only *KüFlGr 506* at List and *KüFlGr 906* at Aalborg. The former was scheduled to convert to landplanes, but the Navy was discovering that this was the first part of *ObdL*'s acquisition process. During the spring of 1940 *ObdL* converted *KüFlGr 606* and *806* to bombers, but during the summer it 'borrowed' them and was soon ominously describing them as *Gruppen 606* and *806*, then as *Kampfgruppen*.[29] *ObdL*'s ownership, and their conversion to conventional bomber units, became a *fait accompli* in January 1941 in exchange for Hitler's agreement to give Dönitz operational control of the Condors, and their fate was shared by the replacement *KüFlGr 106* and *506* within 18 months.

Bruch's only strike force was a single torpedo-bomber *Staffel*, for which the *Luftflotten* refused to provide reconnaissance data. Nevertheless, *SKL* optimistically claimed on 17 October 1940 that the torpedo-bombers had sunk 82,000grt of shipping in 45 missions during a campaign to obtain bombers, with an eye, as *Generaladmiral* Rolf Carls (commander of *Marine Gruppe Nord*) admitted, to the reinstatement of a naval air arm. Certainly, in November *KüFlGr 706* torpedoed seven ships, sinking five (18,085grt) and damaging two.[30] The bleating lamb attracted the wolf and, having previously ignored torpedo-bombing, Jeschonnek at the end of October ordered conversion training for three bomber crews led by former naval officers who were attached to *6./KG 26*, *Leutnant zur See* Helmut Lorenz claiming the first success for these crews on 26 November. With Geisler (and *6./KG 26*) scheduled for transfer to the Mediterranean, an unseemly tussle developed on 26 November when Göring ordered *Generalleutnant* Hans Ritter, the *Befehlshaber der Marinefliegerverbände* and the *Luftwaffe* liaison officer with the Navy (*General der Luftwaffe beim ObdM*) to requisition torpedoes from seaplane bases. When Raeder protested to Hitler he passed the buck to Jodl, who acted like a weathercock in the blasts from the competing parties. An uneasy *status quo* was maintained until the spring, despite an attempt to break the *impasse* with a meeting between Jeschonnek and his opposite number, *Generaladmiral* Otto Schniewind, on 4 January. Exactly three months later Göring grabbed five of Bruch's torpedoes for the *6./KG 26* crews, who had expended their 'eels' in the Eastern Mediterranean. In the face of obstinate naval opposition, Hitler intervened on 21 April in Göring's favour, with the Mediterranean assigned priority for torpedoes and operations off the British coast prohibited until July. But at the beginning of June a British aircraft carrier was spotted and Bruch commandeered three He 111 torpedo-bombers from a training school. These made a successful attack on 2 June, but the ship sunk proved to be a merchantman disguised as the carrier HMS *Hermes*.[31]

51

Table 9. The *Küstfliegergruppen*

Gruppe	Fate
KüFlGr 106	May 1941 became *Kgr 106*. Aug 1942 became *II./KG6*.
KüFlGr 406	*Gruppe Stab* disbanded Dec 1942. *1.* remained *1./406*, *2.* and *3.* to *SAGr 130* and *131* respectively Jul 1943.
KüFlGr 506	Apr 1941 became *Kgr 506*. Jul 1942 became *III./KG 26*.
KüFlGr 606	Apr 1940 became *Gr/KGr 606*. Sept 1942 became *I./KG 77*.
KüFlGr 706	Jul 1943 became *SAGr 130*, absorbing *1.* and *2.* Former *2./KüFlGr 406* became *3.*
KüFlGr 806	Apr 1940 became *Gr/KGr 806*. Sept 1942 became *III./KG 54*.
KüFlGr 906	*Gruppe Stab* disbanded Apr 1942, leaving independent *Staffeln*. *1.* became *8./KG 26* in Nov 1943, *2.* became *2./KGr 506* in Jun 1942, *3.* became *2./SAGr 131*.

Bruch was increasingly marginalised, with the *Küstfliegergruppen* restricted to reconnaissance and anti-submarine operations until Göring could pillage them as he did so many of Europe's art treasures (see Table 9). Fewer seaplane *Staffeln* gave Jeschonnek the excuse in January 1941 to disband the three *Fliegerführerschulen (See)*, the Warnemünde and Stettin establishments becoming basic training (*A/B*) schools while Pütnitz became *FFS (C) 17* with seaplane training responsibilities. Bruch's own allies undermined him, for, without sufficient major warships to justify an air arm, Raeder in early 1941 channelled officers away from the *Küstflieger-gruppen* towards the U-boats. Many officers had already seen which way the wind was blowing and several U-boat commanders, including *Kapitänleutnante* Ralph Kapitzky, Manfred Kinzel, Günther Krech and Jürgen Quaet-Faslem, transferred from the *Seeluftstreitkräfte* around the outbreak of war.[32]

Bruch's fortunes seemed to turn on 7 April 1942 when *FdL* was subordinated to *Luftflotte 3* and in mid-July was assigned three of Coeler's *Kampfgruppen* for attacks upon Great Britain. Three weeks later, on 6 August, he became responsible for anti-shipping operations in the event of an Allied landing, but after the Dieppe raid the *Kampfgruppen* returned to Coeler and, as the autumn storms dispersed the prospects for an invasion, *FdL* was disbanded on 7 September, with *KGr 606* and *806* being formally absorbed into *Kampfgeschwader* to complete the Navy's defeat. Ritter (now a *General der Flieger*), who had been appointed in 1939 to command all naval aviation including carrier-borne units, recognised by March 1941 that he was little more than a liaison officer.[33] However, the following month two *Aufklärungsgruppen (See)* were created for miscellaneous seaplane units, and in July 1943 Ritter reorganised them into six *Seeaufklärungsgruppen* (*SAGr 125–130*) and added *SAGr 131* the following month. His request for the abolition of his command was not implemented until August 1944, at which time *Generalmajor* Karl-Hennig von Barsewisch, *General der Aufklärungsflieger*, assumed responsibility for seaplanes.

Seaplanes, and especially floatplanes, were the most widely travelled of the *Luftwaffe*'s aircraft; indeed, three, aboard the raiders *Michael* and *Thor*, actually reached Japan. *BdFlGr 196* aircraft assisted *Admiral Hipper, Admiral Scheer, Gneisenau* and *Scharnhorst* during these ships' forays in the Atlantic during 1940 and 1941, and many served aboard the raiders which followed in their wake. They were used mostly to detect convoys or warships, but on occasion aircraft carried in raiders bombed or strafed merchantmen seeking to escape. Most of the aircraft were the nimble Arado Ar 196A, but the raiders *Atlantis, Pinguin* and *Widder* carried the Heinkel He 114B biplane while *Stier* had the Ar 231 originally designed for U-boat use. While the U-boats never embarked the Ar 231, the Focke-Achgelis Fa 330 Bachstelze (Water Wagtail) gyro kite was embarked in Type IX submarines on long-distance patrols and was used largely in the South Atlantic and Indian Ocean from mid 1942.[34]

Meanwhile the new *FlFü Atlantik*, Kessler, sought in vain to revitalise the anti-shipping campaign off western Europe as the emphasis swung to the Arctic and the Mediterranean (see Table 10). When he arrived *FlFü Atlantik* was in the doldrums, able neither to support the U-boats on the other side of the Atlantic nor to interdict the convoy routes themselves (see Table 11). The U-boats renewed their assault upon the convoy routes only in the late summer of 1942 when the weather was deteriorating, and consequently during the whole year there were just three attempts at cooperation between the services, the only success being against HG.84 in June. There was also an embarrassing incident on 21 July when *KGr 106*, hunting a convoy earlier reported south-west of Eire by a Condor, mistakenly attacked

Table 10. Merchantmen Losses due to the *Luftwaffe*, 1942

Month	British Waters		Atlantic		Arctic		Mediterranean	
Jan 1942	3	(9,262grt)	–		–		1	(6,655grt)
Feb 1942	2	(3,700grt)	–		–		4	(19,245grt)
Mar 1942	1	(793grt)	1	(1,757grt)	2	(11,823grt)	3	(19,459grt)
Apr 1942	1	(6,305grt)	–		5	(29,419grt)	–	
May 1942	–		1	(928grt)	10	(54,196grt)	2	(3,871grt)
Jun 1942	1	(345grt)	1	(903grt)	–		7	(33,980grt)
Total	8	(20,405grt)	3	(3,588grt)	17	(95,438grt)	17	
Jul 1942	2	(1,460grt)			13	(72,235grt)	–	
Aug 1942	–		–		–		6	(59,932grt)
Sept 1942	1	(1,892grt)	–		10	(54,669grt)	–	
Oct 1942	–		–		–		1	(5,683grt)
Nov 1942	–		–		1	(7,925grt)	6	(53,868grt)
Dec 1942	–		–		–		1	(2,931grt)
Total	11	(23,757grt)	–		24	(134,829grt)	14	(122,414grt)

Sources: British and Foreign Merchant Ships lost or damaged by enemy action during the Second World War (PRO Adm 186/804); and The RAF in Maritime War, Vol. II, App. 17 (PRO Air 41/47).

Table 11. *Fliegerführer Atlantik* **Strength**

Date	Strike Aircraft	Fw 200
26 Jul 1941	90	25
30 Apr 1942	16	20
31 Mar 1943	–	74

Note: Strike aircraft are twin-engine bombers.

Spanish trawlers and sank three. The coastal campaign was largely restricted to night operations, apart from the activities of *Hauptmann* Frank Liesendahl's *Jabos* (*10./JG 2*), which sank two ships (1,460grt), with the prime objective of providing operational training. Consequently, from October 1942 until the Normandy invasion the *Luftwaffe* failed to sink a single ship in British waters. The only effect of the campaign was to pin down Fighter Command, but as the campaign faded away so the British were able to reduce their activity (see Table 12).

Radar might have helped detect convoys in greater safety, but progress was at a snail's pace. A 136MHz *FuG Atlas* was installed in a Fw 200C-3/U3 in July 1941 and later the similar *FuG Neptun-S* was trialled off Norway, but both proved disappointing, and when the latter was compared in July 1942 with the equivalent British metric (200MHz) ASV (Air-to-Surface Vessel) Mk II, from a crashed Hudson in Tunisia, the British sensor was found to be far superior.[35] By this time *FuG Rostock*, operating at 120MHz and with a 30km range, was under development, but production was so slow that by November 1942 only five Fw 200C-4/U3s in the West had radars, and one of these was the captured set! During the autumn, development began of a fourth sensor, the high-resolution *FuG 200 Hohentwiel*, operating at 550MHz and with a range of 80km. Its smaller antennas did not degrade aircraft performance, and it entered service in August 1943 in the Fw 200C-6, but Kessler's low priority meant that by December 1943 only 16 of 26 Condors in *III./KG 40* had radar.[36]

Although his men claimed to have sunk 13 ships (43,000grt), a destroyer and an auxiliary cruiser, Kessler was in despair and, after learning that he was to lose *KG 6*, he proposed to Jeschonnek on 5 September the disbandment of *FlFüAtlantik*, which he described as 'a living corpse'.[37] He peevishly noted that not only had his command not been expanded into a *Fliegerdivision*, but also some units were being used to bomb Britain. 'Often not a single bomb hits the target and frequently hundreds are unloaded on decoys,' he observed. He questioned the value of retaliatory operations and warned, 'The deadliest blow we can deal the British is in shipping space.' He demanded high-altitude *Lotfe 7D* bomb sights for his Condors, the provision of a torpedo-bomber *Gruppe*, and radar. 'If we succeed in reducing enemy tonnage by several hundred thousand a month, then American and British armament potential will be irrelevant.'[38] Despite Dönitz's support,

Kessler's letter had no effect. During the summer the admiral himself pressed for the introduction of the He 177 into the Atlantic battle, and although Milch informed him on 28 October 1942 that Hitler had ordered that the Eastern Front would have priority on this bomber, *I./KG 50* was soon created at Brandenburg-Briest to work up He 177s for operations over the Atlantic. Unfortunately, the need to supply Stalingrad led to its transfer eastwards for transport operations, where it was joined by 20 Condors which formed *KGrzbV 200*.

An ominous feature of 1942 was the provision Kessler had to make for defensive operations, for during *'Paukenschlag'* enemy aircraft were intercepting U-boats crossing the Bay of Biscay in growing numbers, even on the darkest night. In May Dönitz sought *Luftwaffe* protection, and although no night fighters could be spared Kessler did receive six Ju 88C-6s, which arrived in Bordeaux on 10 June and began patrols a fortnight later, becoming a *Zerstörerstaffel* (later *13./KG 40*).[39] On 20 July *Leutnant* Stöffler claimed two Wellingtons, and by the end of August seven victories had been recorded (Coastal Command lost a total of 26 aircraft in the Bay during this period), encouraging representations from Raeder which led Hitler to demand a *Zerstörergruppe*. A *Stab V.(Z)/KG 40* was formed under *Hauptmann* Korthals at the beginning of September, but two months elapsed before it reached establishment, and even by the end of the year there were only 27 aircraft (eight fell to enemy action). As a stop-gap the nimble Ar 196 floatplanes of *5./BdFlGr 196* were pressed into service, claiming eight victories to 6 September. The British reacted by introducing two squadrons of Beaufighters, the heavyweights first clashing on 8 September when *Leutnant* von Hoensbroech claimed a victory, but the biggest threat to the Beaufighters came from the Fw 190s of *8./JG 2*, which claimed most of the 17 Beaufighters which Coastal Command lost by December despite Fighter and Army Co-operation Command sweeps over *JG 2*'s bases, leading Coastal Command to seek P-38 Lightnings. During the second half of 1942 the pace of battle quickened, with the *Luftwaffe* intercepting Coastal Command aircraft on some 70 occasions and claiming 22 victories. The Command's total losses in this period were 98 aircraft.

Table 12. The Maritime War: Estimated *Luftwaffe* Sorties and Fighter Command Shipping Protection Sorties, 1942–43

Period	Anti-ship	Minelayer	Total	Fighter Command
Jan–Jun 1942	3,610	1,210	4,820	25,173
Jul–Dec 1942	3,910	230	4,140	16,336
Jan–Jun 1943	2,990	400	3,390	6,539
Jul–Dec 1943	3,230	425	3,655	3,717

Notes: *Luftwaffe* figures are rounded to the nearest five and probably include *KG 40* and *Küstfliegerstaffeln* sorties.
Source: Roskill, Vol. II, Tables 13, 19, 33; and Roskill, Vol. III, Table 3.

Both sides realised that 1943 would be decisive on the convoy routes, especially Dönitz, who now had a first-line strength of some 200 boats. He became commander-in-chief of the Navy following Raeder's resignation on 30 January, but he continued to act as U-boat force commander and exploited Hitler's high regard for him in order to secure better air support. He arranged a meeting with Göring on 25 February and demanded 12 reconnaissance sorties a day and more very long-range aircraft, but he was informed that the He 177 would not be available until the autumn, while the four-engine Me 264 *Amerika-Bomber* had made its maiden flight only two months earlier. The following day Hitler intervened and ordered the transfer of three six-engine Bv 222 Wiking (Viking) flying boats from transport duties to Kessler, who, with Dönitz, dreamed of using them for 24-hour missions over the central Atlantic, refuelling from U-boat tankers off the Azores. However, Jeschonnek prevaricated and the Wikings did not become available until the summer. As compensation, on 8 March, *ObdL* did agree to provide Dönitz with 10 Ju 88Hs for very long-range reconnaissance and some four-engine Ju 290s, both equipped with *FuG 200 Hohentwiel*. These were heady days for Kessler, with Sperrle talking of expanding his command to 22 *Gruppen* and renaming it *Fliegerkorps III*, while the Condor force was increased in size to 39 aircraft by mid-March to fly more than 100 sorties a month. In a spurt of optimism Kessler informed Sperrle that with all *Luftflotte 3*'s bombers he could sink 500,000 tonnes a month.[40]

The pace of operations accelerated during the spring, and in March Dönitz came close to winning the Battle of the Atlantic by sinking 108 ships (627,377grt), of which 8% were with *Luftwaffe* assistance. During the first quarter of 1943 only six convoys were shadowed, but of the 74,954grt sunk in coordinated air/U-boat operations during the year, 85% were sunk during this period, mostly in actions against SL.126 and XK.2 during March.[41] After March 1943 *FlFü Atlantik* detected only 14 convoys, while during June 1943 none was attacked in the North Atlantic, allowing Coastal Command to reinforce its ASW sweeps in the Bay of Biscay. Meanwhile the British, exploiting 'Ultra' intercepts, re-routed convoys to ensure that Gibraltar traffic passed beyond Condor range. Meanwhile the growing power of ASW forces inflicted 30% casualties on the U-boats in May, while the introduction of new ciphers effectively neutralised the *B-Dienst*, making aerial reconnaissance vital to Dönitz. The admiral sought to withdraw from the Atlantic but was told unequivocally by Hitler on 31 May, 'There can be no let-up in the U-boat war. The Atlantic, Admiral, is my first line of defence in the West.' Nevertheless, he sympathised over the inadequate air support and falsely blamed the *Luftwaffe*'s insistence on a dive-bombing capability for the delay in introducing the He 177. The Condors continued their tedious patrolling, but often flew in formation to and from their sectors for protection not only against Beaufighters but also against Liberator, Fortress and Sunderland ASW aircraft.[42]

Kessler's frustration mounted, and on 4 May he wrote to Jeschonnek that more than 3.75 million gross registered tons of shipping was escaping interception on the Gibraltar route. He requested the He 177 and the new missiles (Hs 293 and PC 1400 X), with which he could sink up to 500,000grt a month, but, while production supremo Milch was sympathetic, none of this equipment was immediately available. The Condors did receive the *Lotfe 7D* bomb sight, which assured accurate bombing from up to 4,000m (13,000ft) with an average error of 20–30m, and this allowed them to resume the offensive role, with 42 attacks by *III./ KG 40* between 23 February and 1 October (26 upon convoys) and 11 ships (79,050grt) sunk. The most spectacular success came on 11 July when the liners *Duchess of York* and *California,* carrying troops to the Middle East, were sunk, matching Jope's feat of three years earlier.[43] But there were rarely more than half a dozen aircraft available (although 21 struck OS.53/KMS.23 on the evening of 15 August) and the cost was high, with 17 aircraft lost (13 to enemy action). Although the Greif was earmarked for stand-off weapons, the lack of aircraft led *ObdL* to authorise the conversion of Fw 200C-3s to carry the Hs 293 (aircraft so modified were designated Fw 200C-6), and shortly after Christmas *III./KG 40* flew a few fruitless missions until its aircraft were diverted to engaged the Anzio bridgehead in January 1944.

In June 1943 four Wikings of *Aufklärungsstaffel See 222 (1. (F)/SAGr 129* from October) arrived at Biscarosse, but a chance raid by Mosquitos destroyed two of the flying boats at their moorings. When patrols began in September they extended reconnaissance to 30°W, or 1,200km west of the British Isles, into the central Atlantic, while the land-based Ju 290s of *Hauptmann* Hermann Fischer's *FAGr 5* (formed in July) could fly even further westward and took over the long-range reconnaissance mission from the Condors. Better air support with new weapons and sensors in his U-boats gave Dönitz hope of an autumnal renaissance in the Atlantic, but this quickly evaporated. There were not enough aircraft: the Wikings flew only seven sorties in the fortnight to 8 October, and their detection of three convoys could not be exploited. During the last quarter of 1943 only a dozen convoys were detected, from which the U-boats sank only one ship (2,968grt). Even with new equipment during the last four months of 1943, the U-boats sank only 67 ships (369,800grt), yet 72 convoys with 2,218 vessels crossed the Atlantic without loss.[44]

With Jeschonnek's suicide, *General der Flieger* Günther Korten became Chief of Staff and ambitious plans were produced on 26 August for prosecuting the maritime war, including upgrading Kessler's command to *Fliegerkorps III* with 42 *Staffeln* (19 with He 177s, 18 with *Zerstörer* and *Jabos*).[45] On 4 September *ObdL* published a new directive for Kessler, but it was little different from the instructions Harlinghausen had received and all the onerous duties of coastal patrol remained.[46] Kessler sought more long-range aircraft, Hs 293 anti-ship missiles for his Condors and Ju

88H-2 *Zerstörer* to strike the anti-submarine aircraft escorting the convoys, but by mid-November he had only 111 aircraft (more than half of them Ju 88C fighters), although he could call upon Fink's *Fliegerdivision 2*, which was under *ObdL* control, to attack shipping in either the Atlantic of the Mediterranean. He tried to remain optimistic and on Christmas Eve claimed that with some 500 aircraft he could sink 500,000 grt a month, but he admitted that his command was being increasingly marginalised, partly because the Allies were tightening their control over the Bay of Biscay, reminding him of the North Sea in the Great War. The matter was certainly being considered at the highest levels, and on 19 December Dönitz's inconclusive conference with Hitler and Göring on the inadequate air support led him to interdict Gibraltar traffic, where Kessler could assist him, to recoup his losses. His hopes were again dashed, for each Gibraltar convoy now had an escort carrier and a fighter direction ship, and the disastrous attack upon MKS.30/SL.129 (see below) saw few U-boats able to exploit the convoy's detection while three were lost together with two reconnaissance aircraft.

Much was expected during 1943 of stand-off weapons, not only torpedoes but also missiles, which began development in 1938. From the spring of 1942 orders were placed for the Rheinstahl PC 1400 X (commonly called Fritz X) radio-guided bomb and the Henschel Hs 293, a rocket-propelled version of the SC 500, both being controlled through dedicated versions of the *FuG 203 Kehl III* transmitter and *FuG 230 Strassburg* receiver.[47] In the spring of 1943 II./KG 100 (Do 217 E-5) was formed around *EK 15* under *Major* Fritz Auffhammer, who became *Kommodore* of *KG 100* in May 1943 and was replaced by *Hauptmann* Franz Hollweck, but the Fritz X *Erprobungskommando* (*EK 21*) was immediately transferred to Stalingrad (as *KGr 21*) for transport duties and was not re-formed until April 1943, when it was absorbed by *Hauptmann* Ernst Hetzel's III./KG 100 (Do 217K-2). After two months' training the two *Gruppen* became operational during July, not in the Atlantic, as Göring hoped, but in the Mediterranean because of the landings in Sicily.[48]

The first Fritz X was launched in vain on 21 August against targets in Augusta harbour, and further missions followed off Sicily. Hollweck's II./KG 100 was assigned to Kessler on 31 July, but instead of a dramatic début against convoys it was to support Dönitz's U-boats, now under severe pressure in the Bay of Biscay from both aircraft and warships. With a large wolfpack scheduled to depart, the Navy demanded *Luftwaffe* action against enemy ASW groups, and between 25 and 27 August Hollweck's men flew 25 sorties which severely damaged two ships, while *Hauptmann* Auffhammer and *Oberleutnant* Paulus sank the sloop HMS *Egret* together with a team of scientists who had embarked to study the Hs 293.[49] The Royal Navy hastily withdrew westwards but returned within a fortnight following the Allied landing in Salerno and Hollweck's transfer to *Luftflotte 2*. On the eve of the landing Italy defected, and on 9 September the Italian battle fleet under Admiral Carlo Bergamini left Spezia for Bône in North Africa, but Bergamini, in the battleship *Roma*, diverted eastwards. German reconnaissance aircraft discovered the fleet east of Sardinia and Fink despatched 11 bombers led by the new *Kommandeur* (*Major* Jope) of *III./KG 100*, which the Italians believed were friendly when they circled his ships. Unchallenged, Jope hit *Roma* with a Fritz X and the battleship blew up with most of her crew, including Bergamini, while *Oberfeldwebel* Kurt Steinborn damaged the battleship *Italia*.[50]

The need to support operations in Italy, and the desire to interdict Mediterranean convoys, prevented this success from being repeated in the Atlantic. Although Kessler received the He 177s of *I./KG 50* (*II./KG 40* from October 1943) with Hs 293s, their début was delayed until 21 November, when 16 aircraft attacked MKS.30/SL.129, sinking a 4,405grt straggler (by *Hauptmann* Nuss) at the cost of 40 missiles (a quarter of which failed) and three aircraft (an 18% loss rate).[51] The *Gruppe* was then switched to the Mediterranean, returning during late December in a vain attempt to save three destroyers from British cruisers. Daylight operations having failed, the He 177s switched to night attacks by pairs of *Ketten*; one would drop 50kg flares to silhouette targets for the other, but after January 1944 they sank only one ship and damaged another.[52] On the evening of 12 February the He 177s and Condors attacked OS.67/KMS.41 in mid-Atlantic, but fighters from the escort carrier HMS *Pursuer* destroyed half the attackers which *FlFü Atlantik* despatched in its last strike mission.

Over the Bay of Biscay Kessler was on the defensive as Coastal Command intensified its ASW patrols to fly some 9,700 sorties (others were flown by US aircraft) during 1943. Flying in formations of up to eight aircraft, the Ju 88C *Zerstörer* of *V./KG 40* (*I./ZG 1* from October 1943) engaged the lumbering Halifaxes, Liberators, Sunderlands and Wellingtons on 137 occasions and shot down 69, as well as a DC-3 airliner on 1 June with the loss of all on board including the British film star Leslie Howard. But the Beaufighter proved superior to the Ju 88C and on 5 March Kessler warned that he could no longer protect the U-boats; indeed, the *Zerstörer* were ordered not to engage Beaufighters unless they had a 2:1 superiority.[53] In May the British tightened their grip on the skies by introducing Mosquito fighters, and although the *Zerstörer* triumphed in the first clash on 11 June the British had the advantage and on 1 December four Mosquitos, outnumbered 2:1 by Ju 88s, destroyed half their opponents. In fact, during the year the British lost only nine aircraft in 27 fighter-versus-fighter engagements.[54] The Fw 190s of *JG 2* and its *Jagdkommando Brest* on the Brittany peninsula were the only fighters which could match the British, and they demonstrated this on 13 June by destroying three Mosquitos off the Isles of Scilly. Six Fw 190s with long-range tanks were assigned to *5./BdFlGr 196* (*1./SAGr 128* from July 1943) and flew escort missions until early 1944, when they were absorbed by *III./ZG 1*.[55] In mid-July Kessler was briefly reinforced by *III./ZG 1* with Me 410s, but within a fortnight the *Gruppe* returned to the Reich for home defence, being briefly replaced by *II./ZG 1* (Bf 110G-2) from the Mediterranean, which also went to the Reich after 10 weeks, during which it lost 12 aircraft. The attempts to clear the skies over the Bay cost 122 aircraft in 1943 (79 to enemy action, including 48 *Zerstörer* and six Fw 190s).

Yet Dönitz complained to Hitler on 5 June that '*Luftwaffe* support is completely inadequate', just as Sperrle was informing *Marinegruppe West* that air–sea rescue of U-boat crews had priority over maritime reconnaissance.[56] The same day Coastal Command reinforced its Bay patrols, while improved coordination allowed the reinforced Allied ASW forces, with Beaufighter and Mosquito support, to slaughter the U-boats. Of 86 which attempted the passage across the Bay between 1 July and 2 August, 16 (18%) were sunk, although their stronger *Flak* armament led to pitched battles between hunter and hunted. The *Luftwaffe* rarely intervened, although on 12 July Ju 88s shot down two aircraft harassing *U441*, and at the end of the month Dönitz informed Hitler that the U-boats would be on the defensive pending the delivery of new equipment. Only by abandoning group surface sailings and relying on slower underwater transit did Dönitz end the slaughter in the Bay, with the result that the British ASW patrols were never as successful again, as the British historian ruefully admits.[57]

A feature of Coastal Command operations was the use of centimetric (3GHz) ASV Mk III, which entered service in February 1943. Almost immediately Bomber Command's H2S navigation radar, also a centimetric sensor, was captured by the Germans, who dubbed it the 'Rotterdam Device' because the first example was found in a shot-down Stirling near the Dutch port.[58] Dönitz quickly realised the implications for his *Metox* radar warning receiver, and Martini (who chaired the *Arbeitsgemeinschaft Rotterdam*, or Rotterdam Commission) agreed to give the U-boat service priority in ESM technology.[59] To discover exactly what radar frequencies the Allies were using, a SIGINT unit, *Sonderkommando Rastädter* (Do 217, He 111, Ju 88), was attached to *KG 40* in June, and tests during July and August appeared to corroborate fears that the enemy were homing on emissions from the *Metox* itself—fears fed by the lies of a talkative Coastal Command prisoner the following month.[60] It was only after a Wellington with the new radar crashed in France in November that the Germans had the key to unlock the problem of their high U-boat losses. Curiously, one German emitter which proved valuable to the Allies was the *Sonne* (Sun) radio navigation system, whose transmitters from 1941 were established from Stavanger in Norway to Seville in neutral Spain. The system, known to the Allies as Consol ('With Sun', in Spanish), provided accurate navigation data and remained in service into the 1970s.

The New Year of 1944 saw Coastal Command maintaining pressure over the Bay of Biscay, flying 4,439 anti-submarine and 796 fighter sorties in the first five months but with decreasing success. Of 169 U-boats which crossed the Bay in the first quarter of 1944, only three were sunk and six damaged (5%), and in May the

British ended their 41-month-old Bay offensive, having sunk 50 boats at a total cost of 350 aircraft.[61] Despite Dönitz's constant bitching to Hitler, the *Luftwaffe* helped where possible, but at great cost; for example, in escorting a Japanese submarine into French waters on 10 March *ZG 1* lost half its aircraft, including the *Kommodore, Oberstleutnant* Janson, while in assuring the safe passage of *U255* a month later the *Zerstörer* lost seven Ju 88s and destroyed four Mosquitos. By D-Day *ZG 1* had destroyed only 10 ASW aircraft (U-boat *Flak* destroyed 12) since the New Year, while the *Luftwaffe* lost 66 aircraft, 28 to enemy action. However, Dönitz decided to conserve his strength from May in anticipation of the Allied invasion, depriving the *Geschwader* of its *raison d'être*.[62]

His decision was influenced by the *Luftwaffe*'s failure to detect targets, despite the U-boats' returning to the Western Approaches in mid-January 1944 after a three-year absence in the hope of exploiting air reconnaissance. During the first two months four convoys were detected, but escort carriers and Beaufighter patrols prevented the *Luftwaffe* from maintaining contact and *FAGr 5* lost three Ju 290s while shadowing ONS.29 to 18 February in what proved to be *FlFüAtlantik*'s last success in locating convoys. Dönitz ordered the U-boats back into the central Atlantic, and when he met Hitler on 26 February he again sought air support, including more long-range aircraft. Less than a month later, on 22 March, heavy losses forced the U-boats out of the central Atlantic; they had sunk only three of 3,360 ships which crossed the ocean in the first quarter of 1944. Dönitz refused to return without improved air support, and this reduced *Luftwaffe* long-range maritime reconnaissance to a token effort until the invasion in June, with missions often flown to acquire meteorological data.[63] Ironically, in January 1944 Kessler received a prototype six-engine Ju 390, which successfully completed a proving flight within 25km of New York city, while there was talk of using the Me 264 to bomb the port. But these plans were overtaken by events.

Kessler's failure was a growing embarrassment for Göring, especially as Hitler favoured Dönitz, and on several occasions in his presence criticised the *Luftwaffe* for delays in developing the He 177. Since the Munich Crisis the *Reichsmarschall* had felt that Kessler was a 'moaning Minnie', and this view was reinforced by *FlFü Atlantik*'s constant, but justified, demands for aircraft. Although Kessler was not informed, *ObdL* decided on 7 February to disband *FlFü Atlantik*, and did so as casually as it had activated the command. At the end of February *Fliegerkorps X* commander *Generalleutnant* Alexander Holle ambled into Kessler's noon conference and informed him of *ObdL*'s decision, although this was not confirmed by teleprinter for several embarrassing hours and Kessler officially retained his command until 15 March.[64] As compensation for his humiliation Kessler was awarded a *Ritterkreuz* and a new assignment as Air Attaché to Tokyo, although nearly a year elapsed before he could begin his journey in a U-boat! This was lucky to avoid the fate of so many of her sisters, but while still in the Atlantic the fall of Germany meant that the crew had to surrender. Holle, for his part, followed Dönitz's example and merely conserved his anti-shipping forces for the Allied invasion.

Meanwhile the Arctic and then the Mediterranean had become the prime ship killing grounds, although the 'strategic' and 'operational' roles became blurred as attacks became extensions of campaigns. During 1942 the emphasis was in the Arctic, as *Luftflotte 5* sought to cut the Allies' shortest supply route to hard-pressed Russia. Even during the Battle of Britain Stumpff's *Kampfgruppen* had roved Britain's northern waters, sinking 67,000grt between September and December 1940, but Geisler's transfer to Sicily had reduced the scale during 1941.With *'Barbarossa'* the *Kampfgruppen* concentrated on supporting the advance on Murmansk, with occasional anti-shipping operations until October (see Table 13).

Norway ceased to be an outpost following a British raid on the Lofoten Islands in December 1941, which increased Hitler's fears of an invasion. The garrison was substantially reinforced with men, warships (including the new battleship *Tirpitz*) and torpedo-bombers, the last sent on the *Führer*'s specific instructions, while half a dozen Condors from *7./KG 40* arrived at Stavanger-Vaernes to extend reconnaissance.[65] Yet during the winter crisis on the Eastern Front the German Navy sank only one of the 103 ships carrying supplies to north Russia, snapping Hitler's patience. On 11 March 1942 he demanded intensive attacks upon Russia-bound convoys by both Stumpff and the Navy.

On paper the task was easy, for the polar ice ensured that enemy shipping sailed no more than 445km from the *Luftwaffe*'s chain of bases within the Arctic Circle, but the region's capricious weather and frequent mists hindered operations. A strike force of 115 aircraft was assembled under *FlFü Lofoten* (*Oberst* Ernst-August Roth), including torpedo-bombers from *KG 26* and *1./KüFlGr 406* (He 115), although *I./KG 26* soon lost its *Kommandeur* (*Oberstleutnant* Hermann Busch) and staff, who became *FlFü Nord (West)*. Roth, aged 44, was an 'Old Eagle' who had been in the naval aviation team at the *RLM* before transferring to the *Luftwaffe*. A former *Kommodore* of *KG 40*, *KG 28* and *KG 26*, he remained in

---

Table 13. *Luftflotte 5* **Maritime Activity, July–December 1941**

Month	Anti-ship	Recon	Coastal	Total	Losses
Jul	113	65	193	371	3
Aug	71	46	385	502	7
Sept	107	242	184	533	4
Oct	8	117	233	358	1
Nov	–	107	446	553	4
Dec	–	92	327	419	3
Total	299	669	1,768	2,736	22

Note: Reconnaissance includes meteorological.
Source: *Luftkrieg Gegen England-Gefechtskalender* (USNA T321, Roll 176).

Table 14. Major Operations against Russian Convoys

Date	Convoy	Sorties/Losses	Ships claimed		Ships sunk	
May 25–30	PQ.16	311/3	7	(31,000grt)	10	(54,196grt)
Jul 9–10	PQ.17	216/7	22	(142,216grt)	14½	(86,469grt)
SepT 13–19	PQ.18	337/20	8	(49,000grt)	10	(54,669grt)

Note: One ship in PQ.17 was abandoned after an air attack but was finished off several days later by a U-boat.
Sources: *Studien zum Luftkrieg: Gedanken zum Einsatz der Luftwaffe im Luftkrieg über See* (USNA T971, Roll 16, fr.325ff); British and Foreign Merchant Ships lost or damaged by enemy action during the Second World War (PRO Adm 186/804); Irving, *PQ 17*; and Plocher, *1942*, pp.34–61.

Norway for the duration, becoming a *Generalleutnant* and *Kommandierender General der deutschen Luftwaffe in Norwegen* in February 1945. Busch was replaced by *Hauptmann* Eicke, then, in July 1942, by *Major* Werner Klümper.

When convoys assembled Stumpff would be alerted by COMINT, spies and prisoner interrogations, and then would increase air reconnaissance between Iceland and Spitzbergen, the southern missions flown by Busch with three *Fernaufklärungsstaffeln* as well as *I./KG 40* and *Wekusta 5*, with sorties (often lasting up to 10 hours) increasing as the convoy's estimated departure time drew near. Once it was detected, one or two Bv 138s or Fw 200s (one with *Neptun* radar), flying up to 1,000km from their bases, would shadow it while the strike force was grounded to conserve strength, taking off only under orders from Stumpff's headquarters. Units would assemble at Bodø, Bardufoss and Banak under Roth, whose reconnaissance aircraft trailed the convoy until it passed the line Spitzbergen–North Cape, whereupon *FlFü Nord (Ost)*, under the able *Oberst* Holle—the Condor Legion's first Chief of Staff, former *Kommodore* of *KG 26* and future commander of *Fliegerkorps X*—would take over and strike forces would move to Kirkenes or Petsamo to begin attacks.

Between late March and mid-May they struck four convoys, but bad weather and poor visibility disrupted operations, with only some 100 fruitless strike sorties at the cost of about 10% of the aircraft. Improving weather combined with an intensive reconnaissance effort to detect potential invasion forces led to ferocious attacks upon PQ.16, PQ.17 and PQ.18 in operations involving some 860 sorties, including 243 by torpedo-bombers, whose attacks began a minute after those of the dive-bombers or horizontal bombers (see Table 14). *Luftwaffe* analysis judged the torpedo to be the most effective means of sinking ships, with one vessel sunk for every eight sorties (compared with 19 bombing sorties), and it was estimated that nearly a quarter of the 340 torpedoes released struck a target.

The massacre of PQ.17 was made possible by the Admiralty's dispersal of the convoy, which, it feared, was about to be attacked by *Tirpitz*, but the *Luftwaffe*'s hopes of repeating this success were dashed when later convoys were more strongly escorted. The escorts included the aptly named escort carrier *Avenger*, whose fighters helped destroy 20 of *KG 26*'s aircraft, including 12 torpedo-bombers, and forced reconnaissance aircraft into the clouds.[66] Operation 'Torch', the Allied invasion of North Africa, ended Stumpff's brief moment of glory for most anti-shipping units were despatched to the Mediterranean and *Luftflotte 5* returned to being a backwater. As convoys sailed through the Arctic winter Stumpff deployed pairs of bombers on ineffectual armed reconnaissance, but the following summer the overstretched Royal Navy abandoned these hazardous missions until September, by which time Stumpff had 13 Condors (*3./KG 40*) but no strike force. During the winter of 1943/44 escort carriers posed a new hazard and those accompanying JW.58 in March 1944 destroyed six reconnaissance aircraft, while from the same month the detection of westbound convoys became more difficult because of aggressive Soviet air patrols. Irritated at *Luftwaffe* impotence, *Marinegruppe Nord* demanded the return of the strike force, but on 2 April 1944 *Luftflotte 5* (now under the former night fighter commander *General der Flieger* Josef Kammhuber) informed the Navy that the threat from carrier fighters meant that it would no longer authorise daytime maritime reconnaissance, and this virtually ended the *Luftwaffe*'s threat to the Arctic convoys.[67]

Its impotence was earlier emphasised during the summer of 1943 when the Home Fleet failed to provoke any reaction after trailing its coat only 275km off the Norwegian coast as a diversion during the invasion of Sicily; yet in the same waters, only three years earlier, *Kampf-* and *Stukagruppen* had decimated the Royal Navy. A perennial problem for *Luftflotte 5* was the threat of carrier raids beginning in July 1941, not only by British ships but also by the USS *Ranger* (which sank 20,000grt of shipping), six being made between April and June 1944 including a 120-aircraft strike against *Tirpitz*, which was hit 14 times. Only the first raid saw any *Luftwaffe* reaction, and this was accidental, when a *Stukastaffel* returning from a mission encountered and strafed the carriers. Other threats came from Britain's Coastal Command and the Soviet Navy's Air Force (briefly reinforced by an RAF detachment in the winter of 1941/42), while Bomber Command's interest was largely confined to minelaying sorties.[68] Stumpff relied upon *ad hoc Jagdgruppen* during 1941, but the New Year saw the creation of *JG 5 'Eismeer'* under the Spanish Civil War veteran *Oberleutnant* Gotthardt Handrick, ultimately with four *Jagdgruppen*, a *Zerstörerstaffel* and a *Jabostaffel*, and half the fighters based in the Arctic Circle protecting coastal shipping. Russian anti-ship sorties doubled every year, with the pressure especially noticeable from 1943, when the Northern Fleet flew 1,974 sorties against convoys, although *JG 5* ensured that no ships were lost between 5 June and 20 October and claimed half of *Luftflotte 5*'s 1,400 victories that year.[69] Outside the Arctic Circle the *Jagdgruppen* faced Coastal Command raids not only upon shipping but also upon ports and airfields, while *I./JG 5* claimed 18 Beaufort torpedo-bombers when defending the cruiser *Prinz Eugen* on 15 May 1942. The most serious threat came on 24 July 1943 when 309 B-17 Fortresses unsuccessfully attacked Bergen in 10/10ths cloud conditions, which prevented both interception and an opportunity to repeat a success of September 1941 when two out of four British Fortress Is attacking the 'pocket battleship' *Admiral Scheer* in Oslo were shot down.

The priority assigned to home defence meant that *JG 5* lost half its strength in November 1943, stretching the remaining fighters to breaking point, and when *Marinegruppe Nord* requested permanent fighter cover for *Tirpitz*'s base in Alta Fjord on 20 March 1944 *ObdL* refused because *JG 5* had a base at nearby Banak, some 80km away by air. This set the scene for *Luftflotte 5*'s biggest scandal, involving *Major* Heinrich Ehrler, *Kommodore* of *JG 5* and its greatest ace with some 200 victories. On 12 November 1944 the RAF's No 617 Squadron bombed and sank *Tirpitz*, but, although the bombers were detected and tracked by radar, *JG 5* failed to intercept, for reasons which are obscure but probably involved an inter-service communications failure. Although the *Jagdgruppen* were some 200km away, Ehrler personally sought out the enemy, but there were vicious rumours that as 1,000 Germans died he was on unofficial leave with a girlfriend in Oslo. There can be little doubt that subsequent events were motivated by political considerations, with Dönitz now in the ascendant over Göring, who court-martialled the ace and found him guilty of dereliction of duty. Ehrler was saved from execution by his exemplary combat record and transferred to the Reich, where he flew Me 262 jets, adding at least five victories before being shot down and killed on 4 April 1945.[70]

The support of German ground forces advancing on Murmansk was *Luftflotte 5*'s other mission from the summer of 1941, with the task assigned to seven *Staffeln*, later reinforced by a *Kampfgruppe*, of *Oberst* Andreas Nielsen's *FlFü Nord* with some 170 aircraft.[71] By December, when Nielsen's command was renamed *FlFü Nord (Ost)* (it was later handed to Holle), the front was static under the newly created *20. Gebirgsarmee*, and the following year Stumpff established a tactical headquarters in Finland to control Holle, Roth and *Luftgau zbV 1* (later *Finnland*), with Nielsen responsible for the remainder of Norway, commanding *FlFü Nord (West)* and *JaFü Norwegen*. Crises in Russia and the Mediterranean stripped Stumpff of his strike force, and by 5 November 1943 he had only 230 aircraft, whose offensive elements consisted of a *Jabostaffel* and *Kette Lappland* with five Ju 88s, while 10 days later the Finland headquarters closed.

By then Germany was aware of Helsinki's peace moves to the Allies, and, in anticipation of Finnish defection, plans were made to retreat to a bridgehead around the North Cape (*Unternehmen 'Birke'*, or Birch), while supplies were built up in bases in northern Norway as those in central Finland dwindled. However, Germany was forced to gamble by reinforcing Finnish forces, including the Air

Force, which had a heterogeneous collection of American, British, French, Dutch and Russian aircraft. Following a visit by Finnish Air Force (*Ilmavoimat*) commander General J. F. Lundquist to Germany on 17 January, Göring authorised the delivery of 159 Bf 109Gs (known as '*Mersus*' to the Finns) and 23 Ju 88A-4s, as well as radar sets, although keeping a wary eye on their allies, whose front remained quiet until June 1944, with *Luftwaffe* activity, as shown in Table 15, at a low level.[72]

From 1943 onwards the Mediterranean was the main venue for *Luftwaffe* anti-shipping operations; these had always been a major *raison d'être* for the *Luftwaffe*'s presence in the theatre since December 1940, although then the priority had been the erosion of the Royal Navy. Only the capture of Tunisia in May 1943 gave the Allies the opportunity to exploit the Mediterranean sea lanes, and until then the *Luftwaffe*'s interdiction of shipping was largely an 'operational' extension of the land campaigns in Greece, Crete and North Africa which provided an anvil upon which the Germans, ably assisted by the *Regia Aeronautica*, could hammer the British mercantile marine. They became 'strategic' only when the Axis sought to prevent supply convoys reaching Malta, the key to the Mediterranean, leading to ferocious air–sea battles, especially in 1942.[73] In June and August 1942 the latter missions involved 29% and 81% of all *Fliegerkorps II*'s strike sorties (see Table 16), but a considerable effort was also expended upon reconnaissance. Shipping in the Gulf of Suez was occasionally interdicted, although the first mission, on 17 January 1941, was a catastrophe since eight He 111s of *II./KG 26*, led by Harlinghausen, encountered headwinds which forced down seven; several pilots landed behind enemy lines, including Harlinghausen, although he was eventually rescued.[74] *Kommando Peterson* was sent to Athens for such missions, and on 3/4 September 1941 *Leutnant* Meyer flew a successful 12-hour sortie, hitting a ship—only to be lost in unknown circumstances two days later.

The presence of torpedo-bombers in *Kommando Peterson* reflected the Mediterranean influence upon German development of the torpedo. The *Regia Aeronautica* had made a considerable investment in this form of attack, and its torpedo-bombers (*aerosiluranti*) earned respect from friend and foe. The *Luftwaffe*

Table 15. *Luftflotte 5* **Activity, 1944**

	Sorties	Lost	Percentage
Fighters	3,376	42	1.24
Day Strike	78	5	6.41
Reconnaissance	3,026	19	0.62
Monthly average	540	5	0.92

Note: Day strikes by *Kampf-* and *Schlachtverbände*.
Source: Luftwaffe Activity, Vol. I (IWM Tin 192, fr. 1044).

Table 16. Anti-shipping Sorties, Mediterranean, 1942

	Jan	Feb	Mar	Apr	May	Jun	Jul	Aug	Sept	Oct	Nov	Total
FlK II	40	55	70	–	5	120	25	270	–	5	5	595
FlK X	70	75	45	15	30	180	5	25	150	–	15	610
Total	110	130	115	15	35	300	30	295	150	5	20	1,205

Note: *Fliegerkorps X* figures include *FlFü Afrika*.

Maritime reconnaissance sorties, Mediterranean 1942

	Jan	Feb	Mar	Apr	May	Jun	Jul	Aug	Sept	Oct	Nov	Total
FlK II	90	75	180	120	70	145	45	125	90	125	55	1,120
FlK X	70	75	45	15	30	180	5	25	150	–	15	610
Total	160	150	225	135	100	325	50	150	240	125	70	1,730

Note: *Fliegerkorps II* figures are rounded out to the nearest 5.
Sources: Santoro, L'Aeronautica Italiana nella Seconda Guerra Mondiale, Vol. 2 pp.295, 357, quoted in Gundelach, Apps 7 and 8.

adopted both the standard Italian torpedo (as the F5a) and the circling torpedo (as the LT350), the latter first being used by *KG 54* during Operation 'Vigorous' in June 1942.[75] The availability of high-performance torpedoes, which ended his dependency upon the Navy, led Göring to plan a three-*Gruppen* torpedo-bomber force based on *KG 26*. From late 1941 *Oberst* Stockman's *KSG 2*, with *IV.(Erg)/KG 26*, was established at Grosseto, south of Leghorn, where it remained until transferred to Riga in 1943, despite the fact training there was impeded by the freezing of the Baltic. As torpedo-bomber supremo, Harlinghausen, a strong advocate of the weapon, was selected in January 1942 to become both *KG 26's* new *Kommodore* and *Bevollmächtigten für das Lufttorpedowesen* (Plenipotentiary for Airborne Torpedoes), with a staff including *Oberleutnant zur See* (later *Kapitänleutnant*) Rolf Thomsen, who later won the *Ritterkreuz* with Oakleaves as a U-boat commander for reasons which are obscure. Harlinghausen produced ambitious plans for two torpedo-bomber *Geschwader*, but his experienced 6./*KG 26* was transferred to the Crimea in January 1942 and within six months reverted to bombing. In courses directed by Klümper, soon to be its *Kommandeur*, I./*KG 26* crews flew five day and three dawn/dusk practice sorties in He 111s to qualify, but in March 1942 they were transferred to Norway, where they were joined by the Ju 88-equipped III./*KG 26* to attack Russian convoys (see above). Both *Gruppen* returned to the Mediterranean to engage the Allies' North African beach-heads in November 1942, just as II./*KG 26* arrived in Grosseto for conversion. At the same time Göring converted Harlinghausen and the *KG 26* staff into *Führer der Luftwaffe in Tunis* (*FdL Tunis*), with Klümper later replacing him.

The torpedo-bombers often staged through Sardinia, but their successes were insufficient to prevent the fall of Tunisia, which allowed the Allies to run convoys

Table 17. Merchantmen Losses due to the *Luftwaffe*, January 1943–May 1944

Month	Atlantic		Mediterranean		Arctic	
Jan 1943	–		5	(25,503grt)	–	
Feb 1943	–		–		–	
Mar 1943	2	(25,150grt)	6	(45,785grt)	1	(7,173grt)
Apr 1943	–		–		–	
May 1943	2	(6,687grt)	3	(14,255grt)	–	
Jun 1943	2	(5,270grt)	1	(813grt)	–	
Jul 1943	6	(66,803grt)	8	(54,306grt)	–	
Aug 1943	1	(6,070grt)	3	(11,567grt)	–	
Sept 1943	1	(7,135grt)	3	(15,770grt)	–	
Oct 1943	–		3	(15,504grt)	–	
Nov 1943	1	(4,405grt)	6	(58,047grt)	–	
Dec 1943	–		17	(75,471grt)	–	
Total	15	(121,520grt)	55	(317,021grt)	1	(7,173grt)
Jan 1944	–		4	(24,237grt)	–	
Feb 1944	1	(7,264grt)	2	(14,352grt)	–	
Mar 1944	–		–		–	
Apr 1944	–		3	(19,755grt)	–	
May 1944	–		1	(2,873grt)	–	
Total	1	(7,264grt)	10	(61,217grt)	–	

Note: The Mediterranean total includes ships lost in harbour and those lost supporting amphibious operations. Excluded are three sailing vessels (253grt).
Sources: British and Foreign Merchant Ships lost or damaged by enemy action during the Second World War (PRO Adm 186/804); The RAF in the Maritime War, Vol. VII, Pt I; and Mediterranean Reconquest and the Submarine War, May 1943–May 1944 (PRO Air 41/75, App. 30).

of more than 100 ships through the Mediterranean, freeing thousands of tonnes of shipping which was no longer forced around the Cape of Good Hope.[76] The strategic implications and the Allies' reliance upon shipping for offensive operations were anticipated in November by the establishment of *Fliegerdivision 2* in Marseilles under Fink (now a *Generalmajor*) as an anti-shipping command, with *KG 26* (torpedoes) and *KG 100* (missiles), while *I.* and *II./KG 77* began converting to torpedo-bombing (see Table 17 for *Luftwaffe* successes). Fink wished to attack every eastbound convoy, but Klümper advocated selective blows and took his campaign to the top, informing Jeschonnek that he would resign if he did not get his way. This led to *Unternehmen 'Paukenschlag'*, when *KG 26* (reinforced by crews from *IV.(Erg)/KG 26*), with 68 aircraft, struck a convoy off Alboran on 13 August, claiming to have sunk 170,000grt for the loss of 12 aircraft (18%) although only two ships were damaged.[77] Having 'proved' his point, Klümper was extremely active between August and October, flying 316 sorties and claiming 64 ships (423,000grt) and 10 warships hit for the loss of 55 aircraft (17%) and 31 crews. According to Allied intelligence, *Major* Klaus Nocken (*Kommandeur* of *III./ KG 26* to February 1944) was shot down five times into the Mediterranean and on the last occasion was in the water for 12 hours before being picked up by a U-boat.[78] Torpedo-bombing was regarded as especially successful, and during August 65 sorties were estimated to have sunk 88,000grt while only 33,000grt was sunk by 1,140 bomber sorties, although this activity attracted American heavy bombers which periodically struck Fink's bases, destroying 106 aircraft in late July and August alone.[79]

ObdL's preference for the Mediterranean, it informed *SKL* on 3 April 1944, was because reconnaissance sorties were more likely to detect enemy shipping than in the Atlantic, yet until early October such reconnaissance was largely defensive, with the objective of detecting invasion attempts.[80] Although the Allies could operate only 75km off the North African coast and the *Luftwaffe* could conceal its approach by flying either down the Spanish coast or between Minorca and Sardinia, the defending Mediterranean Coastal Air Force under Air Vice-Marshal Sir Hugh Lloyd (the former Malta commander) had 52 fighter squadrons to shield the convoys with patrols day and night. The first missile mission appears to have been a dusk attack off North Africa on 4 October by *II./KG 100*, when a freighter was sunk and three others damaged, but the *Kommandeur*, *Hauptmann* Heinz Molinnus, was killed when his aircraft crashed on landing (one of four lost this way), while one bomber was shot down, the sole survivor being captured after swimming for four hours. The *Gruppe*, now under *Hauptmann* Heinz-Emil Middermann, attacked two more convoys in October, sinking a freighter on the 21st, but at the end of the month it was transferred to Greece to support operations against the British in the Aegean Islands (see Table 18). *KG 26* did not join in the offensive until 11 November, when 56 aircraft struck KMS.31, sinking three ships (20,955grt), but the *Löwen Geschwader* lost seven aircraft (17.5%).[81] Shortly afterwards *KG 100* was withdrawn, ostensibly for a rest (having lost 22 aircraft since 1 August) but actually for a *Führer*-inspired (and ultimately abor-

---

Table 18. *Luftwaffe* Anti-Shipping Campaign in the Mediterranean, October 1943–May 1944

Month	Estimated sorties	Losses
Oct 1943	150	3
Nov 1943	100	11
Dec 1943	–	–
Jan 1944	60	7
Feb 1944	40	5
Mar 1944	115	4
Apr 1944	80	19
May 1944	125	20

Notes: Losses exclude *KG 77*, for which no data are available.
Sources: Air Ministry Intelligence Summaries (PRO Air 24/9); Allied Air Forces Intelligence Summary No 65 (PRO Air 24/949.); Balke, *KG 100*; and Schmidt, *KG 26*.

---

tive) surprise attack (*Unternehmen 'Carmen'*) upon the British Home Fleet at Scapa Flow. It did not return until late January, and was immediately committed to containing the Anzio beach-head.

Luckily the He 177s of *II./KG 40* (*Major* Mons) with Hs 293s made their Mediterranean début on 26 November, attacking KMF.26 and sinking the liner *Rohna* (8,602grt) with the loss of 1,000 servicemen, more than half the number embarked, but four of the 14 aircraft (28%) were lost (including Mons') and two were wrecked on landing, leaving the *Gruppe* with seven serviceable machines.[82] Of Mons his enemies wrote: 'He is stated to have been a brilliant pilot, a most likeable man and an inspiring leader.'[83] Consequently Klümper bore the brunt of the campaign during November, his victims including the Dutch liner *Marnix van St Aldegonde* carrying Canadian troops, and usually the airmen sank more ships in the Mediterranean than U-boats. However, by December Allied ship movements in the Mediterranean had increased from 357 in June to 1,012 to exceed Atlantic traffic, although the defenders were hamstrung by the lack of fighter direction ships.[84] The *Luftwaffe* had frequent failures, and on 21 December only eight of 32 Ju 88s intercepted a westbound convoy near Benghazi and two aircraft failed to return.[85]

The peril from Allied fighters meant that from January 1944 strike missions were often escorted by up to 24 Ju 88C *Zerstörer* of *ZG 1*, but casualties, especially in *KG 26*, were heavy from both long-range fighters and AA fire, and Klümper was discredited as the *Löwen Geschwader*'s losses meant that six sorties qualified crews for *Lebensalter* ('Old Hands') or *Häse* ('Hares') status.[86] But Fink did not benefit, for he was relieved on 10 February and succeeded 12 days later by *Generalmajor* Hans Korte, although that latter had no anti-shipping experience— indeed, he had spent the previous year with *Luftwaffenfelddivisionen* and before joining *Fliegerdivision 2* was Chief of Staff of *1. Fallschirmjägerdivision*. Fink became *Kommandierender der Deutschen Luftwaffe in Griechenland* and as consolation was promoted to *General der Flieger*.

Korte's task was further hindered by Lloyd's stationing of long-range fighter wings in Sardinia, and their success in breaking up an attack on 8 March led Korte to replace dusk attacks with night engagements. Pathfinders detected the convoys and laid marker buoys to the north, then, under the direction of the *Verbändesführer* (Master of Ceremonies) flying at 2,700m (9,000ft), illuminators dropped flares to outline the ships, which were then targeted, but the extensive use of smoke-generators during late March and early April enabled four convoys to escape unscathed.[87] Korte reverted to dusk attacks, striking UGS.38 off Algiers on 20 April and sinking or damaging five merchantmen as well as the destroyer USS *Lansdale*, but Lloyd reinforced his combat air patrols and sent his night fighters northwards. On 11 May UGS.40 was shielded by 100 fighters when 62 Ju 88s, with strong fighter escort, attacked without using flares (although it was a moonless night), but none of the 91 torpedoes struck a target while the attackers lost 16 aircraft. The defenders' dominance was underlined in the final mission when 10% of the bombers attacking KMS.51 on 31 May failed to return, and this operation marked the end of the Mediterranean campaign.

The increased dependence upon torpedoes reflected the declining fortunes of missiles since the Salerno landings, when three cruisers and two destroyers were hit and a 6,791grt hospital ship was sunk. The Allies responded by converting some destroyers into electronic warfare vessels. The first appeared at Anzio, and from February 1944 every convoy sailing along the North African coast had at least two jammer ships.[88] On 30 April KG 100 sadly reported the decline of the missiles; the Hs 293 proved more successful, with 357 launched compared with 62 Fritz X 'smart bombs', the former involving 67% of sorties and the latter 55.5%. But III./KG 100 suffered a 10% loss rate (11 aircraft) because the bombers had to launch their missiles close to the target and at minimum speed, while the greater range of the Hs 293 meant that II./KG 100 suffered only a 7% loss rate (27 bombers). Post-war analysis shows that Fritz X sank one battleship and damaged three more warships while Hs 293s sank a cruiser and four other warships (with three damaged) as well as three merchantmen (25,140grt).[89]

Overshadowed by the missions of their colleagues were the mundane minelayer operations of General der Flieger Joachim Coeler's Fliegerdivision 9, which was upgraded to Fliegerkorps IX on 23 October 1940 and from whom Göring demanded in his mid-July 1940 and 20 October directives a major minelaying effort. Coeler had 1,000 mines but lacked aircraft, despite receiving both KG 4 and KG 30, and his efforts were further compromised by the diversion of both to the Blitz, which also consumed a third of his ordnance and gave the British the opportunity to examine the latest sensor technology and then devise counter-measures.[90] Between July 1940 and May 1941 some 6,100 mines were laid in hazardous operations which required alert pilots and accurate navigation as the aircraft flew low over water at night, vulnerable to AA fire although the famous Hauptmann Hans-Joachim 'Hajo' Hermann (Kapitän of 7./KG 30) narrowly escaped becoming a victim of a balloon on 22/23 July 1940.[91] 'Barbarossa' reduced Coeler to three or four Kampfgruppen which were increasingly used for conventional bombing, and there were squabbles with Harlinghausen over anti-ship operations. The British coast was virtually divided into personal fiefdoms, FlFü Atlantik using III./KG 40 to lay mines while Coeler's thinly stretched Gruppen (KG 2, later reinforced by KG 6) were used for anti-shipping sweeps.

Increasingly the minelaying campaign was diluted, especially during the 'Baedecker' campaign of 1942—despite Sperrle's protests to ObdL, OKW and even Göring—with Luftflotte 3's anti-shipping effort in 1942 no better than the latter half of 1941 (see Table 33, Chapter 4). It was planned to revitalise the minelaying campaign by placing it under Greim's Fliegerkorps V, but his staff barely had time to unpack in Brussels during December 1941 when they returned to the east and minelaying (like anti-shipping operations) became more an aspect of operational training. Although Coeler's air strength doubled (from 103 on 30 April 1942 to 205 on 31 March 1943), minelaying virtually ended. There was a corresponding reduction in losses to airborne mines, from 24 ships (41,324grt) in 1942 to seven (19,542grt) in 1943.[92] Göring's interest in minelaying was fading fast as he sought to renew the air offensive against Britain. Coeler's staff provided the means of organising such a campaign, and on 1 April 1943 the *Fliegerkorps* was assigned to *Oberst* Dietrich Peltz's *Angriffsführer England*, Peltz assuming direct command a month later. Coeler, promoted to *General der Flieger* on New Year's Day 1942, was given the newly established transport command, *Fliegerkorps XIV*, which became the staff of *General der Transportflieger* in August 1944.

Meanwhile the Navy's hopes were raised with the development of a pressure fuze to convert the LMB mine into the so-called *Druckdosenmine* (Oyster mine), and in May 1943 Jeschonnek allocated two *Kampfgruppen* to lay them from August. But Hitler, fearing that the enemy would learn the mine's secrets and disrupt training of the new high-underwater-speed U-boats in the Baltic, vetoed the plan at the end of July, commenting, 'If the British should lay those mines in the Baltic we are finished.' Within three weeks of his appointment Korten, Jeschonnek's successor, supported Navy pleas for a renewed minelaying offensive using acoustic and magnetic/acoustic weapons to coincide with the new moon in September. Moreover, on 26 August he published plans for a substantial expansion of the minelayer force to 11 *Kampfgruppen* with Ju 188s and He 177s.[93] The campaign lasted from 15/16 September to 3/4 October, when it was abandoned after the previous night's mission suffered an 8% loss rate, some 600 mines having been laid. Six days later Hitler ordered Sperrle to use Peltz's bombers for a campaign against England (*Unternehmen 'Steinbock'*), and apart from 80 sorties in April and May 1944 the *Luftwaffe* ceased minelaying in the West, the Oyster mines being conserved for the Allied invasion.[94]

In the 46 months following July 1940 the *Luftwaffe* sank 1,988,841grt of merchantmen, mostly in the West, where 1,228,104grt were sunk and 1,953,862grt damaged, while partial figures indicate that in 1942 and 1943 another 60,866grt were sunk by *Luftwaffe* mines.[95] Even these substantial figures merely underline the half-hearted nature of the effort, and the terrible 'if' of history is what might have been achieved had the campaign received wholehearted support. By contrast, the RAF offensive against the smaller German mercantile marine, often with grossly inferior aircraft, destroyed 278,863grt in west European and Scandinavian waters while minelayers sank 462,605grt.[96] To meet the threat from magnetic mines the *Luftwaffe* formed *Sonderkommando Ju 52 (MS)* with Ju 52 (and a few Do 23) *Mausi* (Mice) carrying degaussing rings.[97] The importance of the *Mausi* grew, and in October 1942 *Minensuchgruppe 1* was formed with five *Staffeln*, but 16 months later the *Gruppe Stab* was disbanded and the *Staffeln* became independent.

Even twin-engine bombers would have influenced not only the sea war but also the air one; indeed, the decline of the anti-shipping campaign freed Fighter Command for offensive operations. The failure had many causes: the ubiquity of air power makes it vulnerable to other priorities, and in the *Luftwaffe* the *Kampfgruppen* were transferred almost on a whim. There was certainly a lack of will, partly due to the strain facing the *Luftwaffe* and industry but more because of the priority Germany has traditionally given to land operations, which meant that the sea war was regarded as an irritating diversion. Even the creation of *FlFü Atlantik* was a political expedient, ended when its usefulness ceased, and the *Luftwaffe* was being blamed for Dönitz's defeats. This was the reason why a normally *ad hoc* command (*Fliegerführer*) was not upgraded to permanent *Fliegerkorps* status and a vital strategic role was carelessly neglected.

NOTES TO CHAPTER 2

1. This chapter has greatly benefited from Neitzel's exhaustive study on the *Luftwaffe*'s operations in the Atlantic and North Sea and its relations with the Navy.
2. As Horst Boog has pointed out, the German Navy never produced an aviation doctrine. Howarth and Law, p.304.
3. Balke, *KG 2*, pp.128–9. After visiting Fink's headquarters Kesselring left the bus muttering 'I don't believe it.'
4. For anti-shipping operations over the Channel see Balke, *KG 2*, pp.129–46; and Mason, pp.108–76.
5. BAM, p.108.
6. See Coastal Command Operations Record Book to December 1943 in PRO Air 24/ 364. However, in July 1943 Spanish fishing boats in the Bay of Biscay suspected of passing information to U-boats were warned by Coastal Command to stay out of operational areas or be attacked on sight.
7. Schmidt, *Torpedo Los*, pp.91–3. I would like to thank Mr Alistair Farmer, editor of the *Banffshire Journal*, for publishing my letter seeking further details and Messrs R. T. Carter and Findlay Pirie (the former Postmaster of Banff) for providing further details, including the fact that part of Kuhn's aircraft was salvaged in 1975. Mr Pirie was kind enough to loan me his file on the incident, including correspondence with *Herr* Kuhn.
8. For the Do 26 story see Neitzel, pp.74–6.
9. The most comprehensive description of Condor operations is by Ehrhardt and Benoit.
10. Neitzel, pp.76–8.
11. Poolman, pp.27–34.
12. During the last two quarters of 1940 the *Luftwaffe* accounted for an average 12.5% of shipping lost in the Atlantic and British waters, excluding ships sunk in harbour, or 2% of total shipping losses.
13. Jeschonnek's brother Gert became an Admiral in the post-war West German Navy, while his half-brother Wolf served in U-boats.

14. Neitzel, pp.80–3.

15. In April he was strengthened by *III./KG 40*, formerly *I./KG 1*, with He 111s. It converted to Condors from December 1941 to June 1942 under former *FlFü Atlantik* Operations Officer *Major* Robert Kowalewski.

16. Neitzel, App. 1, provides details of U-boat/*Luftwaffe* cooperation in the Atlantic.

17. Neitzel, Apps 2a, 2d. The Royal Navy had similar problems with Coastal Command during the 1943 Bay of Biscay offensive.

18. The *Luftwaffe* was responsible for 15% of total British shipping losses in the Atlantic and British waters in this period, a figure it never equalled. On 25 March *Hauptmann* Fritz Fliegel, who became *Kommandeur* of *I./KG 40* when Peterson became *Kommodore* of *KG 40*, was awarded a *Ritterkreuz* because his *Gruppe* was officially credited with sinking 39 ships (206,000grt).

19. Poolman, pp.85–8.

20. Two Condors were destroyed by bombs on 22/23 November 1940.

21. To provide meteorological support for this operation, *Unternehmen 'Rheinübung'* (Rhine Exercise), Jope flew a 17-hour mission from Stavanger along the Greenland coast on 24 March to find suitable sites for a covert meteorological station. Ehrhardt and Benoit.

22. Hümmelchen, p.105.

23. Poolman, p.48.

24. Neitzel, p.136. ·

25. The *Kommando* appears to have returned to France in mid-September.

26. Based on Neitzel, p.90 and App. 1. This figure excludes the *Empress of Britain*.

27. See Brütting, *Kampfflieger*, pp.129–30.

28. Ramsey, Vol. I, p.113.

29. From 11 September 1940 *Gr 806* was attached to *KG 54* as its *de facto* third *Gruppe*.

30. Hümmelchen, p.85.

31. For the early days of torpedo-bomber operations see Neitzel, pp.59–66; and Schmidt, *Torpedo Los*, pp.110–12.

32. Air attacks ended the careers of all four. Mr Gus Brittan, of the Royal Navy Submarine Museum, informed me that another U-boat commander, *Kapitänleutnant* Walter Otto, flew bombing missions over Manchester during the Blitz.

33. Boog, op. cit., p.308.

34. For details see Hümmelchen, pp.99–123; and Smith and Kay, pp.606–8.

35. The acquisition of ASV Mk II allowed the Germans to develop the *Metox* radar warning receiver for U-boats.

36. Neitzel, pp.168, 169, 211/n.81, 90; and Pritchard, pp.136–42.

37. Claims from *Studien zum Luftkrieg: Gedanken zum Einsatz der Luftwaffe im Luftkrieg über See* (USNA T971, Roll 16, fr.325ff.).

38. BA MA, RM 35, II/78; USNA T971, Roll 37, fr.902ff; and PRO AIR 20/1101 (translation).

39. On 11 June Dönitz's War Diary noted: 'The Bay of Biscay had become the playground of the British air force.'

40. Neitzel, pp.166–7.

41. During 1943 Kessler's men claimed to have sunk 13 ships (98,000grt) and two destroyers. *Studien zum Luftkrieg: Gedanken zum Einsatz der Luftwaffe im Luftkrieg über See* (USNA T971, Roll 16, fr.325ff).

42. On 8 December a Sunderland shot down the first Fw 200 carrying Hs 293, but six months earlier Condors shot down a Halifax towing gliders to Gibraltar.

43. Neitzel, Table 17. Kessler's airmen had damaged the *Duchess of York* on 14 March.

44. Roskill, Vol. III, Pt 1, p.54.

45. *Ausbildung der Luftwaffe für die Belange des Seekrieges. Planung für den Einsatz der Luftwaffe im Kampf gegen England* (USNA T971, Roll 37, fr.1078ff).

46. The text is in Hümmelchen, pp.129–1.

47. Dual-use versions were introduced in April 1944.

48. For development of the weapons and their units see Balke, *KG 100*, pp.236–8, 245–51; and Smith and Kay, pp.673–8, 679–83, 696–9.

49. Poolman, p.176.

50. Balke, *KG 100*, pp.259–60; and Walt's article.

51. For this mission see Price, *He 177*, pp.270–4.

52. Flares to illuminate shipping targets were used off North Africa from early 1943 and such remained a standard anti-ship tactic until mid-1944. The British used similar tactics against coastal traffic off the Netherlands early in 1944. Roskill, III/I, pp.94, 288.

53. For details of these operations see Franks, *Conflict over the Bay*.

54. Figures from Neitzel, App. 3.

55. Hümmelchen, p.129; and Neitzel p.217/n.300.

56. Boog, op. cit., p.315.

57. Roskill, Vol. III, Pt 1, p.30.

58. See Chapter 8.

59. Price, *Aircraft versus Submarine*, pp.119–20, 142–3, 188–9.

60. Ibid., pp.169–72. The *Sonderkommando* continued operating until April 1944, when it became a full electronic warfare unit as *Horch und Störstaffel 2*. The following month this was absorbed by *4./FAGr 5*.

61. Roskill, III/I, p.262.

62. Figures from Neitzel, App. 3.

63. Since 1941 many Condor crews included a 'weather frog', partly to support their own operations and partly to provide vital meteorological data to the *Wehrmacht* in the West.

64. Neitzel, p.215/n.240.

65. In addition to maritime reconnaissance, until the autumn of 1943 these aircraft were also involved in supporting covert meteorological stations in Greenland. Ehrhardt and Benoit.

66. For *KG 26* operations see Schmidt, *Torpedo Los*, pp.133–47.

67. Boog, p.314.

68. In 1941 and 1942 barely 100 bomber sorties were despatched to Norway.

69. For German-Russian anti-shipping operations see Huan's excellent article 'La bataille aéronavale de l'artique'; and also Plocher, *1943*, pp.210–12.

70. Girbig, *JG 5*, pp.255–60; Hoffmann, III, pp.90–1; and Williamson, pp.108–10.

71. Nielsen was the *Luftflotte 5* Chief of Staff until the end of 1943, then commanded *Luftwaffe* forces in Denmark before becoming, in mid-May 1944, Chief of Staff of *Luftflotte Reich*.

72. For *Luftflotte 5* operations see Girbig, *JG 5*; Plocher, *1941*, pp.178–200, *1942*, pp.18–67 and *1943*, pp.194–220; and *Die Kampführung der Luftflotte 5 in Norwegen* (USNA T971, Roll 6, fr.650ff). During the war the *Ilmavoimat* received 244 aircraft, including 37 trainers, from Germany, but was so short of aircraft that it pressed into service 89 captured Russian machines. See Green's article 'Finland's Modest Air Arm'.

73. See Gerbig, *KG 54*, pp.105–9, 110, 121–5, 127–30; Gundelach, pp.374–5, 406–7; and Shores, *Malta: The Spitfire Years* (hereafter Shores, *Spitfire*), pp.82–4, 138–44, 318–60, 449–516.

74. See Schmidt, *KG 26*, pp.100–4.

75. For details of naval weapons see Campbell, pp. 266, 273–6, 350–1.

76. See Schmidt, *KG 26*, pp.160–70. Poor tactical planning meant that *KG 26* lost 22 crews in November alone.

77. Mediterranean Allied Air Forces Intelligence Summary No 65 (PRO Air 24/949).

78. Mediterranean Allied Air Force Intelligence Summary No 63, week ending 31 January 1944 (PRO Air 24/949).

79. *Studien zum Luftkrieg: Gedanken zum Einsatz der Luftwaffe im Luftkrieg über See* (USNA T971, Roll 16, fr.325ff).

80. Boog, op. cit., p.314.

81. See Balke, *KG 100*, pp. 271–2, for a description of this mission. For the anti-shipping campaign in the Mediterranean see Gundelach, pp.752–4. Between May 1942 and October 1943 *KG 26* flew 2,139 torpedo-bomber sorties, during which it launched 1,653 torpedoes. It was claimed that 21% of these weapons had hit their targets, sinking 77 ships (552,000grt). *Studien zum Luftkrieg: Gedanken zum Einsatz der Luftwaffe im Luftkrieg über See* (USNA T971, Roll 16, fr.325ff).

82. Allied intelligence noted that He 177 crews were enthusiastic about their much maligned engines, 'which appear to function smoothly and efficiently over incredibly long journeys'. Mediterranean Allied Air Forces Intelligence Summary No 65 (PRO Air 24/949).

83. Ibid.

84. Roskill, III/I, p.210.

85. Gundelach, p.1098/n.189.

86. Ibid., p.1098/n.184.

87. See Air Ministry Weekly Intelligence Summary 248, pp.28–9, for a description of the 11/12 April attack on UGS.37 (PRO Air 22/8).

88. See Friedman, pp.128–29. The much-quoted expedient of switching on electric razors and toothbrushes had no effect upon the missile control signals.

89. Balke, *KG 100*, App. 13.

90. Mason, p.105; and Neitzel, pp.70–4, App. 5, based upon *Die Luftmine als Kriegsmittel im Rahmen der Belagerung Englands* (BA MA RM7/826). These figures differ from Table D. See Marchand and Huan, *Achtung Minen!*

91. In July and August 1940 *KG 4* lost five crews. See Gundelach, *KG 4*, pp.87–9; and Mason, pp.145–6.

92. Roskill, III/I, pp.96, 289; and Balke, *KG 2*, Vol. 2, App. 7. During this period 26 fishing vessels and sailing barges as well as four small warships were also sunk by mines. It was claimed that between July 1940 and December 1943 Coeler's mines had sunk 42 ships (167,000grt). *Studien zum Luftkrieg: Gedanken zum Einsatz der Luftwaffe im Luftkrieg über See* (USNA T971, Roll 16, fr.325ff).

93. Maritime operations 1943–1944 (USNA T 971, Roll 37, fr.1078).

94. Neitzel, pp.203–4.

95. These figures exclude fishing vessels.

96. Roskill, various tables.

97. Later Bv 138 and even Ju 88 aircraft were also used.

CHAPTER THREE

Drang nach Osten

*The Mediterranean and Eastern Fronts,
December 1940–January 1942*

The NewYear of 1941 opened ominously for a *Luftwaffe* developed specifically for a single-front war. As it tried to concentrate upon bombing Britain, a theatre developed in the Mediterranean/Balkans while a third was scheduled in the East. Both new theatres were to prove debilitatingly inter-active over the next two years.

Hitler regarded the Mediterranean as an Italian theatre but was sensitive about the Balkans' mineral wealth, especially Romania's Ploesti oilfields, which were Nazi Germany's prime source of black gold. As France fell, Russia seized the Romanian province of Bessarabia and German paratroops were despatched to shield Ploesti until *Generalleutnant* Wilhelm Speidel, formerly Kesselring's Chief of Staff, established the *Deutschen Luftwaffenmission in Rumänien* on 10 October to modernise and to train the FARR (Royal Romanian Air Force) as well as to create a *Luftwaffe* infrastructure. In November he received 9./*JG 52* (soon followed by the remainder of III./*JG 52*) and *Flak* batteries, of which 30 were available by mid-February.[1]

Meanwhile the jackal-like Mussolini entered the war on 10 June, seeking rich pickings from the French and British colonial empires. German liaison missions were established with the Italian services the following day, including *Generalmajor* Maximilian, *Ritter* von Pohl's *Verbindungsstab der Luftwaffe bei der Italienischen Luftwaffe in Rom* (abbreviated to *Italuft*), which initially acted as an intelligence exchange. Pohl, an Army officer who had been Speidel's predecessor, quickly lost confidence in the *Regia Aeronautica* and soon urged Jeschonnek to despatch a *Luftwaffe* expeditionary force to North Africa, a request incorporated on 12 November in Directive 18, which outlined German strategy in the Mediterranean. The linchpin was *Unternehmen 'Felix'*, in which General Franco would help German forces (supported by *Fliegerkorps VIII*) under Richthofen (at the *Caudillo's* insistence) to enter Spain and occupy Gibraltar. Subsequently, the *Luftwaffe* in North Africa would interdict the Mediterranean sea lanes using *Fliegerkorps VIII* and minelayer units, while other aircraft would defend Romania and help occupy Greece. Unfortunately for the Reich, events in the theatre made the directive obsolete before Hitler signed it.[2]

Having established a bridgehead in Egypt, the *Duce* attempted the conquest of Greece, only to suffer during November a humiliating defeat in the Albanian mountains.[3] The RAF returned to mainland Europe to assist the Greeks, although Athens initially refused the offer of an expeditionary force for fear it would incite German intervention, and British pilots using Menidi airfield against the Italians sometimes encountered Lufthansa Ju 52s on regular flights to Greece.[4] On 11/12 November British carriers crippled the Italian battlefleet in Taranto and within a month the British Army had driven the Italians out of Egypt, through Cyrenaica (the eastern part of Italy's Libyan colony) and into Tripolitania (the western part). Axis prestige was shaken, Franco vetoed 'Felix', and Hitler was forced to commit resources both to prop up the cardboard Caesar and to secure the Balkans.

To help the reeling Albanian garrison, Rome reluctantly requested air transport from Berlin on 19 November, leading to the despatch of one of the Luftwaffe's most experienced Gruppen (III./KGzbV 1) with a high proportion of instrument-qualified pilots, who arrived at Foggia on 8 December. Hitler promised Mussolini further support, and on 25 November Milch, Jeschonnek and Generalleutnant Karl Bodenschatz (the Führer's Luftwaffe liaison officer) arrived in Rome to discover that Italian requirements included a strong anti-shipping force. On 4 December Geisler's Fliegerkorps X was nominated both to cut the sea lanes and to mine the Suez Canal, the arrangements being completed in Rome two days later by Milch and Waldau. Geisler received his orders on 10 December and within four days had 14,389 men, 226 combat aircraft and 31 transports on Italian soil, protected by seven batteries of FlakR 102. Meanwhile, on 9 December, III./KGzbV 1 began operations and by 31 March 1941 had flown 4,028 sorties (an average of 35 a day), transporting 28,871 men and 5,680 tonnes of material while evacuating 10,740, including 7,911 wounded and sick. The Gruppe operated under Italian command until the end of February, when it went to Sicily to help the German build-up in North Africa.[5]

Meanwhile the focus of German activity was Malta where, on New Year's Day 1941, Air Vice-Marshal F. H. M. Maynard had 56 aircraft (including 20 fighters). To ease the desperate shortage of supplies both here and in Egypt, convoy MS.6 was despatched from Gibraltar to Alexandria, covered by the Mediterranean Fleet. It was detected on 9 January as Geisler established his headquarters in the Hotel Domenico, Taormina, with only two Gruppen and two Staffeln (II./KG 26, 2./KG 4, III./ZG 26 and 1. (F)/121) in Sicily. He borrowed from Richthofen Stäbe StG 1 and LG 1 (each with two Gruppen), and the following day Hauptmann Paul-Werner Hozzel's I./StG 1 and Major Walter Enneccerus' II./StG 2 made a spectacular début in the theatre by planting six bombs on the carrier Illustrious, after Italian torpedo-bombers drew away her defenders, with further damage inflicted by an evening Stuka mission.[6] The effort temporarily exhausted German bomb stocks, but they were replaced, allowing Enneccerus to pursue MS.6 the following day with an He 111 'pathfinder', attacking two cruisers and mortally wounding HMS Southampton. Illustrious crept into Valletta harbour for emergency repairs and, despite some 200 strike sorties by Geisler with the loss of eight aircraft, she escaped to Alexandria on 23 January, although a year's repairs in the United States awaited the carrier.[7]

When Geisler arrived in Sicily his attempts to crush Malta were initially hindered by cramped airfields, whose lack of revetments made them vulnerable to air attack, as was demonstrated on 12/13 January when three aircraft were destroyed and six damaged, unreliable British bombs preventing greater destruction.[8] He soon began to weaken Malta's defences using small formations of Ju 88s (supplemented from 7/8 February by He 111 night attacks), but the *Zerstörer*, and the fighters of General Renato Mazzucco's *Commando Aeronautica Sicilia,* offered inadequate protection, which was reduced by the transfer of a *Zerstörergruppe* to North Africa. The defenders' complacency was shattered on 12 February with the first sweep by the newly arrived Bf 109s of *7./JG 26* under *Ritterkreuz*-holder *Oberstleutnant* Joachim 'Jochen' Müncheberg, a 23-victory ace. He and two *Kettehunde* shot down two of four Hurricanes and began an aggressive campaign of sweeps which nearly broke the defenders' morale. On 26 February what *OKW* described as 'the elimination of English air power on Malta' began with Müncheberg shooting down Malta's leading scorer, Flying Officer F. F. Taylor, while strike forces destroyed a third of the British bombers. Although relatively light, the offensive quickly halved the defenders' fighter strength and forced the withdrawal of the Wellingtons, then Geisler gradually strengthened the attack until an unwelcome distraction took place in the Balkans.[9] But he lacked an adequate strike force, even using his *Stukas* both day and night, and was never in a position to crush the defenders (see Table 19). Müncheberg's fighters, briefly diverted to the Balkans and augmented from time to time by *Gruppen* from *JG 27*, were increasingly used for escort or even *Jabo* missions, occasional sweeps helping to reduce the defenders to 24 fighters. But in mid-May the offensive was abandoned.

Hitler's concern with the potential British threat from Greece to *'Barbarossa'* (scheduled for May 1941) led on 13 December to Directive 20 for *Unternehmen*

Month	Strike	Fighter Escort	Sweep	Recon	Total	Losses
Jan	285	122	30	14	451	21
Feb	158	66	138	25	387	17
Mar	236	95	158	22	511	10
Apr	383	152	72	30	637	11
May	403	231	80	41	755	6
Total	1,465	666	478	132	2,741	44

Table 19. *Fliegerkorps X*: Campaign against Malta, January–May 1941

Source: *Tätigkeit des X. Fliegerkorps in Italien in der Zeit von 10. Januar bis zum 22. Mai 1941 und erzielte Resultate,* quoted by Gundelach, p.123.

'*Marita*'. Greece was to be invaded in the spring by Romanian-based troops (later *Generalfeldmarschall*Wilhelm List's *12. Armee* and *Generaloberst* Ewald von Kleist's *1. Panzergruppe*), using Bulgaria as a springboard. The *Luftwaffe* was to secure Romania, support the Army, destroy enemy air forces and 'as far as possible . . . seize English bases in the Greek islands with airborne forces'. Hitler briefed List and Richthofen on 8 January and a month later the latter flew to Sofia via Lufthansa to discuss preparations for entering Bulgaria, which had secretly invited in 600 *Flugmeldedienst* personnel wearing mufti. When Bulgaria formally joined the Axis on 1 March, Richthofen sent 120 of his 340 aircraft (mostly fighters and *Stukas*, with a single *Kampfgruppe*) into the country together with some 15 *Flak* batteries. In the meantime the *Luftwaffe*'s *Oberst* Otto Prinz (later *OKW*'s Inspector of Communications) improved the efficiency of the Romanian and Bulgarian aircraft reporting networks to assure the defence of Ploesti.

The '*Marita*' preparations saw moments of high drama, for just as the Balkans seemed set to come under Berlin's influence, with Bulgaria and then the Yugoslav Regent's government signing the Tripartite Pact, there had come a diplomatic blow. Two days before '*Marita*' was set to begin on 1 April, Yugoslavia's Regent, who had signed the unpopular Tripartite Pact, was overthrown in favour of the young King Peter in a *coup* led by air force Chief of Staff General Duson Simonovic and the new government repudiated the agreement. Hitler was furious and his Directive 25 amended '*Marita*' to include an invasion of Yugoslavia using List's and Kleist's armies as well as *2. Armee*, which rapidly assembled in Austria and Hungary. A total of 15 *Gruppen* (most from France) flew 1,500km to bases hastily prepared by Löhr and his Chief of Staff *Oberst* Günther Korten, the only serious incident being the loss of five *KG 51* bombers to bad weather on 1 April, the day planning was completed.[10] Geisler flew some 200 men and urgent material for his two *Gruppen* to new bases, but many units arrived without motor transport and the influx rapidly depleted supplies, yet 87% serviceability was achieved. Richthofen, who received seven *Kampfgruppen*, had the lion's share of the assault force with 392 of the 946 combat aircraft, Löhr retained 200 bombers, and the remaining fighters and *Stukas* were split between the hastily created *FlFü Arad* and *Graz* under the *Kommodore* of StG77 and StG 3.[11]

Brigadier Broivoje Mirkovic's *JKRV* (Royal Yugoslav Air Force), which secretly mobilised on 6 March, was the prime aerial opponent but had only 468 first-line aircraft with 2,000 indifferently trained aircrew. Mirkovic had severe logistical problems, with 11 different types of aircraft (including Bf 109s and Do 17s) and 22 different engines, which were exacerbated by the *JKRV*'s dispersal from 12 March to a network of 100 secret grass airstrips built the previous year. This well-meant attempt at preservation proved counter-productive as few could take bombers, only half were operational (many were covered in snow) and, as the Poles discovered in 1939, inadequate communications compounded control problems for the already fragmented air force. Worse still, a Croatian staff officer betrayed details of the scheme to the *Luftwaffe* just before the invasion.[12] The warning system was rudimentary both here and in Greece, where the *EVA* (Greek Air Force) and RAF had a heterogeneous collection of 230 aircraft, including 152 British (80 serviceable), the *Luftwaffe* estimate being 250. The Greeks were scheduled to receive American-built fighters, including Curtiss-Wright Hawk 75s (P-36s), Hawk 81s (P-40Bs) and Grumman G-36As (F4F-3 Wildcats), but none arrived in time. The Allies were outnumbered by the *Luftwaffe* alone, and its four strike forces were supplemented by 566 Italian and 96 Hungarian aircraft, the Bulgarian Air Force apparently adopting a purely passive role![13] The twin themes of neutralising enemy air power then supporting the Army were the core of Löhr's planning, but there was also a decapitation element called *Unternehmen 'Strafgericht'* (Bench of Judgement). This ultimately proved to be Löhr's death warrant, for it was regarded as another terror attack; indeed, Directive 25 demanded that 'the city of Belgrade . . . be destroyed . . . by continual day and night attack'.[14] Löhr instructed *Oberstleutnant* Clemens, *Graf* von Schönborn (*FlFü Arad*) and his own *Kampfgruppen Kommandeure* to strike the castle and barracks of the Topcider district, the Belgrade Citadel and the Parliament building, as well as communications centres, and use experienced crews, who were to bomb only specific targets. However, he was both a former officer of the Austro-Hungarian Empire and the son of a Croat—sufficient grounds for a traditional enmity of what Hitler called 'the Serb traitor clique'.[15]

Following the Belgrade *coup* there was feverish reconnaissance activity, one aircraft accidentally landing at a Yugoslav airfield, where it was impounded. However, the target folders were full as Palm Sunday (6 April) dawned, and Yugoslavia's Passion began with bombs falling on airfields, communications centres and military positions. Some 800 sorties were flown against the *JKRV* alone and another 484 against Belgrade, where 3,000–4,000 people died as 360 tonnes of bombs and mines started major fires. The *JKRV* reacted vigorously, flying 474 sorties, 93 by bombers, including attacks on Wiener Neustadt, but by dusk it was shattered, having lost 145 aircraft (60% on the ground). The day was a resounding success for the *Luftwaffe*, which lost 37 aircraft, mostly to ground fire, the most prominent casualty being *Hauptmann* Herbert Ihlefeld (*Kommandeur* of *I. (J)/ LG 2* and a Condor Legion ace), who was briefly captured.

Attacks the next day, when there were no enemy fighter sorties, cost Löhr nine aircraft (he claimed 56 victories) and left the *JKRV* with only 177 combat aircraft, although their bombers remained active, flying 60 sorties. However, Geisler's bombers were able to fly unescorted over western Yugoslavia as Belgrade was again pounded. Richthofen supported *12. Armee's* deep thrust from the east as low clouds, sleet and snow appeared, but on Easter Saturday (12 April) the Germans entered the smoking ruins of Belgrade as Yugoslavia rapidly fragmented upon racial fault lines familiar half a century later. The *Luftwaffe* eliminated airstrips, Bjeljina being taken by some 170 airborne troops on 14 April, and drove the surviving *JKRV* aircraft into the south, where most were destroyed, leaving 40–50 survivors which fled the country carrying as many airmen as possible. The Yugoslav Army surrendered on 17 April, but a few squadrons defected to become the air force of Croatia, created only six days earlier. The last days of the campaign saw Löhr using some bombers to assist the Italian advance along the Dalmatian coast.[16]

Palm Sunday also saw the invasion of Greece, with some of Richthofen's aircraft spending the first two days pounding abandoned airfields in northern Greece as well as the Metaxas Line fortifications, whose strength required numerous repeat missions consuming scarce supplies. There was spectacular opening when a routine raid on Piraeus by the Sicily-based *II./KG 30* set ablaze two ships carrying explosives as *2./KG 4* laid mines outside the port. Fearing that the ships would be mined and block the approaches, the authorities refused to tow them away and the inevitable explosion not only wrecked the port but sank nine more ships (bringing the total losses to 41,789grt) and trapped another 20 in the debris.[17] Meanwhile List's troops, supported by *Schlacht-* and *Stukastaffeln* operating from forward fields, drove towards Salonika (Thessaloniki), which fell on 9 April, trapping much of the Greek Army in Macedonia where they surrendered the following day. This allowed Richthofen to bring forces forward, including *Kampfgruppen* such as *I./KG 51*, to launch a major attack upon the port of Volos as *Hauptmann* Hans-Joachim Gerlach, with two *Kettehunde* from *6./JG 27*, wiped out an unescorted No 211 Squadron formation of six Blenheims. Until then air operations were confined to sporadic raids in bad weather against the communications, which were so rudimentary that from 14 April elements of three *Transportgeschwader* began ferrying supplies from Bulgaria to Greek airfields, their crews often flying 10 hours a day. Snow showers grounded Richthofen on 11 and 12 April, giving the Allies time to re-form around Mount Olympus, but the respite was brief, for, as Yugoslavia collapsed, the Germans concentrated in Greece and Richthofen received eight combat *Gruppen* from Löhr, bringing his strength to 653 (including transports) by mid-April.

When the offensive resumed on 15 April in improving weather, he provided overwhelming support for the spearheads while *II./JG 27* and *II./JG 77* smashed an Allied air force confined to a few fields close to the front, destroying some 27 aircraft. Only 46 serviceable aircraft withdrew to Athens, offering token support as the Germans outflanked the Olympus Line, isolating the remainder of the Greek Army in Albania, where it surrendered on 21 April. The *Luftwaffe* hammered retreating British columns, men often abandoning vehicles at the mere appearance of aircraft, although on 19 April two *KG 2* Dorniers fell to small-arms fire. The same day Richthofen began to sweep the skies clear of enemy aircraft, the Allies' new bases having come under attack from 18 April. On that day the

Kommandeur of *I./KG 51, Hauptmann* Heinrich Hahn, was shot down by the RAF ace Squadron Leader Marmaduke Pattle, although *Oberleutnant* Kurt Ubben (*Kapitän* of *9./JG 77*), who force-landed behind Allied lines, was rescued by *Stabsarzt Dr* Stormer in a Storch. Sweeps over bases, largely by *JG 77* and *ZG 26*, with the former's 'Emils' literally hedge-hopping and flying between hangars, accompanied major attacks upon Piraeus by up to 100 aircraft which sank 13 merchantmen (46,413grt) and two destroyers in seven days. However, the bombers were bait for the surviving enemy fighters, of which only five out of 15 returned on 20 April, the victims including Pattle, who was killed fighting *II./ZG 2*.[18] Most of the strike force then roved southwards to the Corinth Canal and Aegean islands as List advanced on Athens, supported by battlegroups drawn from *StG 2, JG 27* and *JG 77*, whose operations were helped by captured British supplies, especially fuel (although with transport crews cigarettes proved a useful medium of exchange for luxuries). Having overwhelmed aerial resistance, the *Luftwaffe* concentrated upon harassing the evacuation of troops, eventually sinking two destroyers and five ships (42,775grt).[19] Under 'Old Eagle' *Major* Alexander von Winterfeldt, even *JG 77* flew *Jabo* operations: running low on fuel after one mission, *Oberleutnant* Wolf-Dietrich Huy's *Rotte* landed behind enemy lines at an abandoned British airfield near Corinth, refuelled from a dump, then flew home.[20]

   The Corinth Canal effectively made southern Greece (the Peloponnese) an island, and the task of taking the key bridge was assigned to *Oberst* Alfred Sturm's *FJR 2*, the core of *Detachment Süssmann* which arrived in Plovdiv on 26 March. The pace of operations and poor weather had restricted airborne operations, and on 21 April a dozen men of *FJR 1* were lost when their transport accidentally strayed into Turkish air space and was shot down by AA fire.[21] Sturm's regiment was given the mission in compensation for the abandonment of an assault on Lemnos Island (*Unternehmen 'Hannibal'*), and on 26 April two battalions dropped on either side of the bridge while a pioneer detachment glided in. But as the pioneers cleared demolition charges the bridge blew up for reasons never fully established, and this accounted for many of the attackers' 237 casualties (29%). Following a show of strength over Athens by 200 aircraft on 27 April, the *Luftwaffe* mopped-up, although there was one tragic incident on the last day of the campaign (28 April) when *Stukas* inflicted 200 casualties upon British troops at Kalamata, unaware that they had surrendered. '*Marita*' secured the Balkans for the Axis and cost the *Luftwaffe* 182 aircraft, of which 164 were lost in action (50 in Yugoslavia), and 292 aircrew. In return the Germans claimed 356 victories (246 on the ground), although this appears to be an underestimate: the *JKRV* lost 400 aircraft (excluding second-line), the *EVA* 162 (130 on the ground) and the RAF 209 (including 55 on the ground and 82 abandoned).[22] On 28 April Suda Bay in Crete was bombed, but a fortnight elapsed before the island felt the full weight of Teutonic fury.

The *Wehrmacht's* rapid advance during *'Marita'* had thwarted *Generaloberst* Kurt Student's dreams of glory for his new *Fliegerkorps XI*, but on 20 April he proposed to Göring an airborne assault upon Crete to secure the eastern Mediterranean and act as a springboard for taking Cyprus and the Suez Canal.[23] In February Hitler discussed with Jeschonnek an *OKW* proposal for using Student's men against Malta, but Student persuaded Göring to support an assault upon Crete, to which the sceptical *Führer* reluctantly agreed on 25 April, largely to strengthen Romania's shield.[24] But, with *'Barbarossa'* in mind, when Directive 28 authorised *Unternehmen 'Merkur'* (Mercury), Student was given a deadline of 16 May, while, at Göring's suggestion, to speed planning and 'keep it in the family' preparations were concentrated in the hands of Student and Löhr, the latter receiving the personal assistance of Jeschonnek, who was apparently on a busman's holiday.

The shattered Greek communications prevented the despatch of *22. Division* from Romania and it was replaced by *Generalleutnant* Julius Ringel's *5. Gebirgsdivision*. Ringel (most of whose men would come by sea) was assigned command of assault *Gruppe Ost*, which was to take Heraklion, while *Gruppen West* and *Mitte* under airborne specialists *Generalmajore* Eugen Meindl and Wilhelm Süssmann would take Maleme airfield and Canea/Suda Bay respectively. Despite the capture of 1,500 tonnes of British petrol, fuel shortages caused the postponement of A-Day to 20 May, and the operation was guaranteed only by the last-minute arrival of a tanker with 9,000 tonnes of petrol which was hastily decanted into 200-litre drums and driven to the four bases around Athens. The delay was exploited by Löhr to build airstrips for single-engine aircraft in the Peloponnese and Aegean islands while the Ju 52 'Iron Annies' were overhauled. Richthofen was responsible for air support and had 552 combat aircraft, supported by 51 Italian, while the transport force had 504 Ju 52s and 100 DFS 230 gliders, more of which might have been used had it not been for a shortage both of experienced pilots and strong towing rope.

The defenders had a collection of some 25 fighters and a few bombers, but even with radar support the shield was weak and after Richthofen's offensive began on 14 May it quickly buckled, the surviving seven fighters departing on 19 May, leaving air defence in the hands of AA gunners (with 30 weapons) and small arms. British bombers vainly sought to disrupt the build-up, destroying 10 aircraft, including the former Lufthansa Junkers G.38 *Generalfeldmarschall von Hindenburg* at Menidi, while German bombers pounded installations and blockaded the island, sinking half the supply ships sent from Alexandria. The 42,000 defenders, predominantly Australians and New Zealanders, escaped the bombs because they had carefully camouflaged their positions, their success being confirmed when the British developed photographs taken by an Hs 126 brought down over Retimo on 16 May. Student's intelligence believed that there were only 5,000 troops in Crete, and the absence of contradictory evidence led to a wave of optimism supported by *ObdL*. While Löhr wanted to take Heraklion then advance eastwards, Student decided to strike three sites simultaneously, thereby fragmenting his forces, for, as Richthofen ominously noted on 16 May, 'Student plans his operations based upon pure suppositions and preconceived notions.'[25]

The airborne assault began at 0700 on 20 May in moderate visibility but with heavy ground haze which further handicapped the attackers. For an hour *KG 2*, *KG 26* and *StG 2* pounded AA sites, then 493 transports began delivering troops, usually at or near airfields. For *Fliegerdivision 7* it was a nightmare from the very beginning, with Süssmann and his command team killed soon after take-off when their glider broke up after its tow rope was cut.[26] The paratroops came under withering ground fire from the moment they leapt out, while the gliders were lashed by machine guns from areas marked 'unoccupied' on their maps, the wounded including Meindl, who was replaced the next day by *Oberst* Bernhard Ramcke.[27] Worse still, the paratroops were often hunted down by Cretans, sometimes armed only with knives, leading to ugly stories of atrocities which post-operation German inquiries proved to be inaccurate or grossly exaggerated; indeed, three airmen who baled out over Crete, *Leutnant* Harald Mann and *Oberleutnant* Otto Grobe (*JG 77*) and *Unteroffizier* Düring (*StG 2*), evaded capture and eventually re-joined their units.[28] Paratroop morale plummeted and there were numerous infringements of the Geneva Convention against captured and injured British troops, while immediately after the island fell Student allowed his men to shoot dozens of civilians as a reprisal for alleged atrocities. In the early hours of '*Merkur*' Student was in an agony of uncertainty because most of the glider-borne radios had been destroyed or damaged, and a liaison officer despatched to Retimo airfield was captured when his Storch landed. Some supplies dropped for isolated detachments fell into the Australians' hands after they had captured both code-books and signal pistols.

Meindl's *Gruppe West* took Maleme airfield, partly because the British commander, General Bernard Freyberg, believed that the main assault would come by sea and failed to garrison it adequately.[29] Having lost only seven aircraft (1.4%) of the assault wave, Student had enough to exploit this success, but follow-up operations were hampered by dusty conditions at the bases and, as Student and Löhr became increasingly desperate, transports crowded into Maleme, where 80 were wrecked.[30] On 21 May a service detachment under *Major* Snowatzki cleared the wreckage using a captured Bren Carrier and British prisoners to make Maleme an airhead for reinforcements. Despite British hit-and-run raids the *Luftwaffe* dominated the skies, and this helped the airborne troops to expand their bridgeheads as reinforcements arrived. By 27 May 23,000 German and 4,000 Italian troops were on the island and steadily tightening their grip on the northern coast.

Richthofen was plagued by his superiors, his diary for 24 May noting 300 radio and 500 telephone messages, while telephone conversations with Jeschonnek sometimes lasted an hour. The Royal Navy bombarded *Stuka* airfields, an extremely risky strategy, as Norway had shown, and one which now provoked the *Luftwaffe's* wrath in a series of one-sided battles. Reinforced by two *Gruppen* from Geisler, and later by *StG 1* and *StG 77*, Richthofen by 23 May had forced the British to abandon the waters north of Crete. Three days later, after attacking *StG 2*'s base at Scarpanto, the aircraft carrier *Formidable* was hit by Enneccerus' *II./StG 2* (which happened to be returning from an abortive anti-shipping operation) while recovering aircraft and was forced to withdraw to America for repairs. Crete was clearly untenable, and on 27 May London authorised an evacuation, which was carried out in the teeth of Axis air superiority, *LG 1*, *KG 2*, *StG 2* and the *Jabos* of *JG 77* distinguishing themselves and inflicting heavy losses on both ships and men. It is worthy of notice, however, that *Stukas* avoided hospital ships, while columns of men retreating under Red Cross flags in Crete escaped attack, and in one case a Bf 109 circled such a column to assure its protection.[31]

By the time the evacuation had been concluded on 1 June the British Mediterranean Fleet was temporarily *hors de combat*, having lost three cruisers and six destroyers while three battleships, a carrier and 16 other warships had been damaged. Crete was Student's second brilliant Pyrrhic victory in two years, with *Fliegerdivision 7* suffering more than 4,500 casualties (including 3,022 dead and missing), leading Hitler to comment, while presenting *Ritterkreuze* for *'Merkur'* on 17 July, that 'the day of the paratrooper is over'. The operation cost 259 aircraft, including 121 transports (48 in accidents), and 438 aircrew, including 311 dead and missing (185 from *Fliegerkorps XI*).[32] The over-extended *Luftwaffe* was unable to exploit the strategic springboard, as was demonstrated weeks after Richthofen made his long-scheduled departure to Poland.

The success of *'Marita'* spurred *ObdL*'s desire to move Geisler eastwards so that he might blockade the Royal Navy and strike Egypt. On the eve of *'Merkur'*, *OKW* published Directive 29 on 17 May ordering *Fliegerkorps X* to Greece and Crete, although Geisler expressed scepticism about the Italians' ability to match

Table 20. *Fliegerkorps X* **Operations (excluding Malta), January–May 1941**

Month	Attacks on Ships	Reconnaissance Armed	Reconnaissance E Med	Minelaying	Escort Ships	Escort A/c	Total
Jan	180	28	40	16	–	–	264
Feb	33	65	120	30	142	33	423
Mar	114	66	149	10	247	46	632
Apr	146	110	123	42	200	24	645
May	61	95	93	41	88	2	380
Total	534	364	525	139	677	105	2,376

Source: *Tätigkeit des X. Fliegerkorps in Italien in der Zeit von 10. Januar bis zum 22. Mai 1941 und erzielte Resultate*, quoted by Gundelach, p.123.

his success in protecting the African sea lanes (see Table 20). On 22 May he formally transferred responsibility for all operations from Sicily to the *Regia Aeronautica*, leaving a small air base organisation and the *Freya* radars of *Oberst* Rosenkranz's *LnRegt 200* at Catania. Four days later, under an agreement with *ObdL*, the *Regia Aeronautica* was given responsibility for air operations west of 20°E (roughly from Corfu to Derna) while Geisler operated to the east. But on 21 May the RAF received substantial reinforcements, including Hurricanes (50 by mid-May), and a week later British torpedo-bombers renewed their operations. The Malta offensive had cost the *Luftwaffe* 44 aircraft, while it claimed 62 victories (42 of them by Müncheberg's *Staffel*, including 19 by the ace himself). Geisler's fears proved well founded, for the *Regia Aeronautica* possessed neither the resources nor the leadership to meet the challenge, and soon both shipping and the air ferry faced a growing British threat, the latter from Maryland reconnaissance bombers.

Geisler moved eastwards, and by 21 June he had 221 combat aircraft (153 bombers and *Stukas*) on Greek territory, but diversions in support of land campaigns, together with inadequate facilities, hindered attacks upon British installations in Egypt. Initially only a third of his strike force was serviceable (the sophisticated Ju 88 being noticeably vulnerable), but vigorous protests to Udet and Waldau rectified the situation, allowing Geisler to improve serviceability and to despatch 723 sorties against Egypt up to mid-September, the most successful raid being on 10/11 July when 100 aircraft were destroyed at the RAF's Abu Sueir depot. With British maritime power confined, Geisler could do little against enemy shipping until the arrival in August of *Kommando Peterson* (see Chapter 2), which used Derna as a forward base to fly half a dozen sorties a night over the Red Sea for about a month, while Geisler's own campaign in October ended after six sorties when on the 6th he was ordered to escort convoys as the British grip on the sea lanes tightened. From July the Germans made increasingly strident protests to the Italians about shipping losses, and a hint of disquiet followed the upgrading of *Italuft* into the *General der Deutschen Luftwaffe beim Oberkommando der Königlichen-Italienischen Luftwaffe* in October.[33] On 12 August *ObdL* informed *OKW* that it was considering returning Geisler to Sicily, and while Italian opposition thwarted this plan, a month later he did extend aerial protection westwards, then assumed responsibility for the main Naples–Tripoli sea route, although with never more than 20 aircraft he had to use *Stukas* for anti-submarine patrols!

Crete's capture came too late for the Germans to exploit British discomfiture in Iraq, where a *coup* led by General Raschid Ali el Ghailani established a pro-Axis government which besieged British military installations from 29 April and sought aid from Fascist friends. *Dr* Grobba, a former Ambassador to Iraq, persuaded Hitler to respond and on 6 May *Oberst* Werner Junck, *JaFü 3* in France, was instructed by Jeschonnek to coordinate the *Luftwaffe* response as *FlFü Irak* (also

Sonderkommando Junck), because the *Führer* wanted 'a heroic gesture'. His two-*Staffeln* expeditionary force found no facilities when it reached Mosul, suffering a drought of aviation fuel in one of the world's largest oilfields! A rickety air ferry, including a few Ju 90s, was established through Vichy-held Syria, but by then a dynamic British response had defeated Raschid Ali's government. Junck returned to Athens on 1 June, ending the *Luftwaffe*'s most easterly excursion, described as the 'Foreign Ministry campaign' by *KG 4*. In losing 19 combat aircraft and two transports, the *Luftwaffe* provided the British with an excuse to invade Syria, in whose support the Germans could fly merely 62 sorties. Misled by Grobba, Jeschonnek had Junck court-martialled, but the 'Old Eagle' was cleared, his offers to resign his commission were rejected and he later distinguished himself in home defence to become commander of *Jagdkorps II* as a *Generalmajor*.[34]

The only beneficiary of the fiasco was former *General der Flieger* Hellmuth Felmy, *Luftflotte 2*'s erstwhile commander, who had become a Party member to shield his sons and brother Gerhard from Göring's wrath.[35] At the instigation of Grobba, his brother-in-law, he was appointed head of an abortive military mission to Iraq but never got beyond Syria.[36] Felmy subsequently held various army commands in Greece, leading to jail for war crimes in 1948, but he served only three of the 15 years' sentence.

The fate of Iraq and Felmy paled into insignificance when compared with North Africa, where there was a wild swing of fortunes. The collapse of the Italian Army in North Africa forced Hitler to despatch a mechanised task force under *General-leutnant* Erwin Rommel, and on 11 January *OKW* Directive 22 extended Geisler's authority into Tripolitania to provide air support. He despatched a *Zerstörer-* and a *Stukagruppe* and promptly lost an aircraft to Italian fighters over Tripoli on 3 February. Despite this inauspicious start, the *Luftwaffe* struck British positions and on 19 February had their first meeting with the RAF, each side losing two aircraft. The following day the *Kommodore* of *KG 76*, *Generalmajor* Stefan Fröhlich, became *FlFü Afrika* to control air operations, and his *Stukas* provided excellent support for Rommel, helping him to recapture most of Cyrenaica at the end of March. An Austrian soldier who joined the *Fliegertruppe* in 1934, Fröhlich was hamstrung by an inadequate infrastructure and a long supply line which denied him essentials, including sand filters, but the situation eased after Waldau's inspection visit on 18 April, reflected in the arrival from Sicily the following day of *I./JG 27* to counter Hurricanes. Rommel blamed Fröhlich for failing to meet his high expectations of air support, although the real villain was Göring, who refused to send reinforcements from the Balkans, while Fröhlich's problems were aggravated by the need to operate both on the Egyptian border and Tobruk with only 170 aircraft.

These helped Rommel defeat enemy offensives in May and June, the 'Emils' taking a heavy toll of Hurricanes while the 8.8cm *Flak* batteries decimated British armour. Ironically, German bombs aggravated Rommel's supply problems: some SC 10s being unloaded from an Italian freighter in Tripoli on 4 May exploded, destroying the freighter and another loaded with fuel. The *Kampfgruppen* had by now abandoned North Africa, after flying some bombing sorties following *KG 26's* catastrophe (see Chapter 2), as *2./KG 4* also laid mines in the Suez Canal, while in February *II./KG 26* dropped a number of agents, two of them Jewish, into Egypt.[37] The second British offensive, 'Battleaxe', was made possible because of another reinforcement operation, 'Tiger', in early May, when only half of Geisler's bombers were serviceable: *LG 1* had lost 30 crews and received such poor replacements that Geisler had to rest and re-train the *Geschwader*. He flew only 31 strike sorties against the convoy, which strengthened the RAF's Middle East Command (Air Marshal Sir Arthur Tedder), whose Western Desert Air Force (Air Vice-Marshal Arthur Coningham) now had more than 200 aggressively handled combat aircraft. From August onwards heavily escorted bombers struck Axis airfields, but it was the appearance of the Curtiss-Wright Tomahawk (Hawk 81, or P-40A/C) which led the *Jagdgruppe* to clamour for Bf 109Fs to replace the 'Emils'. The 'Friedrichs' came from Russia in September with *II./JG 27*, while *I./JG 27* converted to them by December, the new fighters quickly making their mark. Night defence was not neglected, with *Staffeln* from *NJG 3*, then *NJG 2*, protecting Derna from August onwards, but Fröhlich's offensive efforts focused upon Tobruk.

Yet the root of all Rommel's ills in 1941 was Malta, whose 'Ultra'-supported aircraft and submarines decimated shipping (Fröhlich lost 25 DB 601 engines, bombs and fuel in one ship on 2 September) or forced ships into time-consuming diversions. By November 1941 63% of North Africa-bound cargoes were being lost, but relief was already on the way, starting with the extension of Geisler's protection over the central Mediterranean sea lanes. Italian inadequacy was raised with surprising delicacy when Göring met General Francesco Pricolo, the *Regia Aeronautica* Chief of Staff, in East Prussia on 2 October, observing that it was a pity that Malta had not been seized in June 1940. He patronisingly suggested to Pricolo that one solution was to strengthen the *Regia Aeronautica*'s autonomy. German intervention was clearly essential, and Jeschonnek proposed in September simply sending Kesselring, but Göring recognised that even 'Smiling Albert' would need muscle. On 20 October he proposed the despatch of a major command with up to 16 *Gruppen* from the East, and *Luftflotte 2* (with *Fliegerkorps II*) was selected, although it was realised that the move would need several months to complete. Hitler conveyed the decision to Mussolini in a letter 10 days later, and a week after that Waldau was discussing its employment with the *Regia Aeronautica*. Orders for *Luftflotte 2*'s withdrawal, initially for a fortnight's rest and replenishment in Germany, were issued on 10 November, but the situation in Africa deteriorated alarmingly and *KGr 606* and *Hauptmann* Jung's *4./NJG 2* were hastily sent south, coming under the *Kommodore* of *KG 26*, *Oberst* Ernst-August Roth, as

FlFü Sizilien, where they were quickly joined by 10 of Kesselring's *Gruppen*, including *Major* von Maltzahn's *JG 53*.[38]

In North Africa both sides were reinforced during late October in anticipation of new offensives, Fröhlich receiving another *Zerstörer-* and *Stukagruppe* for ground attack missions while *Koluft Libyen* had a *Nahaufklärungsstaffel* and *FlakR 135* with six batteries for new assaults on Tobruk. Tedder assembled 650 aircraft (550 serviceable) and with a new offensive, Operation 'Crusader', imminent he began striking communications and infrastructure from 14 October, then targeted Axis air power for the last six days. By 15 November only half Fröhlich's 171 aircraft, mostly *Stukas*, were serviceable, while *5a Squadra Aerea* had 420 aircraft, of inferior quality although two-thirds were serviceable. Before 'Crusader' began on 18/19 November heavy rain turned the Axis airfields into swamps, and it was four days before Geisler could despatch a *Stukagruppe* and two *Kampfgruppen* with the remainder of *III./ZG 26*, although Fröhlich was demanding a *Stuka-* and a *Kampfgeschwader*. He rarely managed more than 200 sorties a day and the Tomahawks, with newly arrived Kittyhawk Is (P-40Es), matched the 'Friedrichs', which avoided dog fights and picked off stragglers to build up big victory scores while leaving bomber formations to pound the Axis armies remorselessly. On 10 December *I./JG 27* shot down five of six newly arrived Boston bombers, but the RAF dominated the air over Axis columns, where, six days earlier, *Major* Kaschka (*Kommandeur* of *III/ZG 26*) had fallen to 'friendly' fire. There was no such hostile reception for *KGzbV 1*, whose best crews in the Mediterranean flew supplies from Greece to the isolated German garrison at Halfaya Pass until it surrendered on 17 January 1942.[39]

The ground battle became a swirling dog fight in dust clouds, and Fröhlich twice committed his entire strike force in Rommel's support, but the struggle cost him 75% of his strength. The imminent arrival of Kesselring's *Luftflotte 2* made no difference, although 'Smiling Albert' took energetic action to ease the supply crisis, especially the petrol drought. At his instigation *Oberst* Friedrich-Wilhelm 'Fritz' Morzik (*Lufttransportführer beim Generalquartermeister der Luftwaffe und Kommandeur der Blindflugschule*) organised two *Transportgruppen* (*KGr zbV 400* and *500*) on 10 December, and these joined four *Staffeln* flying from Naples-Cancello to Tripoli while a *III./KGzbv 1 Staffel* operated from Athens-Tatoi through Crete to Derna, supplemented by a prototype Bv 222 six-engine flying boat. The units flew in fuel, then evacuated wounded and Italian refugees, but the British, aware of their activities through 'Ultra', successfully intercepted some with Beaufighters, Blenheims and Marylands on 11 December. The following day *III./ZG 26* and *I./NJG 3* flew escort missions and shot down seven would-be attackers.[40] Petrol shortages halved sortie levels to 100 a day and hamstrung reinforcements such as *III./JG 53* (*Hauptmann* Wolf-Dietrich Wilcke) from Russia. Only operational aircraft received fuel, and when Rommel ordered a retreat on 17 December the *Luftwaffe* could move only a handful of aircraft at a time, abandoning 228 with minor mechanical problems or damage to bring total losses since 18 November to 460.[41]

Rommel retained Cyrenaica because the exhausted British were unable to press beyond Benghazi, and the *Luftwaffe* exploited the breathing space to consolidate its infrastructure in the Gulf of Sirte area. Many *Gruppen* were transferred to Sicily and Crete because there were too few airfields in North Africa, while the supply shortages were aggravated by a dearth of vehicles to bring them fromTripoli. The air ferry was weakened on 15 January when *KGr zbV 500* was sent to Russia. The *Jagdgruppen* struggled to contain the RAF, and during the fighting in January the *JG 27 Experte Oberleutnant* Erbo, *Graf* von Kageneck (67 victories) was mortally wounded. The British history of the *Luftwaffe* observes that during the 'Crusader' campaign the Axis air forces acquitted themselves well, despite their supply problems, but were never able to overcome British air superiority.[42]

Meanwhile the first steps to subjugate Malta had begun. Attacks from 19 December resembled RAF 'Circus' operations, with small, but strongly escorted, bomber formations challenging the defenders, who lost 45 aircraft (29 on the ground) and destroyed eight. The tactic was familiar to Malta's new air commander, Air Commodore Hugh Lloyd, for as Senior Air Staff Officer with No 2 Group he had provided 'Circus' Blenheims.[43] It was an ominous moment not only for Malta but also for the *Luftwaffe*, which twice in six months had to strip one front to support another. Barely six months earlier aircraft left the Mediterranean to assist the Nazi crusade against Communist Russia, which was Hitler's supreme political objective.

Planning began even as *'Seelöwe'* was drafted, hastened by the military build-up along Russia's new borders as Stalin secured his ill-gotten gains and countered by the despatch to Poland of *Heersgruppen B* and *C, 4., 12.* and *18. Armees*, with their *Nahaufklärungsstaffeln*. On 1 August an *OKW* conference at Berghof decided that Russia would be attacked the following spring, and deployment plans were drafted as *'Aufbau Ost'* (Construction East), although until December they remained a fall-back strategy pending a decision on *'Adler'/'Seelöwe'*.[44] Outline planning, involving the new Assistant Chief of Staff (Operations), *Generalleutnant* Friedrich Paulus, with whom Richthofen had so often worked, led on 18 December toOKW Directive 21 for *Unternehmen 'Barbarossa'*, whose objectives were the Soviet Army's destruction and pursuit to a line beyond which air attacks upon Germany would be impossible. The main blow was to be delivered in Belorussia by *Heeregruppe Mitte* (*Generalfeldmarschall* Fedor von Bock), which would then help *Heeresgruppe Nord* (*Generalfeldmarschall* Wilhelm, *Ritter* von Leeb) to take Leningrad. In the south *Heersgruppe Süd* (*Generalfeldmarschall* Gerd von Rundstedt) was to destroy the enemy then advance to Kiev. The last phase involved a general advance to a line from Archangel to the River Volga, from which the *Luftwaffe* would eliminate the surviving Russian industries in the Urals.

The *Luftwaffe* was assigned its usual tasks, the enemy air force rather than ground support having priority, while airborne forces were to take key points.[45] Industrial targets would be attacked only during lulls in the main offensive, the directive optimistically adding, 'they will be initially concentrated on the Urals area'. The new strategy provoked unease within the *Luftwaffe* and Göring confronted Hitler with his own arguments against a two-front war in *Mein Kampf*, proposing *'Felix'* as an alternative. Briefly wavering, Hitler then rebuked him— 'Why don't you stop trying to persuade me to drop my plans for Russia? I've made up my mind'—and soon the *Reichsmarschall* became a supporter of the venture.[46] The *Luftwaffe* staff were not formally informed until 13 January, and disquiet was expressed by Milch and Waldau, the latter straining his friendship with Jeschonnek.[47] Only Jeschonnek appears to have been enthusiastic about *'Barbarossa'*, although recognising that it would over-extend the *Luftwaffe*, but, as always, he refused to oppose Hitler, who predicted that the campaign would last only six weeks, possibly because of Schmid's underestimate of enemy strength.[48]

At a joint-services conference chaired by Halder early in January *Generalleutnant* Hans-Georg von Seidel, the *Luftwaffe's Generalquartiermeister*, outlined his preparations and work was soon under way expanding, building and stocking airfields (105 new ones in southern Poland alone), extending the signal service and establishing depots and maintenance facilities. With the thaw in March 1941 the work directed by *Oberst* Löbel accelerated as administrative, supply, transport and *Flak* units were added. The movement of *Staffeln* posed a security headache but exploited the extensive training organisation in the East, where nine schools moved westwards to make room for combat units in late May, the only incidents being crash-landings by four Ju 88s of *KG 77* at Dessau.[49] Transferring three *Fliegerkorps* from the West to *Luftflotten 1* and *4* was easy, while *Luftflotte 2* headquarters reached Posen/Poznan on 22 May to assume control of Richthofen's *Fliegerkorps VIII*, which completed its three-week journey from Greece. As *Oberste* Hermann Plocher (*Fliegerkorps V*) and Kurt Zeitzler (*1. Panzergruppe*) discovered when sharing a Polish hotel, security was tight. The two chiefs of staff were old friends but for a fortnight had to excuse their presence until they learned they would be operating together.[50] To support the *Gruppen* new *Luftgaustäbe zbV* were established, though frequently they were given 'dead wood' and much of the motor transport acquired was in poor condition and required workshop attention.

For this clash of the titans the *Luftwaffe* deployed 2,232 aircraft. The Army and Navy had another 570, while the *Luftgaue* had 237 fighters to shield the Reich from Russian retaliation. *Luftwaffe* planning (in which *Generalmajor* Heinz-Hellmuth von Wühlisch, the *Luftflotte 1* Chief of Staff, evidently played a leading role) fitted the Army matrix. Kesselring's *Luftflotte 2* (1,223 aircraft), supported Bock with more than half the Eastern Front strike force, including all the *Stukas* and *Schlachtflieger*. In addition to Richthofen, who was to support *3. Panzergruppe* and *9. Armee*, Kesselring retained Loerzer's *Fliegerkorps II* for Guderian's *2. Panzer-gruppe* and *4. Armee* while his air defence was strengthened by the presence of *Flakkorps I* (*Generalmajor* Walter von Axthelm). Keller's *Luftflotte 1* (379 aircraft), supporting Leeb from East Prussia, was the *Luftwaffe*'s weakest link, with Förster's *Fliegerkorps I* supplemented, from 21 April, by *Oberst* Wolfgang von Wild's anti-shipping *FlFü Ostsee*. Löhr's *Luftflotte 4* in Slovakia, Romania and Bulgaria had more than a quarter of the *Luftwaffe* strike force (630 aircraft) to support Rundstedt, augmented by more from Germany's allies and satellites, primarily Romania.[51] Löhr received Sperrle's *Fliegerkorps IV* (Pflugbeil) to support the Axis advance from Romania, while Greim's *Fliegerkorps V* and *Flakkorps II* (*Generalleutnant* Otto Dessloch) operated from Poland. Yet, despite the importance of '*Barbarossa*', only 838 bombers were available, half the total deployed for the equivalent *Fall 'Gelb'* a year earlier, partly due to the *Luftwaffe*'s continental commitments and partly because the *Kampfgruppen* had not recovered from their ordeal over Britain.[52] As Jeschonnek informed Halder on 27 February, the low ratio of aircraft to space meant that only key areas could be guaranteed air support, and *OKH* warned field commanders that complete air superiority was unlikely and that they should expect greater exposure to enemy air attacks than in previous campaigns.[53] Kesselring and Keller war-gamed their plans and discussed them with *Heeresgruppen* and *Panzergruppen* commanders, but Löhr was too busy in the Balkans, leaving Rundstedt with a small *Luftwaffe* liaison staff.[54]

Much depended upon an accurate assessment of enemy air strength, and or-ders to photograph up to 300km into the Russian rear were issued on 21 Septem-ber. The following month *Oberst* Theo Rowehl's *Versuchstelle für Höhenflüge* (*Sonderkommando Rowehl*) began operating from Cracow and Budapest, while *AufKlGr ObdL* flew from Romania and East Prussia using He 111s, Do 215B-2s, Ju 86Ps and Ju 88Bs. Often operating between 9,000 and 12,000m (29,500–39,350ft), they initially covered the frontier area but in the absence of opposition (Stalin ordered his fighters not to intercept the intruders) they ranged deeper, although in February they were restricted to the line Murmansk–Moscow–Rostov.[55] One Ju 86P was lost to bad weather near Vinnitsa on 15 April, but its captured crew were later released by advancing German troops.[56] COMINT was conducted from the expanded Reich, Hungary and Finland.

In April 1941 the Russians, who had bought 30 modern German aircraft in 1940, had allowed a delegation led by *Oberst* Heinrich Aschenbrenner (Air Attaché in Moscow) to visit aircraft and aero-engine factories. The delegation was very impressed but Schmid ignored its report, believing that, like the French before Munich, they had been deceived. He estimated the enemy's strength at 23 air divisions (there were actually 79, of which 55 were in the West) with a strength in European Russia of 7,300 aircraft, supported by 3,000 in the interior and 2,000 (actually 4,140) in the Far East (see Table 21). The *VVS-RKKA* (Soviet Army Air

93

Table 21. The *VVS-RKKA* in the West, 22 June 1941

District	Commander	Strength	*Lw* estimate
Leningrad	Major-General A. A. Novikov	1,270	1,400
Baltic	Major-General A. P. Ionov	1,140 }	1,650
Western	Major-General I. I. Kopets	1,472 }	
Kiev	Lieutenant-General Ye. S. Ptukhin	1,672 }	1,300
Odessa	Major-General F. G. Michugin	950 }	
Long Range	Colonel L. A. Gorbatsevich	1,346	None

Note: In the districts 59% of all aircraft were fighters, 31% were bombers and the remainder were assault and reconnaissance aircraft.

Force) actually had 7,850 aircraft in the West complemented by 1,500 *PVO* (Home Defence Force) fighters and 1,445 aircraft of the Navy's western fleets (40% were seaplanes), but Schmid correctly deduced that most Russian aircraft were obsolete. AA strength was estimated at 1,200 heavy and 1,200 light guns, but the *PVO* actually had 3,329 heavy and 330 light AA guns as well as 1,500 searchlights.

However, the Stalinist purges had cursed the *VVS*, which lost its experienced officers, including all who had collaborated with the Germans during the 1920s. Its third commander in three years, Lieutenant-General Pavel Rychagov, who had fought the Condor Legion, was arrested in April 1941 and shot in October together with Lieutenant-General Ivan Proskurov, head of Long Range Aviation.[57] His successor, Lieutenant-General Pavel Zhigarev, was as inexperienced as his major formation commanders, of whom 91% had held their posts less for than six months. Their squadrons had begun to re-equip but the western districts had received only 1,540 modern aircraft by June 1941 and most remained in depots, while only 19 of the 106 regiments scheduled for formation in 1941 had been activated; only one Frontal (light bomber) regiment had modern aircraft (Petlyakov Pe-2) although a quarter had begun conversion. Within the medium/heavy bomber (Long Range Aviation) force, a third of the bombers had no crews and of 520 heavy bombers only 11 were modern (Petlyakov TB-7/Pe 8) although 1,000 were on order, while none of the long-range escort fighter divisions scheduled for each of the four air corps had been formed. Many new aircraft were inferior to their opponents; indeed, of 540 Lavochkin LaGG-1/3, Mikoyan-Gurevich MiG-3 and Yakovlev Yak-1 fighters only the last matched the Bf 109, while the pilots' unfamiliarity with their new mounts created an appalling accident record, 138 aircraft and 141 men being lost in the first quarter of 1941. The expansion of the *VVS* was naturally accompanied by an extension of its facilities and it had 1,100 airfields, but only 200 of these were fully operational.[58]

To neutralise the *VVS*, *ObdL* wished to attack airfields after the artillery bombardment began at dawn, but the Army objected, fearing that the enemy would escape. Hitler agreed and ordered dawn air strikes, although this meant a night take-off and up to 40 minutes' flying time. Kesselring and the other *Luftflotte* commanders compromised by assigning *Ketten* of experienced crews to attack each fighter base, crossing the border at high altitude. Some 66% of the *Luftwaffe* strike force (637 aircraft and 231 fighters) swooped on 31 airfields as the German bombardment began on 22 June and discovered hundreds of aircraft parked in rows because Stalin regarded dispersal as 'provocative'. For the loss of two aircraft, the first wave destroyed an estimated 1,800, while later in the morning the second wave lost 33 aircraft to destroy 700, the pounding continuing throughout *'Barbarossa'*'s first days (see Table 22).[59] In these operations Greim's airmen by 26 June had flown 1,600 sorties against 77 airfields to claim 910 aircraft, including 774 on the ground, where the SD-2 anti-personnel bomb proved especially effective, while *Fliegerkorps II* neutralised every fighter base within a 300km arc. The scale of victory may be gauged from the fact that post-operation analysis confirmed Kesselring's claim of destroying some 2,500 Russian aircraft on the ground. However, the extensive facilities and vast amounts of equipment, probably the foundation for a future offensive, made many ponder.[60]

During the first fortnight of the campaign the bright summer skies became an aerial abattoir as Soviet Frontal Aviation counter-attacked, supported by medium and heavy bombers, the latter flying unescorted to arrive at predictable intervals. On 6 July *Major* Trautloft's *JG 54* (*Luftflotte 1*) shot down 65 out of the 73 bombers attacking a German bridgehead near Ostrov, while two days later *Major* Günther Lützow's *JG 3* (*Luftflotte 4*) was caught on the ground by 27 bombers but took off and claimed all of them. On 12 July *Hauptmann* Richard Leppla shot down *JG 51*'s 500th victim of the campaign. Mölders had his 100th and 101st victories three days later but on 19 July was appointed *Inspekteur der Jagdflieger*. So slow were some enemy aircraft that the *Jagdgruppen* had difficulty adjusting, but then many fighter pilots, such as *Majore* Gerhard Barkhorn (301) and Günther Rall (275), began to build tremendous scores in the East, where the 20-victory qualification for a *Ritterkreuz* was doubled by the end of 1941 then further increased to 50.[61] In the first week *ObdL* estimated total Russian air losses at 4,990 and German losses at 179, while Russian sources indicate that some 3,600 aircraft were lost in three weeks, of which 75% were on the ground, although, given the confu-

Table 22. *Luftwaffe* Losses in the East

Dates	Destroyed	Damaged
22 Jun–5 Jul	491	316
6–19 Jul	283	194
19 Jul–31 Aug	725	n/a
1-27 Sept	878	1,028

Source: USNA T971, Roll 26.

sion, even this figure may be an underestimate.[62] The losses of aircraft, infrastructure and much of its production facilities prevented Russian air power from recovering until late in 1942, although it exercised an active defence which focused upon tactical air support until mid-1943. This helped to shield German and Allied territory, although some 220 sorties were vainly directed against East Prussia while naval bombers struck Berlin. They also damaged Romania's oilfields, but Speidel's forces and the *FARR* made them pay a heavy price, claiming 143 victories by 21 October, including 73 by *Luftwaffe* fighters.

Army support became the *Luftwaffe*'s primary role within three days, with crews flying numerous daily sorties—five to eight for fighter pilots, four to six for *Kampfgruppen* and seven or eight for *Stukagruppen*. Within hours of the invasion Soviet troops found their storage depots laid waste, their land-line communications cut and every movement attracting a rain of bombs, while trains were trapped in sidings or on exposed stretches of line.[63] The Russians soon restricted daylight movement to small groups and entered the brooding forests whenever a reconnaissance aircraft appeared: as in Poland, the *Kampfgruppen* used one or two *Ketten* per *Gruppe* to fly armed reconnaissance missions which attacked targets of opportunity. *Stukas* and bombers disrupted counter-attacks before they could begin, but, unlike in the West, the primitive road system meant that the chokepoints were at river crossings rather than towns or villages. Ground fire was a major hazard and vengeful hands awaited any aircrew who survived, so *Major* Hubertus Hitschold, *Kommandeur* of *I./StG 2*, and his gunner had a lucky escape when they crash-landed near Vilna and were rescued by fellow *Stuka Experte Oberleutnant* Bruno Freitag, *Kapitän* of *3./StG 2*, who landed nearby.[64] '*Merkur*' doomed plans for airborne forces, apart from a drop on the Dvina bridges near Bogdanov on 25 June by 35 members of *Regiment Brandenburg* (the equivalent of the SAS) in two Ju 52s.[65]

In the early battles of envelopment Richthofen performed well, as usual, and liaison with the spearheads was strengthened by a radio-equipped *Flieger-verbindungsoffiziere (Flivo)* in each mechanised division, with the shortest response time generally two hours. On the Bug, Guderian and Loerzer reprised their previous year's success on the Meuse, the Brest-Litovsk Citadel succumbing after *KG 3* dropped an SC 1800 'Satan' on it, but Loerzer soon failed to keep pace with the Panzers. The grumbling Guderian was soothed by Kesselring as the tactical air support task was given to 'Old Eagle' and former Lufthansa pilot *Generalmajor* Martin Fiebig as *Nahkampfführer II*, although he was handicapped by a shortage of radios.[66] To avoid 'friendly fire' incidents the rigid 'bomb lines' of the previous year were abandoned and instead the ground forces displayed signal panels, used pyrotechnics and carried the *Reichsbanner* on their vehicles, yet incidents such as the bombing of *23. Infanterie Division* on 1 August were inevitable because of the fluid situation. There was little strategic reconnaissance once '*Barbarossa*' had begun

and photographic interpretation was sometimes poor; indeed, on 27 June a concentration of horse-drawn vehicles near Orsha was hammered after being mis-
taken for tanks.

With the *Luftwaffe*'s help, Bock's *Panzergruppen* enveloped the Soviet Army at
Minsk and then at Smolensk, where Kesselring's strike force was initially the only
means of stopping the enemy escaping. *Major* Walter Storp's *SKG 210* distinguished itself, flying 1,574 sorties between 22 June and 26 July and claiming 915
aircraft (823 on the ground), 165 tanks, 2,136 vehicles and 60 locomotives. The
Luftwaffe proved an 'equaliser' for the overstretched troops, although on one occasion *Major* Otto Weiss's *II. (Schl)/LG 2* found itself defending its own base as it
had in Arras 13 months earlier, but inevitably the enemy penetrated the cordons
which were often augmented by *Flak* batteries. With overcrowded airstrips under
threat, the 'black men' had the extra burden of defending bases using captured
small arms, although the more ambitious base commanders organised artillery
and anti-tank guns while *Oberst* Gottlob Müller at Bobruisk acquired tanks![67]
Before the Smolensk pocket was reduced, Richthofen was transferred northwards
to *Luftflotte 1* on 3 August with nine *Gruppen* (262 aircraft), leaving Loerzer with
19 *Gruppen* (including two of Richthofen's *Stukagruppen*) and 600 aircraft to support all of *Heeresgruppe Mitte*. The sudden decline of *Luftwaffe* strength, aggravated by bad weather, saw a brief renaissance of Russian air power around the
German salient of Yelna, east of Smolensk. Despite all Kesselring's efforts the
overstretched *Luftwaffe* could do little, and early in September the salient was
abandoned.[68]

Although Hitler always intended to exploit victories in Belorussia by advancing
upon Leningrad, *OKW* directives during July displayed a disturbing strategic incoherence as he sought to destroy the Russians first in the north and then in the
south while *OKH* wished to advance upon Moscow. This did not prevent Halder
peevishly complaining after a meeting with Waldau on 1 July that *ObdL*'s plans
were 'in an absolute muddle'. Directive 33 of 19 July diverted effort away from
Moscow but also demanded that *Luftflotte 2*, reinforced from the West, bomb
Moscow in retaliation for attacks upon allies. The first attack was on 21/22 July by
Fliegerkorps II and Löhr's *Fliegerkorps V*, which were soon joined by *Fliegerkorps I*
after it had been reinforced from the West by *KG 4*. Another three *Kampfgruppen*
(*I./KG 28*, *III./KG 26* and *KGr 100*) joined Loerzer, and together they flew 358
sorties against the Russian capital during July, briefly forcing Stalin's headquarters into underground Metro stations, whence it re-emerged as the bombing faded
away.[69] On 30 July Directive 34 confirmed that Bock was to remain on the defensive and ordered Rundstedt to continue his advance upon Kiev, but the main
effort was to be the advance upon Leningrad by Leeb's *Heeresgruppe Nord*, previously supported by *Fliegerkorps I*. Meanwhile Wild's *FlFü Ostsee* operated over the
Baltic with missions which included minesweeping (dropping bombs in mine-

fields) and attacking the White Sea–Baltic Canal, with several bombers lost when their SC 1000 bombs detonated prematurely. From August Wild interdicted traffic in the Gulf of Finland, sinking nine ships (21,346grt), then assisted the capture of Estonian islands (*Unternehmenen 'Beowulf I/II'*), temporarily operating under Wühlisch who was 'ticket punching' as *FlFü B*. These operations saw the new Me 321 Gigant (Giant) gliders used to bring in supplies. At the conclusion, Wild's command was disbanded on 27 October but the staff were transferred first to Berlin and, early the following year, to the Crimea as *FlFü Süd*.[70]

The arrival of Richthofen and *KG 4* doubled Keller's strength to 24 *Gruppen*, but he was to support *18. Armee* only until it reached the Leningrad–Moscow railway, a decision made by Hitler and Göring without reference to Brauchitsch.[71] Richthofen's new broom swept aside the old concepts of air support and brought in a more professional and effective approach.[72] The attack began on 6 August and Richthofen flew 4,742 sorties in 12 days, dropping 3,351 tonnes of bombs, as the Germans entered Leningrad's suburbs.[73] The price was high, 27 aircraft lost and 143 damaged, proof to some of Richthofen's 'heartlessness', but, with Leningrad's isolation imminent on 6 September, *OKW* published Directive 35 demanding the destruction of the Soviet forces around Kiev and the securing of the line of the Dnieper and warning that Bock's advance upon Moscow (*Unternehmen 'Taifun'*) would then be resumed (see Table 23). Leeb and Keller (who had 1,004 aircraft) were to transfer forces for *'Taifun'* (Typhoon) by 15 September, and Leeb was especially alarmed at the prospect of losing Richthofen's support. He telephoned *OKH* on 12 September demanding retention of *Fliegerkorps VIII*, only to be told that *'Taifun'* had priority, but he was allowed to retain *StG 2* (*Oberst* Oskar Dinort), which helped him isolate Leningrad on 26 September. He was aided by the *Kampfgruppen*, which also struck targets within the city. From 22 September Dinort bombed the Baltic Fleet, sinking three warships and damaging 10, including two battleships and two cruisers. *Leutnant* Hans-Ulrich Rudel (*III./StG 2*) distinguished himself, sinking the battleship *Marat*, but this was overshadowed by the loss of the recently appointed *Kommandeur*, *Hauptmann* Ernst-Siegfried Steen, while attacking the cruiser *Kirov*, which he severely damaged.[74] As Keller helped tighten

Table 23. The *Luftwaffe* in the East, 6 September 1941

	Fighters	Zerstörer	Bombers	Stukas	Recon	Total
Lfl 1	166	39	203	60	13	481
Lfl 2	44	–	141	55	11	251
Lfl 4	85	–	96	71	21	273
Total	295	39	440	186	45	1,005

Notes: Figures are for serviceable aircraft.
Source: Halder's diary, entry for 12 September.

the siege lines, *Luftflotte 1* entered a slow decline during October, although it supported an advance along the Volkhov River to Tikhvin, some 175km east of Leningrad, using the briefly established *FlFüTikhvin* (*Oberst* Hans Raithel, *Kommodore* of *KG 77*). The forward airfield proved inadequate and Tikhvin had to be abandoned on 12 December.[75]

Richthofen's movements reflected the increasing strain of keeping pace with the Panzers: his headquarters had moved 18 times by December, and during the first three weeks five of his *Gruppen* advanced 600km.[76] The *Luftwaffe*'s daily requirement in the East was 14,000 tonnes, but the supply system (aggravated by indifferent staff in the *Luftgaue zbV*) was sluggish and, unlike previous campaigns, few dumps were captured because the retreating Russians destroyed those which survived *Luftwaffe* attack.[77] Communications were a nightmare for the *Wehrmacht* because, in the absence of railways, it had to rely upon a system of fragile dirt tracks which became rutted in dry weather and swamps in wet, with endemic traffic jams.[78] Sometimes the jams were the *Luftwaffe*'s fault: *19. Panzer Division* was halted for hours by a column of *Luftwaffe* trucks which ignored movement orders, and to locate vital supplies *Luftflotte 4*'s staff had to fly along the roads, land, then pull rank in order to assure priority for their trucks.[79] Nine *Transportgruppen* were available to sustain the spearheads, but the shortage of aircraft meant that bombers were sometimes used, the first such missions apparently being flown by *Luftflotte 1* on 23 June. Such actions sustained the advance but only lulls reduced consumption and permitted dumps to be restocked. The scattered reconnaissance units, and especially the Corps squadrons (*Nahaufklärungsstaffeln*), faded away because they were too small to impose their will on the overstretched supply system. Halder noted on 10 July that some of Bock's *Staffeln* had no aircraft while *Nachtaufklärungsstaffel 2* had only two serviceable. The situation was exacerbated by Göring's desire to control the Army's reconnaissance squadrons, with 'takeover bids' being made and rejected before and during '*Barbarossa*'. The crisis continued until the creation in October of *Aufklärungsgruppen* for *Heeresgruppe Nord* and four of the more exposed army headquarters (*2., 6., 11.* and *17. Armees*), and this proved encouraging enough to stimulate the creation three months later of *Nahaufklärungsgruppen*.

In the south, despite the absence of *Stukas*, Greim supported Kleist's *Panzergruppe 1*, which reached the Dnieper opposite Kiev on 10 July but was forbidden to cross. Meanwhile attempts to destroy bridges over the river to impede enemy communications failed because poor airfields restricted bomber loads. Pflugbeil's *Fliegerkorps IV* and its allies had 10 days to eliminate enemy air power before the Romanians and *11. Armee* struck eastwards after *Major* Ulbricht's *KG 27* had mined Russia's southern ports. A month later, on 2 August, the Russian left was enveloped at Uman in heavy rain and thunderstorms, then eliminated within a week after an unseemly dispute between Greim and *Generalfeldmarschall* Walther von Reichenau, whose *6.Armee* held the pocket's northern side. The overstretched Greim rejected Reichenau's requests for support, raising unpleasant memories in *6. Armee* of May 1940 when it was suddenly deprived of air support just as it began its advance.[80] To avert a crisis of confidence, Rundstedt's and Löhr's staffs jointly allocated air support, which Reichenau soon received in full measure to thwart an attempt from Kiev to relieve the pocket. Lützow (*Kommodore, JG 3*) was appointed *Nahkampfführer Nord* with two of his own *Gruppen* and *III./StG 77*, but on his own initiative Greim despatched every aircraft as the defenders were about to be overwhelmed, to pound the enemy for three days despite low cloud, rain and high winds. It was largely through his efforts that the enemy was stopped, the *Luftwaffe* claiming 94 tanks and 148 vehicles.

By now a great enemy salient with 627,000 troops around Kiev was attracting German attention, and, even before Directive 34 was published, *Generaloberst* Heinz Guderian's *2. Panzergruppe* (supported by Fiebig and Loerzer) had turned south with *Generaloberst* Maximilian, *Freiherr* von Weichs' *2. Armee* to cross the River Desna supported by Loerzer's *Fliegerkorps II*.[81] The timely arrival of four *Gruppen* from Richthofen enabled Loerzer to assemble 500 aircraft for this thrust, with the close support *Staffeln* ready to operate from forward landing grounds at short notice. Rundstedt contained the enemy until 10 September, when Kleist struck northwards, supported by Greim's *Fliegerkorps V* with three *Kampf-*, one *Stuka-* and four *Jagdgruppen*, both *Fliegerkorps* hammering the Red Army and the rail network.[82] Within a day the Russians recognised the threat, but Stalin refused to sanction a withdrawal. As the *Panzergruppen* linked up on 16 September Greim outran his supplies and Löhr's own transport difficulties prevented relief, but fortunately there was little aerial opposition, with a daily average of just 300 Russian sorties.[83] As usual *Flak* strengthened the cordon, with *Oberst* Lichtenberger (*FlakR 104*) winning a *Ritterkreuz* for supporting *10. Motorisiert Division* on 18 September, while the *Luftwaffe* thwarted many break-out attempts. By 26 September the last embers of resistance had cooled, the Russians losing 616,300 men in a catastrophe which caused Stalin secretly to offer Hitler terms similar to those of Brest-Litovsk in 1918. Greim's men claimed 23 tanks, 2,171 motor vehicles and 52 trains from 12 to 21 September, having flown 1,422 sorties and dropped some 600 tonnes of bombs for the loss of 17 aircraft (32 casualties) and 14 damaged.[84]

After Kiev, Rundstedt's right drove into the Donetz Basin and the Crimea, supported by Greim and Pflugbeil respectively. Greim's spearhead was *Nahkampfführer Süd* (*Major* Schönborn) with three *Gruppen*, but the *rasputitsa* meant that only a trickle of fuel and ammunition reached the single-engine units, while the *Kampfgruppen* were so far in the rear that only small bomb loads could be carried. Greim was now milked of units: most of his *Jagdgruppen* went to *Luftflotte 2* and the last (*III./JG 52*) went to the Crimea on 22 October although it soon returned.

Kharkov fell on 24 October and Kleist (whose command later became *1. Panzerarmee*) advanced on Rostov, while from the newly captured Taganrog air base, despite numerous *VVS* attacks, *Fliegerkorps V* struck the rail network feeding reinforcements to the city and by 20 November had claimed the destruction of 12 trains and 51 locomotives. On 12 November five of Greim's six *Kampfgruppen* were sent westwards to rest and re-equip, leaving him with nine serviceable bombers, but there was some compensation with the arrival of *KG 27*, which helped Kleist take Rostov on 21 November. Its loss a week later forced Rundstedt's troops behind the River Mius, Reichenau then replacing Rundstedt and praising the *Nahkampffliegerführer* for covering the retreat in low cloud and snow. *ObdL* promptly withdrew *Fliegerkorps V* to Brussels for minelaying operations against Great Britain, but the staff were quickly transferred either to Smolensk to support *Heeresgruppe Mitte* or to the Crimea to become *Sonderstab Krim*.

To the south, Pflugbeil's *Fliegerkorps IV* helped *11. Armee* (now under *General der Infanterie* Erich von Manstein) to blast its way into the Crimea Peninsula on 28 October, although Soviet airmen were extremely active. By 1 November Pflugbeil had 13 *Gruppen*, with the fighters directed by Mölders, but this was to be the *Inspekteur der Jagdflieger's* last campaign. Flying home to attend the funeral of *Generalluftzeugmeister* Ernst Udet, he was killed on 22 November when his He 111 crashed in fog while landing at Breslau-Gandau. Six days earlier the Germans took Kerch, but the Russians prepared an amphibious assault to retake the port, the preparations going undetected because of bad weather and the weakness of Pflugbeil's *Fernaufklärungsstaffeln*. His *Kampfgruppen* remained active against shipping and claimed 16 vessels (18,000grt), as well as striking the Caucasian oilfields.[85]

Kiev cleared the way for the final assault upon Moscow, which *OKH* and *ObdL* were anxious to complete, the latter because Kesselring and Loerzer were earmarked for the Mediterranean. Certain of victory, *ObdL* also drew up plans to garrison the East, and on 8 October Halder noted that there would be a total of 18 *Gruppen*, three *Aufklärungsstaffeln* and five *Flakregimente*. There was something of an end-of-term feel about events, and within a week *StG 2* had lost its *Kommodore*, Dinort, who returned to Germany to act as Udet's Chief of Staff, and Hitschold, who was assigned *Stukaschule 1*. Towards the end of the month Jeschonnek telephoned Richthofen to inform him that *Fliegerkorps VIII* would spend the New Year in Bavaria and Austria.[86] To support 'Taifun', Kesselring welcomed back Richthofen and was reinforced by Löhr to assemble 1,320 aircraft, approximately half the *Luftwaffe* in the East, as well as both *Flakkorps*. Richthofen was not enthusiastic about supporting Bock's left (*9. Armee* and *3. Panzergruppe/Panzerarmee*) because the previous month's operations had halved his strength and he refused to accept responsibility for the outcome.[87] Loerzer's mission was to support Bock's right (Guderian's *2. Panzergruppe/Panzerarmee*), using Fiebig's 14 single-engine *Gruppen*

Table 24. *Luftflotte 2* **Operations**

Date	Fighter	Bomber	Recon	Total
21 Oct	49	168	2	219
22 Oct	123	481	20	624
23 Oct	140	458	17	615
24 Oct	208	441	13	662
25 Oct	173	455	23	651

Source: *Heeresgruppe Mitte* war diary (USNA T311, Roll 288).

for close air support while the *Kampfgruppen* with 400 bombers isolated the battlefield.

The offensive began on 30 September with Guderian striking towards Orel, which fell three days later, allowing Loerzer, on the ball for once, to fly in supplies for Fiebig, including 500 tonnes of fuel, despite opposition from every available Russian bomber.[88] Already the second stage of the offensive was under way as Bock's left punch was thrown on 2 October, with 1,387 sorties and 971 the following day, while on 7 October the Panzer spearheads linked at Vyazma, supported by some 800 bomber sorties.[89] Three days later the pocket was split in two (the second around Bryansk), with *Flak* support helping to reduce both by 20 October, *Flak* batteries alone taking some 4,000 prisoners. Richthofen then moved to Kalinin, where he was exposed to both air and ground threats as supplies were flown in. During the operation the Storch of Richthofen's Chief of Staff and Lipetsk veteran, the schoolmasterly *Oberst* Rudolf Meister, was shot down and burned as he visited *1. Panzerdivision*. By now the temperature was dropping noticeably, with rain and sleet turning Kesselring's airfields into bogs and reducing activity to some 600 sorties a day (see Table 24). The clouds' silver lining was the time they gave the 'black men' to maintain aircraft, and when the weather improved there was a remarkable scale of effort, especially by *Stukas*.

As the *Luftwaffe*'s time ran out, the *rasputitsa* impeded the advance and the Russians resisted every inch of the way. On 5 November Kesselring prepared to withdraw his forces, despite Bock's vigorous protests to Halder emphasising the demoralising effect of such a move. Yet on 11 November he received formal notice that Kesselring would be withdrawing units within a week; indeed, the next day Loerzer began handing over his sector to Fiebig as Bock desperately attacked to exploit the air power which was fading before his eyes. Loerzer's withdrawal involved 13 *Gruppen* which had flown 40,000 sorties since the beginning of the campaign, as he proudly proclaimed in an order of the day which also noted the expenditure of 23,150 tonnes of bombs and the destruction of 3,826 aircraft (2,169 in the air), 789 tanks and 14,339 vehicles. There had been 3,579 attacks upon railways in which 159 complete trains and 304 locomotives had been de-

stroyed. He did not forget his signallers, who had laid 3,000km of wire and transmitted 40,000 radio and 30,000 teletype messages—which may be taken as typical of all the *Fliegerkorps* in the East.

On 29 November Kesselring departed for Dresden and the next day Richthofen
assumed control of the *Luftwaffe*'s Moscow front, having taken control of Fiebig
four days earlier, but progress on the ground was slow as the weather restricted
operations and froze the muddy German airfields (see Table 25). The *VVS*, which
lost 293 aircraft to 5 December, was more active and had the advantage of using
all-weather airfields around Moscow.[90] On 6 December *'Taifun'* ended, and two
days later Directive 39 was issued ordering the *Wehrmacht* on to the defensive
because of 'the severe winter weather which has come surprisingly early'. The
Luftwaffe, which had lost 489 aircraft destroyed and 333 damaged since 28 September, was ordered to create a defensive infrastructure and to disrupt the recovery of enemy forces 'as far as possible'. No action by the Russians was anticipated
before March 1942 owing to their severe losses (some 2,500,000 men dead and
missing and 20,000 tanks lost, plus 6,100 combat and 11,800 second-line aircraft, according to Russian documents), but Stalin demanded an active defence
from his equally exhausted forces and on 5 December his skeletal armies took the
initiative, supported by 1,376 aircraft (859 serviceable), which flew an average
480 sorties a day. The featherweight push was a psychological hammer-blow to
the equally exhausted Germans, and, with little air support, Bock's overextended
defences collapsed, bringing down the other *Heeresgruppen* in a broad retreat.

As the wings of panic beat in many headquarters, Hitler issued his famous
stand-fast order on 16 December and three days later replaced Brauchitsch as
head of the Army. The depression extended into the *Luftwaffe*, and the *Fliegerkorps*

Table 25. *Luftwaffe* **Operations on the Moscow Front, November to mid-December
1941**

Date	*Flkorps VIII*	*Nakafu II*
Nov 30	269	65
Dec 1	227	123
Dec 2	423	185
Dec 3	18	2
Dec 4	303	117
Dec 5	152	7
Dec 6	175	92
Dec 8	3	41
Dec 9	2	22
Dec 12	79	23
Dec 13	36	11
Dec 14	144	95

Note: On 12 December there were also seven transport sorties.
Source: *Heeresgruppe Mitte* war diary, USNA Microfilm T311, Roll 288.

VIII account notes that Richthofen tried in vain to rouse *Generalmajor* Rudolf Eibenstein (*12. Flakdivision*) and *Generalleutnant* Veit Fischer (*Luftgau Moskau*) with a stirring exhortation.[91] While 'black men' and *Flak* units were organised into battlegroups to plug gaps, Richthofen was reinforced by four *Kampfgruppen* and, in addition to the five *Transportgruppen* he had already received under Morzik's command, he was sent another four on Hitler's orders to fly in an SS regiment from Cracow while Löhr sent other *Transportgruppen* with an *ad hoc* infantry battalion. These were aspirins to cure cancer, for the *Wehrmacht* was driven further westwards in the forthcoming weeks.

The disaster was caused by the German High Command's strategic incoherence, from which the *Luftwaffe* suffered worst, although the *VVS* remained a broken reed. Yet the superhuman efforts of the *Luftwaffe* had contributed much to Germany's earlier success. A British study notes that, although the *Luftwaffe* rarely had more than 2,500 aircraft between June and October, it averaged 1,200 sorties a day, and sometimes 2,000, with *Stukagruppen* displaying an average sortie rate of 75% of unit establishments, *Jagdgruppen* 60% and *Kampfgruppen* 40–45%.[92] Jeschonnek's pessimistic views to Halder in February 1941 were borne out and exacerbated by *ObdL*'s constant shuffling of units between sectors, which further eroded strength. By 1 November the *Luftwaffe* in the East, whose average monthly strength was 2,462 aircraft (1,119 strike), was losing every month 741 aircraft and 318 aircrew, with exhaustion reflected by December in a growing accident rate.[93] Neither factories nor schools could produce sufficient replacements, and with schools deprived of fuel to compensate for high consumption in the East there was an inevitable effect upon *Kampfgruppe* efficiency.

NOTES TO CHAPTER 3

1. See Dickfeld, pp.28–43.
2. For the background see Gundelach, pp.28–77. Gundelach is essential reading for anyone studying the *Luftwaffe* in the Mediterranean, while Shores' works provide much fascinating detail.
3. This was especially irritating as Pohl was able to give only a week's notice of the *Regia Aeronautica*'s intentions. Gundelach, pp.59–61.
4. Shores, *Air War for Yugoslavia, Greece and Crete* (hereafter Shores, *Balkans*), p.120.
5. Gundelach, pp.38–9, 81–3, 88–102; and Morzik, pp.101–3.
6. Hozzel eventually became *Kommodore* of StG 2 and distinguished himself during the Kharkov riposte in 1943. Enneccerus, a *Stuka* pioneer, became *Kommodore* of StG 77 and later a staff officer. After the war both joined the *Bundesluftwaffe*.
7. Shores, *Malta: The Hurricane Years* (hereafter Shores, *Hurricane*), pp.109–11, 114–15, 119–36.
8. During the spring *1./NJG 3* was transferred to shield Sicily, but it met with little success.
9. See Hermann, pp.71–100, 121–8.

10. Foreman, *1941-1*, p.296.

11. For German preparations see Gundelach, pp.150–66.

12. For the *JKRV* see Shores, *Balkans*, pp.173–4, 177,187–91.

13. For the *Luftwaffe* build-up see *Fall 'Marita'—Wehrmachtberichte über die Tätigkeit der Luftwaffe in Jugoslavia und Greichenland*, USNA T971, Roll 3, fr.751ff.

14. Found guilty of war crimes by a Yugoslav court, Löhr was executed on 26 February 1947.

15. For the background to *'Strafgericht'* and a well-argued apologia which ignores both Löhr's ancestry and the use by *Kampfgruppen* of both mines and incendiaries, see Gundelach, p.168.

16. For operations over Yugoslavia see Gundelach, pp.170–7; and Shores, *Balkans*, pp.179–229.

17. 'Hajo' Hermann of *KG 30* hit one of the ships and barely reached safety in Rhodes after AA fire damaged an engine. Hermann, pp.101–20.

18. The decision to evacuate British forces was made on 20 April and two days later the RAF withdrew to Crete, leaving a few Hurricanes.

19. One of the ships dive-bombed, but not sunk, was carrying 40 *Luftwaffe* prisoners. Beevor, pp.50–1.

20. Shores, *Balkans*, pp.289–97.

21. Ibid., pp.273–4.

22. For the Greek campaign see Gundelach, pp.177–98; and Shores, *Balkans*, pp.230–309.

23. *Fliegerkorps XI* was established on 15 December 1940 to command the paratroops of *Fliegerdivision 7* and the airborne soldiers of *22. (Luftlande) Infanteriedivision*.

24. Beevor, pp.73–4.

25. Six months before *'Merkur'* the local British commander deduced every potential airborne objective and landing zone. Ibid., p.72.

26. He was replaced by *Oberst* Richard Heidrich, commander of *FJR 3*.

27. Meindl was flown out by a transport pilot called Köntiz, who flew to a nearby beach on his own initiative. Beevor, p.152.

28. However, a Cretan woman did hack off the engagement ring finger of a *JG 77* pilot before British troops arrived. Beevor, pp.235–7; and Shores, *Balkans*, pp.341–50.

29. Freyberg had access to 'Ultra' material but was handicapped by the large number of administrative troops on the island as well as a lack of weapons and ammunition, especially for the 10,000 Greek soldiers.

30. Waldau noted in his diary a 'morbid nervousness' at *ObdL* on 20 May (BA MA Msg 1/141). See also Bekker, p.193.

31. Shores, *Balkans*, p.393.

32. For *'Merkur'* see Beevor, pp.59–232; Bekker, pp.184–200; Gundelach, pp.200–21; Kuhn, pp.56–131; and Shores, *Balkans*, pp.314–16, 320–402.

33. It was still known as *Italuft*.

34. For Iraq see Gundelach, pp.235–54. One of the casualties was *Major* Axel von Blomberg, son of *Generalfeldmarschall* Werner von Blomberg, who secured Nazi control of the *Luftwaffe* in 1933. Axel was accidentally shot dead by Iraqis on 11 May as he landed to become *Luftwaffe* liaison officer to the Iraqi Air Force.

35. Gerhard Felmy ended the war as a *Generalmajor* in charge of *1. Fallschirmarmee* supplies.

36. He held the rank of *General der Infanterie* from the date of his appointment.

37. Gundelach, *KG 4*, pp.119–26; and Schmidt, *KG 26*, pp.108–9.

38. *FlFü Sizilien* was disbanded on 12 January 1942 and Roth went to Norway. For the background see Gundelach, pp.329–38.

39. See Morzik and Hümmelchen, App. 12.

40. See Green, p.94; and Morzik and Hümmelchen, pp.110–13. Yet in the first month *KGrzbV 400* lost 11 aircraft.

41. For this campaign see Gundelach, pp.300–26; and Playfair, Vol. III, p.99.

42. BAM, p.138.

43. Shores, *Hurricane*, pp.349–63.

44. Taylor, pp.72–5.

45. From late February there was a hare-brained scheme, originating with Göring and later taken up by Keitel, for an airborne assault upon the Baku oilfields, but wiser counsels prevailed. Leach, pp.145–9.

46. See also Irving, *Göring*, pp.307–9, 317–19.

47. See also Irving, *Milch*, pp.114–17.

48. On 22 June Jeschonnek is reported to have exclaimed, 'At last, a proper war.' Irving, *Göring*, p.328.

49. Foreman, *1941-2*, pp.266, 268.

50. *Generalleutnant* Hermann Plocher, *The German Air Force versus Russia, 1941* (hereafter Plocher, *1941*), p.21.

51. Aircraft were supplied by Hungary (52), Romania (302), Italy (84 from August) and Slovakia (63) as well as Finland (307).

52. Their total strength dropped from 1,760 in May 1940 to 1,338 in June 1941. See also Murray, pp.76–7.

53. Leach, pp.99, 129–30.

54. Ibid., p.130.

55. Reinhardt, p.8. The sectors covered were *Luftflotte 2 (1./ObdL)*, *Luftflotte 1 (2./ObdL)* and *Luftflotte 4 (3./ObdL)*. Rowehl covered the area between Minsk and Kiev as well as flying deep-penetration missions. Hoffmann, Vol. II, p.81.

56. Only one of the three cameras provided damaging evidence. Kozhevnikov, p.24.

57. For the circumstances see Volkogonov, p.375; and Shukman pp.97, 161, 362.

58. Data on the Soviet air forces is based upon Andersson, pp.23ff; Erickson, *Stalingrad*, pp.64–5; Hardesty, Apps 3, 11, 12; Kozhevnikov, pp.13, 18, 20–3; Shukman, p.161; and Tyushkevich, pp.231, 242.

59. The fate of German aircrew who fell into Russian hands was extremely uncertain, as demonstrated by that of two *Kapitäne* who failed to return on 22 June. *Oberleutnant* Rudolf Naumann's crew (*3./KG 54*) was murdered five days later, while that of *Hauptmann* Willi Stemmler (*4./KG 51*) survived with the help of Ukrainian peasants and reached German lines during July (Dierich, *KG 51*, p.163; and Radktke, *KG 54*, p.289). *Oberleutnant* Fritz Bliesner and his crew of *5./KG 55* were twice shot down during 1941 and successfully evaded capture. Bliesner's luck ran out on 25 November 1942.

60. Waldau noted in his diary on 15 July that 63 major bases were being constructed (BA MA MSg 1/1410). See also Rudel, p.29.

61. Both survived the war and eventually joined the *Bundesluftwaffe*. Barkhorn flew 100 sorties before his first victory on 2 July 1941, while Rall was *hors de combat* for most of 1942 after breaking his back when shot down. The career of the greatest *Experte*, *Major* Erich 'Bubi' Hartmann, is especially interesting because, although he laid the foundations of his 352 victories in the East, it was not until the summer of 1943 that he began to build a respectable score. Like Barkorn and Rall, he joined the *Bundesluftwaffe*. See Williamson, pp.99–100, 117–19, 136–7; and Bekker, pp.220–1.

62. A declassified Russian study states that the *VVS* lost 3,670 aircraft to *Luftflotten 1* and 2 by 10 September; another 1,218 were destroyed in *Luftflotte 4's* area of operations to 6 July (Glantz and House, Table B). *Der Luftkrieg in Osten* (USNA T971, Roll 18, fr.793) states that the *Luftwaffe* lost 160 aircraft in the first week and destroyed 4,017.

63. The 7th Soviet Tank Division lost 63 of 368 tanks and all its transport in a 14-hour march (Glantz, *Initial Period*, pp.197, 200, 202, 259). However, on 26 June *StG 2* attacked 60 tanks near Grodno and later discovered that only one had been knocked out (Smith, *Stuka*, p.68).

64. Both men won the *Ritterkreuz* and survived the war. Their contemporary in the '*Immelmann*' *Geschwader*, the great *Stuka Experte* Hans-Ulrich Rudel, rescued six crews in this fashion. Brütting, pp.133, 196.

65. Kuhn, p.133.

66. The British learned of '*Barbarossa*' when a Polish countess with the RAF's Y-Service overheard communications between *Fliegerkorps V* bombers and *1. Panzergruppe* columns and recognised names of the villages they mentioned (Clayton, pp.139–41). For the *Nahkampfführer* and *Flivos* see Muller, pp.48–51.

67. Müller held several *Luftgau* commands and was killed during the Battle of Berlin in April 1945.

68. For *Luftflotte 2* operations to the Battle of Kiev see Plocher, *1941*, pp.79–116.

69. Moscow was last bombed on 5/6 April 1942, by which time there had been 11 day and 76 night attacks. Bekker, pp.223–4; and Muller, p.51.

70. See Plocher, *1941*, pp.146n,157–77; and Rohwer and Hümmelchen, pp.69–81.

71. *II./JG 27* was transfered to the Mediterranean and *StG 1*, under *Oberst* Walter Hagen, a former Heinkel test pilot, remained with Kesselring.

72. Muller, p.56.

73. Russian sources state that 1,702 Soviet aircraft were lost between 10 July and 30 September.

74. Brütting, p.252; and Rohwer and Hümmelchen, p.87.

75. For *Luftflotte 1* operations to the New Year see Murray, p.84; and Plocher, *1941*, pp.136–58.

76. BAM, Map 15. *StG 3* moved some 600km in a month.

77. A British intelligence document noted (probably through 'Ultra' intercepts) that *Luftgau zbV 4* reported average daily fuel consumption each month between July and October at 50, 167, 111 and 85 tonnes (Russian Campaign Papers, PRO Air 40/2037). See also Murray, pp.83–4.

78. Russian railways had to be converted to the European standard gauge before the *Reichsbahn* could use them. Railways were essential not only because of the quantity of supplies they could move but also because they were the only reliable all-weather transport system. During the autumn and spring, rain and/or thaw turned roads to swamps in a period known to the Russians as the *rasputitsa*, or 'the time without roads'.

79. Plocher, *1941*, p.60; and Seaton, p.118.

80. See Hooton, pp.250–1.

81. Between 9 and 13 September Loerzer provided Fiebig with three *Jagdgruppen* to augment his two *Gruppen*, but he retained seven *Kampf-*, three *Stuka-*, one *Jagd-* and one *Jabogruppen*.

82. On 14 September Greim received a *Stukagruppe* from Pflugbeil.

83. Greim's men claimed only 107 aircraft, including 65 on the ground.

84. For the Battle of Kiev see Plocher, *1941*, pp.117–35, and a captured report in German Air Force operations against the USSR (PRO Air 40/1925). The British, in a document dated 1 October 1941, estimated that Greim's men flew 846 sorties from 15 to19 September and consumed 472 tonnes of fuel. Russian Campaign Papers (PRO Air 40/2037).

85. For *Luftflotte 4* operations see Plocher, *1941*, pp.46–78, 117–35, 202–24.

86. *Fliegerkorps VIII Einsatz Russland-Mittelabschnitt* (BA MA RL8/49).

87. Muller, pp.57–8.

88. The Russians had only 364 Frontal aircraft, backed by 344 aircraft of the *PVO*.

89. During *'Taifun'* Loerzer had 40 *Flivo*s to ensure smooth cooperation. Muller, p.49.

90. The *VVS* appears to have flown 51,300 sorties in the defence of Moscow, 14% by the *PVO*.

91. *Fliegerkorps VIII Einsatz Russland-Mittelabschnitt* (BA MA RL8/49).

92. BAM, p.174.

93. Murray, Table XIII. The *Luftwaffe* lost 371 aircraft in the East in December. Reinhardt, p.370.

CHAPTER FOUR

The Western Shield

October 1940–December 1942

The autumn of 1940 did not end *Luftwaffe* daylight offensive operations but changed their nature from massed bomber to harassing attacks which kept the British on their toes for the next three years. By the time most of the *Kampfgruppen* went east in the summer of 1941, RAF pressure in western Europe was mounting, yet the *Luftwaffe* was able to withstand this pressure comfortably until mid-1943.

As the days shortened during the last quarter of 1940 the *Luftwaffe* tried to erode enemy fighter strength through large fighter/*Jabo* sweeps supplemented by a 300-plane mission, *Unternehmen 'Opernball'* (Opera Ball), against Fighter Command's infrastructure on 20 October. The *Kampfgruppen* relied upon surprise attacks, or *Seeräuber/Pirat-angriffe* ('Pirate Raids'), upon factories and harbours with tragi-comical support by the 103 aircraft of the *Regia Aeronautica*'s *CAI*, the German raids worrying those responsible for war production until well into 1941. Specialists in these raids included *Ritterkreuz*-winners *Oberleutnant* Erich Heinrichs (*II./KG 54*), *Leutnant* Karl Höflinger (*III./KG 77*) and *Hauptmann* Alfred Kindler (*II./KG 2*), but all eventually fell to the defences.[1] *ObdL*'s November 1940 directive for the conduct of air operations indicated that London remained the primary target, with day attacks by escorted *Jabos* from high altitude (5,000m; 16,500ft) and by individual bombers exploiting cloud cover. *Jagdgruppen* sweeps continued, although the weather increasingly restricted operations, with the last big dogfight on 28 November off the Isle of Wight, where Wick, clearly suffering from combat fatigue, was killed barely a month after becoming *Kommodore* of *JG 2*. He was succeeded by *Major* Wilhelm Balthasar.

Fighter Command also saw radical changes at this time, with the replacement of Park at No 11 Group by Leigh-Mallory, who, encouraged by Douglas, followed the German example of reorganising squadrons into larger tactical units (Wings) of three squadrons. Just after noon on 27 December two Spitfires of No 92 Squadron strafed targets at Abbeville to herald Fighter Command's more aggressive role in the New Year (see Table 26). These low-level fighter sweeps, later designated 'Rhubarbs', were part of the 'leaning forward' policy to erode the German war machine and *Luftwaffe* strength. On 10 January the policy's second element began when 'Circus 1' was flown with a small bomber formation trailing its coat to attract enemy fighters, which its strong escort would engage, and this was

Table 26. RAF Offensive Operations, 1 October 1940–30 June 1941

| Month | Day Operations | | | | Night Operations | | | |
	Fighter Cd		Bomber Cd		Fighter Cd		Bomber Cd	
Oct 1940	–		82	(2)	–		455	(3)
Nov 1940	–		55	(1)	14	(–)	352	(5)
Dec 1940	2	(–)	16	(–)	14	(–)	470	(7)
Jan 1941	234	(3)	40	(1)	24	(2)	171	(–)
Feb 1941	850	(17)	60	(2)	8	(–)	504	(7)
Mar 1941	599	(6)	124	(1)	51	(2	467	(7)
Apr 1941	640	(17)	534	(16)	58	(1)	750	(7)
May 1941	596	(12)	275	(14)	78	(–)	438	(3)
Jun 1941	3,956	(57)	153	(3)	56	(–)	1,277	(15)
Total	6,875	(112)	1,186	(37)	303	(5)	3,607	(39)

Note: In March and April intruders destroyed another bomber at night.
Sources: Monthly Operational Summaries Fighter Command, Air Defence Great Britain and 2nd Tactical Air Force (PRO Air 16/1036); Middlebrook and Everitt; Day Bombing Raid Sheets (PRO Air 14/3361–3362); Night Bombing Raid Sheets (PRO Air 14/2666–2672).

soon followed by 'Rodeo' massed fighter sweeps and 'Ramrod' fighter escort missions for bombers. An aggressive officer, Leigh-Mallory was repeating Trenchard's offensive patrol policy of the Great War which might be likened to the bull-like tactics of early bare-knuckle boxers. Like the more scientific boxers, the *Jagdgruppen* responded with the principles established by Manfred von Richthofen in the Great War of striking as, and when, they wished, avoiding the attackers' wild swings, as *Oberleutnant* Georg Michalek's *II./JG 3* demonstrated during 'Circus 1' by shooting down one of the escorting Hurricanes. A few days later *JG 3* shot down seven fighters (two more collided) escorting 'Circus 3', suffering only minor damage to two Bf 109s. On 2 July 1941 four out of 12 Blenheims participating in 'Circus 29' were shot down, together with eight fighters, at a cost of four Bf 109s destroyed or badly damaged, including *Oberleutnant* Martin Rysavy, *Kapitän* of *2./JG 26*, killed in error by *Flak*. The RAF's only significant success occurred on 15 May when Grauert, the *Fliegerkorps I* commander, whose reputation had been built in Poland, met his nemesis when Polish pilots from No 303 Squadron shot down his transport near Aire.

During June the scale of Douglas's offensive increased massively, yet Leigh-Mallory's assumption that the *Jagdgruppen* would automatically meet the challenge proved to be wishful thinking, with the scales further tipped against him by qualitative inferiority (see Table 27). None of his single-engine aircraft, even the Spitfire IX introduced in 1942, had an operational radius beyond 300km, and if the pressure grew too great (as in 1944) the *Jagdgruppen* could have been withdrawn beyond that. However, this was unnecessary, for, having learned the advantages of radar-based air defence, the Germans used them to outweigh their numerical inferiority (see Table 28). Early in 1941 they began augmenting the

Flugmelde- and *Funkhorchdienst* with a radar network which by March 1942 extended from Heligoland to the Biscay coast, with 32 *Freya (FuMG 80)* and 57 *Würzburg (FuMG 62A)* sets in a command and control system headed by the *JaFü* headquarters with *Flugwachkommando* reporting centres.[2] When *Luftflotte 2* was withdrawn it left behind Osterkamp's *JaFü 2*, responsible for the sector from the Schelde to the Seine, while *Oberst* Werner Junck's (then *Oberst* Max-Josef Ibel's) *JaFü 3* defended air space to the west. *JaFü 1* was re-formed on 1 April to defend the Netherlands, being renamed *Mitte* on 9 August under the baby-faced 'Old Eagle' *Generalmajor* Karl-Bertram von Döring, who had just been relieved by Mölders as *Inspekteur der Jagdflieger*.[3] Each *JaFü* controlled a *Jagdgeschwader*, from west to east *Major* Walter Oesau's *JG 2 'Richthofen'*, *Oberstleutnant/Oberst* Adolf Galland's *JG 26 'Schlageter'* and *Oberst* Carl Schuhmacher's (later *Major* Erich von Selle's) *JG 1*, but re-equipment and rest meant that the shield was weak: in

---

Table 27. RAF Offensive Operations, Western Europe, July–December 1941

| Month | Day Operations | | | | Night Operations | | | |
	Fighter Cd		Bomber Cd		Fighter Cd		Bomber Cd	
Jul 1941	5,961	(112)	499	(53)	115	(–)	423	(5)
Aug 1941	6,271	(108)	418	(17)	65	(3)	319	(3)
Sep 1941	3,153	(78)	227	(10)	39	(1)	457	(3)
Oct 1941	2,719	(50)	177	(13)	34	(–)	428	(13)
Nov 1941	1,644	(48)	17	(–)	27	(–)	419	(6)
Dec 1941	747	(20)	68	(9)	31	(1)	642	(9)
Total	20,495	(416)	1,406	(108)	311	(7)	2,688	(39)

Notes: Bomber Command night sorties exclude minelaying and leaflet operations. Army Co-operation Command 'Rhubarb' and bomber sorties are included with Fighter and Bomber Command figures. Figures in parentheses are failed to return.
Sources: Monthly Operational Summaries of Fighter Command (PRO Air 16/1036); Middlebrook and Everitt; Night Bombing Raid Sheets (PRO Air 14/2673–2675); Day Bombing Raid Sheets (PRO Air 14/3363–4); and Army Co-operation Command Operational Year Book 1942, Appendix (PRO Air 24/100).

Table 28. The *Luftwaffe* in the West

| Date | Fighters | | Bombers | Recon | Total | |
	Day	Night				
27 Sept 1941	430	n/a	226	105	761	(+)
27 Dec 1941	527	n/a	130	140	797	(+)
30 Mar 1942	532	213	208	130	1,083	
30 Jun 1942	564	243	233	148	1,188	
30 Sep 1942	599	346	276	145	1,366	
30 Dec 1942	636	379	205	128	1,348	

Notes: Excludes seaplanes and transports.
Source: *Luftwaffe* first-line strength is based on German documents. PRO Air 40/1207.

July 1941, for example, *II./JG 26* (*Hauptmann* Walter Adolph) began converting from the Bf 109E-7 to the Fw 190A-1 Würger (Shrike) while *7./JG 26* was in Sicily.[4] An unusual *Rottehund* in *JG 1* during 1941 was *SS-Sturmbannführer (Major)* Reinhard Heydrich, a cashiered naval officer who was as evil as he looked. Heydrich, one of Himmler's deputies, was ultimately banned from flying by Hitler, but as compensation he was promoted *SS Gruppenführer (Generalleutnant)* and became Protector of Bohemia-Moravia, where he was assassinated a few months after leaving *JG 1*.[5]

Like Park, or the 'Red Baron' a generation earlier, the *Jagdgruppen* held the initiative and selected their own moments to strike. During the good flying months of the summer and early autumn most of their missions were scrambles (*Alarmstarts*), which accounted for up to 93% of all sorties, but as the weather deteriorated they flew more patrols and intercepted fewer missions (see Table 29). Early warning of major operations came from the *Funkhorchdienst*, whose detection of pre-flight testing of radios gave clues to the imminence and scale of the attack, leading to radar stations being placed on higher alert. The *Freya*s would observe formations assembling and alert both *Jagdführer* and *Geschwader*, the latter placing their *Gruppen* on standby. Once the attackers' direction was known, the *Jagdgruppen* would take off and, while observing radio silence, receive a running commentary, often by the *Geschwader* signals officer, using *Freya* and *Flugmeldedienst* information with *Wurzbürg* giving the altitude. The *Kommandeure* would break radio silence to place formations in an advantageous tactical position, then lead the attacks, which the *Jagdfliegerführer* and *Stäbe* followed through radio chatter

Table 29. *Luftflotte 3 Jagdgruppen* Activity, 1941

Month	Scrambles	Patrols	Escort
Jul 1941	4,385	–	127
Aug 1941	4,258	–	77
Sept 1941	2,534	–	105
Oct 1941	2,553	–	65
Nov 1941	1,287	683	77
Dec 1941	1,133	334	56

Source: *Luftkrieg gegen England* (USNA T321, Roll 176).

Table 30. Flak Batteries in the West

Year	Heavy	Light/Med	Searchlight	Total
1940	368	353	78	799
1941	97	146	71	314
1942	122	183	99	404

Source: Koch, p.144.

Table 31. *Luftflotte 3* Activity/Losses, July–December 1941

Month	Bomber		Fighter		Reconnaissance	
Jul 1941	1,388	(42)	5,319	(42)	182	(1)
Aug 1941	990	(21)	4,663	(18)	196	(–)
Sep 1941	981	(13)	2,915	(15)	143	(2)
Oct 1941	1,106	(21)	2,740	(8)	200	(4)
Nov 1941	1,086	(15)	2,202	(5)	195	(2)
Dec 1941	858	(17)	1,696	(5)	192	(4)

Note: Losses are in parentheses.
Source: *Luftkrieg gegen England* (USNA T321, Roll 176).

and ground observer reports.[6] The odds against the 'Tommies' were further stacked by the *Luftwaffe*'s qualitative superiority, first with the introduction of the Bf 109F in March and then by the Fw 190A in July, the latter aircraft proving superior to the newly introduced Spitfire V. Although the 'Friedrich' used 87-octane (B4) fuel, it was superior over 6,000m (20,000ft) to the Spitfire V, which used 100-octane fuel. It was one of these fighters which brought down the British ace Wing Commander Douglas Bader on 9 August (Bader was later entertained by Galland in the *JG 26* mess and was shown the cockpit of a Bf 109F, but the one-legged Huth, recently appointed *JaFü 2* and now a *Generalmajor*, had his pistol ready to prevent the legless Briton from flying away).[7] The Fw 190 would prove superior in every respect to the Spitfire V, but design faults meant that it was plagued by engine problems which *JG 26* had to resolve and did not become fully operational until September, after which it began to demonstrate its superiority.[8] Adolph had the misfortune to be the first combat victim and was replaced by Malta ace 'Jochen' Müncheberg, who led *II./JG 26* to their first victory (four Spitfires over Boulogne on 21 September). By the end of the year *JG 26* had completely re-equipped with the Fw 190, with *Major* Gerhard Schöpfel becoming *Kommodore* after Galland was appointed *Inspekteur der Jagdflieger* following Mölders' tragic death. Mention should also be made of the formidable *Flakwaffe*, whose numbers halved in the summer but were still adequate to take a steady toll of the attackers (see Table 30).

The British suffered badly during 1941: Fighter Command's daytime loss rate was around 2%, while Bomber Command's (largely No 2 Group) was 7.68%, excluding anti-shipping missions, with ominous increases during the last quarter. From 14 June 1941 until the end of the year, Fighter Command lost 411 aircraft over the Channel, 14 during the last 'Circus', and although its pilots claimed 731 victories, the *Jagdgruppen* lost only 103, leading a post-war RAF staff study to observe that every *Luftwaffe* aircraft destroyed cost the RAF 2.5 pilots.[9] By contrast, the *Jagdgruppen*, whose loss rate was less than 1% (see Table 31), destroyed four fighters for every one they lost, and many *Experten* honed their skills over western Europe, including the diminutive *Oberleutnant* Josef 'Pips' Priller, who claimed 19 aircraft (17 Spitfires) in 26 days from 16 June 1941, his 20th victory on 14 July bringing his total to 40. Yet, curiously, when the RAF Air Staff began to conserve resources from October by reducing the scale of the offensive, morale in Fighter Command apparently declined, especially when 'Rodeos' and 'Circuses' were abandoned at the end of the year as the overstretched RAF faced demands not only from the Mediterranean but also the new Far Eastern theatre.

During 1941 Bomber Command occasionally risked its growing four-engine bomber force in small-scale surprise daylight raids on French harbours, notably Brest, but rarely with any success, while the majority of night attacks on western European targets were conducted by crews who were completing their operational training. The need to protect Brest was a major headache for Sperrle because it became the refuge first of the battlecruisers *Scharnhorst* and *Gneisenau* and later also of the cruiser *Prinz Eugen*. As part of a campaign to prevent these ships from returning to the Atlantic, Bomber Command began a 10-month offensive on 29 March 1941 which involved 2,928 sorties, 171 of them in daylight, but at great cost, partly at the hands of *Oberst* Engel's *FlakR 100* but increasingly from *JG 2*, which was concentrated in Brittany and inflicted 12% losses during raids on 24 July. Night bombing was safer in the absence of night fighters and *Flak* claimed only 18 victims, but few bombs hit the ships, although the night of 7/8 December saw the first use of the Oboe electronic navigation aid.

Raeder pressed for the ships' return to German waters, winning Hitler's agreement because he wanted them to underpin the defence of Norway, and it was he who advocated exploiting the short winter days for a dash through the Channel, *Unternehmen 'Cerberus'*. *ObdL* was not happy about providing air cover, with Jeschonnek remarking to Galland that if *'Cerberus'* failed the *Luftwaffe* would be made the scapegoats, and when they met Hitler, Keitel, Raeder and the task force commander *Vizeadmiral* Otto Ciliax on 12 January to discuss the *Luftwaffe* element, he was soon proved right. The Navy demanded massive fighter protection and again won Hitler's support, but Jeschonnek stood his ground and refused to give any guarantees or to reinforce the western fighter forces. Galland was given executive power for the *Luftwaffe* operation, *Unternehmen 'Donnerkeil'* (Thunderbolt), which was prepared in conditions of such security that he and Jeschonnek signed secrecy pledges before leaving Hitler's headquarters. He worked out the details with *Oberst* Karl Koller, Sperrle's Chief of Staff, and to assemble sufficient strength they had to mobilise some training units. The route was subdivided into three sectors based upon the three existing *JaFü* boundaries, but to ensure local control Ibel (who had defended the Maastricht bridges so magnificently as *Kommodore* of *JG 27* in May 1940) embarked in *Scharnhorst* as *JaFü Schiff* with a signals team led by *Oberst* Elle. Eight dummy escort runs involving 450 sorties were made between 22 January and 10 February to perfect the arrangements, while

Martini prepared to jam British radio-telephone frequencies; further, a subtle jamming programme created 'atmospheric interference' which degraded the performance of British coastal radars. In addition 15 Do 217s of *III./KG 2* were to fly electronic deception missions over the western Channel to divert enemy fighters. Coeler's *Fliegerkorps IX* was to strike British bases in south-west England and to be prepared to strike at naval forces which might operate in the eastern Channel (with five *Ergänzungsgruppen* in reserve), while *FAGr 123* and Bruch divided responsibility for reconnaissance in the west and the east respectively. To ensure constant air support some *Jagd-* and *Nachtjagdgruppen* would keep pace with the task force as it made its way up the Channel, and the 'black men' had to ensure that refuelling and re-arming the fighters took no more than 30 minutes.

On 7 February the *Luftwaffe* completed its preparations after the 'weather frogs' had indicated suitable meteorological conditions for the mission from 11 February, on which day a joint-service conference confirmed that the task force would leave within hours. Galland flew to *JG 26*'s command post in the Pas de Calais to direct the operation and to brief the *Kommodore*. Anticipating *'Cerberus'* through 'Ultra' intercepts, the British assembled 100 bombers and several torpedo bomber squadrons to thwart it, but their hopes were dashed through a combination of bad luck, bungling and inertia. The bad luck was that a bomber raid delayed the task force's departure for three hours, then airborne radar malfunctions prevented Coastal Command from detecting the ships rounding Brittany.

To avoid alerting Fighter Command's radars, night fighters did not appear until 0800 on 12 February, and they remained on station at low level for three hours, some 19 sorties being flown before *JG 2* appeared. From then onwards four *Schwärme* covered the task force for 30 minutes at low level and in conditions of absolute radio silence, each relief arriving 10 minutes before the end of the patrol to assure an overlap. It was during one such relief that two Spitfires returning from a 'Rhubarb' shot past the warships, but they did not alert the defences until they reached base. Despite interference British radars spotted both the fighters and the task force, but Fighter Command waited two hours before investigating and failed to alert either the Royal Navy or Coastal Command (whose anti-shipping forces had stood down) until the task force entered the Strait of Dover. Meanwhile, to occupy British fighters, *III./KG 2* flew some 25 sorties against British airfields.

The British riposte began just as *JG 2* was being relieved by *JG 26*, whose *Kommodore*, Schöpfel, led *III. Gruppe*'s Fw 190s against six Swordfish torpedo bombers escorted by 11 Spitfires. As Galland lifted radio silence the Swordfish, led by Lieutenant-Commander Eugene Esmonde, vainly sought to penetrate the battlecruisers' shield, but all were destroyed and only five of the 18 men survived. By then the task force was through the Strait. As the cloud ceiling slowly descended like a curtain to a layer of a sea mist and snowstorms, the humiliated

British strove desperately for success, but with the *Jagdgruppen* now close to their bases Galland was able to double the umbrella and to stage his fighters at various levels. In vain the RAF despatched 242 bomber sorties, including some by new Douglas Bostons which were not officially operational, but the vigilant fighter pilots (some flying their fourth sortie) and *Flak* crews inflicted 7% casualties upon them.[10] The situation became chaotic, with both side's bombers attacking their own ships in error, one *'Holzhammer'* crew bombing Ciliax as he transferred flags after *Scharnhorst* had struck a mine. The admiral demanded more fighter protection, but as dusk fell and Galland flew north to Jever to supervise the last stage of *'Donnerkeil'* the air battle ended, and even the night fighters sent to cover the task force's entry into the Elbe had to be withdrawn. The ships reached sanctuary by midnight. *'Donnerkeil'* was a tremendous success, the *Luftwaffe* flying more than 300 fighter and 40 bomber sorties and losing 17 fighters and five bombers (including two from *III./KG 2* which collided while returning to base), or some 5–6% of sorties flown, as well as 23 men. The Germans claimed some 60 British aircraft but actually shot down 41; nevertheless, Galland later described *'Donnerkeil'* as the greatest hour in his career.[11] But within a fortnight *Prinz Eugen* had been torpedoed by a submarine and *Gneisenau* had been crippled during a bombing raid on Kiel.[12]

'Donnerkeil' proved to be a watershed in electronic warfare, for by using jammers Martini removed British inhibitions concerning the use of ECM against the German defensive system and paved the way for the devastating début of 'Window' chaff in June 1943. One step in this campaign was a paratroop raid on 27/28 February on the *Würzburg* station at Bruneval operated by *23./Luftgau LnRgtWest Frankreich*. The defenders, whose commander, *Hauptmann Prinz* Ferdinand Alexander von Preussen, was on leave, were overwhelmed and the British removed key components which helped them to develop counter-measures.[13] To prevent a repetition of the raid *ObdL* fortified all radar stations in the west, making their detection easier by photographic reconnaissance, but in the meantime the British began occasional airborne jamming of *Freya* ('Moonshine') from 6 April, although this was not apparently recognised by the *Luftwaffe* until September.[14] The Germans, too, used offensive jamming to support new *Jabo* operations against southern England designed to maintain pressure upon the enemy, who described them as 'a real menace'.

Since December 1941 fighters had made strafing attacks, augmented by the new *Jabostaffel JG 2* (*Hauptmann* Frank Liesendahl), which was renamed *10. (Jabo)/ JG 2* on 10 March, when a similar unit under *Hauptmann* Karl Plunser was formed by *JG 26* at Sperrle's direction, each with a cadre of experienced *Jabo* pilots. From 19 April Liesendahl's men began attacking shipping while Plunser's struck coastal utility and rail targets, both using Bf 109s, each aircraft carrying a 250kg bomb, until they re-equipped in July with the Fw 190, which could carry a 500kg bomb.

In contrast to the 1940 campaign, they made very low-level approaches below radar coverage, and most of their targets were on, or near, the coast. In the first two months 94 attacks were made, initially in *Rotte* strength but gradually increasing and penetrating deeper inland with fighter escorts, culminating on 31 October in a *Jabo* reprisal raid on Canterbury by 49 Fw 190s escorted by 62 fighters of *JG 2* and *JG 26* under Priller's command. Sweeping in under the radar, which Martini's men were jamming, the *Jabos* achieved complete surprise and the defenders accounted for only two, although one was *Leutnant* Paul Galland, the *Inspekteur der Jagdflieger*'s youngest brother. The offensive involved some 775 sorties during 1942 with the loss of 38 aircraft (including those of two *Kapitäne* of *10./JG 26*), some due to the tail-trimmer which could flip the Fw 190 into a high-speed stall. Nevertheless they undermined the whole British defensive system, forcing it to return in September to the wasteful system of standing patrols, with limited effect, although the light AA batteries (despite being short of 40mm guns) had more success. The solution was a new chain of Chain Home Extra Low (CHEL) radars, based upon a naval sensor and capable of detecting a target flying at 15m (50ft) some 65km away, but these were not ready until the following year, while the new Hawker Typhoon was plagued with technical problems until the same period. Although 80% of the *Jabos* aimed their bombs at recognisable military targets, their high-speed, low-level tactics made aiming difficult, frequently causing bombs to hit the ground and then skip over the target. On two occasions they hit crowded schools.[15]

From the autumn of 1942 the *Jabos* were increasingly flying pure reprisal raids, which had become the norm for the western *Kampfgruppen* from the spring of 1942. During 1941 the remaining *Kampfgruppen* in the West—not only Sperrle's forces but also Stumpff's—flew anti-shipping missions, with occasional token attacks upon industry, their losses being cut to some 2% by reducing their exposure to the defences (see Tables 32 and 33). In January 1942, with 274 bombers, Sperrle tied down some 2,000 fighters (including 450 night fighters), 600,000 personnel and some 2,800 AA guns, but during the spring events in the Reich led to de-

---

Table 32. Breakdown of *Luftflotte 3* Bomber Activity

Month	Day Bombing	Night Bombing	Other	Ordnance HE tonnes	BSK/AB 36
Jul 1941	–	641	747	1,171	1,400
Aug 1941	3	135	852	672	71
Sept 1941	4	162	815	619	34
Oct 1941	–	329	777	755	53
Nov 1941	–	142	944	533	139
Dec 1941	–	115	743	286	117

Source: *Luftkrieg gegen England* (USNA T321, Roll 176).

Table 33. *Luftflotte 3* **Sorties, July–December 1941**

Month	Bomber (over land)	(over sea)	Fighter	Recon	Total Sorties	Losses	Claims
Jul 1941	1,639 total		n/a	n/a	n/a	87	445
Aug 1941	1,108 total		927	61	2,096	46	405
Sept 1941	166	670	2,936	264	4,036	31	202
Oct 1941	331	638	2,755	314	4,038	35	133
Nov 1941	142	709	2,216	390	3,463	23	100
Dec 1941	115	591	1,729	301	2,736	27	84
Jan 1942	42	341	1,049	333	1,765	19	32
Feb 1942	26	383	1,352	431	2,192	27	57
Mar 1942	226	343	1,744	405	2,723	28	74
Apr 1942	909	275	3,456	403	5,043	38	193
May 1942	637	295	2,916	484	4,332	49	110
Jun 1942	791	402	3,509	632	5,334	42	207
Jul 1942	639	150	2,010	643	3,642	70	122
Aug 1942	254	139	4,018	838	5,249	84	245
Sept 1942	240	18	1,577	536	2,371	34	87
Oct 1942	207	52	2,405	485	3,149	35	78
Nov 1942	99	30	1,236	381	1,746	28	101
Dec 1942	208	56	1,534	297	2,095	22	99

Note: August 1941 figures for fighters and reconnaissance sorties (and therefore overall sorties) are incomplete.

Source: *Einsatz gegen England: Übersicht zur die Zeit vom 26.8.1941 bis 3.4.1943* (IWM AHB 6, Tin 29, fr.2826).

mands for greater activity.[16] On Palm Sunday (28/29 March) Bomber Command burned the heart out of Lübeck, causing 200 million Reichsmarks' worth of damage (equivalent to $500 million at the 1939 exchange rate), and similar devastating raids followed, leading the German press to christen them 'terror attacks'. With Party officials baying for vengeance, Hitler's headquarters ordered *ObdL* on 14 April to give the air war against England 'a more aggressive stamp', adding, 'when targets are being selected, preference is to be given to those where attacks are likely to have the greatest possible effect on civilian life'. Minelaying was to be replaced by what were described as 'terror attacks of a retaliatory nature'.

The backbone of the offensive remained *Oberst* Dr Georg Pasewaldt's *KG 2*, which was reinforced by two *Kampfgruppen* from Sicily, anti-shipping and *Ergänzungsgruppen* (the last under *Stab KG 111*), to give 429 bombers by 30 April, of which half were serviceable. On 23/24 April 60 bombers attacked Exeter, but only one managed to hit the city, and poor navigation remained noticeable throughout the year. Following an attack upon Rostock, Hitler declared in a speech on 26 April that he would eradicate all British cities for each RAF attack, and the German press referred to selecting targets from a Baedeker's Tourist Guide and marking off each destroyed British city. That night the first of the 'Baedeker Raids' was made on poorly defended Bath, where the attackers flew as low as 180m (600ft) to cause tremendous damage. Such success, repeated in cities of Lübeck's vintage such as Exeter, Norwich and York, achieved higher levels of concentration because crews flew double sorties. However, the need to keep the enemy off balance meant that they had to shuttle between bases, increasing wear upon man and machine, yet the defences coped with the threat and by inflicting a 5.3% loss-rate helped conclude the offensive on 8/9 May after 716 sorties, partly also because 16 of the 38 lost aircraft came from the *Ergänzungsgruppen*. Sharp blows continued to fall at night upon British cities until the autumn, notably a series of tit-for-tat raids in late July upon Birmingham after attacks upon Hamburg, but there was an air of desperation about these operations, reflected in the use of *III./KG 26*, which had barely completed a torpedo-bombing course. By the end of the year some 2,400 night bomber sorties had been flown by *Luftflotte 3* against British targets for the loss of 244 aircraft (10.16%), many of them from the *Ergänzungsgruppen*; indeed, during the Birmingham raids *IV./KG 55* lost a quarter of its instructors![17] The policy of tit-for-tat raids was opposed by Kessler in his letter to Jeschonnek of 5 September 1942, when he demanded more bombers for the anti-shipping campaign than for what he described (in a phrase more common in Germany before 1945 than afterwards) as 'You thrash my Jew and I'll thrash your Jew', arguing that the ship was 'The British Jew'.

The *Kampfgruppen* also flew *Pirätenangriffe* during 1942 on cloudy days, the defenders using night fighters against them, while *EK 17* flew operational trials with various navigation aids. The intention was to cause the maximum disturbance with the minimum number of aircraft, and while the physical damage was small, much time was wasted by stopping work on account of air raid warnings. Experimental high-altitude raids began on 24 August when two Ju 86Rs of *Versuchsstelle für Höhenflüge* (Rowehl's former command) each dropped a 250kg bomb on Camberley and Southampton from 12,200m (40,000ft). A few more sorties were flown until 12 September, when *Feldwebel* Horst Götz had to abort a mission as modified Spitfires closed in, and this led to the abandonment of the missions. Götz's high-altitude experience no doubt became useful after the war when he flew Lufthansa airliners.[18] During the year *Luftflotte 3*'s *Kampfgruppen* flew 7,039 sorties over Britain and dropped 6,584 tonnes of bombs, but this effort had little or no effect upon either British morale or war production.[19]

By contrast, Bomber Command's threat to the Reich grew steadily from 1941, despite an erratic start the previous summer when the absence of navigators, navigation and bombing aids meant that its crews could neither hit a barn door nor even find the barn (see Table 34). Yet the Command became the instrument of retribution not only for the British Empire but also Occupied Europe, although at a terrible cost: of the 125,000 men, one boy, one woman and one dog who flew with the Command during the war, more than 57,000 were shot down, about

Table 34. Bomber Command Operations against the Reich, 1 July 1940–31 December 1942

Month	Sorties Despatched			Failed to Return		
	Day	Night		Day	Night	
Jul 1940	156	1,419		15	33	
Aug 1940	14	1,646		3	42	
Sept 1940	–	1,162		–	32	
Oct 1940	30	1,575		–	21	
Nov 1940	3	1,352		1	29	
Dec 1940	4	808		1	14	
Total	207	7,962		20	171	
Jan 1941	3	768		1	11	
Feb 1941	1	992		–	10	
Mar 1941	1	1,248	(6)	–	27	
Apr 1941	84	1,233	(18)	6	41	
May 1941	23	1,812	(21)	1	35	
Jun 1941	120	2,537	(108)	5	75	
Jul 1941	75	2,666	(109)	11	85	(6)
Aug 1941	74	2,962	(173)	12	121	(12)
Sept 1941	4	1,752	(78)	–	71	(8)
Oct 1941	–	1,856	(119)	–	62	(2)
Nov 1941	1	1,272	(40)	–	72	(4)
Dec 1941	4	702	(17)	1	16	(2)
Total	390	19,801	(689)	37	797	(34)
Jan 1942	–	851	(46)	–	35	(–)
Feb 1942	–	582	(46)	–	11	(1)
Mar 1942	18	1,370	(171)	–	56	(7)
Apr 1942	16	2,553	(362)	7	96	(6)
May 1942	8	1,813	(558)	1	87	(27)
Jun 1942	12	3,973	(1,423)	1	195	(79)
Jul 1942	171	3,302	(1,405)	14	143	(54)
Aug 1942	39	1,926	(1,002)	4	117	(54)
Sept 1942	49	2,987	(1,665)	3	157	(68)
Oct 1942	103	1,448	(942)	9	68	(53)
Nov 1942	31	435	(302)	–	25	(18)
Dec 1942	17	812	(684)	1	58	(45)
Total	464	22,052	(8,606)	40	1,048	(412)

Note: Figures in parentheses refer to four-engine bombers. Sorties from July 1941 are major missions only. Aircraft which returned to base and were written off through damage are not included.
Sources: Middlebrook and Everitt; Night Bombing Raid Sheets (PRO Air 14/2666–75); and Day Bombing Raid Sheets (PRO Air 14/3361–4).

one-third of them in the 18 months before D-Day.[20] Although most aircrew were white, a few black West Indians shared the danger, with men drawn not only from the Empire and Occupied Europe but also from the United States and even from Germany itself, the last flying in 'ABC' (Airborne Cigar) COMINT jamming missions from late 1943.[21]

Despite enthusiastic claims during debriefing, the average British bomber crew's bombs until 1942 hit homes and fields, leading the Germans to assume that these raids were purely terror attacks, although Goebbels did not use this phrase until after Lübeck had been wrecked. Despite the trivial military damage in 1940, the *Luftwaffe* naturally wished to protect the population and restore its prestige. However, the Reich's night defences were not strengthened until after the fall of France with measures which mirrored those of the British, although the *Luftwaffe* was slower developing both GCI techniques and airborne radar. The pre-war *Nachtjagdstaffeln* had been absorbed by *Jagdgruppen*, and, despite *Würzburg* radars, which claimed their first victory near Essen in September, *Flak* proved a weak shield for the Reich, with batteries scattered among the *Luftgaue* and lacking target acquisition equipment such as *Kommandogerät 36* predictors—even at the end of 1942 about 30% of the heavy batteries had none while only 25–30% had radar fire control. Command and control improved with the creation of *Luftverteidigungskommandos (LvKdo)*, which were renamed *Flakdivisionen* on 1 September, with two more created in *Luftflotte 3* and a third in Romania. The number of batteries rose from 756 (423 heavy) in 1940 to 932 (537) the following year and 1,182 (744) in 1942, with a more modest expansion in searchlight batteries from 143 to 174. However, there was a tendency to deploy batteries outside the Reich: in December 1942 120 batteries (100 heavy) were transferred to Italy and did not return until the spring of 1943.[22]

The need for aircraft was obvious, and the key figures in developing the night fighter system were *Leutnant* Hermann Diehl, *Hauptmann* Wolfgang Falck and *Oberst* Joseph Kammhuber, although Milch may well have been the *eminence grise*. Diehl had developed radar-controlled GCI for daylight operations during the Phoney War and with *Freya* could bring interceptors to within 500m of their target, demonstrating it with devastating success in December 1939 when he helped decimate a Wellington formation. Falck (*Kommandeur* of *I./ZG 1*) used *Würzburg* in night interceptions during April 1940, recommending development of the technique to *ObdL*, and, possibly at Milch's instigation, on 22 June his *Gruppe* was transferred to Düsseldorf to become *I./NJG 1*. He became *Kommodore* of *NJG 1*, was given tactical control of *Luftgau VI*'s *FlakSwR 1* (*Oberstleutnant* Fichter) in Westphalia near Münster and initially adopted the pre-war method, *Hellenachtjagd* (Bright Night Fighting), using the *Flugmeldedienst*, searchlights and fighters, but the division of responsibility between *Luftflotte 2* (aircraft) and *Luftgau VI* (ground element) created anomalies.[23] This problem was overcome on 17 July with the creation of *Nachtjagddivision 1* under Kammhuber (former *Kommodore* of *KG 51* and, briefly, *KG 1*), one of the most experienced *Luftwaffe* officers, who had recently returned from a French prison camp. In the Great War he had enlisted in the Bavarian Army, where he became an officer, qualifying as a staff officer with the post-war *Reichsheer*, and by 1933 he was Director of Operations. He had won his wings at Lipetsk in 1930 and then transferred to the *RLM*, and, after commanding the airship *Graf Zeppelin* when it flew to South America in 1935, he became head of organisation, only to resign in 1938 in disgust at Jeschonnek's grandiose plans for *Luftwaffe* expansion. His sojourn as *Luftflotte 2* Chief of Staff ended with the Mechelen Incident in February 1940, but, while his superior *General der Flieger* Hellmuth Felmy was made a scapegoat, Kammhuber was transferred to *KG 51*.[24]

Three nights after his appointment, on 20/21 July, *Oberleutnant* Werner Streib (*Kommandeur* of *I./NJG 1*) claimed the first of his 66 victims using *Hellenachtjagd*, and the following night five more were claimed, including a second by Streib.[25] These successes allowed Kammhuber to extend the *Hellenachtjagd* system with the newly created *1.* and *2. Flakscheinwerferbrigaden* under *Obersten* Luczny (Stade) and von Rantzow (Arnhem), and within eight months he had established a belt (*Gürtel*) of six *Scheinwerfer-Grossräume*, each with a searchlight regiment (*FlakSwR*) subdivided into 17 *Räume* or battalion zones (originally 30km long and 20km deep but later expanded) from Lübeck to Liége with a separate *Raum* in Schleswig-Holstein covering Kiel. He also created a dozen night fighter bases, such as Venlo-Herongen, where 18,000 men had built two 1,450m and one 1,200m concrete runways, a command post, workshops and accommodation linked by 48km of road by 18 March 1941.[26] The fighters were usually cramped Bf 110s, crudely converted with flame dampers, but they were supplemented by other *Zerstörer*, including the roomy Ju 88C and the underpowered Do17Z-6/10 Kauz (Screech Owl) I/II. The shortage of aircraft meant that some Bf 109s were inherited, and *10./NJG 1* retained theirs until October. Manpower was more difficult to obtain, and, despite using retrained *Zerstörergruppen* crews supplemented by men from *Kampf-* and *Fernaufklärungsstaffeln*, transport units, *Lufthansa* and schools, all anxious to become fighter pilots in an arm which emphasised experience and maturity rather than youth, by the New Year there were only 60 operational aircrew in 16 *Nachtjagdstaffeln*.[27]

Hellenachtjagd could operate only to 5/10ths cloud conditions because the searchlights were unable to penetrate the vapour, while the addition of *Würzburg* to the searchlight battalions from October did little to improve efficiency. Kammhuber did not have Falck's experience of radar, and his scepticism about the sensor was strengthened by exercises near Berlin during the autumn. However, in six of the RAF's prime targets Kammhuber had established *Kombinierte Nachtjagdgebeite* (Combined Night Fighting zones) in which fighters were supposed to cooperate with *Würzburg*-supported *Flak*. Initially using Bf 109s of the *Versuchs Nachtjagdstaffel* (redesignated *Ergänzungsstaffel/NJG 1* in August) at Cologne-Osterheim and later Bf 110s, the system had little success, but Falck was given a demonstration with *Freya* by Diehl early in July and encouraged the signaller to w.·te a memorandum on radar-supported GCI to *RLM*. Kammhuber received the memorandum on 19 August (his 44th birthday) and, while sceptical, he assigned Diehl a zone south of the Ijssel Meer (Zuider Zee) in which a *Freya* was coupled with a searchlight in what was called a *Parasitanlage* (parasite installation). This became operational on 26 September. A second was established and on 2/3 October helped *Leutnant* Ludwig Bekker in a Do 17Z-10 Kauz II shoot down a bomber.[28] The new system, *Dunkelnachtjagd* (Dark Night Fighting), was expanded into six coastal *Gebiete* (zones) some 140km in front of the *Scheinwerfergürtel* from the Danish border to the Scheldt estuary, but this proved painfully slow due to production delays with *Freya* and a shortage of experienced ground controllers. Kammhuber was interested in airborne sensors, and the failure of *Spanner* (PeepingTom) infra-red searchlights led him in the autumn of 1940 to consider radar. Göring opposed the idea, observing that 'a fighter cannot have things sprouting from its head', but Martini and *RLM* were more supportive. Telefunken had developed a derivative of a radio altimeter as *Lichtenstein B/C*, and by the summer of 1941 experiments with this sensor were proving extremely promising.

The reorganisation of Germany's night defences took its toll and pushed British loss rates between July 1940 and June 1941 to twice those of the *Luftwaffe* during the Blitz, despite a smaller scale of operations. The longer distances flown by British pilots, the inadequacies of many bomber designs, especially with regard to endurance, and the RAF's pre-war neglect of navigation proved just as deadly as Kammhuber and Falck. During the second half of 1940 more than 170 British aircraft failed to return from night bombing operations against the Reich (excluding minelaying sorties), yet the defenders claimed only 72 (30 by *Flak*). While the shortfall may partially be explained by 'winged birds' which later succumbed to their injuries, it is clear that many aircraft simply ran out of fuel.

The situation continued to improve for Germany during the spring of 1941, when a further reorganisation of the defences took place. To coordinate Berlin's defences *Luftwaffe Befehlshaber Mitte* was created on 24 March 1941, controlling the resources of *Luftgaue III* (Berlin) and *IV* (Dresden) under the former's commander, *Generalmajor* Hubert Weise. To provide depth, in May Weise extended his empire into *Luftgaue VI* (Münster) and *XI* (Hanover) when Kesselring's *Luftflotte 2* moved eastwards, but Sperrle refused to relinquish control of his *Luftgaue VII* (Munich) and *XII/XIII* (Wiesbaden). Even if Weise had succeeded, the system would have been less efficient than the British, for the *Flugmeldedienst*, which supported the *Flakwaffe*, was one of four autonomous warning services, the others being under the Navy, the Nazi Party and the railway (*Reichsbahn*). However, there was little coordination, and none provided information about the types of aircraft attacking the Reich. Despite these inadequacies, British loss rates rose: on 1/2 March 1941 4.58% of the force despatched to Germany failed to return, while accidents brought total losses to 15.26%.[29] The following month saw rates exceed 8% but then decline as the British concentrated upon coastal targets. The defences also proved effective on the occasional cloud-cover daylight raids, when the overall loss rate was 6.37%, or nearly three times that of night operations.

By the summer of 1941 the strategic air war had reached an *impasse*, with neither side capable of inflicting major damage upon the other, but gradually the balance tipped firmly in favour of the British, and while there were occasional cloud-cover and even deep-penetration raids during the day, until late 1942 the main effort was at night. Here the weight of British bombs falling on Germany increased as more four-engine bombers entered service, rising from 4% of total sorties in July 1941 to 12% by March 1942 and 84% by the end of the year. Although the new generation of British bombers (Halifax, Lancaster, Manchester and Stirling) could often fly higher and faster than the Bf 110, they were plagued by mechanical problems, giving the *Luftwaffe* time to adjust to the threat. The summer of 1941 also saw a brief threat to Berlin from an unexpected source, starting on 7/8 August when Russian bombers struck the capital. Three more attacks followed up to 3/4 September, mostly by naval bombers but including some four-engine TB-7/Pe-8s, the campaign ending after 21.5 tonnes of bombs had been dropped when the forward bases in the Baltic states were lost after some 100 sorties had been flown at a cost of four aircraft.[30]

The *Luftwaffe's* defensive system expanded to meet the threat, and on 9 August the *Nachtjagddivision* was expanded into *Fliegerkorps XII* under *Inspekteur der Nachtjagdflieger Generalleutnant* Kammhuber, with five *Gruppen*, two *Flakscheinwerferdivisionen* (formerly *Brigaden*) and three signal regiments. *Hellenachtjagd* with searchlight support remained the backbone of night fighter operations during 1941, and by the end of the year there were 14 *Räume* in a belt running from the base of the Jutland peninsula to Metz. In addition to the coastal *Dunkelnachtjagdgebiete*, increasingly reliant upon radar alone, a seventh covered the central Rhine, while eight *Kombiniertes Nachtjagdgebiete* supplemented the northern end of the *Hellenachtjagd* system as well as prime targets such as the Ruhr and Berlin. During 1942 work began developing a belt of *Hellenachtjagdräume* and *Dunkelnachtjagdgebiete* to protect Berlin, while the original system benefited from the introduction during the autumn of *Würzburg-Reise (FuMG 65)* radars and improved *Freya AN*. The spring of 1942 also saw the introduction of long-range (200–300km) *Mammut (FuMo 51)* and *Wasserman (FuMG 402)* radars to provide earlier warning. Each *Hellenachtjagdräum* received two *Würzburgen* to control searchlights, and a *Freya* to detect approaching targets, but from the autumn of 1941 the control posts within each *Räume* increasingly used the radars as the prime sensors with *Seeburg* automated plotting tables in a system designated *Himmelbett Verfahren* (Four-Poster Bed Procedure). The development of airborne radars remained slow, but a prototype *Lichtenstein* was installed in a Do 215B of *4./NJG 1* and flown by *Oberleutnant* Ludwig Bekker, who shot down a Wellington on 8/9 August and claimed four more to 1/2 October, coming up below his prey until he could see it then making a climbing attack which automatically forced the bomber to fly through a cone of fire. These tactics later became standard within the *Nachtjagdwaffe*, but Bekker's run ended when his radar became unserviceable and could not be repaired.[31] Nevertheless his success encouraged *Projekt 'Adler'*, in which *NJG 1*'s Bf 110Es were to receive the radar, but shortages of technicians at Telefunken delayed production of *FuG 202 Lichtenstein B/C* and only in February 1942 were the first four Bf 110s of *II./NJG 1* equipped. The sensor proved unpopular because the 'antlers' (antenna) reduced speed by 40kph (25mph) and the set was temperamental. Indeed, there were no victories for four months.[32]

With new equipment and dedicated men Kammhuber's organisation steadily expanded, splitting in March 1942 into two *Nachtjagddivisionen* formed under Döring and 'Old Eagle' *Generalmajor* Walter Schwabedissen (former Chief of Staff of *I. Flakkorps*). They were converted into *Jagddivisionen* following another reorganisation on 1 May 1942 which gave the command eight *Nachtjagdgruppen*, increasingly operating within specific regions, and seven signal regiments.[33] This reflected the steady success of the organisation, which claimed 421 victories in 1941 and 687 the following year, indicating that the *Nachtjagdwaffe* was accounting for some 60% of Bomber Command's casualties. On 27/28 June 1941 the Command first recorded 'intense night fighter attacks' and a third of the 35 Whitleys despatched were lost together with three Wellingtons.[34] Four aircraft fell to *Oberleutnant* Reinhold Eckhardt of *NJG 1*, who became an instant *Experte* but was killed a year later, while other successes were registered during the year, notably on 7/8 November when 12.4% of the mission against Berlin was lost, although the night's overall loss was 9.4% partly due to severe icing conditions.[35] Nevertheless, Bomber Command eased its operations to conserve forces until the spring.

The leading night fighter ace in 1941 was Streib (22 victories), exploiting *Dunkelnachtjagd* as the most efficient defence, even without airborne radar: it required less than nine sorties per victory in the final quarter of 1941 (52% of all victories), compared to 41 with *Hellenachtjagd*.[36] The following year Streib was overtaken by former *Zerstörer Experte* Helmut Lent (8 victories), who had doubled his score to 40, while other *Experten* in both years' top five were Paul Gildner and Egmont, *Prinz* zur Lippe-Weissenfeld, who each had 38 victories in 1942. All were members of Falck's *NJG 1*, which ended the war with 2,311 victories—over 1,400 more than the next formation, *NJG 5*, of which Lent became *Kommodore*. The Prince would command *NJG 3*, but only Streib survived the war, with 66 victories (one in daylight). Gildner (44 night victories) fell on 24 February 1943, while the Prince (51) and Lent (102) fell on 12 March and 7 October respectively. Streib's successes, like that of his fellow *Experten*, owed as much to his status as *Kommandeur* of *I./NJG 1* as to his own skills (and those of his controllers), for he could select when, where and with whom to fly. The *Experten* could 'poach' active areas, leaving less favoured crews futilely orbiting beacons in fallow sectors, with the result that a small number of crews accumulated great experience at the expense of the majority. Indeed, of 118 night fighter *Ritterkreuz* holders, only 12 joined the arm after July 1942.[37] The inevitable losses of *Experten* had an impact out of all proportion to their numbers, yet there were always ambitious pilots of whom it was said 'They've got a sore throat', meaning that they wanted a *Ritterkreuz* which was worn around the neck.[38]

Lack of aircraft was a major problem for Kammhuber, whose strength dropped from 263 on 9 September 1941 to 255 on 30 June 1942, when it was only 63% of establishment. Numbers gradually rose, and by the end of the year there were some 375 fighters, but generally only two-thirds were serviceable until late 1942. Part of the problem was the continued demand for *Zerstörer* from the Eastern and Mediterranean Fronts for long-range operations, while during the summer of 1941 Messerschmitt AG ran down the Bf 110 production line to ensure acceptance of the diabolical Me 210. This policy was reversed only in the late autumn of 1941, leading to the Bf 110G which entered service during the summer of 1942. Although the only dedicated fighter design, the Bf 110 did have one drawback in that it was difficult for the radio/radar operator to escape from his position quickly. The Dornier alternatives (including the Do 217J introduced in March 1942) were inadequate, while Milch, whose grip on production grew tighter, obstinately refused to sanction increased production of the Ju 88C on the grounds of cost. Learning of Kammhuber's predicament, the ever resourceful Ernst Heinkel proposed his *Projekt 1060 Zerstörer*, rejected by both *ObdL* and the *RLM*, for the night fighter role and the *Inspekteur der Nachtjagd* used his plenipotentiary powers to inaugurate the design of the He 219 Uhu (Owl) in January 1942. The beginning of the year also saw a slight surplus in night fighter crews as losses were reduced and more students completed their course.

By then Bomber Command was growing in effectiveness as navigation became a recognised profession and electronic navigation aids such as Gee (resembling *Knickebein*) and Oboe (known to the Germans as *Bumerangverfahren*, or Boomerang Procedure) entered service. RAF electronic intelligence gradually developed a detailed picture of what they called the Kammhuber Line, and mission planning sought either to avoid it or reduce the attackers' exposure. The radical overhaul of Bomber Command was symbolised by the appointment of Air Chief Marshal Sir Arthur Harris as its commander-in-chief on 22 February 1942. Harris, a fighter squadron commander in the Great War, was one of the Douhet crusaders who believed that aerial bombardment almost alone would defeat Germany.[39] By now the British had analysed the impact of the Blitz and were concluding that conventional bombing—attacks upon individual targets within cities largely with high explosive—should be replaced by area attacks, with an emphasis upon incendiaries, which would be more likely to disrupt regional production. Harris inherited from his predecessor a directive to strike at civilian morale, especially industrial workers, and the new bombing tactics allowed this objective to be attained also, with the result that he began to target German city centres. His operational research section addressed the problem of assuring higher bomb concentrations and reduced exposure to the defences, and the bombers would now fly in a tight stream, similar to the *Krokodil* tactics, up to 100km long and 40–50km across by the spring of 1944, which could saturate any night fighter sector.[40] To improve effectiveness more, the bombers would be sent against one target per night, although for much of the year Harris concentrated on re-equipping his forces and developing further tactical improvements.

The first signs of Harris's tactics came from 8/9 March, when he used a third of his 450 night bombers to strike Essen on three nights in succession, using pathfinder techniques with flares and incendiaries to mark the target area in the same way as the *Luftwaffe* had operated during the Blitz. Although unsuccessful, these raids reduced casualties to 2.86% and demonstrated a need for a higher ratio of incendiaries. On the night of 28/29 March 1942, as already noted, 234 aircraft outflanked the Kammhuber Line by flying through the northern edges of *Dunkelnachtjagdgebiet 'Wolf'* and *Hellenachtjagdraum 1* to strike the medieval streets of Lübeck. The bombers dropped 400 tonnes, including 266 tonnes of incendiaries, which burned out the heart of the Hanseatic city and its half-timbered buildings at the cost of 12 aircraft (5.12% of the attackers). Initially it appeared that this Coventry-style success would be unique, and nine conventional raids followed, but from 23/24 April to 26/27 April there were four attacks upon Rostock which emulated the Lübeck *Terrorangriff* and, as Goebbels noted in his diary, virtually ended community life. The British flew some 525 sorties and lost just eight aircraft (1.5%). Only eight of Kammhuber's fighters were able to intercept the raiders, although 13 victories were claimed.[41]

There were vain attempts to repeat the success in the Ruhr and Hamburg, and pressure grew on the RAF to transfer bomber squadrons both to overseas theatres and to the Battle of the Atlantic. To demonstrate what might be achieved, Harris planned a publicity stunt in which 1,000 bombers would wipe out a German city. By mobilising operational training units (which provided a third of his strike force), he despatched 1,047 aircraft against Cologne on 30/31 May. Harris expected to lose 50 aircraft, but Bomber Command actually lost only 41 (3.9%), more than on any previous mission, with about half falling to night fighters, of which 25 made contact. However, the centre of Cologne was devastated and industrial activity paralysed for a week, although within six months the city had recovered.[42]

Similar attacks were carried out against Essen and Bremen during June, but Harris could not maintain the momentum and during the rest of the year smaller attacks were made though in growing strength. The Bremen raid saw 55 aircraft lost (4.9%), of which *II./NJG 2* (some of whose Bf 110s had *Lichtenstein*) claimed 16.

The new British tactics accelerated the demise of *Hellenachtjagd* and its replacement by *Himmelbett* and *Dunkelnachtjagd. 1.* and *2. Flakscheinwerfer Divisionen* were disbanded on 31 July 1942 and their searchlight batteries transferred to help protect the cities, largely as a result of Party demands. *Himmelbett/Dunkelnachtjagd* remained cumbersome because only one fighter at a time could be controlled, while tracking proved difficult until the introduction of *FuG 25 Erstling* IFF systems, when it became possible to hold a second fighter in reserve orbiting a radio beacon. The problem was eased by allowing a 50% overlap in radar coverage and adding more sectors, the reliability of interception being another reason why airborne radars remained unpopular. To improve the defences Kammhuber demanded 600 *Würburg-Reisen* by September 1942, the creation of three more *Nachtjagdgeschwader* and another 150,000 men. While these demands may have been justified, they also demonstrated his belief that the solution to the problem was to throw money at it rather than seek new approaches, to which he sometimes reacted with arrogant dismissiveness. This further stirred resentment against '*Wurzelsepp*' (Bavarian Turnip Head), as some called him, feelings partly aroused by the fact that he was an abstemious non-smoker; indeed, the views of his critics—no doubt detected from the secretly recorded conversations of prisoners—were reflected in a comment by RAF intelligence that he was 'a small, insignificant-looking man . . . of the type who does not drink or smoke much because he cannot stand it'.[43]

In the longer term he sought new ground and airborne radars but encountered opposition from both Göring and Jeschonnek, who regarded his demands as excessive. Kammhuber then went around them by appealing to the Nazi Party's organisations for manpower, and by August 1942 he had 30,000 male and female auxiliaries in his signals establishment, which was expanded as *Dunkelnachtjagdgebieten* were added behind the *Himmelbett* line to provide a total of 96 signal companies, each supporting one night fighter station. But during the Cologne raid dozens of crews were uncommitted and subsequently there was a groundswell of opinion seeking more flexible tactics. Kammhuber's response was to improve coordination, and at about the time *Jagddivision 3* was formed at Metz under Junck on 1 October the *Jagddivisionen* formed three *Nachtjagdraumführer*, each responsible for a *Himmelbettraum* and a couple of *Dunkelnachtjagdgebieten* on either side of it.

The *Nachtjagdwaffe* adapted to Harris's new tactics and the pattern of operations was maintained until the end of the war. Alerted by *Funkhorchdienst* interceptions under the direction of *Major* Kuhlmann of enemy radio activity, the crews

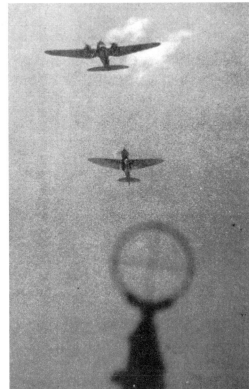

Above left: As a Do 17 flies low over an East Grinstead street the inhabitants duck for cover.

Above right: A Spitfire closes on an He 111 while the gunner of another Heinkel engages it.

Right: The pilot of a doomed Spitfire rolls the aircraft on to its back so that he can drop out and parachute to safety.

Above: A Bf 110 of
V.(Z)/LG 1, damaged
by Spitfires of No 609
Squadron off
Portland on 9 July
1940, ditches in the
Channel. (Alex
Vanags-Baginskis)

Left, upper: As the
fighter sinks and a
Seenotdienst rescue
boat approaches it,
the crew scramble to
safety. They were
picked up by an He
59, possibly from
Seenotkommando 3.

Left, lower: The view
from the bomb-
aimer's position as a
Ju 88 taxis out for
take-off.

Right, upper: The front gunner/bomb-aimer of an He 111 waits as the engines are run up.

Right, lower: An He 111 enters British airspace.

Left, upper: A low-level attack upon an RAF fighter base by Do 17s.

Left, lower: Two Bf 109Es fly low down the English coast. They have *II. Gruppe* markings.

Below: A burned-out Ju 88 of *I./KG 77* under guard after being shot down during an attack on Hatfield on 3 October 1940. (Alex Vanags-Baginskis)

Right: 'Black men' work on the engine of an He 111.

Below left: People in glass houses shouldn't fly through AA fire, as this Ju 88 demonstrates.

Below right: A downed fighter pilot grabs a boat hook prior to being hauled to safety.

Above left: An Fw 200 Condor prowls the Atlantic.

Above right: A near miss for a Condor during an attack upon a convoy.

Left, upper: A Condor makes another low-level pass on a fatally damaged freighter.

Left, lower: An He 115 torpedo-bomber of *KüFlGr 706*. The success of these aircraft in 1940 stimulated *ObdL* interest in torpedo-bombing but led to a fierce inter-service battle which the *Luftwaffe* won.

Right, upper: A successful attack by *KG 26* on a Murmansk convoy is marked by the explosion of an ammunition ship.

Right, lower: A Do 18 flying boat of *KüFlGr 406* patrols over a German convoy off the French coast. The protection of these convoys was one of the responsibilities of *FlFü Atlantik*.

Below left: A Coastal Command Whitley falls to the guns of an Ar 196 in the Bay of Biscay. (Alex Vanags-Baginskis)

Below right: A *Luftflotte 3* He 111 attempting to attack a convoy is fatally damaged by a Hudson escort and falls with its starboard engine ablaze. (Alex Vanags-Baginskis)

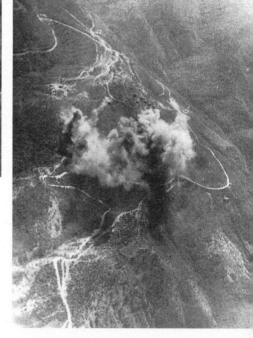

Top: One of two *SAGr 130* Bv 138s destroyed by Beaufighters off the Scottish coast in the summer of 1943. (Alex Vanags-Baginskis)

Above: A remarkable photograph of a bomb as it is released from a *Stuka*.

Right: Bombs fall upon retreating British and Australian troops in Greece.

Right: A Bf 110 on guard as *Stukas* pound British positions in Cyrenaica.

Left: A Ju 87B of *FlFü Afrika* lands after a mission over Tobruk in 1941.

Below: Burning Belgrade after *Unternehmen 'Strafgericht'*.

Above left: A brief rest for paratroops during *Unternehmen 'Merkur'*.

Above right: Barracks are bombed on the opening day o[f] *Unternehmen 'Barbarossa'*.

Left, upper: An airfield unde[r] *Luftwaffe* attack.

Left, lower: The *Luftwaffe*'s greatest achievement on the opening days of *'Barbarossa'* was to destroy the *VVS* with attacks such as this. The Russians took nearly two year[s] to recover from the disaster.

Above left: Wrecked Russian TB-1 bombers.

Above right: A navigator checks his map as an He 111 formation flies over the Russian steppes.

Left: The railways were vital to both sides on the Eastern Front and the *Luftwaffe* formed rail-busting *Staffeln* from late 1942. Here a direct hit cuts a Russian railway line.

eft, top: A *Stuka* flies in triumph over an astern Front battlefield.

ar left, centre: The *Flak* batteries' deadly 8cm guns were used as substitute artillery nd anti-tank weapons to support Army perations in the East and the South.

ar left, bottom: A bridge destroyed at itebsk. The *Luftwaffe* played a vital role in olating Russian forces during the summer of 941.

eft, below: An observer makes a last-minute neck of his maps before a Henschel Hs 126 orps aeroplane takes off. The *Nahaufklärungs-affeln* were so decimated by the Russian

campaign that they required substantial reorganisation.

Above: Russian marshalling yards under attack. From 1942 to 1944 similar targets were periodically bombed by the *Kampfgruppen,* and the so-called 'strategic' offensive of *Fliegerkorps IV* in 1944 was directed almost exclusively against this sort of target.

Below left: Road and rail communications were prime targets for the *Luftwaffe* during the 1941 and 1942 campaigns in Russia.

Below right: A final briefing before a *3.(F)/ 123* Do 17 leaves for a winter reconnaissance over England.

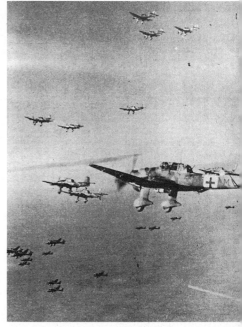

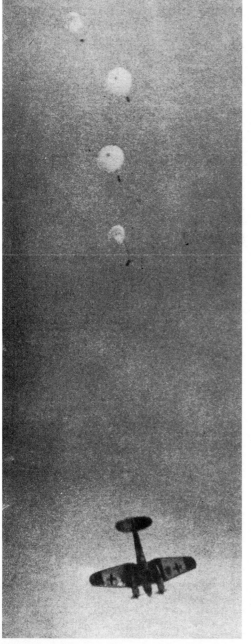

Top left: The 8.8 *Flak 36* was the backbone o
German anti-tank defence in North Africa an(
its shells were capable of blowing apart even th
strongest tank.

Top right: The Ju 87Ds of *II./StG 3 en route* t(
attack British positions during 1942.

Above: A crude attempt to camouflage a Bf
109F on the Eastern Front during the winter (
1941/42.

Left: A supply drop by a *KG 4* He 111 to an
isolated Eastern Front garrison. This became
an ever more frequent task for the
Kampfgruppen after 1941.

Top left: The freezing temperatures of a Russian winter meant that even the robust Ju 52 had to be freed from ice and snow before it could take off. These 'black men' are pushing a transport free.

Above: The view from a Ju 88 as it dives towards a target.

Above right: An *LG 1* Ju 88 prepares to dive on positions in North Africa. The *Geschwader* distinguished itself in the Mediterranean between 1941 and 1943.

Below left: Pilot and observer study a map during a reconnaissance sortie over Britain.

Below right: The Bf 110 was increasingly used for ground attack duties both in the Mediterranean and in Russia. Here a *ZG 1* aircraft is bombed up at an Eastern Front airfield during the winter of 1941/42.

Left: Twice a year rain or thaw created the *rasputista* or muddy season on the Eastern Front. The problems at *Luftwaffe* airfields are graphically shown in this picture.

Above: Refuelling a Ju 87D of *7./StG 1* on the Eastern Front. The familiar 'spats', or mudguards, have been removed from the aircraft.

Below left: An *StG 1 Staffel* is shielded by Bf 109s on the Eastern Front.

Below right: A last-minute briefing at a *Stukagruppe* command post on the Eastern Front.

would assemble for a briefing by the *Kommandeur* or his deputy in the *Bereit-schaftsraum* (ready room) during the late afternoon. They would then sit in arm-chairs or play chess, *Skat* or *Doppelkopf*, until the first crews went to *Sitzbereitschaft* (cockpit alert) and taxied their aircraft from dispersal bays to the runway, await-ing the green flare which was the order to take off. They would then fly to a navigation beacon, which they would orbit until a target was found. The greatest dangers came from the weather or friendly fire, but the 7.69mm (0.303in) ma-chine guns of the bombers, much derided after the war, were also a hazard since most interceptions took place within range of these weapons, yet the bombers' most effective defence was the violent corkscrew manoeuvre.[44] By the end of the year there were 15 *Nachtjagdgruppen*. Kammhuber retained overall control from a bomb-proof bunker, while the *Jagddivisionen* did not receive a similar facility until July 1943. The expanded system ensured that from August until December the RAF's main attacks were losing an average 5.76% a month compared with 3.98% from January to July, while in December the figure rose to 7.14%, the RAF attrib-uting half of its losses to fighters.[45]

Kammhuber was not content with a passive defence, arguing, 'If you want to render a wasp swarm harmless it is better to destroy the nest along with the wasps.'[46] Attacks upon enemy airfields began in mid-August 1940 with probing flights aimed at attacking bomber bases. *Feldwebel* Peter Laufs claimed a Hurricane on 16/17 August, but it was not until late September that enemy bombers were hunted over their own airfields. The task was assigned to *I./NJG 2* under Condor Legion vet-eran *Major* Karl-Heinrich Heyse, and their first success came on 24/25 October when *Oberleutnant* Kurt Herrmann damaged a Blenheim and *Feldwebel* Hans Hahn shot down a Whitley. Heyse was lost on 9/10 October and replaced by *Hauptmann* Karl Hülshoff, and four months later, on 10/11 February, the *Gruppe* succeeded in intercepting returning bombers, for which they had been waiting. Five victories were claimed, but two bombers were only damaged, although a third was aban-doned after running out of fuel and being denied permission to land.

Hülshoff's campaign continued intermittently, and while victories were rela-tively few they had a psychological effect upon tired bomber crews, with the added bonus of disrupting British night training; indeed, from late July 1941 the latter was assigned higher priority (see Table 35). The crews, who flew 'cat's eyes' mis-sions, found that they shared the usual dangers of night fighting—and a few, more noticeably, the risk of falling into the North Sea—and when *Oberleutnant* Paul Bohn, *Kapitän* of *4./NJG 2*, was killed by fire from a Whitley gunner his flight engineer *Unteroffizier* Walter Lindner had to fly the aircraft home, although he had been declared unsuitable for pilot training.[47] Several aircraft flew into the ground while pursuing victims and collisions were not unknown, *Experte Leutnant* Heinz Völker (7 victories) falling this way on 21/22 July. Hahn, a *Leutnant* with 11 victo-ries, perished when colliding with an Oxford on 11/12 October, but the following morning, when the *Gruppe* was paraded for Kammhuber, there was more depressing news.

The intruders' initial success led Göring in December 1940 to authorise three *Geschwader*, but unfortunately this was strongly opposed by the *Fliegerkorps* and senior elements in *ObdL*, especially Jeschonnek, who resented what they regarded as Kammhuber's 'empire building'. Jeschonnek constantly refused the *Gruppe* reinforcements, and its strength dropped from 15 in November to seven two months later (including some purpose-built Do 215B-4s), although from February 1941 it rose. In the backbiting atmosphere of Nazi Germany the complaints filtered upwards through Göring's political enemies until they reached the sympathetic ears of Hitler himself. But Hitler believed—and it would appear that neither Göring nor Jeschonnek sought to dissuade him—that the *Gruppe*'s claims were exaggerated and that it was better to shoot down bombers over German territory. He ordered the abandonment of intruder operations, and this was the news Kammhuber delivered at the parade, adding that the *Gruppe* would be going to Sicily for conventional night fighter operations. Nevertheless, one last mission was flown that night, and in August 1942 the unit briefly returned to resume intruder operations against both the British and American bomber force. However, for reasons unknown these operations did not take place and in November the *Gruppe* returned to Sicily. Part-time intruder operations were flown by *Kampfgruppen* against airfields, while there were some chance encounters with enemy aircraft—indeed, *Luftflotte 3* records 210 sorties in November and December 1941. However, the absence of a concerted effort allowed Harris to expand his bases and

Table 35. *NJG 2* Intruder Campaign

Month	Sorties	RAF Losses		*Luftwaffe* Losses	
		Claims	Actual	FTR	Accident
Oct 1940	36	5	2	–	5
Nov 1940	111	3	–	3	1
Dec 1940	61	4	–	1	1
Jan 1941	56	6	3	1	–
Feb 1941	25	12	6	1	1
Mar 1941	53	6	2	3	–
Apr 1941	205	23	12	1	1
May 1941	216	13	4	1	–
Jun 1941	245	20	1	6	–
Jul 1941	223	17	8	4	–
Aug 1941	187	12	8	1	1
Sept 1941	104	4	3	2	–
Oct 1941	81	3	3	1	–
Total	1,603	128	52	25	10

Note: German losses are 60% on operational missions. RAF losses are shot down, crashed, crash-landed and damaged beyond repair.
Sources: Parry, Appendices; *Einsatz gegen England* (IWM AHB 6, Tin 29, fr.2798); and *Luftkrieg gegen England* (USNA T321, Roll 176).

conduct night training without interference, and it was not until August 1943 that *V/KG 2* began semi-official intruder operations, although never on the scale of, or with such success as, Hülshoff's men. What might have been achieved was indicated by *Unternehmen 'Gisela'* on 3/4 March 1945 when 142 night fighters struck British bombers, of which 21 were lost, three crash-landed and six were damaged, but the *Luftwaffe* did lose 23 aircraft (nearly a third to fuel shortages).[48]

The growing power of Bomber Command was not the only problem facing Germany's defenders. It was reflected in the decision to give the *Jagddivisionen* a day as well as a night role and also to expand Selle's *JG 1* to three *Gruppen* by April 1942 in anticipation of powerful attacks not only from the RAF but also the newly arrived US Eighth Air Force under Major-General Carl A. Spaatz. From 31 May Mosquitos occasionally flew daylight missions (striking Berlin on 19 September), while throughout the year there were daylight missions by bombers, including *Viermöte* (literally, 'four-motors'), as far east as Danzig. Meanwhile in western Europe, despite the Air Staff's ban on offensive operations, Douglas sent his fighters eastwards to restore morale, but it was not until 13 March that the Air Staff authorised the resumption of 'Circus' operations, specifically to erode *Luftwaffe* strength.[49] The *Jagdgruppen* (which had 311 fighters in March) and *Flakwaffe* responded vigorously, and the first fortnight of April saw the RAF suffer four times the losses of the *Luftwaffe*. Within a month Douglas (who had lost many experienced pilots to overseas theatres) had decided to abandon deep-penetration 'Circus' operations, but on 24 April he opted for bigger 'Super Circus' ones. There was no improvement, and during 'Circus 178' on 1 June nine Spitfires of the Debden Wing, including the commander, were shot down by *JG 26*; the following day the latter jumped the inexperienced No 403 Squadron (RCAF) and destroyed seven out of 12 fighters.[50] Fighter Command consoled itself with the belief that it had inflicted equal casualties, but in fact the *Jagdgruppen* usually escaped unscathed. During June this unwelcome truth began to dawn. On 13 June the Air Ministry informed Douglas that the balance of casualties was turning against him: in the four months to the end of June Fighter Command's losses were 264 while the *Jagdgruppen* lost only 58, largely because most of their 332 fighters were the superb Fw 190. On 17 July Douglas admitted that he was in an inferior position (see Table 36). The superiority of the Fw 190 was not fully appreciated until a *JG 2* officer accidentally landed one in England on 23 June, and after evaluating it against the Spitfire V the Fighter Development Unit could conclude only that the best chance for the British pilots was to circle as close as possible to the English coast until the enemy pilots ran short of fuel and withdrew! The Hawker Typhoon continued to be plagued with engine and structural problems, and the only gleam of hope occurred in July 1942 when No 64 Squadron re-equipped with the Spitfire IX, whose performance equalled that of the Fw 190 below 7,600m (25,000ft) but whose supercharger made it superior over that

131

Table 36. RAF Offensive Sorties, Western Europe, 1942

Month	Day Operations				Night Operations			
	Fighter Cd		Bomber Cd		Fighter Cd		Bomber Cd	
Jan 1942	284	(4)	12	(–)	36	(–)	1,029	(8)
Feb 1942	949	(27)	344	(4)	34	(–)	203	(3)
Mar 1942	2,087	(32)	143	(2)	69	(-)	456	(6)
Apr 1942	7,719	(104)	218	(6)	204	(6)	658	(11)
May 1942	5,835	(65)	100	(–)	198	(4)	288	(7)
Jun 1942	5,855	(63)	190	(4)	342	(10)	143	(1)
Jul 1942	3,532	(63)	113	(5)	312	(6)	–	
Aug 1942	6,676	(129)	136	(9)	158	(7)	39	(2)
Sept 1942	2,120	(30)	85	(2)	111	(4)	–	
Oct 1942	2,818	(20)	177	(3)	78	(–)	9	(–)
Nov 1942	2,686	(30)	110	(12)	111	(3)	4	(–)
Dec 1942	2,778	(20)	166	(15)	108	(1)	33	(1)
Total	43,339	(587)	1,794	(62)	1,761	(41)	2,862	(39)

Notes: Bomber Command night sorties exclude minelaying and leaflet operations. Army Co-operation Command 'Rhubarb' and bomber sorties are included with Fighter and Bomber Command figures. Figures in parentheses are 'failed to return'.
Sources: Monthly operational summary of Fighter Command (PRO Air 16/1036); Middlebrook and Everitt; Night Bombing Raid Sheets (PRO Air 14/2673–5); Day Bombing Raid Sheets (PRO Air 14/3363–4); and Army Co-operation Command Operational Year Book 1942, Appendix (PRO Air 24/100).

altitude. The first clash between the two was in 'Circus 200' on 30 July, when No 64 Squadron shot down a Fw 190 without loss, but the joy was muted by the knowledge that 14 Spitfire Vs failed to return. In any event, the limitations of the Fw 190 over 7,500m were anticipated, and from late May top cover was provided through the introduction of the Bf 109G in the newly created *Höhen* (High) *Staffeln* (*11./JG 2 and 11./JG 26*) which were attached to *JG 26*.

Although Douglas was again urged in June to avoid deep-penetration missions, they continued until August, a vain attempt being made to use radar for ground-controlled interception during offensive operations. It seems likely that Leigh-Mallory was the *eminence grise* in this policy of 'leaning forward': his strong escorts provided the only crumb of comfort, with the daylight bomber loss rate in 1942 more than halved compared with 1941 to 3.45%, partly through the introduction of better aircraft. American factories had been producing a stream of excellent bomber designs for the Allied cause since 1939, including the Douglas Boston (which the French had used as the DB-7 and which the USAAF designated A-20), the North American B-25 Mitchell and the Lockheed Ventura, all superior to the Blenheim (though only marginally in the Ventura's case). However, without the stimulus of the bomber threat, American fighter design lagged behind that in European countries, forcing the Eighth Air Force fighter squadrons to adopt the Spitfire V. The bizarre Bell P-39 Airacobra and P-63 Kingcobra and the conventional Curtiss P-40A/B (Tomahawk) and P-40D/F Kittyhawk were all inferior to the Spitfire, while British purchasing commissions were not enamoured of the new generation of fighters, including the twin-engine Lockheed P-38 Lightning, the massive Republic P-47Thunderbolt and the Allison-powered North American P-51A Mustang, which could not dogfight with the Fw 190.

The Americans' baptism of fire occurred on 29 June when Captain Charles C. Kegelman and his crew from the 15th Bombardment Squadron flew with Bostons of No 226 Squadron against marshalling yards at Hazebrook. On 26 July six Spitfires of the 31st Fighter Group flew a sweep over the Pas de Calais area but Lieutenant-Colonel Clark was shot down, possibly by *Oberfeldwebel* Walter Meyer of *JG 26*, and became a prisoner of war. During 'Jubilee' (see below) the Group lost eight aircraft (6.5% of sorties).[51] Poor weather meant a significant decline in enemy offensive activity, but *Luftflotte 3* was not complacent. It was a matter of public knowledge that the British and Americans had been forced to pledge relief for their hard-pressed Russian allies by opening a Second Front in western Europe. German intelligence, assisted by the *Fernaufklärungsstaffeln*, was aware that a third of the British divisions were in south-eastern England and there was an increase in commando raids during the summer. From mid-July *Jagdgruppen* at forward airstrips were withdrawn inland on most evenings to avoid such raids—not that members of *II./JG 26* were too upset, for they often moved to the Cambrai area, where there was a school for air women (*Luftwaffehelferinnen*), commonly called *Blitzmädchen* (Lightning Girls).

On 19 August *5./JG 26*'s early morning duty pilots, *Oberleutnant* Horst Sternberg and *Unteroffizier* Peter Crump, were ordered to conduct a reconnaissance over Dieppe and returned with news of an invasion fleet! Operation 'Jubilee' was a reconnaissance in force by a Canadian division with British and American commandos at Dieppe, but an alert defence contained the main thrust on the beach, where half the assault force became casualties. In the short term 'Jubilee' was a disaster, but the lessons learned ensured that the full-scale invasion ('Overlord') would be a success. For Leigh-Mallory 'Jubilee' provided the opportunity he had long sought to bring the *Luftwaffe* to battle in conditions of absolute numerical superiority, with 56 fighter or fighter-bomber squadrons (four with Spitfire IXs), four tactical reconnaissance squadrons (Mustang) and five bomber squadrons (Boston and Blenheim), which flew 2,604 operational sorties (including 120 by the USAAF). In this aim he succeeded, but the results nowhere matched his optimism, although Sperrle had only 356 fighters and 175 bombers.

For the first four hours *JG 26* battled the air armada alone until joined by *JG 2*, and another hour elapsed before offensive sorties began to be flown by *KG 2*, which contributed 63. It lost 14 bombers, for the western *Jagdgeschwader* had forgotten how to escort bombers, but during the afternoon the two *Jabostaffeln* swept in and *JG 2*'s unit severely damaged the destroyer *Berkeley*, which sank later in the day. In the absence of bomber targets (the British flew 62 sorties and lost six aircraft to enemy action), the *Jagdgruppen* sniped at enemy fighter formations and many pilots flew three or four sorties during the day, but, while the British defensive umbrella was not shredded, it was hardly 'waterproof', and although Leigh-Mallory claimed success and 96 victories the truth was more sobering. The *Luftwaffe* had flown some 945 sorties (377 by *JG 26*) and lost 48 aircraft (more than 5%), including 23 fighters (six from *JG 26*, including all the pilots) and 25 bombers (representing more than 17% of sorties), the most distinguished casualty being *Oberleutnant* Erich Leie, *Kommandeur* of *I./JG 2*, who successfully baled out. The Germans claimed more than 100 victories and actually destroyed 91 British aircraft (3.52% of sorties) as well as eight American, while Fighter Command, which flew 2,427 daytime sorties (94% of the operation), lost 81 aircraft.[52]

In the aftermath of 'Jubilee' Fighter Command operations were more restricted pending re-equipment with the Spitfire IX, although 'Circus' and 'Rhubarb' sorties continued. Douglas was replaced on 28 November by Leigh Mallory, but by the end of the year the two of them had been partly responsible for the loss of 587 fighters, the equivalent of more than 30 squadrons, while total *Jagdgruppen* losses had been 198.[53] Worse still was the loss of many experienced pilots, including 'aces' such as Brendan 'Paddy' Finucane and Robert Stanford Tuck; the latter was forced down by *Flak* damage on the day Galland received the Diamonds to his *Ritterkreuz* and, like Bader, was entertained by the *Inspekteur der Jagdflieger* in *JG 26*'s mess.[54] Moreover, during the year *Jagdgruppen* strength increased to 457 in September with 71% serviceability, and with improved command and control thanks to the introduction of IFF into formation leaders' fighters, but a new challenge was emerging. Having made its first major contribution to the Allied air offensive in 'Jubilee', the USAAF began its heavy bomber campaign on 17 August when Fortresses of the 97th Bombardment Group struck marshalling yards at Rouen/Sotteville, with two aircraft slightly damaged by *Flak* (see Table 37).

The Fortress was no stranger to the western *Jagdgruppen*, having been operated in small numbers by the RAF since 1941, but the British had been critical of the

---

Table 37. Eighth Air Force Operations over Western Europe, 1942

Month	Sorties			Failed to Return		
	Heavy Bomber	Lt/Med Bomber	Offensive Fighter	Heavy Bomber	Lt/Med Bomber	Offensive Fighter
Jul 1942	–	12	6	–	2	1
Aug 1942	120	–	324	–	–	8
Sept 1942	205	35	341	–	1	–
Oct 1942	264	12	373	7	–	–
Nov 1942	464		180	9		1
Dec 1942	341	–	164	13	–	–
Total	**1,394**	**59**	**1,081**	**30**	**2**	**10**

Source: Freeman, *Mighty Eighth War Diary*.

bomber's poor defensive armament, especially in the tail. This was rectified in the new B-17E/F with 10 12.7mm (0.50-cal) machine guns which out-ranged the MG 17 cannon and which were included in a tail gun position. Operating at 7,600m (25,000ft), the Fortresses posed a serious problem since the Fw 190 was hard-pressed to operate over 7,500m, and for this reason the *Luftwaffe* had to place greater reliance on the Bf 109 'Gustav'. However, the first successful interception was with Fw 190s on 21 August when *Oberleutnant* Robert Olejnik led *4./ JG 1* and met Fortresses attacking shipyards at Rotterdam. The *Staffel* failed to shoot any down and one damaged fighter had to make a belly landing.[55]

The *Ami* (American) *Viermöte* or *Möbelwagen* (Furniture Vans) were formidable opponents, not only because of their armament but also because of their size, which filled the gun sights before the bombers were in range, leading many pilots to break off attacks too early. Conventional beam and stern attacks meant running the gauntlet of numerous machine guns—one pilot likened it to opening a wasp's nest—and a *4./JG 26* pilot was mortally wounded on 2 October, but, having noted the absence of a nose armament, *Hauptmann* Egon 'Conny' Mayer, *Kommandeur* of *III./JG 26*, who had shot down one Fortress in September while with *II./JG 26*, led a head-on attack on 23 November which brought down four near St Nazaire.[56] The B-24 Liberator, which operated at slightly lower altitudes than the Fortress, suffered its first loss on its début over Lille on 9 October, although victor *Hauptmann* Klaus Mietusch, *Kapitän* of *7./JG 26*, identified it as a Stirling! During this mission there occurred, west of Dunkirk, the first of 48 collisions suffered within Eighth Air Force bomber formations to June 1944, although the two B-17s of the 92nd Bombardment Group miraculously returned home.[57] The 'green' leadership of the USAAF believed that its bombers were decimating the *Jagdgruppen*, shooting down six fighters for every bomber lost, although they sometimes showed less confidence when they flew missions. Brigadier-General Haywood S. 'Possum' Hansell, one of the USAAF's leading bombardment philosophers, spent his first combat sortie flight huddled in fear on the floor of the radio operator's compartment (he later led several missions), while on his first mission the commander of the 97th Group, Colonel Frank A. Armstrong, panicked when the bomber's cockpit was hit by 20mm fire and tried to take the aircraft out of formation, the pilot having to elbow him to the floor.[58]

As Eighth Air Force strength increased from 104 heavy bombers with 39 crews on 31 August to 296 bombers and 128 crews two months later, it began to conduct a new campaign. From 21 October U-boat bases in France were attacked in missions which frequently encountered *JG 2*, both sides suffering losses. However, by this time the Allied build-up for Operation 'Torch', the landings in North Africa, meant that men and aircraft were being transferred southwards (many Eighth Air Force units joined the Twelfth Air Force). Activity declined noticeably, and by the end of the year there were only 219 bombers with 176 crews.[59]

Although 'Torch' began on 8 November, Hitler waited three days to determine French intentions, then informed the Vichy government that the *Wehrmacht*, including Sperrle's *Luftflotte 3*, would occupy the Mediterranean coast. Contingency planning for an unopposed occupation of Vichy France had begun in December 1940 with *OKW* Directive 19 for *Unternehmen 'Attila'* (renamed *'Anton'* in May 1942) and been anticipated with Gallic pessimism, for Vichy ordered its forces to offer no resistance as *Heeresgruppe D* advanced. The *Luftwaffe* element of *'Anton'* was *Unternehmen 'Stockdorf'*, and by coincidence *ObdL* reviewed its arrangements on 27 October, allocating a major role to *Ergänzungsgruppen* both as a potential strike force and for reconnaissance. The task was assigned to Coeler's *Fliegerkorps IX*, Kessler's *FlFü Atlantik* and two new commands, Fink's *Fliegerdivision 2* and Ibel's *FlFü Rhône*, with *KG 2 (I., II., III.* and *IV. Erg), KG 6 (I.* and *II.)* and *II./KG 40* and the *Jabostaffeln* of *JG 2* and *JG 26*, supported by *IV. (Erg)/KG 4* and *IV. (Erg)/KG 76*. Fighter/*Jabo* support was to be provided by two *Gruppen (III./ZG 2* with Fw 190s and *I./JG 2)*, supported by the *Höhen* and *Jabostaffeln* of *JG 2* and *JG 26*, while four *Aufklärungsstaffeln* (two resting from the Eastern Front) would act as the task force's eyes. On 30 October Sperrle placed his strike force under Coeler but replaced *KG 40* with *IV. (Erg)/KG 55* and *IV. (Erg)/KG 77* and drafted his final orders on 2 November. *Luftflotte 3* was to protect the advancing columns, provide tactical air support and destroy the *Armée de l'Air de l'Armistice* on the ground if the French offered resistance. Most of the strike force was assigned the last task, and the *Ergänzungsgruppen* of *KG 55* and *KG 4* were to strike supply dumps.

During 7/8 November the *Gruppen* took up position, *KG 2* moving from bases in the Netherlands to Cognac and Bordeaux-Mérignac, with each bomber carrying one or two 'black men', and some demonstration flights were flown on the morning of 12 November, *KG 2* conducting 70 sorties but encountering heavy AA fire near Marseilles. However, there was no resistance from the *Armée de l'Air*, which had nine *groupes* (six bomber/assault) with a first-line strength of some 400 aircraft. Its bases were quickly occupied, with *KG 2*, a couple of *Ergäunzungsgruppen* and the *'Zerstörergruppe'* moving into coastal bases while the *Aufklärungsstaffeln* concentrated at Avignon, the remainder of the *Gruppen* returning to their bases in mid-November when the initial fears of an Allied landing in France were allayed. With the coast secure the *Wehrmacht* then prepared for *Unternehmen 'Lila'*, the seizure of Toulon and the French fleet. This was set for 27 November but the previous evening *KG 2*, minus *III. Gruppe* (which failed to receive the order), mined the waters around the port, helping to alert the French, who scuttled their ships as the *Wehrmacht* stormed into the naval base.[60]

'Anton' proved to be a mixed blessing for the *Luftwaffe*, on one hand providing new bases for Fink's *Gruppen* to strike shipping in the Mediterranean and on the other demonstrating the paucity of *Luftwaffe* resources, Sperrle being left with only four *Jagdgruppen* to defend northern and western France, and when *I./JG 2*

departed for Tunis an *Ergänzungsgruppe* had to be upgraded to become *Jagdgruppe Süd*. New training space was acquired and hundreds of French aircraft were captured, most being transferred to *Luftwaffe* training units although some were given to the Romanian and Italian Air Forces, the latter using 80 Lioré et Olivier LeO 451 bombers and Dewoitine D.520 fighters in front-line units. The LeO 451 and Caudron C.445 remained in production for transport and courier duties. Yet these measures could not compensate for further strains on the *Luftwaffe,* which had worrying implications for the air defence of western Europe and the Reich itself.

NOTES TO CHAPTER 4

1. Höflinger failed to return on 18 April 1941 and Heinrichs a month later on 28 May. Kindler was shot down during a night attack upon Birmingham on 31 July/1 August and was captured.
2. See Hoffman, Vol. III, Map 6.
3. On 31 January 1942 *JaFü Mitte* was split into *JaFü Deutsche-Bucht* and *Holland-Ruhrgebiet* as Döring assumed command of the new *Nachtjagddivision 1*.
4. For *JG 26* see Caldwell. The name 'Shrike' or 'Butcher Bird' was only briefly allocated to the Fw 190, which remained anonymous for the remainder of the war (as did the Bf 109).
5. Despite the ban, Heydrich flew several sorties with *JG 52* in late 1941. See Dickfeld, pp.66–7.
6. See Caldwell, pp.106–8, for a typical day in 1942.
7. See Baker, pp.172–3; Caldwell, pp.100–1; and Toliver and Constable, pp.304–5.
8. See Price, *World War II Fighter Conflict*, pp.106–7.
9. AHB, *The Air Defence of Great Britain, Vol. V: The Struggle for Air Supremacy, January 1942–May 1944*, p.88; and Caldwell, pp.93, 103, 105.
10. Fighter Command flew 416 sorties during '*Donnerkeil*'.
11. Caldwell, p.113.
12. For '*Cerberus/Donnerkeil*' see 'Studien zum Luftkrieg: Gedanken zum Einsatz der Luftwaffe im Luftkrieg über See', dated 23 January 1944 (USNA T971, Roll 16, fr.325); Aders, p.50; Baker, pp.181–90; Balke, *KG 2*, pp .84–90; Caldwell, pp.110–13; Galland, pp.91–116; and Middlebrook and Everitt, pp.234–5.
13. Hoffmann, Vol. III, pp.46–50. One of the *Luftwaffe* 'casualties' was a *Luftnachrichtenhelferin* who proved so rude to her captors that an exasperated British paratrooper put her over his knee and spanked her. Private information.
14. Price, *Instruments*, pp.88–9.
15. AHB, *The Air Defence of Great Britain*, Vol. V, pp.16–36; BAM, p.196; Caldwell, pp.135–6; and Saunders, 'Jabo Attack'.
16. AHB, *The Air Defence of Great Britain*, Vol .V, p.14/n.1.
17. For the night offensive see AHB, *The Air Defence of Great Britain*, Vol. V, pp.39–67; Balke, *KG 2*, Vol. 2, pp.103–83; Collier, pp.305–8; and Wakefield, 'The Baedeker Raids'.
18. Wakefield, 'The Danger by Day'; and Bowyer, 'High-Flying Raiders'.
19. Figures from Balke, *KG 2*, p.183.
20. WAAF Iris Price flew an unofficial mission with No 153 Squadron on 13/14 March 1945 while the dog Antis flew semi-officially with Czech aircrew from 1941 (*Daily Mail*, 9 May 1994 and 9 October 1995). Thomas Dobney, aged 15, flew several missions as a

pilot in Whitleys until his real age was discovered and he was discharged. Two women flew with American heavy bombers, *Life* photographer Margaret Bourke-White, unofficially with the 97th Group in North Africa, and RAF COMINT specialist Section Officer M. K. 'Rusty' Goff, officially with an Eighth Air Force mission to Wilhelmshaven (Perret, p.188; and Clayton p.323n).

21. Brookes, p.101.

22. Koch, p.427.

23. For Falck's account of his new assignment see Hinchliffe, pp.40–1.

24. See Hooton, pp.195–6.

25. Both of Streib's kills were confirmed after the war, his second being the only Bomber Command aircraft lost that night. On 9/10 July *Oberfeldwebel* Förster of *8./JG 1* claimed a Whitley near Heligoland, but no Bomber Command aircraft were lost that night. Aders, p.18; and Middlebrook and Everitt, pp.63, 66.

26. Aders, p.29.

27. Ibid., pp.28–9.

28. Ibid., p.24. Bomber Command records show the loss of a Blenheim and a Whitley on that night (Middlebrook and Everitt, p.89).

29. On 12/13 March the first RAF four-engine bombers attacked Germany, which had been struck by a single French aircraft on 7/8 June 1940. See Hooton, p.250.

30. I am indebted to Alex Vanags-Baginskis for this information and for a copy of his article 'Red Stars Over Berlin'.

31. *Hauptmann* Ludwig Bekker, who achieved 44 victories, was lost on 26 February 1943 during a daylight mission against US heavy bombers. He should not be confused with another night-fighter *Experte*, *Hauptmann* Martin 'Tino' Bekker of *NJG 3*, *4* and *6*, who survived the war with 58 victories.

32. For *Himmelbett* and electronics see Aders, pp. 57–8, App. 10; Hinchliffe, pp. 64–5, 68–70, 98; Price, *Instruments*, pp.65–70; and Streetly, pp.214–16, App. 1.

33. While several sources show *Jagddivision 3* incorporated in this reorganisation, the most authoritative ones indicate that this did not occur until 1 October 1942 and it is possible that *JaFü Holland-Ruhrgebiet* is meant.

34. Middlebrook and Everitt, p.168.

35. Ibid., pp.217–18.

36. Aders, p.54. A typical *Dunkelnachtjagd* interception, directed by *Oberleutnant* Walter Knickmeier and leading to Streib's 27th victory, is in Hinchliffe, pp.95–7.

37. Aders, p.47. The arrogant *Experte Major* Heinrich, *Prinz* zu Sayn-Wittgenstein (usually called plain Wittgenstein), who was the *Nachtjagdwaffe*'s top scorer at the time of his death on 21/22 January 1944 with 83 victories, was one of those who pulled rank to increase his score. When he knew that a raid was due he would fly to the most favourable beacon and if another fighter was orbiting would radio, 'Wittgenstein here—bugger off' (Hinchliffe, p.142, but with my translation).

38. Hinchliffe, p.82.

39. In 1938 Harris was scheduled to take over No 11 Group but swapped assignments with Park. Probert and Cox, p.37.

40. A *Krokodil* stream tended to be less than 15km wide.

41. Aders, p.51; and Middlebrook and Everitt, pp.251–61. Following an agreement with the Red Cross, which shipped supplies through the port, Lübeck never received another major attack.

42. Aders, p.56; and Middlebrook and Everitt, pp.269–73.

43. PRO Air 22/79 Weekly Intelligence Summary 214 (9 October 1943). In his diary Knocke, who was given a rocket by Kammhuber for bombing American bombers in 1943 (see Chapter 8), described him as a 'poisonous little twerp' (Knocke, p.96).

44. Based upon Hinchliffe, pp.207–8; and Parry, p.20. For a typical mission see Price, *Bf 110*. For corkscrew also see Price, *Battle Over the Reich*, p.98.
45. BAM, pp.185, 278.
46. The best account of *Luftwaffe* intruder operations is by Parry.
47. At Göring's orders this decision was revoked. Parry, pp.66–77.
48. Ibid., Apps VI, VII.
49. For RAF offensive operations in 1942 see AHB, *The Air Defence of Great Britain*, Vol. V. pp.87–134.
50. Caldwell, pp.117–19.
51. For early USAAF operations see Freeman, *War Diary*, pp.6–7. See also Caldwell, p.122, which makes no mention of Clark.
52. For air operations over Dieppe see Balke, *KG 2*, Vol. 2, pp.147–57; Caldwell, pp.124–9; Franks, *The Greatest Air Battle*; and Freeman, *War Diary*, p.11.
53. AHB, *The Air Defence of Great Britain*, Vol. V, p.132.
54. Baker, pp.190–1.
55. In October 1943 Olejnik's final victory while serving with *JG 1* was a B-17. Mombeek, pp.65, 185.
56. Head-on attacks were made against German bombers by Nos 111 and 132 Squadrons in July 1940 and often forced the bombers to swerve out of formation, but they were an extremely risky tactic which required both experience and courage. There were several collisions with German aircraft, and as the veterans were lost RAF Fighter Command largely abandoned the tactic. Mason, p.121; Freeman, *War Diary*, p.15; and Caldwell pp.133, 139.
57. The figure excludes collisions with enemy aircraft.
58. The pilot in both cases was Major Paul W. Tibbets, who went on to drop the atomic bomb on Hiroshima. Perret, pp.247, 250.
59. Freeman, *The US Strategic Bomber*, pp.153–4, and *War Diary*, pp.19–22.
60. For 'Stockdorf' see Balke, *KG 2*, pp.172–8; BAM, pp.147–8, Map 10; and Caldwell, pp.136–7.

CHAPTER FIVE

The Feet of Clay

The Sinews of Air War

The paradox of the Battle of Britain was that the *Luftwaffe*'s leadership displayed the casual amateurism associated with the English while the RAF leaders demonstrated the ruthless professionalism associated with the Germans. This unhappy situation persisted until mid-1943, when the *Luftwaffe* finally acquired the professional leadership it needed, but until then it was also blighted by a combination of bad luck and ill-feeling.

Göring personified the amateurism, combining the posts held in Britain by Sir Archibald Sinclair (Secretary of State for Air) and Air Chief Marshal Sir Charles Portal (Chief of the Air Staff) yet being capable of filling neither due to a mixture of ignorance, laziness, poor health and alternative interests. Although frequently briefed by his Chief of Staff *General der Flieger* Hans Jeschonnek, he was generally content to leave matters in the hands of his subordinates but would half-heartedly participate in periods of crisis, behaving rather like the grit in the oyster which produces the pearl. Such intervention sometimes followed conversations with his inner circle, drawn largely from cronies of the Great War, including Loerzer, Bodenschatz (who headed his private office and was the *Luftwaffe* liaison officer at Hitler's headquarters) and Keller as well as Paul 'Pilli' Körner, his deputy both in the Four-Year Plan and in Prussia. Upon their advice Göring would impulsively make decisions which he would communicate directly to the commands or units involved, sometimes without even the courtesy of consultation with Jeschonnek or the commanding officer.[1]

Göring's cavalier attitude to his responsibilities had fatal consequences when Hitler asked him to guarantee the air supply of 6. *Armee* at Stalingrad. The matter was intensely debated after the army's isolation on 19 November, with Jeschonnek providing ambiguous replies, evidently hedging his bets, but Göring the politician saw the opportunity to strengthen his prestige with the *Führer*, whom he met on 22 November at Berchtesgaden *en route* to visit Paris art dealers. Preoccupied with thoughts of acquiring new treasures, he assured the *Führer* that the *Luftwaffe* could meet 6. *Armee*'s daily requirement for 600 tonnes of supplies by flying 300 sorties a day. When Hitler returned to his Rastenburg headquarters with this news, Plocher's old friend *General der Infanterie* Kurt Zeitzler, who had replaced Halder two months previously and was probably primed by Richthofen, again advocated a break-out and warned that Göring was lying. However, Hitler stated, 'The

Reichsmarschall has reported to me that the air supply operation will work. I must believe his reports.' Later, Hitler recognised that Göring had deceived him, but he refused to make his intended successor a scapegoat and on 5 February 1943 informed his generals that he alone was responsible for the fatal decision.[2]

Nevertheless, Stalingrad marked a watershed in their relations, for it cast a shadow over the *Luftwaffe*—which lengthened as Bomber Command's offensive grew in strength and was then joined by that of the US Eighth Air Force during the summer of 1943. As German cities collapsed into ruin and death tolls grew, Hitler publicly rounded upon his deputy, tongue-lashing him mercilessly during their infrequent meetings. When Göring scuttled away, his representatives bore the brunt to such a degree that Bodenschatz took to spending nights in hotels rather than stay in *Führer* headquarters and be flayed.[3] Ironically, Göring appears to have made a greater attempt during 1943 to meet his responsibilities, but, in the face of mounting hostility from both the *Führer* and Party leaders (but, surprisingly, not the German people, with whom he remained popular), he would vent his humiliation upon his subordinates. Yet frequently he was the architect of his own misfortune, adopting an ostrich-like approach to critical news such as the development of radar-jamming chaff and the extended range of American fighters. His efforts to take personal control sometimes generated moments of high farce, as on 22/23 October 1943 when he helped to confuse his night fighters and allowed the RAF to devastate Kassel.[4]

Jeschonnek was caught between the truculence of Hitler, whom he greatly admired, and Göring, leading to a desperate desire to escape into the field during the summer of 1943. Of the triumvirate at the head of the *Luftwaffe*, Jeschonnek was the most professional, but the tragedy was that his character had been stunted by having spent the whole of his adult life in uniform. He had volunteered for the Great War when aged 15½, then became a fighter pilot, and when the war ended he served first in the *Freikorps* and then the *Reichsheer*, in which, as a staff officer, he joined a camouflaged air organisation under Felmy. Although possibly under the shadow of his distinguished older brother Paul (who was killed in an air crash in 1929), he was hard-working, quick and intelligent, and he proved to be an asset to the *Luftwaffe*, which he joined in 1933. He rose swiftly to become the Director of Operations (*Chef des Führungsstabs*), but his rise was too rapid and his appointment as Chief of Staff owed as much to his enmity with Göring's deputy, *Generalfeldmarschall* Eberhard Milch, as to his own talents. His youth and immaturity may have appealed to Göring, but they were handicaps when dealing with more experienced leaders such as Greim, Richthofen and Kesselring, to whom he frequently deferred.

His lack of social graces meant that Jeschonnek's relations with the moody Göring gradually deteriorated as the *Reichsmarschall* lost confidence in him, while he was unable to create his own court within the *Luftwaffe* staff, although he did seek the advice of young *Experten* as well as the new generation of *Waffeninspekteure*, such as Galland (*Inspekteur der Jagdflieger*) and Dietrich Peltz (*Inspekteur der Kampf- und Sturzkampfflieger*), who were responsible for developing equipment and tactics for their services. These tasks required maintaining contact with the front, then carefully analysing and evaluating the results in the light of new technology, but the men selected were rarely innovative tacticians (in 1939 Galland had opposed radios for fighters). They were brave men and skilled pilots, but desk work was anathema to them and they frequently exploited the undeniable need to communicate with the men at the front to re-enter the familiar world of the unit mess, and immaturity clouded their advice. With subordinates Jeschonnek was abrasive, frequently brusque and often sarcastic, which made him difficult to approach with new ideas, while relations with the astute, but caustic, head of the supply and administration branch, *General der Flieger* Hans-Georg Seidel, were especially bad. There were few officers who could discourage Jeschonnek's short-term solutions, partly encouraged by his belief in Hitler's infallibility; indeed, only 331 qualified staff officers had served in the *Luftwaffe*'s ranks to 1 March 1944, and by that date 87 were either dead or in captivity.[5] There was also the problem that fewer technically aware officers were available owing to sociological change, for, since the beginning of the century, increasing numbers were drawn from the *Humanistische Gymnasien* with their classics-based education rather than the technically based *Real Gymnasien*. In fact, of the *Luftwaffe*'s generals and trained staff officers only 5% had technical degrees.[6] With no one to remove the blinkers, Jeschonnek was unable to take a broad view of the air war, and although the failure at Moscow meant that the *Luftwaffe* faced the dreaded prospect of a four-front war, the opportunity presented during the winter of 1941/42 to create a central reserve as 26 *Gruppen* were withdrawn from the Eastern Front to rest and re-equip was thrown away. Five *Gruppen* were briefly assembled in Prussia, but only for use in the East, and subsequently Jeschonnek simply robbed Peter to pay Paul. The training organisation in particular was treated like a medieval peasant, starved and regularly plundered, initially to provide transport facilities and later to provide bombers.[7]

Jeschonnek's immaturity had a malign effect upon the other dilettante influence within the *Luftwaffe*, the *Generalluftzeugmeister*, *Generaloberst* Ernst Udet. As a judicial inquiry noted in 1942, neither Jeschonnek's staff nor the *RLM*'s *Technisches Amt* (responsible for development) set specific requirements for performance in issuing their requirements, confining themselves to generalities and leaving the amiable Bohemian prey to the ravenous manufacturers, like a lion-tamer without the whip. Udet was selected in 1937 to supervise the development and production both of aircraft and of all their equipment, succeeding the technocrat Milch, who had formerly led Lufthansa and had masterminded aircraft development and production during the *Luftwaffe*'s early days. The doyen of the Great War aces (62 victories), Udet was a brilliant barnstormer who had flirted briefly with production, lost interest and watched his company absorbed by the Bayerische Flugzeugwerk (later Messerschmitt). His new position required dedication, a thorough knowledge of the aircraft industry and the ability to comprehend the potential of new technology—all features lacking from Udet's character. Indeed, his reaction to the French Armistice was one of relief: 'The war's over! All our plans can be tossed into the waste-paper basket. We don't need them any more.' In fairness, his task was made more complex by conflicting demands from Jeschonnek for aircraft and from industry for resources, with Udet at a severe disadvantage competing with the Army, since Germany was essentially fighting a land war. Briefly Hitler decreed on 13 July 1940 that the *Luftwaffe* and Navy had priority, but as planning for *'Barbarossa'* began he reversed his decision in the Army's favour. Although 16 production programmes were produced by Udet from the outbreak of war to his death (one every six weeks), none could be implemented, and even after his death the planning kaleidoscope continued to turn, reaching *Liefer-Plan* (Production Plan) 225 by New Year's Day 1944, and this, too, was uncompleted.[8] Incoherent planning led to a spectacular own goal when a Ju 88 contract for Henschel was cancelled in favour of the Hs 129 ground attack aircraft, which was itself cancelled when production tooling was half-complete, first in favour of the Ju 188 then, just as production was about to begin, of the Me 410 and finally of the Ju 388. In the event the last contract was also cancelled in 1944 because the production emphasis switched to fighters, and the company failed to produce a single bomber.

Proper support by his officials and engineers might have compensated for Udet's inexperience and technical ignorance, but from 1938 the organisation of the *Generalluftzeugmeisteramt* was compartmentalised, largely through the persuasion of the engineers, who sought to enhance their relatively lowly status. This blinkered view hindered development, for there was little coordination either within or without the organisation, and the Focke-Wulf Flugzeugbau seemed especially cursed. The Fw 191 contender for the high-altitude *Bomber B* requirement was forced to incorporate extensive electrical systems which would have doomed the design even if it had successfully completed development.[9] The Fw 190 suffered major problems with overheating when introduced into service, leaving the lowly *JG 26* Technical Officer, Ernst Battmer, to coordinate the industrial response which solved these problems and produced one of the outstanding designs of the war. Udet's lack of authority neutralised the state's growing control of the industry, which meant that designers such as Dornier, Heinkel and Messerschmitt often had only nominal control of the companies which bore their names. Consequently there was little control over their activities, allowing them to produce designs which were frequently flights of fancy with no relevance to the war effort, while much of Udet's time was taken up with convivial visits to factories to see or to fly the new designs. The surprising lack of control, with civilians excluded from production decision-making, extended into raw materials, where manufacturers received over-generous quotas of aluminium and copper, little of which was used in production, allowing them either to hoard the material or use it in other work.

The wayward and wasteful aircraft industry also reflected the *Wehrmacht*'s distrust of mass production in the belief that it meant equipment of lower quality. The services continued to demand very high technical standards in both design and workmanship, which was one reason why the *Generalluftzeugmeisteramt* opposed moves to simplify designs or to reduce types. Even with established projects there were frequent calls for minor changes to the basic design—and at times for specialised models, often of marginal value—which hindered mass production: the Bf 109E/F and G, for example, had 60 sub-types, while in 1942 it was estimated that design changes had cost 20% of total aircraft production.[10] Such attitudes encouraged the retention of craft-based production, despite Milch's earlier attempts to modernise production, and these proved both time-consuming and wasteful; for example, more than half a tonne of metal was lost in engine-machining. New factories built and operated by the state were poorly designed and reflected the traditional ethos: even in 1944, when the British had a dozen factories employing more than 10,000 people (two with 25,000), the Germans had only four (the largest with 14,000)—a situation caused not by the need to disperse to smaller sites but by poor planning. While the British mobilised the motor and electrical industries as well as passenger transport depots, there was a marked reluctance in Germany to exploit production facilities from outside the traditional aircraft industry such as those of the Volkswagen and Opel works. These features all combined to create near stagnation in the aircraft industry, and while the number of workers rose between 1939 and 1941 by some 50% to 1.85 million, production rose by only 15% to 11,776, including gliders. In the first half of 1941 the average monthly production of fighters and twin-engine aircraft was 301, while in the second half it was 322.[11]

As the Blitz neared its climax and *'Barbarossa'* loomed on the horizon, it became obvious even to Göring that something was seriously wrong. Indeed, from March 1941 production actually declined. Both Milch and Göring tried in vain to persuade Udet to reorganise, and on 20 June 1941, when Hitler, anticipating the success of *'Barbarossa'*, authorised a quadrupling of the *Luftwaffe*, the task was assigned to Milch, who received plenipotentiary powers and tackled it with his usual enthusiasm and skill. In September he began cutting out the dead wood, including Udet's Chief of Staff *Generalmajor Dipl.-Ing.* August Ploch, and replacing it with his own men, including his able friend *Oberst* Carl-Henrich, *Freiherr* von Gablenz (the *Lufttransportführer*).[12] Udet's worries were aggravated by aircraft development problems, partly because he had accepted his engineers' advice and sought to truncate the development programme between prototype and pre-production by a year. Since many designs had been selected for production schedules before they were fully assessed, this was a high-risk policy, especially when manu-facturers such as *Professor* Willi Messerschmitt and Junkers' *Dr* Heinrich Koppen-berg sought to minimise the problems, and by early 1941 it was clear that the He 177 Greif, the Me 210 *Zerstörer* replacement, the Me 209 day fighter and the sophisticated Ju 288 (which had been selected for the *Bomber B* requirement) were all in serious trouble.

The professional worries were aggravated by personal ones. Udet's health was declining due to vitamin deficiency (he rarely ate vegetables or fruit) and the excessive use of alcohol, cigarettes and narcotics. He was also under *Gestapo* sur-veillance, apparently at Heydrich's instigation, partly because of the defection of Deputy *Führer* Rudolf Hess on 10 May 1941 and partly because of intercepted correspondence with an *emigré* friend in Sweden.[13] His telephone calls were being monitored through Göring's interception service in the *RLM* building, and in August 1941 he was forbidden from flying himself, although he sometimes took the controls in mid-flight. The strain became too much, and on 17 November he shot himself. The bullet helped kill two more senior *Luftwaffe* figures, for while flying to his funeral first *General der Flieger* Helmuth Wilberg (who had laid the foundations for a renaissance of German air power after the Great War) and then Mölders were killed in air crashes within two days of each other.[14] The shock brought Jeschonnek to the verge of collapse: he took to his bed for three days and briefly banned his staff officers from flying.[15]

Milch immediately became *Generalluftzeugmeister*, resuming the work for which he was superbly qualified, and it must have been an immensely satisfying moment for the *Staatssekretär der Luftfahrt und Generalinspekteur der Luftwaffe*, who had been in a limbo of his own making only three years earlier. His talent made Milch ambitious and arrogant, yet this masked an insecurity which made him acutely conscious of slights both real and imagined. He sought to undermine rivals through intrigues, and following the tragic death of the *Luftwaffe*'s first Chief of Staff, the immensely capable *Generalleutnant* Walther Wever, feuds with the *Staatssekretär* caused the rapid departure of his successors Kesselring and Stumpff. In appoint-ing first Udet and then Jeschonnek (the latter once a friend of Milch but later a bitter enemy), Göring clipped his deputy's wings, but his undoubted skills could not be overlooked for long and by the outbreak of war he was essentially in charge of the *Luftwaffe*'s rear echelon, '*Kurfürst*', which included training and production as well as Martini's signal service. In November 1940 Milch assumed temporary command of the *Luftwaffe* (Jeschonnek promptly went on leave), but it was in the field of production where the *Staatssekretär's* talents reigned supreme. Having replaced Udet, he rationalised the *Generalluftzeugmeisteramt* into three *Haupt-ausschüsse* (Supervisory Boards)—for airframes, engines and accessories. Below them were *Sonderausschüsse*, under a director producing one type of aircraft, and *Ausschüsse*, under a chief engineer with one or more large assembly centres supported by component factories. Focke-Wulf's facilities were transferred to Kassel and Marienburg from Bremen, Messerschmitt's were at Brunswick, Leipzig, Regensburg andWiener Neustadt while Junkers' were based at Bernberg, Halberstadt and Oschersleben. Milch's brief fear of rivalry with Albert Speer, who from February 1942 headed the *Reichsministerium für Rüstung und Kriegsproduktion* (State Ministry for Armament and War Production), were quickly allayed for the two were soulmates and Speer was happy to leave Milch in control of aircraft production while he supported the other services, especially the Army. Milch improved organisation and efficiency, introducing flow-production techniques first into the components industry and then into Messerschmitt for aircraft production, with that company's example followed the next year by BMW, Henschel, Heinkel and Junkers. Plant construction was severely curtailed and the 48-hour week (excluding weekends) was replaced by shift work, with a more rational use of space. The number of individual companies in manufacture was reduced and output was concentrated at the most efficient, with efficiency also dictating the allocation of raw materials.

While the workforce increased it was considerably diluted, reducing the emphasis upon craft-work, and between 1941 and 1944 the percentage of skilled male workers at Messerschmitt dropped from 59 to 21, with skilled workers used in a supervisory role as new processes enabled semi-skilled workers, including women, to operate specialised equipment. By the summer of 1944 manpower in the industry had risen by 24% since 1941 to 2.3 million (450,000 in airframe assembly, of whom 23% were women), who produced during the year 39,788 aircraft (nearly 65% of them single-engine fighters/*Jabos*), and although the amount of aluminium available had increased by only 5% since 1941 there was 120% more structure weight.[16] The effects of Milch's reforms were quickly felt: at Junkers, between 1941 and 1942 production of aircraft increased by 42%, while 75% more engines were made, although the labour force grew by only 7%. The reorganisation saved both time and material. By 1944 there was a 53% saving in Bf 109 production time, man-hours had been halved and there was a 25% saving in raw materials; and between 1940 and 1944 the amount of metal for each BMW 801 radial dropped from 5.14 tonnes to 2.79 tonnes, and man-hours had been reduced from 3,260 to 1,250 per engine.[17]

Although Germany supplied aircraft and manufacturing equipment to her friends and satellites, as a result of Milch's efforts the *Luftwaffe*'s strength increased from 4,882 in June 1941 to 4,942 a year later, and by the beginning of June 1944 it was 6,504.[18] Yet until 1944 the Reich's aircraft production was exceeded by that of Great Britain, and it was able to surpass the British only by concentrating upon single-engine aircraft; both were dwarfed by the rapidly mobilised US industry. Moreover, Milch had to rely essentially upon the designs he himself had developed in the mid-1930s, for the new generation of aircraft proved disappointing. The performance of the Me 210 and Ju 288 was inadequate; the former was also extremely dangerous, while the latter required replacement engines which were not forthcoming and development was formally abandoned in June 1943, ostensibly due to a shortage of strategic materials. The decision to abandon production of the Me 210, whose design faults had by now been overcome, was taken in April 1942, Messerschmitt AG having spent 30 million Reichsmarks (US $12 million) while the war effort lost some 600 aircraft, providing Milch with an excuse to force Messerschmitt's resignation as chairman of the company.[19] Curiously, with some relatively minor design changes the aircraft emerged as the Me 410 Hornisse (Hornet) in January 1943 and became the German equivalent of the Mosquito in the light bomber, reconnaissance and heavy fighter roles. Development problems with the He 177 persisted since the *Luftwaffe* refused to consider the obvious solution of installing four separate engines. It eventually resolved the difficulties and the heavy bomber provided satisfactory service from the latter half of 1943.[20]

The failure to produce new designs meant that the *Luftwaffe* had to rely largely upon improved versions of pre-war designs: the Ju 88 and the Fw 190 accounted for 80% of production, while the long-obsolete He 111 remained in production despite Milch's wishes because it was easy to manufacture, was economic in manhours and material and remained effective in the less demanding Eastern Front, where it could also double as a transport. A few designs could be 'stretched', the Ju 88 evolving into the Ju 188 and Ju 388 (as substitutes for *Bomber B*) and the Fw 190 into the Ta 152, but such evolutionary work depended upon new engines. Here, too, development was plagued with problems. Those involving the 12-cylinder, liquid-cooled DB 603 were eventually overcome, but production of the Do 217M and Do 217N, which were to receive them, had continued and numerous airframes were at the factory awaiting engines. Eventually production of the Do 217N night fighter had to be abandoned as the engines were switched to the He 219 Uhu (Owl). Development of the 12-cylinder, liquid-cooled Junkers Jumo 213 (selected for the He 277) was also protracted, delaying the introduction of the Ju 188, but it too eventually entered service, unlike the 24-cylinder Junkers Jumo 222 (selected for the Ju 288 and Ju 488), which had to be abandoned at the test stage. Production was therefore concentrated on the proven BMW 801, Daimler Benz DB 601 and 605 as well as the Junkers Jumo 211, but this created bottlenecks, and plans to equip later versions of the Ju 88 with the BMW 801 were compromised by the priority assigned to the Fw 190.

There were also limits to what Milch could achieve. Although he tightened state control of the industry, it still remained wilful, and Messerschmitt even continued development of the Me 209 fighter, rolling out the Me 209HV1 prototype after the programme had been officially abandoned. Milch's efforts to improve fighter production to meet an anticipated massive air assault following the entry of the United States into the war were widely opposed, and when the *General-luftzeugmeister* scathingly dismissed Göring's request for 360 fighters on 21 March 1942 and offered 3,600, Jeschonnek caustically observed, 'I do not know what I should do with more than 360 fighters.'[21] Neither Hitler nor Göring would authorise any dilution of offensive capability; indeed, the Fw 190 was produced for the *Jabo* as well as the fighter role, and from late 1943 it gradually re-equipped the *Stukagruppen*. A further complication was Hitler's demand for a strong transport arm, but here Milch had to continue relying upon the Ju 52, its replacement the Ju 352 Herkules appearing too late. Hopes that powered versions of the Me 321 Gigant and Go 242 glider might supplement the 'Tante Ju' were dashed, for the Me 323 and Go 244 proved too vulnerable to enemy action, forcing the *Luftwaffe* to use bombers in the transport role. Moreover, for all Goebbels' talk of defending Europe, there was little attempt to exploit aircraft manufacturing facilities outside the Reich, even in Bohemia. French factories which had received millions of francs-worth of American-made machine tools before the Armistice had most of them seized and transported to Germany, where they were simply stockpiled. Up to 100,000 French workers were eventually employed in German factories, while their own factories were largely reduced to repairing *Luftwaffe* aircraft, refurbishing *Armeé de l'Air* combat aircraft for allies and producing second-line aircraft for the Germans, although development of the four-engine Ju 488 began at the former Latécoère factory in Toulouse in 1944. This was an exception, however, and most foreign aircraft industries suffered a similar fate to the French.

Milch's career was wrecked on the rock of his own character. Although a jet aircraft had appeared before the Great War, it required significant development before practical engines appeared in the late 1930s, the He 178 making the first jet flight on 24 August 1939 and being followed by Italian Caproni N.1 and British Gloster E.28/39 in 1940 and 1941 respectively. Two operational jet designs would eventually emerge from German industry, the Arado 234 Blitz (Lightning) reconnaissance bomber and the Me 262 Schwalbe (Swallow), but as American raids pushed deeper into Germany it was the latter which attracted high-level attention. Jet engine technology was immature, with German development and production hamstrung by acute shortages of nickel and chrome. Even when its design was frozen in June 1944, the Junkers Jumo 004 proved extremely temperamental, with an average life of 25 hours, which meant frequent engine changes. In January 1944 only two Me 262s were available for service testing, and even in their heyday towards the end of the year no more than a dozen ever participated in a single mission. Yet Hitler, like many semi-educated people, was fascinated by technology and perceived in the Me 262 a means of overcoming Allied air superiority and striking the beach-heads when the anticipated invasion of western Europe occurred. From November 1943 he stressed the importance of jet *Jabos*, and Milch, ever the courtier, had acquiesced while concentrating upon producing Me

262 fighters: he was aware of the development of the Ar 234 jet bomber and the Feisler Fi 103 ramjet-powered surface-to-surface missile (officially designated *Flakzielgerät* 76 and which later became the V-1), both of which would be operational the following summer.[22]

The need for the Me 262 fighter was underlined from February 1944 when the Americans began pounding the aircraft industry, hitting 26 factories and causing the loss of at least 1,000 aircraft (including 700 Bf 109s) by the end of March, the vulnerability confirming an earlier decision by Milch and Speer's deputy, Karl-Otto Saur, to disperse the aircraft industry. Saur was a rival who had stolen key personnel from the aircraft industry, and Milch was determined to pay back the stocky engineer, whom he had placed at the head of an organisation dedicated to fighter production, the *Jägerstab* (Fighter Staff). Milch remained a key player, and together the two men achieved miracles of organisation, as well as introducing a 72-hour working week, so that from April 1944 a monthly production of 2,000 fighters was achieved. On 23 May Milch gave a *Jägerstab* progress report to Hitler but in mid-flow was asked how many *Jabo* versions of the Me 262 had been produced and had to reply that only fighter versions were being built. Milch, as one observer commented to Peterson (the former *KG 40 Kommodore* and now Director of Research), had 'crashed in flames' and found himself alone facing the *Führer's* fury, with both Saur and Peterson supporting Hitler's contention that the aircraft could be adapted to the strike role. Speer quickly moved to take over the aircraft industry, and an embarrassed Göring (who sought in vain to change Hitler's mind) was unable to resist this occurring on 20 June. The unhappy Milch initially did not realise that he, too, was being cast aside, although he retained the largely ceremonial post of *Generalinspekteur der Luftwaffe*. From July 1944 fighter production was given absolute priority and bomber production largely faded away, helping to neuter the *Luftwaffe*, whose few *Kampfgruppen* continued to rely upon the He 111, the Ju 88 and the Do 217, the Heinkel also being used to launch V-1 missiles.

Yet the emasculation of the *Kampfgruppen* had begun some 30 months earlier and was becoming apparent in April 1942 when Jeschonnek's former friend Waldau was replaced by Richthofen's former Chief of Staff Meister, now recovered from his injuries, as Director of Operations. Meister was 45 years old and had volunteered for the Army as soon as he was 17, serving as an observer during the Great War, after which he joined the *Reichswehr* and served for two years at Lipetsk. He joined the *Luftwaffe* and held various posts until replacing Seidemann in mid-October 1940, remaining with *Fliegerkorps VIII* until he was wounded. Meister took office as an insidious malaise crept into the *Luftwaffe* from the East like a plague virus—one which proved fatally debilitating and undermined Wever's key achievement. When Wever joined the *Luftwaffe* he was a conservative, favouring tactical air support, but after extensive reading he proposed focusing on the *Operativ*

149

level (operational level) and successfully 'sold' this concept to the Army's leaders, although they were never completely convinced. The concept included attacks upon enemy industry to disrupt the short-term supply of munitions to the front and undermine resistance to a German offensive. Operational air support was one of the keys to *Blitzkrieg* success, but the Army's loss of heavy weapons in the East during the winter of 1941/42 led to growing pressure for the *Luftwaffe* to be used as flying artillery, and one of its generals observed after the war, 'Air support became, in fact, the basic prerequisite upon which depended the success of efforts to repel major Soviet attacks.'[23] Another factor was the Army's crisis of confidence as overstretched troops became psychologically dependent upon air support, the absence of which led to withdrawal symptoms expressed in bitter complaints up the chain of command. *Luftwaffe* officers still considered themselves 'soldiers' and, therefore, duty-bound to respond to their comrades' pleas even though these violated their service's prime doctrine and undermined its autonomy.[24] Hitler became a strong advocate of tactical air power; indeed, when *Heeresgruppe Nord* was preparing a counter-offensive by *16.* and *18. Armees* in March he insisted that it should have thorough air preparation as 'escort artillery', attacking enemy troop concentrations and positions with the heaviest possible bombs.[25] The *Luftwaffe* military history organisation in 1944 calculated that 60–80% of the *Luftwaffe*'s effort in 1942–43 went to tactical air support, and there is no indication that Jeschonnek opposed the process. Yet he was not the only one, and while Richthofen later lamented that the *Luftwaffe* had become 'the army's whore', events in 1942 made him the leading pimp.[26]

Meister was more 'virtuous' and may have had time to consider other uses for air power, for it was also during his tenure that he and Jeschonnek nurtured the concept of strategic bombing as a symbol of *Luftwaffe* autonomy. Wever had not been blind to the potential of strategic bombing (seeking to defeat the enemy by attacking the means of production), but he certainly influenced the 1936 *Luftwaffe* book on doctrine, *Luftwaffendienstvorschrift 16*, whose Paragraph 22 stated that such operations 'normally produce results very slowly and carry the inherent risk that their effect upon Army and Navy operations comes too late'. Because they required the commitment of large forces for long periods of time they were to be undertaken only to break an *impasse* in the land (and/or sea) war. Nevertheless the *Luftkriegsakademie*, where staff officers were trained, displayed an increasing interest in the concept of strategic bombing after his death.

However, the *Luftwaffe* lacked a strategic bombing philosophy and the Blitz was essentially a succession of half measures, while later attacks upon Great Britain were of an increasingly retaliatory nature. *ObdL*'s renewed interest in genuine strategic, as distinct from operational, bombing originated in the East with Greim, whose *Fliegerkorps* ultimately became *Luftflotte 6*. During lulls in ground operations in 1942 he used his under-employed *Kampfgruppen* (with 180 aircraft) to

Table 38. *Fliegerkorps XIV*

New designation	Old designation	New designation	Old designation
Stab TG 1	*Stab KGzbV 1*	*Stab TG 4*	New
I./TG 1	*I./KGzbV 1*	*I./TG 4*	*KGrzbV 105*
II./TG 1	*II./KGzbV 1*	*II./TG/4*	*KGrzbV 500*
III./TG 1	*III./KGzbV 1*	*III./TG 4*	*KGrzbV 400*
IV./TG 1	*IV./KGzbV 1*	*IV./TG 4*	*KGrzbV 700*
Stab TG 2	*Stab KGzbV 3*	*Stab TG 5*	*Stab KGrzbV*
I./TG 2	*KGrzbV 600*		*Wittstock*
II./TG 2	*KGrzbV 800*	*I./TG 5*	*I./KGzbV 323*
III./TG 2	*KGzbV 106*	*II./TG 5*	*II./.KGzbV 323*
Stab TG 3	*Stab KGzbV 2*	*III./TG 5*	*III./KGzbV 323*
I./TG 3	*KGrzbV 9*	*TGr 10*	*KGrzbV 5*
II./TG 3	*KGrzbV 50*	*TGr 20*	*KGrzbV 108*
III./TG 3	*KGrzbV 102*	*TGr 30*	*KGrzbV 23*
IV./TG 3	*KGrzbV 172*	*ErgTransGr*	*KGrzbV 300*

attack industrial targets as far east as Gorki (900km east of Greim's main base at Smolensk), which in turn stimulated an interest in strategic bombing, leading to an outline plan of campaign which was sent to *ObdL*. It arrived when the Stalingrad operation seemed on the verge of success and was pigeon-holed, but, with the triumph of Russian arms, Jeschonnek began reappraising the situation during the spring of 1943, when he also rationalised the transport forces for which *Fliegerkorps XIV* was created under Coeler on 15 May with 21 *Transportgruppen* (formerly *Kampfgruppen zbV*) (see Table 38). He also began to appreciate the value of strategic bombing to counterbalance the Soviet Union's numerical superiority. Germany had clearly lost the strategic initiative everywhere and was on the defensive, devoid of any means of changing the situation, but, while Milch advocated an improvement in the *Luftwaffe*'s defensive capability, to both Hitler and Göring this smacked of 'defeatism' and they continued to demand an offensive posture.

A week-long conference in Berlin from 28 January 1943 had concluded that the *Luftwaffe* would face its biggest test in the Mediterranean, where increasing quantities of aircraft, men and equipment were despatched in the first half of the year. On the Eastern Front it was clear that the Red Army was too strong for the *Wehrmacht* to destroy, but as the *rasputitsa* of March 1943 brought a lull to the front and the *Kampfgruppen* were conserved, Greim's plans were re-examined and *Luftwaffe* intelligence, which Schmid had surrendered in mid-October 1942, began assembling target folders with Speer's advice. Gorki, with its tank producing plants, became the El Dorado of German strategic bombing, but there were also other targets, and Greim assumed control of all the *Kampfgruppen* in the East for a month-long night offensive starting on 4/5 June and involving some 1,000 sorties and 1,520 tonnes of bombs. Losses were light—six aircraft in the Gorki missions (0.87%)—and this boosted morale in the *Kampfgruppen*, which were also glad to get back to real bombing. Greim had to end his campaign to support *Unternehmen 'Zitadelle'* (Citadel), the *Wehrmacht's* summer offensive in the East, but even as his first campaign was under way he made proposals for another. Jeschonnek replied on 18 June that he 'fully and entirely agreed' with these plans, and requested speedy implementation of them, although recognising the need for better intelligence. This problem was addressed five days later when, at Speer's instigation, a target selection committee was established under *Dr. Ing.* Rudolf Carl, Chief of Electrical Power Planning, while further indications of Jeschonnek's attitude were shown on 20 June when Greim's Chief of Staff, *Oberst* Friedrich Kless, visited him to discuss details and was informed that *ObdL* planned to establish a *Generalkommando* under a separate authority to supervise strategic bombing.[27]

Tragically, it was strategic bombing which prevented Jeschonnek from seeing the plans implemented. Furious at British attacks, and with the *Reichsmarschall* having retired to his estates, Hitler railed against the Chief of Staff, who received insults rather than sympathy from Göring. The miserable Jeschonnek attempted suicide, and this may have stimulated Göring's search for a replacement, with both Richthofen and Greim being considered. Far from being downcast at the prospect of exclusion from the stormy Olympus, Jeschonnek eagerly anticipated it, for he would be given a *Luftflotte* command in exchange, but Hitler vetoed the appointment of Richthofen, who went to *Luftflotte 2*. On 21 June, the day after meeting Kless, Jeschonnek briefly reported sick, leaving Göring to face the *Führer's* wrath in the wake of further RAF attacks, but returned to watch the opening of *'Zitadelle'* from *Luftflotte 4's* headquarters, which he hoped soon to occupy. Unfortunately these hopes were dashed by the horrific British bombing of Hamburg from 24/25 July, accompanied by the use of 'Window' chaff which wrecked the night fighter system. Göring was now considering either Richthofen or *General der Flieger* Günther Korten, but when the former rejected the idea the 'Fat Man' decided to retain Jeschonnek, whose professional despair was tinged by personal grief with the recent loss of his father, brother and brother-in-law. The final straw was on 17/18 August when the RAF wrecked the missile research base at Peenemünde, Hitler telephoning Jeschonnek the following morning and bluntly telling him, 'You know what to do!' Jeschonnek, who had spent the previous evening toasting his daughter's birthday, now dictated a memorandum to Göring complaining about the *Reichsmarschall's* failures, then walked into a small hut and shot himself.[28]

With Richthofen again pushing aside the poisoned chalice, the mantle fell upon Korten's shoulders. The 45-year-old Korten looked like a prosperous official but was a good staff officer with a winning personality. He had served as a gunner in the Great War and his first experience of flying had come when he was trained at Lipetsk in 1928. He joined the *Luftwaffe* as a member of the Army Co-operation

Command (*Kommando des Heeresflieger*) but then served with Milch and was an instructor on the first *Luftkriegsakademie* course. The *Luftwaffe* had, for the first time, an experienced and mature leader who had held senior staff posts then commanded in succession *Fliegerkorps I/Luftwaffe Kommando Don* and *Luftflotte 1*, and the leadership was strengthened by the appointment of his close friend *Generalmajor* Karl Koller as Director of Operations in succession to Meister but with a directorate given greater autonomy, control of the quartermaster (Seidel) and Martini's signallers and stronger intelligence support. The Bavarian Koller was the same age as Korten, had volunteered for the Army when he was 16 and later became an 'Old Eagle'. He served as a *Polizeiflieger* after the war and remained with the police until he joined the *Luftwaffe*, where his entire career was spent in staff posts. He was not happy about leaving *Luftflotte 3*, where he had been Chief of Staff since January 1941, and even the prospect of working with a friend did not stifle his opposition to the transfer, Sperrle supporting him by signing an unfavourable report on him to Göring. When he did arrive he and Korten worked as a team, using the 'hard-man/soft-man' approach with Koller in the former role until both were injured in the July Bomb Plot. Korten died a few days later, whereupon Göring promptly dismissed Koller, only to install him as *Luftwaffe* Chief of Staff in November until the war's end.

The two friends rapidly introduced more rational policies into the direction of the *Luftwaffe* but had to recognise that since the autumn of 1942, and especially the North African landings, it could neither seek to defeat its opponents in detail nor exploit the advantage of interior lines of communication. Despite Milch's efforts the *Luftwaffe*'s leaders had to seek the most cost-effective means of operation, even if this meant weakening one or more theatres. The Berlin Conference in January had already established this principle, which was most strongly espoused by Galland, who also pressed for top priority for the strengthening of his arm. Jeschonnek's 'Mediterranean first' strategy was clearly not cost-effective and was the first victim of the new pragmatism, and as the German Army retreated up the Italian peninsula *Jagd-* and *Zerstörergruppen* were withdrawn to defend the Reich while *Kampfgruppen* were used to strengthen *Luftflotte 3*. Partly this was in preparation for a renewed air offensive on England, *Unternehmen 'Steinbock'* (Ibex), but it also anticipated *OKW* Directive 51, which demanded the strengthening of the defences in western Europe and Scandinavia in anticipation of an Allied invasion. The infrastructure was to be decentralised 'so that . . . our own units will not be exposed to enemy bombing at the beginning of large-scale operations . . .' Arrangements were to be made for a major reinforcement of the threatened area, and if the invasion took place in western Europe or Denmark then air and *Flak* forces would be taken from Reich defence. During 1943 the latter received a dozen *Jagd-* and *Zerstörergruppen*, mostly from the Mediterranean and Russian theatres, while other *Jagdgruppen* were created within Germany.

153

Nevertheless, there were also ambitious plans for anti-shipping forces and bombers, with Peltz now pleading in October for a 24-*Geschwader* force, including three with Ju 290s, a total of 840 four-engine and 2,120 twin-engine bombers (Ju 188, 288 and 388), although the total bomber force at that time was less than 1,100 aircraft.[29] Such a plan was beyond Germany's resources, but the work of Jeschonnek and Meister in preparing a strategic bombing force was not neglected; indeed, Meister was given command of *Fliegerkorps IV*, which was the *Generalkommando* that Kless had been promised. Korten was a supporter of strategic bombing, as was Koller's intelligence organisation, although the latter was hamstrung by the absence of any long-range photographic reconnaissance aircraft which could have provided more detail on Russian industry, forcing it to rely upon agents' reports and prisoner-of-war interrogation. With their reports and the considerations of the Carl Committee, Koller produced an outline plan in November 1943 but acknowledged that the German retreats during the summer and autumn meant that 'we have let slip our most favourable opportunity and . . . the difficulties have become great'. Work on targeting began just before Christmas and involved a wide range of personalities, including Himmler, while the activities of the US heavy bomber force in Italy (later Fifteenth Air Force) also had a strong influence. In fact, it was a suggestion by *Oberst* Rudolf Wodarg, head of intelligence, that they follow the Allies' example in Italy and strike the rail system that proved to have the greatest impact.[30] Meanwhile *Kampfgruppen* were assembled under Meister for re-training and re-equipment, but during the first months of 1944 the German retreat meant the abandonment of more bases, especially in the Ukraine, making attacks upon industrial targets more difficult. Moscow remained the only industrial target within practical range, and for this reason Wodarg's proposals for attacking the rail system grew in prominence, the attacks commencing on 27/28 March.[31] Although four-engine bombers were later committed, the campaign was more of an operational than a strategic exercise and proved a failure in both roles.

Korten and Koller also sought to reduce air support for the Army but in this they were less successful. However, Meister did conclude in August 1943 that the need to make this support more effective, especially against Russian armour, required significant reorganisation of the existing resources. On 10 October 1943 the close support organisation was rationalised with the removal of *Stuka*- and *Schnellkampfgruppen* from the *General der Kampfflieger* and the *Schlachtgruppen* from the *General der Jagdflieger* and the creation of a *General der Schlachtflieger* under *Major* Otto Weiss (see Table 39).[32] It was hoped to re-equip most of the 20 *Schlachtgruppen* with the Fw 190 *Jabo* and transfer their Ju 87s to the *Nachtschlachtgruppen* formed at the same time from the *Störkampfgruppen*, but by the summer of 1944 the process was far from complete.

Yet there was a worm in the apple, for the *Luftwaffe*'s quantitative and qualitative improvements were not matched by the training organisation, although Korten

Table 39. The new *Schlachtflieger*, October 1943

New designation	Old designation	New designation	Old designation
Stab SG 1	Stab StG 1	II./SG 4	II./SKG 10
I./SG 1	I./StG 1	III./SG 4	III./SKG 10
II./SG 1	II./StG 1	I./SG 5	I./StG 5
III./SG 1	III./StG 1	IV./SG 9	Führer der Panzerjäger-
Stab SG 2	Stab StG 2		staffeln
I./SG 2	I./StG 2	Stab SG 10	Stab SKG 10
II./SG 2	II./SchG 1	I./SG 10	I./SchG 2
III./SG 2	III/StG 2	II./SG 10	IV./SKG 10
10. (Pz)/SG 2	Panzerjägerstaffel/StG 2	III./SG 10	II./StG 77
Stab SG 3	Stab StG 3	Stab SG 77	Stab StG 77
I./SG 3	I./StG 3	I./SG 77	I./StG 77
II./SG 3	II./StG 3	II./SG 77	I./SchG 1
III./SG 3	III./StG 3	III./SG 77	III./StG 77
Stab SG 4	Stab SchG 2	10. (Pz)/SG 77	Panzerjägerstaffel/StG 1
I./SG 4	II./SchG 2		

continued the reforms belatedly initiated by Jeschonnek. In the summer of 1940 one of the most experienced of the 'Old Eagles', *General der Flieger* Bernhard Kühl, was *Chef des Ausbildungswesens* and nominally controlled an organisation of 60 flying and 16 operational training schools, together with induction units (*Flieger Ausbildungregimenter*) and specialist training establishments.[33] In practice training was controlled by the *Luftgaue*, whose myriad other duties made them neglect the subject and left Kühl with only a monitoring and supervisory role, which limited his influence. When *Unteroffizier* Peter Stahl, a pre-war test pilot and reservist, was transferred to one school early in 1940 he noted that there was little flying and that most of the administrative personnel gave the impression of 'clumsiness, arrogance, laziness and shirking of duty'.[34] There was some expansion of schools a year later, and while a few moved to eastern France the majority were in Poland and the eastern part of the Reich. The first modification to the organisation arose from concerns among the combat units about the poor quality of aircrew reaching them from the combat training schools, where they usually trained in obsolete aircraft such as the Do 23.[35] From 1940 each *Geschwader* created an *Ergänzungs-gruppe* (Operational Training Group) which allowed newcomers to become familiar with the aircraft they would operate in first-line service and provided a degree of operational training.[36] However, as instructors often had little recent combat experience, the students continued to display fatal inadequacies, and after the war Galland told his captors that newcomers' radio discipline was so poor that in *JG 26* he introduced a two-button switch to operate the radios.[37]

Because both *ObdL* and the *Luftgaue* tended to neglect training while Udet was more interested in producing combat aircraft, the schools were starved of resources. In 1942 the need to support the front meant a 44% reduction in the monthly fuel allocation for training to 15,000 tonnes, but when Kühl protested Jeschonnek replied, 'First we've got to beat Russia, then we can start training!', while when Milch proposed to produce 500 trainers a month during that year his offer was rejected. Consequently the schools were hard-pressed to produce sufficient numbers with adequate training: *FFS (C) 15* at Gablingen had on 21 March 1941 34 instructors (eight of them auxiliaries) against an establishment of 40, 48 trainers instead of 78, but 209 students rather than 160, giving a instructor/pupil ratio of 1:6 instead of 1:4.[38] Loot helped make up the schools' shortfall in aircraft, with large numbers of Czech (Avia Ba 122, Praga BH 39, Zlin 212) and French (Morane MS.230, MS.430, North American NA.57) machines augmenting German designs, but with so many aircraft maintenance was difficult, while trainee pilots had to adapt to a confusing variety of mounts. From 16 March 1943 the foreign aircraft were gradually phased out.[39] By that time the operational training schools were receiving a quota of modern German combat aircraft and *Nachtjagdschule 1* had even received its first airborne radars!

The shortage of aircraft and instructors was one cause of the high accident rate not only in training units but within the *Luftwaffe* as a whole (see Tables 40 and 41). During the last three quarters of 1941 accidental aircraft losses averaged 21.5% of total losses in front-line units, then rose steadily in 1942 and 1943 to 22.8% and 23.5% before dropping in 1944 to 15.5%. Within the training units

Table 40. Breakdown of Aircraft Losses, April 1941–June 1944

Quarter	Front-line Units				Training Units	
	Enemy Action		Not Enemy Action			
	Destroyed	Damaged	Destroyed	Damaged	Destroyed	Damaged
II/1941	1,243	711	330	508	490	366
III/1941	1,651	981	347	468	421	298
IV/1941	877	553	319	363	324	216
I/1942	1,000	634	291	350	250	224
II/1942	1,535	977	433	636	326	295
III/1942	1,676	1,117	474	695	201	186
IV/1942	1,392	623	457	471	397	318
I/1943	1,769	791	585	805	676	676
II/1943	2,397	1,360	723	1,161	497	589
III/1943	3,187	1,713	913	1,365	638	679
IV/1943	2,452	1,241	767	884	640	494
I/1944	3,209	1,761	838	1,226	880	755
II/1944	4,464	2,319	1,137	2,054	1,614	1,428

Notes: 'Destroyed' relates to aircraft damage of 60% or more; 'damaged' relates to aircraft damage of 59% or less. The original documents are cumulative, and the figures may not include second-line units such as transports. Training unit casualties include aircraft mobilised for front-line service.
Source: RAF Air Staff Post-Hostilities Studies, Book 21: 'Luftwaffe Activity I' (IWM Tin 192, fr.1071–85). Figures extrapolated from 'Einsatzbereitschaft der fliegende Verbände'.

Table 41. Personnel Losses, April 1941–June 1944

Quarter	Front-Line Units				Training Units	
	Dead and missing		Wounded		Dead and missing	Injured
II/1941	2,267/	319	514/	161	369	300
III/1941	2,532/	273	981/	155	341	245
IV/1941	1,387/	349	510/	105	307	207
I/1942	1,642/	324	396/	136	264	178
II/1942	2,376/	422	653/	185	330	210
III/1942	2,427/	406	843/	192	225	156
IV/1942	2,134/	912	435/	182	440	299
I/1943	2,525/	586	702/	321	524	417
II/1943	3,216/	805	1,028/	430	513	333
III/1943	3,455/	982	1,260/	490	557	364
IV/1943	3,001/	988	1,169/	310	714	364
I/1944	3,390/	1,017	1,331/	381	904	533
II/1944	4,111/	1,083	1,482/	592	1,170	681

Note: In front-line units the first casualty figure is for operations and second for non-operations.
Sources: Monthly operational summary of Fighter Command (PRO Air 16/1036); Middlebrook and Everitt; Night Bombing Raid Sheets (PRO Air 14/2673–5); Day Bombing Raid Sheets (PRO Air 14/3363–4); and Army Co-operation Command Operational Year Book 1942, Appendix (PRO Air 24/100).

the fatal accident rate was approximately 2–3% of sorties, although in combat training this rose to 8%, with 14% of training aircraft lost annually, while the failure rate was 30–40% in flying schools and about 10% in operational schools.[40] The Munich-based *Luftgau VII* reported 506 accidents between April and November 1942 with 194 casualties, 1,944 accidents the following year with 416 casualties and in January 1944 131 accidents with 66 casualties. *Grosskampf-fliegerschule 2* lost 24 dead in accidents between May and June 1940 alone, while in 1940 and 1941 *Jagdfliegerschule 5* suffered 29 casualties.[41]

The quality of training continued to decline during 1942; indeed, the observer course, which had once been so important, was concentrated at *Grosskampf-fliegerschule 2*, which could produced 90 a month, and slashed to six months or less. One observer captured by the British had flown only 68 hours, including 12 in a Ju 88.[42] Twice during the year training units were mobilised to augment the transport forces, and it would appear that in the winter of 1942/43 training units lost up to 350 aircraft and some 400 instructors and advanced students, bomber training being especially badly affected. Worse still, the fuel allocated for training was cut so that during the year the average hours per student dropped to 260 from some 300. A report stated that in the two years following the invasion of Russia an average of 11,000 aircraft were held by the training units, of which 60% were serviceable, but of these fewer than 2,400 were in use because of fuel shortages. Nevertheless, during the year 14,530 men qualified as pilots.[43]

The crisis could not be ignored, and on 21 July 1943 Kühl was retired and replaced by 39-year-old *Generalmajor* Werner Kreipe, who was appointed *General der Flieger-Ausbildung*. Born in Hanover, Kreipe had joined the *Reichsheer* in 1922 and the following year had participated in the Beer Hall *Putsch*, although this did not prevent him from receiving a commission a couple of years later, followed by flying training in Germany. He transferred to the *Luftwaffe* in 1934 and served alongside luminaries such as Milch and Sperrle before reaching the front, where he served as Chief of Staff to *Fliegerkorps I*, then *Luftwaffekommando Don*. An outspoken man, he became Kühl's Chief of Staff in November 1942, and this provided him with the insight to reform the organisation. Unable to acquire more instructors or aircraft, he rationalised the organisation, especially the basic training schools (*A/B Schule*), nine of which became *Doppelschule* by absorbing others, allowing him to provide an instructor/student ratio of 1:5—the same as in the RAF and USAAF.[44] The advanced flying (*C-Schule*) and instrument training schools were largely unaffected, because Kreipe observed that they were 'the most important aspect of the entire air training process', but they became more specialised. This enabled him to produce 29,050 pilots during the year, but the quality continued to decline because Kreipe, despite improving his petrol allocations after arguing with Göring, had to cut flying hours per student to 110 to meet the growing losses. One prisoner reported students going solo after 10 flights instead of the previous 50.[45] By contrast, USAAF pilots in September 1944 qualified after 140 hours' flying training, with bomber pilots receiving a further 105 hours' conversion training to heavy bombers before joining an operational training unit.[46] To conserve petrol, more use was made of glider training by the paramilitary *Nationalsozialistisches Fliegerkorps* (*NSFK*) for boys: between 1943 and 1944 the Austrian *NSFK Gruppe 17* made 44.5% of the 780,000 glider launches carried out between 1939 and 1944, as well as taking 56.5% of the 20,860 proficiency tests.[47]

There was also a rationalisation of operational training with the creation of training *Jagd-* and *Kampfgeschwader*, usually by renaming the schools, in January 1943.[48] The process was extended to *Zerstörerschule* in March (see Table 42), then dive-bombing, with the creation of *StG* (later *SG*) *101*, *102* and *151* in May followed by *NJG 101* and *NJG 102* in June, while in the winter of 1943/44 the greater emphasis upon fighter and *Jabo* operations saw the creation of *JG 109* (Stolp-Reitz), *JG 110* (Altenburg) and *SG 103* (Metz). Just as live-firing is used in Army training, so the new schools were given more realistic experience, for they were often given second-line operational duties such as the defence of targets less likely to be attacked, or supporting counter-insurgency forces. Bomber crews were sometimes employed for such duties in Russia, while *StG 151* (later *SG 151*), which was formed from *Ergänzugsgruppen* of five *Stukageschwader*, augmented the Croatian Air Force fighting Tito's partisans under *FlFü Kroatien*. Only the front-

Table 42. Operational Training Schools, July 1943

New title	Old title	Main base
JG 101	Jagdfliegerschule 1	Pau
JG 102	Jagdfliegerschule 2	Magdeburg-Zerbst
JG 103	Jagdfliegerschule 3	Châteauroux
JG 104	Jagdfliegerschule 4	Herzogenaurach
JG 105	Jagdfliegerschule 5	Chartres
JG 106	Jagdfliegerschule 6	Eschborn
JG 107	Jagdfliegerschule 7	Nancy
JG 108	Jagdfliegerschule 8	Völsau
KG 101	Grosskampffliegerschule 1	Tours and Foggia
KG 102	Grosskampffliegerschule 2	Hörsching-bei-Linz
KG 103	Grosskampffliegerschule 3	Landsberg
KG 104	Grosskampffliegerschule 4	Torun (Thorn)
KG 105	Grosskampffliegerschule 5	Parow-bei-Stralsund
NJG 101	Nachtjagdschule 1	Munich-Schleissheim
NJG 102	Nachtjagdschule 2	Stuttgart-Echterdingen
StG 101	Stukaschule 1	Wertheim
StG 102	Stukaschule 2	Graz-Thalerhof
StG 151	Stuka Ergänzungsgruppen	Zagreb (Agram)
ZG 101	Zerstörerschulen 1 & 3	Rheims

Sources: Ketley & Rolfe; and Rosch.

line *Kampfgeschwader* retained their *Ergänzungsgruppen*, which were frequently used to augment the main bomber force to complete the operational training of crews. However, the new operational training organisation was fatally flawed for it received few experienced airmen as instructors—many had been rejected for front-line duties—while the output barely made up losses. In 1943 3,276 fighter pilots left the schools, but the *Jagdgruppen* lost 2,870.[49]

The failure to provide experienced instructors from combat units reflected not only the *Luftwaffe*'s neglect of training but also the neglect of personnel. In the last years of the Great War doctors studying aerial medicine in Great Britain recognised the great mental strain of air warfare, which led not to collapse but rather to combat fatigue, a debilitating condition which caused fatal mistakes. A system was introduced in 1917 of withdrawing pilots from squadrons and sending them to schools where they could both rest and impart their knowledge to a new generation, leading to a double improvement in overall operational efficiency. In the Second World War this system was formalised as the tour: in February 1944 the US Eighth Air Force increased those for bombers from 25 to 30 combat sorties while in fighter squadrons the 200-flying-hour tour was replaced by one with 200 combat hours.[50] The RAF had similar criteria, although the British had the luxury of rotating fighter squadrons to non-operational sectors, which enabled them to rest the pilots, senior officers being rotated between staff/training and operational duties.

Allied bomber aircrew performed such duties for up to a year after a tour, then they could (and frequently did) volunteer for further tours, but it was a rare Allied bomber airman who flew more than 100 full sorties. By contrast, *Hauptmann* Kurt Seyfarth (*KGr zbV 9, KG 2*) flew 532 sorties, *Leutnant* Hellmuth Kahle (*KG 4*) flew 526 and *Oberleutnant* Benno Hermann (*KG 76*) flew 520, while at least 13 other *Ritterkreuz Kampfflieger* flew more than 400; most of these men, surprisingly, survived the war.[51] The Germans were slow to recognise the value of resting front-line personnel, and the short-term views meant that many men stayed with their units until they literally dropped out of the sky. The *Luftwaffe* felt that this was the most cost-effective means of using its limited manpower in the face of frequent and multiple crises, but some *Experten*, such as Rudel, were occasionally sent to the operational schools for a few months. One advantage of the German system was that those who remained at the front might become *Experten*, and this was one reason why 106 day fighter pilots had scores of 100 or more (15 had more than 200) and 24 night fighter pilots had 50 or more.[52] Many did not survive the war, and a considerable number, such as Wick in 1940, succumbed as much to combat fatigue as enemy action, and short-term solutions such as providing a fortnight's leave per year or giving men suffering from combat fatigue a month's medical leave were no solution. The *Jagd-* and *Kampfflieger* had rest homes south of Munich to which each *Geschwader* would send a quota of pilots who could hunt, fish, swim and climb in an informal atmosphere akin to a first-class hotel. However, as the men recovered they gave vent to their high spirits and the riotous activity led to complaints from the local authorities, while the atmosphere at the bomber establishment was restricted because, in contrast to the practice at the fighter rest home, wives and girlfriends were allowed to stay and sometimes remained when their loved ones had been killed.[53]

Post-war personal accounts would suggest that it was not until the odds became truly crushing in the last year of the war that individual morale began to decline, but generally men were proud to fight for their country and to protect their loved ones. Even when all hope of victory had vanished, the men fought on, maintained by the twin factors of nationalism and élitism which are found in every air force, in the hopes of reducing the burden on their countrymen and possibly of winning a favourable peace.[54] Crew spirit helped many men endure, while personal as well as unit aircraft markings helped to provide a stamp of individualism in an age of impersonal total warfare. From 1943 there was the occasional desertion, the most notable of which was that of Condor Legion veteran *Oberleutnant* Heinrich Schmitt of *NJG 3*, who, with his crew, defected (apparently by prior arrangement with the British secret service) in May 1943 with a Ju 88R-1 night fighter, giving the enemy a complete *Lichtenstein* radar. A year later *Oberfeldwebel* Karl Wimberger, an Austrian nationalist, defected in a two-seat Bf 109G-12, although whether this was from political conviction or some other reason is impossible to discover. Interestingly, there were few defections to nearby Sweden, although a number of aircraft and men ended up on Swedish territory as a result of navigational mistakes.[55] One reason was the presence of the *Gestapo*, and when *Oberleutnant* Wim Johnen of *NJG 6* accidentally landed in Switzerland after his new Bf 110G-4 had been damaged by enemy fire the families of all the crew were arrested and jailed, being released only when their menfolk returned after the fighter had been blown up by agreement with the Swiss.[56] A noticeable feature during the winter of 1943/44 was that shot-down aircrew provided far less information, because in fighting the Eighth Air Force the *Luftwaffe* became aware from US prisoners how much could be gathered from slack security, the Americans sometimes carrying cameras whose films provided details of their bases. The uncommunicative nature of *Luftwaffe* aircrew may be judged from a *JG 4* pilot shot down over Anzio who assured his captors that he was only a ferry pilot who had lost his way![57]

Apart from the inevitable temporary crises, unit morale remained high and crews or pilots returning after completing a milestone would usually be greeted by 'black men' bearing a placard surrounded by a celebratory garland. Relations between them and 'their' crew/pilot were as close in the *Luftwaffe* as in other air forces, as was demonstrated especially at the end of the Tunisian campaign when evacuation by air was the only means of escaping captivity. Armour plate and radios were removed from fighters and 'black men' squeezed into the spaces, or crouched over the pilot's seat, for a short flight to safety: *JG 77*'s *Obergefreiter* Schomaker reached Sicily carrying *four* men in his Bf 109G-2 on 8 May 1943.[58] Undoubtedly there was a celebration after this feat as well as for victories, promotions, awards and milestones as in any air force. However, the noisy parties to let off steam which were a feature of RAF and USAAF mess life were excluded from the *Luftwaffe* mess (*Kasino*) and tended to be limited to off-base bars or unit clubs, the only restriction at the latter being a ban on dancing for the duration of the war. If the clubs were on base, women were prohibited from entering them for security reasons.[59] Drinking did cause disciplinary problems, but even the most riotous parties had a measure of decorum, with no attempt to 'debag' superior officers. Some of the latter, such as *Major* Heinrich, *Prinz* zu Sayn-Wittgenstein (*Kommodore* of *NJG 2*), could be extremely aloof, and when *Hauptmann* Wilhelm-Ferdinand 'Wutz' Galland became *Kommandeur* of *II/JG 26*, his older brother Adolf advised him to adopt attitudes of absolute discipline and loyalty to his *Kommodore*, though added, 'You must not be too familiar with your brother officers; nevertheless, they can be your best friends.'[60] However, pranks would be played upon officers, such as one *Jagdgruppe Kommandeur* whose New Year present was a deep purple smoke candle tossed through his window to stain his uniform, while members of *Oberstleutnant* Erich Bloedorn's *KG 30* would jokingly complain in song that there was no one dumber (*bloedorn*) than their *Kommodore*.[61]

In the field life was more serious and accommodation was often in a tent. When *Major* Hans Philip became *Kommodore* of *JG 1* in April 1943 he established his command post in a tent near the concrete bunker housing *Jagddivision 3*'s headquarters at Arnhem-Deelen to show those pilots 'spoiled by their comfortable quarters' what life was like in the East.[62] In fact alternative accommodation in the East could range from verminous wooden huts to trailers or even Czarist palaces, and in sectors where the front moved sluggishly aircrew would be housed in hotels, requisitioned farms or even *châteaux*. The *Luftwaffe* tended to ensure that its airmen had the best food and many bases in the field were menageries, with cattle, pigs and chickens mingling with the ever-present dogs which were the pilots' pets and were sometimes were taken on sorties. However, the *Wehrmacht*'s surprisingly poor standards of field hygiene meant that in the East and the Mediterranean consumption of local fruit and vegetables might require men to pass time (and much more) on the 'thunderbeam'. Between sorties the airmen might play cards or sports, go hunting, take saunas (in the East) or carve to pass the time, but the constantly busy 'black men' spent what little spare time they had catching up on lost sleep. Anyone with talent and an instrument would be persuaded to join a unit band, while films might also be shown. At one point *JG 54* was seeing a new feature film every evening! Occasionally there were classical concerts by touring parties or troupes of entertainers, such as film star Heinz Rühmann, the beautiful actress Carola Höhn and the corpulent composer Ludwig Schmidseder. All ranks were allowed to see these stars, and especially the pretty actresses, but Galland's view that the officers were not allowed to monopolise them was not always accurate.[63] Away from the front, nurses, *Luftwaffehelferinin* and women delivery pilots might be encountered, while the men could use the *Wehrmacht*'s brothels, with separate establishments for officers and other ranks, which were staffed by professional and amateur ladies of negotiable affection as well as by shanghaied girls. Some units, such as *III./JG 52* when it was stationed in Romania in 1940–41 and *Fliegerkorps VIII*, made their own arrangements and sometimes flew in the girls to operational bases. Galland considered that the advantage of the brothel system was that it reduced the incidence not of venereal disease but of homosexuality.[64] As for the most senior officers, they occasionally arranged for their mistresses to accompany them or meet them on tours of inspection, especially to elegant cities such as Rome or Paris.

At home and in western Europe there was less of a requirement for professional service for the airmen's glamour was itself a potent attraction. Girlfriends and wives visited many bases, but as casualties mounted in the *Jagdgruppen* some of these girls became what the British called 'Spitfire widows', moving from pilot to pilot as their lovers fell, and perhaps it was for this reason that the one-eyed *Oberleutnant* Günther Specht of *JG 11* (32 victories) banned them from his station.[65] One advantage of western, and even Reich, bases was the access to farms, whose produce could be smuggled to loved ones when on leave, but such journeys were not without hazard. The *Kommodore* of *NJG 1*, *Major* Hans-Joachim 'Achim' Jabs (50 victories, 28 at night), was carrying a side of bacon in his Bf 110 when it was shot down on 29 April 1944 by Spitfires led by Wing Commander Geoffrey Page. Years later, victor and vanquished met and Jabs jokingly complained that Page had robbed him of a side of bacon, so he was astonished to receive shortly afterwards another side of bacon. In his letter of thanks Jabs, tongue-in-cheek, added, 'By the way, I forgot to tell you about the case of cognac!'[66] Unlike some of his superiors, Jabs was not involved in commercial smuggling or theft, but the taint of corruption rose to the highest level, with Göring looting art treasures and gems from all over Europe. Loerzer, the *Fliegerkorps II* commander and former cigar salesman, was involved in smuggling train loads of oranges into the Reich, and this may have been a reason for his losing his command, although he was promptly given control of the Personnel Department. The Austrian *General der Flieger* Bernard Waber exploited his command of *Luftgaue* in Poland, the Ukraine and Yugoslavia to indulge in wholesale looting as well as black market activities, but he may have over-indulged for in November 1944 he was court-martialled (possibly for not handing over some loot to the right people) and three months later shot.[67]

By 1944 corruption was the least of the *Luftwaffe*'s problems, for a universal petrol drought was in prospect during the summer. Monthly fuel production from both natural and synthetic sources had risen considerably, from 20,000 tonnes in 1939 to 50,000 tonnes in 1941, although consumption also rose, and by mid-1942 restrictions on non-essential flying were being imposed at the front while the allocation for training was reduced. Synthetic fuel became ever more important, but the *Luftwaffe* had failed to appreciate the need for high-octane, high-energy petrol, which required tetraethyl lead and ethylene dibromide additives that were produced in only three German and one Italian plants. By 1943, when 130-octane fuel was being used by Allied fighters, the *Luftwaffe* had only 100 octane C4, and many fighters still relied upon the 87-octane B4 fuel. In January 1944 159,000 tonnes of synthetic aviation fuel was produced, rising to 181,000 tonnes in March, but the following month the USAAF began striking the fuel plants. By June only 152,000 tonnes was produced, and the figure was steadily declining as the tonnage of bombs dropped on the plants increased. In May 1944 the *Luftwaffe* had a reserve of 420,000 tonnes of fuel (a further 120,000 tonnes was held by *OKW*), little more than it had at the beginning of the war, but this would be quickly drained in the coming months.[68]

Shortage of manpower was also a German problem. It became more acute as the war continued, and the *Luftwaffe* could not escape. In July 1940 the service had 2.2 million men (including civilian officials), of whom 588,000 were in the air units and 571,000 in the *Flakwaffe*. This strength was maintained until the beginning of 1942, by which time the Army had suffered some 750,000 casualties in the East, and by April 1942 the total was 1,118,000. During the desperate winter the 'black men', signallers and *Flak* personnel had been mobilised into *ad hoc* battle groups to defend bases and installations, then to help prop up the front with paratroops led by former mountain gunner *Generalmajor* Eugen Meindl, now recovered from his wounds in Crete. Battle groups participating in these desperate conflicts included *Luftwaffe Kampfverband Meindl, Luftwaffenfeldbrigade Schlemm* and the *Luftwaffe Lehr-Infanterie Regiment*, and these were joined by seven all-volunteer *Feldregimenter der Luftwaffe*. During the summer four of these regiments became *Division Meindl*, which fought with distinction in *Heeresgruppe Nord*, but the focus of operations at that time was in the south, where the acute shortage of troops was causing serious concern. Inevitably the *Luftwaffe*'s large numbers of 'idle' hands were sought by the Army, but Göring refused, observing, 'You can't expect me to hand over these men to the Army so that some general . . . can make them attend church parade.' His solution, influenced by Meindl's success, was to create an 'army' of 22 *Luftwaffefelddivisionen*, which were organised from 17 September by Meindl under *Fliegerkorps XIII* using a pool of 46,000 men already assembled. This was expanded by subjecting other branches, including Signals, to an arbitrary 10% cut, while *Fliegerausbildungsregimenter* found themselves emphasising infantry training. Some 180,000 officers and men were mobilised, many with more ambition than experience, including unsuccessful pilots, and placed under four *Luftwaffe Feldkorps* attached to *Luftflotten 1* and *4* as well as *Luftwaffekommando Ost*. Although the divisions were supposed to have only garrison duties, many were committed to the front from December 1942 without adequate equipment or training, and what followed was a *Kindermord* (Massacre of the Innocents) until the Army took them over in November 1943, replacing most officers.[69] The specialised training of some men meant that they were retained by the *Luftwaffe*, as were all *Flak* units, while some 10,000 men were transferred to the paratroops, whose expansion created a formidable body of infantry. In addition, Göring also expanded the formation which bore his name from a regiment to a brigade, and by mid-October 1942 to a division under 'Beppo' Schmid. The *Luftwaffefelddivisionen* absorbed some 300,000 men, of whom only half survived to the end of 1943, but the adverse effects upon air operations were being felt by May that year. Many mechanics and technicians had been killed or taken prisoner in the Mediterranean and Eastern theatres, while the loss of so many would-be replacements to Göring's military folly adversely affected serviceability rates. It became difficult to create new *Gruppen* or to develop new airfields, while the weakening of the signals organisation, which had played so important a role in the *Luftwaffe*'s victories, invariably had an adverse effect upon efficiency.

The transfer of men to the front eased acceptance of the *Luftwaffehelferinin*, while for labouring duties which required no skill 100,000 Russian prisoners of war became *Hilfswillige* (*Hiwis*) rather than starve to death in prison camps. Also mobilised in the aftermath of Stalingrad were thousands of 15- and 16-year-old schoolboys as *Luftwaffenhelfer*, of whom some 200,000 were enlisted, later being joined by girls. Parents were reluctant to allow their children to live away from home because of concern about their schooling, and, while teachers did visit the sites, the parents' fears proved well-founded, leading to a constant stream of complaints to the authorities. The children were usually attached to home defence *Flak* batteries, forming up to 50% of each battery's strength, with regular (but older) Germans and *Hiwis* forming 20% and the remainder made up of paramilitary *Reichs-Arbeits Dienst* (*RAD*) personnel and *Luftwaffehelferinin*, the latter to the disgust of *General der Flakartillerie* Walther von Axthelm (*General der Flakwaffe*), whose prejudice led Hitler to describe him as 'an idiot'. Such was the mix at batteries by 1944 that one commander addressed the assembled personnel as 'Ladies and gentlemen, fellow workers, schoolboys and *Tovarischi*'.[70] Within the signal service the girls worked very well, and their soprano and contralto voices proved clearer than men's in directing fighters in the babel of conversation and jamming which otherwise filled the earphones.[71]

There was little attempt to recruit foreigners into the *Luftwaffe*, although Spanish and Croatian *Staffeln* did serve with *Gruppen* on the Eastern Front. Few airmen were recruited from western Europe, the exceptions including the Danish *Hauptmann* Paul Sommer, who had three victories with *JG 27*, and the Belgian *Feldwebel* Guido Rombaut, who perished in September 1943 soon after joining *JG 1*.[72] There was far greater success in the East, especially in the Baltic states, where many young men still seethed with resentment after their countries had been 'liberated' from independence by the Soviet Union in 1939 and 1940. The occupation of their countries, the suppression of their national heritage and the 'pauperisation' of their society by the Russians made many of these men wish to strike back, although initially the Germans were reluctant to harness this rage. A *Sonderstaffel Buschmann* was established with Estonian personnel early in 1942 and was later expanded into *SAGr 127*. As the Germans retreated during the autumn of 1943 their desire to turn the former subjects of the Soviet Union against their masters grew and *SAGr 127* became *NSGr 11 (Est)*, while other night attack units were created from Latvians (*NSGr 12*) and Russians (*Ostfliegerstaffel 1*). There was little active recruiting for the Baltic states' units, although there were sufficient volunteers, but German doubts as to their reliability grew as the Eastern Front collapsed in the second half of 1944 and in October the two *Nachtschlachtgruppen* were disbanded, the Russian unit having been dissolved three months earlier.[73]

On 1 June 1944 the *Luftwaffe* comprised 2,870,300 personnel (120,000 officers), but this figure included 510,700 auxiliaries and 450,000 civilians. Some 80,000 paratroops remained under direct *OKL* command, mostly recruits undergoing training or men recovering from injury, while there were a further 35,000 construction personnel attached to *Organisation Todt*.[74] Materially the *Luftwaffe* was at the height of its powers, with 6,504 aircraft and 45,545 anti-aircraft guns (26,369 light, 4,945 medium and 14,231 heavy guns, the latter including 10,224 8.8cm), yet, as its leaders would quickly discover during the catastrophic summer, it was capable only of pygmy blows.

NOTES TO CHAPTER 5

1. In the summer of 1943, for example, Göring proposed giving *Wilde Sau* exponent Herrmann command of the night fighter force (*Fliegerkorps XII*) in place of Kammhuber. Hinchliffe, pp.166–7.
2. Zeitzler's post-war claim that there was a confrontation between him and Göring is contradicted in Irving's biography of the *Reischsmarschall*. See Irving, *Göring*, pp.367–9, and *Milch*, pp.176–7; Plocher, *1942*, pp.274–9, 346–7; and Ziemke and Bauer, p.476.
3. Irving, *Göring*, p.401.
4. Nevertheless the main force suffered 7.6% losses. Irving, *Göring*, p.408; and Middlebrook and Everitt, p.440.
5. Nielsen, p.47.
6. See Hooton, p.151.
7. The fact that the *Kommandeur der Blindflugschulen*, *Oberst* Morzik, was also *Lufttransportführer* facilitated the mobilisation of training units.
8. It should be noted that on 15 September 1941 Production Plan 20/2 was published. See Gundelach, pp.711–60, for reactions to Plans 223 and 224 with their increasing emphasis upon defence.
9. See Green, p.198.
10. Feist, App. 1.
11. It is interesting to note all the ills of German aircraft production had also occurred in the Great War. For the German aircraft industry see BAM, pp.205–6, 208, 211–12, 215–16; Cooper, pp. 259–86; Irving, *Milch*; Murray, pp.88–103, 136–9, 182–91, 251–5; Overy, *Air War*, pp.191–236; Overy, *War and Economy*, pp. 29–30, 212, 280–1, 346, 350–1; and articles by Morrow and Boelcke.
12. Ploch was replaced by *Stuka Experte* Dinort but he proved unsatisfactory and was relegated to training duties from February 1942 until the end of the war. Gablenz was killed in an air crash on 21 August 1942.
13. Of the defection Waldau commented that it was 'A black day' (entry of 12 May 1941, BA MA MSg 1/1410). For Udet's last months see Ishoven, *Ernst Udet*, p.434ff.
14. At the time of his death the half-Jewish Wilberg had a training command.
15. Waldau's diary, 23 November 1941. BA MA MSg 1/1410.
16. Of this workforce 36% were foreign nationals, including political prisoners and prisoners of war. German production figures included severely damaged (up to 59%) aircraft which had been repaired at the factory.
17. Overy, *War and Economy*, pp.358–72, Tables 11.2, 11.3.
18. Between 1940 and 1944 Germany supplied some 1,300 combat aircraft to allies, friendly neutrals and satellites. Aircraft supplied to allies enabled the *Luftwaffe* to concentrate in the important sectors.
19. The two men had loathed each other since Milch's days at Lufthansa, and Messerschmitt's subordinates spread rumours about Milch being half-Jewish after the Nazis

came to power. Some Me 210s were rebuilt and saw service in North Africa. The Me 210Ca-1 was manufactured for the Hungarian Air Force by Duna Repüplögépgyár and appears to have caused no problems.
20. As a private venture Heinkel did develop an He 177 with four separate engines as the He 277 (originally as the He 177B), which appears to have had few problems. In late May 1944 Göring demanded production of 200 per month, but within six weeks the decision was reversed (Green, pp.359–61). It should be noted that when the twin-engine Manchester heavy bomber proved a failure the British redesigned it with four engines to become the legendary Lancaster.
21. Irving, *Milch*, pp.147–8.
22. For the Me 262 and the fall of Milch see Karl Toll's article; and Irving, *Milch*, pp.265–86. Toll makes the point that the Me 262 could be adapted for the *Jabo* role without significant problems, especially on the production line.
23. Plocher, *1942*, p.171.
24. In many personal accounts and autobiographies by airmen, and sometimes sailors, the author uses the word *'soldat'* to describe himself and his comrades. This can be translated as 'serviceman', yet it is noteworthy that *Luftwaffe* post-operation staff reports often allocate much space to descriptions and critiques of ground operations. In his diary Waldau wrote reams about the 1940 western campaign with little or no reference to *Luftwaffe* operations, while Richthofen's diary often criticised ground operations.
25. Ziemke, *Decision in the East*, pp.190–2.
26. Muller, pp.103, 270/n. 1.
27. See Muller, pp.113–22.
28. Irving, *Milch*, pp.376–83, 388–99.
29. Gundelach, pp.711–60.
30. In German terms the Fifteenth Air Force was less a 'strategic' bombing force and more an 'operational' one, with half its monthly missions involving targets in Italy or air bases in nearby countries.
31. For the background to German strategic bombing planning see Muller, pp.149–202.
32. In November 1943 Weiss joined Greim's staff and was replaced by *Oberstleutnant Dr* Ernst Kupfer. He promptly died in an air crash and was replaced by *Oberst* Hubertus Hitschold.
33. For details of the schools and their syllabuses see Ketley and Rolfe; and Ries, *Flugzeugführerschulen*. See also Ernst Hartmann's article 'Eine Flugzeugführerausbildung im 2.Weltkrieg'.
34. Stahl, p. 12.
35. In addition to worn-out *Luftwaffe* aircraft, would-be combat crews would fly foreign aircraft such as the Czech Avia B.534 and French Dewoitine D.520 fighters and the Czech Aero Ab.101 and B.71 (Tupolev SB) bombers.
36. In 1942 Galland replaced the *Jagdgeschwader Ergänzungsgruppen* with three regional *Ergänzungsjagdgruppen*, which acted as training pools for the western, southern and eastern theatres.
37. For the radios see Interrogation of General Galland, 16 August 1945 and 26 August 1945 (IWM Tin 195, fr.3321ff). See also Steinhilper, p.303.
38. Ries, *Flugzeugführerschulen*, p.185.
39. In his article 'Fliegerische Grundausbildung und Jagdfliegerschulung', *Generalmajor Dr* Jürgen Schreiber notes that fighter pilot Heinrich Schild, who qualified in 1940, flew 11 different types of aircraft, while four who qualified in 1943 each flew seven or eight different types.
40. Based upon data in a *Luftwaffe* training report of 27 January 1944 (IWM Tin 192, fr.1517ff). See also Tuider, p.26; and USNA T321, Roll 102, fr.408ff.

41. Tuider, p.104/n. 69.

42. Luftwaffe Training and Organisation (PRO Air 40/1473).

43. *Luftwaffe* training report of 27 January 1944 (IWM Tin 192, fr.1517ff; and USNA T 321, Roll 102, fr.408ff).

44. Luftwaffe Organisation for Training (PRO Air 40/1134).

45. Mediterranean Allied Air Force Intelligence Summary 63, PRO Air 24/949. Schreiber, op. cit., gives the number of flying hours for seven fighter pilots who were trained at *A/B Schule* between 1943 and 1944. Their average was 105.27 hours, but individuals varied between 90 and 136 hours. Four who followed them averaged 98 hours, with one flying only 75. By mid-1943 a German fighter pilot received 70 hours at *A/B-Schule*, 70 at *C-Schule* (including 30 hours' instrument training), 60 at a *Jagdschule* and 50 at an *Ergänzungsgruppe*. RAF Weekly Intelligence Summary 231 (PRO Air 22/ 79).

46. Freeman, *The US Strategic Bomber*, pp.143–5.

47. Tuider, p.23.

48. *JG 108* was formed in May 1943.

49. Murray, p.254.

50. McFarland and Newton, p.166.

51. Based upon Brütting, *Kampfflieger-Asse*. Benno Hermann should not be confused with 'Hajo' Herrmann.

52. Tolliver and Constable, pp.386–9.

53. Interrogation of General Galland, 16 August 1945 and 26 August 1945 (IWM Tin 195, fr.3321ff).

54. See the diary entries of an *NJG 1* radio operator for late August and early September 1944 in Hinchliffe, pp.300–2.

55. See articles by Widfeldt.

56. Hinchliffe pp.135–6, 269–72; and Bob Collis, 'Escape to Britain'. In the winter of 1942/43 Göring interrogated Galland about his mother's loyalty after Himmler reported that the lady had signed a petition requesting that her childhood Catholic school be allowed to remain open (Baker, p.211).

57. Mediterranean Allied Air Forces Intelligence Summary 68 (PRO Air 24/949).

58. Prien, *JG 77*, pp.1561, 1565; and Shores, *Tunisia*, pp.352–3, 381.

59. Interrogation of General Galland, 16 August 1945 and 26 August 1945 (IWM Tin 195, fr.3321ff).

60. Letter of 11 January 1943, quoted by Baker, pp.213–14. 'Wutz' was killed on 17 August 1943 by escorting P-47s when intercepting a US Fortress formation.

61. Clayton, p.269; and Weal, *Fw 190 Aces of the Western Front*, pp.51–2.

62. Weal, p.45.

63. See Hermann, p.100; Scutts, *JG 54*, App. 1; Steinhilper, p.320; and Interrogation of General Galland, 16 August 1945 and 26 August 1945 (IWM Tin 195, fr.3321ff).

64. Interrogation of General Galland, 16 August 1945 and 26 August 1945 (IWM Tin 195 fr.3321 ff); and Dickfeld, pp.31–2, 58–9.

65. Knocke, pp.133–4.

66. *The Times*, 18 August 1994.

67. See Irving, *Göring*, p.451; and Mitcham, p.296.

68. 'Entwicklung der Flugkraftstoffluge der deutschen Luftwaffe' (USNA T 971, Roll 13, fr.32).

69. For a brief but adequate history of *Luftwaffefelddivisionen* see Ruffner. *Kindermord* was the German term for the First Battle of Ypres (1914), when thousands of newly enlisted students perished.

70. Rumpf, p.197.

71. See Schreiber, 'Luftwaffen- und Marinehelfer (Flak)'; and Luftwaffe Training and Organisation (PRO Air 40/1473).

72. Mombeek, p.182; and Shores, *Tunisia*, p.254.

73. The author would like to thank Mr Alex Vanags-Baginskis, formerly of *NSGr 12*, for his assistance in understanding the background to the creation of *NSGr 11* and *12*.

74. Luftwaffe Training and Organisation (PRO Air 40/1473).

CHAPTER SIX

Crusaders in Retreat

The Eastern Front, January 1942–June 1944

With Siberian winds chilling the air to –46°C, freezing Russian soil and burying it under metres of snow during the winter of 1941/42, exhausted and starving men, the remnants of divisions, clawed at each other as extensions of dictators' wills. The battle maps became a surreal picture of salients and gaps, which panicked many commanders, whom Hitler ruthlessly purged until the untidy German line was secured by the thaw and his boundless self-confidence had returned.

The *Luftwaffe* played an important part in the resolution of the crisis, but not as Douhet's disciples would have anticipated, since transfers and withdrawals had aggravated the perennial shortage of aircraft and by the spring there were fewer than 1,800 aircraft available (see Table 43). The strike units helped to restrict the Russian advance during the 1941/42 winter, not only with close air support but also by eroding the enemy's limited transport resources. In the first 20 days of February 1942 8,170 vehicles and 59 railway locomotives were claimed, while *JG 52*'s winter score sheet included several manure sleds which proved to be carrying ammunition![1] Yet the price had been heavy, and between 7 December 1941 and 8 April 1942 859 aircraft in the East were destroyed and 636 damaged.[2]

Winter compounded the problems, for in low temperatures untended engines froze, their lubricating oil and hydraulic liquids acquired a glue-like consistency while rubber crumbled. To ensure that the aircraft would fly, their engines had either to be turned over regularly (especially during the night), consuming scarce fuel and oil, or to be encased in heated sheds ('alert boxes'). As with the rest of the *Wehrmacht*, there were problems of inadequate clothing and accommodation (although quickly overcome by Milch), while aircraft maintenance in intense cold and deep snow declined and overall serviceability dropped to some 30%. The 'black men' wore gloves when working or risked their fingers being instantly frozen to the metal, and because metal becomes brittle in sub-zero conditions they were unable to trust their tools unless they were pre-heated.[3] Snow had to be cleared from runways or rolled to provide a firm surface, while frozen vapour frequently snapped the telephone and teleprinter lines which were vital to *Luftwaffe* operations.

Luftwaffe signallers and truck drivers faced threats from guerrillas (partisans) and even Russian advanced patrols, and to protect themselves local commands organised ground crews, administrative personnel and *Flak* units into battalion-

Table 43. *Luftwaffe* **Strength in the East**

Date	Fighters/ Zerstörer	Bombers	Close Support	Reconnaissance LR	Tactical	Total
30 Mar 1942	454/ 57	621	299	184	151	1,766
30 Jun 1942	580/193	937	358	245	377	2,690
30 Sept 1942	611/ 81	771	288	209	364	2,324
30 Dec 1942	395/ 50	383	206	213	254	1,501
31 Mar 1943	549/ 56	475	448	196	269	1,993
30 Jun 1943	612/ 52	552	578	224	274	2,292
30 Sept 1943	531/ 92	258	469	207	208	1,765
31 Dec 1943	473/ 82	226	519	179	204	1,683
31 Mar 1944	513/ 88	163	612	178	231	1,785

Note: Excludes seaplanes and transports. LR = Long-Range.
Source: *Luftwaffe* first-line strength based on German documents (PRO Air 40/1207).

or even regimental-strength battle groups. As the crisis on the ground deepened these units were increasingly committed to the front line, and *Luftwaffenfeldbrigade Schlemm* (*Generalmajor* Alfred Schlemm) was used to protect the boundary of *Heeresgruppen Nord* and *Mitte* with support from *FliegerkorpsVIII*. Motorised *Flak* batteries played a major part in pinning the whole German front line together since they combined mobility and lethality. The 8.8cm *Flak 36* could tear apart even the formidable T-34 tank, while the lighter 2cm and 3.7cm automatic weapons laid down a curtain of fire through which no one could pass.

The Eastern Front pivoted in the centre, where Richthofen's *Fliegerkorps VIII* struggled manfully to support *Heeresgruppe Mitte* with 10 under-strength *Gruppen,* and during the first quarter of 1942 his *Nahkampffliegerkommando Nord* (*General der Flakartillerie* Otto Dessloch, who also commanded *Flakkorps II*) flew more than 5,000 sorties supporting the northern flank (see Table 44 for senior officers in the East). Yet the key events were in *Heeresgruppe Nord*'s sector following the envelopment of *Generalleutnant* Walter, *Graf* von Brockdorff-Ahlefeldt's *II. Armee Korps* with 95,000 men around Demyansk on 9 February 1942, while simultaneously 5,000 of *Generalmajor* Theodor Scherer's *281. Sicherung Division* were surrounded at Kholm to the south-west. Ironically *KG 4*, which bore Wever's name, was ordered to fly supplies to Scherer, thus setting an ominous precedent for the *Kampfgruppen*. There was some uncertainty over whether or not to begin a full-scale airlift, but on 13 February Halder requested it in a telephone conversation with Jeschonnek and in doing so instituted the *Transportgruppen*'s first real test.

Generaloberst Keller, the *Luftflotte 1* commander, had begun the airlift the previous day using his own *Transportgruppe,* but Hitler promised him 337 transports within a week and on 18 February ordered Morzik (*Lufttransportführer beim Generalquartiermeister der Luftwaffe* and *Kommandeur der Blindflugschulen*) to transfer his forces to *Luftflotte 1* from *Fliegerkorps VIII*. Morzik was no stranger to Rus-

171

Table 44. *Luftwaffe* Commands, Eastern Front, 1 January 1942–1 June 1944

Command	Commander	Dates
Lfl. 1	*Genobst* Alfred Keller	1 Jan 42–25 Jun 43
	Gen d Fl Günther Korten	26 Jun–20 Aug 43
	Gen d Fl Curt Pflugbeil	4 Sept 43–1 Jun 44
	CoS *Obst* Herbert Rieckhoff	1 Jan 42–23 Feb 43
	CoS *Obst* Hans-Detlef Herhudt von Rohden	1 Mar–7 Aug 43
	CoS *Obst* Klaus Uebe (*Genmaj* from 1 Jan 44)	8 Aug 43–1 Jun 44
Lfl. 4	*Genobst* Alexander Löhr	1 Jan–1 Jul 42
	Genobst Wolfram von Richthofen (*GFM* from 16 Feb 43)	4 Jul 42-12 Jun 43
	Gen d Flak Otto Dessloch (*Genobst* from 1 Mar 44)	13 Jun 43–1 Jun 44
	CoS *Genmaj* Günther Korten (*Genlt* from 1 Aug 42)	1 Jan–23 Aug 42
	CoS *Obst* Hans-Detlef Herhudt von Rohden	24 Aug 42–28 Feb 43
	CoS *Obst* Karl-Heinrich Schulz (*Genmaj* from 1 May 44)	14 Mar 43–1 Jun 44
Lfl. 6	*Genobst* Robert, *Ritter* von Greim	5 May 43–1 Jun 44
	CoS *Obst* Friedrich Kless	5 May 43–1 Jun 44
LwKdo Don	*Genlt* Günther Korten (*Gen.d.Fl* from 30 Jan 43)	26 Aug 42–17 Feb 43
LwKdo Kaukasus	*Gen d Flak* Otto Dessloch	25 Nov 42–6 Feb 43
LwKdo Kuban	*Gen d Flak* Otto Dessloch	7 Feb–? Mar 43
Lwkdo Ost	*Gen d Fl* Robert, *Ritter* von Greim (*Genobst* from 16 Feb 43)	1 Apr 42–4 May 43
FlK I	*Gen d Fl* Helmut Förster	1 Jan–23 Aug 42
	Genlt Günther Korten	2 Apr–25 Aug 42
	Gen d Fl Günther Korten	18 Feb–11 Jun 43
	Genlt Karl Angerstein	15 Jun–8 Nov 43
	Genmaj Paul Deichmann (*Genlt* from 20 May 44)	8 Nov 43–1 Jun 44
FlK IV	*Genlt* Curt Pflugbeil (*Gen d Fl* from 1 Feb 42)	1 Jan 42–3 Sept 43
	Genlt Rudolf Meister	4 Sept 43–1 Jun 44
FlK V	*Gen.d.Fl* Robert, *Ritter* von Greim	1 Jan–31 Mar 42
FlK VIII	*Genobst* Wolfram von Richthofen	1 Jan–3 Jul 42
	Genlt Martin Fiebig (*Gen d Fl* from 1 Mar 43)	4 Jul 42–18 May 43
	Genmaj Hans Seidemann (*Genlt* from 1 Jan 44)	19 May 43–1 Jun 44
FlD 1	*Genlt* Martin Fiebig	12 Apr–31 May 42
	Genlt Alfred Schlemm	1 Jun–30 Sept 42
	Obst Hermann Plocher	1–31 Oct 42
	Genmaj Alfred Bülowius (*Genlt* from 1 Mar 43)	1 Nov 42–11 Jun 43
	Genmaj Paul Deichmann	26 Jun–6 Nov 43
	Genmaj Robert Fuchs	7 Nov 43–1 Jun 44
FlD 2	*Genmaj* Stefan Fröhlich	12 Apr–28 Dec 42
FlD 3	*Obst* Herbert Rieckhoff	23 Feb–25 Sep 43
	Genmaj Werner Zech	26 Sept 43–19 Jan 44
	Genmaj Walter Boenicke	20 Jan–1 Jun 44
FlD 4	*Genmaj* Hermann Plocher	1 Jul–26 Aug 43
	Genmaj Franz Reuss	29 Aug 43–1 Jun 44
FlD Donez	*Genlt* Alfred Mahnke	2 Jan–31 Mar 43

Note: This list ignores minor *ad hoc* commands. *GFM* = *Generalfeldmarschall*; *Genobst* = *Generaloberst*; *Gen d Fl* = *General der Flieger*; *Gen d Flak* = *General der Flakartillerie*; *Genlt* = *Generalleutnant*; *Genmaj* = *Generalmajor*; *Obst* = *Oberst*.

sian skies, having been a pilot with a Russian airline in the 1920s, and from Pskov-West he began assembling a force of 15 *Gruppen* within three weeks, mostly by mobilising schools. Initially there was friction between him and Keller, while the Army supply organisation's bumbling bureaucracy also proved a hurdle. The aircraft flew in *'pulks'* of 20–40 at 1,800–2,400m (6,000–8,000ft) and the Demyansk airfields were organised to ensure that they could always receive transports.[4] This guaranteed a flow of supplies until a corridor was established to the pocket from 18 May, when the airlift was reduced, although three *Gruppen* continued to bring in men to *II. Korps* until the pocket was evacuated in January 1943. By then Morzik's *Gruppen* had flown 33,086 sorties, bringing in 64,844 tonnes of supplies and 30,500 men (24,303 tonnes and 15,446 men by 18 May), while 35,400 men, most of them sick or wounded, were taken out of the pocket.[5] With no airfield, Kholm depended upon Go 242 and DFS 230 gliders towed by *KGrzbV 5* and landing in the gloom of dawn or dusk until it too was relieved in May after a 103-day siege. The gliders were supplemented by supply drops from as low as 200m (1,300ft) using bombers and transports, which provided 1,024 tonnes in one three-day period. The success boosted Army and *Luftwaffe* morale while convincing Hitler that airlifts would ensure that any isolated garrison could hold out against the Bolshevik hordes. The weakness of these 'hordes' and the neutralisation of Malta enabled the *Transportgruppen* on this occasion to operate effectively in two separate theatres at once, a fact unappreciated by Jeschonnek at the time, while the mobilisation of training units proved extremely short-sighted.

As the *rasputitsa* brought relief, the *Luftwaffe* prepared for the inevitable summer campaign. There was an urgent need to rationalise the *Aufklärungsstaffeln*: the *Nahaufklärungsstaffeln* were reorganised into *Nahaufklärungsgruppen* during January to provide each major Army command with tactical reconnaissance, while the spring saw a third of the 55 *Nahaufklärungsstaffeln* disbanded. This marked the demise of traditional air support in which each *Armee Korps* and *Panzer Division* had a *Staffel* of slow corps aeroplanes for reconnaissance and artillery fire direction. In the face of intense Russian AA, high-performance aircraft were required and the *NAGr* became largely tactical photographic reconnaissance units with a secondary ground attack capability, although corps aeroplanes such as the Fw 189 remained in service until the end of the war. The Army also lost its long-range and night reconnaissance *Staffeln*, whose roles became purely a *Luftwaffe* responsibility and led to the creation in July of *Fernaufklärungsgruppe* to centralise reconnaissance.

The *Wehrmacht's* severe losses restricted Hitler's strategic options, as was clear when the strategic blueprint, *OKW* Directive 41, was published on 5 April making the economising of manpower a priority by smoothing the front line. In the Crimean Peninsula *11. Armee* (*Generalfeldmarschall* Erich von Manstein) was to eliminate the Kerch bridgehead (*Unternehmen 'Trappenjagd'*), then take Sevastopol.

173

The Russian salient around Izyum was then to be eliminated by Bock's *Heeresgruppe Süd* in *Unternehmen 'Fridericus'* using *6. Armee* and *Armeegruppe Kleist* (*17. Armee* and *1. Panzer Armee*). When these preliminaries were completed, the main campaign, *Fall 'Blau'*, would take the *Wehrmacht* to the Volga at Stalingrad and the Don at Rostov through a series of envelopments which would open the way to the occupation of the Caucasian oilfields. Once these objectives were achieved Manstein and *Fliegerkorps VIII* would be transferred north to *Heeresgruppe Nord* and take Leningrad.

The *Luftwaffe* was assigned its usual operational roles, although the directive noted that 'The possibility of a hasty transfer of *Luftwaffe* units to the central and northern fronts must be borne in mind, and the necessary ground organisation for this must be maintained as far as possible.' Richthofen's *Fliegerkorps VIII* would play a major role in the new offensive, although first it needed a rest, and in April its whole sector was taken over by Greim's *Fliegerkorps V*, which had returned from Brussels in February to assume responsibility for *Heeresgruppe Mitte*'s southern flank. On 10 April Greim's command was upgraded to *Luftwaffenkommando Ost*, supported by *18. Flakdivision*, as *Generalmajor* Richard Reimann's *Flakkorps II* was redesignated.[6] In May Richthofen joined Löhr's *Luftflotte 4*, which already had Pflugbeil's *Fliegerkorps IV* and *Oberst* Wolfgang von Wild's *FlFü Süd*, for the summer campaign.

The *rasputista* allowed the *Luftwaffe* to withdraw units to Germany for rest and re-equipment while the restored rail network brought in stocks of fuel, spares and ammunition when the *Gruppen* returned for the summer. Some *Kampfgruppen* remaining in the East during April conducted half-hearted strategic bombing as far east as Stalingrad, using only a few aircraft at a time and achieving little. In a revealing comment, Plocher wrote, 'Since none of these attacks resulted in the actual destruction of the source of enemy power, it would have been far more advisable to have committed these few planes in support of the Army. Because these unsystematic attacks made no tactical impact whatever at the front, they were literally senseless and could be considered a typical example of inefficiency and waste in military operations.'[7]

With A-Day scheduled for 18 May, Pflugbeil and Kleist prepared for *'Fridericus'*, until Hitler revised the plan to make *6. Armee* (*General der Panzertruppe* Friedrich Paulus) the spearhead. Then, six days before A-Day, the Russians began a double envelopment of Paulus using 640,000 men and 926 aircraft. Despite support from Pflugbeil and *9. Flakdivision* (the latter claiming to have destroyed 107 tanks by 20 May), Paulus gave ground and the Russians expanded the Izyum salient, exposing themselves to a riposte by Kleist from the south. The plan was coordinated at a noon conference on 15 May which included Paulus, Löhr and Pflugbeil, and, with nine *Gruppen* from Richthofen, it began two days later in bright, clear weather. Kleist was supported by Pflugbeil's *Gefechtsverband Süd*, created the previous day with 11 *Gruppen* (seven strike), which provided air support 'most effectively' as *1. Panzer Armee*, and within 20 minutes of a request for air support the *Landsers* would hear the sound of German aircraft. On 19 May the rest of Pflugbeil's forces supported Paulus's counter-offensive which struck the northern face of the salient's base, the two spearheads meeting within five days. The *Luftwaffe* was extremely active. *KG 51* flew 294 sorties on 20/21 May while *III./JG 77* claimed 35 victories, and on 28 May the flames of Russian resistance were extinguished with 170,958 men (nearly a quarter of the manpower committed to the offensive) dead or prisoners, largely because Stalin was reluctant to evacuate the salient. *I. Flak Korps* claimed hundreds of tanks and 33 aircraft destroyed.[8]

The irony of Hitler's decision to withdraw Richthofen's aircraft from the Crimea was lost on Manstein, for the *Führer* himself had demanded massive air support for *'Trappenjagd'* (Bustard Hunt). Although Directive 41 offered no strategic justification for the Crimean campaign, there was a general recognition that it would eliminate a potential thorn in the side, yet, as one observer notes, it became a focal point of German operations.[9] While on leave, Richthofen had persuaded Hitler of the value of air power in the Crimea, and when the *Führer* discussed the campaign with Manstein on 16 April he announced that he would personally oversee air support and, despite Jeschonnek's protests, ordered the transfer of *Fliegerkorps VIII* (originally earmarked for *'Fridericus'*) to the Crimea to provide, in the words of the *XXX. Armee Korps* war diary, 'concentrated air support the like of which has never existed'. The decision also offered Richthofen an opportunity to play armchair general, albeit under *ObdL* control, and he constantly interfered with Manstein's preparation.[10] Although the *Landsers* were still denied direct contact with the airmen, the air support plan greatly eased their advance upon Kerch from 8 May, with Richthofen's men flying 3,800 sorties until the last defender surrendered on 15 May.[11]

Although Kharkov had delayed *'Blau'*, Hitler decided not to proceed with the main offensive until Sevastopol had been stormed in *Unternehmen 'Störfang'* (Sturgeon Trap). Richthofen's *Gruppen* returned and, while Wild's *FlFü Süd* used its anti-shipping force in the operational role, *Fliegerkorps VIII* began reducing the defences from 2 June with the 390 aircraft acting as flying artillery.[12] Despite the lack of opposition (only 31 aircraft were lost) and the scale of operations (23,751 sorties and 20,528 tonnes of bombs, including SC 1400 and SC 1800), air support did not prove the panacea the Army officers, but not Richthofen, had anticipated, and mopping up continued until 4 July, bringing the total 'bag' of prisoners in the Crimea to 260,000. Richthofen's beguiling success at Sevastopol and Kerch proved to be another poisoned chalice, raising Army expectations of similar levels of support, which ensnared the *Luftwaffe* in a trap of its own making. An overlooked factor in the Crimean victories was the activity of the 'black men', whose 'incredible speed' in re-arming aircraft between routine maintenance duties both day and night, sometimes without sleep, permitted eight sorties a day per aircraft at Sevastopol, where a 64% serviceability rate was maintained.[13]

Even before Sevastopol fell, *Fliegerkorps VIII* began assembling around Kursk to support *4. Panzer Armee*'s advance towards Voronezh in the first phase of *'Blau'*. Beforehand there were two preliminary operations, *Unternehmen 'Wilhelm'* and *'Fridericus II'*, for which *ObdL* had originally earmarked Richthofen. Jeschonnek decided to allow Richthofen to complete *'Störfang'* while Pflugbeil took up the slack; Bock, tugging at the bit to begin *'Blau'*, was informed that 'the *Luftwaffe* cannot be spared from *"Fridericus II"'*, further delaying the summer campaign. Rain hindered both preliminary operations, and when *'Fridericus II'* was completed on 25 June only 70,000 prisoners were taken, a disappointing swansong for Löhr. *'Störfang'* had highlighted the fact that Richthofen was overdue for promotion, and Löhr was assigned *12. Armee* in the Balkans, where the former Austrian officer could exploit his familiarity with the region and his linguistic skills. He later became *Oberbefehlshaber Südost* (*OB Südost*) but had little direct contact with the *Luftwaffe* for the rest of the war, after which he was accused of war crimes by Yugoslavia, found guilty and executed on 16 February 1947.

For the new campaign the *Luftwaffe* assembled its largest concentration in the East since 'Barbarossa', and one never later equalled, with 2,690 aircraft (including three *Staffeln* from Spain and Croatia), while the *VVS* had a total of 2,800 front-line combat aircraft (including 700 Polikarpov Po-2 night bombers and R-5 corps aircraft) and 900 aircraft in reserve, as well as 1,200 *PVO* fighters. Tactical air support was strengthened through the creation of *Schlachtgeschwader*, with *Jabos* supplemented by the Hs 129, some in *Luftflotte 4,* which had 52% (1,400 aircraft) of the *Luftwaffe*'s Eastern Front strength. This would be supplemented by 265 Hungarian, Italian, Romanian and Slovak combat aircraft, and they faced 23% of the *VVS* (640 aircraft) in the South-Western Theatre.[14] To the north Greim, with 500 aircraft, helped *Heeresgruppe Mitte*'s deception operation, *Unternehmen 'Kreml'* (Kremlin), convince the Russians that the main thrust would be towards Moscow. There was an extensive building programme to produce new airfields and expand existing ones, while from mid-June Greim demonstrated over the front and increased reconnaissance flights around Moscow.[15]

Heeresgruppe Süd opened *'Blau/Braunschweig'* on 28 June with *Fliegerkorps VIII* sweeping the way clear in front of *4. Panzer Armee*'s tanks while Pflugbeil struck enemy headquarters, reserves and communications.[16] In the tense early days of the offensive Richthofen relieved Löhr but retained Korten (who had worked with Löhr since the *Anschluss*) and was, in turn, relieved in *Fliegerkorps VIII* by Fiebig. Meanwhile Stalin, fearing a new threat to Moscow, put heavy pressure upon the boundary between *Heeresgruppen Mitte* and *Süd*, forcing Fiebig to divert aircraft and leading to fierce air battles which brought Russian losses in the Voronezh operation to 783 aircraft by 24 July without the compensation of saving the city.

Fiebig then supported the next phase, *Unternehmen 'Clausewitz'* (formerly *'Blau II'*), which began on 9 July, and as it became increasingly difficult for him to support the hard-pressed *Landsers* around Voronezh on 2 August Richthofen created *Gefechtsverband Nord* under Bülowius, with *Nahaufklärung-*, *Jagd-* and *Kampfgruppen* and *Stukas* on an *ad hoc* basis being joined later by Hungarian and Italian squadrons as their armies took up positions along the Don south of Voronezh. Bülowius was an 'Old Eagle' who had been a *Staffelführer* in the *'England Geschwader'* (*Bogohl 3*), then served in *Freikorps* and *Polizeiflieger* units before settling into the *Reichsheer*. He had joined the *Luftwaffe* in 1934, but his career had received a setback when, as *Kommodore* of *LG 1*, he had been shot down and wounded just before the Armistice, and until his latest appointment he had had training responsibilities.

'Clausewitz' struck thin air for on 6 July Stalin ordered his troops to retreat and avoid envelopment by Bock's newly created *Heeresgruppe B* (*2.* and *6. Armees* with *4. Panzer Armee* and the 2nd Hungarian, the 3rd Romanian and the 8th Italian Armies) in the north and *Generalfeldmarschall* Wilhelm List's *Heeresgruppe A* (*11.* and *17. Armees* with *1. Panzer Armee* and the 4th Romanian Army) in the south. Fiebig and Pflugbeil supported *4. Panzer Armee* and *6. Armee* respectively, with units moving forward so rapidly that their new airfields were sometimes still under artillery fire, Fiebig being especially affected because he had most of the single-engine units, having transferred most twin-engine aircraft to Pflugbeil, who could maintain them more effectively from his established bases. The *Luftwaffe* was very active operationally, striking airfields and communications (especially bridges), although the usual combination of extreme activity and lengthening supply lines reduced sortie levels. The *Transportgruppen* remained active and on 12 July flew more than 200 tonnes of fuel to the Panzer divisions.[17] Both *Fliegerkorps* and *I. Flakkorps* (*9.* and *10. Flakdivisionen*) supported List's capture of Rostov on 15 July, shielded by Weichs, who pushed *6. Armee* and *4. Panzer Armee* towards Stalingrad to secure the Don River, reaching its subsidiary the Chir on 17 July. Two days later Paulus's *6. Armee* was ordered to take Stalingrad 'by a daring high-speed assault', but then *OKW* issued Directive 45 on 23 July which split the German advance. Weichs was to secure the Don and take Stalingrad, assisted by Fiebig, who was to undertake the 'timely destruction of Stalingrad'. List was to drive into the Caucasus with Pflugbeil's aid, secure the Black Sea coast then seize the Caucasian oilfields. The directive demanded attacks upon the Caucasian oilfields despite opposition from *Luftwaffe* intelligence, but, in the event, no bombers could be spared for this task until October. As Richthofen complained to *ObdL* about supporting two diverging *Heersgruppen* with inadequate resources, he had lost some 350 aircraft to enemy action since the campaign began. Fiebig interdicted rail and river traffic around Stalingrad, where the Germans were encountering fierce resistance despite the commitment of about 1,000 aircraft.[18]

Table 45. *Luftwaffe* **Distribution in the South, July 1942–January 1943**

		JGr	*ZGr*	*KGr*	*StGr*	*SchGr*
17 Jul	LwKdo Don	1	–	2	–	–
	Lflt 4	6⅓	2	13	7⅓	2
13 Aug	LwKdo Don	1	–	2	1	–
	Lflt 4	8	2	14	7	2
22 Aug	LwKdo Don	1	–	2	1	–
	Lflt 4	6⅓	2	11⅔	6⅓	2
13 Oct	LwKdo Don	1	–	2	1	–
	Lflt 4	8⅓	2	14	7⅓	2
31 Jan	LwKdo Don	1	–	3⅓	1⅓	⅓
	Lflt 4	2	2	8⅓	3	2

Note: ⅓ = one *Staffel*; ⅔ = two *Staffeln*.

On 21 August Paulus thrust towards Stalingrad and within two days his northern spearhead, supported by a regiment of *9. Flakdivision*, reached the Volga after 1,000 tonnes of bombs were dropped in 1,600 sorties. When the spearhead was briefly isolated his men were sustained by airdrops of fuel and ammunition. Meanwhile Korten assumed command of the Kharkov-based *Fliegerkorps I* (withdrawn from *Luftflotte 1* a month earlier), which was upgraded to *Luftwaffenkommando Don*, supported by *Luftgau Charkow*, to secure the line of the River Don and its allied garrisons, including the newly arrived 3rd Romanian Army, which took position between the Italians and *6. Armee*. He absorbed Bülowius's *Gefechtsverband*, although it retained a semi-autonomous status until it was disbanded in November, and while it was later suggested that Korten's appointment owed more to favouritism than necessity, he had an important responsibility. The 500km line was under constant pressure, and he rarely had more than four *Gruppen*, augmented by 110 aircraft of the 2nd Hungarian Air Brigade and *Regia Aeronautica*, strengthened in crises by Fiebig's forces (see Table 45). He established command posts at each end of his sector, and these proved useful during October when the Russian probes pushed back allied forces in many places, putting much of the responsibility for securing the front upon the *Luftwaffe*.[19]

Meanwhile the assault upon Stalingrad was heralded on 3 September with an unremitting 24-hour bombardment by Fiebig and Pflugbeil, who dropped thousands of incendiaries from as low as 2,000m (6,600ft), turning the log-cabin suburbs into a forest of stone chimneys. As German troops fought their way into the city against fierce resistance, Fiebig established a command post with a panorama of the battlefield, while a neighbouring army observation battalion helped to provide an up-to-the-minute picture of the situation. Yet the next two months' operations were a regression to the *Schlachtflieger* tactics of the Great War, with aircraft used as an extension of the infantry. At Stalingrad, *Stukas*, flying four sorties a day in *Staffel*-size missions, struck targets selected from small-scale maps; Richthofen was to comment in his diary on 1 November that his bombers were dropping bombs within grenade-throwing range.[20] Attacks by *Gruppe*-size formations were confined to major efforts by 6. *Armee*, which agreed in late September that the *Kampfgruppen* should be confined to striking the massed artillery batteries on the far side of the Volga and interdicting river traffic. Paulus had to supplement his batteries with those of *Oberst* Wolfgang Pickert's 9. *Flakdivision* and *FlakR 91*, but these lost four battery commanders in one day due to the confined nature of the battle, which exposed the men to snipers and mortar fire, especially when guns were used not only against armour and artillery but also against infantry units.[21] Richthofen, an inveterate intriguer who seized every opportunity to criticise Paulus's leadership and to play the armchair general, even persuaded *OKH* that the despatch of five combat engineer battalions would turn the tide of battle, complaining as late as 16 November to Army Chief of Staff *Generaloberst* Kurt Zeitzler (who replaced Halder on 25 September) in a long telephone conversation.[22]

The *VVS*'s feeble response eased Fiebig's problems, for it was contained by *Major* Wolf-Dietrich Wilcke's *JG 3 'Udet'*, by Pickert's gunners and by occasional attacks upon its airfields; indeed, on the Stalingrad front the Russians lost 2,063 aircraft between 17 July and 18 November. The open steppes made it easy for Fiebig to build airstrips for his own units, with *Stuka*- and *Schlachtgruppen* established between the Don and the Chir within sound of the battle and *Jagd*- and *Zerstörergruppen* within the Don bend, while the *Kampfgeschwader* operated from Morozovskaya and Tatsinskaya, 200–250km from Stalingrad. Richthofen's burden was eased from mid-September with the arrival of the Romanian Air Corps (180 combat aircraft) to support the 3rd Romanian Army and interdict Russian communications north-west of Stalingrad.[23] By 6 October Paulus had secured central and southern Stalingrad, but he was exhausted and paused to await reinforcements and supplies, as did Richthofen. However, *Luftwaffe* strength in the East had dropped by nearly 14% after four months of continuous operations, and some units, especially *Kampfgruppen*, were withdrawn for re-equipment.[24] *ObdL* had nothing to spare, so Richthofen, displaying the child-like wilfulness so prevalent in German officers, went south to support *Heeresgruppe B* until Paulus renewed his attack. Göring promptly issued a directive re-emphasising the supremacy of the Stalingrad front, but Richthofen stubbornly refused to return. This stimulated a discussion about *Luftwaffe* resources, leading to a meeting with Hitler on 15 October involving Göring, Jeschonnek and Richthofen. A good-humoured *Führer*, who had personally directed operations in the Caucasus since List's resignation on 9 September, rubber-stamped Richthofen's decision, partly because he believed that the Stalingrad battle was in its last phase.

Despite the strategic importance of the oilfields, the advance into the Caucasus had been the poor relation for air support. On 20 August Richthofen regretfully informed List that he was transferring most of his aircraft to Stalingrad on Hitler's orders, and when List's Chief of Staff, *Generalleutnant* Hans von Greiffenberg, asked *OKH* on 28 August when the *Heeresgruppe* would receive air support he was tersely told, 'When Stalingrad is taken or given up as impossible'. Pflugbeil's units were overstretched, and hard-pressed to maintain pace with the spearheads; indeed, *3. (H)/14* of *NAGr 3* had eight bases in the four weeks from 28 July. Richthofen's armchair-general tactics meant that it was his views of the Army's prospects which decided where air power was to be focused, and when this was provided it proved 'adequate, but not lavish', with a few extra sorties to bomb the Grozny oilfields.[25] Mountainous terrain and heavy rain meant that the Panzer units could not exploit *Luftwaffe* attacks and, in a fit of pique, Richthofen refused to increase air support.[26]

Meanwhile on 14 October, as the evenings grew chillier and rain showers became more common, Paulus renewed his assault upon Stalingrad. Richthofen returned with most of his *Gruppen* to find that Soviet pressure along the whole front was forcing him constantly to shuffle units around to meet real or imagined threats, giving them no time to rest.[27] Nevertheless, *Luftwaffe* support helped to ensure that by 7 November the Russians were left with their legs dangling in the Volga, though this effort created a supply crisis. The extended German rail network stopped short on the Chir River, 100km from Stalingrad, but Richthofen and Korten's four trains a day had priority over Army traffic. On 1 November Richthofen proposed to *Generalfeldmarschall* Maximilian von Weichs (who had replaced Bock) and Paulus relinquishing railway space for Army ammunition, because with fighting at such close quarters 'the *Luftwaffe* cannot be very effective any more'. He was, in fact, better served than the Army, for since August 10 *Transportgruppen* (one with He 111s) had ferried urgent supplies, although five were sent to the Caucasus when the railway finally reached the Chir, and by mid-November they had brought 42,630 tonnes of supplies and 27,044 personnel while evacuating 51,018 casualties. Most of these supplies were for the *Luftwaffe*, which received 20,173 tonnes of fuel and 9,492 tonnes of bombs and ammunition, but 9,233 tonnes were for the Army, half of it vehicle fuel. The distribution of this manna was eased by Richthofen's early rationalisation of his motor-transport resources, which not only allowed him to create a reserve but also increased the 'lift' of supplies from 2,000 tonnes to 5,000 tonnes.[28]

An ominous feature of this phase was the growing activity of the *VVS*: an *OKH* liaison officer noted on 15 October that their night air superiority was assuming 'intolerable proportions'. The *VVS* was benefiting from organisational and leadership reforms initiated by General Aleksandr Novikov, who became its commander in April 1942. Frontal aviation was reorganised into well-balanced air armies of several fighter, attack-bomber and light bomber divisions, each roughly equivalent to a *Geschwader*, while the medium bomber and transport force came under the *ADD*. More capable aircraft such as Lavochkin La-5 and Yakovlev Yak-9 fighters and a two-seat version of the Il-2 *'Ilyusha'* attack bomber, the Il-2m3, were being produced, while from Russia's allies came Hurricane, P-39 Airacobra (later joined by the P-63 Kingcobra), Spitfire, Tomahawk and Warhawk fighters as well as A-20 Boston and B-25 Mitchell bombers. The Russian night attacks began as a means of using obsolete aircraft from October 1941 onward, although the night bomber regiments increasingly relied upon the nimble Po-2 biplane trainer to harass the German rear, bombing dumps, headquarters, batteries and even individual vehicles. The Po-2's distinctive engine noise earned them the German nickname *'Nähmaschinen'* (Sewing Machines). To counter them *'Flak* Circuses', mobile battle groups of light/medium batteries, were created, and these proved more successful than *Nachtjagdstaffeln*, whose crews found their targets too slow. The damage inflicted by the 'Sewing Machines' was limited, although *Major* Alfons 'Ali' Orthofer (*Kommodore* of *StG 77*) was killed by one while taking off from Belorezhenskaya on 12 October, but they were an irritation for the long-suffering soldiers and on 7 October 1942 the *Luftwaffe* authorised similar units. Most commands created *Befehlskampfstaffeln* with Fw 58s, Go 145s, He 46s, Hs 126s and Junkers W.34s, but the wilful Richthofen assigned the task to *Verbindungs-staffeln*, which had a wide variety of trainers and liaison aircraft (including Ar 66s, Ar 96s, Bf 108s, Caudron C.445s and Fi 156s). A month later the *Staffeln* were reorganised into *Störkampfgruppen*, with one to each major command (*Luftflotte 5* formed a *Störkampfstaffel*), operating up to 60km behind enemy lines with considerable success.[29]

While the Germans dissipated their strength, Stalin conserved his, feeding the fire within the city which bore his name while his staff prepared a double-envelopment, Operation 'Uranus', to exploit the enemy's exposed position. The Germans were at the tip of a long salient whose flanks were held by allied forces whom the Russians recognised were of dubious effectiveness. 'Uranus' was approved at the end of September, and in the following weeks forces assembled, shielded by rain, sleet and snow showers together with fog, which sharply reduced *Luftwaffe* activity. *FAGr 4* produced evidence that a major blow would strike the 3rd Romanian Army on Paulus's northern flank, but Fiebig was unable to respond to Hitler's demands for major air strikes, especially after the transfer of *Major* von Friedburg's *KG 76* to the Mediterranean. Richthofen intensified reconnaissance and reinforced the Romanians with five *Flak* batteries while improving liaison with both them and *XLVIII. Panzer Korps*. Supplies for two *Gruppen* were assembled at Bokovskaya airfield near the junction of the 8th Italian and 3rd Romanian Armies, while stocks of ammunition for *9. Flak Division* were increased (when it surrendered it still had 10,000 8.8cm shells unused). There was contingency planning for Pflugbeil to move north in the event of a crisis, leaving Caucasian air support under *General der Flakartillerie* Otto Dessloch, a 53-year-old 'Old Eagle' who was commander of

181

I. Flakkorps, but Richthofen ignored ominous signs south of Stalingrad opposite the 4th Romanian Army and *4. Panzer Armee*. By mid-November Axis airfields were being struck by *Ilyusha*s as Richthofen's *Kampfgruppen* interdicted communications, but the Allied landings in North Africa earlier in the month and transfers of 10 *Gruppen* to that theatre, together with losses, meant that overall strength in the East had dropped by about a quarter, with *Luftwaffekommando Don* and *Luftflotte 4* down from about 1,000 to some 700 aircraft.[30]

'Uranus' began on a snowy, overcast 19 November with low cloud and in temperatures just above freezing. The 3rd Romanian Army collapsed and within a day the Russians were approaching Fiebig's forward airfields, which were hurriedly abandoned, sometimes under tank fire. *Oberstleutnant* Paul-Werner Hozzel's *StG 2* was left with the strength of a weak *Gruppe*, while *Oberstleutnant* Hubertus Hitschold's *SchG 1* escaped westward only at the last minute. More ominously, a momentary break in the clouds allowed a *Nahaufklärungsflieger* flying at 90m (300ft) to spot huge tank columns driving through the 4th Romanian Army as *4. Panzer Armee* escaped encirclement with difficulty. The weather grounded most of *Fliegerkorps VIII*, causing Richthofen to write in his diary, 'We must have good weather soon, otherwise there can be no hope.' There was no improvement in the weather and the *Luftwaffe* response was weak, with most missions in *Kette* strength, and on 23 November the Russians linked up east of the Don bend.

The Germans cobbled together a line along the Chir using *15. Luftwaffenfelddivision* (*Generalleutnant* Alfred Mahnke) and the ad hoc battle groups, including one of *Luftwaffe* ground personnel under *Oberst* Reiner Stahel, while *Flak* from *Luftgau XXV/Rostow* added strength as *FlakR 99* (*Oberst* Eduard Obergethmann) shielded Fiebig's remaining airfields. Behind this line the *Luftwaffe* regrouped at Morozovskaya, Tatsinskaya and nearby Oblivskaya, where the stocks assembled through Richthofen's foresight enabled the Axis air forces to fly 150 sorties a day on 22 November. In fact it was the weather which restricted operations rather than an absence of supplies—a situation Richthofen described as 'a crying shame'. Some supply drops were flown to isolated groups of Axis troops struggling westward, while the *Luftwaffe* signals network ensured that Fiebig's headquarters could monitor the situation in the chaos and at a time when Paulus decamped to a new command post nearer Stalingrad. By 24 November he had 250,000 men (including 13,000 Romanians and 19,000 Russian *Hiwi*s) encircled in a pocket 50km long and 40km wide which included 12,000 *Luftwaffe* personnel, of whom 10,000 were from Pickert's *9. Flak Division* with 251 guns (including 37 8.8cm weapons). There were also two *Gruppen* of *JG 3* and the remnants of a *Stukagruppe*, as well as *NAGr 12, 14* and *16* operating from four airfields, primarily Pitomnik and Gumrak.[31]

The isolation of *6. Armee* stunned the German High Command, then national prestige and experience of the previous winter's campaign created a consensus that Paulus, already making pessimistic noises to gain Hitler's permission for a break-out, should await relief, although this view was opposed by Manstein, whose newly created *Heersgruppe Don* was assembled to relieve the pocket. Those closest to the front recognised that the Soviet Army was far stronger than a year earlier; indeed, the *VVS* had committed 1,414 aircraft (426 obsolete U-2s), while a further complication had been the transfer westwards a month earlier of most of the 6. *Armee*'s horses, which not only restricted army mobility but also deprived the men of a source of food. As at Demyansk, everything depended upon an airlift, but when Paulus raised this prospect with Fiebig on the evening of 21 November the latter replied with considerable perception: 'Impossible! Our aircraft are heavily engaged in Africa and on other fronts. I must warn you against exaggerated expectations.'[32] The corps commanders were unwilling to rely upon an airlift and demanded a break-out, but the obstinacy of the army Chief of Staff, *General der Panzertruppe* Rudolf Schmidt, stiffened Paulus's resolve to follow Hitler's instructions and await relief.[33] Hitler's decision was underlined by Göring's assurances, evidently following discussions with Jeschonnek and *General der Flieger* Hans-Georg von Seidel, the *Generalquartermeister*, who convinced him that the airlift was indeed practicable.[34]

Even in ideal circumstances the task was beyond the *Luftwaffe*, but 11 of the 23 *Transportgruppen* were already committed to supplying North Africa and *Gruppen* sent eastwards had to call at Berlin-Staaken for adaptation to the Russian winter. The task required at least 500 Ju 52s, but on 25 November Richthofen had only 298, and to make up the shortfall 600 aircraft were mobilised from the *Fliegerschulen* and *Kampfgruppen* and pressed into service. Snow, sleet, low cloud and fog restricted operations, while transports reaching Pitomnik and Gorodyzhe in the pocket suffered from an absence of navigation aids (some pilots made seven attempts to land). The latter airfield was suitable only for single-engine aircraft, and Paulus rejected *Luftwaffe* requests to expand Gumrak because of its proximity to his new headquarters. While justifiably complaining about the failure to provide sufficient supplies, neither he nor Schmidt organised reception or distribution but dumped the responsibility upon Pickert's shoulders. From *FlakR 104*, Pickert (formerly Chief of Staff to *Luftwaffe Befehlshaber Mitte*) created *Luftversorgungsstab Stalingrad* (Air Supply Staff, Stalingrad), who began to create order from the chaos, while Pitomnik's air traffic control officer, *Oberstleutnant* Kolbenschlag, and signaller, *Major* Freudenfeld, lashed together a navigation system which operated in the face of Russian jamming.

Once again Morzik arrived, but the task of organising the airlift was assigned on 26 November to *Generalmajor* Viktor Carganico (*Kommandeur, Flughafenbereichs 1/VI Tazinskaya*), an 'Old Eagle' since before the Great War, after which he had helped to establish the Mexican Air Force. Most of Fiebig's *Kampfgruppen* were tied up in the airlift, which exploited bases around the railway. All He 111 transports were assigned to *Oberst* Ernst Kühl's *KG 55* at Morozovskaya, while the Ju 52s (and newly arrived Ju 86s) were assigned to *Oberst* Hans Förster's *KGzbV 1* at Tatsinskaya, each *Geschwader* having four or five *Gruppen*. The transports flew day and night, escorted whenever possible by Wilcke's *JG 3*, until the *Jagdgruppen* were diverted to support the relief operation, *Unternehmen 'Wintergewitter'* (WinterThunderstorm), leaving the transport *'pulks'* at the mercy of massed AA as well as enemy fighters. Bases were also attacked, with four transports and 75 tonnes of fuel destroyed at Tatsinskaya on 9 December alone. Fiebig was pessimistic about the airlift's prospects yet desperate for success, and he wrote in his diary on 17 December, '. . . it must succeed! The alternative is unthinkable.'

But that alternative soon had to be faced, for *'Wintergewitter'*, which began on 12 December spearheaded by *4. Panzer Armee* and supported by Pflugbeil's *Fliegerkorps IV*, ran out of steam within a dozen days. Hitler still rejected Fiebig's and Manstein's pleas to authorise Paulus to break out, while Richthofen was at his wit's end, confiding in his diary on 18 December that he had been unable to speak to anyone and had given up telephoning Jeschonnek because he was being ignored and promises were being broken. Meanwhile Göring was in Italy, having gone on a 'tour of inspection'. This was completed on 10 December, when he went to Hitler's headquarters at Rastenburg, where, 11 days later, he received such shocking news that he sobbed throughout an interview with Kesselring.[35]

When *6. Armee* was isolated Stalin demanded a new offensive 'in the general direction of Millerovo and Rostov'. Planning was disrupted by *'Wintergewitter'*, and Operation 'Small Saturn' envisaged smashing through the 8th Italian Army in a double envelopment of Manstein's *Heeresgruppe Don*, with the spearheads meeting at Tatsinskaya and Morozovskaya. These bases were vital to the *Luftwaffe* to supply Stalingrad and prop up the Chir River line (under *General der Infanterie* Karl Hollidt). Close air support resources were extremely limited, and most of the 'black men' from the single-engine *Gruppen*, as well as the signallers, had been driven into the pocket with their vehicles and equipment (see Table 46 for *Luftwaffe* strength in the East). A new clutch of muddy airfields was established west of the Chir, but the lack of equipment such as tools led to much squabbling over the limited human and material resources, while the restricted number of aircraft

---

Table 46. Comparative Figures for *Luftwaffe* Strength, 1942/43

	Mid-October		Early December		Mid-January	
Luftfl 1	485	(25%)	270	(16%)	195	(11%)
LwKdo Ost	425	(22%)	480	(27%)	380	(22%)
Don front	545	(28%)	700	(39%)	900	(53%)
Crimea/Caucasus	495	(25%)	330	(18%)	240	(14%)
Total	1,950		1,780		1,715	

Source: BAM, p. 224.

were extensively used, sometimes flying 14 sorties a day. The disruption of the signal network by enemy advances meant that orders were either transmitted by radio (making them vulnerable to interception by the enemy) or delivered by Storch, a time-consuming business.

On 16 December 'Small Saturn', supported by 415 aircraft (a third of them R-5s and Po-2s) pulverised the Italians and four days later Millerovo, home of *Major* Mans-Henning, *Freiherr* von Büst's *KG 27*, was hastily abandoned, but Hitler authorised the evacuation of other bases in the Russians' path only if they were under fire. On Christmas Eve rockets rained down on Tatsinskaya, which received no warning due to the destruction of a local telephone exchange. There were wild scenes as 180 aircraft took off in all directions (one collided with a tank) amid clouds of snow, the last aircraft carrying Fiebig's staff. A third of the aircraft were lost, and the 108 Ju 52s and 16 Ju 86s which escaped took two days to assemble at Salsk (300km south-west of Stalingrad). Ironically the Russians were isolated by a prompt counter-attack and survived on supply drops, made at Stalin's insistence, before breaking out northwards on 29 December with tanks fuelled partly by *Luftwaffe* aviation fuel. Tatsinskaya was reoccupied, but much vital material and supplies had been lost; worse still, *4. Panzer Armee* was driven back, making the relief of *6. Armee* impossible.

New Year's Day brought no end to the Russian advance, and soon both Tatsinskaya and Morozovskaya were abandoned for bases 350–400km from the pocket, ending Ju 86 operations and reducing the He 111s to one sortie per day. *FlFü Atlantik* was stripped to provide four-engine aircraft, but there were too few to take up the slack and the Ju 52s were unable to operate in daylight because there were insufficient fighters (the Eastern *Jagdgruppen* had only 375) and they had lost their forward airfields. Wastage was abnormally high during the last weeks of 1942, partly due to adverse weather conditions, so that during December *Luftwaffe* strength in the East dropped by some 150 aircraft.[36] The collapse of the Don line and the need to reorganise the transport effort meant that on 2 January Fiebig transferred his single-engine units to *Fliegerdivision Donez*, under the *15. Luftwaffenfelddivision* commander, Mahnke. A 54-year-old 'Old Eagle' since before the Great War (during which he largely held staff posts), Mahnke had later served in the *Freikorps,* then the police, before entering the *Luftwaffe* in 1935, since when he had worked mostly in staff positions. His new command received increasing support from *Kampfgruppen* which were reverting to their traditional mission under the recently established *Kampfführer, Luftflotte 4*. Mahnke covered the retreat westwards as Salsk was abandoned in mid-January for Cherekovo behind the Donetz, but this stretched the air ferry to breaking point and there remained a desperate shortage of equipment. In the fluid situation many 'black men' had last-minute escapes from the enemy vanguard, while at Oblivskaya *Oberleutnant* Heinz Jungclausen's *6./StG 2* prevented a Russian cavalry-mecha-

185

nised group overrunning their base, the last tank being knocked out on the edge of the airfield![37] There was a narrower escape for *KG 51*'s *Leutnant* Geruschka and his crew, who faced Soviet captivity when their He 111 force-landed after being damaged by ground fire but were rescued by *Leutnant* Winkel, who landed in the snow beside them.[38]

Paulus's position was now desperate as a new Russian offensive compressed 6. *Armee* tighter into its tomb, and by 13 January Fiebig was writing in his diary, 'The 6. *Armee* is fighting its last battle.' From 16 January Pitomnik was under artillery fire, forcing the remaining combat aircraft under Pickert's command to Gumrak. This base was itself lost five days later, leaving the Stalingradskiy airfield in the suburbs although this was also under artillery fire and was too small for transports.

It was against this background that Milch took over the transport operation after Hitler briefed him on 15 January and demanded the supply of 300 tonnes daily to help 6. *Armee* tie down the largest possible Soviet force.[39] Claims that Milch might have achieved more if he had been brought in earlier seem exaggerated, and Plocher later claimed that the weather was the greatest obstacle.[40] On 18 January *Sonderstab Milch* relieved Carganico of his onerous burden and he retired into the comfortable obscurity of running airfields. But he could not escape Russian vengeance, for he was captured at the war's end and shot on 27 May 1945. Milch brought his remarkable organising skills and energy to bear and by 29 January he had assembled 363 aircraft and even considered exploiting a glider fleet which Richthofen had acquired from *Fliegerkorps XI* before recognising that without fighter escort they could not be used.[41] To provide token fighter cover Milch had nine Bf 109s and five Bf 110s equipped with long-range tanks and placed under Wilcke's command. On 30 January 11 of these aircraft flew a sweep over the pocket, claiming two victories on their return but losing a *Zerstörer* of I./ ZG 1. Low cloud and poor serviceability precluded further offensive actions, and with Richthofen's airfields under frequent attack all the fighters were assigned to conventional operations. It was too late in any case, for on 23 January the pocket was split into two and these could be supplied only by parachute or by simply throwing food and ammunition out from as low as 50m (165ft). Nothing could prevent the inevitable, and on 31 January Paulus was captured, followed, three days later, by the last of 91,000 Germans as a dozen He 111s flew forlornly overhead.[42]

The *Luftwaffe* delivered 8,250 tonnes of supplies and evacuated some 11% of the German troops, 24,760 wounded and 5,150 key personnel or experts, including Pickert and *Generalleutnant* Hans-Valentin Hube, the latter apparently shanghaied at gun-point on Hitler's instructions. It was an impressive effort but amounted to only 19% of Paulus's requirements because only 11 *Transportgruppen* were available, compared with 15 for Demyansk, forcing Fiebig to press the *Kampfgruppen* into service, largely to carry fuel, while *ObdL* cobbled together some more bomber-equipped *Gruppen*. Even these desperate means failed to raise the daily average number of sorties to more than 81; overall it was only 68 (see Table 47). An average 111 tonnes of supplies came in each day, and only on four days was Paulus's 300-tonne requirement reached, partly because the airlift's organisation was poor and the lessons of Demyansk do not appear to have been applied (Morzik appears to have been sidelined). Yet Paulus cannot escape blame for abrogating his responsibilities to prepare airfields and distribute supplies. The cost was high, with a 5.72% loss rate (279 aircraft destroyed or failing to return, 89 at night); 215 were damaged, while personnel losses were also heavy (114 between 28 December and 5 January). The greatest toll was among the 'Tante Jus', of which 174 were lost, many of them drawn from schools with instructors and advanced students, leading Göring later to comment that their destruction and the loss of 67 He 111s from the *Kampfgruppen* meant that 'There died the core of the German bomber fleet.' It also doomed hopes of effective participation by *FlFü Atlantik* in Dönitz's spring campaign by disrupting the introduction into service of the He 177.

The *VVS*'s growing strength meant that the *Luftwaffe* could not disengage units for refitting, and its strength was down to 1,600 aircraft while there was an acute shortage of long-range reconnaissance aircraft to cover a 300km-long front. The loss of forward airfields helped the enemy to achieve local air superiority, while the frequency of moves meant that *Gruppen* abandoned many unserviceable aircraft. Resources were strained due to intensive operations, numerous technical

---

Table 47. Stalingrad Airlift Weekly Performance, 24 November 1942–3 February 1943

Dates	Aircraft	Sorties	Supplies	Wounded
24–29 Nov	53	204	397	1,740
30 Nov–6 Dec	132	355	612	2,920
7–13 Dec	137	572	1,244	3,470
14–20 Dec	106	567	1,023	4,380
21–27 Dec	97	415	801	2,590
28 Dec–3 Jan	64	524	968	4,700
4–10 Jan	98	564	1,237	4,500
11–17 Jan	74	445	767.5	460
18–24 Jan	69	431	422.5	–
25–31 Jan	102	614	600.5	–
1–3 Feb	87	181	179	–
Total	–	4,872	8,250	24,760

Notes: Aircraft are daily average available. Sorties are those which reached Stalingrad and supplies delivered, with figures adjusted to 0.5 tonne.
Sources: Muller, pp.96–8, quoting *Sonderstab Milch* war diary (USNA T321, Roll 207); 'Aufzeichnungen des Genemaj Pickert, Kommandeurs der 9. Flak-Division und Generals der Lw bei der 6. Armee aus der Zeit vom 25.VI.42–23.I.43' (IWM AHB 6, Tin 20, fr.K1976–2080).

defects and inadequate repair facilities, while most men were exhausted, leading to low serviceability. As *6. Armee* died Manstein's *Heersgruppe Süd* (as it was renamed on 13 February) slowly retreated, but from 29 January it was threatened with envelopment as a new Russian offensive, 'Gallop', fragmented the remnants of *Heersgruppe B* in the north, with Korten able to provide only token air support. Manstein created *Armeeabteilung Kempf* to meet this threat, supported by Mahnke, while Hollidt anchored the *Heeresgruppe*'s right on the River Mius as Pfugbeil and the Romanian Air Corps covered the withdrawal of *1.* and *4. Panzer Armees* through Rostov. The vital enemy rail system was also struck by *Kampfgruppen*, supplemented since December by three dedicated Railway (*Eisenbahn*) *Staffeln* which produced several 'train-busting' *Experte*, including *Leutnant* Edo Cordes of *9. (Eis)/ KG 3*, who claimed 41 locomotives and 19 trains in three weeks while his *Kapitän*, *Hauptmann* Ernst Fach, claimed 216 locomotives before he crashed to his death in May 1943.[43]

To the south, *Heeresgruppe A* retreated from the Caucasus with air support provided since 25 November by Dessloch's *Luftwaffenkommando Kaukasus* (later *Kuban*) and with 7,000 men and some 250 guns of *Oberst* Eduard Muhr's *15. Flakdivision*, supported by *FlFü Krim* (*General der Flieger* Konrad Zander) with seaplanes and a few anti-shipping aircraft. Although *1. Panzer Armee* cut its way through to join Manstein, with the support of *4. Panzer Armee* and *Armeeabteilung Hollidt* (later *6. Armee*), *17. Armee* was pushed towards the sea until it established a bridgehead in the Kuban River valley behind the *Gotenkopfstellung* (Goth's Head Position). Immediately after Stalingrad's fall, the Condors of *KGrzbv 200* were assigned the task of supporting Dessloch and provided him with 254 tonnes of supplies while returning with 1,887 men and 12 tonnes of copper. They were replaced from mid-February by five veteran *Transportgruppen* from the Stalingrad airlift (whose losses were made up from other units), a *Gruppe* of Ju 52 floatplanes and three glider *Gruppen* of *Oberstleutnant Dr* Eggert's *LLG 1*. With some 180 transports, of which 120 were serviceable, these flew up to three sorties a day until the end of March, bringing in 5,418 tonnes of supplies and, despite Hitler's avowed intentions, flying out 15,500 men.[44]

As his front seemed on the verge of collapse Manstein perceived in the crisis an opportunity for a counter-stroke on his left. For once there was no opposition from Richthofen, who reined in subordinates previously fighting private wars and began to organise support for Manstein's grand design. He already had the lion's share of air support in the East (see Table 48), and he brought in the *Generäle der Kampf-* and *Jagdflieger* (*Oberstleutnant* Peltz and *Generalmajor* Galland, respectively) to help reorganise his forces with eight of the weakest *Gruppen* withdrawn to rest and re-equip, leaving their aircraft for redistribution (the bombers of *I./KG 100* went to *KG 55*). This move strengthened the remaining units while simultaneously reducing the strain on the infrastructure and congestion at airfields. Serv-

Table 48. Distribution of the *Luftwaffe* in the East, January–March 1943

		JGr	*Zgr*	*Kgr*	*StGr*	*SchGr*	*FAufSt*	*NahAufSt*
31 Jan	*Lfl 1*	1	–	2	1	–	4	4
	LwKdo Ost	1⅓	–	1	1⅓	–	5	9
	LwKdo Don	1	–	3⅓	1	⅓	3	3
	Lfl 4	2	2	8⅓	3	2	5	11
20 Feb	*Lfl 1*	2⅔	–	2	1⅔	–	4	4
	LwKdo Ost	2⅓	–	1	–	–	6	10
	Lfl 4	4	1⅓	11⅔	6	1⅔	8	11
10 Mar	*Lfl 1*	3⅓	–	1	–	–	4	4
	LwKdo Ost	3⅓	–	1	2	–	6	11
	Lfl 4	3	1	11⅔	5	2⅔	6	11

Note: ⅓ = one *Staffel*; ⅔ = two *Staffeln*.

iceability rapidly increased, and by February 23 Richthofen was congratulating the 'black men' upon their 'self-denying and meticulous work', helped by the fact that the *Luftwaffe* was returning to excellent bases built the previous year near major supply depots, such as Nikolaiev and Poltava, which accelerated re-equipment (especially of *Stuka-* and *Schlachtgruppen*). This ensured that within three weeks *Luftflotte 4* regained much of its effectiveness from its own resources, with the *Stukas* placed under Hozzel (*Kommodore* of StG 2) as *Gefechtsverband Hozzel*.

These were hectic times for Richthofen, who also had to attend conferences, one with Göring and Hitler on 11/12 February, giving him the opportunity to relax by hunting and catch up on lost sleep. He kept most of his forces in the Rostov area until 10 February before regrouping to support Manstein, moving his command train near Zaporozhye on 18 February. He retained control of the *Kampfgruppen*, whose bases were defended by *17. Flakdivision* (*Oberst* KarlVeith), but moved Korten's *Fliegerkorps I* (formerly *Luftwaffenkommando Don*) from Borispol, near Kiev, to Poltava to support Kempf with *10. Flakdivision* (*Generalleutnant* Johann Seifert). Fiebig was transferred to the Kuban, while Pflugbeil was at Dnepropetrovsk in the centre as Mahnke, his subordinate since the beginning of February, moved to Stalino with Hozzel and powerful close support forces to support *1. Panzer Armee*, aided by Muhr's *15. Flakdivision*. The *Funkhorchdienst* discovered that 'Gallop' had slowed to a shuffle, for the Russians were tired, with overstretched supply lines threatened by an early thaw. Indeed, in mid-February intercepted messages indicated that fuel shortages were crippling both *VVS* units and the offensive's spearhead, Lieutenant-General M. M. Popov's Mobile Group.

On 19 February *4. Panzer Armee*, now on Manstein's left, and Korten began the counter-stroke towards Kharkov, while Pflugbeil used Mahnke as his spearhead to help *1. Panzer Armee* isolate and crush Popov, Richthofen's men flying 1,145 sorties of 21 February and 1,486 the following day. As the situation improved Richthofen had time for a lie-in on 27 February while Manstein advanced upon Kharkov and Belgorod. The former was recaptured on 15 March and the latter three days later, but the *rasputitsa* then ended German ground operations, leaving the Russians with a huge salient around Kursk and bridgeheads over the lower Donetz. In supporting Manstein, Korten and Pflugbeil concentrated upon tactical air support and were encouraged to operate across command boundaries, the daily average sortie rate reaching 1,000 compared with 350 in January. They displayed extreme flexibility, which allowed Richthofen to direct the main effort and switch it between sectors with Hozzel supporting the army spearheads; the word 'concentration' frequently appeared in Richthofen's orders. Richthofen also had the advice of *Schlachtflieger Major* Otto Weiss, who led his *Versuchskommando für Panzerbekämpfung* (popularly known as *Panzerjägerkommando Weiss*) with Ju 87Ds and Hs 129Bs against armour with more success than the *Stukas* had achieved.[45] The Germans were aided by the relative absence of the *VVS*, which lost only 420 aircraft between 13 January and 3 April, and this also helped the *Luftwaffe* regain its old verve for mobile warfare.[46]

Richthofen set the pattern for *Luftwaffe* operations in the East until the end of the war. The usual response to break-throughs was tactical strikes aimed at blunting the spearheads (detected by the *Nahaufklärungsstaffeln*), but new crises would often draw away the *Gruppen* before they succeeded. The close support (*Schlacht* from October 1943) units, flying at 1,800m (6,000ft), would make shallow dive attacks with anti-personnel and armour-piercing bombs against weapons, armour concentrations, transport and signal centres. Ground fire was a growing hazard and, with reports that light AA batteries were often manned by women, the German crews referred to missions as 'a date with the *Flak* girls' and each formation would allocate crews to 'entertain' the ladies with bombs and automatic weapons. Yet, despite the dangers, there was never any shortage of pilots, because the *A/B-Schule* would often 'nudge' promising students in the 'right' direction. Anti-tank units would usually operate in *Staffel* formation while *Nachtschlachtgruppen* would fly individually to strike batteries, transport and troop concentrations. The *Schlachtgruppen* usually operated within 150km of their bases, and from late in 1943 they benefited both from radio beacons and improvised radio telephone communications.[47] With close support forces overextended, the *Kampfgruppen* were also involved in these missions and were used more rarely in their traditional operational role of interdicting communications and striking airfields, supply dumps and headquarters. Despite the growing physical and qualitative strength of the *VVS*, the *Luftwaffe* continued to operate largely in the daytime until almost the end of the war, while against the RAF and USAAF it became largely a night time force by 1944.[48] However, the time actually spent behind the enemy lines was short: *Leutnant* Elmar Börsch of *KG 4* noted after the war that, of the first 100 of his 312 sorties, only 7% involved more than 10 minutes over enemy territory, and there was a similar ratio for his second century.[49]

190

Manstein's success at Kharkov was clearly a momentary one, for Soviet military power had increased substantially and soon Stalin would resume the offensive. The *VVS*, for example, had 8,290 combat aircraft (including Po-2s, reserves and the *PVO*), while *Luftwaffe* first-line strength had risen from 1,993 combat aircraft in March to 2,330 (excluding *Luftflotte 5*) and 209 transports by the end of May, out of an overall strength of some 6,000.[50] There was also some qualitative improvement as new aircraft such as the Fw 190 arrived. Moreover, the Allied and satellite formations benefited from growing German production, and while they remained of uneven quality, they covered secondary sectors, allowing the *Luftwaffe* to concentrate in the key sectors.

Meanwhile Hitler, seeking to regain the initiative, developed Manstein's proposals for pre-emptive strikes into a double envelopment of the Kursk salient as *Unternehmen 'Zitadelle'* with an outline order published on 13 March. *'Zitadelle'* was intended to begin around May Day, but delays, largely instigated by *Generalfeldmarschall* Günther von Kluge of *Heersgruppe Mitte*, thwarted this plan. Jeschonnek vainly objected to any delay at a conference on 3 May, noting that it would not benefit the *Luftwaffe*, which was completely prepared, and that Richthofen was already countering an enemy air offensive.

The prospect of offensive operations was especially pleasing for the former fighter ace Greim (*Luftwaffekommando Ost*) who had spent 1942 efficiently supporting the noisy, but secondary, central front, using excellent command and control with a well-organised infrastructure.[51] Recognising that he could not control the untidily extended front, Greim divided it in mid-April 1942 between *Fliegerdivision 1*, initially under Fiebig, in the north and *Fliegerdivision 2*, under former *FlFü Afrika Generalleutnant* Fröhlich, in the south. Greim's resources were adequate, although he faced threats from partisans in the rear and his *Kampfgeschwader* used their *Ergänzungsgruppen* against them.[52] His most serious test came in late November 1942 when a diversionary operation in support of the Stalingrad operation isolated the 7,000-man garrison at Velikiye Luki, which was sustained through supply drops and later by gliders which brought into the contracting pocket supplies and heavy weapons, including anti-tank guns. A month elapsed before any relief was attempted, and on 15/16 January the survivors broke out, although only 176 reached the German lines and the *Luftwaffe* lost 55 aircraft.[53] The siege demonstrated *Heersgruppe Mitte*'s exposure, and in the aftermath of Paulus's surrender Hitler reluctantly sanctioned the abandonment of the Rhzev salient, which shortened the line by mid-March, releasing much-needed resources. The *Luftwaffe* withdrew to airfields around Smolensk after blowing up the abandoned ones and Greim then supported *2. Panzer Armee* and *2. Armee* holding Orel on the right.

Rather than lose his *Kampfgruppen* in the maelstrom around Stalingrad, Greim ensured that they were constantly active, even when the armies were licking their wounds. His bases around Smolensk were well placed to strike industry, and during the spring of 1942 he flew small-scale raids (sometimes little more that *Störangriffe* by individual bombers) against targets up to 900km east of Smolensk until an upsurge in Russian military activity in June brought these operations to an end. They resumed in October, but Greim's staff used the intervening period to begin a study for a strategic bombing campaign, assisted by *1./ObdL*, which included Ju 86P high-altitude reconnaissance aircraft, and by military intelligence agents (*Abwehr V-Männer*), many of whom flew out of Greim's bases.[54]

Because of the delays to '*Zitadelle*' Greim was again able to indulge his interest in bombing, and within a week of his command being renamed *Luftflotte 6* his *Kampfgruppen* began a campaign on 12 May against targets, especially railways, up to 300km behind the lines.[55] It was subsequently claimed that these attacks disrupted the enemy's preparations and forced him to move his railheads eastwards, but the German rail system also came under severe pressure as the Russians, well aware of German intentions, retaliated in kind.[56] This provoked fierce air battles, during which *Oberstleutnant* Karl-Gottfried Nordmann's *JG 51 'Mölders'* claimed more than 170 victories between 5 and 10 June. During June Greim's airmen flew 8,995 combat sorties and suffered a 0.66% loss rate (60 aircraft, the majority to fighters), but concern over enemy night harassing operations led Kammhuber to reinforce the *Luftflotten's Nachtjagdschwärme* with two *Staffeln* of *NJG 5* and also rail-mounted radars.[57] The night threat from the *ADD* (which had 950 bombers and transports) became serious enough for the *Luftwaffe* to establish nine mobile *Himmelbett* stations in *Luftflotten 6* and *4*, supporting nine *Nachtjagdstaffeln*.[58] In early June Greim coordinated a month-long bombing campaign involving 1,813 sorties which was essentially operational in nature but had sufficient success to encourage hopes for a more ambitious campaign later.[59] It also led the Russians to make a substantial reorganisation of the *PVO*, dividing it into two sectors, the Western and Eastern Fronts, with 1,459 fighters and 7,400 AA guns, the former covering Moscow and potential targets to the north and the latter the Urals, the Volga and the Caucasus.[60]

Richthofen also used the enforced delay to good effect, striking airfields and communications as far east as the Volga between March and July. From late March he also supported *Heeresgruppe A*'s defence of the Kuban bridgehead, which was ostensibly held as a springboard for a renewed offensive against the Caucasian oilfields. The task was 'subcontracted' to Fiebig's *Fliegerkorps VIII*, supported by the maritime reconnaissance *SeeFlFü Schwarzesmeer* based on *SAGr 125* and operating largely from the Crimea, for there were few airfields in the bridgehead. Air defence was provided by the re-formed *9. Flakdivision* with 78 batteries under its old commander Pickert, who was also responsible for coast defence. On 1 April Fiebig was transferred to the 'mainland' and replaced by Korten's *Fliegerkorps I*, whose six *Gruppen*, with Romanian and Slovak support, were to crush beach-heads established at Novorossiysk in February. The attack began on 17 April and Korten, with 600 aircraft, flew an average 400 sorties per 24 hours while his *Stukas* flew up to 1,000 sorties, but the Russians held on and matched the build-up with one of their own to 800 aircraft, which soon forced the *Luftwaffe* on to the defensive. The Russians used these battles as a tactical proving ground and, like the RAF, developed tactics of mutually supporting layers. *Panzerjägerkommando Weiss* also operated over the Kuban with an assortment of aircraft, including the Hs 129 B-2 with 30mm cannon, anti-tank versions of the Bf 110G-2 (R1, R2 and and R4) and the Ju 87G with 37mm guns. Rudel and *Hauptmann* Hans-Karl Stepp developed the Ju 87G into a formidable weapon, but from early May the fighting died down because most of Korten's *Gruppen* were transferred north-wards for *'Zitadelle'*.[61]

This had continued to be plagued by delays, and only on 20 June did Hitler set A-Day for 5 July. Since late March Greim had prepared for the offensive with reinforcements from within theatre by stripping quiet sectors. *Fliegerdivision 1*, now under Deichmann, was to support Kluge's thrust, but ominous signs of an impending Russian offensive against the Orel salient led Greim to allocate a small staff with a few *Staffeln* and two signal regiments as a contingency headquarters. Meanwhile Richthofen transferred *Fliegerkorps VIII*, now under Seidemann fol-lowing Fiebig's departure to *Luftwaffenkommando Südost*, from the Crimea to sup-port Manstein and assigned it the 2nd Hungarian Air Brigade. Yet Richthofen was on borrowed time, for Göring planned to have him and Jeschonnek exchange places, a prospect more pleasing to the *Luftwaffe* Chief of Staff than to Richthofen, who viewed both the prospect of entering *'Robinson'* and leaving his *Luftflotte* at a critical time with considerable alarm. An unsatisfactory solution was provided by the increasingly tense strategic situation in the Mediterranean, where Kesselring could no longer exercise personal command of *Luftflotte 2*. Richthofen was offered the command, and, although extremely pessimistic about the prospects, he evi-dently regarded it as the lesser of two evils and departed in June, taking with him Bülowius and Mahnke. Jeschonnek, who visited *Luftflotte 4* headquarters on sev-eral occasions to familiarise himself with the sector, eagerly anticipated his depar-ture from *'Robinson'*, but to mollify Manstein, who was alarmed at the prospect of lower quality air support, Göring appointed Dessloch as Richthofen's replace-ment. Dessloch was a Bavarian officer who became an 'Old Eagle' during the Great War and received refresher training while serving with the *Reichsheer*. He had held a variety of posts after joining the *Luftwaffe* in 1933 and commanded *Fliegerdivision 6* in 1939; he had then held *Flak* commands, but from June 1943 until the end of the war he returned to commanding air units. Curiously, he never officially become commander-in-chief (*Oberbefehlshaber*) of *Luftflotte 4*, and even from 4 September he was officially only acting commander (*Chef*)—indeed, until that date Richthofen was officially *Oberbefehlshaber* of both *Luftflotte 2* and *Luftflotte*

4.[62] Jeschonnek retained faint hopes of succeeding Richthofen well into July, and was at Dessloch's command post for the beginning of *'Zitadelle'*. As it became clear that *'Robinson'* was a prison from which he would never escape, Jeschonnek became increasingly depressed.

Meanwhile preparations for *'Zitadelle'* had continued, but with every summer week the *Aufklärungsstaffeln* brought photographs and reports showing the Russians fortifying the salient. Greim, whose aircraft flew 1,638 sorties photographing the entire 18,600 sq km salient from early April, also reported much traffic from the interior to Kursk and Kharkov, while in the following weeks COMINT reported a growing number of *VVS* units within the salient, including the 2nd, 16th and 17th Air Armies, which had 2,900 aircraft (including 400 Po-2s). By the beginning of July the *Luftwaffe* had concentrated 80% of its Eastern Front force around the Kursk salient, although at 1,830 aircraft this was only 66% of the

Table 49. *Unternehmen 'Zitadelle'* **Operations**

Luftflotte 6

Date	Fighter	Bomber	*Stuka*	*Schlacht/Jabo*	Recon	Night	Total	Losses
5 Jul	522	582	647	168	141	15	2,075	7
6 Jul	317	164	289	93	139	92	1,094	7
7 Jul	307	454	582	123	195	134	1,795	3
8 Jul	291	274	378	73	100	6	1,122	2
9 Jul	255	138	181	52	164	22	765	5
10 Jul	266	220	375	66	134	51	1,112	7
11 Jul	283	226	249	20	111	21	910	2
12 Jul	345	173	419	89	85	15	1,126	13
13 Jul	320	234	415	59	85	–	1,113	18
14 Jul	208	210	410	55	96	7	986	20
15 Jul	200	36	250	96	121	211	914	10
Total	3,059	2,711	4,195	894	1,371	574	13,012	94

Luftflotte 4

Date	Fighter	Bomber	*Stuka*	*Schlacht/Jabo*	Recon	Night	Total	Losses
5 Jul	371	536	1,071	335	74	–	2,387	19
6 Jul	253	323	793	240	77	–	1,686	7
7 Jul	297	498	746	200	88	64	1,893	10
8 Jul	229	493	701	681	77	28	2,209	5
9 Jul	248	384	699	183	97	–	1,611	11
10 Jul		682 day			18	700	3	
11 Jul	176	197	447	176	62	61	1,119	14
12 Jul	191	13	150	248	52	–	654	11
13 Jul	204	60	239	103	50	28	684	5
14 Jul	238	486	510	135	83	40	1,492	9
15 Jul	132	282	191	68	33	111	817	5
Total	2,339	3,272	5,547	2,369	693	350	15,252	99

Notes: Losses are probably only aircraft which failed to return.
Sources: Klink, Apps II/7, II/8.

strength of the force which supported 'Blau'. Deichmann had 730 aircraft supported by *Generalleutnant* Ernst Buffa's *12. Flak Division* and *Generalmajor* Paul Pavel's *10. Flak Brigade*, with a total of 140 batteries, while Seidemann had 1,100 aircraft supported by *Generalleutnant* Richard Reimann's *I. Flak Korps (10., 15. and 17. Flak Divisions)*. Supplementing Dessloch's forces were the 2nd Hungarian Air Brigade and 1st Romanian Air Corps with a total of 275 aircraft. Ammunition stocks were adequate, but the East was receiving a monthly allocation of only 160,000 tonnes of fuel when consumption was 350,000 tonnes: during the offensive Greim consumed 9,713 tonnes and received 6,163, forcing him to mould missions on the basis of fuel availability.

The last *Gruppen* reached their bases on the evening of 4 July and attacks began at dawn the following day, Seidemann's being delayed as the *Jagdgruppen* smashed a pre-emptive bomber attack detected by radar, with Jeschonnek witnessing some of the 120 victories claimed. Excellent summer weather and long days ensured good support, some pilots flying up to eight sorties a day. Deichmann initially struck airfields and artillery but encountered stronger fighter resistance than Seidemann, who concentrated on tactical air support for first the *SS Panzer Korps* and then *XLVIII. Panzer Korps* and responded enthusiastically to requests from *Flivos*. On the first day the *Luftwaffe* was more active than its enemies, flying 4,462 sorties against 3,385, but Deichmann could not compensate for Kluge's bulldozer approach, which was effectively stopped on 8 July. Manstein infiltrated the fortifications, aided by the *Luftwaffe*'s anti-tank *Staffeln*, including the redoubtable Rudel, who claimed 12 tanks on the first day. Although Manstein almost broke through, the men were exhausted and by 11 July both 'Zitadelle' and the *Luftwaffe* were running out of steam, with declining serviceability and sortie rates (see Table 49). The strength of the *VVS* prevented the Germans from controlling the skies and the *Landsers* were attacked up to 25km behind their own lines, although radar and the *Funkhorchdienst* provided partial compensation for the *Jagdgruppen*'s numerical weakness.

The long-anticipated Russian offensive against the Orel salient began on 12 July, diverting most of Greim's forces, including Deichmann's headquarters, although with little effect as the enemy exploited the cover of the woods, forcing Greim to concentrate against railheads. With Seidemann's help Deichmann had 450 aircraft, which flew up to six sorties a day, and when the Russians left the woods the *Luftwaffe* helped to slow their advance until heavy rain turned the battlefield into a quagmire in late July, allowing the Germans to occupy positions at the base of the Orel salient. By mid-August Deichmann had flown 37,421 sorties, dropped more than 20,000 tonnes of bombs and claimed 1,733 victories (1,671 by the *Jagdgruppen*), for the loss of 64 aircraft (a 0.17% loss rate). *Flak* had played an important part in the defence, and *12. Flak Division* claimed the destruction of 383 aircraft and 229 tanks. But of greater concern to Hitler was the Allied landing in Sicily, and on 13 July he ordered the abandonment of '*Zitadelle*'. The Russians in the salient were exhausted, having lost 14% of their men and nearly half their armour as well as 459 aircraft (nearly 16% of their initial strength). The *VVS* had flown as many sorties as the *Luftwaffe*, but the situation in the Mediterranean and growing Russian pressure along the southern half of the front forced Hitler's hand. During late July there were ominous signs of another Russian offensive around Belgorod and Kharkov, but threats to Orel and on Manstein's right meant that Seidemann was stripped of aircraft to reinforce Deichmann and Pflugbeil. When *Oberst* Helmut Bruck's *StG 77* went to the latter on 16 July, Seidemann became dependent upon the Hungarians (with 70 aircraft) until, a fortnight later on 3 August, the Russians broke through at Belgorod, which fell within two days. Pflugbeil hastily returned Bruck as Seidemann vainly strove to defend Kharkov, which fell on 21 August, the *Fliegerkorps* flying up to 1,000 sorties a day and even using SC 1800 'Satan' blockbusters.[63]

The loss of Orel and Kharkov unlocked the Eastern Front: during the next eight months the Germans were driven westwards and the *Luftwaffe*, which had lost 1,030 aircraft in July and August, could not help.[64] In the northern and central sectors a new series of fortifications, the *Pantherstellung* (Panther Position), would underpin the line until the following summer, but work on its southern equivalent, the *Wotanstellung* (Wotan Position) along the Dnieper, had barely begun when Manstein entered it with the Russians hard on his heels supported by 2,850 aircraft. The *Wotanstellung* was broken and the Russians flooded into the Ukraine, leaving Manstein clinging to the wreckage of his command, which eventually came to rest during the spring of 1944 in Poland, Slovakia, Hungary and Romania. Despite occasional brilliant ripostes, Manstein, and his southern neighbour List, could do nothing to stem the flow of the enemy, who was constrained only by exhaustion.

The *Luftwaffe* was the spearhead of the *Wehrmacht*'s efforts to contain enemy thrusts, being committed whenever there was a break-through in what came to be called '*Feuerwehr Taktik*' (fire fighting tactics). The 'firemen' claimed numerous local successes, but these were temporary at best, and with Reich defence leading to the withdrawal of five *Jagd-* and *Zerstörergruppen* during the autumn, including the whole of *JG 3*, the strike force often flew without escort in daylight and suffered heavy wastage without significantly affecting the course of ground operations. Worse still, the airmen were frittered away through incoherent solutions to local crises. By the New Year the *Luftwaffe*'s first-line strength in the East had dropped to 1,683 combat aircraft, while in January 1944 the *VVS* had 8,818 with 313 reserves.

In the centre Greim anticipated the threat during the summer of 1943 by creating Plocher's *Fliegerdivision 4* to cover the Smolensk sector. During the latter half of September he successfully covered the retreat into the *Pantherstellung*, us-

Table 50. *Fliegerdivision 4* Sorties

	Day	Night	Total	Strength
10 Oct	714	88	802	960
11 Oct	552	114	666	747
12 Oct	488	81	569	908
13 Oct	519	47	566	829
14 Oct	441	99	540	722
15 Oct	473	85	558	752
Total	3,187	514	3,701	–

Source: '*Einsätze der Luftwaffe in der Zeit 10.10-31.10.1943*', *Luftwaffenführungsstab Ic*, quoted by Plocher, pp.114–16.

ing daylight delaying actions complemented by systematic night harassing operations against communications. The Germans destroyed 303 aircraft but could not prevent the loss of Smolensk on 24 September, and they had barely reached the *Pantherstellung* when pressure grew between Vitebsk and Orsha which lasted until early January 1944. *Fliegerdivision 1*, later under Fuchs, who had become the first *Kampfflieger* to win a *Ritterkreuz* during the 1940 Norwegian Campaign, helped stiffen the defence, while some idea of *Luftwaffe* activity can be gained from a report of Reuss's *Fliegerdivision 4* covering just six days (see Table 50). With a daily average strength of 819 aircraft, he flew an average 617 sorties every 24 hours, of which some 12% were, unusually, against partisan bands. Here, as everywhere else on the Eastern Front, *Flak* batteries were an integral part of the defence, and, to tighten control of them throughout the *Heersgruppe*'s operational depth, *II. Flak Korps* (*Generalleutnant* Job Oldebrecht) was assigned on 3 November 1943.

In the Ukraine *Luftwaffe* operations were compromised by the frequent abandonment of bases and command posts with their landline networks. *ObdL* insisted that abandoned airfields should be thoroughly destroyed while simultaneously demanding operations until the last possible moment. To square the circle, buildings were generally demolished and most runways ploughed up, then mined, leaving one in commission until the final sorties took off, often as shells fell on the boundary; *Flak* batteries would then hold off the enemy until demolition was completed. However, thrusts deep into the German rear meant that the *Luftwaffe*'s infrastructure of depots, repair shops and aircraft parks kept moving westward, disrupting the supply system. The mud and fast-moving Russian armour were also threats, and between February and May of 1944 *Flak* units supporting List lost 4,000 of their 9,000 vehicles.

In the retreat to the Dnieper during August and September, Seidemann's *Fliegerkorps VIII* tried to shield the retreating troops while Meister's *Fliegerkorps IV* remained in the Crimea supporting the shrinking Kuban bridgehead. The strain was considerable, and only after a new attack upon *Heeresgruppe A* began on 9

October were changes made, Seidemann flying 867 day and 158 night sorties on 10 October alone. Meister took over the southern sector of Manstein's front and was then relieved on 14 October by Angerstein's *Fliegerkorps I* and withdrawn to control *Kampfgruppen* in anticipation of becoming a strategic bomber force. Seidemann now shielded Manstein's northern flank while Angerstein supported List's *Heeresgruppe A* from the Crimea as the Kuban bridgehead was evacuated, the *Transportgruppen* moving 15,661 men and 1,154 tonnes of equipment by the time the last troops had been withdrawn on 9/10 October. Angerstein then moved to the 'mainland' to cover List and Manstein's southern flank, leaving the Crimea's defence to *FlFü Krim* (*Oberst* Joachim Albrecht Bauer) and *SeeFlFü Schwarzesmeer* (now under *Oberstleutnant* Schalke), supported by *9. Flak Division* (55 batteries). The defenders had a rare success on 9 October when *Stukas* sank three destroyers bombarding Yalta.

List's retreat during October isolated the Crimea, while on Manstein's front the *Luftwaffe*'s excellent bases at Krivoi Rog were under threat from 20 October, but Dessloch exploited the *Kampfgruppen* mercilessly with two sorties a day here and a third some 300km to the north in the defence of Kiev. Exploiting other airfields, the *Luftwaffe* flew up to 1,200 sorties a day to support a timely counter-attack which saved the bases until February, but attempts to interdict communications by bombing bridges over the Dnieper and using *14. (Eis)/KG 55* against railways had limited effect. The *rasputista* hindered single-engine aircraft operations and the 'black men' often had to use horses or oxen to move aircraft around the muddy forward airfields. Barely had the threat to Krivoi Rog ended when a Russian offensive took Kiev on 6 November after Seidemann's *4. (F)/Nacht* reported major Russian movements towards their bridgehead north of the city. Unfortunately, Manstein was convinced that the threat would come from the south, and Seidemann, who had been stripped to reinforce Meister, concentrated his strike force there, with *Kampfgruppen* using *Y-Verfahren* for some night attacks. The Russians came close to dividing *Heersgruppen Mitte* and *Süd* until they were temporarily stopped on 23 November with the support of all available *Luftwaffe* units despite rain, low cloud and fog. Seidemann was reinforced and was fortunate that the *VVS* did not exploit the congestion at his handful of all-weather airfields. The uncertain weather conditions grounded the *Luftwaffe* for nearly a month and Meister's *Kampfgruppen* were finally withdrawn for conversion to a strategic bombing force. Deichmann's *Fliegerkorps I* now covered the southern sector, but when Deichmann reached Kirovgrad as the Russians were approaching he discovered that a snowstorm had trapped more than 100 aircraft. Fortunately the enemy ran out of fuel, the weather improved and the aircraft managed to escape. By the New Year Dessloch had 1,150 aircraft, 68% of the *Luftwaffe*'s first line strength in the East, as the situation in the Ukraine verged on the catastrophic.[65]

On Christmas Eve the Russians resumed their attempt to envelop Manstein and List. A lack of aircraft restricted the *Luftwaffe* response, although Dessloch correctly anticipated that the main blow would come from Kiev and reinforced Seidemann, who received tactical control of Deichmann's *Kampfgruppen* (which remained in their southern bases) as well as 100 *Schlachtflieger* from *Fliegerkorps I*. Bad weather, poor airfields, frequent moves and the transfer to central Poland (650km away) of the infrastructure adversely affected maintenance, and with serviceability rates low there were barely 300–350 sorties per day. The effort wore down the *Schlachtgruppen* and dashed hopes of re-equipping both the *Stukagruppen* and the Fw 189-equipped *Nahaufklärungsstaffeln*, the latter confirming on 28 January 1944 that a Russian thrust, supported by 768 aircraft, had isolated 56,000 men of *XI*. and *XLII. Armee Korps* near Cherkassy. The following day three *Transportgruppen* began flying in supplies, but fog and snow restricted operations and when the weather cleared the temperature rose, turning the airfields to marshes and causing the loss of 44 transports in the first five days. A new airfield was built on firmer ground by 9 February, but only 100–185 tonnes a day could be flown in as a relief operation began which helped 30,000 men escape on 16/17 February. The *Transportgruppen* flew 1,500 sorties to bring in 2,026 tonnes of supplies and to evacuate 2,400 wounded, but 32 aircraft were lost and 113 damaged.[66]

The Russians now carved great gaps in the German line and, as at Cherkassy, the *Luftwaffe*'s primary role increasingly became one of transport. With Russian pressure along the whole front, the *Luftwaffe* was unable to concentrate in one sector and frittered its resources in penny packets to provide the illusion of air support.[67] The *Stukagruppen*, especially, struggled for survival, and many *Experten* failed to return, including the great *Major* Rudel, *Kommandeur* of *III./SG 2*, whose aircraft stuck in the mud on 20 March when he attempted his seventh rescue of a downed crew. Rudel narrowly escaped capture and had to flee across country, reaching German lines in rags but without his trusty radio-operator/gunner *Feldwebel* Erwin Hentschel, with whom he had flown 1,200 sorties and who was drowned crossing a river.[68] *Hauptmann* Alwin Boerst, *Kommandeur* of *I./SG 2*, did not have Rudel's luck and failed to return from a mission 10 days later. The *Luftwaffe* was too weak to provide serious opposition to a secondary Russian advance eastwards towards Poland which cut Manstein's rail link to the Reich early in March, although the Russians were unable to use it until they took Ternopol on 15 April after a month's siege. The 4,000-man garrison held out, aided by air supply initially from five *Transportgruppen* (one with He 111s) and a glider *Gruppe*, supplemented by Meister's *Kampfgruppen*, but soon only the gliders of *Schleppgruppe 2* were used because of a greater crisis in the south, where Korten's applications of the lessons of both Stalingrad and Cherkassy helped bring triumph from adversity. Following the isolation of *Generaloberst* Hube's 300,000-strong *1. Panzer Armee*, Manstein decided on 25 March that it should escape westwards rather than to the south, and to sustain it *Generalmajor* Morzik was sent to control all transport operations in *Luftflotte 4* as *Transportfliegerführer 2* (*TFF 2*). He arrived at Krosno in Poland on the day of Manstein's decision, and to support the moving pocket he relied upon the 150 transports which had been supplying Ternopol as well as 100 of Meister's bombers, the large transport fleet at Odessa being too far away for practical use. The ferry began in ominous conditions, snow, low cloud and poor visibility, but the weather rapidly improved, while the preparations for supporting the aircraft and receiving and distributing supplies were far better because Hube, a Stalingrad veteran, had also appreciated the lessons. The Russians were too weak to stop the pocket moving or to prevent the laying down of airstrips to bring in the previous food, fuel and ammunition which helped it to reach German positions on 6 April, where it quickly established a firm new defensive front. Tragically, while flying back to his troops after receiving the Diamonds to his *Ritterkreuz*, Hube was killed in a crash on 21 April.[69]

Manstein's right, *8.* and *6. Armee*, retreated south-westwards towards the Romanian border on the Dniester from early March, assisted by the move of part of *3. SS Panzer Division 'Totenkopf'* in Me 323 Gigant transports of *Major* Günter Mauss's *I./TG 5* at the instigation of *8. Armee* commander *General der Infanterie* Otto Wöhler.[70] Dessloch, flying an average of 700 sorties each day (and more than a 1,000 on five occasions), used Deichmann and Seidemann to support *8. Armee* from 17 March, leaving the 2nd Romanian Air Corps (120 aircraft) to protect *6. Armee*, but Nikolaev fell on 28 March followed by Odessa on 10 April (see Table 51 for operations). The *Luftwaffe* was almost exhausted, Dessloch had fewer than 1,800 aircraft at the end of the month and his *Jagdgruppen* had only 42 serviceable fighters on 20 March, but the Dniester provided the necessary breakwater and by mid-April the Russian fury had abated. However, Manstein and Kleist were both relieved on 30 March, their commands being renamed *Heersgruppe Nordukraine* and *Südukraine* respectively.[71] The Russians' losses were heavy, 1.9 million dead in the year after July 1943 and at least 4,100 combat aircraft, but they were well placed to renew the offensive along the whole front during the summer and the Germans had few natural defences.[72]

Table 51. *Luftflotten 4* and 6 Operations, March 1944

Date	Luftflotte 4		Luftflotte 6		Total
	Day	Night	Day	Night	
1–10 Mar	5,008	57	2,406	348	7,819
11–20 Mar	8,608	351	1,112	102	10,173
21–30 Mar	6,766	78	2,255	276	9,375
Total	20,382	486	5,773	726	27,367

Source: 'Lagekarten Ost, Marz 1944', USNA T321, Roll 86, fr.411.

Meanwhile the loss of Odessa disrupted the air ferry to the Crimea, for Morzik's *TFF 2* had based seven *Transportgruppen* there under *Oberst* Walter Erdmann's *TG 2* and *Oberstleutnant* Fritz Schroeder's *TG 3*, as well as a glider *Gruppe*.[73] These moved to Foscani in Romania to maintain the airlift, whose importance grew when a Russian offensive from 8 April drove the garrison into Sevastopol. Bauer's *FlFü Krim*, with only 160 German and Romanian aircraft (85 serviceable), flew 2,400 sorties, while Fuchs' *Fliegerkorps I* provided *III./SG 3* and some fighters, the former claiming 160 tanks, but neither could change the course of events and by 20 April artillery fire had rendered the naval base's main airfield unusable.[74] Morzik's men took out 21,457 wounded and essential experts (Romanian aircraft removed a further 3,056) as Hitler dithered about an evacuation. He gave permission only on 6 May, by which time the final assault had commenced, and within two days the last airstrip had been lost as the German and Romanian Navies, covered by 70–80 aircraft, managed to evacuate 38,000 of the 64,700-strong garrison. Between 4 and 14 May Fuchs' men (including Bauer) flew 2,010 combat sorties, 332 of them maritime reconnaissance and air–sea rescue. Bauer's men lost 87 aircraft (76 abandoned) while Fuchs lost 10, but they largely succeeded in shielding the evacuation from enemy air and naval interference and destroyed 179 Russian aircraft. But *9. Flakdivision* was again destroyed, with most of its men and 490 guns, and while Bauer and his staff were evacuated by flying boat on 10/11 May only 430 of his men had similar fortune.[75]

On Greim's northern flank *Luftflotte 1* flew over what was a backwater following the relief of the Demyansk pocket, and on 19 July 1942 *Fliegerkorps I* was transferred to *Luftflotte 4*; a month later, almost in exchange, came a small staff under *Oberstleutnant* Torsten Christ (the Condor Legion's Operations Officer in mid-1938) to prepare air support for Manstein's projected assault upon Leningrad. Christ returned to the south in November to become *Fliegerkorps IV* Chief of Staff, but his staff became *Fliegerdivision 3* under Rieckhoff in February 1943 after the Russians had raised the siege. Rieckhoff continued to act as Keller's Chief of Staff until relieved by Rohden a month later, the first in a remarkable turnover at the *Luftflotte*'s headquarters. Keller was replaced by Korten and then Pflugbeil, while Rohden was given responsibility for *Luftwaffe* history and replaced by Uebe. The shortage of resources meant that *Major* Rudolf Jenett's *Nachtschlachtgruppe* was used in daylight to support counter-insurgency operations on the boundary of *Heersgruppen Nord* and *Mitte* as well as being a factor in the creation of the *Luftwaffe*'s 'Foreign Legion'.

The value of harnessing nationalist and anti-Communist sentiments in the Baltic states was recognised throughout the *Wehrmacht*, but the first use of airmen in February 1942 was under naval auspices. *Hauptmann* Buschmann created *Sonderstaffel Buschmann* from Estonian airmen flying German trainers and light aircraft as well as De Havilland DH 89As, Miles Magisters and Stampe SV-5s on anti-submarine and liaison missions, with *Luftflotte 1* providing technical assistance. In April 1943 the *Staffel* was expanded into *Aufkl. Gr 127 (See)* (later *SAGr 127*), with such success that it was decided to give it a more active role. In October it became *NSGr 11 (Est)*, while recruiting also began in Latvia for what became *NSGr 12 (Lett)* four months later. Meanwhile attempts were made to recruit Russian troops under General Andrei Vlassov, and as part of this movement *Ostfliegerstaffel 1* was created in December 1943. Plans existed for a Russian air force, and the former head of the Aeroflot sanatorium in Yalta, *Oberst* Viktor Ivanovich Malcev, headed a *Fliegergruppe* under *Oberstleutnant* Holter training Russian airmen. Malcev became *Befehlshaber der Luftstrietkräfte der Völker Russlands im Verband der deutschen Luftwaffe* as a *Generalmajor* in March 1945, fell into Russian hands at the end of the war and was shot.[76]

In mid-January 1944 the unwelcome spotlight fell once again on *Luftflotte 1* with a massive offensive supported by 1,140 Russian aircraft which drove *Heersgruppe Nord* back to the *Pantherstellung*. The Russians encountered a feeble but gallant air defence which inflicted a 1.5% loss rate (260 aircraft) but received few reinforcements due to the greater crises in the Ukraine and Italy. Army enthusiasm was muted, especially when *Stukas* helping to thwart a small amphibious operation near Narva accidentally hit a German divisional headquarters and knocked out some Tiger tanks. The lack of reinforcements was unfortunate, for the *Luftwaffe* lost bases which were scheduled to play an important role in Meister's planned strategic bombing campaign.[77]

The retreat to the *Pantherstellung* proved to be a severe setback for German hopes during the winter of 1943/44 for a strategic bombing campaign from the spring. The first step was on 26 November when Göring authorised the concentration of eight Eastern *Kampfgruppen* under *Fliegerkorps IV* (which was often referred to simply as *Korps Meister*), to operate from bases in Greim's sector but under *ObdL's* direct control. The *Gruppen* concentrated in the rear during December under *Auffrischungsstab Ost* (Eastern Replenishment Staff) to rest and recover their strength then began rigorous training for their new assignment, which they accepted with relish. Most missions would have to be at night, and Meister imitated Bomber Command tactics with *KG 4* providing what proved to be a very proficient Pathfinder force, although plans to re-equip it with Ju 188s fell foul of the priority assigned to the new attack on England, *Unternehmen 'Steinbock'*. Detailed planning began in February 1944 with a comprehensive programme for striking production and material reserves, worked out with the *Reichsministerium für Rüstung und Kriegsproduktion* and *Luftwaffe* Intelligence. It was calculated that 50–80% of productive capacity (estimated at 3,500 tanks and 3,000 first-line aircraft per month) could be eliminated.

Although training was disrupted by the use of *KG 53* and *KG 55* for supply drops in the northern Ukraine and most of the key bases had been lost through

Heeresgruppe Nord's retreat, a mission began to appear in late February. Preparations for an offensive were observed around Kovel, 130km from Meister's headquarters at Brest-Litovsk, and these reports, together with the desire of both Korten and Meister for operational training, led to a plan to strike the enemy rail network in the western Ukraine. The campaign, *Unternehmen 'Zaunkönig'* (Wren), began on 27/28 March when 50 bombers struck Sarni with some success, and another 44 missions involving some 7,000 sorties were flown against railway stations until mid-June. The assessment was that 17 missions had 'very good' or 'good' results, while losses appear to have been about 1%. Despite the provision of radio navigation systems in Warsaw and Pinsk, the *Kampfgruppen* (as in the Blitz) preferred to operate in bright moonlight, but they encountered few night fighters. In late May *Oberstleutnant* Horst von Riesen's *KG 1* began high-altitude daylight operations with the He 177 from East Prussia in formations of up to 87 aircraft, but battlefield interdiction, an operational rather than a strategic objective, remained Meister's sole role.[78]

Meanwhile the Germans used the spring and early summer to rebuild and re-equip units: the *Schlachtgruppen* began passing their Ju 87s to the *Nachtschlachtgruppen* while more *Nahaufklärungsgruppen* received Fw 190s. Air–ground liaison was improved, with *Fliegerleittruppe* (air control teams) providing direct radio contact with the aircraft from an armoured half-track or even a command tank.[79] Some 200 aircraft had been added in the East, but the redistribution of forces reflected the belief at *Führer* Headquarters that the Russians would exploit their spring successes and strike either in Poland or in Romania, partly because the acute shortage of long-range reconnaissance aircraft made it difficult to discern enemy intentions (see Table 52). Dessloch, with headquarters at Rzeszow (160km west of Lvov), had to defend half the front supported by *15. Flakdivision* with 56 batteries, but his forces were largely concentrated in Romania, where Seidemann

Table 52. The *Luftwaffe* in the East, 31 May 1944				
	Lftl 1	**Lftl 6**	**Lftl 4**	**Total**
Jagdgruppen	100/ 88	104/ 86	186/139	390/ 313
Zerstörer- and	29/ 23	32/ 21	43/ 32	104/ 76
Nachtjagdgruppen				
Kampfgruppen	11/ 8	369/263	46/ 34	426/ 305
Schlachtgruppen	70/ 45	125/106	446/300	641/ 451
Nachtschlachtgruppen	122/107	75/ 58	88/ 70	285/ 235
Reconnaissance	56/ 42	80/ 51	101/ 74	237/ 167
Observation	12/ 6	51/ 38	23/ 13	86/ 57
Seaplanes	15/ 10	–	15/ 10	30/ 20
Total	415/329	836/623	948/672	2,199/1,624

Note: First figure is strength, second is numbers serviceable.
Source: Based upon Price, *Luftwaffe Data Book*.

had 520 aircraft, leaving Deichmann in southern Poland with 320. Moreover, Seidemann could also call upon *Luftwaffekommando Südost* with 185 aircraft and 5. *Flakdivision* with 14 German heavy batteries. In central Russia Greim had some 470 aircraft, mostly fighters and *Jabos*, although he could call upon Meister's 370 bombers and he also had five *Flakdivisionen* and two *Flakbrigaden* with 416 batteries.[80]

Despite intensified *Luftwaffe* bombing against both his industry and its rail network, Stalin was well satisfied with German dispositions. The main blow, Operation 'Bagration', was scheduled not south of the Pripet Marshes but north of them, against *Heersgruppe Mitte*. To confuse the enemy and further disperse his resources, Stalin first struck Finland on 10 June with 260,000 men and 1,547 aircraft. The Finns, with 75,000 men and 118 aircraft, were hard pressed, and to support them the *Luftwaffe* hastily despatched two *Gruppen* of *Luftflotte 1* with 51 aircraft as *Gefechtsverband Kuhlmey* under *Oberstleutnant* Kurt Kuhlmey (*Kommodore* of *SG 3*), but despite valuable COMINT assistance from the Finns they could not prevent their allies suing for an armistice. This was signed on 19 September, whereupon they turned on the Germans.[81]

Meanwhile Greim intensified his efforts to disrupt the enemy. A third of the 8,989 sorties flown in May (compared with 6,777 the previous month) were reconnaissance, while night attacks accounted for nearly 37% of sorties. The scale increased during the first 15 days of June, when 5,995 sorties were flown.[82] On the eve of 'Bagration' Meister had his most spectacular success when he struck the recently established USAAF bomber base at Poltava on 21/22 June: 180 aircraft dropped 46 tonnes of bombs to destroy 43 B-17s which had arrived a few hours earlier on a shuttle-bombing mission. The blow shook Allied confidence in shuttle-bombing, and although a few more missions were flown up to September this never proved as serious a threat as the Americans had hoped.[83]

Yet it was irrelevant to the course of 'Bagration', which was launched on 23 June with 2.4 million men supported by 6,334 aircraft, including 1,007 medium/ heavy and 431 night bombers. Greim's *Luftflotte 6* had already lost a *Jagdgruppe* to Germany (replacing fighters transferred to France after D-Day), and with only 3,800 tonnes of fuel he could do little to prevent the envelopment of the *Heersgruppe*.[84] As the front collapsed, the heavy bombers of *KG 1*, like the *VVS*'s three years earlier, were used for tactical air support, flying low-level missions in pairs and losing 10 aircraft. Three *Jagdgruppen* arrived from Germany or *Luftflotte 4*, another two came from *Luftflotte 1* and Richthofen surrendered his last strike forces of *SG 4*, but they could do nothing to change the situation, and out of 165,000 troops barely 15,000 escaped and 57,000 were taken prisoner.

Even as *Heersgruppe Mitte* was in its death agonies, the disaster spread to the flanks, mirroring the events of the summer of 1941. The *Luftwaffe* fought (see Table 53), but it could only reduce the degree of *VVS* air superiority, which never

Table 53. *Luftwaffe* **Activity on the Eastern Front, 1944**

	Luftflotte 1		Luftflotte 4		Luftflotte 6	
	Sorties	Lost	Sorties	Lost	Sorties	Lost
Day Fighters	12,143	133	29,426	336	20,206	260
Night Fighters	436	–	621	19	1,731	16
Day Strike	29,932 }	260	88,057 }	582	48,416 }	458
Night Strike	27,559 }		15,399 }		13,183 }	
Day Recon	9,649 }	67	19,313 }	118	19,519 }	171
Night Recon	1,086 }		1,648 }		4,159 }	

Notes: Day strikes by *Kampf-* and *Schlachtverbände*. Night strikes by *Kampf- and Nachtschlachtverbände*
Source: Luftwaffe Activity, Vol. I, IWM Tin 192, fr.1041.

achieved the domination which the RAF and the USAAF imposed. It was the price the *Luftwaffe* paid for its blinkered attitude to air power, especially the obsession with tactical air support, as well as for its failure to invest sufficient resources.

NOTES TO CHAPTER 6

1. 'Die Kampfhandlungen im Osten während des Jahres 1942'; and Dickfeld, pp.73–4.
2. Luftwaffe Losses (USNA T971, Roll 26).
3. Airmen often sat on the tails of aircraft taxiing through snow to provide a firmer grip for the tailwheel. However, one *Gefreiter* of 7./StG 1 was frozen to the tailplane and the *Stuka* took off with him still attached. The crew quickly realised what had happened and returned to base, where the unfortunate *Gefreiter* was freed, complaining about losing his cap (Brütting, pp.39–40).
4. 'Pulk', the Russian word for regiment, was *Luftwaffe* slang for an aerial formation and was used from the first days of 'Barbarossa'.
5. Figures from Morzik, p.145; and Plocher, pp.97–100. Note that Plocher, p.86, gives a figure of 302 tonnes for 18 February to 19 May.
6. Until 12 February *Fliegerkorps V* was under its Chief of Staff, *Oberst* Hermann Plocher, while Greim and some of his staff were in the Crimea as *Sonderstab Krim* from 15 January helping *11. Armee* defensive operations. Once the crisis had passed *Sonderstab Krim* was disbanded. See Plocher, *1942*, pp.159–67. *Flakkorps*, which had previously been division-sized units, were now formed to control the new *Flakdivisionen* and *Flakbrigaden*.
7. Plocher, *1942*, p.97.
8. For the Kharkov operation see Dierich, *KG 51*, pp.177–80; Dierich, *KG 55*, pp.242–4; Plocher, *1942*, pp.171–7; Prien, pp.1004–37; and *6.* and *17. Armee* war diaries (USNA T312, Rolls 1676 and 693). Curiously, the *Luftwaffe* contribution is largely ignored by German sources except for unit histories.
9. Muller, p.70.
10. For the background see Ziemke and Bauer, p. 264; Muller, pp.70–2; and Plocher, *1942*, pp.178–81.

11. For *'Trappenjagd'* see Muller, pp.72–3; Plocher, *1942*, pp.177–84; and Prien, pp.977–1010.

12. Richthofen appears to have been critical of Wild during this operation, for when they met in the Italy a year later relations between the two were tense. See entry in Richthofen's diary for 22 June 1943 (BA MA N671/11).

13. For *'Störfang'* see Muller, pp.75–82; and Plocher, *1942*, pp.184–206.

14. Details of Soviet air forces from Ziemke and Bauer, pp. 302, 308; and Tyushkevich, pp.66, 271.

15. For *'Kreml'* see Ziemke and Bauer, pp.328–30.

16. The code-name was changed because of a serious security breach by a divisional operations officer whose Storch landed behind enemy lines with plans for *'Blau-I'*. The documents reached Stalin's hands but were dismissed as forgeries. Ziemke, pp.330–2.

17. For air operations from late June 1942 see Plocher, *1942*, pp.212–23, 338.

18. Between 2 July and 25 August the *Luftwaffe* in the East lost 647 aircraft while 536 were damaged (Luftwaffe Losses, USNA T971, Roll 26; and 'Der Einsatz der Luftwaffe vom 1. Juli 1942', IWM AHB 6, Tin 20, fr.K1478–503). German total losses in the East rose from 350 in June to 438 and 436 in the next two months and then dropped to 200 and 224 in October–November (Murray, Table XXV).

19. BAM, p.178; Plocher, *1942*, pp.231–2, 245, 340–2.

20. BA MA N 671/9.

21. Pickert was promoted to *Generalmajor* on 1 October.

22. See Muller, pp.90–1.

23. Axworthy, p.293; and his article 'Flank Guard: Romania's Aerial Advance on Stalingrad.'

24. BAM, p.179.

25. Muller, p.88; and Ziemke and Bauer, p.381.

26. For air operations in the Caucasus see BAM, p.182; Dierich, *KG 51*, pp.185–6; Plocher, *1942*, pp.223–30, 337–8, 343–4; Ziemke and Bauer, pp.375, 376; and 'Der Luftkrieg in Osten', IWM AHB 6, Tin 21, fr.K1604–61.

27. BAM, p.182.

28. For air operations during the German Stalingrad offensive see Axworthy; Balke, *KG 100*, pp.117–25; BAM, p.179; Dierich, *KG 51*, pp.186–90; Kozhevnikov, pp.81–94; Muller, pp. 89–91; Plocher, *1942*, pp. 231–42, 337–8, 348–51; Prien, pp.1080–221; Sarhidai, Punka and Kozlik, pp.20–7; Ziemke and Bauer, pp. 460, 463, 464; 'Luftflotte 4 vor Stalingrad unter Verwendigung des Tagebuchs Gen.Obst. Frh. v. Richthofen', BA MA RL7/482; 'Der Einsatz der Luftwaffe vom 1. Juli 1942', IWM AHB 6, Tin 20, fr.K1478–503; and 'Der Luftkrieg in Osten', IWM AHB 6, Tin 21, fr.K1604–61.

29. See Weal, 'A Nocturnal Miscellany'; and Plocher, *1942*, pp.145,147. For later *NSGr* operations see Smith, *Stuka*, pp.102–3.

30. BAM, p.182.

31. For air operations during 'Uranus' see Kozhevnikov, pp.95–7; Plocher, *1942*, pp.243–59; Rudel, pp.81–92; and Ziemke and Bauer p.470.

32. Plocher, *1942*, p.261, quoting Fiebig's diary.

33. One of Paulus's corps commanders was *Generalmajor* Walter von Seydlitz-Kurzbach, whose corps had relieved Demyansk.

34. After the catastrophe Göring blamed both men and threatened them with courts-martial, but Seidel retained his post until the end of June 1944 and was then promoted commander of the training *Luftflotte 10*.

35. *Luftflotte 4*'s *Quartermeister, Generalmajor* Karl-Heinrich Schulz, praised Göring for his efforts to ensure that Richthofen had sufficient aircraft, auxiliary units and equipment as well as fuel to supply *6. Armee*. Plocher, *1942*, p.349.

36. BAM, pp.182–3.

37. Jungclausen's *Staffel* was the last *Stuka* unit to operate from the Stalingrad pocket. He was killed off Hela in December 1944 flying a torpedo-bomber mission in a Ju 87. Brütting, *Stuka-Asse*, p.215.

38. Dierich, *KG 51*, pp.198–9.

39. The *VVS* lost 706 aircraft in the offensive operations against Stalingrad and flew 35,920 sorties.

40. Plocher, *1942*, pp.320–1.

41. Their transfer was stopped on 24 January, by which time 349 had been assembled, including 10 Gigants. USNA T971, Roll 8.

42. For air operations in Stalingrad after the isolation see Axworthy; Bauer and Ziemke, p.479; Erickson, *Berlin*, pp.18–22; Kozhevnikov, pp.97–101; Irving, *Milch*, pp.183–96; Morzik and Hümmelchen, pp.150–66, Anlage 15; Muller, pp.91–101; Plocher, *1942*, pp.260–330; Rudel, pp.91–8; Lufttransportführer Oberst Morzik, 'Erfährungsbericht Stalingrad', USNA T971, Roll 18; and 'Sonderstab GFM Milch Kriegestagbuch', BA MA RL30/1–7.

43. See Dierich, *KG 55*, pp.335–8, 346–8.

44. Morzik and Hümmelchen, pp.166–76; and Tiecke, pp.315–16.

45. Weiss had led the Hs 123s of *II. (Sch)/LG 2* with distinction, then become *Kommodore* of *SchG 1*. Subsequently he was appointed *Inspekteur der Schlachtflieger* under Galland and became the first *General der Schlachtflieger*.

46. For operations to the recapture of Kharkov see BAM, pp.224–32; Plocher, *1943*, pp.14–23; Sarhidai, Punka and Kozlik, pp.27–8; 'Der Einsatz der Luftflotte 4 im Jahr 1943', USNA T971, Roll 18, fr.719; IWM AHB 6, Tin 20, fr.K1525–70); 'Luftflotte 4 vor Stalingrad unter Verwendigung des Tagebuchs Gen.Obst. Frh. v. Richthofen', BA MA RL7/482; and Richthofen diaries, BA MA N671/10.

47. For details of ground attack operations see Rudel and the interrogations of Hitschold in 1945 (IWM AHB 6, Tin 195, fr.3385–9, 3411–14, 3418–22, 3424–6). See also Brütting, pp.16–39.

48. For a German view of the *VVS* see Dierich, *KG 55*, pp.318–35.

49. Murray, p.249, quoting BA/MA RL10/544.

50. The *Luftwaffe* lost some 500 aircraft in February and March, mostly in the Manstein counter-offensive. Murray, p.156.

51. Göring provided his old friend Greim with a train to act as a mobile command post. Some idea of the activity may be gauged from the fact that in battles around Rzhev during early August the *Luftwaffe* claimed 1,572 tanks and 547 aircraft for the loss of 25 aircraft. 'Der Einsatz der Luftwaffe vom 1. Juli 1942'.

52. On 17 August Greim had 11 *Kampf-*, three *Stuka-* and five *Jagdgruppen* and a *Schlacht-*, a *Panzerjäger-* and a *Jagdstaffel*.

53. Murray, p.156.

54. One Ju 86P was shot down in the first action by Russian-operated Spitfire VBs. Bombing in the East was assisted by the introduction during 1942 of the *Lotfe 7D* bomb sight, which permitted more accurate high-altitude attacks. For air operations over *Heersgruppe Mitte* between January 1942 and May 1943 see Aders and Held, *JG 51*, pp.107–25; Diehl, *KG 53*, pp.191–6; Plocher, *1942*, pp.101–50; Plocher, *1943*, pp.51–66; and 'Der Luftkrieg in Osten'.

55. See Plocher, *1943*, pp.61–3. for a description of a raid on the Kursk marshalling yards by *Major* Friedrich Lang, *Kommandeur* of *III./StG 1*.

56. Plocher, op. cit., p.66. Kozhevnikov, pp.121–3, states that the Long Range Bomber force (*ADD*) flew 9,400 sorties between April and June.

57. In Kluge's rear areas *18. Flakdivision* claimed 617 victories at night between April and June and only 130 during the day (Plocher, *1943*, p.64). During June 45 night fighter sorties were flown ('Einsatz, Luftflotte 6, Juni 1943–Juni 1944', BA MA RL7/521). For night fighting in the East see Aders, pp.63–5, 90–2, 118–21, 139, App. 21.

58. Aders pp.163–5, App. 21; and *Tätigkeits und Erfahrungsbericht des Gen. Kdo XII. Fl.Korps*, BA MA RL8/88.

59. See Dierich, *KG 55*, pp.304–9; Gundelach, *KG 4*, pp.233–8; and 'Einsatz, Luftflotte 6, Juni 1943–Juni 1944', BA MA RL7/521

60. Tyushkevich, p. 323.

61. For operations over the Kuban bridghead see BAM, pp.232–3; Bateson; Kozhevnikov, pp.10–17; Muller, pp.109–11; Plocher, *1943*, pp.17, 24–50; and Rudel, pp.106–8. For details of aircraft see Green.

62. See Hildebrand's entries on Dessloch and Richthofen, which must raise questions about whether or not the snub was Jeschonnek's revenge. In August 1944 Dessloch succeeded Sperrle as *Oberbefehlshaber, Luftflotte 3*.

63. For air operations around Kursk see BAM, pp.233–6; Dierich, *KG 55*, pp.309–10; Glantz and House, pp.163, 296; Klink, p.184, 160, 246; Kozhevnikov, pp.121–44; Muller, pp.112–46; Plocher, *1943*, pp.56–107, 121–5; Ziemke, pp.128–9; 'Der Einsatz der Luftflotte 4 im Jahr 1943', USNA T971, Roll 18, fr.719, and IWM AHB 6, Tin 20, fr.K1571–82); and Richthofen diary, BA MA 671/10.

64. Murray, p.159.

65. For *Luftflotte 4* operations from September to December 1943 see BAM, pp.240–2; and Plocher, *1943*, pp.45–50, 133–71.

66. Morzik and Hümmelchen, pp.176–81.

67. The *Kampfgruppen* had only 165 bombers.

68. Rudel, pp.151-170. Two months later the crew of *Feldwebel* Justin of *14. (Eis)/KG 55* were brought down 150km behind enemy lines near Staraya Russa but escaped to friendly lines after a 12-day odyssey (Dierich, *KG 55*, pp. 340–6).

69. For transport operations see Gundelach, *KG 4*, pp.265–6; and Morzik and Hümmelchen, pp.193–205.

70. Ziemke, p.284. During March 1,149 transport sorties were flown by *Luftflotte 4* ('Lagekarten Ost, Marz 1944', USNA T321, Roll 86, fr.411).

71. Casualties may be gauged from the fact that between August 1943 and April 1944 *JG 51 'Mölders'* lost 72 pilots killed or failed to return, while *KG 53 'Legion Condor'* lost 33 crews and *KG 55 'Greif'* lost 64. Aders and Held, *JG 51*, p.140; Dierich, *KG 55*, App. 1; and Kiehl, *KG 53*, App. 6.

72. BAM, pp.243–5; and Ziemke, p.231.

73. Many of these *Gruppen* had previously been in the Mediterranean.

74. The *Luftwaffe* had some 1,730 men in the Crimea infrastructure and 8,000 *Flak* personnel.

75. For the Crimea operation see BAM, pp.244–5; Gundelach, *KG 4*, pp.266–9; Hümmelchen, p.136; Morzik and Hümmelchen, pp.193–205; *Einsatz, Auflockerung und Ausbau der Festung Sewastopol*, IWM AHB 6, Tin 21, fr.K1662–87); and Report on Operations in Crimea, IWM AHB 6, Tin 21, fr.2129–39.

76. Hildebrand; and Rosch, pp.147, 325, 326 335.

77. The Germans reported that the Russians were operating Fw 190s and Ju 88s against their former owners on Pflugbeil's front. For air operations in *Luftflotte 1* and *Luftflotte 6* in the autumn and winter see Muller, p.199; Plocher, *1943*, pp.108–19, 172–82; Ziemke, pp.262–3; and Reports on *Luftwaffe* Operations in the East, IWM AHB 6, Tin 21, fr.2139ff.

78. Engine fires were a rarity in *KG 1* because pilots had learned to avoid them by careful use of the throttles, *KG 40* having similar success in western Europe—see Price and Smith's article 'He 177'. For *Fliegerkorps IV* operations see BAM, p.240; Dierich, *KG 55*, pp.312–14, 348–59; Gundelach, *KG 4*, pp.252–7, 270–84, 293; Hoeffding, pp.36–55; Muller, pp.180–208; Murray, pp.246–7; Price and Smith, 'He 177'; Reports on *Luftwaffe* Operations in the East, IWM AHB 6, Tin 21, fr.2139ff.
79. Muller, pp.222–4.
80. For preparations see BAM, pp.245–6, 357–8; and Koch, p.447ff.
81. The *Gefechtsverband* was withdrawn on 12 August after flying 1,998 sorties and losing 27 aircraft. The Russians lost 311 aircraft. Kuhlmey earned his *Ritterkreuz* in July 1942 with *StG 3* in North Africa, where he was known as 'The Prince of El Hachin'. After the war he joined the *Bundesluftwaffe* and was the first German to receive jet training in the United States. For Kuhlmey's operations see Stenmann, 'The Short Saga of Battle Unit Kuhlmey'; and BAM, p.358.
82. Reports on Luftwaffe Operations in the East, IWM AHB 6, Tin 21, fr.2139ff.
83. Dierich, *KG 53*, pp.271–4; Dierich, *KG 55*, pp.359–68; Gundelach, *KG 4*, pp.283–92; and Muller, pp.208–14.
84. BAM, p.358; and Muller, p.215.

CHAPTER SEVEN

Full Circle

The Mediterranean and Balkans, January 1942–June 1944

New Year's Day 1942 saw preparations continue in Sicily for the neutralisation of Malta, which Kesselring would direct from his headquarters in Taormina. The *Kampfgruppen* had begun probing attacks in *Kette* strength from December, but Loerzer's *Fliegerkorps II* was still recovering from its Russian experience and the *Gruppen* needed to be fleshed out from 118 aircraft in January to 390 in mid March, when a full-scale offensive became practicable.[1]

The gradual increase in strength (see Table 54) meant that the *Kampfgruppen* operated in *Staffel*-size formations, attacking AA batteries and also acting as bait to help the fighters, three for every bomber, to destroy the defending fighters. Surprisingly, although Loerzer was a former fighter pilot he kept his *Jagdgruppen* on a very short rein throughout the campaign against Malta, with relatively few autonomous sweeps (see Table 55). The Bf 109Fs outclassed Malta's 80 Hurricanes, of which barely 20 were serviceable by the beginning of March as Loerzer assembled 425 aircraft, 190 of them bombers, for the main attack. By 27 February Malta's air commander, Lloyd, was demanding more fighters, and within a week the first Spitfires arrived from the aircraft carrier *Eagle*.[2]

Meanwhile Hitler and Mussolini had agreed a strategy in which Malta was to be exhausted by air attack and then finished off with an airborne assault, *Unter-*

Table 54. The *Luftwaffe* in the Mediterranean

Date	Fighters SE/TE	Bombers	Close Support	Reconnaissance LR	Tactical	Total
27 Dec 1941	194/ 92	208	83	36	n/a	613 (+)
30 Mar 1942	271/ 90	215	110	53	13	752
30 Sept 1942	260/ 61	246	95	67	14	743
30 Dec 1942	212/ 68	434	50	56	23	843
31 Mar 1943	336/140	277	66	78	24	921
30 Jun 1943	380/142	268	150	40	48	1,028
30 Sept 1943	136/ 32	337	84	31	49	669
31 Dec 1943	191/ 43	82	16	42	74	448
31 Mar 1944	146/ 59	154	62	47	77	545

Note: Excludes seaplanes and transports. SE = single-engine; TE = twin-engine; LR = Long-Range.
Source: *Luftwaffe* first-line strength based on German documents (PRO Air 40/1207).

Table 55. *Fliegerkorps II* Sorties against Malta, January–November 1942

Month	Fighter Escort	Sweep	Airfield	Strike Day	Night	Recon	Total
Jan	541	429	–	248	216	34	1,468
Feb	964	488	–	284	167	32	1,935
Mar	1,958	945	165	859	330	43	4,300
Apr	2,681	1,451	203	4,082	256	115	8,788
May	1,029	844	102	277	133	91	2,476
Jun	424	171	9	2	291	59	956
Jul	1,030	216	–	328	191	54	1,819
Aug	552	210	–	8	54	38	862
Sept	150	229	–	–	–	12	391
Oct	1,651	413	206	394	149	55	2,842
Nov	51	39	–	–	10	3	103
Total	10,975	5,435	698	6,482	1,797	536	25,940

Notes: Strike sorties include *Kampf-* and *Stukaflieger.*
Source: Based upon L'Aeronautica Italiana nella Seconda Guerra Mondiale, Vol. 2, p.295, quoted by Gundelach, App. 7.

nehmen 'Herkules' (formerly *C3*), planned by Student and *Generalmajor* Bernhard Ramcke. This envisaged paratroops establishing a bridgehead during late July in south-west Malta which would be expanded by airborne forces.[3] An air offensive would first reduce the island, and Kesselring's plan, drafted by Loerzer's Chief of Staff *Oberst* Paul Deichmann and agreed with the Italians at Catania on 12 March, was to destroy the fighters and AA guns, then launch a sustained assault upon the naval base and airfields. The Germans would spearhead the operation because most Italian aircraft were obsolescent: between February and April the latter contributed only 2,455 sorties. On 20 March the offensive formally opened with German aircrew sometimes flying three sorties a day, a third of all sorties being against airfields, which would suffer a *Jagdgruppen* sweep 30 minutes before the *Kampfgruppen* arrived. Takali was so severely cratered that it reminded Lloyd of the Western Front battlefields of the Great War. It attracted 841 tonnes of bombs because the Germans mistakenly thought that it had an underground hangar, against which they used some rocket-assisted PC 1800RS Panther bombs. The outnumbered British fighters concentrated upon the bombers, *Major* Arved Cruger (*Kommodore, KG 77*) being lost, but the *Jagdgruppen* generally thwarted them and during April 94% of all strike sorties were in daylight. However, there were higher losses in the Ju 88 *Gruppen* until early April, when formations learned to make dive-bombing attacks simultaneously rather than individually.

On 20 April *Luftflotte 2*'s efforts reached a peak of 325 sorties (140 strike) as 46 Spitfires arrived from the American carrier *Wasp*.[4] This attempt at reinforcement was promptly nipped in the bud, leaving only 27 Spitfires serviceable the following dawn, but the British learned from their mistakes and the next batch of Spitfires, on 9 May, was shielded and succoured, allowing the aircraft to strike their own blows for the defence.[5] Simultaneously a minelayer with supplies including AA ammunition and smoke generators slipped in and was unloaded before the *Luftwaffe* could react. By 25 April Kesselring began striking troop positions and supply dumps, but three days later the offensive was ended, although bloody fighting continued. Between 20 March and 28 April the *Luftwaffe* flew 11,819 sorties, dropped 6,557 tonnes of bombs (3,150 tonnes on Valletta) and lost 173 aircraft in an assault which aroused ugly passions on both sides: a mob of Maltese civilians beheaded a German who had parachuted down, while pilots often strafed opponents in dinghies. Nevertheless *Major* Gruhne's Syracuse-based *Seenotbereichskommando X* was always ready to attempt to rescue friend or foe, and during May the 'customers' included Maltzahn, now *Kommodore* of *JG 53*, and *Unteroffizier* Dr Felix Sauer, who had spent eight days in his dinghy.[6]

The arrival of reinforcements in May was a watershed in Malta's defence—which never again reached the nadir of the previous months—but by then '*Herkules*' had been postponed until August. The decision was influenced by the easing of Rommel's supply situation, which encouraged the 'Desert Fox' in early April to seek permission for an offensive within two months. Kesselring was shocked at the request and on 13 April warned *ObdL* that he did not have the strength to support operations in Malta and Africa simultaneously. At the end of April the Italians, who would not be ready for '*Herkules*' until August, reluctantly supported Rommel, and with *OKW* having uneasy memories of the '*Merkur*' bloodbath and *OKH* concerned about the diversion of resources away from '*Blau*', the decision was rubber-stamped when Hitler and Mussolini met at Berghof. A formal postponement was delayed until 21 June, Student hearing the news from Hitler's lips and then being banned from returning to Rome. Loerzer's forces were dispersed during May, leaving two *Kampf*- and one *Jagdgruppen* in Sicily. '*Herkules*' remained a contingency plan until Rommel's summer victories appeared to make it redundant and it was pigeon-holed.[7]

An unwelcome diversion of Kesselring's air power was the need to impose a blockade upon Malta (see Table 16, Chapter 2). During the first half of the year *Hauptmann* Joachim Helbig's *LG 1* in Crete was the primary obstacle to British attempts to break the blockade, intercepting three convoys from Alexandria to sink four ships (28,970grt) as well as three out of four task group destroyers, and the waters south of Crete were dubbed 'Bomb Alley' by the Royal Navy.[8] When major relief attempts (Operations 'Harpoon' and 'Vigorous') were made in June, British commandos blew up seven of Helbig's bombers at Heraklion, but with the assistance of *StG 3* he sank two ships (12,915grt) and two destroyers, although there was no success for the Italian circling torpedoes (LT 350), which made their German combat début with *KG 77*.[9] When the British made a major new effort from Gibraltar in August (Operation 'Pedestal'), the *Luftwaffe* transferred Helbig to Sicily, bringing its strike force to 75 aircraft. The convoy was discovered by a radar-equipped Ju 88 of *1. (F)/122* on 11 August, leading to four days of ferocious attacks which cost the *Luftwaffe* 16 aircraft. Although they had the lion's share of success against shipping (five ships totalling 52,416grt), sufficient supplies (including aviation fuel) reached the island to end the threat of starvation.[10]

By that time Loerzer had made a second assault upon Malta which, despite intermittent *Regia Aeronautica* bombardment since May, had rebuilt its strike force to threaten Axis communications. Reluctantly, in early July the *Luftwaffe* despatched to Sicily two *Gruppen* of *KG 77* from France and a *Jagdgruppe* from Russia, the latter under the great *Experte Hauptmann* Heinz 'Pritzl' Bär, so that Kesselring might reprise his earlier success, but he had only 150 aircraft, of which half were serviceable. The defenders, too, were reinforced with the arrival of the former No 11 Group commander Air Vice-Marshal Park, who replaced the abrasive Lloyd and prepared 'Big Wing' tactics, grouping his fighters and meeting the *Kampfgruppen* north of the island to inflict a 5.8% loss rate upon them during the month. The German radar system, still operated by *LnR 200*, appears to have been of little assistance to the *Jagdgruppen*, which were unable to devise countermeasures. Nevertheless, by the end of the month only 80 of the 275 Spitfires delivered to Malta since the beginning of March were left. Loerzer's bombing effort faded away and vanished completely in September, while more ominous was the decline in reconnaissance activity after June, with the task increasingly assigned to the *Jagdgruppen*.[11]

The Malta boil remained unlanced and Axis shipping suffered the pain from both air and submarine attack. Under Navy and *OKW* pressure, in late September *ObdL* reluctantly authorised the resumption of attacks upon the island after Loerzer had been reinforced by five *Kampf-*, one *Schlacht-* and two *Jagdgruppen*. The Italians contributed eight groups when the offensive commenced on 11 October, but the defenders were too strong, inflicting a 7.5% loss rate on the *Kampfgruppen* despite the presence of the new Bf 109G, of which Kesselring had had such high hopes. On 16 October he abandoned the operation.[12] This was the *Luftwaffe*'s ultimate attempt to beat Malta into submission, and the need to support operations in Africa prevented any repetition. The campaign against the island cost the Germans 357 aircraft in two years and the *Regia Aeronautica* 175.[13]

In North Africa, when British troops reached *JG 53*'s base at Derna in December 1941 they found, scrawled on a blackboard, the message 'We come back. Happy Christmas!'[14] Within two months the prophecy was fulfilled as Rommel, his seaborne communications temporarily secure, recaptured Benghazi in February and drove the British back to the Gazala Line to begin compromising Kesselring's offensive against Malta. During May he soundly defeated the British in *Unternehmen 'Theseus'*, driving them into Egypt, taking Tobruk on 21 June and earning him a *Generalfeldmarschall*'s baton. He had planned to await *'Herkules'* on

213

the Egyptian border, but his hunter's instincts were awakened by the fleeing prey and he impetuously pursued the enemy until stopped at new fortifications in the First Battle of El Alamein (2–17 July). His attempts to outflank the position were thwarted at Alam Halfa in early September, and on 23/24 October the British opened a massive attack upon the Axis positions in the Second Battle of El Alamein. A week later, on 2 November, they forced Rommel to retreat into Tripolitania, where his hopes of repeating his success of February were dashed by the Allied landings in French North Africa (Operation 'Torch').

Rommel's early advance exacerbated his relations with Fröhlich, who began avoiding meetings with him and was relieved by Kesselring in March to find better prospects on the Eastern Front. The 'Desert Fox' quickly discovered that the new *FlFü Afrika*, Waldau, was no doormat, for as a former Director of Operations he possessed the experience and authority to stand up to Rommel, although the latter's egocentric command style meant that *Luftwaffe* operations were often based upon guesswork regarding his intentions and activity. Waldau also could do little to end the petrol drought, for he and his successor rarely had more than 1,400 tonnes (sufficient for a month), a figure which dropped to 160 tonnes by 8 November.[15] There were also severe maintenance problems since only essential spares were brought to Africa, while it was difficult to transport large components such as wings, propellers and undercarriages. Devoid of equipment and a recovery organisation, the *Luftwaffe* usually cannibalised badly damaged aircraft in forward airfields.[16]

Despite the capabilities of the Bf 109, Waldau was unable to achieve air superiority, notwithstanding the great skill displayed by his *Jagdgruppen*. The latter were drawn principally from *JG 27*, initially under *Major* Bernhard Woldenga and from 8 June under *Oberstleutnant* Eduard 'Edu' Neumann, which claimed 1,165 victories in Africa during 1941 and 1942. This skill was underlined on 14 January when *Unteroffizier* Horst Reuter 'bounced' and shot down six Hurricanes, but this paled before the achievements of *Leutnant* Hans-Joachim Marseille, 'The Star of Africa', who equalled Reuter's feat twice and claimed 17 fighters on 1 September! After an inauspicious start in France, Marseille's star had waxed in Africa, where he claimed his 40th victim in February 1942 and his 101st four months later, despite a brief sojourn in Europe on a training course. Like the legendary Boelcke's, his victories were marked by excellent marksmanship and parsimonious expenditure of ammunition, but there was also a tragic similarity because Marseille, too, died as a result of an accident, on 30 September. He had a score of 158. The natural rivalry among pilots meant that, with some *Experten*, high scoring appears to have become an object in itself, while the hit-and-run tactics adopted to compensate for numerical inferiority meant that it was enemy fighter squadrons which tended to suffer.[17] The bomber squadrons were rarely mauled, pounding both airfields and Axis communications almost unopposed, while the *Jagdflieger* pursued their private war, leaving the *Landsers* of all ranks cowering under enemy bombs.[18]

From late June the *Jagdgruppen* encountered stiffer opposition from Spitfire Vs and USAAF P-40F Warhawks, which evolved tactics to counter the qualitative superiority of the Bf 109F. Consequently, during September *JG 27* lost not only Marseille but also another 14 pilots killed or failed to return, including *Leutnant* Hans-Arnold Stahlschmitt (59 victories), *Oberfeldwebel* Günther Steinhausen (40) and *Leutnant* Karl von Lieres (24).[19] The *Jagdgruppen*'s most significant contribution to the ground war came during a sweep on 7 August when *Unteroffizier* Bernd Schneider (*II./JG 27*) shot down a Bristol Bombay transport carrying the recently appointed commander of the 8th Army, Lieutenant-General W. H. E. Gott, who was killed and replaced by Lieutenant-General Bernard Montgomery. The British struck not only during the day but also at night, leading *ObdL* to despatch *I./ NJG 2*, which took a steady toll of the raiders.

Neither Fröhlich nor Waldau possessed a significant long-range strike force, although the former did despatch an He 111 flown by *Hauptmann* Theo Blaich on a successful 2,500km mission against the French base at Fort Lamy on Lake Chad on 21 January. The bomber ran out of fuel on the return leg but after a week was discovered by a *Wüstennotstaffel* aircraft, refuelled and returned. The strike force of *FlFü Afrika* was based upon the *Stukas* of *Oberstleutnant* Walter Sigel's *StG 3*, which performed with distinction and formed the core of *Gefechtsverband Sigel* which spearheaded Waldau's operations in support of '*Theseus*' in May.[20] The enemy rear was sporadically raided by *Fliegerkorps X* with up to 10 bombers under Geisler to 23 August and then Waldau, but the introduction of radar-equipped Beaufighters made such operations costly and when a detachment of Ju 86P high-altitude reconnaissance aircraft began to probe Egyptian skies during the summer the British responded by stripping down Spitfires in August, which effectively blinded the Axis.[21]

As *FlFü Afrika*, Waldau (and his successor Seidemann) never had more than 300 aircraft and operations were plagued by an inadequate infrastructure and long lines of communication (see Table 56). Airfields were frequently attacked not only from the air but also the ground, the SAS destroying eight at Quasaba on 27/28 July (three from the visiting *12. (Erg)/LG 1*) and damaging 11, while rain sometimes turned landing grounds into swamps, notably in mid-October. With 278 aircraft (and 340 Italian), Waldau played an important part in '*Theseus*', where Sigel's airmen flew 1,400 sorties, eliminating the Free French stronghold of Bir Harcheim to allow Rommel to outflank the Gazala Line, although the casualties included *Hauptmann* Heinrich Eppen (*Kommandeur, I./StG 3*). With Rommel's subsequent advance the *Luftwaffe*'s 'tail' had a hard time catching up to the 'head', and to provide the forward units with fuel, spares and ammunition a glider unit, *Sonderkommando Dora*, was established in July with DFS 230s and Go 242s.[22]

Table 56. *Fliegerfuhrer Afrika/Fliegerkorps X* **Sorties over Land, January–December 1942**

Month	Fighter	*Jabo*	Strike	Recon	Total
Jan	1,210	65	765	105	2,145
Feb	590	245	365	80	1,280
Mar	740	180	365	65	1,350
Apr	1,080	160	265	65	1,570
May	2,060	155	1,250	105	3,570
Jun	3,410	550	2,225	140	6,325
Jul	3,060	175	1,500	145	4,880
Aug	2,055	195	255	100	2,605
Sept	2,550	615	635	100	3,900
Oct	1,870	575	370	125	2,940
Nov	1,100	355	510	70	2,035
Dec	470	115	385	50	1,020
Total	20,195	3,385	8,890	2,770	33,620

Notes: Fighter sorties includes sweeps, combat air patrols (*Sperrefliegen*) and convoy escort. Strike includes *Kampf-* and *Stukaflieger*. Reconnaissance excludes *Nahaufklärungsstaffeln*.
Sources: Based upon L'Aeronautica Italian nella Seconda Guerra Mondiale, Vol. 2, p.357, quoted by Gundelach, App. 8.

With their aid Seidemann, who replacedWaldau on 24 August having been Kesselring's Chief of Staff, strengthened his strike force with *Jabos*, creating *Jabogruppe Afrika* from independent *Staffeln* and adding the Bf 110Es of *III./ZG 1*. StG 3 received Ju 87Ds, but these had no effect on the outcome of Alam Halfa.[23]

From 9 October the Allies' Western Desert Air Force (Air Marshal Sir Arthur Coningham) and US Ninth Air Force (Major-General Lewis H. Brereton) began to pound the Axis air bases in preparation for Montgomery's offensive At this time Seidemann had 324 aircraft and the Italians 250, while the Allies had about 1,000. Throughout the offensive Allied fighters shielded the battlefield, inflicting heavy losses on Axis close support forces, *Hauptmann* Kurt Welter (*Kommandeur, III/StG 3*) becoming one of the casualties on 26 October. The despatch of *Major* Joachim Müncheberg's *JG 77* failed to prevent Allied strike forces from hammering every Axis counter-attack, and *Luftwaffe* sorties dropped dramatically as forward fuel stocks were exhausted. Rommel's retreat was covered by *Luftwaffe* close support forces, but at great cost. *I./StG 3* was mauled on 11 November, its *Kommandeur, Oberleutnant* Martin Mossdorf, being taken prisoner, while the African débuts of the Me 210 (in a re-equipped *III./ZG 1*) and Hs 129 failed to slow the British advance. Frequent movements meant the abandonment of many aircraft as overall strength fell to 194 aircraft by 20 December, less than half of which were serviceable, with 11,200 men. The defence increasingly devolved upon *Generalleutnant* Heinrich Burchard's *19. Flakdivision* (*Generalmajor* Gotthard Franz from 21 December), but this had lost 63% of its 174 guns by 17 November, partly because they had been deployed too far forward at El Alamein.[24] As the year ended and Rommel's troops withdrew westwards through Tripolitania, Seidemann sought to deny his airfields to the enemy by ploughing and mining them, and the ploughs became prime targets for British fighter-bombers despite their strong *Flak* shield.[25]

Throughout the North African campaign the *Luftwaffe* played an important part in securing the supply lines to Africa. Protecting the convoys from submarines was the responsibility not only of *Oberstleutnant* Herbert Kaiser's Athens-based *SAGr 126*, whose 40 seaplanes included some Dutch Fokker T.VIIIWs, but also any bomber which *Fliegerkorps X* could spare (see Table 57). The ubiquitous seaplanes, described as 'a girl in every port', helped sink the British submarines *Taku* and *Upholder* during 1942, the latter with the submarine ace Lieutenant-Commander David Wanklyn on board. Axis convoys were discovered by 'Ultra' but were targeted only if 'discovered' by judicially aided reconnaissance, and in November 1941 Italian COMINT intercepted instructions to an aircraft but failed to recognise the significance.[26]

There was also the threat from air attack, which could break the monotony of a patrol at any time. The need for quick reactions led to a tragedy on 29 April when an aircraft which appeared near a convoy returning to Sicily was shot down by *Unteroffizier* Georg Schleich (*III./ZG 26*) but proved to be an Italian airliner. Realising his mistake, and full of remorse, Schleich dropped the survivors his dinghy before plunging his Bf 110 into the sea, killing himself and *Bordfunker Unteroffizier* Werner Beck.[27] British fighters were a threat to the airlift, as was demonstrated on 12 May when Kittyhawks and Beaufighters intercepted 13 Ju 52s escorted by Bf 110s of *9./ZG 26*, shot down eight transports and badly damaged a ninth. Of 175 men only 39 were rescued, and the death toll increased when the *Kapitän* of *Wüstennotstaffel 1*, father-of-six *Hauptman* Heinz Kroseberg, who had rescued many airmen from the desert, went missing over the sea after flying over the survivors and dropping his own lifejacket.[28]

The airlift was directed by *Oberst* Rudolf Starke, former *Kommandeur* of *III./ KGzbv 1*, as *Lufttransportführer Mittelmeer*, with half a dozen *Gruppen* and the gliders of *LLG 1*. The *Transportgruppen* flew a total of 4,425 sorties to Benghazi

	Jan	Feb	Mar	Apr	May	Jun	Jul	Aug	Sept	Oct	Nov
FlKorps II	145	235	330	560	585	155	120	620	905	580	110
FlKorps X	30	30	10	40	110	60	155	640	815	590	190
Total	175	265	340	600	695	215	275	1,260	1,715	1,170	300

Table 57. *Luftwaffe* Convoy Escort Sorties, January–November 1942

Notes: Figures are rounded out to nearest 5 and include *FlFü Afrika*.
Sources: Based upon L'Aeronautica Italiana nella Seconda Guerra Mondiale, Vol. 2, pp.295 and 357, quoted by Gundelach, Apps 7 and 8 respectively.

from Greece or Crete by 30 June, operating in *'pulks'* of 25 aircraft, the acute shortage of crews (due to sickness) and transports (despite the impressment of signals and ambulance aircraft) limiting mission sizes and compelling crews to fly two sorties a day. They delivered 28,200 men and 4,400 tonnes of supplies and returned with wounded (10,700 to June 1942), mail, empty fuel containers and worn-out aero-engines (up to 10 per transport). An extra burden on the *Gruppen* until the fall of Tobruk was the need to fly up to 1,000 men and 25 tonnes of material daily to Rommel's troops as well as 300 tonnes of fuel to Waldau's airmen. Tobruk became the southern terminus from June, but Brindisi in Italy became the northern one with three *Gruppen* because there were better rail communications there than in the Balkans. In mid-August there were only 161 aircraft, half of them serviceable, but by 19 November they had flown 11,500 sorties to deliver 42,000 men and 15,000 tonnes of supplies while evacuating 9,000 sick and wounded. An unusual operation on 21 July saw 30 Ju 52s under *Major* Walter Hornung land behind the lines to help capture the British-occupied Siwah Oasis.[29] From October Allied fighters exerted growing pressure upon the airlift, with 70 Ju 52s destroyed in six weeks, despite the Crete-based escorts provided by 7. and 9./ZG 26 and *Jagdkommando Kreta* being increased from three to five aircraft and *'pulk'* size rising to 60. All the transports were 'Tante Jus', including a refrigerated one which brought in meat and vegetables, with a limited capacity of 18 men or 3.2 tonnes, but during the autumn a *Gruppe* of Gigants and the Wiking flying boats of *Transportstaffel (See) 222* increased the Mediterranean 'lift' just in time to support Rommel's retreat. To sustain this, Wild, the anti-shipping specialist, came from the Black Sea to Athens and established *Lufttransportführer I (Südost)* on 1 November to control Balkans-based transports, while schools, and even *Mausis*, were mobilised in Italy to create *KGzbV S (Sizilien)*, raising total transport strength in the Mediterranean theatre to 514 (including seven Wikings and nine Gigants) by 10 November, half the *Luftwaffe*'s transport force. Yet *Kampfgruppen* were also pressed into transport duties. With the fall of Tobruk on 13 November temporary termini were created, but within a week the Axis forces were beyond the range of Wild's transports, which were transferred westwards together with assembled supplies.[30]

The increase in transport strength was timely since Operation 'Torch' created a new front in French Morocco and Algeria on 8 November.[31] The Germans reacted with their legendary audacity, first occupying Vichy France then entering the protectorate of Tunisia from 9 November and beginning an airlift and a sealift for every available man, including paratroops, who were quickly organised into *Generaloberst* Jürgen von Arnim's *5. Panzerarmee*.[32] The airlift was conducted in *'pulks'* of up to 100 transports, with journeys to forward bases such as Gabès (Qabes) and Sfax in central Tunisia being made at night, and from 8 November to 31 December they brought in 41,768 men and 10,086 tonnes of material.[33] The

Axis defensive web contained the enemy on the Tunisian border, and by early December exhaustion and heavy rain (it was the worst winter for many years) brought a stalemate in northern Tunisia which lasted until the spring. At the Axis front's other extremity, Rommel, later given command of *Heeresgruppe Afrika*, consisting of Arnim's troops and his old command, renamed the 1st Italian Army, withdrew into the former French Mareth Line on the Tripolitania border, abandoning Tripoli to the British on 22 January. He sought to regain the initiative by striking the Allies' weak point, the Franco-American front around the Kasserine Pass, which was probed in December then struck by Arnim in mid-February's *Unternehmen 'Frühlingswind'* (Spring Breeze). Despite initial success the *Wehrmacht* was driven back within a fortnight and a riposte against Montgomery failed at Medenine on 6 March, the British then enveloping the Mareth Line, which was abandoned on 25/26 March. Arnim replaced Rommel at the head of *Heeresgruppe Afrika* as the British and Americans linked on 6 April, and a fortnight later the Allies began the final advance upon Tunis, which fell on 7 May. Two days earlier Hitler recognised that Tunisia was lost, but only half-hearted attempts at evacuation were made as the surviving Axis forces retreated to Cape Bon, and when Arnim surrendered on 13 May only 800 of his 200,000 men had escaped.

'Torch' led to substantial reinforcements to the *Luftwaffe* in the Mediterranean, where its strength rose to 1,646 aircraft by 12 November, of which 850 were assigned to Kesselring. *Luftflotte 4* lost six *Gruppen* (mostly from *KG 77* and *JG 77*) at what proved to be a critical time and *Luftflotte 5* was stripped of its anti-shipping force, while from the West came *Einsatzgruppen* of *KG 6* and *KG 66*.[34] The *Kampfgruppen* were assigned to Loerzer for operational-level missions against communications, but tactical air support was given to the torpedo-bomber specialist Harlinghausen, who was appointed *Führer der Luftwaffe in Tunis* (*FdL Tunis*) on 9 November. He immediately flew to Tunis-El Aounia air base in an He 111 escorted by two Bf 109s of *Oberstleutnant* Maltzahn's *JG 53* and was followed by *I./JG 53* and *II./StG 3* with 51 combat aircraft. This quickly rose to about 140, which were used extensively: by the end of the year they had flown 4,620 sorties (1,200 strike), for the loss of 126 aircraft. Most of the attacks were on enemy positions and communications, American columns driving bunched up during the day and with lights on at night, while Bône's harbour and all-weather air base were also struck. But the *Stukas'* growing vulnerability meant that the *Richthofen Geschwader*'s small Fw 190 force was increasingly pressed into service as *Jabos* against harbours and installations, although from 13 January they were joined by *SKG 10*. The *Regia Aeronautica* assisted, having assembled 288 aircraft (excluding tactical reconnaissance types) in Tunisia by 15 November, with another 379 in Sardinia and Sicily (excluding seaplanes), representing 47% of its combat strength. The Allies had 600 aircraft in French North Africa, but this numerical superiority was neutralised by a lack of airfields and of an early warning network, the inexperience of the aircrews and the obsolescence of most of the aircraft, especially the American fighters. The *Jagdgruppen* exploited conditions similar to those in Russia a year earlier and inflicted heavy losses: on 4 December *Oberleutnant* Julius Meimberg's *11./JG 2* annihilated 11 Blenheim V bombers of Nos 18 and 614 Squadrons and on 13 March *JG 77* wiped out seven P-39s, while the experienced US 33rd Fighter Group was reduced from 75 to 13 fighters and withdrawn to Morocco.[35] Harlinghausen was also supported by the formation of *Generalmajor* Georg Neuffer's *20. Flakdivision*, which benefited from Hitler's decision to despatch 100 heavy batteries, including the latest 8.8cm *Flak 41* guns, to Tunis and Italy.[36] Yet it was its light guns which had the greatest impact, forcing American twin-engine bombers to abandon low-level close air support in favour of attacks from 3,000m (10,000ft).[37] However, a shortage of spares, supplies and motor transport as well as the poor infrastructure all restricted Harlinghausen's options, with serviceability at about 50%.[38] Nevertheless he handled his aircraft aggressively in support of German probing operations, flying 3,142 sorties (475 strike) in January.

The delicate balance which existed on the battlefield at the beginning of 1943 was tipped in the Allies' favour by their success in overcoming supply difficulties, which also reflected the waning power of the *Luftwaffe*. Within hours of discovering the Allied landings, Loerzer's *Kampfgruppen* were attacking shipping off Algiers, the French colonial government's formal defection on 11 November bringing the port itself under attack, with aircraft staging through Sardinia or flying directly from Sicily using long-range tanks and carrying reduced bomb loads. In the first week Loerzer, who had 311 bombers by 10 November, claimed 183,000grt of shipping sunk and 234,000grt damaged, but the Allies lost only five ships (55,305grt). The greatest success was at Bône, occupied on 12 November by British paratroops who literally beat German paratroops to the drop but were unable to exploit the success because the *Kampfgruppen* sank half the four ships (28,707grt) bringing in supplies, including high-octane fuel for fighters at the all-weather air base. Other ports in eastern Algeria, including Bougie and Philippeville, which were closer to the bases, were struck, but there was little attempt to focus the effort, which encountered fierce resistance from AA and the fighters of the US Twelfth Air Force and RAF Eastern Command. In the 20 days from the end of November Loerzer's bomber strength declined by 25% to 298, but the number of crews fell 29% to 289, of whom the number fully operational—those who had flown 10 or more sorties in enemy air space—was down 44% to 127.[39] Loerzer's haphazard direction of bombing operations so infuriated the distinguished pilot *Major* Werner Baumbach (*Kommandeur, I./KG 30*) that he wrote a protest letter to Jeschonnek on 12 December. He was promptly relieved of his command and sent to Berlin for special operations, later becoming the second *Kommodore* (as an *Oberstleutnant*) of *KG 200*, which was created for such missions in February 1944.[40]

Bases in Sardinia might have been more useful, and on 9 December Wild established *FlFü Sardinien* there from *Gefechtsverband Major Kleyenstüber* with 110 aircraft (half of them strike including *II./KG 26*), but expansion was hindered by the shortage of technically trained men such as signallers and ground crews. The defences grew stronger, and *Kampfgruppen* operations declined during December because of losses and the difficulties of finding replacements. Kesselring had to withdraw three *Kampfgruppen* for rest and re-equipment and only two were replaced, so that by New Year's Day overall strength had dropped from 310 to 270, of which 55% were serviceable, while replacement crews were so poorly trained they could not find Algerian ports. The strike force was increasingly used to escort maritime convoys, attacking communications on only 14 days between December and January but escorting convoys on 48 days. Between January and May they attacked shipping on only 54 of the 149 days they were active, while a third of all sorties involved convoy escort, allowing the Allies to ship in men and supplies. The only highlight was on 30/31 December, when seven Condors of *III./KG 40* from Bordeaux-Mérignac celebrated the forthcoming New Year by striking Casablanca on the initiative of the *Kommandeur, Major* Robert Kowlewski. Each dropped four 250kg bombs, which caused consternation because, unknown to Kowlewski, Churchill and Roosevelt were scheduled to arrive within a fortnight for a conference. However, the *Kommandeur* was 'given a rocket' because four Condors were damaged by AA fire and made emergency landings in Spain, where one was written off and another was requisitioned as an airliner.[41]

The loss of the Mareth Line marked a change in bomber tactics, with the *Kampfgruppen* now concentrating upon the enemy rear at Kesselring's insistence (see Table 58 for activity). The Ju 88s were especially active as Sigel's *Stukas* were driven from the skies, but Kesselring had an ulterior motive since Göring was seeking resources from *Luftflotte 2* for a new bombing offensive against Great Britain which would earn him political kudos from the *Führer*. During April the *Kampfgruppen* had only 180 bombers, but they flew 1,332 sorties, of which 45% were Army support/airfield attack and 31% were convoy escort; the remainder were against shipping or harbours, and they suffered a 2.5% loss rate. Even the

---

Table 58. *Luftwaffe* **Activity in the Mediterranean, January–May 1943**

Month	Fighter	Strike	Recon	Total	Losses
Jan	4,452	3,199	762	8,413	105
Feb	4,840	2,604	821	8,265	99
Mar	7,294	3,427	1,024	11,745	160
Apr	8,786	3,272	415	8,786	n/a
May	4,375	1,664	688	6,829	n/a

Note: Fighter includes *Zerstörer* and night fighter; strike includes *Kampf-, Stuka-* and *Schlachtflieger*.

Fernaufklärungsstaffeln were pressed into anti-shipping and convoy escort missions, although to a lesser extent. As the airlift came under increasing pressure the *Kampfgruppen* were pressed into service to bring in fuel, 42 Ju 88s bringing in 51 tonnes to El Djem on 8 April, while during the month 204 tonnes were brought in 133 sorties, mostly by *KG 1*.

By contrast, almost as soon as the Germans arrived in Tunisia their bases and communications came under remorseless air attack which inflicted heavy losses, wore the nerves, disrupted the supply organisation and led to a sharp decline in serviceability. The daylight attacks were spearheaded by B-17s, which made their Mediterranean début over Tunis on 16 November, and on 22 January they caught 35 Ju 52s at Tunis-El Aounia, destroying 13 (with seven Bf 109s) and damaging 15. The disaster was due to the failure to establish an effective early-warning network in the 100km deep bridgehead as well as the need to provide the Army with fighter support—indeed, only four fighters met the Fortresses—and consequently more fighters had to be retained for defensive duties. The Allied sword stabbed into southern Italy, but it was deadliest between Cape Bon and Sicily, where the sea route was nicknamed 'Death Row' by the Axis and 67% of all supplies were lost to air attack. Belated protection was offered by Osterkamp's appointment as *JaFü Sizilien* on 7 April, with four *Gruppen* to protect maritime traffic into Tunisia, and with a maximum of 148 aircraft he flew 3,521 sorties during April alone, but, despite the loss of 22 fighters, 70,000grt of shipping was sunk by Allied aircraft. British night attacks were met by *II./NJG 2*, whose *Kommandeur, Hauptmann Dr* Horst Patuschka, was killed in a crash on 6/7 March after scoring 23 victories.

Although most *Luftwaffe* activity was in northern and central Tunisia, it was the *FlFü Afrika*, Seidemann, in the south who was to play the prominent role, despite a decline in strength from 201 to 123 aircraft during January. To protect his rear from possible American attack two *Gruppe*-size task forces, *FlFü Mitte* (Sfax) and *FlFü Gabès*, were established early in January, with the latter disbanded at the end of the month when Seidemann moved his headquarters to Gabès. His arrival gave Kesselring the opportunity to rationalise the organisation in Tunisia, possibly spurred by dissatisfaction with the corrupt and incompetent Loerzer, who was replaced at *Fliegerkorps II* on 6 February by Harlinghausen and returned to become head of personnel at *RLM* until the end of the war. Seidemann and his *FlFü Afrika* headquarters were renamed *Fliegerkorps Tunis*, with three *Fliegerführer, Tunis, Mitte* and *Gabès*. Seidemann had the equivalent of 12 *Gruppen*, which maintained a strength of some 300 aircraft until mid-April and benefited from an expansion of the infrastructure and the introduction of a rudimentary, radar-supported early-warning network. His first task was to support *'Frühlingswind'* with 600 sorties on the first two days before Allied air power and bad weather neutralised *Luftwaffe* activity. In mid-February the Allies, too, reorganised their air forces, with the North-West African Air Force (Major-General Carl A. Spaatz) divided into Strategic (General James H. Doolittle), Tactical (Air Marshal Sir Arthur Coningham) and defensive Coastal (Air Vice-Marshal Sir Hugh Lloyd) Air Forces. By mid-March Doolittle and Coningham had 1,500 combat aircraft and Coningham's bombers began pounding the German rear while his fighter squadrons were re-equipped and used in strong, coordinated operations which swamped the *Jagdgruppen*. During one of these *JG 77*'s *Kommodore*, Müncheberg (135 victories), was killed in action with American Spitfires on 23 March.[42]

With the loss of the Mareth Line the two southern *Fliegerführer* were merged as *FlFü Süd*, but even bombing attacks by Harlinghausen and Waldau could not prevent the remorseless British progress. The *Stukas* now required strong escorts, while the Hs 129 failed to match the hopes placed in it owing to its vulnerability to dust and ground fire. As the bridgehead was compressed on to the Tunis plain, the supply of spares dried up and fuel arrived erratically, Seidemann's staff took personal control of air operations on 15 April, disbanding the *Luftgau* and sending the *Fliegerführer* staffs to Sardinia and Sicily. But it was becoming, in the words of the British study, 'an effete force', incapable of competing with Allied material superiority as airfields became ever more vulnerable.[43] *Gruppen* were gradually being withdrawn, *III./StG 3* after a mauling by American Spitfires on 3 April, and the infrastructure manpower became infantry, but the end was clearly in sight as *Fliegerkorps Tunis* visibly wilted under the blast and Allied aircraft smashed all opposition, leading to wholesale surrenders by German as well as Italian troops.

As the sea lanes became more hazardous, greater reliance was placed upon the airlift, which had declined in importance after November, allowing Kesselring to despatch three *Transportgruppen* to *Luftflotte 4* and reducing the fleet from 551 on 30 November to 172 on 31 January. To coordinate operations 'Old Eagle' fighter pilot and former *Freikorps* man *Generalmajor* Ulrich Buchholz (*Kommodore, KGzbV 3*) was appointed *Lufttransportführer II, Mittelmeer* on 15 January, with his forces organised under the Naples-based *KGzbV N (Neapel)* and the Trapani-based *KGzbV S. KGzbV S* had two daily missions and *KGzbV N* had one, with transports flying in *'pulks'* of 80–120 aircraft at 45m (150ft), arriving around noon when the Allies were supposed to be at lunch. On average the Ju 52s brought in 90 tonnes daily and the Me 323s carried 30 tonnes, the unloading parties including Indian prisoners of war (see Table 59). The Sicilian-based units picked up their escort, one fighter for every five transports, after take-off while the Naples units were met near Trapani, and on the return journey fighters and *Zerstörer* appeared at the coast. The end of the Stalingrad and Kuban airlifts permitted a timely expansion of transport forces to 185 on 10 March, 263 a month later and 426 by the beginning of April, mostly flying in fuel and ammunition to replenish *Heeresgruppe Afrika*'s exhausted stocks, the task being facilitated by *KGzbV N*'s transfer to Sicily in late March. Through 'Ultra' intercepts the Allies had detailed

Table 59. The Tunisian Airlift, 1943

Month	Tonnes	Men
Jan	4,665	14,523
Feb	4,954	12,803
Mar	7,651	11,819
Apr	4,327	18,128
May	587	292
Total	22,184	57,565

Note: May figures are to 10 May only.
Source: Gundelach, p.1054/n.328, based upon Army records.

knowledge of enemy air traffic and occasionally intercepted *'pulks'* of transports, but they planned a massive offensive, Operation 'Flax', to end the airlift completely. Originally scheduled for February, 'Flax' was postponed until April because of bad weather and for maximum impact, with fighters intercepting *'pulks'* on six occasions to bring the total losses during the month to 123 Ju 52s, four S.82s and 14 Me 323s, forcing the transports to operate individually at night, when they were harried by night fighters.

By early May only *JG 77* and an Italian fighter group remained in Africa, and with barely a toe-hold in Africa on 11 May Kesselring gave Osterkamp's *JaFü Sizilien* responsibility for providing tactical air support. Three days earlier *I.* and *II./JG 77* had withdrawn from Africa, and, given the dangers facing transports (16 men of *JG 77* were lost in a crash on 29/30 April), pilots tried to take out their own ground crews and, sometimes, those of other pilots. While carrying two passengers in his Bf 109 on 8 May *JG 77's Leutnant* Ernst-Wilhelm Reinert claimed his 51st African victory.[44] The last transport missions were flown on 4 May, when 117 tonnes of fuel and ammunition were brought in, while the last key personnel, such as 'Beppo' Schmid, commander of the *Hermann Göring Division*, were flown out. In the next few days *II./KG 1* made a few supply drops, but the vast majority of the *Flak*, signals, transport and administrative staff left in Africa were destined for prison camps.[45]

The defeat in North Africa was a disaster for the *Luftwaffe*, for, in addition to thousands of trained and experienced men, it lost 2,422 aircraft, the equivalent of 67 *Gruppen*, in the theatre between 1 November and 30 April. Yet there was to be no respite, and Harlinghausen's desire to rest and rebuild his *Kampfgruppen* was overruled by Göring, leading to a month-long night offensive from mid-May, with 38 missions against Algerian harbours, usually by 30–40 aircraft, the navigational skills of whose crews showed no improvement. Harlinghausen's complaints to Kesselring proved to be counter-productive and on 16 June he was relieved of his command. He briefly went into limbo, then joined the *General der Kampfflieger's* staff in October before commanding first a *Luftgau* and then *Luftwaffenkommando*

Above: An important role for the *Transport-truppen* was the delivery of fuel. Here drums of petrol are rolled off a truck towards a Ju 52 transport. On return flights Ju 52s would often bring back fuel containers, both drums and jerrycans.

Below: A *'pulk'* of Ju 52s from *KGrzbV 700 Wittstock* approaches Tunisia.

Left: In the absence of a bowser this Ju 88 must be refuelled by hand-pump from a drum—a clumsy and time-consuming operation for the 'black men'.

Above: The fluid situation in the East meant that both *Luftflotten 4* and *6* headquarters operated from command trains. In this picture a Storch flies low over *Luftflotte 4*'s train.

Below left: As the *Luftwaffe* retreated it demolished its installations. Here an airfield magazine in the East is blown up.

Left: Servicing a 3.7cm *Flak 18* gun of a *Panzerjägerstaffel* Ju 87G-1.

Top: Gliders were used extensively by the *Luftwaffe* for transport not only to isolated garrisons but by units moving from base to base. This Go 242 is pictured over the Eastern Front.

Above: Preparing to load wounded into an Me 323 Gigant transport of *TG 5*.

Right: A *Panzerjäger* Ju 87 uses its 3.7cm guns to strafe a Russian footbridge.

Left, upper: Light and medium *Flak* weapons such as this Sd Kfz 251/10 self-propelled 3.7cm gun, were used extensively by batteries in the East against infantry as well as against night-harassing aircraft.

Left, lower: Tunis-El Aouina airfield was full of wrecked transports when it was occupied by the Allies in May 1943. The aircraft in the background has the tactical designation 'T2', indicating that it was with *KGrzbV 800*. The piece of rudder in the foreground carries the tactical designation 'P2', indicating that it is from a *KGrzbV 400* transport. (Alex Vanags-Baginskis)

Below: An unusual collection of wrecked aircraft at Stalingrad in the spring of 1943. In the foreground is a *KG 53* He 111H bomber beside a He 111F 'hack', behind which is an H 123 close support aircraft, probably also a personal 'hack'. (Alex Vanags-Baginskis)

Right, upper: A smashed transport surrounded by the bodies of those its crew tried to support at Stalingrad. (Alex Vanags-Baginskis)

Right, lower: A *Lufttransportstaffel 290* Ju 90 under attack from RAF Marauders off Corsica in the summer of 1943. The transport was shot down near Bastia. (Alex Vanags-Baginskis)

Below: During the autumn of 1942 the *Nahaufklärungsgruppen* probed the Russian rear. This Fw 189 was shot down in October. (Alex Vanags-Baginskis)

Above: He 72 Kadetts of *Luftkriegschule 2*, which was closed at Reinsdorf in October 1944

Left: Briefing crews for *Unternehmen 'Steinbock'*, the 'Little Blitz' of 1944.

Top left: A Ju 88 begins to taxi towards the runway during *Unternehmen 'Steinbock'*.

Above left: An Fw 190 makes a low-level pass in 1942 as a blazing Spitfire falls behind it.

Top right: A Bf 109 pursues a Spitfire near the Channel in 1941.

Above right: Celebrations at a fighter field in western Europe as a *Feldwebel* is cheered for winning his *Jagdgeschwader*'s 1,000th victory.

Right: A *Jagdgruppe Adjutant* prepares to take off in an Fw 190.

Left: As the *Jagdgruppen* were driven back during 1943 and 1944, *Flak* batteries such as this one became *Luftflotte 3*'s primary defence.

Below left: A returning night fighter pilot is congratulated by a member of his ground crew.

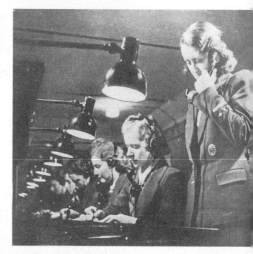

Above: *Luftwaffehelferinnen* released men from second-line duties such as those at telephone exchanges and were used extensively in the signals service. Not everyone welcomed them: when one answered *Generalfeldmarschall* Sperrle he would throw a tantrum.

Left: A scene at a *Jagddivision* headquarters, dubbed by Galland 'battle opera houses'.

Right: Like the British, the Germans used wrecked enemy aircraft as a source of scrap metal. Although Wellingtons dominate this photograph, on the right appear to be a Dewoitine D.520 and a Breguet 693, while behind are a LeO 451 and a Fairey Battle.

Left: COMINT operations not only allowed the *Luftwaffe* to deduce trends in enemy operations but actually provided early warning of bombing attacks on the Reich. Before each mission British and American ground crews would tune bombers' radios several hours before take-off, and this upsurge of traffic was intercepted by the *Funkhorchdienst* who then alerted the defences.

Below left: An Fw 190 gives the *coup de grâce* to a blazing B-17 Fortress.

Right: Using models demonstrating the defensive cones of fire in a B-24 Liberator, a *Kommandeur* indicates the best means of attack to newly arrived fighter pilots.

Above left: Preparing an FzG 76 (V-1) missile for firing. Much was expected by *OKL* of these missiles, but the British, who had actually smuggled one out of Poland, had time to prepare counter-measures.

Top right: Bombs from a USAAF Martin B-26 Marauder just miss an Fw 190. (Alex Vanags-Baginskis)

Above right: A successful fighter pilot describes his victory to fellow pilots. (Alex Vanags-Baginskis)

Below: *Unternehmen 'Steinbock'* cost Peltz the equivalent of his whole force, including this Do 217 which landed in East Anglia after being abandoned over London. (Alex Vanags-Baginskis)

Right: He 177 Greifs being strafed by Mustangs. (Alex Vanags-Baginskis)

Below: A Bf 109G pictured by a gun camera as it bursts into flames over Germany. (Alex Vanags-Baginskis)

Below left: In the face of American long-range fighters the *Zerstörer* were doomed over Germany. With their starboard engine ablaze, this Me 410 Hornisse crew have ejected the canopy before baling out. (Alex Vanags-Baginskis)

Below right: *Generalfeldmarschall* Hugo Sperrle, right, with *Generalleutnant* Gustav Kastner-Kirdorf, who headed the Personnel Department until replaced by Loerzer in February 1943. He committed suicide at Berchtesgarten in May 1945.

Below: Fighter aces from two world wars: *Generaloberst* Ernst Udet (left) and *Oberst* Werner Mölders. Mölders was killed while flying to Berlin to attend Udet's funeral.

Above right: *Generaloberst* Robert, *Ritter* von Greim succeeded Göring as commander of the *Luftwaffe* in 1945. He spent most of the Second World War on the Eastern Front, and although a fighter 'ace' in the Great War he was at the forefront of the strategic bombing debate.

Below left: *Generaloberst* Hubert Weise, a *Flak* specialist, spent most of the war directing

Germany's air defences as commander of *Luftwaffe Befehlshaber Mitte* until relieved by Stumpff in 1944. (Alex Vanags-Baginskis)

Below right: *Generalleutnant* Theodor 'Uncle Theo' Osterkamp, who directed the *Jagdgruppen* during the Battle of Britain and in the latter stages of the Tunis campaign.

Above left: *General der Flieger* Günther Korten had no air experience in the Great War but he became one of the best staff officers in the *Luftwaffe* and in August 1943 became Chief of Staff. He was mortally wounded by the bomb meant to kill Hitler in July 1944.

Above right: *Generalleutnant* Karl Koller was Korten's friend and became his Director of Operations. Ultimately he succeeded Korten as Chief of Staff, a position he held until the end of the war. (Alex Vanags-Baginskis)

Below left: *Generaloberst* Hans Jeschonnek was too immature, and perhaps too soft, to be Chief of Staff, and when his masters grew tired they ordered him to dispose of himself.

Below right: *Generaloberst* Otto Dessloch was a *Flak* specialist who commanded *Luftflotte 4* from the summer of 1943, briefly becoming the last commander of *Luftflotte 3* in late August 1944.

Left: *Generalmajor* Martin Harlinghausen was the first *FlFü Atlantik*, but injury and the Tunisian campaign broke his link with the anti-shipping campaign. He commanded *Fliegerkorps II* but fell foul of Kesselring. He became the last commander of *Luftwaffekommando West* in 1945 and later had a distinguished career in the *Bundesluftwaffe*.

Below left: *General der Flieger* Martin Fiebig, seen here with *Oberst* Stahel when commanding *Fliegerkorps VIII*, was a close air support specialist. He and Löhr were both executed in Yugoslavia for war crimes. (Alex Vanags-Baginskis)

Below right: Göring and Jeschonnek consider strategy. As criticism of the *Luftwaffe* mounted, Göring increasingly left Jeschonnek to face Hitler's fury—an abandonment which greatly contributed to the younger man's suicide. (Alex Vanags-Baginskis)

Above: *Generalmajor* Adolf Galland was *General
er Jagdflieger* from 1942 to 1944, when he quit
1 anger. With him here are *Oberst* Johannes
Hannes' Trautloft, his right-hand man, and
Oberst Walther Oesau, *Kommodore* of *JG 1*, who
vas killed by American fighters in 1944.
Galland and Trautloft later served in the 'ace'
et unit *JV 44*. (Alex Vanags-Baginskis)

Below: 'Smiling Albert' prepares for an
inspection flight. *Generalfeldmarschall* Albert
Kesselring commanded *Luftflotte 2* from
February 1940 to June 1943, when his duties as
OB Süd forced him to hand over to Richthofen.
(Alex Vanags-Baginskis)

Above left: *Oberst* Werner Baumbach, *Kommandeur* of *I./KG 30*, was an anti-shipping specialist relieved of his command in 1942 after protesting to Jeschonnek about Loerzer's incompetent direction of such operations. He ended the war as *Kommodore* of the special duties unit *KG 200*. He was killed in an air crash in Argentina. (Alex Vanags-Baginskis)

Above right: *Stuka Experte Major* Hans-Ulrich Rudel was fanatical about keeping fit and was famous for his abstinence—hence the doggerel *'Major Rudel trinkt nur Sprudel'* (Major Rudel drinks only mineral water). (Alex Vanags-Baginskis)

Left: *Oberst* Werner Streib was *Kommodore* of *NJG 1* in early 1944 before becoming *General der Nachtjagdwaffe* until the end of the war. An *Experte* with 65 night and one day victory, he is believed to have shot down the Stirling whose H2S radar (*Rotterdamgerät*) revolutionised German electronic development. (Alex Vanags-Baginskis)

West (the former *Luftflotte 3*). After the war he became one of the few *Reichsluftwaffe* senior officers to hold high rank in the *Bundesluftwaffe*, retiring in 1961 as commander of NATO's Air Force North. The dismissal of Harlinghausen was Kesselring's Parthian shot, for on the same day Richthofen reluctantly assumed command of *Luftflotte 2*, telling Göring that 'This is a theatre where I can lose my honour and reputation.'[46] He established amiable relations with Kesselring, who was now totally preoccupied with his responsibilities as *OB Süd*, but Richthofen was evidently Göring's watchdog on 'Smiling Albert', to whom, in his own words, 'the whole *Luftflotte* still pays homage'. To establish his authority he placed his own men into the key commands, Bülowius at *Fliegerkorps II* and Mahnke as *FlFü Sizilien*. Wild (*FlFü Sardinien*) was justifiably suspicious when he met Richthofen, the two having clashed during the Sevastopol campaign.[47] On 19 June the former was sidelined into a staff post with responsibilities for convoys (*Geleitzugführer Mittelmeer*) and on 26 June replaced by the erstwhile *Kommodore* of *SchG 1*, *Oberstleutnant* (*Oberst* from 1 July) Hitschold.[48] Wild's departure saw close support specialist Weiss (newly promoted to *Oberst*) arrive in Sicily to join his superior, Galland, in a vain attempt to 'fire up' the *Schlachtflieger*. Galland had been in the theatre since April to monitor and support fighter operations, but while he was a brave and skilful pilot he was no staff officer. The lure of action proved too great, and on 22 June he replaced Osterkamp as *JaFü Sizilien*, having appointed *Oberst* Günther 'Franzl' Lützow as *Inspekteur der Jagdflieger (Süd)* on 17 May to relieve him of many staff problems.[49] An addition to Richthofen's staff, appointed by *ObdL*, was *Oberst* Peltz, who had helped Richthofen reorganise *Luftflotte 4*'s bombers in January before becoming *Angriffsführer England*. His new appointment as *Fernkampfführer Luftflotte 2* (also *Fernkampfführer Mittelmeer*) was similar to that of Galland and evidently reflected *ObdL*'s agreement over Harlinghausen's earlier concerns about the *Kampfgruppen*.[50]

Relations between these officers were soon to be sorely tested as the Allies prepared to invade Sicily. Between 11 May and 10 July *Luftflotte 2*'s strength increased 17% from 725 to 838, half in Italy, while serviceability improved from 52% to 60% (see Table 60). Within the strike forces there was a 63% increase in bombers, while close support strength doubled, Peltz bringing with him from western Europe *KG 2*, *KG 6* and half of *SKG 10*. The strengthening of *SKG 10* was an acknowledgement that the *Kampf-* and *Stukagruppen* were no longer an effective day strike force, and the *Stukagruppen* now went to the Balkans. Yet fighter strength was unchanged, although Milch diverted 40% of total production between 1 May and 15 July to the theatre while Galland stripped even the Fatherland and added a *Zerstörer-* and two new *Jagdgruppen* for what he believed would be the decisive confrontation with the Allies. Facilities in Sardinia and Sicily were also improved, the latter work directed by *Generalmajor* Gottlob Müller's *Luftgau zbV Sizilien* (later *Feldluftgau Sizilien*). Most of the bombers were in Italy and the

Table 60. *Luftflotte 2*, May 1943–June 1944

Date	Fighters	Bombers	*Schlacht*	Recon	*Zerstörer*	Total
11 May 1943	290/166	180/ 91	63/ 26	60/ 27	123/ 64	725/374
10 Jul 1943	298/165	294/186	131/ 79	45/ 25	70/ 52	838/507
31 Aug 1943	181/ 91	260/110	90/ 51	48/ 30	–	579/282
30 Sept 1943	111/ 67	195/113	32/ 20	25/ 16	–	358/216
20 Oct 1943	108/ 43	198/141	49/ 29	38/ 15	–	393/228
31 Dec 1943	184/ 78 (24/ 19)	–	28/ 10	31/ 25	–	243/113
20 Jan 1944	200/136 (24/ 24)	–	60/ 37	31/ 22	–	291/195
10 Feb 1944	213/138 (33/ 17)	165/103	54/ 28	40/ 32	–	472/301
31 Mar 1944	155/109 (24/ 24)	100/ 58	99/ 57	40/ 26	–	394/250
10 May 1944	197/146 (57/ 45)	96/ 74	75/ 40	40/ 24	–	408/284
10 Jun 1944	161/ 93 (69/ 27)	–	84/ 69	40/ 25	–	285/187

Note: *Zerstörer* includes night fighter and *Schlacht* includes *Nachtschlacht*. Figures in parentheses are for *ANR*. First figure is operational strength and second is aircraft serviceable.
Source: Gundelach, various pages, based upon strength returns.

fighters and *Jabos* were in Sicily, where there were 282 aircraft on 10 July. However, serviceability was poor (less than 50% in many cases) due to the loss of spares and tools, while the 8.8cm *Flak 41* guns, which unlike the *Flak 36* could reach the American Fortresses, had all been lost, having been committed to Tunisia on Hitler's orders, and no replacements were available. For its part the *Regia Aeronautica* was a broken reed, having lost 2,190 aircraft between 2 November and 30 June 1943, leaving 620 aircraft (387 fighters) to defend Sicily. In February Rome requested 500 aircraft from the Germans, who despatched only 20 Ju 88 and a few modern fighters, although the supply of DB 601 and DB 605 engines enabled Italian industry to provide fighters such as the Macchi MC.205 Veltro, the Regianne Re.2005 Sagittario and the Fiat G.55 Centauro, all of which could hold their own with enemy aircraft. Yet the country was demoralised following the fall of Tunis, and an air of lethargic defeatism hung everywhere, feeding German distrust.

Even before Arnim had surrendered Allied bombers had been attacking mainland and offshore Italy. In mid-May 1943 the battle for Sicily's outposts began over the islands of Pantelleria and Lampedusa, which came under sustained air bombardment in a successful effort to blast them into surrender following the appearance of the Allied assault force on 11 June. The prisoners included 78 *Flugmeldedienst* personnel. *Luftwaffe* reconnaissance spotted the ships, but Peltz allowed them unhindered passage until Pantelleria surrendered, whereupon *SKG*

10 and *SchG 2 Jabos* attacked them, *SKG 10* flying 200 sorties between 5 and 15 June. Pantelleria marked the beginning of a four-phase offensive by Allied air forces, which had 3,462 aircraft (including transports), of which 2,510 were serviceable. Between 16 May and 9 July they flew 42,147 sorties over the western Mediterranean, gradually concentrating upon Sicily, where, on 9 July, Liberators struck Bülowius's headquarters at Taormina, destroying his central telephone exchange and rendering all the airfields in the Catania-Gerbini complex non-operational.[51] The six-week offensive cost the Allies 250 aircraft and the Axis some 325 in the air, but at Italian bases the *Luftwaffe* lost another 122. With hindsight, one German historian said that *ObdL* should have anticipated the impossibility of conducting a successful air defence of Sicily.[52]

The *Kampfgruppen* in return struck potential invasion harbours on seven occasions from 7 June, with Peltz introducing the low-level approach and last-minute-climb tactics used against Great Britain. Poor navigation undermined the offensive, together with declining serviceability rates (55% on average), while the shortage of fully trained crews ('Old Hares') meant that only half the serviceable bombers could be despatched. The efficient defences aggravated the situation by inflicting an average 5% loss rate, rising to nearly 13% on the last mission (6/7 July). During June the bomber bases came under Allied air attacks which pushed the *Kampfgruppen* out of Sicily into central Italy or even southern France.[53]

The air assault on Sicily tested the *Luftwaffe* leaders: Kesselring's optimism grated on the nerves and Richthofen was carping at Peltz's lack of success but was content to allow the moody Galland sufficient rope to hang himself. The *Jagdgruppen*'s failure was an acute personal disappointment and Galland would tongue-lash unsuccessful pilots, earning a quiet rebuke from *Major* Johannes 'Macki' Steinhoff (*Kommodore, JG 77*). Galland was himself under pressure from Göring, who sent hysterical and insulting teleprinter messages, demanding on 25 June that pilots who returned with undamaged aircraft or without victories be court-martialled for cowardice. Having lost 70 fighters since the beginning of the month, a furious Galland was summoned to Berlin on 9 July to explain his 'failure'.[54]

While he winged his way northwards, *Luftwaffe* reconnaissance discovered convoys sailing towards Sicily, but no action was taken and they began unloading unhindered the following dawn. *Major* Günther Tonne's *Stab SchG 2* immediately became *Gefechtsverband Major Tonne* to control *Jabo* attacks upon shipping off the western (American) beach-heads, and was joined by the *Kampfgruppen* during the evening. Attacks on the western beachhead switched to the eastern (British) waters from 13 July, with the *Jabos* striking in the day and the bombers at night (apart from a disastrous daylight mission on 11 July). The latter used circling torpedoes (the waters were too shallow for conventional torpedo attacks) as well as bombs in missions which proved both hazardous and fruitless because the targets were obscured by smokescreens. Although the US 1st Division suffered serious damage on 10/11 July the *Luftwaffe* failed to disrupt the flow of supplies and during July sank only seven merchantmen and auxiliaries (48,685grt), a destroyer and six smaller vessels (see Table 61). Allied fighters smothered the Axis response and on the first day destroyed 27 aircraft (16 German), while only 25 Allied aircraft were lost. The *Kampfgruppen*'s greatest successes were accidental, their presence causing nervous Allied naval AA gunners to shoot down 37 of their own transport aircraft on three nights.

Richthofen spent long hours on the telephone with Göring and Jeschonnek demanding more anti-shipping units and reinforcements, but there was neither sympathy nor understanding. The airfields were a shambles and 36 fighters despatched by Milch burst their tyres on bomb splinters upon landing and were damaged. Yet the defenders still had teeth, *JG 77* claiming 27 victories from 10 to 31 July while losing 51 fighters and 12 pilots killed.[55] But Italian resistance collapsed as the Allies expanded their beach-heads, screened daily by 1,100 fighter sorties, and within three days these fighters were operating from Sicilian airfields, forcing even the normally optimistic Kesselring to seek permission for a timely evacuation. Yet Richthofen was reinforced: Sperrle provided three *Gruppen* (including Fink's missile units) while Fiebig transferred four, his strength having been doubled before 'Husky' because deception measures had convinced the German High Command that the landing would be in Greece.[56] However, Richthofen sadly noted on 13 July that an attack upon Naples had destroyed two-thirds of his Bf 110s and he observed, 'We are playing cat and mouse in Sicily.' With no more than 150 serviceable aircraft each day and his airfields under threat, Richthofen's *Gruppen* were pushed into southern Italy, staging through airfields in northeast Sicily during the day. On 14 July Galland was recalled to Germany, leaving *Oberst* Viek in charge of fighter operations, and the following evening Bülowius flew his last serviceable aircraft to the mainland. Viek, Tonne and *2.(H)/14* remained, but the next day they too quit the island.[57] There were so few *Luftwaffe* fighters that between 14 and 20 July the *Nahaufklärungsflieger* Bf 109s had to fly unescorted as *Flak* assumed responsibility for air defence.[58]

Table 61. Axis Air Response to Operation 'Husky'

Date	Luftwaffe	Italian
10 Jul	370	141
11 Jul	283	198
12 Jul	202	171
13 Jul	164	197
14 Jul	156	88
15 Jul	85	76

Source: Molony, V, p.97/n.1, based upon Italian documents.

As Galland departed Richthofen's air strength faded away from 120 aircraft (30 serviceable) in Sicily on 16 July to barely a dozen operational aircraft two days later. By dawn on 22 July the *Luftwaffe* had lost 273 aircraft (the Italians 115) since the invasion and the Allies only 100. Due to *SKG 10*'s crippling losses against shipping, *Jagdgruppen* were pressed into the ground attack role, and *Oberleutnant* Wolf Ettel (124 victories) of the newly arrived *8./JG 27* was killed by ground fire near Catania on 17 July. Preparations were under way for the evacuation, and to shield the Straits of Messina *Oberstleutnant* Fischer was assembling *Flak* batteries, 14 heavy on 19 July and 65 (including 22 Italian) by 2 August to produce the *Flakglocke von Messina* (Messina Anti-Aircraft Bell).[59] The fall of Palermo on 22 July saw preparations for an evacuation accelerate, covered by a rearguard around Mount Etna which included *1. Fallschirmjägerdivision*, part of which was flown from France to Catania, arriving in transports, in gliders or by parachute between 11 and 16 July. They were supplied by Ju 52s both day and night using rough landing strips, despite day and night attacks (25 aircraft were destroyed on 14/15 July). The biggest disaster occurred on 25 July when Spitfires caught a *'pulk'* landing at Milazzo and shot down 10 as well as two of the three escorts from *JG 77*.

Bowing to the inevitable, Hitler authorised the evacuation of Sicily, *Unternehmen 'Lehrgang'* (Instruction Course), which began on 11 August shielded by Fischer's gunners. Bülowius supported them with 74 Bf 109s of *JG 77*, *I./JG 53* and *IV./JG 3*, which flew up to 150 sorties a day while the rearguard was supported by 50 *Jabos* and 50–60 fighters from the 'toe' of Italy, but with limited airfield facilities and Allied air superiority they averaged only 60 sorties a day. As the infrastructure contracted, most signallers were used to flesh out *22. Flakbrigade*, while radars, spares, fuel and equipment were evacuated in the chaos of civilian refugee columns. The Allies were slow to respond, and their 838 bombers and 1,001 fighters and fighter-bombers flew only 1,170 sorties, held off by Fischer's gunners. The Germans managed to evacuate 39,569 men (including 4,444 wounded), 17,075 tonnes of supplies and other equipment including 47 tanks by the time the operation was completed on 17 August, ensuring an effective defence of Italy.

It was a small consolation in a disastrous campaign for the *Luftwaffe*. Between 10 July and 17 August *Luftflotte 2* flew 7,354 sorties over Sicily, including 2,971 (41%) fighter and 2,411 (33%) bomber, losing more than 600 aircraft (262 in the air), while *Fliegerdivision 2* lost another 106 in southern France. In the same period the Allies flew some 27,400 sorties and lost 140 aircraft (a 0.5% loss rate compared with 3.5% for the *Luftwaffe*). Throughout the Sicily campaign Richthofen's airfields in Italy were under attack: the Americans' 15 July raid on Foggia so disrupted the *Kampfgruppen* that hardly an aircraft flew the following night's mission; five days later most of Richthofen's *Jabos* and night fighters were destroyed at Aquino; and when *IV./JG 3* lost a third of its fighters at Leverano on 23

July Richthofen ordered a court of inquiry to see if the disaster could be ascribed to negligence by local headquarters. To neutralise the threat new bases were designed to accommodate no more than two *Gruppen*, whose aircraft were well dispersed.[60]

Italian war weariness led to Mussolini's arrest on 25 July, and while the new government under Marshal Pietro Badoglio pledged to remain by Germany's side the Germans soon intercepted a telephone call between Churchill and Roosevelt which showed that Rome was seeking an armistice. The mistrustful *Führer* had been under no illusions, and when Mussolini was arrested he summoned Student to Rastenburg and ordered him to transfer *2. Fallschirmjägerdivision* to Rome as insurance and to prepare an airborne rescue mission, which would be placed under *SS Obersturmbannführer (Oberstleutnant)* Otto Skorzeny.[61] Kesselring drafted a contingency plan, *Unternehmen 'Achse'* (Axle), to disarm his allies if they defected, yet, ever the optimist, he accepted Badoglio's assurances, although he and a sceptical Richthofen frequently discussed the situation with Jeschonnek, who was increasingly concerned both with the Reich's air defences and the failures in the East. Richthofen himself was increasingly irritated by the failure of Peltz's bombers, which he wished to control himself, but the *Fernkampfführer* remained a favourite of Göring. On 1 August the *Kampfgruppen* had a rare victory when *KG 26* and *KG 100* wrecked Palermo's main dock, but follow-up raids could not prevent the enemy's remorseless advance. A post-operation report claimed that 516,850grt of shipping had been sunk or severely damaged, but only 54,306grt was actually sunk and the lack of success gave Richthofen the excuse to remove Peltz on 6 August and replace him with the 43-year-old former sailor *Oberst* Walter Storp (*Kommodore KG 6*). Foggia became the primary bomber base (with seven *Kampfgruppen* at the beginning of September) under *KG 54*'s *Kommodore, Major* Volprecht Riedesel, *Freiherr von und zu* Eisenbach (*Führer des Gefechtsverbandes Foggia*) and *Oberstleutnant* Bloedorn (*Kommodore, KG 30*), and extensive training became a matter of urgency.

Although Storp was reinforced the *Luftwaffe* effectively abandoned the struggle for the Mediterranean skies, conserving its strength by reducing operations. By 3 September its strength in the theatre had dropped by 370 to 880 aircraft in just two months, and with an invasion of Italy imminent Richthofen dissolved *Italuft* and dispersed its functions under *Luftgau zbV Süd* (now under Mahnke) and *General der Flakartillerie Süd* (the former *Italuft General der Flieger* Maximilian, *Ritter* von Pohl) in southern Italy with *22. Flakbrigade* while *Flakführer Oberitalien* (later *3. Flakbrigade*) defended the northern Italian infrastructure. Sicily's loss made Calabria untenable, and the *Luftwaffe*'s forward elements moved to Puglia (the 'heel') as five *Gruppen* were withdrawn either for refitting or to defend the Reich. For long-range daylight reconnaissance 300-litre drop-tanks were provided for *Nahaufklärungsstaffel* Bf 109s, enabling them to cover first Bougie and later

Algiers, flying up to 14 sorties a day. They discovered a large amphibious force with 500,000grt of shipping in Bizerta, but delays forwarding reports and strong fighter shields ensured that there were no attacks upon convoys.

During the last fortnight of August communications and airfields in southern Italy came under a systematic attack involving 3,500 sorties which so buckled Richthofen's infrastructure that by 31 August less than half of his 579 aircraft were serviceable. He was convinced that the Allies would land in Sardinia, but Kesselring believed (correctly) that it would be in Calabria, and this led to a heated argument between them on 20 August. That day Storp's bombers were ordered to launch pre-emptive night attacks on shipping, although they were already conducting missions of up to 60 aircraft against harbours, supplemented by *Jabo* attacks on Augusta. Casualties were heavy, at 5–10% per mission, and a B-17 raid destroyed 28 aircraft at Foggia on 25 August, thwarting plans for a major raid upon Algiers. On 30 August Storp rested his crews, especially new ones who had suffered such heavy losses, allowing him to despatch 80 bombers at Bizerta a week later though with little effect. Four days later the British 8th Army landed in Calabria, as Kesselring had anticipated, although he had no intention of fighting under the shadow of an Allied supremacy enforced by 2,721 combat aircraft when he had only 120 fighters and 50 *Jabos* immediately available at inadequate airfields. Instead he wished for a rearguard action including *Luftflotte 2*, but Richthofen refused to risk his exhausted men's lives when Italian resistance was again collapsing. Rather than flout Kesselring's instructions he 'interpreted' them by committing limited forces.[62]

The wisdom of Richthofen's action quickly became apparent when reconnaissance on 5 September indicated large shipping movements towards the Naples area, an attack upon a convoy by 80 aircraft suffering 10% losses. Early on 8 September reports came of a landing at Salerno, south of Naples, in Operation 'Avalanche', but more stunning was the simultaneous news broadcast by the Allies that Rome had secretly signed an armistice. The German implementation of '*Achse*' was hindered by the bombing on 8 September of Kesselring's headquarters at Frascati and Richthofen's at Grotta Ferrata (where 30 men were killed), which left only *Fliegerkorps XI*'s headquarters operational. The paratroops played a key role in disarming the defecting Italians and there were two parachute operations, by *II./FJR 6* (*Major* Walther Gericke) on the 2nd Italian Army headquarters at Monte Rotondo, south-west of Rome, on 8 September and by *II./FJR 7* (*Major* Friedrich Hübner) on Elba 10 days later. Meanwhile on 12 September Mussolini was rescued from his prison in the skiing resort of Gran Sasso in an operation involving 10 gliders carrying 90 men of the *Fallschirm Lehrbataillon* (*Major* Mors) and 16 SS troops. *Il Duce*, accompanied by Skorzeny, was then flown out in a Storch piloted by *Hauptmann* Gerlach (Student's personal pilot) to become head of the puppet *Republica Sociale Italiana* (*RSI*).[63] Elsewhere *Flak* batteries at Foggia disarmed and captured an Italian division, while both *JG 77* and *TG 5* also helped disarm their former allies.

Simultaneously the *Luftwaffe* met the threat at Salerno and had hopes of gaining air superiority as the beach-head was 280km from the Allies' Sicilian airfields. Richthofen had increased serviceability to 58% and now made concentrated attacks as he had long desired, ignoring the advance of the British 8th Army. Bülowius's fighters and *Jabos* flew 108 sorties (82 escort) on the first day, and from dusk on 8 September Storp's bombers took up the attack, flying 150 sorties but never posing a serious threat to shipping. However, the Allies were able to cover the beach-head with P-38s, Spitfires with long-range tanks and carrier-borne Seafires. Richthofen failed to dent this shield, while enemy air superiority crushed every land threat to the beach-heads and even permitted the Allies to parachute in a regiment. Bülowius attacked daily for 10 days, sometimes twice a day supporting counter-attacks, with a peak of 100 *Jabo* sorties on 10/11 September; even escorting Bf 109s of *IV./JG 3* participated in ground attacks, using 21cm *Nebelwerfer* rocket-launchers. Richthofen demanded two sorties per crew at night from his *Kampfgruppen*, which achieved up to 100 sorties between dusk and dawn, while Fink's missile *Gruppen* joined the fray from 11 September. Operating during the day, they posed a serious threat because their high-speed weapons were launched beyond AA range into crowded anchorages where there was no room to manoeuvre. They maintained a daily offensive until 17 September in missions involving four to five bombers, often covered by *'pulks'* of 14–20 Bf 109s, to damage several warships, cripple the battleship HMS *Warspite* and sink the hospital ship *Newfoundland* (6,791grt), but suffered 20% losses. Conventional anti-shipping forces claimed another two merchantmen (14,326grt).[64]

Sustained attacks from 16 September on his main bomber base at Foggia marked the beginning of the end for Richthofen. The following day Kesselring broke off the Salerno battle and withdrew north, his troops receiving only token support from the *Luftwaffe* with barely 30 *Jabo* sorties a day, often with weak escorts. Within a couple of days the *Kampfgruppen* flew to winter bases in northern Italy while single-engine *Gruppen* withdrew to central Italy. The enemy occupied the Foggia airfields on 28 September and promptly began creating the strike bases which Peltz had always desired; indeed, within three days American bombers flew from there to Wiener-Neustadt. This added to Richthofen's worries, for he now became responsible for protecting the southern approaches to Austria. To this end Steinhoff reorganised the defences of northern Italy and established three fighter control posts (*Jägerleitstände*), *West* (Turin), *Mitte* (Pontecchio, near Bologna) and *Ost* (Udine). Richthofen would have preferred Maltzahn (*Kommodore, JG 53*), but he had been transferred to Germany for two months and did not return until 13 December, to become *JaFü Oberitalien*. Steinhoff had only 149 fighters by the end of October and could achieve little against American heavy bomber formations droning into Austria or smashing Italian targets. The lack of success irritated both Richthofen and Göring, the latter expressing his displeasure with the usual stream of hysterical teleprinter signals. Meanwhile Richthofen met*Kommodore* and *Kommandeure* at Guidonia on 17 November to determine the problems. It became clear that these included physical exhaustion and combat fatigue as well as the poor training of new pilots, whose morale collapsed when they realised that they had been thrown in at the deep end.[65] Richthofen ordered a thorough retraining of all *Jagdgruppen* with the intention of gradually committing them in morale-building set-piece battles, and under Maltzahn the policy appeared to bear fruit when three *Jagdgruppen* intercepted US heavy bombers on 28 December and claimed 20. Meanwhile the defence was further strengthened by some 100 *Flak* batteries, of which half had Italian equipment.

With the Reich unable, or unwilling, to support him, Richthofen was forced back on to his own resources. On 23 November he authorised the creation of an *RSI* air force (*Aeronautica Nazionale Republicana*, or *ANR*). This was initially under *Generalmajor* Müller's command, but his talents lay in diplomacy and administration and he became *Deutschen Bevollmächtigten beim italienischen Luftfahrtministerium*, to be replaced by Bloedorn. It was decided to create a group each of fighters, torpedo-bombers and transports, but, on Hitler's instructions, they were to receive only Italian equipment. Macchi MC.205s were supplied to the 1st Italian Fighter Group, which flew its first patrol on 2 January 1944 and the following day claimed two American bombers, but poor German aircraft recognition sometimes led to the *Jagdgruppen* shooting down Macchis and eventually resulted in the re-equipment of the Italian units with Bf 109s.[66] The group was expanded and its performance encouraged Richthofen to form two more with Fiat G.55s and Macchi MC.205s as well as an independent fighter squadron.[67] Strike and support arms were created with Torpedo Bomber (S.79-II/III) and Bomber (Z.1007*bis*) Groups as well as two transport groups with Savoia aircraft. Richthofen had hoped to recruit 50,000 Italians for the *ANR* but by mid-May 1944 there were only 5,000—reduced by occasional defections.

The Salerno landings drew German attention to Corsica. Kesselring feared that the seizure of its airfields would extend the range of Allied medium bombers and reinforcements were ordered to the island. Using *TG 5*, Hitschold (*FlFü Sardinien*) organised an airlift to Corsica from 10 September, but then the Free French landed on the island at Ajaccio and began expanding their beach-head. With southern Italy being abandoned and Corsica threatened with isolation, Kesselring reversed policy and on 18 September ordered the evacuation of the 30,000-man garrison by sea and by air. The latter task was the responsibility of *Transportfliegerführer 1* (*TFF 1*), as Buchholz's *Lufttransportführer II, Mittelmeer* had been renamed on 15 May, with four *Gruppen* and 156 aircraft, including 21 Gigants, but operations were immediately threatened by Beaufighters which destroyed 18 aircraft and damaged six between 21 and 24 September, leading Buchholz to suggest what the *TG 5* war diary described as 'a wonderfully simple' solution of better formation discipline when threatened with fighters.[68] Initially only Ar 196 floatplanes were available to protect the transports, but from 25 September they were supplemented by two *Gruppen* of *JG 77*, although enemy air superiority restricted transport operations to dawn or dusk until the airlift ended on 2 October. In 1,580 sorties the *Transportgruppen* evacuated most of the garrison (23,192 men and 618 tonnes of material) in *Unternehmen 'Schlussakkord'* (Final Contract) for the loss of 32 transports, while the Navy evacuated most of the equipment. Buchholz's command continued to control large transport forces until the New Year and was disbanded only on 30 January 1944, most of the transports moving to Odessa.[69]

Richthofen received only 309 replacement aircraft for his battered units in October and November and was no doubt glad that the autumn rains restricted flying as the war of movement dissolved into positional warfare, but he was concerned about the 'extremely questionable morale' of the *Schlachtgruppen* and at the beginning of November the *Inspekteur der Tagsschlachtflieger, Oberst* Alfred Druschel, visited the Italian-based *Gruppen*.[70] Meanwhile the German Army retreated into fortifications south of Rome, where they were to hold the Allies throughout the winter. Richthofen had only 290 combat aircraft in Italy (including 82 bombers and 111 fighters), of which 60% were serviceable, but he also possessed a large transport force of 238 aircraft, of which 79 were for the paratroops of *Fliegerkorps XI*.[71] Naples, liberated on 1 October, became another port in the *Kampfgruppen*'s target folders as a *Führer* directive of 12 October demanded an offensive against both harbours and shipping. Between 10 October and 5 December the bombers flew about 800 sorties with 10 major night attacks, mostly on Naples (where the Allies were unloading 9,000 tonnes of supplies a day), but night fighters inflicted heavy losses—13% in the first major raid on Naples on 12/13 October. *'Düppel'* chaff (the German equivalent of 'Window') had been used since a raid on Bizerta on 6/7 September, but when it was first used in Italy on 23/24 October Richthofen noted in his diary 'inexplicable losses'. He was as dissatisfied with Storp as he had been with Peltz and on 28 October abolished the position of *Fernkampfführer*, a decision which 'profoundly offended' Storp.[72] The *Kampfgruppen* now returned to Bülowius, whose headquarters had been established north of Milan at Merate, and he also controlled the single-engine units (three to five *Jagdgruppen*, two *Schlachtgruppen* and a *Nahaufklärungsstaffel*) in central Italy, although tactical air support for *10. Armee* was the responsibility of Hitschold as *Fliegerführer, Luftflotte 2* (later *FlFü 2*). The change of command could not compensate for the bomber crews' inadequate training: by the end of November, of 222 crews only 75 were 'Old Hares' and a third were rated 'not combatworthy'. Bülowius planned heavy, but short-duration, attacks, with the first opportunity on 2/3 December following reports of the arrival of a convoy at Bari. He despatched 105 aircraft, and while only 88 found the target they achieved a rare but spectacular success for the loss of two aircraft. The Allies' early warning system failed, the bombers had *'Düppel'* support to distract the AA gunners and (as at Piraeus in 1941) a ship hit and set ablaze, the SS *John Harvey*, was carrying ammunition. The resulting detonation sank 16 ships (69,712grt) with 38,000 tonnes of supplies and damaged seven (26,217 grt), but the *John Harvey* was also carrying poison gas shells and the deadly fumes killed 1,000 people in what the British naval historian described as a 'most serious blow'.[73]

But this proved to be a swansong, for that day Richthofen was informed by Koller that he would have to hand over *Kampfgruppen* to *Luftflotte 3* for use by his *bête noir* Peltz. A month earlier, on 3 November, *OKW* Directive 51 assigned strategic priority to the west European theatre while *ObdL* was preparing *Unternehmen 'Steinbock'* against England. Some *Kampfgruppen* went to France, one returned to Fiebig and three were transferred to Germany for conversion, two (*I./KG 1* and *II./KG 1*) into heavy bomber units for *Korps Meister* and the third (*II./KG 77*) into a torpedo-bomber unit. Worse still, on 11 December *Fliegerkorps II* was transferred to *Luftflotte 3* and many *Schlachtstaffeln* were also withdrawn, so that by the end of the month Richthofen had only 243 aircraft, his strike force reduced to 28 *Jabos* and *Nachtschlacht* aircraft, the latter including Caproni Ca.314s. This left Fink as the only remaining long-range offensive element in the Mediterranean attacking convoys in accordance with the 12 October directive. A snapshot of activity around the New Year (Table 62) shows what a backwater the Mediterranean was becoming for the *Luftwaffe*. It was essentially a defensive force, with the *Jagdgruppen* largely committed to defending air bases, communications and Italy's industrial north, with occasional jabs at the Allied armies in southern Italy. It is worthy of notice that virtually all the 'bomber' activity consisted of raids by German and Croatian He 46s and Hs 126s against Tito's partisans in Yugoslavia.

With little else to occupy him, Richthofen went on leave in late December and spent most of the time hunting, once as Göring's guest at Carinhall. He returned

Table 62. *Luftwaffe* **Mediterranean Activity, 13 December 1943–16 January 1944**

Week	Fighter	Bomber	Attack	Recon	Transport	Total
13–19 Dec	489	22	87	133	98	871
20–26 Dec	151	16	–	55	44	391
27 Dec–2 Jan	721	14	9	88	27	685
3–9 Jan	514	19	57	115	65	861
10–16 Jan	632	13	96	106	68	1,002

Notes: Data for 21 December missing. Total sorties include convoy escort, minesweeping and pamphlet missions.
Source: *Luftflotte 2* war diary, 12 December 1943–19 January 1944 (USNA T371, Roll 178).

on 17 January, but four days later went hunting again at the Italian royal hunting preserve of Peretti. After bagging 180 pheasants he returned to the lodge at mid-day on 22 January to learn that the Allies had landed at Anzio.[74] The landing (Operation 'Shingle') was to outflank the German defences at Monte Cassino and was accompanied by US 5th Army's renewed assault upon the German right, against which Hitschold's replacement, *Major* Georg Dörffel, threw 158 *Jabo* sorties. It had been heralded by a six-day air offensive against communications and airfields involving 1,500 bomber sorties, Richthofen's fighters flying 221 sorties against them and claiming only 13 victories, while reconnaissance was difficult in the face of Allied air superiority. By 20 January the number of serviceable aircraft in the *Fernaufklärungsstaffeln* dropped to two, and none visited Naples after 11 December, with maritime reconnaissance confined to routine weather patrols and missions over fixed routes. Although there was a marginal increase in *NAGr 11*'s serviceable strength from 18 to 20 after 16 January, it was impossible to produce adequate photographic coverage of the front, while on 21/22 January fog prevented the only operational night reconnaissance Ju 88 taking off.[75] The *Luftwaffe* faced overwhelming odds, having only 291 combat aircraft, two-thirds serviceable, on 20 January including a strike force of 60 *Jabos* and Ca.314 night attack aircraft, while the Allied air forces, renamed on 10 December the Mediterranean Allied Air Force (formerly Mediterranean Air Command and North West African Air Forces) and Mediterranean Allied Tactical Air Force (formerly North West African Tactical Air Force), now under General Ira C. Eaker, had some 2,500 combat aircraft, of which 1,100 were in western Italy with 850 in the Naples area.

Nearly five hours elapsed before a Bf 109 reconnaissance aircraft flew over the bridgehead and the pilot reported, 'My God! It looks like another Salerno.'[76] Once alerted, the *Luftwaffe* swung into action with 40 *Jabo* and 54 escort sorties against Anzio, the escorts losing four aircraft, including that of *Hauptmann* Hans 'Gockel' von Hahn (*Kommandeur, I./JG 4*), one of 14 casualties in his *Gruppe* over a six-week period. A *Schlachtgruppe* and two *Jagdgruppen* were moved closer to the front line from 24 January, but during the first few days there were rarely more than 100 sorties in each twenty-four hour period, of which 60 were by fighters. Richthofen was given operational control of Fink's *Fliegerdivision 2*, although the missile *Gruppen* were slow into action because of the need to repair airfields while Helbig's *LG 1* was transferred from Greece with two *Gruppen*. Fortunately, the ultra-cautious Allied commander failed to exploit his success, giving the Germans time to rush in troops under *I. Fallschirmjägerkorps* (*Generalmajor* Ernst Schlemm, the former *Fliegerkorps XI* Chief of Staff) who quickly sealed the beach-head to dash the Allies' hopes. Yet, having contained the Anzio threat against all expectations, Kesselring was now urged by Hitler to crush the beach-head. Several attempts were made during February, including a full-scale counter-offensive, *Unternehmen 'Fischfang'* (Fishtrap), which was launched on the 16th and lasted four days, but all withered away in the face of Allied fire power, especially from the air forces, which flew 17,000 sorties on 17 February alone. Allied interdiction of his roads forced Kesselring to postpone his first counter-attack, scheduled for 30 January, as Richthofen joined the chorus of protest at the lack of preparation. The *Luftflotte* commander learned of the plan only from Dörffel and not only sent his Chief of Staff, *Oberst* Torsten Christ, to deliver a protest to Kesselring but also went over his head by complaining to Korten.[77]

Although the counter-attacks were scheduled for poor weather, to deprive the enemy of his air superiority, Richthofen provided as much air support as possible, with planning conducted by Christ and executed by Dörffel as *Nahkampfführer der Luftflotte 2*. However, with the Eastern Front on the verge of collapse no more *Schlachtgruppen* could be spared, and their absence became a striking feature of subsequent operations.[78] Although by the beginning of February Richthofen had increased his strength by 106 aircraft, only half were serviceable, none of the *Jagd-* and *Schlachtgruppen* having more than half of their aircraft operational, while a third of the fighters were held back to shield Austria, leaving the remainder dangerously overstretched. Much depended upon the *Flak* forces, which were reorganised: the 35 batteries of *3. Flakbrigade* (*Generalmajor* Johann Edler von Krziwanek) were assigned to *14. Armee* on the right, holding the Cassino and Anzio sectors, while *22. Flakbrigade* (*Oberst* Müller) supported *10. Armee* opposite the British 8th Army, its operations coordinated by Pohl. For 'Fischfang' Richthofen had not only increased his strength to 479 aircraft but improved serviceability to nearly 64%; fighter numbers rose to 213 (33 Italian), while the strike forces had 165 bombers and 54 *Jabos*. The *Flak* batteries, increasingly used as artillery substitutes, had 172 heavy and 519 light/medium guns.[79]

Dörffel provided fighter and *Jabo* sweeps, supplemented by probes from individual reconnaissance aircraft, *NAGr 11*'s Bf 109s operating in daylight with dangerous high-speed, low-level missions. They were also used to direct artillery fire, but it was risky and during eight 'shoots' in April 15 Bf 109s were lost. There were only 120 sorties during the first counter-attack due to the weather, but for 'Fischfang' 170 *Jabo* and 350 fighter sorties were flown on the first two days, the *Schwarm*-size formations of the first day (at Kesselring's suggestion) quickly being replaced by more effective sweeps by up to 80 fighters and 20–40 *Jabos* once or twice a day. Nevertheless, the effort was restricted by waterlogged forward airfields.[80] The *Jabos* were a major tactical problem for the Allies as little warning could be given to the defenders and they were difficult targets for ships' AA gunners. By the end of February Richthofen had 607 aircraft, of which 75% were serviceable, increasing overall *Luftwaffe* strength in the Mediterranean by a third. However, the USAAF's all-out offensive against the *Luftwaffe*'s fighters ('Big Week') not only denied Richthofen more fighters but led to the diversion of his *Jagdgruppen* northwards, so the last counter-attacks were supported by only 120 fighter and

Jabo sorties. As the *Luftwaffe* faded the *Flak* batteries blazed away in support of the hard-pressed troops, and ammunition expenditure rose prodigiously from 8,000 rounds a day to 20,000 by 18 February.

Throughout this period the beach-head and enemy shipping were also under bomber attack, mostly at night although the missile *Gruppen* continued to operate in the gloom of dusk or dawn. Richthofen had the satisfaction of depriving Peltz of three *Kampfgruppen* with some 140 bombers, although '*Steinbock*' began just as the Allied fleet arrived off Anzio and some of the crews had last flown over London. *Fliegerdivision 2*, soon under Korte, staged through Piacenza (*KG 26*) and Bergamo (*KG 100*), with operations coordinated in a command post established in the old *Fliegerkorps II* headquarters in Merate, while Helbig controlled the remaining *Kampfgruppen* which were based around Udine. The missile *Gruppen* sank the British cruiser *Spartan*, forcing the cruisers to withdraw from the beach-head every afternoon, then 'an inexperienced and over-excited crew' attacked three British hospital ships, brightly illuminated in accordance with the Geneva Convention, on 24 January, damaging two and sinking the third.[81] To neutralise the threat the Allies deployed three electronic warfare ships with ESM and ECM systems which gradually took the measure of the missiles and reduced their effectiveness, although Korte's men did sink an American destroyer and two freighters (14,327grt). Torpedo-bomber missions were hampered by a shortage of 'eels' and *KG 26* reverted to conventional bombing—and was decimated. The defenders' AA forces both on shore and at sea were reinforced, with the latter usually facing attack around dusk when the Germans sought to illuminate the anchorage with flares, but, as the task force commander, US Rear-Admiral F. J. Lowry, commented, 'smoke, silence and slow speed' neutralised them, those ships with poor fire discipline often being hit. Helbig's forces struck the beach-head itself, but bomber losses were heavy and successes few as the increasing number of inexperienced crews meant that the proportion of hits or even near misses per sortie dropped severely.

Although the port of Anzio was attacked regularly in the first month, with a maximum 150 sorties on the first two nights, the Allies landed a daily average of 3,400 tonnes of supplies; indeed, by 29 March there was almost no more space to store supplies. By late February Helbig's bombers could manage only harassing attacks on battlefield targets, rarely with more than 10–15 aircraft, although about this time the Germans were using radio target beacons dropped by reconnaissance aircraft and transmitting on 48Mc for up to six hours, while *NSGr 9* exploited Egon radar control.[82] In late January the USAAF retaliated by striking Fink's and Helbig's bases. Attacks upon Udine, on 30 January, saw the Republic P-47 Thunderbolt make its Italian combat début, mauling a '*pulk*' of Ju 52s. The defending fighters were overwhelmed and Axis losses both on the ground and in the air totalled 140 aircraft; the Americans lost only nine.

While the Anzio battle raged, pressure built up around Cassino, and during March the *Luftwaffe* flew up to 150 sorties a day in support of the hard-pressed troops. However, following a third hard winter in the East the *Wehrmacht* increasingly regarded Italy as a sideshow and during March only 88 new fighters (6.7% of production) and 27 *Jabos* were sent south as Richthofen's 'coat' was increasingly cut and patched with Italian cloth. He had to transfer 279 aircraft to Sperrle, who was also given sole control of Korte's anti-shipping force; one *Jagdgruppe* was rested and another was transferred to the Balkans. A second *Nachtschlachtstaffel* was formed with Italian aircraft, but the more robust Ju 87 was introduced in increasing numbers, so that by the end of March Richthofen had 394 aircraft (63% serviceable), nearly half in his strike force. The return of one *Kampfgruppe* to Peltz did not prevent renewed raids upon Naples involving up to 120 sorties, but without significant effect, while some 600 mines were laid off Anzio and the Italian Torpedo-Bomber Group flew its first mission over the beach-head on 11/12 March.

An extra burden for Richthofen was the opening in mid-March of Operation 'Strangle', an attempt to cut the German communications system throughout Italy. Maltzahn defended it as best he could with 125 fighters (including 62 Italian) and personally controlling *Jägerleitstand Süd*, while Steinhoff controlled *Jägerleitstand Ost*, but by the end of the month Richthofen was describing the situation as 'extremely difficult'. At the beginning of April he again reorganised his forces, giving Pohl responsibility for tactical air operations through the creation of a *Nahkampfkorps*, Pohl's former staff becoming 25. *Flakdivision* (*General der Flakartillerie*, later *Generalmajor*, Walter von Hippel). With improved weather at the beginning of April Allied air superiority was strengthened as the *Jagdgruppen* struggled to defend communications. There was a burst of *Luftwaffe* activity on 20/21 April at Anzio to help a naval miniature submarine attack, while the beach-head remained under attack from close support units both day and night, although the latter were at greater risk from Allied night fighters. At the end of the month a *Jagdgruppe* was transferred to Romania, and with fighter strength declining light *Flak*, especially quad 2cm *Flak 38* batteries, assumed a greater responsibility for protecting communications. The German rear now appeared as a ghost zone devoid of activity during daylight as Allied air dominance brought disaster to anything which moved, while the lack of any air threat meant that the Allies' rear zones pulsated with life. The dangers became apparent to Richthofen on 7 May when, three days into an inspection tour of the front, his limousine was twice attacked by fighter-bombers on the Rome–Viterbo road. He never completed the tour, for on 11/12 May the Allies began to break the German mountain defences and advance on Rome.

Luftwaffe reconnaissance was unable to produce a clear picture of the battlefield situation as an avalanche of tactical air power crushed the German positions.

Pohl struck back with formations of 20–30 *Jabos* with escorts of 50 fighters, which took such heavy losses that Richthofen had to withdraw the *Jagdgruppen* northwards on 14 May, leaving only *NSGr 9* to hit enemy gun positions and crossing points. At the start of the offensive Richthofen had 408 combat aircraft with 69% serviceability. It was largely a defensive force, although on 13/14 May Helbig personally led a long-planned bomber mission against Allied air bases in Corsica which destroyed 23 aircraft and damaged 90, preventing air operations from there the next day. But on 14 May the *Luftwaffe* was bombed out of first Piacenza then Viterbo, with heavy losses, while Hitler demanded that the *Kampfgruppen* be used for tactical air support, and this edict was obeyed for the next three weeks despite heavy losses. Richthofen retained the *Kampfgruppen* only because *OKL* feared new Allied landings behind their retreating armies and also as a reserve for rapid transfer to France. In the aftermath of the D-Day landings the *Kampfgruppen* departed, *LG 1* to join Sperrle in France and *KG 76* to convert to Ar 234 jet bombers, and were replaced by the *Schlachtgruppen*.

On 19 May, the day after Monte Cassino fell, Richthofen requested a conference with Korten to discuss the *Luftwaffe*'s future in Italy. He was extremely pessimistic, agreeing with Steinhoff that *Flak* (concentrated in Hippel's *25. Flakdivision*

Table 63. The *Luftwaffe* in the Mediterranean, June 1944

	Luftflotte 2	LwKdo Südost	Total
Jagdgruppen	87/ 75	61/ 51	148/126
	(60)	(360)	
Nachtjagd- and *Zerstörergruppen*	13/ 11	31/ 27	44/ 38
		(25)	
Kampfgruppen	67/ 48	–	67/ 48
		(50)	
Schlachtgruppen	44/ 15	7/ 7	51/ 22
		(65)	
Nachtschlachtgruppen	37/ 23	29/ 25	66/ 48
Reconnaissance	34/ 17	54/ 28	88/ 45
		(25)	
Observation	–	4/ 2	4/ 2
		(60)	
Seaplane	6/ 5	48/ 37	54/ 42
		(10)	
Total	288/194	234/177	522/371
***Flak* batteries (guns)**			
Heavy	167	107	274
	(812)	(485)	(1,297)
Light/Medium	91	68	159
	(1,932)	(1,396)	(3,328)

Note: First figure for aircraft is strength and second is the number serviceable. Figures in parentheses are for Allied aircraft.
Sources: Based upon Price, *Luftwaffe Data Book*; Koch, Anlage 6; and USNA T971, Roll 2.

Table 64. *Luftflotte 2* Activity, 1944

	Sorties	Lost
Fighters	16,189	479
Strike (day and night)	7,606	209
Reconnaissance	4,869	128

Source: Luftwaffe Activity, Vol. I (IWM Tin 192, fr.1044).

since 1 April) would have to bear the burden of defence because the air battles were too weighted in the enemy's favour, and when the conference began on 22 May he demanded to be relieved of his command or its disbandment unless he received more aircraft and supplies. The following day Richthofen met Hitler and Göring, who smoothed his ruffled feathers by assuring him that the theatre remained important, yet during May he received only 134 replacement aircraft—a drop of water on a hot stone.[83] The situation continued to deteriorate with a break-out from the Anzio beach-head. Kesselring's demands for increased *Schlacht-flieger* effort were countermanded by Richthofen when he returned on 25 May, although the following day the highly decorated Dörffel was lost on his 1,004th sortie. Only the bombers and *NSGr 9* could provide tactical air support, flying 50–60 sorties a night, but the front collapsed, the *Flak* batteries losing 56 8.8cm guns on 29 May, and on 6 June American troops entered Rome.[84] By then Richthofen was reduced to 285 combat aircraft (see Table 63) and Hippel's *25. Flakdivision*, but *JG 77*, the *Kampfgruppen* and the *Schlachtgruppen* would soon depart, together with many *Flak* batteries, for other theatres, reducing him further to 100 aircraft.[85]

Fuel shortages now restricted operations, and Richthofen's primary task, apart from air defence, was maritime reconnaissance of the Adriatic and Ligurian Seas. Occasionally harassing units made weak and ineffective moonlight attacks on Allied communications, while fighters vainly intercepted heavy bombers striking targets in central Europe. During August Richthofen decided to disband the *ANR* and in *Unternehmen 'Phönix'* (Phoenix) to absorb the Italian units into a *Luftwaffe* legion, and this proved to be his undoing.[86] With protests from Mussolini and a deteriorating situation, *Luftflotte 2* was disbanded on 27 September, with Richthofen going into limbo as a brain tumour pursued its relentless course, leading to his transfer to the reserve two months later and his death in July 1945. The remaining units were placed under the *Kommandierende General der deutschen Luftwaffe in Italien* (the former *Fliegerdivision 2*) and contributed little if anything to the future conduct of the campaign (see Table 64).

Although overshadowed by *Luftflotte 2*, the *Luftwaffe* forces in the Balkans gained in importance from the latter months of 1943. On New Year's Day Waldau's *Flieger-korps X* staff became *Luftwaffenkommando Südost*, with a new *Fliegerkorps X* and

Feldluftgau XXIX (Südost/Griechenland) to support Löhr's *OB Südost* and also to defend the Ploesti oilfields, which had been under the *Deutschen Luftwaffenmission Rumänien* since the end of 1941. Tragically Waldau was killed in a plane crash on 15 May, depriving the *Luftwaffe* of one of its best staff officers. He was succeeded a week later by Fiebig, who wore a second hat as commander of *Fliegerkorps X* and was also responsible for supporting the air forces of Germany's allies as well as counter-insurgency and operational training commands such as *Luftwaffenstab Kroatien*.

Although Helbig's bombers harassed the enemy's African bases, *Luftwaffen-kommando Südost* was largely a defensive backwater relying upon *JG 27*'s fighters and *SAGr 125*'s floatplanes.[87] The highlights for the command were on 23 July, when *Flak* destroyed 18 of 104 (17%) aircraft attacking Crete, and 1 August, when 163 Liberators made a daring low-level attack upon Ploesti and the defenders of *JaFü Rumänien* (*Oberst* Douglas Pitcairn) and *Oberst* Julius Kuderna's 5. *Flakdivision* helped to ensure that 51 failed to return.[88] Romania's defenders flew 148 sorties (59 Romanian) and lost seven fighters (five German), and the night defences were equally formidable with a *Nachtjagdgruppe* and six *Himmelbettraume*.

The defection of Italy a month later saw the *Luftwaffe*'s dynamism play a key role in solving the herculean problem of disarming the former allies and securing the region, including the Aegean islands. With 40 *Stukas* of *StG 151*, Fiebig helped the *Wehrmacht* capture the islands of Kephallenia and Corfu, each aircraft flying three sorties daily. In the Aegean the small German garrison secured Rhodes and its airfields on 12 September, yet, despite this setback, and American objections, the following day the British began landing at nearby Kos and Leros islands: Churchill hoped to secure the Dodecanese islands and induce Turkey to enter the war on the Allies' side in what proved a blunder reminiscent of Gallipoli.

Both Dönitz and Weichs (who had replaced Löhr as *OB Südost* in August) proposed abandoning Crete and the Aegean, but Hitler feared the effect upon Turkey and demanded prompt action to thwart Churchill's ambitions.[89] Air support came from *Luftwaffen Stab Griechenland*, established on 15 June in Athens under Holle (now a *Generalmajor* and also commander of *Fliegerkorps X*) with two *Stuka-* and one *Jagdgruppe*, but seven *Gruppen* and an *Einsatzstaffel* of *KG 100* were despatched from as far afield as the Reich and France. By 30 September Fiebig had 290 aircraft (168 serviceable), including a strike force of 145 bombers and *Stukas*, while *Oberst* Paul Pavel's *19. Flakdivision* had 71 batteries including naval units. Within the Aegean Holle had 114 aircraft, including a strike force of 32 bombers and *Stukas*, which could dominate the Dodecanese from excellent bases in Rhodes (110km away) and Crete (240km), the former occupied by *Stukas* from 27 September. Cyprus, the Allies' nearest base, was 560km away and even the long-legged Lightnings operating from Benghazi could remain over Kos and Leros for only 20 minutes. General Eisenhower, the Supreme Allied Commander in the Mediterranean, refused to allocate air forces permanently to the operation and the vital American heavy bombers and Lightnings were available only on an *ad hoc* basis. Meanwhile Holle's strike forces dominated the skies, annihilating a Kos-based Spitfire squadron by the end of the month. On 3 October the assault on Kos, *Unternehmen 'Eisbär'* (Polar Bear), began with an amphibious landing by *General der Infanterie* Friedrich-Wilhelm Müller's *22. Luftlande Division* while *Fallschirmjäger Kompanie, Regiment Brandenburg* dropped in the centre of the island, which was swiftly captured with 3,100 prisoners (600 British) at the cost of 85 German casualties (15 dead). There were light *Luftwaffe* losses during the operation, in which *JG 27* flew some 70 sorties and the strike forces flew 134, dropping 110 tonnes of bombs.

Within four days Holle, now with 95 bombers and 65 fighters following the arrival of *5./KG 100*, began isolating Leros. By 11 November he had flown 984 strike sorties, dropping 1,096 tonnes of bombs on the island, while heavy losses upon shipping were inflicted by a further 447 sorties which expended 334 tonnes of bombs and 12 Hs 293 missiles.[90] On 12 November Müller's troops landed in *Unternehmen 'Leopard'*, supported by a drop in a stiff breeze of 470 men of *I./FJR 2* (*Hauptmann* Martin Kühne), later reinforced by a drop of *Brandenburger*, although fighting continued for another three days, during which time there were 705 strike sorties. At the cost of some 4,000 men and 45 aircraft, the *Wehrmacht* retained control of the Dodecanese in a campaign which cost the British 4,800 men, 115 aircraft, five destroyers (two to missiles) and a merchantman. The British naval historian is especially critical of the campaign, which repeated the mistake of trying to operate when the enemy had air superiority.[91]

Yet the Aegean proved an albatross, with the *Luftwaffe* increasingly on the defensive under mounting British pressure. With the departure of Holle and *Fliegerkorps X* to France, Fink was brought in on 10 February 1944 as *Kommandierender General der deutsches Luftwaffe in Griechenland*, being promoted to *General der Flieger* on 1 April. He had only a *Jagdkommando*, *SAGr 126* and *Generalmajor* Pavel's *19. Flakdivision*, but the appearance of Spitfire IX and Mustang fighters gave control of the air to the RAF by the summer. The isolation of the Dodecanese meant that urgent supplies had to be flown in using two Condors under *Oberleutnant* Karl-Heinz Stahnke, though Athens was also used for other long-range operations.[92] From September part of *2./Versuchsverband ObdL*, which included two captured B-17s, was at Athens-Kalamaki flying agents into the Middle East and even using S.75 transports to insert, extract and re-insert a team into Tripolitania; one of these aircraft was captured there on 14 March 1944.[93] Special and counter-insurgency operations were also conducted against Tito's partisans, support which cost Fiebig his life for after the war he was tried and shot by the Yugoslavs on 24 October 1947. Most missions were flown by *StG 151* and the unreliable Croatian Air Force, initially under former *KG 3 Kommodore Oberst*

Table 65. Air Operations in the Balkans, January–May 1944

Month	US Bomber		US Fighter		RAF Bomber		Luftwaffe	
Jan	792	(24)	657	(14)	111	(5)	n/a	
Feb	193	(–)	–		87	(7)	n/a	
Mar	70	(–)	–		293	(13)	n/a	
Apr	3,478	(85)	1,539	(16)	544	(14)	481	(53)
May	3,116	(58)	1,474	(16)	407	(17)	541	(77)
Total	7,649	(167)	3,670	(46)	1,442	(56)	1,022	(130)

Note: Figures in parentheses are losses.
Sources: Wolfe, p.151; and Mediterranean Allied Air Forces operational record, Appendices (PRO Air 24/937 and 938).

Wolfgang von Chamier-Glisczinski, who came from a training school to establish *FlFü Südost Kroatien* on 1 April 1943. He was killed in a crash on 12 August and the command was renamed *FlFü Kroatien* under *Generalmajor Dipl.-Ing.* Wolfgang Erdmann, former commander of *18. Luftwaffenfelddivision,* on 26 August 1943.[94] For the most part these were simple strafing and bombing missions, but during February 1944 an attempt was made to decapitate the Yugoslav Communists during *Unternehmen 'Rösselsprung'* (Knight's Move), when *500.* (later *600.*) *SS Fallschirmjägerbataillon* made a daring glider-borne assault on Tito's headquarters near Drvar on 25 March, the Yugoslav leader literally escaping through a back door and fleeing to Italy. Despite this setback, partisan control in Yugoslavia grew and there was a trickle of defections from the Croatian Air Force.[95]

As preparations for *'Rösselsprung'* were complated Fiebig had to divert forces northwards since, with the Russians nearing their borders, all three of Germany's Balkan allies sought to defect. The powerful German forces retreating into Romania ensured that that country would remain in the Axis camp, while Bulgaria kept her options open, but Hungary was a different matter and her loss would sever communications with the Reich. It was decided to take over the country in *Unternehmen 'Margarethe',* but, with the *Luftwaffe* fully committed, Fiebig relied upon the fighters of *JaFü Balkan* (as Pitcairn's command was renamed on 7 February), *SG 151* and a few *Kampf-* and *Ergänzungskampfgruppen* assembled in Austria. Operations were directed by the *General der deutschen Luftwaffe in Ungarn,* the monocled *Generalleutnant* Kuno Heribert Fütterer, who had been Attaché in Budapest since 1938. In the event the occupation on 19 March was unopposed, the Hungarian Air Force and AA batteries coming under German command (the latter under *Oberst* Trost's new *17. Flakbrigade*), and on May Day the *Kommandierende General der deutschen Luftwaffe in Ungarn* (Fütterer) and *Jagdabschnittsführer Ungarn* were incorporated in *Luftflotte Reich* as part of *JaFü Ostmark.*[96]

The strengthening of the Balkans defences was timely, for since the beginning of the year the Allies had exploited Foggia to increase their pressure upon the production and distribution of Romanian oil, with side-swipes at Hungarian (and Yugoslav) industry (see Table 65). The Allies were preoccupied by operations in Italy and Austria, and their blow did not fall until April, but soon American bombers, with P-51 escorts, were smashing the refineries while British bombers mined the Danube to reduce traffic by 60% in May, despite 46 *Mausi* sorties. On 2 June the American Fifteenth Air Force began shuttle-bombing, landing in Russia after striking Ploesti, which was hit again on the return journey. The campaign continued until the Red Army took Romania in August to find the oil industry wrecked. The scale of the destruction was a major factor in the Russian decision to develop both nuclear weapons and their own post-war strategic defensive system.[97]

In January 1942 the *Luftwaffe* was on the verge of controlling the Mediterranean, but 30 months later it was incapable of controlling its own air space. The débâcle was as much due to *ObdL*'s irresolution and incoherent strategic thought as to Germany's overall weakness.

NOTES TO CHAPTER 7

1. This chapter owes much to Gundelach's research on the *Luftwaffe* in the Mediterranean.
2. The most detailed account of air operations in and around Malta during 1942 is Shores, *Malta: The Spitfire Years* (hereafter Shores, *Spitfire*).
3. Details in Shores, *Spitfire*, App. IV.
4. The American contribution to Malta's defence was not confined to this warship. As Shores points out, a number of Spitfire pilots were Americans who had joined the RCAF.
5. Half the new pilots in March had never fired their guns in anger and the Spitfires were wrecks when they arrived. Shores, *Spitfire*, pp.195–206, 242–51.
6. Kühn, pp.128–9; and Shores, *Spitfire*, pp. 260–6, 271–4.
7. For the air operations over Malta to mid-May 1942 and *'Herkules'* see Gundelach, pp.338–66, 376–86; Radtke, pp.100–20; and Shores, *Spitfire*, pp.29–266. There was later an outline plan for an airborne assault in Egypt, *Unternehmen 'Kleopatra'*.
8. For Helbig, who became a brewery manager in Berlin after the war, see Brütting, *Kampfflieger-Asse*, pp.81–100. For operations see Shores, *Spitfire*, pp.45–56, 82–4, 138–44.
9. The Germans in Sicily, reinforced by *IV.(Erg)/KG 54* and *ad hoc* units, sank three ships (20,978grt) from the eastbound convoy. Shores, *Spitfire*, pp.324–59.
10. For the convoy battles see Gundelach, pp.374–5, 406–7; Radtke, pp.126–30; and Shores, *Spitfire*, pp.45–6, 82–4, 138–44, 318–60, 449–55.
11. For the July offensive see Gundelach, pp.399–406; Radtke, p.126; and Shores, *Spitfire*, pp.379–447.
12. For the final offensive see Gundelach, pp.431–7; Scutts, pp.34–5; and Shores, *Spitfire*, pp.569–643.
13. Shores, *Mediterranean Air War*, Vol. 3, p.84.
14. Scutts, *Bf 109 Aces*, p.18.
15. Figures in BAM, p.216/n.2.
16. Gundelach, p.396.

17. See Shores, *Mediterranean Air War*, p.75. For *JG 27* in 1942 see Ring and Gerbig, *JG 27*, pp.142–248.
18. During Alam Halfa air attacks wounded the commander of *Deutsches Afrika Korps*, *General* Walter Nehring, while Rommel had a vehicle destroyed only 10m from his own slit trench.
19. On 27 February Stahlschmidt failed to return after being shot down for the second time in two days. He was captured, but escaped and walked 80km to reach German lines on 1 March. Ring and Gerbig, *JG 27*, pp.160–71.
20. Sigel became *FlFü 5* in Norway and perished on 8 May 1944 when his Storch crashed into Trondheim Fjord. Brütting, *Stuka-Asse*, pp.143–4; and Held and Obermaier, p.71.
21. AHB, *The Middle East Campaign, Vol. IV: Operations in Libya, the Western Desert and Tunisia, July 1942 to May 1943*, App. 2 (PRO Air 41/50).
22. The author would like to thank Mr Dave List for drawing his attention to the use in Africa of gliders.
23. For *FlFü Afrika* operations see Gundelach, pp.366–73, 386–91, 413–25, 437–49, 484–503; Scutts, pp.20–34, 54–5; and Shores, *Fighters Over the Desert*, pp.114–216.
24. Koch, p.164.
25. AHB, *The Middle East Campaign*, Vol. IV, pp.487, 516.
26. Bennett, p.75.
27. Shores, *Spitfire*, pp.224–5.
28. Held and Obermaier, p.139; Morzik and Hümmelchen p.113; and Waldau's diary, 13 May (BA MA MSg 1/1410).
29. Morzik and Hümmelchen, Anlage 13. The author would again like to thank Mr Dave List for drawing his attention to this incident.
30. Wild's command was disbanded on 8 December. For transport operations see AHB, *The Middle East Campaign*, Vol. IV, App. 1; BAM, pp.153–5, 158–9; Gundelach, pp.409–12; Morzik and Hümmelchen, pp.112–16; and information from Mr Dave List.
31. The *Luftwaffe* had believed that the 'Torch' convoys were to sustain Malta and prepared to intercept them in *Unternehmen 'H'*, for which Kesselring had 150 aircraft. For 'Torch' see Gundelach, pp.450–5.
32. The heroes of Ebem Emael, Walter Koch and Rudolf Witzig, both led battalions to Tunisia and the former prevented members of *10. Panzer Division* from murdering British paratroops. He was killed in a car accident in October 1943. Quarrie, pp.52, 54.
33. For the airlift see Morzik and Hümmelchen, pp.116–17.
34. BAM, pp.145–7, 220, Map 10; and Gundelach, pp.450–72.
35. On 18 December *Feldwebel* Anton 'Toni' Hafner (*II./JG 51*) shot down a P-38 and was photographed with the pilot, Lieutenant Norman Widen. Hafner was himself shot down and injured in February, then returned to action but was killed in East Prussia in October 1944 after 204 victories. After the war his brother, a successful businessman, met Widen and gave him some mementoes of 'Toni' (Held and Obermaier, p.187; and Shores, *Fighters over Tunisia*, p.106). *Major* Kurt 'Kuddel' Ubben of *JG 77* claimed his 100th victory in January and went on to become *Kommodore* of *JG 2*, eventually taking his score to 110.
36. Koch, pp.166,171.
37. Mortensen, p.66.
38. In late April *II./JG 27* had only one petrol bowser which could provide each Bf 109 with just 300 litres of fuel for each mission when each fighter had a 400-litre internal tank. Shores, *Fighters over Tunisia* (hereafter *Tunisia*), pp.344–5.
39. During November *KG 26* lost 22 torpedo-bomber crews while that month *KG 54* lost 11 aircraft to enemy action.

40. Brütting, *Kampfflieger-Asse*, p.60. Baumbach survived the war but was killed an air crash in 1954. *KG 200* was created by expanding *Gruppe Gartenfeld.*

41. Erhardt and Benoit; and Smith, *Fw 200.*

42. Fighter Command was stripped of Spitfire IXs in favour of North African squadrons. Information from Mr Ted Hooton.

43. BAM, p.254.

44. He survived the war with a score of 154. Shores, *Tunisia*, p.375.

45. For operations in Tunisia see Aders and Held, *JG 51*, pp.126–32; BAM, pp.148–9, 152, 159, 249–54; Galland, pp.152–3; Mark, pp.21–50; Prien, pp.1328–565; Radtke, pp.160–81; Ring and Gerbig, *JG 27*, pp.254–66; Scutts, pp.55–8; Schmidt, *KG 27*, pp.160–70; Shores, *Tunisia*; Gundelach, pp. 455–584; 'Ablauf des Krieges im Mittelmeer 1.1-31.3 1943', IWM AHB 6, Tin 19, K334–86; 'Einsatz Afrika, Mittelmeerraum, FdL Tunis. 11 November 1942–10 Februar 1943', BA MA RL 7/30–33; 'Einsatz Afrika, Mittelmeerraum, Lft 2. 28 Marz–11 Mai 1943', BA MA RL 7/632–5; and German Air Force Activities in the Mediterranean, PRO Air 40/2437.

46. Gundelach, p.593, from correspondence with Deichmann.

47. Richthofen's diary, 22 June 1943 (BA MA N671/9).

48. Wild fell ill two months later and subsequently had minor staff posts. At the end of the war he was under orders to fly across the North Pole to Japan but was captured by the British.

49. Baker, p.197; and Gundelach, pp.592–3.

50. The new appointments are inaccurately given in BAM, pp.254, 257; and Molony, p.47/n.1.

51. See Weekly Intelligence Summary 213 for German documents on the availablity of airfields in Sicily and 215 for replacement aircraft (PRO Air 22/79).

52. Gundelach, p.616; and Molony, V, pp.48/n.1, 51, 74–5. See Molony, V, pp.127–8 for examples of attacks on airfields in Sicily and Italy.

53. Gundelach, pp.617–18.

54. For a typical day in the operations room and a worm's eye view of the leaders see an interview with a captured *Flugmeldedienst* officer in Weekly Intelligence Summary 218. See also Baker, p.218; Gundelach, pp.614, 617–18, 1062/n.92, 1063/n.98; and Richthofen diary, 11 June, 25 June.

55. For *JG 77* see Prien and Steinhoff.

56. BAM, pp.258–9.

57. It appears that Osterkamp was appointed *JaFü Luftflotte 2* at about this time (Gundelach, p.640). Tonne, a former *Zerstörer* ace with 20 victories, was killed at Reggio later that day when his engine failed on take-off.

58. On 20 July III./JG 27 had only 20 fighters.

59. In early August Hamburg had only 58 heavy *Flak* batteries. For a map of the *Flak* defences see Roskill, Vol. III, Pt I, Map 11.

60. The *Regia Aeronautica* lost some 400 aircraft, including 136 in the air. For operations over Sicily see Galland, pp.153-154; Gundelach, pp. 585–651 and 644 quoting OB Süd 'Bericht über die Kämpfe in Sizilien' (BA RH 19 X/12); Mark, pp.53–79; Molony, Vol. V, pp.128–9, 169–70; Prien, pp.1570–704; Radtke, pp.179–89; Scutts, pp.59–61; Shores, *Pictorial History of the Mediterranean War*, p.107; II/KGzbV 1/TG 1 history, pp.187–90; and AHB, *The RAF in the Maritime War, Vol. VII, Pt I: Mediterranean Re-conquest and the Submarine War, May 1943–May 1944*, App. 15 (PRO Air 41/75).

61. Typically, Richthofen opposed the occupation of Rome by Student, whom he described as an 'absolute idiot'. Irving, *Göring*, pp.394–5.

62. See Gundelach, pp.670–1.

63. For airborne operations in Italy see Kuhn, pp.194–202.

247

64. For the Salerno campaign see Balke, *KG 100*, pp.205–66; Gundlach, pp.653–87; Mark, pp.81–108; Radtke, pp.191–3; Schmidt, *KG 26*, pp.181–2; and Scutts, p.61.

65. Gundelach, pp.734–5.

66. For *ANR* fighter operations see Scutts, pp.64–9.

67. Gundelach, pp.742–4.

68. Ibid., p.1082/n.140.

69. For the Sardinia-Corsica operations see Balke, *KG 100*, p. 267; Gundelach, pp.687–94; Morzik and Hümmelchen, p.119; II/KGzbV 1/TG 1 history, pp.195–7; and AHB, *The RAF in the Maritime War. Vol. VII, Pt I: Mediterranean Re-conquest and the Submarine War, May 1943–May 1944*, Apps 20, 21 (PRO Air 41/75).

70. Druschel went missing over Belgium as *Kommodore*, *SG 4* during *Unternehmen 'Bodenplatte'* on New Year's Day 1945. His opposite number was *Major* Boris von Maubeuge.

71. Between July and October *Luftwaffe* strength in the Mediterranean dropped by 40%.

72. Gundelach, p.1092/n.67. Storp became *Fliegerkorps IV*'s Chief of Staff, then *Kommodore* of *KG 76*, and in October 1944 *General der Kampfflieger*.

73. Radtke, *KG 54*, pp.196–7; and Roskill, Vol. III, Pt 1, p.210.

74. Richthofen diary (BA MA N671/12).

75. Gundelach, pp.765, 766. Dörffel, *Kommodore* of *SG 4*, became *Nahkampfführer der Luftflotte 2* in January 1944.

76. Clayton, p.327.

77. Gundelach, pp.774–5.

78. BAM, p. 267.

79. Gundelach, pp. 779, 1106/n.103.

80. Ibid., p.781.

81. Ibid., p.772.

82. Mediterranean Allied Air Force Intelligence Summary 63, PRO Air 24/949; and Interrogation of Hitschold, 20 September–4 October 1945, IWM AHB 6, Tin 195, fr.3385–9.

83. Gundelach, pp.804, 807.

84. The previous day Richthofen's son Wolfgang was lost in Romania with *SG 2*. Weal, *Fw 190 Aces of the Russian Front*, p.44.

85. For operations in 1944 see Balke, *KG 100*, pp.275–301; Gundelach, pp.761–811; Mark, pp.179–209; Schmidt, *KG 26*, pp.184–8; and Scutts, pp.62–4.

86. See Scutts, p.68.

87. While flying home from Crete to his wedding *Oberleutnant* Werner Schröer (*III./JG 27*) shot down two Marauders on 15 February 1943. He survived the war with 114 victories. Ring and Gerbig, *JG 27*, p.330; and Shores, *Tunisia*, p.206.

88. Pitcairn, a Condor Legion veteran, was of Scottish descent and after the war became head of his clan. See also Axworthy, p.311; and Ring and Gerbig, *JG 27*, pp.269–72.

89. Löhr became commander of *Heersgruppe E*.

90. During an inspection tour of Greece the *General der Schlachtflieger*, *Oberstleutnant Dr* Ernst Kupfer, was killed when his He 111 crashed near Salonika on 6 November.

91. For Kos and Leros see Holland, 'The Aegean Mission'; Balke, *KG 100*, pp.270–3; Gundelach, pp.694–710; Ring and Gerbig, *JG 27*, pp.275–9; and Roskill, Vol. III, Pt 1, pp.203–5.

92. For Stahnke see Pete Brown, 'KG 200: Fact and Fiction'.

93. For details of this operation see Mediterranean Allied Air Force Intelligence Summary No 75 (PRO Air 24/949). This stated that the B-17s were designated Do 288. In February 1944 *2./Versuchsverband ObdL* became *1./KG 200* and in May *4./KG 200*.

94. Erdmann committed suicide in a British PoW camp after the war.
95. For *'Rösselsprung'* see Fatutta's article. The *SS* paratroops made the last German glider attack in the West against French guerrillas at Vaisseux on 21 July 1944. The battalion was destroyed after being dropped on Bucharest the following month. For the Croatian Air Force see articles by Amico and Valentini and by Frka.
96. Koch, p.156; and Tuider, p.166.
97. For Bulgarian operations see Bateson, 'Bulgaria at War', p.177; and Green and Swanborough, 'Balkan Interlude', pp.71–3. For Hungarian operations see Sarhidai, Punka and Kozlik, pp.35–6, 40. For Romanian operations see Axworthy, pp.313–15. On 30 August the German Air Attaché, *Oberst* Clemens, *Graf* von Schönborn, former *Kommodore* of *StG 77*, was killed in a crash while flying out from a defecting Bulgaria.

CHAPTER EIGHT

Tempest in the Heavens

The West, January 1943-June 1944

The beginning of 1943 saw a great storm brewing over Britain ready to break over the heads of all the Reich's subjects. In sheltering them, the *Luftwaffe*'s fortunes changed dramatically, with success and failure riding neck-and-neck in a campaign which destroyed more than 5,000 Allied aircraft to D-Day but failed to prevent cities and industries from being reduced to ruins.

Leading the attack was Harris's Bomber Command, increasingly an instrument of retribution rather than retaliation. As more squadrons received four-engine heavy bombers with H2S on-board navigation radar and as bombing support systems such as Oboe and Gee were perfected, the British were able to strike cities with a high degree of precision, delivering 1,000 tonnes of bombs per night, a figure doubled within a few months. Harris pursued the Douhet goal of ending the war through the industrial destruction, yet area-attack, based upon Blitz experience, proved as much a mirage for the RAF as for the *Luftwaffe*, although successful raids did disrupt regional production for weeks and sometimes months. The problem for Germany's aerial defenders was a mirror image of the one they had posed to Britain three years earlier. In 1940 conquest had given the Reich bases along most of Europe's western coast, but every attack was channelled inward by geography; in 1943 geography allowed the attacker to fan out and the defenders could never be sure where the blow would fall. The bombers no longer flew individually to targets in almost leisurely attacks but now proceeded in a *Krokodil*-like bomber stream 250km long, 10km wide and 2,000m deep whose stragglers could broaden it by 50km, making interception even more difficult, especially as the target would be bombed for no more than 40 minutes. The purpose of the bomber stream was to saturate the defences, which employed 40,000 people (including 14,000 women) in an infrastructure with some 600 fighters spread evenly over a wide area and operating in sectors where 76% of interceptions resulted in kills.

The success of the tactics was demonstrated at Cologne, but Harris then had to support the Battle of the Atlantic and was also experimenting with tactics and techniques pending the wholesale re-equipment of his squadrons with four-engine bombers. This provided Kammhuber with the opportunity to extend his system to meet Harris's revitalised squadrons when they returned to Germany on 5/6 March 1943 in the Battle of the Ruhr, which lasted until 23/24 July and involved 38 Main Force missions, mostly against targets in the Ruhr, Hessen and Bavaria although a few deep-penetration missions were made against targets as far east as Czechoslovakia (see Table 66). Like the curate's egg, the Kammhuber system proved good in parts—unable to stop the British smashing German cities but capable of making them pay a terrible price, for the system was organised in depth, with new defences added to cover Berlin from October 1942 when *Jagddivision 4* was carved from *Jagddivision 2*. However, when the Battle of the Ruhr began the British usually flew through *NJRF 102*, creating such pressure that Kammhuber reinforced *I./NJG 1* with experienced crews from other *Gruppen*, to which the British responded by diverting bomber streams through other *Nachtjagdräume*. The unpredictability of the British offensive meant that it was impractical to reinforce other *Nachtjagdraumführer* temporarily, while the inflexibility of the system prevented the concentration of fighters against one stream, even if all of Kammhuber's 28 bases had been adequately equipped with night-landing aids.[1]

The defences inflicted losses of more than 5.8% on 12 missions (11% on an attack on Pilsen on 16/17 April) and from April the monthly loss rate over Germany averaged more than 5%, yet Kammhuber was plagued by the uneven nature

Table 66. The Air Assault upon the Reich, 1943–1944: Bomber Sorties

Month	Bomber Command		Eighth Air Force		Fifteenth Air Force	
Jan 1943	1,237	(57)	55	(3)	–	
Feb 1943	2,399	(68)	74	(7)	–	
Mar 1943	3,868	(129)	225	(10)	–	
Apr 1943	4,279	(216)	107	(16)	–	
May 1943	4,600	(219)	542	(32)	–	
Jun 1943	4,806	(266)	750	(68)	–	
Jul 1943	5,066	(167)	839	(87)	–	
Aug 1943	5,591	(234)	558	(85)	–	
Sept 1943	3,821	(178)	357	(25)	–	
Oct 1943	4,413	(158)	1,909	(175)	–	
Nov 1943	4,002	(149)	2,013	(80)	112	(11)
Dec 1943	3,389	(166)	3,552	(128)	140	
Total	47,471	(2,007)	10,981	(716)	252	(11)
Jan 1944	5,010	(314)	3,429	(154)	137	(–)
Feb 1944	3,813	(186)	5,264	(227)	929	(91)
Mar 1944	5,738	(228)	6,177	(278)	519	(17)
Apr 1944	4,008	(121)	7,004	(333)	1,441	(50)
May 1944	2,427	(99)	8,574	(267)	1,576	(87)
Total	20,996	(948)	30,448	(1,259)	4,602	(245)

Notes: Figures in parentheses are aircraft which failed to return. Bomber Command sorties are Main Force and diversions conducted by 10 or more aircraft which entered the Reich.
Sources: Middlebrook and Everitt; Freeman, *Mighty Eighth War Diary*; Mediterranean Allied Air Forces operational record, appendices (PRO Air 24/937 and 938).

of the force both in personnel and equipment: the *Experten* received preferential treatment both in aircraft and in hunting sites, leaving the 'new boys' to patrol sterile areas in obsolete aircraft.[2] The Battle of the Ruhr saw the first success of an upward-firing twin 20mm gun installation, *Schräge Musik* (Hot Music), developed from the spring of 1942 by a former intruder pilot, *Oberleutnant* Rudolf Schoenert, *Kommandeur* of *II./NJG 5*. The weapon permitted an unobserved approach from below and the near certain destruction of the target where the aiming point was between two engines to strike the fuel tank. *Schräge Musik* kits appeared in June 1943, but it was only when a Ju 88 accidentally landed in England a year later that the RAF learned of it; in the meantime many crews had observed the sudden destruction of their comrades, and the legend grew that the Germans were firing 'scarecrow shells' designed to look like exploding bombers to frighten them.[3] A major shortcoming, caused by the failure to expand the electrical and electronics industries, was a shortage of *Lichtenstein B/C* airborne radars, and even by the summer of 1943 they were absent from 20% of night fighters, with priority assigned to *I./NJG 1* and *II./NJG 2* shielding the approach to the Ruhr. Low production standards meant that many sensors were returned to the manufacturers for repairs, while the shortage of spares (especially valves) meant that serviceability was low, unless the 'black men' made a super-human effort.[4] Kammhuber's solution to all his problems—an expansion of the night fighter force from 18 to 72 *Gruppen*, with 2,100 first-line aircraft—received Göring's approval in May 1943 but proved to be a poisoned chalice. During a formal presentation to Hitler on 25 May Kammhuber was cut off in mid-sentence when Hitler stated that his proposals were unnecessary as he was overestimating the enemy's air strength (the estimates were separately confirmed by *OKW* but Keitel remained silent). The unhappy Bavarian's star began to wane when Göring afterwards accused him of being a megalomaniac. Kammhuber had certainly overplayed his hand and might have achieved greater things with more moderate proposals.

The Battle of the Ruhr saw improvements to the *Flak* arm which Kammhuber's success had greatly overshadowed, to such an extent that many batteries during 1942 were sent eastwards to support the Army. There was a lack of modern range-finding equipment: in December 1942 some 30% of the heavy batteries had none while no more than 30% had *Würzburg*. The *Luftgaue*'s batteries were scattered around potential targets, but this piecemeal distribution was no match for the bomber stream, even if a city had 40–60 batteries (240–360 guns). The solution during 1943 was to make each battalion (*Abteilung*) of three batteries (12–18 × 8.8cm guns) into a *Grossbatterie* with centralised fire control based upon two *Würzburg* radars, while battery strength was increased from six to eight heavy guns with the 8.8cm supplemented by 10.5cm *Flak 38/39* and the 12.8cm *Flak 40*.[5] *Flakregimenter* and larger formations increasingly became headquarters for

Table 67. *Flak* **Battery Strength in the Reich**

Date	Heavy	Light/medium
13 Jan 1943	659	558
15 Jun 1943	1,089	738
8 Jan 1944	1,402	721
8 Mar 1944	1,431	581

Source: Koch, Anlage 6

Table 68. Reich *Flak* **Battery Disposition, June 1944**

Luftgau	Heavy	Light/Medium	Major *Flak* Units
I (Konigsberg)	56	16	*11. Bde*
III/IV (Berlin)	318	107	*1.,14. Div; 2. Bde*
VI (Münster)	309	134	*4.,7.,22. Div*
VII (Munich)	308	122	*21., 26 Div; 20.Bde*
VIII (Breslau)	114	33	*15.Bde*
XI (Hamburg)	163	73	*3.,8.Div; 8.,15.Bde*
XII/XIII (Wiesbaden)	116	147	*21.Div; 21.Bde*
XVII (Vienna)	167	38	*24.Div; 7.,16.,17.Bde*
Total	1,551	670	

Source: Koch, Anlage 6.

the defence of areas—for example, *FlakR 24* was also *Flakgruppe Düsseldorf*—in an extremely flexible organisation which was steadily expanded during 1943 (see Table 67) to meet the threats from both Bomber Command and the Eighth Air Force, and by January 1944 the *Reich* had 70% of the arm's personnel (900,000 men), 75% of the heavy weapons and 55% of the light/medium weapons. By June 1944 there were 8,755 heavy guns (including 1,490 × 10.5cm and 324 × 12.8cm) and 14,276 light/medium guns defending the *Reich* (see Table 68), yet their effectiveness was limited and the Germans themselves calculated it that cost 3,343 rounds of 8.8cm, worth the equivalent of US $107,000, to bring down one heavy bomber.[6]

Kammhuber's fighters remained the backbone of the defence, yet during April his system came under mounting criticism. A few pilots exploited *Himmelbett* to dive into the bomber stream which they then pursued using *Lichtenstein*, and with the improved *FuG 212 Lichtenstein SN-2* under development *Oberleutnant* (later *Oberst*) Viktor von Lossberg, now head of night fighters in the *RLM Technische Amt*, proposed formal adoption of these tactics. As a *protegé* of Milch, Lossberg was able on 30 April to win Göring's approval in principle, but Kammhuber was sceptical of the fighters' ability to remain in the stream without ground control and fearful of 'friendly fire' casualties. Meanwhile bomber *Experte Major* 'Hajo' Herrmann had noticed that the increase in searchlight batteries around the cities together with illumination created by British pyrotechnics silhouetted the bombers and proposed using day fighters to intercept them.[7] He persuaded Galland in April to authorise experiments with an *ad hoc* force of pilots 'moonlighting' from the *Fluglehrschule* (Flying Instructors' School) at Brandenburg-Briest, and this led to the creation of a *Nachtjagdversuchskommando* in late June. On 3/4 July, during a raid on Cologne, Herrmann's fighters claimed 12 victories (they were credited with six), and the following day Göring, with Milch's enthusiastic backing, ordered their expansion to a *Gruppe*, with Herrmann as *Kommodore* of the newly formed *JG 300*, whose tactics were dubbed *Wilde Sau* (Rogue Elephant).[8] A conference chaired by Milch on 16 July clearly demonstrated that the night fighter force was developing more flexible tactics, although Milch was worried about the prospect of some new Allied advance in electronic warfare, and the meeting led to the establishment of the *Reichsstelle für Hochfrequenz-Forschung* (Reich High-Frequency Research Establishment) with some 3,000 scientists.[9] To support the new tactics, which were to complement *Himmelbett*, Milch requested from Telefunken on 21 July new airborne radars, for he hoped to inflict 20–30% losses.[10] Kammhuber, too, was seeking greater flexibility and in February 1943 introduced a modified *Y-Verfahren* system which allowed *Himmelbettträume* to have two fighters in aerial reserve while a third engaged the enemy, and by the summer he was also examining automated control for the fighters, semi-active radar guidance and radar data links between the command posts and sensors.[11]

By the beginning of July Kammhuber had 149 *Räume* in a *Himmelbett* system which covered the western and northern approaches to Germany[12] and almost circled Berlin.[13] Attacks by the Soviet *ADD* in April involving 920 sorties (700 tonnes of bombs) against East Prussian targets meant that a similar system was being created in East Prussia and would be completed in mid-August with 18 *Räume* under *NJRF 104* and *112*.[14] Kammhuber planned to complete the system in Germany with another 13 *Räume* along the Baltic coast (to protect Berlin) and in southern Germany, then extend it into western Europe with 27 *Räume* in Belgium and down the Rhône valley.[15] He and Martini were half-aware of the enemy's growing electronic threat, for during an otherwise unsuccessful raid upon Mannheim on 6/7 December 1942 the British jammed *Freya* radars and the night fighter radio system. The former was overcome by stretching radar operating frequencies and the defenders took refuge in complacency, congratulating themselves that *Würzburg* was unaffected and that their lead in radar remained.[16] To strengthen this lead *Dr* Plendl, who developed *Y-Verfahren*, had become responsible for radar research in mid-November and secured a *Führer* order to release 1,500 scientists from the services for special research centres, yet even as the order went out Telefunken abandoned research into centimetric radars because its scientists concluded that nothing could be achieved except at very great cost and resources were more urgently needed to improve the existing family of sensors. Plendl was the third leg on the stool of German radar technology, but neither Milch nor Martini were willing to accept full responsibility and the lack of clear leadership bedevilled the *Luftwaffe* until Milch became radar supremo on 6 July. German complacency was pricked when a Pathfinder Stirling was shot down at Hendrik-Ido-Ambracht near Rotterdam and its 10cm (3GHz) H2S navigation radar, with cavity magnetron, was recovered intact by *Luftwaffe* intelligence. Dubbed '*Rotterdamgerät*' (Rotterdam Device), it proved startlingly advanced when tested by Telefunken in Berlin, and though the original was destroyed when the factory was bombed out on 1/2 March another was found the following morning in the wreck of a Halifax. By now Martini had established the *Arbeitsgemeinschaft Rotterdam* (Rotterdam Commission) to investigate the technology and develop ESM systems, the first being *FuG 350 Naxos Z*, which could home on H2S, but after studying the first report in May Göring commented, 'We must frankly admit . . . the British and Americans are far ahead of us. I expected them to be advanced but, frankly, I never thought that they would get so far ahead.'

The *Luftwaffe* already had good reason to seek alternative technologies for since the spring of 1940 Rechlin had been aware that *Würzburg* could be jammed by chaff (called '*Düppel*' by the Germans because it was tested on the Düppel estate), but Göring thwarted Martini's attempts to develop counter-measures for fear the research would alert the enemy to the sensors' vulnerability. The introduction of centimetric radars helped allay similar British concern and they decided to use the chaff, dubbed by them 'Window', offensively, especially after the defection of *Oberleutnant* Heinrich Schmitt and his crew of *10./NJG 3* on 9/10 May gave them a brand-new Ju 88R-1 with a *Lichtenstein B/C* radar.[17] On 15 July, the day before the establishment of the *Reichsstelle für Hochfrequenz-Forschung*, Churchill himself hosted a conference authorising the use of 'Window' by Bomber Command, which deployed it from 24/25 July in a series of devastating attacks upon Hamburg (Operation 'Gomorrah') and the Ruhr which continued until 2/3 August. The second Hamburg raid (27/28 July) created a firestorm which killed some 40,000 people, the teleprintered reports chilling Göring's blood and leading him by midday to notify Milch that 'the [*Luftwaffe*'s] main effort is to be focused forthwith on the defence of the Reich'.[18]

A radical overhaul of the night defences was the priority, and on 29 July Milch chaired a conference at which Lossberg presented proposals for new tactics. The investment in *Himmelbett* could not be abandoned so the system was not dismantled, but the spare fighters would be assembled behind the *Räume* and *Fühlungshälter* (contact-keepers), using *Y-Verfahren*, would pick up the leaders of the bomber stream, which were not covered by 'Window', and would pace them, broadcasting location and direction data over a common frequency to bring the rest of the night fighters into the stream. The new tactics depended upon the rapid introduction of airborne radar for all night fighters, but as an interim measure Herrmann's

Wilde Säue, which had engaged the enemy over Hamburg on their own initiative, were to become officially operational over the cities two months earlier than planned. Kammhuber and Weise remained sceptical and two days later Lossberg made another presentation to them, but the generals' objections were overruled by *Oberst* Bernd von Brauchitsch, Göring's adjutant and the son of the former Army Chief of Staff, who reminded them that the system was to be accepted 'on the *Reichmarschall*'s orders', and it was formally adopted on 1 August.[19]

'Gomorrah' proved to be a catalyst for the German night fighters, accelerating changes which had already begun, but the speed of the recovery surprised Harris. The first use of 'Window' cut his loss-rate to 1.5% (12 aircraft), but the next night, when Essen was attacked, the rate doubled to 3.7% (26 aircraft) and five nights after that reached 5.5%. In the short term Bomber Command's overall losses on major missions dropped from 5.53 to 3.29%, but they then climbed rapidly and by September were 4.65%. The Lossberg system, dubbed *Zahme Sau* (Pet Lamb), appears to have been used from 9/10 August, but its first real test was against a Nuremberg mission on 27/28 August which suffered 4.9% losses (33 aircraft, although 48 were claimed).[20] Yet until the early winter Herrmann's *Wilde Säue* dominated the defence and helped inflict 6.7% losses during an attack which wrecked the Peenemünde missile research base on 17/18 August, and 7.9% upon bombers attacking Berlin on 23/24 August. At one point Göring impetuously informed Herrmann that he was making Kammhuber his subordinate, but Herrmann observed the proprieties while establishing his own command posts within the *Luftgaue*, which supported him with optical signals as his pilots, answerable to no one, rushed around the skies.

Their success led to Herrmann being given his own, autonomous *Jagddivision 30* on 26 September, to which were added two new *Geschwader*; *JG 301* in Bavaria and *JG 302* in Brandenburg, as well as a *Beleuchter* (illuminator) unit (*III./KG 3*), and as public acclaim grew more pilots joined, including *Kampfflieger Ritterkreuz*-holders Arnold Döring, Iro Ilk, Gerhard Stamp and Helmut Weinreich. However, as each *Jagdgeschwader* had only sufficient fighters for one *Gruppe*, they tended to 'borrow' fighters from the *Jagdgruppen*. Unfortunately, as *Nachtjagdgruppen* aircrew observed, most of Herrmann's pilots had more parachute jumps than victories to their credit, and upon hearing one *Wilde Sau* pilot report that he was about to bale out a conventional *Nachtjagdflieger* commented unsympathetically, '*Arme Sau*' ('Poor bastard').[21] Even when fighters were returned they were often badly damaged, usually from *Flak* fire as batteries rarely took notice of limitations imposed by headquarters. The situation grew worse from the autumn when Herrmann recklessly demanded that his men take off in conditions where, as one observed, 'even the birds were walking'. This led to a demoralising increase in casualties, including *Oberleutnant* Weinrich (*Kommodore*, *JG 301*) who was killed when his damaged Fw 190 crash-landed at Frankfurt/Rhein-Main on 18 November.

Herrmann led from the front and often flew with the *JG 300* Operations Officer, *Oberleutnant* Friedrich-Karl Müller (known because of his proboscis as *'Nasenmüller'*), and was shot down and injured on 2/3 January, but this was no compensation for the *Jagdgruppen*, who began allocating the *Wild Säue* worn-out or even unserviceable fighters.[22] With the Reich under growing threat from American heavy bombers and the *Jagdgruppen* ill-fitted for bad-weather operations, the *Wilde Säue* were absorbed by the day fighter force on 16 March 1944 and *Jagddivision 30* was disbanded. Herrmann was given command of *Jagddivision 1*.[23]

Wilde Sau tactics were widely adopted by the conventional *Nachtjagdgruppen*; *Himmelbett* continued to be used extensively, but increasingly against occasional individual targets such as minelayers (see Table 69). From early November the decline in *Nachtjagdwaffe* strength (390 serviceable fighters on 20 September, 221 on 20 October and 244 on 20 November) appears to have dictated a decision to concentrate effort against the Main Force. During this period *Zahme Sau* was practised more rarely, justifying Kammhuber's scepticism and perhaps reinforcing his belief in *Himmelbett*, which claimed only 48 of the 250 victories during August. Kammhuber was clearly yesterday's man.[24] In fact *Zahme Sau* remained plagued by a shortage of airborne radars, while plans to provide a running commentary from *Fühlungshälter* were abandoned for fear of attracting intruders. Meanwhile the American attacks meant that Germany required an integrated air defence system, and on 15 September *Fliegerkorps XIII* was renamed *Jagdkorps I* and placed under *Generalmajor* Schmid, while Kammhuber became *Kommandierender General der Nachtjagd*.[25] 'Beppo' was apparently a stop-gap, and the position was offered to Lossberg, who rejected it, possibly because Göring still remained dissatisfied with the night fighter system.

Table 69. *Jagdkorps I* Night Fighter Operations

Week	Wilde Sau	Zahme Sau	Sectors	Other	Losses
20–26 Sept	383	18	56	2	9
27 Sept–3 Oct	401	19	145	–	16
4–10 Oct	298	–	175	1	15
11–17 Oct	–	–	4	1	–
18–24 Oct	310	56	82	–	17
25–31 Oct	38	–	20	–	1
1–7 Nov	33	25	31	–	2
8–14 Nov	–	–	2	2	–
15–21 Nov	83	3	53	21	11
22–28 Nov	284	78	118	–	7
6–12 Dec	–	–	14	–	–
13–19 Dec	30	28	42	–	6

Notes: 'Other' includes *Freijagd* and *Y-Verfahren* missions. Data for 1–5 December is incomplete.
Source: *Jagdkorps I* war diary (BA MA RL 8/91–2; and IWM AHB 6, Tin 165).

By now each *Jagddivision* had an underground *Grossgefechtsstand* (large command post), at the heart of which was a glass screen upon which the situation was displayed by 30 *Luftwaffehelferinnen*. These sat in rows of tables behind the screen, linked by telephone to a radar station and using a light projector to mark the position of friendly and hostile aircraft. In front of the screen, in double rows of seats, sat representatives of the signal service, *Flugmeldedienst* and *Flak* as well as *Jägerleitoffiziere* (fighter control officers), while supervising this whole 'battle opera house' (to use Galland's words) were the senior operations officers and the *Jagdfliegerführer* himself. From these command posts there came a running commentary on the location, altitude and direction of the enemy formations and the meterological situation, as well as instructions to fighter formations, which were given specific initial headings to avoid confusion with the enemy. A similar general commentary was issued by corps headquarters, while the Anne-Marie forces' radio station was also later conscripted into the night defence system by broadcasting music to indicate the areas under threat, for example dance music for Berlin and beer cellar songs for Munich.[26] To disrupt this command and control system from the late summer onwards the British introduced diversionary raids and a series of electronic counter-measures to jam radar, communications and even *Y-Verfahren* signals (see Table 70). One of the most startling was 'Corona', first used on 22/23 October, in which a Canterbury-based transmitter provided a false commentary, in the middle of which the German pilots heard one man say, 'The Englishman is now swearing', whereupon the genuine controller retorted, 'It is not the Englishman who is swearing, it is me.' The false commentaries were often provided by German Jewish emigrés, including women, to match the intro-

---

Table 70. Support Missions for the Assault upon the Reich, October 1943–May 1944

| Month | Royal Air Force | | | | Eighth AF | | Fifteenth AF | |
	NF		E/W					
Oct 1943	–		–		3,033	(10)	–	
Nov 1943	–		4	(–)	2,800	(49)	–	
Dec 1943	11	(–)	26	(–)	4,926	(41)	–	
Jan 1944	40	(1)	51	(–)	6,187	(63)	100	(4)
Feb 1944	75	(2)	20	(–)	9,914	(92)	568	(9)
Mar 1944	99	(2)	54	(–)	13,584	(167)	115	(–)
Apr 1944	171	(2)	90	(–)	14,811	(189)	692	(6)
May 1944	305	(4)	96	(1)	13,768	(162)	1,309	(12)
Total	701	(11)	341	(1)	69,023	(773)	2,784	(31)

Notes: RAF sorties are in support of main force attacks and those operations where 10 or more aircraft were despatched to the target. All USAAF sorties are day fighter. Eighth Air Force figures include missions over Occupied Europe as well as the Reich while Fifteenth Air Force figures are purely for missions over the Reich. Figures in parentheses are failed to return.
Sources: Middlebrook and Everitt; Freeman, *Mighty Eighth War Diary*; Mediterranean Allied Air Forces operational record, appendices (PRO Air 24/937 and 938).

duction of *Luftwaffehelferinnen*, and on occasion the women would exchange invective like fish-wives. As a result of these and other activities only five of 28 missions despatched by Bomber Command (joined on a few occasions by the Eighth Air Force) against Germany between 2/3 August and 17/18 November suffered losses in excess of 5.8%, one of these being the attack upon Kassel, where Göring intervened, while losses in major missions during October and November averaged 3.65%.[27]

Within three days of the first Hamburg raid Plendl developed 'de-lousing' (ECCM) systems for the air and ground radars, although the modifications often reduced sensor range, while the *FuMG 404 Jagdschloss* (Hunting Lodge) panoramic radar with 120km range was introduced, together with the *Egon* navigation system, exploiting 70 *Freya-Gemse* emitters to control fighters up to 200km away. Telefunken completed development of *Lichtenstein SN-2*: although production was initially slow, with 49 sets delivered by November, by May 1944 1,000 sets had been delivered to provide immunity to 'Window', improved short-range resolution and a simplified display.[28] Yet the growing effectiveness of *Zahme Sau* did not depend just upon the new radars: the old *Lichtenstein* could be used to home in on 'Window' clouds which acted as a trail for experienced pilots, while passive sensors were even more useful. The H2S navigation and Monica tail-warning radars carried by the bombers could be tracked by *Naxos-Z* and the new *FuG 227 Flensburg* at distances of 50 and 100km respectively; indeed, the use of *Naxos* was one reason for the high British casualties in the Kassel raid. By incorporating *Naxos* in *Würzburg* to create *Naxburg* during the autumn, the bomber-stream's progress could be followed from the ground at distances of up to 256km. Reports from *Naxburg*, code-named *'Flammen'*, were intercepted through 'Ultra', and it was calculated that between January and February they were responsible for the destruction of 42% (210) of the 494 heavy bombers lost over Germany in the same period, yet the British refused to believe that the bombers could be tracked through H2S transmissions.[29]

Harris prepared for a new trial of strength, having intended to strike hard at Berlin immediately after Hamburg, believing that the capital's destruction would cost up to 500 bombers and Germany the war. But he then waited until new navigational aids and longer winter nights had arrived, by which time the defenders were on the verge of recovery. On 18/19 November Harris opened the Battle of Berlin, a series of deep-penetration missions mostly aimed at Germany's capital, which lasted until 30/31 March. Initially losses were light, partly because the length of the stream was reduced to slash times over the target to 15–20 minutes, but losses of Stirlings and Halifax IIs/Vs soon rose because their poor performance exposed them to the full fury of the defences. Within a week the Stirlings were withdrawn from Main Force operations, followed, in late February, by the poorer-performing Halifaxes, reducing Main Force strength by 250 aircraft. The night fighter force had only 258 serviceable aircraft when the offensive started and 247 a month later, but the new sensors and tactics began making their presence felt—unfortunately not in time to save Kammhuber. The fires from the first Berlin raid, which cost the British 2% of their force, were still burning when he was dismissed as *Kommandierender General der Nachtjagd* and attached to *Luftflotte 5* for a month before becoming its commander on 23 December. He remained for less than a year, and in October he was transferred as a supernumerary to the *RLM* until February 1945, when he became responsible for jets to *OKL* and *RLM* (*Sonderbeaufträger und General Bevollmachung für Strahlflugzeuge*).[30] He joined the *Bundesluftwaffe* in June 1956, retiring in 1962 as its Inspector (beating Galland to the post), although he remained a figure of controversy for his selection of the Lockheed F-104 Starfighter as the *Luftwaffe*'s primary combat aircraft in the 1960s. Galland reluctantly accepted responsibility for night fighters, but he relied heavily upon Herrmann until the appointment in March 1944 of *Oberst* Werner Streib (*Kommodore, NJG 1*) as *General der Nachtjagd* and Galland's subordinate.[31]

Meanwhile the defences gradually became deadlier, especially to deep-penetration raids, and by 30/31 March 1944 13 (39%) of the 33 Main Force attacks upon Germany suffered losses in excess of 5.8%. The establishment by *Jagddivision 3* in December of *Luftbeobachtungstaffel 3* marked an extension of the *Fühlungshalter* concept, using Ju 88s equipped with the latest electronics, including *Lichtenstein SN-2*, and flown by experienced night fighter crews to follow the bomber stream, dropping marker flares and giving a running commentary. In January *Jagddivision 3* received *III./KG 3* (renamed *I./KG 7*) from Herrmann to help mark the route, and within two months other *Jagddivisionen* were creating *Luftbeobachtungstaffeln* and *Behelfsbeleuchterstaffeln* with Ju 88s supplemented by Bf 110s, He 111s, Me 210s and Me 410s.[32] *Zahme Sau* now came into its own, partly as more *Lichtenstein SN-2* sets became available and partly with the demise of the *Himmelbett* system, heavily criticised as inefficient since early November, which no longer controlled fighters. The main night fighter force now orbited radio and visual beacons like moths, until the *Fühlungshälter* made contact with, and trailed, the bomber stream, calling in the fighters to exact bloody retribution upon the '*Terrorflieger*'. Wittgenstein celebrated his appointment as *Kommodore, NJG 2* by shooting down six bombers on 2/3 January; it was the second time he had achieved this feat, and he was well on the way to achieving it once again when he was shot down and killed by an intruder on 21/22 January with his score on 83. This was to be overtaken by *Major* Heinz-Wolfgang Schnaufer, a man with film-star looks who survived the war with 121 kills only to perish afterwards following a bizarre road accident in France. The increasing flexibility of the *Nachtjagdgruppen* meant that they were no longer territorially bound, and it was not unknown for units based in Denmark to intercept bombers over Stuttgart. As the *Nachtjagdwaffe* took the measure of Harris there was some reorganisation of the air defence establishment, with *Generaloberst*

Stumpff relievingWeise on 6 January as commander of *Luftwaffe Befehlshaber Mitte*, the latter being upgraded on 9 February to *Luftflotte Reich*, with its headquarters moved within a month to a more central location in Brunswick-Querum. Stumpff, aged 55, was the son of an Army officer who had followed in his father's footsteps when he was 18 and become a staff officer during the Great War. His abilities ensured that he joined the *Reichsheer*, and his first significant contact with aviation occurred when he was one of the handful of qualified staff officers transferred to the *Luftwaffe* in 1933. This placed him on the fast track for promotion: he was briefly Chief of Staff before falling foul of Milch, and for most of the war he was in Norway. Immediately after the upgrading Stumpff reformed the *Flugmeldedienst*, which he placed under *Jagdkorps I* control, then centralised the observer system to provide simplified overland tracking, which was also improved by upgrading COMINT facilities. These and other electronic support measures were organised by *Oberst* Alfred Bonner, who had been *Höherer Nachrichtenführer* to Weise since 16 February 1943 and retained his position under Stumpff until the end of the war, receiving a well-deserved promotion to *Generalmajor* in August 1944.

Meanwhile Harris remorselessly pursued his objectives despite the growing butcher's bill, with losses in excess of 5% inflicted in seven out of nine Main Force missions during January, although in the first quarter of 1944 the number of serviceable night fighters varied from 179 to 273 aircraft.[33] Dense cloud, diversions and counter-measures as well as a growing commitment to targets in France brought some relief to Harris's hard-pressed airmen during February, but on 30/31 March the defenders had their greatest success against a Nuremberg-bound mission. The controller ignored all attempts to divert his attention and the bomber stream flew past the beacons where the night-fighters were assembling, allowing them to pursue the enemy aircraft through a brilliant moonlit night. The British Y-Service intercepted numerous *'Pauke-Pauke'* (boom-boom) calls, the equivalent of the British 'Tally-ho', followed by *'Sieg Heil'* or *'Horrido'* to indicate a victory. The *Nachtjagdgruppen* destroyed 95 bombers, 11.9% of the force, to inflict Bomber Command's worst losses of the war, forcing Harris to end the 'Battle of Berlin', ostensibly to pursue an operational role preparing for D-Day. The battle had cost Harris not 500 bombers but more than 1,000, and he had failed totally in his objectives.[34] Between December and April the night fighters of *Jagdkorps I* and *Jagddivision 30* flew 7,000 sorties and claimed 1,200 victories, but at a high price: losses during the first quarter of 1944 rose from 3.5% to 6% of sorties, the victims including 18 *Experten* (see Table 71). Wittgenstein died having achieved his ambition of overtaking Lent's score, and on the same night*Hauptmann* Manfred Meurer (*Kommandeur, I./NJG 1*) also perished with 65 victories—in fact, the same quarter saw the *Nachtjagdwaffe* lose nearly 15% of its crews.[35] The constant movement between beacons took its toll: between 15 and 26 March *I./NJG 6* lost six

Table 71. *Jagdkorps I* Night Operations, October 1943–July 1944

	Luftwaffe			**Estimated Allied**		
	Sorties	**Losses**	**(%)**	**Sorties**	**Losses**	**(%)**
Oct	1,381	38	(2.8)	n/a	n/a	
Nov	756	20	(2.6)	n/a	n/a	
Dec	771	24	(3.1)	n/a	n/a	
Jan	1,651	58	(3.5)	4,200	283	(6.7)
Feb	1,243	53	(4.3)	4,000	182	(4.6)
Mar	1,676	101	(6.0)	4,150	310	(7.5)
Apr	1,640	63	(3.8)	4,000	144	(3.6)
May	1,001	34	(3.4)	3,300	153	(4.6)
Jun	540	10	(1.8)	950	126	(13.3)
Jul	1,323	60	(4.5)	4,000	112	(2.8)

Notes: Excludes *Jagddivision 30*. Figures for December may be incomplete.
Source: 'Luftwaffenkommando Führungsabteilung: Bericht über den Alliierten Luftkrieg gegen das Reich' (incomplete report) (USNA T971, Roll 2, fr.82–3); and *Jagdkorps I* war diary (BA MA RL 8/91–2; IWM AHB 6, Tin 165).

aircraft which ran out of fuel and two in action and there were further casualties due to bad weather, while an increasing number of aircraft were falling to intruders, known to the *Luftwaffe* as *Indianer* (Red Indians), which prowled the bomber streams like wolves in sheep's clothing. In January each *Gruppe* was ordered to disband a *Staffel* to strengthen the remainder, yet at the same time a tactical evaluation unit (*NJGr 10*) was created. The threat from intruders grew from October 1943 when long-range Mosquitos began operating over central Germany, leading to the development of the *FuG 216 Neptun-R* tail-warning radar as well as an ECCM system, *Freya-Halbe*, although most of the latter were assigned to *IV./NJG 5* protecting the U-boat pens in western France.

The 'area attack' policy has aroused great, and understandable, emotion, but while it is usually dismissed as merely terror bombing, a recent study indicates that it helped restrict the gains German industry made through rationalisation. Facilities were destroyed and the random nature of the attacks (from the German perspective) disrupted the supply of components and material, forcing companies to carry larger stocks than they required and making them vulnerable. At a time when concentration was beginning to prove profitable, the authorities had to disperse industry, forcing a growing dependency upon transport and reliance upon skilled labour at small firms. By the beginning of 1945 Speer calculated that the bombing had caused a 35% shortfall in tank production compared with potential, 31% in aircraft and 42% in trucks, meaning that in 1944 German aircraft production could have been 55,000 and tank production 30,000, while it was one reason why only 50% of the aircraft scheduled in 1942 to be produced in 1944 emerged from the factories. Part of this shortfall was due to poor morale, displayed in high levels of absenteeism, among German workers (especially among female workers, who comprised 51% of the industrial workforce in 1944). This increased from 4% to 25% between 1940 and 1944 in some (non-aviation) factories compared to 3% with foreign workers (these under-performed German workers by 50–80%), who could be more easily 'disciplined'.[36]

In April and May Harris's Main Force visited German cities on 14 occasions, restricting themselves to targets in western Germany, yet the defences remained formidable: in missions against Stuttgart and Hamburg on 28/29 July the main forces lost 7.9 and 7.2% of their aircraft, Halifax casualties reaching 9.6% in the latter operation.[37] During the spring Stumpff transferred four of his 24 *Nachtjagdgruppen* to Sperrle, but in May two were driven back into Germany by Allied air power, to give Schmid 484 night fighters by the end of the month, of which 320 were serviceable.[38] Meanwhile the Germans continued to improve their electronic defences, and by the summer development was well advanced on the wide-angle *FuG 228 Lichtenstein SN-3* and centimetric *FuG 240 Berlin N1a* airborne radars. However, ambitious plans for automated control and data links were abandoned at Milch's instigation in February 1944 in order to focus on more pragmatic technology. One problem for which there was never any solution was the Mosquito bomber, which, although classified as 'light' by the British, could carry a similar bomb load to Berlin as the B-17 and was often used to mark targets as well as for harassing attacks. Night fighters lacked the performance and day fighters lacked the sensors to catch their irritating foe, making the destruction of a Mosquito at night almost an act of God. It was as difficult intercepting the Mosquito in daytime, and two units created for this purpose in July 1943, *JGr Nord/25* (*Major* Herbert Ihlefeld) and *JGr Süd (Ost)/50* (*Major* Hermann Graf) had so little luck that they were disbanded within four months.[39]

Success for the *Nachtjagdgruppen* was achieved just as the battle for Germany's skies during daylight became more desperate. American heavy bombers appeared first over Wilhelmshaven on 27 January 1943 and their formations proved to be veritable hedgehogs.[40] The *Jagdgruppen* had barely 160 fighters, and when the second American raid on Germany was made against Emden on 4 February *Hauptmann* Hans-Joachim Jabs led *Alarmrotten* (Alert Sections) of *IV./NJG 1* against it, the night fighter pilots claiming three bombers but losing two of eight aircraft. Despite the risk of losing valuable crews and aircraft—*Hauptmann* Ludwig Bekker, *Kapitän* of *12./NJG 1* and a 44-victory *Experte*, was lost on 26 February—the *Nachtjagdgeschwader* were forced to maintain *Alarmrotten* until the end of January 1944, although the order was amended to exclude the most experienced crews.[41] Day bombing was the core of USAAF philosophy, based upon the confidence placed in the Norden bomb sight and the bombers' armament. The bombers operated in tight, mutually supporting formations known as 'boxes' (the Germans, naturally, called them '*Pulks*'), each aircraft carrying up to a dozen 12.7mm (0.50-calibre) machine guns, with a ballistic performance similar to the 20mm Oerlikon carried by most German fighters, and more than half a tonne of ammunition.[42] So tight were the 'boxes' that some aircraft were lost to 'friendly' bombs, while many suffered damage from a rain of spent cartridges, but the Americans were confident that their bombers would brush away opposition en route to their targets.[43] The 'Pulks' posed a major tactical challenge to the Jagdgruppen, not only because of their formidable, interlocking firepower but also because they operated at 6,000–7,600m (20,000–25,000ft), close to the limits of the practical high-altitude performance of the Bf 109 and Fw 190. Worse still, fighter armament proved inadequate, an average 20 rounds of 2cm ammunition being required to shoot down a B-17, but an analysis of gun camera film showed only 2% of rounds aimed at a bomber actually hit it, so that 1,000 rounds of ammunition (23 seconds' firing time) were actually fired to achieve a result.[44] The introduction of 3cm Mk 108 cannon (augmented by 15mm MG 151 heavy machine guns) meant that only three hits were required to destroy an 'Ami Viermot' (American four-engine bomber), but often the new weapons had to be installed in underwing gondolas ('Bathtubs'), which degraded performance.

Questioned by Hitler after these early raids, Galland requested an expansion of the Jagdgruppen and warned that he would require a 3:1 fighter/bomber ratio, and if the bombers were escorted then a 4:1 ratio. Meanwhile the Jagdgruppen inflicted thought-provoking losses over France and, as the Eighth Air Force penetrated ever deeper into German skies, 7% on the first mission over the Ruhr on 4 March. Conventional beam or tail attacks, made by Schwärme formations, proved costly, but the Luftwaffe quickly noticed that the 'Dicke Auto/Möbelwagen' ('Big Cars/Furniture Vans') lacked adequate nose armament and by 5 April head-on attacks were being undertaken.[45] The previous tactics of individual Schwarm attacks had been abandoned by 17 April when waves of coordinated Staffeln had struck a mission attacking Bremen and destroyed almost 14% of the bombers, with the 306th Group suffering 38% casualties, double those of previous missions and leading to the first doubts being expressed about the ability of the heavy bombers to conduct unescorted missions successfully.[46] One solution was to have some bombers modified as dedicated escorts with increased armament and ammunition, but experiments with the YB-40 (a converted B-17) over France were unsuccessful, as noted later. The Luftwaffe experimented with stand-off attacks to break up enemy formations, retarded bombs being reported by returning units after the 14 May mission to Kiel, while on 28 July the 4th Bombardment Wing en route to the Oschersleben aircraft factory was hit by 21cm Nebelwerfer rockets (WfrGr 21) being used as 'Pulk Zerstörer', one missile striking a 385th Group Fortress which promptly collided with another two.[47] More ominously for the Luftwaffe, single-engine fighters penetrated German air space for the first time in three years when P-47s of the 4th Fighter Group, using two 75 US gallon (284-litre) jettisonable fuel tanks to extend their radius of action to 545km, claimed nine victories for the loss of one aircraft.[48] Galland had anticipated this, but when Göring heard the news his response was, as usual, to disbelieve it. When told that wrecked American fighters had been found near Aachen, he claimed that they had glided eastward after receiving fatal damage. When Galland objected, Göring blustered, 'I hereby give you an official order that they weren't there' and stormed off.[49]

In response to the growing threat the *Luftwaffe* expanded the day fighter force in the West (see Table 72): between the end of February and the beginning of July 1943 the *Jagdgruppen*'s strength rose by some 114% and in the next six months increased by a further 66%, augmented by *Zerstörergruppen*. By New Year's Day 1944 the Reich had 1,650 day and night fighters as well as *Zerstörer* (68% of total fighter strength), when the total strength of the *Jagdwaffe* a year earlier had been 1,770. The net losers were the Eastern Front, where fighter strength dropped from 590 in April to 414 in September, and the Mediterranean, where numbers fell from 355 in June to 115 in September. Moreover, by sucking in *Jagdgruppen* to the Reich the *Luftwaffe* opened the skies to the enemy, especially in western Europe, laying the foundations for the Allied air superiority over the Normandy beach-head.[50] Galland did not neglect the infrastructure and organised a network of camouflaged airfields away from the main bases where fighters could be re-fuelled, rearmed and repaired, but were there were also refreshment rooms and medical, meteorological and briefing facilities. The network ensured that pilots could pursue the enemy and still fly two or even three sorties a day.

By mid-August the Eighth Air Force (Brigadier-General Ira C. Eaker) had successfully flown 21 missions against peripheral German targets while building its strength. In Washington and in England there was an impatience to begin deep-penetration missions, although monthly loss rates over Germany had been climbing remorselessly since May, averaging 6.4% per month—and nearly 10% per month in the first two quarters of 1943 (with peaks of nearly 9.5% and 15% in February and April respectively). In real terms 248 bombers had been lost to an efficient, well-oiled defensive system which was exploiting the aircraft's weakness. The American planners ignored the need for strict fire-discipline by the gunners,

Table 72. German Fighter Force Expansion, 1943

Date	Lw Befh. Mitte	Luftflotte 3	Total	
20 Jan	163/126	241/183	1,090/	771
20 Apr	188/144	232/191	1,328/	980
20 Jun	343/259	353/305	1,704/	1,261
20 Sept	677/525	222/152	1,500/	1,055
20 Dec	572/366	312/216	1,558/	1,085

Note: Figures are total/serviceable.
Source: Gundelach, p.716.

who had to use their weapons sparingly to conserve ammunition and to avoid long bursts which could jam their guns temporarily or even permanently.[51] On the afternoon of 17 August Schweinfurt and Regensburg were struck by 315 bombers of the 1st and 4th BombardmentWings who were escorted across the German border by Thunderbolts, but the moment they departed the *Jagdgruppen* waded in, striking *'Pulk'* lead and low squadrons from the front and the high squadrons from the rear. Soon bombers were falling everywhere, with 60 failing to return (19%) and four damaged beyond repair, German pilots often holding their fire as crews began to bale out. The 100th Bombardment Group (soon to be dubbed 'The Bloody Hundredth') suffered nearly 43% casualties, and losses might have been heavier still had the 4th Wing not flown south to North African bases rather than return to England.[52] The *Luftwaffe* lost 42 aircraft (including nine night fighters and *Zerstörer*) and a score of aircrew killed, including Galland's brother 'Wutz'. Yet Göring, who received another tongue-lashing from Hitler because of the damage inflicted, remained dissatisfied and blamed both the absence of a centralised day fighter organisation and 'skulking' fighter pilots, leading to the establishment of *Jagdkorps I* and some purging of senior officers (see Table 73).[53] For the pilots the defence of Germany had advantages and disadvantages. On 4 October *Oberstleutnant* Hans 'Fips' Philipp (*Kommodore, JG 1*) warned friends that the air battles were extraordinarily hard, not because of enemy numerical superiority or the defensive armament of the Fortress 'but more because one is suddenly torn from the comfort of a deep armchair and the almost relaxed atmosphere of the field.[54] Four days later he was dead, shot down by a Thunderbolt.

Three weeks later, on 6 September, a mission against Stuttgart by 111 bombers saw 16% losses in what 'proved to be one of the most costly fiascos in 8AF history'.[55] A crisis of confidence developed within the USAAF, which then toyed with the idea of converting to night operations. One squadron flew 27 shallow-penetration night sorties from 15/16 September for the loss of two bombers before reverting to leaflet missions, while 90 B-17s of the 3rd Bombardment Division began conversion to night operations until confidence in day bombing was restored.[56] While the Americans did not follow the British example over tactics they did adopt British technology to deal with targets obscured by cloud, haze

Table 73. *Jagdkorps I*, 15 September 1943

New Division	Old Title	New Commander	Old Commander
JD 1	*JD 4*	*Oberst* Lützow	*Genmaj* Huth
JD 2	*JD 2*	*Genmaj* Ibel	*Genlt* Schwabedissen
JD 3	*JD 1*	*Oberst* Grabmann	*Genmaj* v.Döring
JD 4	*JD 3*	*Genmaj* Junck	*Genmaj* Junck
JD 7	*JD 5*	*Genmaj* Huth	*Oberst* v. Bülow
JD 8	*JaFü Ostmark*	*Oberst* Handrick	–

and smoke, and on 27 September a mission against Emden saw the first use of H2S (known to the Americans as H2X) radar. As more electronic aids were used for blind-bombing techniques, the Eighth Air Force also adopted, in all but name, the British policy of area attack. Electronic support was not ignored, and from October at least two groups in each combat wing carried 'Carpet' jammers for use against *Würzburg* radars, which cut *Flak* damage by 50%. The problem of head-on attacks was met from September by the introduction of the B-17G with a twin-gun chin turret originally developed for the YB-40. The presence of some 260 sorties by P-47s, exploiting the first use of the single 108 US gallon (409-litre) drop tank, ensured that only 3% of the bombers failed to return, and there were similar results with a repeat mission on 2 October, which encouraged the Americans to begin striking targets as far east as the Rhine from 4 October.[57] The presence of the Thunderbolts forced Schmid to withdraw *Jagdgruppen* from western Holland to the German border, and as confidence returned the Eighth Air Force flew further into Germany. On 9 October Eaker struck Danzig/Gdynia using the B-24s on only their second mission against the Reich, yet, despite heavy losses (4.9%, and nearly 22% the following day when the 3rd Division struck Münster), pressure to renew deep-penetration missions mounted.[58] With the problems unresolved Eaker flew another mission against Schweinfurt on 14 October, but this was as catastrophic as the first, the *Luftwaffe* flying 567 sorties (some pilots flying three missions) and, for the loss of 21 fighters (3.7%), shooting down another 60 bombers (18.75%) and damaging seven beyond repair.[59]

The disaster created a crisis of confidence within the Eighth Air Force and in Washington over Eaker, while the inability of the RAF to assist led to Anglo-American friction. An escort fighter was the prime requirement, for even with two 150 US gallon (568-litre) drop tanks the backbone of the USAAF fighter groups, the Thunderbolt, had a radius of just 725km. Much was expected of the P-38 Lightning, which began operating from 15 October, for with a single 150 US gallon drop tank it could escort bombers some 725km (to between Hanover and Berlin) into Germany and with two tanks as far as Berlin. But deliveries were slow, it was no match for nimble single-engine fighters and when shackled to the bombers it was forced to operate below optimum performance. Worse still, the cold, moist European air played havoc with the Allison engines; indeed, half the Lightning losses during the winter of 1943/44 were to engine failure.[60] The solution was found in the P-51B Mustang, which, with two 75 US gallon drop tanks, could fly close escort missions all the way to Berlin. The Mustang escort fighter began operations from 5 December, when only one group was available, but the employment of escorts became as much a matter of debate in the Eighth Air Force as it had been for the *Luftwaffe* in 1940. Attacks upon Germany continued to December but were restricted to within fighter range and were confined to the Rhine valley and the coast in order to reduce average monthly bomber losses to

Table 74. *Jagdkorps I* Day Operations, 15 September 1943–31 July 1944

Month	*Luftwaffe* Sorties	Losses	(%)	Estimated Allied Sorties	Losses	(%)
Sept	497	11	(2.2)	n/a	n/a	
Oct	3,840	119	(3.1)	n/a	n/a	
Nov	2,531	102	(4.0)	n/a	n/a	
Dec	1,153	88	(7.6)	n/a	n/a	
Jan	3,315	177	(5.4)	6,600	362	(5.5)
Feb	4,242	379	(8.2)	10,000	661	(6.6)
Mar	3,672	347	(9.4)	14,700	394	(2.7)
Apr	4,505	469	(9.2)	18,400	657	(3.6)
May	3,805	446	(11.7)	27,000	562	(2.1)
Jun	1,264	187	(14.9)	11,550	224	(1.9)
Jul	2,583	336	(13)	26,000	359	(1.4)

Source: 'Luftwaffenkommando Führungsabteilung: Bericht über den Allierten Luftkrieg gegen das Reich' (incomplete report) (USNA T971 Roll 2, fr.82–3); *Jagdkorps I* war diary (BA MA RL 8/91–2; IWM AHB 6, Tin 165).

3.78%, compared with 9.16% in October (see Table 70 for escort operations). As it became obvious that the Mustang was the solution to the problem, Eaker, although a fighter specialist, dragged his feet when under pressure once again to return to deep-penetration missions. In January he was 'kicked upstairs' to become commander of the Mediterranean Allied Air Forces and replaced by Major-General James H. Doolittle, who inherited a slowly improving escort situation as Mustang strength expanded and he was willing to exploit the technology to the hilt and destroy German fighters.[61] Yet in a mission against aircraft factories in Oschersleben and Halberstadt on 11 January Doolittle encountered the fiercest fighter opposition since the last Schweinfurt mission, although the *Jagdgruppen* flew only 239 sorties. Nevertheless they shot down another 60 bombers (nearly 11%), one formation losing 19%. Schmid later commented that this was the last *Luftwaffe* victory over the US Army Air Force, but he lost 40 aircraft, representing nearly 17% of the aircraft despatched.[62]

Even when Eaker was making peripheral attacks upon the Reich, the defenders' losses almost doubled between November and December 1943 (see Table 74). Yet public confidence declined: people would wryly state that if the fighters appeared the raid must be over.[63] Göring continued to carp and to criticise, and his complaints in early October about the fighter pilots' failure to press home their attacks had some justification, although to blame *Kommandeure* and *Kapitäne* a month later was grossly unfair.[64] Schmid was meeting his divisional commanders and *Kommodoren* almost on a daily basis by November, and one problem, highlighted at a conference on 4 November, was the *Jagdgruppen's* poor bad-weather capability, which meant that fighters had been grounded even when enemy bombers were striking German cities. Not only did few fighter bases have navigation aids, but fewer pilots, especially the newer ones, were experienced in instrument flying, and in the coming months a depressingly high accident rate would be the result.[65] The problem became increasingly acute as Koller, at Göring's behest, demanded that the *Jagdgruppen* move from one divisional area to another to pursue bomber formations—a policy which exhausted both man and machine.[66] In the face of American fighter escorts Weise believed that the *Zerstörer* should revert to their original bomber-destroyer role while the single-engine fighters tackled the escorts, but most people recognised that this was only a short-term solution. Earlier in the year *Major* Hans-Günther von Kornatski had proposed a *Staffel* of volunteers willing to ram American lead aircraft, and, although rejecting this, Galland agreed to the formation in June 1943 of *Sturmstaffel 1* under Kornatski to press home attacks in tight formations.[67] The success of this unit, which was absorbed into *IV./JG 3* in October, led on 7 November to a proposal to form heavy and light single-engine units.[68] It was decided the following day to form five light *Gruppen* with Bf 109Gs to engage the escorts while the three Fw 190-equipped heavy *Gruppen* struck the bombers. For reasons which are obscure, the plan was delayed and substantially modified. *JG 3 'Udet'* was selected to implement it, *IV./JG 3* (*Hauptmann* Wilhelm Moritz) becoming the *Sturmgruppe* in April equipped with heavily armoured Fw 190A-8s, whose pilots signed a declaration to bring down one bomber per sortie if necessary by ramming. The remainder of the *Geschwader* consisted of light *Gruppen*, but the first mission did not take place until 7 July.[69] Meanwhile by 29 December another *Jagdkorps I* conference depressingly concluded that the weather, but mostly German numerical inferiority, would neutralise new tactics to engage escorted formations.[70]

The impact of the long-range fighters was felt slowly but with growing power. Surprisingly, it had only a limited effect upon monthly bomber losses, which averaged 4.5% from January to April and showed a sharp fall to 3.11% only in May, when Mustangs began to fly the majority of escort missions. The real success of the American long-range fighters was in forcing the *Jagdgruppen* into a battle of attrition they could not win, with loss rates rising alarmingly from February to undermine the *Luftwaffe*'s plans for expansion (see Tables 75 and 76). In four months the equivalent of seven *Jagdgeschwader* became casualties at an ever-in-

Table 75. *Jagdkorps I* Casualties

Month	Killed/Missing	Wounded
Dec 1943	76	34
Jan 1944	127	48
Feb 1944	172	49
Mar 1944	154	51
Total	529	182

Source: *Jagdkorps I* war diary (BA MA RL 8/91–2; IWM AHB 6, Tin 165).

Table 76. Representative *Jagdgruppen* Casualties

Month	*I./JG 1*	*II./JG 1*	*III./JG 1*	*I./JG 27*	*II./JG 27*
Aug 1943	1	2	4	–	–
Sept 1943	1	2	5	–	3
Oct 1943	7	2	5	1	2
Nov 1943	10	6	11	–	2
Dec 1943	2	2	2	3	9
Jan 1944	9	4	9	1	5
Feb 1944	13	9	8	4	4
Mar 1944	7	10	3	1	9
Apr 1944	9	10	15	7	16
May 1944	12	15	14	7	14

Notes: Casualties are killed or missing.
Sources: Prien, *JG 1*; Ring and Gerbig, *JG 27*.

Table 77. 'Big Week': US Sorties/Losses

Date	Bombers B-17	B-24		Fighters P-47	P-38	P-51
Feb 20	314/ 6	–	}	668/ 2	94/ 1	73/ 1
	417/ 7	272/ 8	}			
Feb 21	617/ 13	244/ 3		542/ 2	69/ –	68/ 3
Feb 22	622/ 38	177/ 3		535/ 8	67/ –	57/ 3
Feb 24	304/ 5	–	}	609/ 4	70/ 4	88/ 2
	266/ 11	239/ 33	} –	139/ 2		
Total	3,098/ 105	1,133/ 53		3,041/ 21	373/ 5	425/11

Notes: In addition 14 B-17s, seven B-24s, four P-47s, three P-38s and one P-51 were damaged beyond repair. Bomber sorties are totals despatched.
Source: Freeman, *Mighty Eighth War Diary*.

creasing pace, as Table 76 indicates, but it was the erosion of quality which was as serious as the numerical loss. In March four *Experten* with more than 100 kills fell, including Wilcke, who had led *JG 3* at Stalingrad, Egon 'Conny' Mayer (*Kommodore, JG 2*) and Anton 'Toni' Hackl; two more fell in April and another two in May, including *Oberst* Walter Oesau (*Kommodore, JG 1*) and Friedrich-Karl 'Tutti' Müller.[71] The loss of friends was an added strain, and many days, like 8 March for *Leutnant* Heinz Knocke (*Kapitän, 5./JG 11*), were ended chain-smoking in crew-room armchairs surrounded by photographs of dead comrades.[72] In April the *Jagdgruppen* throughout Europe lost 489 pilots, the majority over Germany, but received only 396 replacements. Despite *Wilde Sau* escort, the *Zerstörergruppen* were frequently massacred by American fighters: 11 out of 16 Bf 110s from *ZG 26* were destroyed on 22 February, including leading *Zerstörer Experte Hauptmann* Eduard Tratt (*Kommandeur, II./ZG 26*; 38 victories); 26 of 43 *ZG 76* Bf 110s were lost on 16 March; and a dozen Hornisses of *II./ZG 26* went down near Poznan/Posen on 13 May. The night fighters lost so many aircraft to escorts that on 30 January they were ordered to attack only unescorted bomber formations, which effectively ended their suicide missions, and by the summer Galland had to abandon the use of *Fühlungshälter* in daytime, for the ground organisation was more than adequate for tracking.

Worse still from the German viewpoint was that, while maintaining a strong escort, from 24 January Doolittle loosened the reins on his long-range fighters by assigning some patrol areas in which they would protect all passing bombers and then be free to raise mayhem, with airfields a favourite target. On 8 March, for example, after two sorties the Bf 109 of *Leutnant* Knocke was destroyed as it was being prepared for a third and two 'black men' were seriously wounded.[73] However, the airfields were well defended by the deadly 2cm and 3.7cm guns, and during such operations in the Berlin area on 5 April the 4th Fighter Group lost four Mustangs, including the ace Duane Beeson. Harried in the air and on the ground, it is little wonder that the less experienced fighter pilots developed *Jägerschreck* (Fighter Fear), which made them break off engagements upon spotting Thunderbolts or Mustangs. On 21 May the Mustangs began autonomous offensive sweeps against the overstrained German rail network, and on the first day of 'Chattanooga' operations they attacked 225 locomotives and claimed 91 destroyed (in fact 105 were damaged). On the same day 36 airfields were attacked: 57 aircraft were destroyed (38 of them trainers) and 52 were damaged.[74] The effect of enemy fighters upon training was profound, creating a *Kindermord* in the schools which lost dozens of students and instructors to the marauders, which in turn contributed further to a declining standard in fighter pilots despite all Galland's efforts to raise them.

A defensive routine was now established: the *Funkhorchdienst* would provide warning of an imminent attack, which would be detected by radar and reported to the *Jagdfliegerführer*, who informed his neighbours. When the formation crossed the coast its progress would be followed from the ground in the same way as a bomber stream and as the *JaFü* calculated the formation's direction and likely target the *Jagdgruppen* would be placed on 20-minute and then 10-minute alert. By this time the pilots would be seated in their aircraft at dispersal bays, listening to a running commentary on the *Reichsjägerwelle* which would continue after they took off. They would be scrambled by the *Jägerleitoffizier* (usually a signals officer or a fighter pilot unfit for active service), who would direct the formation (*Gefechtsverband*) to the best interception point, whereupon the *Gefechtsverband* leader directed the attack. Interceptions were made in ever greater strength, with *Staffel* attacks succeeded later by *Gruppen* formations. Koller demanded *Geschwader*-size attacks, although only *JG 1*'s Oesau seemed capable of achieving this. After the attack the pilots would land at their nearest airfield for debriefing while their aircraft were refuelled and rearmed for another mission or, at the *Jagddivision*'s discretion, return to base. At the base there would be a further debriefing and the *Kommodore* would telephone his report to the division.[75]

The bombers were well shielded, then, when the Eighth Air Force began its campaign against the German aircraft industry, 'Big Week' or Operation 'Argument' (see Table 70 for escort sorties in 1944). More than 8,300 tonnes of bombs were dropped and severe damage was caused to the German aircraft industry, for the loss of 158 bombers (3.73%) and 37 fighters (see Table 77).[76] The *Jagdgruppen* could still bite deep, and on 6 March the bombers suffered their highest loss, 69 aircraft (10.26%), while nine days later 'The Bloody Hundredth' were decimated for the third time, with 15 aircraft failing to return (one was interned in Sweden)—the heaviest casualties ever suffered by one unit on a mission. Yet American confidence grew and from March olive green camouflage paint was increasingly removed in favour of a bare metal finish. However, missions against the central German aircraft industry targets on 11 April suffered 6.97% losses despite 819 escort fighter sorties, the 3rd Bombardment Division suffering nearly 11% losses.[77] The *Jagdgruppen* tended to concentrate upon stragglers and 'winged birds', and the growing awareness of this among American crews meant that some sought sanctuary in neutral Switzerland or Sweden rather than fight the odds and make a solo journey home. On 24 April 14 bombers (35% of those which failed to return) flew to Switzerland, yet, despite the terrible strain, it appears that few crews sought the easy option of deserting.[78]

During May the Americans increasingly demonstrated their air superiority, striking targets in eastern Germany and even western Poland with a 2,360km, Mustang-escorted mission to Poznan/Posen on 13 May. Both mission and overall loss rates were declining, only to rise again as Doolittle struck the raw nerve of the oil industry: the first mission, on 12 May, lost 5% despite 735 escort fighter sorties, while the 3rd Bombardment Division again bore the brunt, losing nearly 14%.[79] The escorts had greater success during the next two oil missions, on 28 and 29 May, with losses cut to 2.38% and 3.42% respectively, but a mission against Berlin on 24 May suffered 6% losses.[80] The Americans were able to absorb these casualties for, from 27 May, the Eighth Air Force was able to despatch more than 1,000 bombers on a mission as its strength rose from 2,647 bombers (2,496 crews) on 30 April to 3,137 (3,225) a month later.[81] By that time Schmid was increasingly placing his hopes on new technology: *III./ZG 26* was beginning to receive the Me 262, of which Galland observed, 'the engines were everything claimed for them, except for their performance on take-off and landing', while *I./ JG 400*, formed in January, had 10 of the new Me 163 Komet rocket-propelled fighters.[82] Galland increasingly sought to use his conventional fighters in one great blow, and to this end during May he planned to exploit increased production to expand *Staffel* strength to 16 aircraft and add a fourth *Staffel* to each *Gruppe*. However, the expanded *Jagdwaffe* was not ready until the winter, and it was massacred in *Unternehmen 'Bodenplatte'* (the New Year's Day offensive against Allied air forces). With the fighters increasingly held at bay, *Flak* returned to its own, and while Eighth Air Force records show that some 30% of monthly bomber losses were due to *Flak* up to May (including missions over western Europe), subsequently the figure rose to 66%.[83]

Flak had slightly more success against the Fifteenth Air Force, which faced lighter fighter opposition, accounting for 36% of monthly losses until May and nearly 71% afterwards (see Tables 66 and 70 for operations). American bombers first visited Austria on 13 August when the Messerschmitt works at Wiener Neustadt was bombed, the factory being defended by 10 Fw 190s, although it was the more experienced fighters of Richthofen's *Jagdgruppen* who avenged the slight. On Hitler's orders an emergency strengthening of the Reich's southern defences began from 11 September, with six radars established in cloud-swathed mountains, and when the Americans struck again on 1 October they lost 14 bombers.[84] With the creation of the Fifteenth Air Force the Americans extended their attacks into southern Germany, beginning on 19 December with a raid on Augsburg, and during the following year missions against Austrian, Bavarian and Czech targets became more common, further stretching the defences. The effectiveness of the latter may be gauged from the fact that while less than 12% of the Fifteenth Air Force's bomber sorties were flown against targets in the Reich between January and June, these cost them 46% of their losses (245 bombers), but, even here, the monthly loss rate halved from 9.8% in February to 5.5% in May.[85]

While the *Luftwaffe* continued to mount a dynamic defence in the West, its offensive capabilities had become terminally feeble and largely retaliatory, most missions being at night although there were some unsuccessful *Pirätangriffe* during 1943 which exploited cloud. Less than 4,000 bomber sorties were flown against Britain during 1943, and the *Jabo* offensive was curtailed in the summer by a mixture of higher casualties (the equivalent of two *Gruppen*) and the need to reinforce the Mediterranean theatre (see Table 78). The real contribution was to force the British to maintain strong fighter patrols, for little significant damage was inflicted. The year opened with small-scale night raids by Coeler's *Fliegerkorps IX*, but these were pathetically weak compared with Bomber Command's efforts: on 3/4 May only 117 sorties were flown against London while Harris flew a 400-bomber mission against Hamburg. Hitler's patience snapped and on 6 March his adjutant, *Oberstleutnant* Nicholas von Below, teleprintered a demand to Jeschonnek for the appointment of an officer to coordinate attacks upon the British. The same evening Göring echoed his master's whim. It would appear that *Stuka Experte Oberst* Dinort was the initial candidate. The need for a coordinator increased with the beginning of the Battle of the Ruhr, and on 24 March *Oberstleutnant* Dietrich Peltz, the *General der Kampfflieger*, was selected for the task directly under *ObdL*, and following promotion to *Oberst* on 1 April he became *Angriffsführer England*

Table 78. German Operations over Britain, 1943

Month	Day Bomber	Night Bomber	Bomber Losses	Day *Jabo* (Losses)		Tonnage	Recon (Losses)	
Jan 1943	16	311	8	146	(12)	321	3	(2)
Feb 1943	28	176	10	81	(2)	175	23	(2)
Mar 1943	–	415	38	146	(9)	631	38	(3)
Apr 1943	–	260	19	36	(16)	191	26	(3)
May 1943	7	395	29	232	(19)	680	25	(4)
Jun 1943	–	287	7	83	(7)	268	12	(4)
Jul 1943	10	326	12	4	(–)	276	14	(6)
Aug 1943	–	308	19	–		233	17	(4)
Sep 1943	–	386	8	–		77	25	(4)
Oct 1943	3	537	21	–		408	3	(1)
Nov 1943	1	324	11	–		205	–	
Dec 1943	2	190	9	–		111	1	
Total	**67**	**3,915**	**191**	**728**	**(65)**	**3,576**	**187**	**(33)**

Note: Night bomber includes *Jabo* sorties.
Sources: Balke, *KG 2*, p.183; AHB, *The Air Defence of Great Britain. Vol. V: The Struggle for Air Supremacy, January 1942–May 1944* (PRO Air 41/49), p.187, App. 24.

and commander of *Fliegerkorps IX* as Coeler was assigned *Fliegerkorps XIV*.[86] Peltz, aged 28, was born under a lucky star for as *Kapitän* of *1./StG 76* he had survived the Neuhammer disaster in 1939 when 13 *Stukas* ploughed into the ground, and he later transferred to *Kampfgruppen*, becoming *Kommandeur* of *I./KG 60*.[87]

His arrival made no difference to the *Luftwaffe*'s offensive capabilities—205 bombers (of which 55% were serviceable) and 175 crews of *KG 2* (*Major* Bradel) and *KG 6* (*Hauptmann* Kästner)—but almost immediately a new *Gruppe* was formed from the *Jabostaffeln* of *JG 2* and *JG 26*, giving *Major* Tonne's *SKG 10* a total of 119 Fw 190G *Jabos*. The introduction of centimetric Type 273 radars and the deployment of stronger light AA batteries were already restricting *Jabo* daytime activity, and while only 15% of the 26 raids in January were intercepted, during the following month the success rate rose to 33% from 18 raids, and Tonne's men then turned their attention to East Anglia. Unable to increase his strength, Peltz concentrated upon new tactics to beat the radar screen and pressed for new aircraft while maintaining his predecessor's policy of striking ports and towns near the coast. On 16/17 April 1943 the first night *Jabo* mission was launched at London, but of 47 aircraft despatched five (10.6%) failed to return. Although night missions were repeated, Tonne's men tended to make daylight attacks. With the Allies increasing pressure over France, *SKG 10* was withdrawn to Amiens but returned to the English south coast in June and suffered 8.4% casualties, while meaconing led several aircraft to land in southern England, their pilots believing that they had reached Amiens![88] During May and June *KG 2* began to receive the Do 217M and two *Gruppen* received the Hornisse. Peltz followed Bomber Command's example by creating a pathfinder force, *I./KG 66*, the first step being the redesignation of the pathfinder *15./KG 6* as *1./KG 66*. It appears that an electronic warfare unit (*Horch und Störstaffel*) was also formed within *KG 66*, although details are lacking.[89] In attacking Britain, Peltz's bombers flew at 50–100m (165–330ft) across the Channel and then across England, spiralling up to 4,000m (13,100ft) to make a dive-bomber attack then a low-level withdrawal, with SD 2 anti-personnel bombs used to hinder fire-fighting. His preparations were disrupted by the crisis in the Mediterranean, leading to the despatch of Tonne and some *Jabos* in May, followed by Peltz and two of Kästner's *Kampfgruppen*, former *FlFü Afrika Generalleutnant* (*Generalmajor* from 1 July) Fröhlich assuming command of *Fliegerkorps IX* to maintain pressure.

Fröhlich's tenure was marked by the growing use of pathfinders and the re-introduction of intruder operations. The former would line up on a visual beacon then make a low-level approach, dropping flares to mark turning points (as the RAF did at that time), then the *Zielfinder*, usually the *Kommandeur* or a *Kapitän*, would mark the target and a trio of *Beleuchter* (illuminators) would strike it with incendiaries and drop flares for the remainder of the bombers. Electronic support for the pathfinders included the use of *Knickebein*, *Elektra* and *Sonne*, but the British retaliated by switching from spot to area jamming with considerable success.[90] On 18 August *Leutnant* Hans Altrogge marked the combat début of the Ju 188E with a *Pirätangriff* on Lincoln by three aircraft of *I./KG 66*, the Hornisse having been initially used for *Störangriffe*. Sporadic attacks upon targets around the coast, and occasional *Störangriffe* on London, continued until 3 September, when Peltz (with Kästner's *Gruppen*) returned as *Angriffsführer England* and Fröhlich departed for Vienna to command *Luftgau XVII*, where he ended the war.[91] After an uncomfortable few months under Richthofen, Peltz was anxious to resume his bombing campaign, although his strength grew slowly from 222 bombers to 335 in November and 501 in December—still based upon *KG 2* and *KG 6*—while in mid-September he had barely enough fully qualified crews to man his serviceable aircraft. At the beginning of the month two nights were wasted and 148 sorties flown on *Unternehmen 'Nordwind'* (North Wind), in which a defensive minefield had to be laid off Boulogne in anticipation of an enemy landing.

His responsibilities were also extended into intruder missions, which had been resumed on 13/14 July using the Hornisses of *Hauptmann* Friedrich-Wilhelm Methner's *V./KG 2* over Bomber Command bases, but within two nights Methner was lost, either to a night fighter or to friendly AA fire, and replaced by *Major* Wolf-Dietrich Meister. Although the *Gruppe* claimed 10 aircraft it shot down only four, and because Peltz feared that his strike force would be diluted during the autumn he restored the *Gruppe* to bombing duties. Despite harassment by German night fighters *ObdL* had little interest in intruding, and when, in December, Schmid proposed pursuing a bomber stream across the North Sea with *Naxos* then striking its bases with every night-fighter and bomber available he was rebuffed by Göring on the grounds that Peltz was responsible for intruders! Schmid tried again when Stumpff assumed command of the Reich defences, but fears of compromising *Lichtenstein SN-2* again led to rejection.[92]

Peltz's overworked crews continued to harass the British during the late summer and early autumn, assisted by the return of *I./SKG 10*. *'Düppel'* chaff was used from 7/8 October, to little effect, but the attack upon London was renewed from 12/13 October using the new Ju 88S and Ju 188 which began to re-equip *KG 6*. New tactics saw the low-level approach maintained, but instead of spiralling as the bombers approached their target they would climb to 4,500m (14,700ft) and make a shallow-angle dive-bombing attack which would lead directly into a low-level withdrawal. Most missions were against ports or targets near the coast to reduce exposure to night fighters, while, to confuse the enemy, aircraft would be frequently moved around bases. However, when two *KG 2 Unteroffiziere* were ordered to fly from Beauvais to Soesterberg they decided to mark their departure. They 'beat up' Beauvais a couple of times, then bid *adieu* to a *Blitzmädchen* girlfriend with a third pass firing flares. Their arrival at Soesterberg was distinctly unwelcoming, for one flare had passed through the station commander's office. The result was a rapid court-martial, reduction to the ranks and jail.[93] Peltz now planned an offensive involving devastating, short-duration raids led by pathfinders in emulation of the British, but the need to assemble the necessary forces meant that it was delayed until January 1944.[94]

Throughout Harris's air assault Hitler and Göring had sought retaliation, and the thirst for vengeance grew as the Battle of Berlin got under way. On 3 December Göring issued orders for *Unternehmen 'Steinbock'*, whose objective was 'to avenge the terror attacks of the enemy'. Richthofen was to provide Peltz with six *Kampfgruppen* while *ObdL* would provide another three which had been resting, and they were to carry 'English Mixture' loads of 70% incendiaries and 30% high explosive, including 1-tonne bombs and mines. On the eve of the operation Peltz had 522 bombers (87% serviceable) and 25 *Jabos*, the largest strike force assembled in the West since the Blitz. A feature of the offensive was the extensive electronic support: to beat meaconing navigation beacons operated in pairs; the Oboe-equivalent, *Egon*, was used in association with *Freya* and *Mammut* radars (but would fall prey to jammers); and Gee was also copied, with bombers using captured equipment (*Hyperbel*) and new systems (*Truhe*).[95] *'Steinbock'* began on 21/22 January with repeated attacks on London and lasted until 20/21 April, but the defences took a steady toll, and while damage was caused during the 'Little Blitz' it had no significant effect upon the British war effort—indeed, the *Kampfgruppen* had difficulty even finding London (see Table 79). Peltz ignored Göring's orders to strike on moonlit nights, a wise move for the defences had been strengthened with the Mosquito NF.XVIII with the AI Mk X radar. While *'Düppel'* was used it was powerless against the new Type 21 GCI radars, but it did cause a 15.5%

Table 79. The 'Little Blitz', 1944

Month	Bombers Sorties/Losses	Jabos Sorties/Losses	RAF NF Sorties
Jan	813/ 32	52/ –	n/a
Feb	1,468/ 53	78/ 5	1,136
Mar	989/ 82	60/ 4	1,501
Apr	666/ 50	20/ –	948
May	490/ 26	17/ 1	827
Totals	4,426/243	227/ 10	4,412

Notes: Losses are to enemy action. RAF sorties are defensive night fighter.
Sources: Based on Balke, *KG 2*; Radtke, *KG 54*; and Ramsey Vol. III.

failure in interceptions by night fighters with older radars, according to RAF figures, and was supplemented from May by jammer aircraft. In late April the offensive switched to eastern and western ports, but night photo-reconnaissance on 25 April brought in photographs of large shipping concentrations in Portsmouth and these came under attack from 25/26 April, with 428 sorties (including minelaying) to the end of the month. The loss rates, at an acceptable 3.77% for the first six weeks, rocketed to 8.29% in March and at 7.5% in April were little better, and by that time 591 aircraft had been lost to enemy action and accidents (31%), the equivalent of all *Fliegerkorps IX*.[96] During May Portsmouth remained the primary target, but from 27/28 May other southern ports came under attack. However, '*Steinbock*' was an obvious failure, although bomb-damage assessment was difficult, and even when the Hornisses of *1. (F)/121* accompanied the raiders they were still vulnerable and in four months lost seven crews.[97] Despite Peltz's doubts, intruder operations were resumed on 30/31 March 1944 by *Hauptmann* Herbert Voss's *II./KG 51* (formerly *V./KG 2*) and destroyed 13 British aircraft (one collided with an Me 410) to the beginning of June. Their greatest success was against the Eighth Air Force on 22 April, when the *Gruppe* met a returning mission over its bases and 14 bombers were either shot down or forced to crash-land.[98]

Even as Peltz began his planning for '*Steinbock*' the *Luftwaffe* was preparing an alternative means of offensive action, FzG 76 surface-to-surface missiles, and had begun building launchers and storage facilities for them in western France. The British were aware of German surface-to-surface missile developments, which included the Army's A-4 (later V-2) rocket, and had begun extending their radar system to detect rocket launching sites as well as preparing evacuation plans for some 120,000 people from London and the southern ports. To operate the missiles the *Luftwaffe* assigned *FlakR 155 (W)* under *Oberst* Max Wachtel, who planned to join in '*Steinbock*' using 96 launcher sites in December. Delays in production thwarted this plan, and the problems which he might face were demonstrated on

277

Table 80. Allied Day Operations against Western Europe, January 1943–May 1944

Month	Lt/Med Bombers		8AF Bombers	Bomber Cd	Fighter/Fighter-Bombers		
	RAF	USAAF			RAF Day	NF	USAAF
Jan 1943	324	–	186	692	3,033	124	192
	(8)		(15)	(13)	(34)		(1)
Feb 1943	444	–	146	1,505	2,977	141	212
	(10)		(10)	(21)	(47)		(1)
Mar 1943	223	–	388	1,089	2,327	153	180
	(4)		(12)	(4)	(29)		(1)
Apr 1943	314	–	245	146	4,578	290	515
	(12)		(12)	(2)	(60)		(6)
May 1943	341	11	675	104	5,410	483	2,084
	(17)	(–)	(35)	(–)	(46)		(11)
Jun 1943	251	–	372	455	5,974	414	1,834
	(7)		(17)	(4)	(52)		(9)
Jul 1943	267	184	777	293	8,204	431	2,208
	(6)	(2)	(22)	(5)	(65)		(13)
Aug 1943	409	637	1,129	205	10,612	634	2,250
	(16)	(3)	(21)	(1)	(62)		(10)
Sept 1943	783	2,009	1,704	1,069	14,900	405	2,859
	(6)	(6)	(58)	(8)	(80)		(14)
Oct 1943	334	1,070	–	127	7,046	625	–
	(14)	(–)		(–)	(44)		
Nov 1943	709	1,568	388	605	8,644	329	–
	(6)	(6)	(10)	(5)	(48)		
Dec 1943	837	2,067	1,137	288	6,922	116	415
	(1)	(2)	(34)	(1)	(32)		(7)
Total	3,590	7,543	7,147	6,578	80,384	3,845	12,749
	(103)	(19)	(246)	(65)	(590)		(73)
Jan 1944	1,137	1,711	1,232	554	7,618	129	370
	(2)	(3)	(21)	(–)	(54)		(4)
Feb 1944	1,167	3,881	1,842	205	8,291	145	1,966
	(5)	(14)	(23)	(2)	(41)		(16)
Mar 1944	833	4,067	2,346	2,138	4,885	280	5,080
	(7)	(10)	(21)	(8)	(32)		(36)
Apr 1944	1,166	7,346	3,001	4,501	6,831	89	7,914
	(2)	(30)	(28)	(68)	(26)		(39)
May 1944	1,399	11,947	5,874	7,526	17,495	219	21,074
	(2)	(43)	(53)	(155)	(97)		(78)
Total	5,702	28,952	14,295	14,924	45,120	1,459	36,404
	(18)	(100)	(146)	(233)	(250)		(173)

Notes: US fighter/fighter-bomber figures are 8th AF January–September 1943 then 9th AF. Bomber Command figures exclude minelaying and leaflet missions but September 1943 figures include 8th AF night sorties. RAF light/medium bomber and fighter/fighter-bomber figures are for Army Co-operation Command and No 2 Group RAF to June, then 2TAF. All night fighter (intruder) figures are RAF, for which no losses are available. In addition to the above losses 9th AF had 97 aircraft damaged beyond repair between October 1943 and May 1944. Figures in parentheses are failed to return. Reconnaissance sorties in 1943 were 573 (Army Co-operation Command), 1,526 (2 TAF) and 48 (9th AF), while the figures until the end of May 1944 were 3,814 and 2,269 for 2 TAF and the 9th AF respectively, apparently without loss to enemy action.
Sources: AHB, *The Air Defence of Great Britain* ,Vol. 5, Apps 19, 28 (PRO Air 41/49); Freeman, *Mighty Eighth War Diary*; Middlebrook and Everitt; Army Co-operation Command Operational Rcord Book 1943, Apps (PRO Air 24/101); Statistical Summary of 9th Air Force Operations (PRO Air 40/1096).

27 August when 224 Fortresses of the Eighth Air Force wrecked the Army site at Watten. It was not until October that Allied photographic reconnaissance (alerted by the French Resistance) discovered the first FzG 76 launchers near Abbeville, and from 4 December a photographic survey began of all potential sites within the missile's anticipated range from London. Most had already been identified, and on 5 December the Allied tactical and strategic air forces began pounding them, dropping 3,216 tonnes of bombs by the end of the month.

Luftflotte 3 assembled 297 *Flak* batteries (164 heavy) to protect the sites, and during the New Year *ObdL* added another 114 (85 heavy); indeed, by June 54% of the *Flak* in France was protecting the missile sites. From early January Wachtel began to build simpler, less recognisable launcher sites and planned 150 as well as underground storage facilities. The original sites acted as decoys, attracting some 24,000 tonnes of bombs to D-Day and diverting a significant part of the Allied air effort between December 1943 and June 1944: a total of 528 sorties were flown without loss by Bomber Command (reaching a peak in January then rapidly falling off, although Pathfinder sorties were provided for the 2nd Tactical Air Force), while the Eighth Air Force flew 5,363 sorties, losing 50 aircraft, mostly to *Flak*, and another 58 damaged beyond repair. But the new sites were unmolested, apart from an unsuccessful fighter-bomber attack on 27 May, and Wachtel commenced his offensive on 12 June, launching more than 4,200 missiles in the first month.[99]

Yet the *Luftwaffe*'s blows were puny compared with the thunderbolts launched by the Allied air forces throughout 1943 and in preparation for Operation 'Overlord', the long-awaited invasion of Europe (see Table 80). The success of these operations was largely due to the USAAF, not only because of its growing strength but also because American industry was producing both for its own forces and its allies medium bombers such as the North American B-25 Mitchell, the Douglas A-20 Havoc and the Martin B-26 Marauder, superior to almost anything Europe could design in performance, payload and defensive capability with the exception of the Mosquito. However, American fighter design lagged behind that of Europe in terms of dogfight capability until the P-51 Mustang airframe was matched with the Merlin engine late in 1943. In air-to-air combat, therefore, the Allies relied upon the Spitfire as the RAF policy of 'leaning forward' into Europe remained the basis of the Allied campaign, with numerous 'Circus' and 'Rhubarb' ('Rodeo' to the USAAF) style operations. Equipped with American bombers and, increasingly, with the improved Spitfire IX and XII (as well as the Typhoon), the RAF spearheaded the Allied assault, whose qualitative and quantitative superiority posed a serious problem for the *Luftwaffe*. The *Jagdgruppen*, equipped largely with the Fw 190A, were outnumbered and increasingly outclassed, and this was one reason why plans to exchange *JG 26* and *JG 54* were abandoned after each temporarily exchanged a *Gruppe* during the spring, the *Grünherz* pilots requiring almost complete re-training.

On 8 April the Thunderbolt made its combat début in western Europe, but German pilots were able to exploit their experience and a week later *II./JG 1* shot down three without loss, although only two were claimed.[100] The Thunderbolt pilots often paid for their inexperience, and on 26 June the 56th Fighter Group lost five to *JG 2* while another four were badly damaged. Yet the robustness of the Thunderbolt was an unwelcome discovery for the *Jagdgruppen*: after the 26 June battle a *JG 26* pilot who had used all his ammunition to convert Lieutenant Robert Johnson's fighter into a colander flew alongside shaking his head in amazement, then flew off.[101] The British were handicapped by the short 'legs' of their fighters—the Spitfire IX had only a 320km radius—although the limited number of Mustang IIIs could fly 645km. Consequently some bomber formations flew unescorted, and on 3 May 1943 a fighter conference in Amsterdam-Schipol broke up as pilots rushed to machines to intercept an unescorted British bomber attack. A total of 69 fighters engaged 11 American-made Venturas of No 487 Squadron and wiped them out, only two members of the squadron surviving.[102] Eleven days later the Eighth Air Force began medium bomber missions using the Marauder, whose units were able to strike European targets twice in one day on 31 July.[103] The Allies' air threat was not confined to the Channel coast, and during the first quarter their strategic bombers were involved in a futile offensive against the U-boat's French bases—an unwelcome diversion for the bomber barons but useful operational training for the Eighth Air Force. For *JG 2* and *JG 26* the bomber *'Pulks'* continued to pose a serious tactical problem, and on 16 February two Fw 190s were observed unsuccessfully trying to bomb the B-17s of the 91st Group during a mission against St Nazaire. The 'soft kill' option was preferred by the *Luftnachrichtentruppe*, who turned back the 305th Group with a bogus recall message on 27 February when it was within sight of its Brest target.[104] During the first four months of 1943 the Americans' average monthly loss rate of bombers which crossed the French coast was 5.72%, shaking confidence in the belief that the bombers would blast their way to and from the target. Some B-17s were converted into escort aircraft with heavier armament and increased ammunition as YB-40s and flew with a St Nazaire mission on 29 May, but its charges suffered 12.5% losses. The Americans persevered, flying 47 sorties with the YB-40, but there was no benefit and the last YB-40 mission was flown against Le Bourget airfield on 16 August.[105]

During August the pace of air warfare increased significantly as the USAAF began flying the majority of bombing missions, the Eighth Air Force handing over the task on 16 October to Lieutenant-General (later Major-General) Lewis H. Brereton's Ninth Air Force.[106] Of greater significance on the Channel Front was the Americans' ability to extend fighter ranges with the introduction of 75 gallon drop tanks, increasing the Thunderbolt's combat radius to 545km.[107] This meant that the bombers could now be escorted throughout the Operational Zone in

Table 81. The *Luftwaffe* in the West

Date	Fighters Day	(Reich)	Night	Bombers	Recon	Total
31 Mar 1943	513	(185)	460	265	176	1,414
30 Jun 1943	791	(387)	421	148	168	1,528
30 Sep 1943	983	(643)	853	159	140	2,135
31 Dec 1943	875	(562)	781	689	165	2,510
31 Mar 1944	1,019	(853)	720	451	150	2,340

Notes: Excludes seaplanes and transports. From June 1943 night fighters includes *Zerstorer*.
Source: *Luftwaffe* first-line strength based on German documents (PRO Air 40/1207).

France, the Low Countries and even Germany, making it increasingly difficult for the *Jagdgruppen* to shield *OB West*'s communications and installations. The task was hindered by the demands of Reich defence, and from a peak of 400 fighters in June 1943 *Luftflotte 3*'s fighter strength dropped to some 315 within six months; by March 1944 only 166 were available (see Table 81). In attempting to shield France and Belgium the *Jagdgruppen* had a gypsy-like existence, roaming from airfield to airfield intercepting Eighth Air Force missions as well as defending German military power in western Europe. One solution to the problem was the creation on 15 September of *Jagdkorps II* with *Jagddivision 4* and *Jagddivision 5* to improve command and control, but without reinforcements the reorganisation had little effect and during the year the Allies increasingly attacked the *Jagdgruppen*'s airfields, allowing their formations freedom of the skies. As the defence weakened, British fighter and fighter-bomber loss rates declined steadily throughout 1943, from a quarterly average of 1.24% to 0.54%, but the day bombers (which attracted more *Flak* and fighter attention) had heavier losses, although the average monthly loss per quarter also fell, from a peak of 3.8% in the second quarter to 1.71% in the last—an indication of growing Allied air superiority. Curiously, the American medium/light day bomber force, although flying twice as many sorties, had a far lower casualty rate during this same period. Some idea of the scale of operations may be gauged from the fact that during 1943 *JG 26* claimed a total of 385 victories in the West but lost 151 pilots killed. Daytime flying of all sorts became increasingly hazardous, and on a formation training flight *3./KG 2* was attacked by British fighters which shot down eight of the 11 Do 217s near Eindhoven.[108]

Although resourceful and dynamic leadership was required, Sperrle did not meet the challenge. The chaos of *ObdL* direction infuriated him, but his only response was bitter sarcasm and he was too vain or too lazy to make a stand, increasingly turning to the pleasures of the table. His moods were hardly helped by his misogyny as women were increasingly employed for second-line duties, and if a female telephone operator answered on a military line he would throw a tantrum.[109] With such uninspirational leadership it is little wonder that when *Luftflotte 3* was driven from France he was relieved of his command on 23 August and sent into limbo. Acquitted of war crimes at Nuremberg, he went into a lonely and bitter retirement in Munich, where he died in 1953.

As the New Year dawned the Allied air preparations intensified, with the USAAF bearing the lion's share of the burden from February 1944. The Allies regularly struck airfields. Fighter-bombers left five Do 217s in flames at *III./KG 100* at Toulouse-Francazal on 15 April, while fighters shot down an He 177 of *II./KG 100* at Aalborg-East on 17 May, and with their airfields under frequent attack the German strike forces were driven further away from potential beach-heads.[110] Factories which might support the German forces in the forthcoming campaign, railway marshalling yards and bridges were systematically smashed, and a campaign began against German radars. Bomber Command increasingly, but reluctantly, was committed to the campaign, but the Eighth Air Force gave priority to the German aircraft and oil industries as strategic targets and missile sites as operational targets, which were sometimes hit twice in a day, until 9 May, when 823 bombers struck *Luftwaffe* and rail targets covered by 668 fighters, 13 aircraft being lost. The threat to railways led to the despatch of *Oberst* Born's *FlakR Stab 159* with 23 rail batteries, and these claimed their 1,000th victory during the summer, but from 26 May daylight rail movement in France ceased. Nevertheless rail, missile and costal defence targets around the Pas de Calais were also struck until 6 June, while on 31 May 116 Thunderbolts and Lightnings were despatched to attack *Luftwaffe* bases at Gütersloh and Rheine-Hopsten. On 29 May *Fliegerkorps X* headquarters at Angers was bombed and it had to be transferred to Château Serrant, 15km outside the city. Attacks were made at night as well, and while

Table 82. *Luftflotte 3* **Day Fighter Sorties, 1944**

Jan	Feb	Mar	Apr	May	Jun
3,239	2,142	1,349	1,192	1,704	9,471

Source: 'Zusammenstellung der Ersätze und Verluste der Luftflotten' (US NA T971, Roll 32, fr.3330).

Table 83. *Luftflotte 3 Flak* **Batteries**

Date	Heavy	Light
29 Jan 1943	189	271
15 Jun 1943	206	292
26 Nov 1943	224	331
23 May 1944	349	407

Source: Koch, Anlage 6

282

Table 84. *Luftflotten 3* and *Reich*, June 1944

	Luftflotte 3	*Luftflotte Reich*	Total
Fighters	168/ 115	815/ 451	983/ 566
Night fighters	103/ 57	484/ 320	587/ 377
Zerstörer	53/ 37	192/ 81	245/ 118
Bombers	486/ 247	202/ 78	688/ 325
Schlacht	73/ 49	34/ 31	107/ 80
Reconnaissance	116/ 53	23/ 3	139/ 56
Seaplane	16/ 12	–	16/ 12
Total	1,015/ 570	1,750/ 964	2,765/1,534

Note: Figures are aircraft available/serviceable.
Source: Based upon Price, *Luftwaffe Data Book*.

Sperrle's *Nachtjagdgruppen* were substantially reinforced, pressure upon their bases forced many eastwards. Two returned to Germany, forcing Sperrle to train the intruder *Gruppe* of *KG 51* and the *Jabos* of *I./SKG 10* in *Wilde Sau* tactics.

From 16 March 1944 the Allied air forces began systematically to blind *Jagdkorps II*, which had 22 battalions with 46 long-range radars such as *Wassermann* and *Mammut*; indeed, of the 300,000 personnel in *Luftflotte 3*, some 56,000 were in the signal units. The fortification of the radar sites after Dieppe helped highlight them, and by D-Day, of 92 radar sites identified, 76 had been put out of action, including all the *Wassermann* and *Mammut* sets, whose narrow beams were difficult to jam. The last raid, on 2 June, struck *15./LnR 52*'s site at Dieppe. Sperrle's *Jagdgruppen* struggled in vain, losing 102 aircraft in April and 119 in May to represent an average 7.76%. It was little wonder that COMINT reported in the spring that *II./JG 26* formations seemed distinctly nervous of enemy fighters, but it should be remembered that *JG 26* lost 106 pilots, including 11 *Kapitäne*, between January and May (see Table 82).[111] Consequently the *Luftwaffe*'s defence increasingly relied upon *Flak* batteries, whose strength was steadily increased until by June there were 10,481 guns (1,502 heavy), and *III. Flakkorps Stab* was attached to control units supporting *Panzergruppe West*, which would direct the German riposte to the landing (see Table 83). Plans were made to transfer *Jagd-* and *Kampfgruppen* from the Reich the moment the code-word (*Dr Gustav Wilhelm* for *Drohende Gefahr West*, or Imminent Danger, West) for the invasion was received, and dozens of airfields were prepared with supplies, communications and accommodation, some reportedly having dispersal bays up to five kilometres from the runway.[112] On 31 May *Luftflotte 3* had more than 1,000 combat aircraft and *Luftflotte Reich* had 815 day fighters (of which only 55% were serviceable), 192 *Zerstörer* and 259 strike and reconnaissance aircraft, some in units which were being re-equipped (see Table 84). By contrast the 2nd Tactical and Ninth Air Forces had 4,029 aircraft, while another 5,514 aircraft of the strategic air forces and the Air Defence of Great Britain were available.[113]

The threat of an Allied invasion loomed great in German eyes but the RAF clouded them from 1943 onwards. During the summer of 1943 there was a series of high-altitude reconnaissance sorties, possibly by Ju 86s, but from August 1943 fighters prevented daylight photographic-reconnaissance over Great Britain until March 1944. In October *FAGr 123* (*Major* Hans Wolff) had to abandon high-altitude daylight reconnaissance in favour of low-level missions in cloud, but even these failed to succeed and the only images acquired were at night. By the spring of 1944 Sperrle, under considerable pressure from *Führer* headquarters, was demanding reports and photographs of inland England from Wolff. The task was especially hazardous from mid-April 1944, when the RAF had standing fighter patrols over shipping assembly areas, and even the Bf 109H of *5. (F)/121*, which could operate at 12,200m (40,000ft), encountered Spitfires, so most photographs were of targets within 40km of the coast. Shortly before D-Day one of Wolff's Bf 109s succeeded in photographing Portsmouth harbour, but the Area Controller of No 11 Group, Squadron Leader Eric Holmes, had made a study of *FAGr 123* operations and correctly deduced that it would return to Cherbourg, where a Free French Spitfire destroyed it as it rolled along the runway. Nevertheless the Germans did acquire some pictures, apparently by using a captured Thunderbolt in Allied markings, while *1. (F)/121* conducted daylight patrols of the Channel and the Ju 188Ds of Kammhuber's *1. (F)/120* probed northern Britain to detect shipping movements.[114]

When the landing took place German aircraft were far from the beach-heads, most of the *Jagdgruppen* being dispersed all over France to assure their survival. *Luftwaffe* confirmation of the landing came from *Leutnant* Adalbert Bärwolf of *3./ NAGr 13*, but although Normandy was covered by *Major* Kurt Bühlingen's *JG 2* the initial response on 6 June was a quick pass along 'Sword' Beach by the *Kommodore* of *JG 26*, 'Pips' Priller, and his *Rottenhund, Unteroffizier* Heinz Wodarczyk, who flew from Lille-North in the first of 121 *Luftwaffe* fighter sorties that day.[115] In the following weeks Sperrle received 670 aircraft, but his airfields

Table 85. *Luftwaffe* Activity in the West, 1944

	Luftflotte Reich			West		
	Sorties	Lost	%	Sorties	Lost	%
Day fighters	36,006	3,706	10.29	44,255	2,634	5.95
Night fighters	20,284	664	3.27	3,091	142	4.59
Day strike	–	–	–	4,499	212	4.71
Night strike	–	–	–	21,796	1,074	4.92
Reconnaissance	–	–	–	5,470	150	2.74
Monthly average	4,690	364	7.76	6,592	351	5.32

Notes: Day strike by *Kampf-* and *Schlachtverbände*, night strike by *Kampf-* and *Nachtschlacht-verbände*.
Source: Luftwaffe Activity, Vol. I (IWM AHB 6, Tin 192, fr.1052).

were constantly harassed, and the deployment of 190 *Flak* batteries (140 heavy) did little to relieve the situation as casualties mounted steadily and the anti-shipping forces failed completely to disrupt the build-up. During June some 1,200 anti-shipping and nearly 900 minelaying sorties were flown, but the following month the ratio was reversed. However, losses were so heavy that as the German Army retreated from France during August only 250 sorties were flown, of which about 80 were minelaying.[116]

It was all in vain, and by August the *Luftwaffe* was covering the wreck of the *Wehrmacht* as it departed from France. Sperrle's *Luftflotte* was disbanded and a series of minor commands replaced it, but their sole contribution to the defence of the nation's borders was the devastating *Unternehmen 'Bodenplatte'* on New Year's Day which virtually finished off the *Luftwaffe* (See Table 85 for *Luftwaffe* activity in the West). As the *Reichsbanner* fluttered down from occupied towns the *Luftwaffe* fought a rearguard action which cost it 7,957 dead and missing (1,280 in non-operational missions) and another 3,260 wounded and injured (687 in non-operational missions) from July to the end of December 1944. During the same period they lost 10,362 aircraft destroyed (1,698 in accidents) and 6,787 damaged (2,919 in accidents). The training units lost 1,314 dead and 672 injured while their material losses were 2,052 aircraft destroyed and 1,986 damaged.[117]

In the months after D-Day air warfare reached new heights of technical sophisticaton: the *Luftwaffe* used jet fighters and bombers, its He 111s launched air-to-surface missiles against English targets and its scientists developed surface-to-air and air-to-air missiles.[118] The British, in turn, also used jet fighters and a crude form of airborne early warning, while their home-defence radar chain was used to detect ballistic missile launching sites. For all their technical sophistication the Germans were still misusing air power at the end of the war, having treated it like children playing marbles with diamonds. It has been fashionable to blame this misuse upon the Nazis, but the roots are to be found in an earlier generation. The German Empire's General Staff lost the Great War because they sought to chain twentieth century technology to nineteenth century philosphy, and their misuse of air power through the failure to concentrate forces, the inability to persevere with worthwhile strategies and persistent interference with industrial organisation was repeated by the Nazis with even more devastating results. Ultimately, the Germans could not beat their own history and the end of the war left them with a ruined and divided land.

NOTES TO CHAPTER 8

1. Aders, p.60.
2. In the spring of 1944 *NJG 1* was still using the Do 215B-5, in which Ludwig Bekker achieved his first radar victory in August 1941. Aders, p.135.

3. For *Schräge Musik* see Hinchliffe, pp.137–8.

4. For German night fighter technology see Aders, pp.75–9.

5. BAM, p.284.

6. Rumpf, p.62; and USNA T971, Roll 2.

7. Galland observed, with only slight exaggeration, that during night raids it was possible to read a newspaper in the street. Galland, p.172.

8. *Wilde Sau* literally means 'Wild Boar' or 'Savage Boar' but the colloquial English equivalent is 'Rogue Elephant'.

9. The British had created the equivalent Telecommunications Research Establishment some three years earlier. For changes in night fighting see Aders, pp.61–3, 85–7, 101; Herrmann, pp.160–70; Hinchliffe, pp.127–33; and Price, *Instruments*, pp.145–8.

10. Hinchliffe, p.159.

11. Aders, pp.127–8.

12. NJRF, 1–12, 100–3, 105–8, 111.

13. NJRF, 10–12, 105.

14. During the previous summer the *ADD* flew 212 sorties against Berlin and other targets in eastern Germany. Kozhevnikov, pp.87, 123.

15. 'Fliegerkorps XII: Organisation der Nachtjagd Juni 1943' (BA MA RL 8/84).

16. *Würzburg* was not jammed because the Allies did not wish to alert the enemy until after the invasion of Sicily. Yet, according to Aders, pp.79–81, *Würzburg* radars in western France reported jamming from March 1943.

17. For the electronic warfare situation see Aders, pp.79–81; Hinchliffe, pp.135–6; Price, *Instruments*, pp.128–42; and Price, *Ju 88 Night Fighters*, p.6.

18. See Hinchliffe, pp.143–58; Irving, *Goring*, pp.395–6; Middlebrook and Everitt, pp.411–16; Middlebrook, *The Battle of Hamburg*; and Price, *Instruments*, pp.151–65.

19. Aders, pp.101–2; Herrmann, pp.176–7; and Hinchliffe pp.159–60.

20. The exact translation of *Zahme Sau* is 'Tame Boar', but the colloquial English translation would be 'Pet Lamb'.

21. Hinchliffe, p.212.

22. Müller was officially credited with 30 victories and was the leading *Wilde Sau Experte*.

23. For *Wilde Sau* see Aders, pp.97–101, 106–7, 141–2, 147; Herrmann, pp.177–214; Hinchliffe, pp.150–1, 166–7, 179–92, 211–15; and Middlebrook and Everitt, pp.422–4.

24. Aders, p.104.

25. At the same time *Jagdkorps II* was formed to perform a similar function under *Luftflotte 3*. Plans existed for a *Jagdkorps III* in Bavaria and Austria but were later abandoned.

26. For a detailed description of the headquarters and commentaries see Hinchliffe, pp.163–6, 191.

27. For operations from July to November 1943 see Aders, pp.146–7; Hinchliffe, pp.187–9, 196–7, 200; and Middlebrook and Everitt, pp.415–43.

28. The *Jagdkorps I* war diary reports the first victory for *Lichtenstein SN-2* as taking place on 13 December. For the new generation of sensors see Aders, pp.122–8.

29. Hinsley, App. 21.

30. Stumpff, the commander of *Luftflotte 5*, went into the reserve on 6 November but after a fortnight's leave held a watching brief on Kammhuber, who became *Befehlshaber, Luftflotte 5* on 23 December (based upon Hildebrand).

31. The Rotterdam Stirling may have been one of Streib's 66 victims.

32. In March *I./KG 7* was redesignated *I./NJG 7*.

33. *Jagdkorps I* war diary (BA MA RL 8/93).

34. For the Battle of Berlin see Aders, pp.111–14, 148–58; BAM, pp.277–9; Hinchliffe, pp.203–57; Hinsley, App. 21; Middlebrook and Everitt, pp.446–88; Middlebrook, *Berlin*

Raids and *Nuremberg Raid*; Price, *Instruments*, pp.179–98; Streetly, pp.35–50; 'Geschichte des I. Jagdkorps', BA MA RL8/91–3; and IWM AHB 6/165.

35. Murray, p.221.

36. Based upon Overy, *War and Economy*, pp.280/n.71, 373.

37. Middlebrook and Everitt, p.552; and BAM, p.279.

38. Sperrle later requested the transfer of *Jagddivision 3* to his command but Stumpff refused.

39. The *Gruppen* were numbered in August and distinguished themselves against American bombers. Ihlefeld, a Condor Legion *Experte*, ended the war with 130 victories while Graf had 212.

40. On 31 January the Americans had 214 heavy bombers and 155 crew in England. Freeman, *The US Strategic Bomber* (hereafter *Strategic Bomber*), pp.153–4.

41. Jabs himself was shot down during daylight.

42. A B-17F carried 4,430 rounds or more than half a tonne. Freeman, *Strategic Bomber*, p.120.

43. The box, based upon the Bombardment Group, had the following dimensions:

Date	Length	Width	Depth	Aircraft
Mar 1943	715m	200m	275m	18
Apr 1943	200m	350m	275m	18
Jan 1944	250m	475m	180m	12

Three vertically stacked boxes would form a wing formation at intervals of 9.5km and later 6.5km. Price, *Bomber*, pp.124–34.

44. Price, *Fighter Conflict*, p.83.

45. See notes of Brigadier-General Frank A. Armstrong (then commander of the 101st Provisional Combat Wing and later of the 1st Bombardment Wing), published in Freeman, *Mighty Eighth War Diary* (henceforth Freeman, *Diary*), pp.50–1. Middlebrook points out that while all the other gunners in the bomber were professionals, those in the nose tended to be the bombardier and navigator who had no gunnery training (*Schweinfurt-Regensburg*, pp.101–2). For *Jagdgruppe* tactics see Baker, pp.211–12.

46. Freeman, *Diary*, p.54.

47. The *Luftwaffe*'s first attempt at bombing the Fortresses was over St Nazaire on 16 February 1943. It is unclear whether or not *JG 1*'s *Leutnant* Dieter Gerhard knew about the St Nazaire attempt but he began similar experiments about a fortnight later. He was mortally wounded while attacking Liberators on 18 March, but his closest friend, *Leutnant* Heinz Knocke, continued with the work and dropped the first bomb in action four days later to claim a Fortress. He was praised by Göring and 'given a rocket' by Kammhuber. Knocke, pp.88–97.

48. Freeman, op. cit.

49. Baker, p.235; and Murray, p.231.

50. BAM, pp.274–5

51. Middlesbrook, *Schweinfurt-Regensburg*, p.244.

52. Middlebrook's excellent account indicates that only four bombers fell to *Flak* and eight were damaged by *Flak* and finished off by fighters (App. 1).

53. For the first Schweinfurt/Regensburg mission see Aders, p.110; Bekker, pp.320–1; Caldwell, pp.184–91; Freeman, *Diary*, pp.89–95; Irving, *Göring*, p.397; and Middlebrook, *Schweinfurt-Regensburg*. On 24 August the 4th Wing struck Bordeaux-Mérignac airfield on its return journey and lost another three bombers (Freeman, *Diary*, p.99).

54. Quoted in Weal, *Fw 190 Aces of the Western Front* (hereafter *Fw 190 Aces*), p.49.

55. Freeman, *Diary*, pp.106–7.

56. Ibid., pp.112–13, 116, 119.
57. Ibid., pp.118–21, 239.
58. In the Münster mission the 100th Group lost 12 out of 14 bombers, one bomber being damaged beyond repair. Freeman, *Diary*, p.125.
59. Caldwell, pp.200–2; Freeman, *Diary*, pp.126–9; and McFarland and Newton, pp.129–30. Despite the losses, between 31 August and 31 October Eighth Air Force heavy bomber strength rose from 907 to 1,138 and the number of crews from 806 to 1,116 (Freeman, *Strategic Bomber*). The figures include replacements and non-operational second-line aircraft.
60. Freeman, *Diary*, pp.123–5, 173–4, 183.
61. For the issue of US fighter escorts see McFarland and Newton, especially pp.140–1, 144–50, 160–237.
62. Freeman, *Diary*, p.165; McFarland and Newton, p.158; and *Jagdkorps I* war diary.
63. Irving, *Göring*, p.404.
64. Irving, *Göring*, p.406; and Murray, p.226.
65. Between September and November 1943 Schmid's and Sperrle's *Jagdgruppen* lost 967 aircraft to enemy action and 1,052 to accidents and 'friendly fire'. McFarland and Newton, p.135.
66. Baker, p.220–1.
67. Weal, *Fw 190 Aces*, pp.52–3, 77–8.
68. Murray, pp.231–2.
69. About the same time Kornatski's *II./JG 4* also became a *Sturmgruppe*.
70. *Jagdkorps I* war diary.
71. However, *Oberfeldwebel* Adolf 'Addi' Glunz, of *II./JG 26*, flew 574 sorties in four years without once being either shot down or wounded and scored 68 victories, all in the West. Weal, *Fw 190 Aces*, p.50.
72. Knocke, pp.149–50.
73. Ibid., p.148.
74. Freeman, *Diary*, p.246; and 'Bericht über den Allierten Luftkrieg gegen das Reich' (USNA T971, Roll 2, fr.1).
75. For German day fighter defence see Baker, pp.225–9; Feist, pp.66–77; Fighter Operations of the German Air Force (IWM AHB 6, Tin 195, fr.3296–311); Interrogation of *Oberstleutnant* Dahl (IWM AHB 6, Tin 195, fr.3443–5); and Galland's 'Tactical Regulations for Fighters in Home Defence' of 3 September 1943 (translation in IWM AHB 6, Tin 195, fr 3525–7).
76. Freeman, *Diary*, pp.169, 183ff; and McFarland and Newton, pp.141–2, 157–92.
77. Freeman, *Diary*, pp.217–18.
78. Ibid., pp.195, 226.
79. Ibid., pp.242–3.
80. Ibid., pp.248–9, 252–4.
81. For Eighth Air Force operations after 'Big Week' and the *Luftwaffe*'s reactions see McFarland and Newton, pp.193–237.
82. In August *ZG 26* was redesignated *JG 6*, while the following month *III Gruppenstab* became *Kommando Nowotny* under *Major* Walter Nowotny. The Komet-equipped *EK 16* flew individual sorties against American bombers from 13 May, but without success. See Späte and Bateson.
83. Freeman, *Strategic Bomber*, pp.155–6.
84. Tuider, p.231ff.
85. On 30 April the Fifteenth Air Force had 1,375 heavy bombers (1,436 crews) and a month later 1,499 bombers (1,537 crews). Freeman, *Strategic Bomber*.
86. For the background see Balke, *KG 2*, pp. 215–19.

87. For the Neuhammer disaster see Bekker, pp.42–3.
88. BAM, p.198.
89. This may have been *3./KG 66*, formed in April, which, unusually, became *6. (F)/ AufKlGr 123* a year later, at which time a *Horch- und Störstaffel 2* was also created from *Sonderkommando Rastedter* (Rosch, pp.253, 334). For Peltz's operations see Balke, *KG 2*, pp.219–41.
90. Hinsley, App. 21.
91. For operations under Fröhlich see Balke, *KG 2*, pp.242–62.
92. Schmid's plan sowed the seed for *Unternehmen 'Gisela'* in March 1945. For intruder operations see Parry, pp.87ff.
93. German report translated in Air Ministry Weekly Intelligence Summary 265 (PRO Air 22/8).
94. For offensive operations against Britain see Balke, *KG 2*, pp.262–86; Wakefield, 'The Fiasco of 1943'; and AHB, *The Air Defence of Great Britain.Vol.V: The Struggle for Air Supremacy, January 1942–May 1944*, pp.171–228 (PRO Air 41/49).
95. Navigation beacons had operated in quartets during 1943, but this proved too complicated for the *Kampfgruppen* (Mediterranean Allied Air Force Intelligence Summary 66, PRO Air 24/949). See also Hinsley, App. 23.
96. *Obergefreiter* Emil Imon, the tail gunner of a *KG 100* Greif, was doubly lucky to survive. When the aircraft crashed on 22/23 February he was the only survivor, but he was trapped with broken legs for 10 hours until found by a civilian, who gave him tea from a flask before seeking help. Ramsey, Vol. III, p.340.
97. For *'Steinbock'* see Balke, *KG 2*, pp.287–342; Brooks, p.171; Delve, pp.159–61; Neitzel, pp.205–7; Ramsey, Vol. III; Wakefield, 'The Steinbock Raids'; and AHB, *The Air Defence of Great Britain*, Vol. V, pp.208–28. For the diary of a radar operator with *2./KG 6* during the 'Little Blitz' see Air Ministry Intelligence Summary 240 (PRO Air 22/8).
98. All based upon Parry and Dierich, *KG 51*, pp.220–3.
99. For FzG 76 see Koch, p.129; Price, *Luftwaffe Handbook*, pp.85–9; and Air Ministry Intelligence Summary 265 (PRO Air 22/8).
100. Based upon Caldwell, p.169; and Freeman, *Diary*, pp.53–4. Surprisingly, Mombeek's otherwise detailed account makes no mention of this clash.
101. Caldwell, p.175.
102. Middlebrook and Everitt, p.383.
103. Freeman, *Diary*, pp.58–84.
104. Ibid., pp.39, 41.
105. Ibid., pp.64–89.
106. From 1 June the spearhead of RAF operations over western Europe was the 2nd Tactical Air Force.
107. With the same drop tanks the P-38's radius was 835km and the P-51's 1,045km.
108. Balke, *KG 2*, pp.282–3.
109. Mitchell, pp.249–50.
110. Balke, *KG 100*, pp.292, 296.
111. Statistics from 'Luftwaffenkommando Führungsabteilung: Bericht über den Allierten Luftkrieg gegen das Reich' (incomplete report) (USNA T971, Roll 2, fr.82–3). For *JG 26* see pp.236, 241.
112. Air Ministry Intelligence Summary 250 (PRO Air 22/8).
113. For the Allied air offensive from 1943 to D-Day, and the German reactions, see Bowyer; Caldwell, pp.150–241; Hoffmann, Vol. III, pp.253–63; Lacey-Johnson; Mark, pp.211–63; Mombeek, pp.113–240; Price, *Instruments*, pp.199–201; Weal, *Fw 190 Aces*; Air Ministry Intelligence Summaries 252, 254, 256, 259, 262 (PRO Air 22/8); AHB, *The Air Defence of Great Britain*, Vol. V, pp.255–98; and 'Befehl des Luftflottenkommandos 3

für die Kampfführung in der Küstenverteidigung' (USNA T971, Roll 51, fr.273). Air Ministry Intelligence Summary No 254 has a vivid description of the activities of *8./LnR 53* and the Douvres radar station.

114. Bushby, pp.168–9; Brooks p.171; AHB, *The Air Defence of Great Britain,* Vol. V, pp.171–88; and Air Ministry Weekly Intelligence Summary 247 (PRO Air 22/8).

115. On D-Day the *Luftwaffe* flew 319 sorties, of which 139 were strike, 24 were reconnaissance and 35 were night fighter ('Dokumente, Auszüge, Entwürfe u/w für das Thema Invasion in Frankreich 1944', USNA T 971, Roll 8, fr.464). The Allies flew 14,075 sorties and lost 127 aircraft (Buffetaut, p.37). The *Luftwaffe* transferred to France 14 *Jagdgruppen* (475 fighters), two *Nachtjagdgruppen* (68 night fighters), four *Kampfgruppen* (108 bombers) and two *Fernaufklärungsstaffeln* (19 reconnaissance aircraft).

116. Neitzel, Table 19.

117. RAF Air Staff Post-Hostilities Studies, Book 21: 'Luftwaffe Activity I' (IWM AHB 6, Tin 192, fr.1071–85). Figures extrapolated from 'Einsatzbereitschaft der fliegende Verbände'.

118. For *Luftwaffe* operations in the last year of the war see the excellent account in Price, *The Last Year of the Luftwaffe.*

Appendices

APPENDIX 1
LUFTWAFFE ORDER OF BATTLE,
BATTLE OF BRITAIN, 13 AUGUST 1940

Luftflotte 5 (Generaloberst **Stumpff)**

Fliegerkorps X (General der Flieger Geisler)

KG 26	*Stab, I., III.*	He 111H, He 111P *(Stab)*
KG 30	*Stab I., III.*	Ju 88A
ZG 76	*I*	Bf 110C/D
JG 77	*Stab, I., II.*	Bf 109E
KüFlGr 506		He 115B/C
AufKlrGr 22		
3./ObdL		Do 215B, Bf 110C, He 111P
1./(F) 120		He 111H, Do 17P
1./(F) 121		He 111H, Do 17P
2. (F)/22		Do 17M/P
3. (F)/22		Do 17M/P
Westa Kette		He 111H

Luftflotte 2 (Generalfeldmarschall **Kesselring)**

Wekusta 26		Do 17P, He 111H

Fliegerkorps I (Generaloberst Grauert)

KG 1	*Stab, I., II., III.*	He 111H, Ju 88A *(III.)*
KG 76	*Stab, I., II., III.*	Do 17Z, Ju 88A *(II.)*
5./(F) 122		Ju 88A, He 111H, Do 17P
4./(F) 123		Ju 88A, He 111H, Bf 110C

Fliegerkorps II (General der Flieger Loerzer)

KG 2	*Stab, I., II., III.*	Do 17Z
KG 3	*Stab, I., II., III.*	Do 17Z
KG 53	*Stab, I., II., III.*	He 111H
II/StG 1		Ju 87B
IV./(St) LG 1		Ju 87B
EprGr 210		Bf 109E, Bf 110C/D

Fliegerdivision 9 (*Generalleutnant* Coeler)
KG 4	*Stab, I., II., III.*	He 111H, Ju 88A (*III.*)
KG 40	*Stab, I.*	Fw 200C
KGr 100		He 111H
KGr 126		He 111H
KüFlGr 106		He 115C, Do 18G
3./(F) 122		Ju 88A, He 111H

Jagdfliegerführer 2 (*Oberst* von Döring)
JG 3	*Stab, I., II., III.*	Bf 109E
JG 26	*Stab, .I, II., III.*	Bf 109E
JG 52	*Stab, I., II., III.*	Bf 109E
JG 54	*Stab, I., II., III.*	Bf 109E
ZG 26	*Stab, I., II., III.*	Bf 110C

Nachtjagddivision (*Oberst* Kammhuber)
NJG 1	*Stab, I., II., III.*	Bf 110B/C, Ju 88C, Do 17Z, Bf 109D/E

Luftgau VI (Münster)
Luftgau XI (Hanover)
Lufgau Holland (Rotterdam)
Luftgau Belgien-Nord Frankreich (Brussels)

Luftflotte 3 (*Generalfeldmarschall* Sperrle)

Wekusta 51	Do 17U, He 111H

Fliegerkorps IV (*Generaloberst* Keller)
LG 1	*Stab, I., II., III.*	Ju 88A
KG 27	*Stab, I., II., III.*	He 111D/P/H
I./StG 3		Ju 87B
Gr 806		Ju 88A

Fliegerkorps V (*General der Flieger* Greim)
KG 51	*Stab, I., II., III.*	Ju 88A
KG 54	*Stab, I., II.*	Ju 88A
KG 55	*Stab, I., II., III.*	He 111H
4. (F)/14		Do 17P, Bf 110C
4. (F)/121		Ju 88A, Do 17P

Fliegerkorps VIII (*General der Flieger* Richthofen)
StG 1	*Stab, I., III.*	Ju 87B, Ju 87R (*I.*), Do 17M (*Stab*)
StG 2	*Stab, I., II.*	Ju 87B, Do 17M (*Stab*)
StG 77	*Stab, I., II., III.*	Ju 87B, Do 17M (*Stab*)
II. (Sch)/ LG 2		Bf 109E
V.(Z)/LG 1		Bf 110C
2. (F)/11		Do 17P, Bf 110C
2. (F)/123		Ju 88A

Jagdfliegerführer 3 (*Oberst* Junck)

JG 2	*Stab, I., II., III.*	Bf 109E
JG 27	*Stab, I., II., III.*	Bf 109E
JG 53	*Stab, I., II., III.*	Bf 109E
ZG 2	*Stab, I., II., III.*	Bf 110C

Luftgau VII (Munich)
Luftgau XII (Wiesbaden)
Luftgau XIII (Nuremberg)
Luftgau West Frankreich (Paris)

FdL West (*Generalmajor* Ritter)

KüFlGr 606		Do 17Z
KüFlGr 406	*Stab*	
2./106, 3./406, 2./906		Do 18G
KüFlGr 706	*Stab*	
1., 2./406		Do 18G
1./BordFlGr 196		Ar 196A
Transozeanstaffel		Do 26A

Army units

Coastal Artillery

	3. (F)/10	Do 17P, Bf 110C
	3. (F)/11	Bf 110C
	4. (F)/11	Bf 110C

Koluft Heeresgruppe A

	2. (F)/11	Do 17P

Koluft 9. Armee

	3. (F)/31	Do 17P, Bf 110C
AK VIII	*1. (H)/31*	Hs 126
AK X	*4. (H)/26*	Hs 126
AK XXIV	*4. (H)/21*	Hs 126
AK XXXVIII	*2. (H)/21*	Hs 126
Mot AK XV	*4. (H)/31*	Hs 126
5. Pz Div	*2. (H)/31Pz*	Hs 126
7. Pz DiV	*3. (H)/14Pz*	Hs 126

Koluft 16. Armee

	3. (H)/22	Do 17M/P, Bf 109E
AK IV	*1. (H)/41*	Hs 126
AK V	*3. (H)/13*	Hs 126
AK VII	*2. (H)/13*	Hs 126, Do 17M
AK XIII	*5. (H)/13*	Hs 126

AK XLII	*2. (H)/10*	Hs 126
Mot AK XLI		
8.Pz Div	*3. (H)/41*	Hs 126
Koluft Heeresgruppe C		
	1. (F)/22	Do 17P
Koluft 6. Armee		
AK II	*1. (H)/21*	Hs 126

APPENDIX 2
LUFTWAFFE ORDER OF BATTLE,
BATTLE OF BRITAIN, 4 SEPTEMBER 1940

Luftflotte 2 (*Generalfeldmarschall* Kesselring)

Stab AufKlGr 122

1. (F)/22		Do 17P, Bf 110C
2. (F)/122		Ju 88A
4. (F)/122		Ju 88A, He 111H, Bf 110C
Wekusta 26		Do 17P, He 111H

Fliegerkorps I (*Generaloberst* Grauert)

KG 1	*Stab, I., II., III.*	He 111H, Ju 88A (*III.*)
KG 30	*Stab, I., II.*	Ju 88A
KG 76	*Stab, I., II., III.*	Do 17Z, Ju 88A (*II.*)
KG 77	*Stab, I., II., III.*	Ju 88A
5. (F)/122		Ju 88A, He 111H

Fliegerkorps II (*General der Flieger* Loerzer)

KG 2	*Stab, I., II., III.*	Do 17Z
KG 3	*Stab, I., II., III.*	Do 17Z
KG 53	*Stab, I., II., III.*	He 111H
StG 1	*Stab, II.*	Ju 87B, Do 17M (*Stab*)
IV. (St)/LG 1		Ju 87B
II. (Sch)/LG 2		Bf 109E
EprGr 210		Bf 110C, Bf 109E
1. (F)/122		Ju 88A
7. (F)/LG 2		Bf 110C

Fliegerkorps VIII (*General der Flieger* Richthofen)

StG 1	*I., III.*	Ju 87B, Ju 87R (*I.*)
StG 2	*Stab, I., II.*	Ju 87B, Ju 87R (*I.*),
		Do 17M (*Stab*)
StG 77	*Stab, I., II., III.*	Ju 87B, Do 17M (*Stab*)
2. (F)/11		Do 17P, Bf 110C

Fliegerdivision 9 (Generalleutnant Coeler)

KG 4	*Stab, I., II., III.*	He 111H, Ju 88A (*III.*)
Stab KG 40		Ju 88A
KGr 126		He 111H
KüFlGr 106		He 115C, Do 18G
3./(F) 122		Ju 88A, He 111H

Jagdfliegerführer 1 (Oberst Osterkamp)

JG 27	*Stab, I., II., III.*	Bf 109E
JG 76	*Stab, II.*	Bf 109E
V.(Z)/LG 1		Bf 110C

Jagdfliegerführer 2 (Oberst von Döring)

Stab JG 51		Bf 109E
JG 3	*Stab, I., II., III.*	Bf 109E
JG 26	*Stab, I., II., III.*	Bf 109E
JG 53	*Stab, I., II., III.*	Bf 109E

Luftgau VI (Münster)

Schwärme	*III./JG 53 I./JG 52*	Bf 109E

Luftgau XI (Hanover)

Stab JG 1		Bf 109E
II./JG 51		Bf 109E
II./JG 52		Bf 109E

Luftgau Holland (Rotterdam)

Schwärme	*II./JG 51, I., II.* and	Bf 109E
	III./JG 54	

Luftflotte 3 (Generalfeldmarschall **Sperrle**)

Stab AufKlGr 123

1. (F)/123	Ju 88A, Do 17P
2. (F)/123	Ju 88A, Do 17P
3. (F)/123	Ju 88A, Do 17P
Wekusta 51	Do 17P, He 111H

Fliegerkorps I (Generaloberst Grauert)

KG 1	*Stab, I., II., III.*	Ju 88A, He 111H (*I.*)
KG 30	*Stab, I., II.*	Ju 88A
KG 76	*Stab, I., II., III.*	Do 17Z, Ju 88A (*II.*)
KG 77	*Stab, I., II, III.*	Ju 88A
5. (F)/122		Ju 88A, He 111H

Fliegerkorps IV (Generalleutnant Pflugbeil)

LG 1	*Stab, I., III., Erg.*	Ju 88A
KG 27	*Stab, I., II., III.*	He 111P/H
KGr 100		He 111H
Gr 606		Do 17Z

Gr 806		Ju 88A
I./KG 40		Fw 200C
Erg./KG 40		Fw 200C, He 111H
I./StG 3		Ju 87B

Fliegerkorps V (*General der Flieger* Greim)

KG 51	*Stab, I., II., III., Erg.*	Ju 88A
KG 54	*Stab, I., II., Erg.*	Ju 88A
KG 55	*Stab, I., II., III., Erg.*	He 111H
4. (F)/14		Bf 110C, Do 17P
4. (F)/121		Bf 110C, Do 17P

Jagdfliegerführer 3 (*Oberst* Junck)

JG 2	*Stab, I., II., III.*	Bf 109E
ZG 26	*Stab, I., II., III.*	Bf 110C
ZG 76	*Stab, II., III.*	Bf 110C

APPENDIX 3
LUFTWAFFE ORDER OF BATTLE, WESTERN EUROPE, JANUARY 1941

Luftflotte 2 (*Generalfeldmarschall* Kesselring)

Stab AufKlGr 122

1. (F)/122		Ju 88A
2. (F)/122		Ju 88A/D
4. (F)/122		Ju 88A/D
7. (F)/LG 2		Ju 88A/D, He 111H
Wekusta 26		Do 17P, He 111H

Fliegerkorps II (*General der Flieger* Loerzer)

KG 2	*Stab, I., II., III., Erg.*	Do 17Z
KG 3	*Stab, I., II., III., Erg.*	Do 17Z
KG 53	*Stab, I., II., III., Erg.*	He 111H

Fliegerkorps IX (*Generalleutnant* Coeler)

KG 4	*Stab, I., II., III., Erg.*	He 111H, Ju 88A (*III.*)
KG 30	*Stab, I., II., III.*	Ju 88A
KüFlGr 106		He 115C
3. (F)/122		Ju 88A/D, He 111H

Jagdfliegerführer 2 (*Oberst* von Döring)

JG 3	*Stab, I., II., III.*	Bf 109E
JG 26	*Stab, I., II., III., Erg.*	Bf 109E
JG 53	*Stab, I., II., III.*	Bf 109E
56th Italian Fighter Gp		Fiat G.50
StG 1	*Stab, I., III.*	Ju 87B, Ju 87R (*I.*)
Attached:	*II. (Sch)/LG 2*	Bf 109E

EprGr 210		Bf 110C

Nachtjagddivision (*Oberst* Kammhuber)

NJG 1	Stab, I., II., III.	Bf 110C/D
I./NJG 2		Ju 88C, Do 17Z
I./NJG 3		Bf 110C

Luftflotte 3 (*Generalfeldmarschall* **Sperrle**)

Stab AufKlGr 123

1. (F)/123		Ju 88A/D
2. (F)/123		Ju 88A/D
3. (F)/123		Ju 88D, Do 17P, Bf 110C
2./ObdL		Do 215B
Wekusta 5		Do 17P, He 111H

Fliegerkorps I (*Generaloberst* Grauert)

KG 1	Stab, I., II., III.	Ju 88A, He 111H (I.)
Attached:	III./KG 26	He 111H
KG 77	Stab, I., II., III., Erg.	Ju 88A
5. (F)/122		Ju 88A

Fliegerkorps IV (*Generalleutnant* Pflugbeil)

LG 1	Stab, I., II., III.	Ju 88A
KG 27	Stab, I., II., III.	He 111P/H
KGr 100		He 111H
Gr 606		Do 17Z
I./KG 40		Fw 200C
JG 77	Stab, II., III.	Bf 109E
3. (F)/121		Ju 88A/D

Fliegerkorps V (*General der Flieger* Greim)

KG 51	Stab, I,. II., III., Erg.	Ju 88A
KG 54	Stab, I., II., Erg.	Ju 88A
Attached Gr 806		Ju 88A
KG 55	Stab, I., II., III., Erg.	He 111H
StG 77	Stab, I., II., III.	Ju 87B
JG 2	Stab, I., II., III., Erg.	Bf 109E
4. (F)/121		Bf 110C, Do 17P

APPENDIX 4
LUFTWAFFE ORDER OF BATTLE, MAY BLITZ 1941

Luftflotte 2 (*Generalfeldmarschall* Kesselring)

Fliegerkorps II (*General der Flieger* Loerzer)

KG 2	Stab, I., II., III., Erg.	Do 17Z

KG 3	Stab, I., III.	Do 17Z

Fliegerkorps IX (*Generalleutnant* Coeler)

KG 4	Stab, I., II., III., Erg.	He 111H, Ju 88A (*III.*)
KG 30	Stab, I., II., III.	Ju 88A

Jagdfliegerführer 2 (*Oberst* von Döring)

StG 1	Stab, I.	Ju 87B
Attached:	EprGr 210	Bf 110C

Luftflotte 3 (*Generalfeldmarschall* Sperrle)

Fliegerkorps I (*Generaloberst* Grauert)

KG 1	Stab, I., II.	Ju 88A
Attached:	III./KG 26	He 111H
KG 53	Stab, I., II., III., Erg.	He 111H
KG 76	Stab, I., II., III.	Ju 88A
KG 77	Stab, I., II., III., Erg.	Ju 88A
5. (F)/122		Ju 88A

Fliegerkorps IV (*Generalleutnant* Pflugbeil)

LG 1	Stab, I., II., III.	Ju 88A
KG 27	Stab, I., II., III.	He 111P/H
KGr 100		He 111H
Gr 606		Do 17Z

Fliegerkorps V (*General der Flieger* Greim)

KG 54	Stab, I., II., Erg.	Ju 88A
Attached:	Gr 806	Ju 88A
KG 55	Stab, I., II., III., Erg.	He 111H

APPENDIX 5
LUFTWAFFE ORDER OF BATTLE, UNTERNEHMEN '*MARITA*', 5 APRIL 1941

ObdL Command

KGzbV 2

I./KGzbV 1	Ju 52/3m
II./KGzbV 1	Ju 52/3m
KGrzbV 60	Ju 52/3m
KGrzbV 101	Ju 52/3m
KGrzbV 102	Ju 52/3m
KGrzbV 172	Ju 52/3m
KGrzbV Babekuhl (part)	Ju 52/3m
I./LLG 1 (one *Staffel*)	Ju 52/3m, DFS 230

Luftflotte 4 (*General der Flieger* Löhr)

Austria

4. (F)/121		Ju 88A, Bf 110C
Wekusta 76		He 111H, Ju 88A, Bf 110F
KG 2	Stab, I., III.	Do 17Z
Attached:	III./KG 3	Do 17Z, Ju 88A
KG 51	Stab, I., II., III.	Ju 88A
Attached:	II./KG 4	He 111P

Fliegerführer Graz (*Oberstleutnant* Christ)

StG 3	Stab, II.	Ju 87B, He 111H (*Stab*)
JG 54	Stab, 4., 6.	Bf 109E
Attached:	I./JG 27	Bf 109E

Romania: *Fliegerführer* Arad (*Oberstleutnant* von Schönborn)

StG 77	Stab, I., III.	Ju 87B, Bf 109E (*Stab*), Bf 110C (*III.*)
Attached:	III./JG 54	Bf 109E
I./ZG 26		Bf 110C/E
JG 77	Stab, II., III.	Bf 109E

Bulgaria: *Fliegerkorps VIII* (*General der Flieger* von Richthofen)

2. (F)/11		Do 17P
IV./KGzbV 1		Ju 52/3m
StG 2	Stab, I., III.	Ju 87B/R, Do 17P (*Stab*)
Attached:	I./StG 3	Ju 87B/R
I./StG 1		Ju 87R
II./ZG 26		Bf 110C/E
II. (Sch)/LG 2		Bf 109E
10. (Sch)/LG 2		Hs 123A
JG 27	Stab, II., III.	Bf 109E
Attached:	I. (J)/LG 2	Bf 109E

Koluft 1. Panzergruppe

	7. (F)/LG 2	Bf 110F
Mot. K XIV	2. (H)/31Pz (and 5. Pz Div)	Hs 126
11. Pz Div	3. (H)/21Pz	Hs 126

Koluft 2. Armee

	3. (F)/11	Bf 110F
Mot. K XLI	4. (H)/13Pz	Hs 126
Mot. K XLVI	6. (H)/31	Hs 126
8. Pz Div	3. (H)/41Pz	Hs 126
14. Pz Div	2. (H)/32Pz	Hs 126
AK XLIX, AK LI	3. (H)/13	Hs 126

Koluft 12. Armee

	3. (F)/22	Ju 88D
	1. (F)/22 (part)	Ju 88D
16. Pz Div	5. (H)/14Pz	Hs 126
Mot. K XL	4. (H)/22	Hs 126
9. Pz Div	3. (H)/12Pz	Hs 126
Geb. K XVIII	2. (H)/10	Hs 126
2. Pz Div	1. (H)/14Pz	Hs 126
AK XXX	5. (H)/13	Hs 126

Allied Units in German Area of Operations

Hungarian Air Force

1st Fighter Regiment	1./I and II Gps	Fiat CR.42
1st Long Range Recon Gp		He 170
Five Corps sqns		He 46; WM 21 Sólyom
Parachute Transport Sqn		Savoia S.75

APPENDIX 6
LUFTWAFFE ORDER OF BATTLE, *UNTERNEHMEN 'MERKUR'*, 20 MAY 1941

Fliegerkorps VIII (Generalmajor von Richthofen)

	2(F)/11		Do 17P, Hs 126
	7(F)/LG 2		Bf 110F
	Aufklärungsstaffel Fliegerkorps XI		Bf 110F
Menidi:	KG 2	Stab, I., III.	Do 17Z
Eleusis:	LG 1	I., II.	Ju 88A
	Attached:	II./KG 26	He 111H
Argos:	StG 1	Stab, II.	Ju 87B/R
	Attached:	I./StG 3	Ju 87B/R
	StG 77	Stab, I., II., III.	Ju 87B, Bf 109E (Stab), Bf 110C (III.)
	ZG 26	Stab, I, II	Bf 110C/E
	Attached:	II./ZG 76	Bf 110C/E
Molaoi:	StG 2	Stab, I.	Ju 87B/R, Do 17P (Stab)
	JG 77	Stab, II., III.	Bf 109E
Scarpanto:	III./StG 2		Ju 87B
Scaramanga:	2./SAGr 126		He 60

Fliegerkorps XI (General Gerhard)

Megara and Corinth:	KGzbV 1	I., II.	Ju 52/3m
	KGzbV 172	I., II.	Ju 52/3m

Topolia:	*Stab KGzbV 2*		
	Attached:	*KGrzbV 60*	Ju 52/3m
		KGrzbV 101	Ju 52/3m
		KGrzbV 102	Ju 52/3m
Tangara:	*Stab KGzbV 3*		
	Attached:	*KGrzbV 40*	Ju 52/3m
		KGrzbV 105	Ju 52/3m
		KGrzbV 106	Ju 52/3m
		I./LLG 1	Ju 52/3m, DFS 230

Regia Aeronautica

Comando Aeronautica Egeo (Rhodes)

Gadurra, Rhodes:	II./KG 4 (attached)	He 111H
	39th Bomber Wing	
	92nd Bomber Gp	Savoia S.79
	41st Torpedo Bomber Gp	Savoia S.84
	281st Torpedo-Bomber Sqn	Savoia S.79
	163rd Fighter Sqn	Fiat CR.32/CR.42
Maritza, Rhodes:	50th Bomber Gp	Cant Z.1007*bis*
	172nd Reconnaissance Sqn	Cant Z.1007*bis*
Leros:	161st Seaplane Fighter Sqn	Romeo Ro.43/Ro.44
Scarpanto:	162nd Fighter Sqn	Fiat CR.42

APPENDIX 7
LUFTWAFFE ORDER OF BATTLE,
UNTERNEHMEN 'BARBAROSSA', 22 JUNE 1941

Luftflotte 1 (*Generaloberst* Keller)

2. (F)/Obdl		Do 215
Wekusta 1		He 111, Ju 88D, Do 17Z, Ju 52/3m
KGrzbV 50		Ju 52/3m

Fliegerführer Ostsee (*Oberstleutnant* von Wild)

KGr 806		Ju 88A
KüFlGr 125	1.	He 60
	2.	He 114
	3.	Ar 95

Fliegerkorps I (*General der Flieger* Förster)

5. (F)/122		Ju 88D, Bf 110F
KG 1	*Stab, II., III.*	Ju 88A, He 111H (*Stab*)
KG 76	*Stab, I., II., III.*	Ju 88A
JG 54	*Stab, I., II., III.*	Bf 109F
Attached:	*4., 5./JG 53*	Bf 109F

Luftgau I (Königsberg)
Erg. Jagdgruppe 52   Bf 109E
Erg. Jagdgruppe 54   Bf 109E

Luftgaustäbe zbV 1, 10

Luftflotte 2 (*Generalfeldmarschall* Kesselring)

JG 53	*Stab, I., III.*	Bf 109F
Stab Aufklärungsgruppe 122		
Attached:	*2. (F)/122*	Ju 88D, Bf 110F, Bf 109E
Attached:	*Wekusta 26*	Bf 110F, He 111P, Do 17Z
IV./KGzbV 1, KGrzbV		Ju 52/3m

Fliegerkorps II (*General der Flieger* Loerzer)

1. (F)/122		Ju 88D, Bf 110F
KG 3	*Stab, I, II*	Ju 88A/Do 17Z, Ju 88A (*I.*)
KG 53	*Stab, I., II., III.*	He 111H/P
StG 77	*Stab, I., II., III.*	Ju 87B, Bf 110C (*Stab, II.*)
SKG 210	*Stab, I., II.*	Bf 110E
JG 51	*Stab, I., II., III., IV.*	Bf 109F

Fliegerkorps VIII (*General der Flieger* von Richthofen)

2. (F)/11		Do 17P
KG 2	*Stab, I., III.*	Do 17Z
Attached:	*III./KG 3*	Do 17Z
StG 1	*Stab, II., III.*	Ju 87B, Bf 110C (*Stab*)
StG 2	*Stab, I., III.*	Ju 87B (*Stab/I.*), Bf 110C (*Stab*), Ju 87R (*III.*)
Attached:	*II. (Sch)/LG 2*	Bf 109E
	10. (Sch)/LG 2	Hs 123A
ZG 26	*Stab, I., II.*	Bf 110C/E
JG 27	*Stab, II., III.*	Bf 109E
Attached:	*II./JG 52*	Bf 109F

Flakkorps I (*Generalmajor* von Axthelm)
Luftgau II (Posen/Poznan)
Erg. Zerstörergruppe 26   Bf 110C/D
Erg. Jagdgruppe 51   Bf 109E
Luftgaustäbe zbV 2, 20

Luftflotte 4 (*Generaloberst* Löhr)

4. (F)/122	Ju 88D, Bf 110F
Wekusta 76	He 111H, Ju 88A, Bf 110F
KGRzbV 106	Ju 52/3m

Deutsche Luftwaffen-Mission Rumänien (*Generalleutnant* Speidel)
    JG 52   *Stab, III.*   Bf 109E

Fliegerkorps IV (*Generalleutnant* Pflugbeil)
    3. (F)/121   Ju 88D, Bf 110F
    KG 27   *Stab, I., II., III.*   He 111H
        Attached: *II./KG 4*   He 111H
    JG 77   *Stab, II., III.*   Bf 109E
        Attached: *I. (J)/LG 2*   Bf 109E

Fliegerkorps V (*General der Flieger* von Greim)
    4. (F)/121   Ju 88D
    KG 51   *Stab, I., II., III.*   Ju 88A
    KG 54   *Stab, I., II.*   Ju 88A
    KG 55   *Stab, I., II., III.*   He 111H, Bf 110C (*Stab*)
    JG 3   *Stab, I., II., III.*   Bf 109F

Flakkorps II (*Generalleutnant* Dessloch)
Luftgau VIII (Breslau)
    Erg. Jagdgruppe 3   Bf 109E
    Erg. Jagdgruppe 27   Bf 109E
Luftgau XVII (Vienna)
    Erg. Jagdgruppe 77   Bf 109E
Luftgaustäbe zbV 4, 40

Army Co-operation

Koluft Heeresgruppe Nord

                1. (F)/22   Ju 88D
                3. (F)/ Nacht   Do 17P

Koluft 18. Armee

                3. (F)/10   Do 17P, Bf 110C
AK I: 7. (H)/21   Hs 126
AK XXVI: 4. (H)/21   Hs 126
AK XXXVIII: 2. (H)/21   Hs 126

Koluft 16. Armee

                3. (F)/22   Ju 88D
AK II: 2. (H)/13   Hs 126
AK X: 4. (H)/23   Hs 126
AK XXVIII: 1. (H)/12   Hs 126

Koluft 4. Pangergruppe

                4. (F)/33   Bf 110F
PzK XLI: 4. (H)/31   Hs 126

1.PzD:	2.(H)/23	Hs 126
6.PzD:	3.Pz (H)/23	Hs 126
PzK LVI:	8.(H)/32	Hs 126
8.PzD:	3.(H)/41	Hs 126

Koluft Heergesgruppe Mitte

4.(F)/14	Ju 88D
2.(F)/ Nacht	Do 17P

Koluft 3. Panzergruppe

	2.(F)/33	Bf 110F
PzK LVII:	7.(H)/13	Hs 126
12.PzD:	3.(H)/12	Hs 126
19.PzD:	2.(H)/32	Hs 126
AKV:	4.(H)/10	Hs 126
PzK XXXIX:	4.(H)/12	Hs 126
7.PzD:	1.(H)/11	Hs 126
20.PzD:	1.Pz (H)/13	Hs 126
AKVI:	2.(H)/12	Hs 126

Koluft 9. Armee

	1.(F)/33	Ju 88D
AK XLII:	2.(H)/10	Hs 126
AK XX:	5.(H)/41	Hs 126
AKVIII:	1.(H)/31	Hs 126

Koluft 4. Armee

	4.(F)/11	Ju 88D
AK XLIII:	7.(H)/12	Hs 126
AK IX:	2.(H)/41	Hs 126
AKVII:	1.(H)/10	Hs 126
AK XIII:	5.(H)/12	Hs 126

Koluft 2. Panzergruppe

	3.(F)/31	Bf 110F
PzK XXIV:	7.(H)/32	Hs 126
3.PzD:	9.(H)/LG 2	Fw 189A
4.PzD:	6.Pz (H)/41	Hs 126
AK XII:	1.(H)/21	Hs 126
PzK XLVII:	5.(H)/23	Hs 126
17.PzD:	6.(H)/32	Hs 126
18.PzD:	6.Pz (H)/13	Hs 126
PzK XLVI:	6.(H)/31	Hs 126
10.PzD:	3.(H)/14	Hs 126

APPENDICES

Koluft Heeresgruppe Süd

2. (F)/11	Do 17P, Fw 189A
1. (F)/ Nacht	Do 17P

Koluft 1. Panzergruppe

	7. (F)/LG 2	Bf 110F
PzK XLVIII:	5. (H)/32	Hs 126
11.PzD:	5.Pz (H)/11	Hs 126
PzK III:	4. (H)/22	Hs 126
14.PzD:	4. (H)/13	Hs 126
9.PzD:	1. (H)/23	Hs 126
13.PzD:	3. (H)/21	Hs 126
16.PzD:	5.Pz (H)/14	Hs 126

Koluft 6. Armee

	3. (F)/11	Bf 110F
AK XLIV:	4. (H)/41	Hs 126
AK XVII:	6. (H)/21	Hs 126

Koluft 17. Armee

	3. (F)/33	Ju 88D
AK LII:	4. (H)/32	Hs 126
AK IV:	1. (H)/41	Hs 126

Koluft 11. Armee

	2. (F)/22	Ju 88D
AK LIV:	3. (H)/13	Hs 126
AK XXX:	5. (H)/13	Hs 126
AK XI:	6. (H)/12	Hs 126

Slovak Air Force
    1st Observation Gp   Letov S-328
    2nd Fighter Gp   Avia B 534

Hungarian Air Brigade
    1./3 Sqn   Fiat CR.42
    Héja Flight   Reggiane Re.2000
    Detachment 4./IV Gp   Ju 86K
    Detachment 4./III Gp   Caproni Ca.135
    I Short Range Recon Sqn   He 46
    III Short Range Recon Sqn   Weiss WM 21

Romanian Air Group
    1st Sqn   Bristol Blenheim I

1st Bomber Flotilla	1st Bomber Gp	Savoia S.79B
	4th Bomber Gp	PZL 37

	5th Bomber Gp	He 111H
1st Fighter Flotilla	5th Fighter Gp	He 112B
	7th Fighter Gp	Bf 109E
	8th Fighter Gp	IAR 80
2nd Bomber Flotilla	2nd Bomber Gp	Potez 63B, Bloch 210B, IAR 37
2nd Army Co-op. Flotilla	11th, 12th, 13th, 14th Sqns	IAR 38/39

3rd Romanian Army
4th Sqn		Bristol Blenheim I
19th, 20th, 21st Sqns		IAR 39

4th Romanian Army
3rd Sqn		Bristol Blenheim I
15th, 17th, 22nd Sqns		IAR 39

Regia Aeronautica
22nd Fighter Gp		Macchi MC.200
61st Observation Gp		Caproni Ca.311
Transport Gp		Savoia S.81

APPENDIX 8
AXIS ORDER OF BATTLE, SICILY, JANUARY 1942

Fliegerkorps II (*General der Flieger* Loerzer)

KG 54	*Stab, I.*	Ju 88A
Attached:	*KGr 806*	Ju 88A
KG 77	*Stab, II., III.*	Ju 88A
KGr 606		Ju 88A
StG 3	*Stab, II., III.*	Ju 87D
JG 53	*Stab, I., II., III.*	Bf 109F
Attached:	*II./JG 3*	Bf 109F
III./ZG 26		Bf 110C/D/E
4./NJG 2		Ju 88C, Do 17Z
2. (F)/122		Ju 88D

Flakbrigade VII (*Generalmajor* Schulze)
Luftgau zbV Sizilien

Regia Aeronautica

10th Bomber Wing	30th, 32nd Gps	Savoia S.79
278th Torpedo- Bomber Sqn		Savoia S.79
54th Fighter Wing	7th Gp	Macchi MC.200
	16th Gp	Fiat CR.42
377th Fighter Sqn		Reggiane Re.2000

172nd Escort Fighter Sqn	Fiat CR.25
75th Observation Gp	Romeo Ro.37, Caproni Ca.311
83rd, 85th Seaplane Gps	Cant Z.501/506
612th Seaplane Sqn	Cant Z.506

APPENDIX 9
LUFTWAFFE ORDER OF BATTLE, *UNTERNEHMEN* *'CERBERUS/DONNERKEIL'*, 11–12 FEBRUARY 1942

Jagdfliegerführer Deutsche Bucht (*Oberst* Junck)

9./JG 1	
III./NJG 3 (attached)	Bf 110, Do 217
5./NJG 1 (attached)	Bf 110, Do 217
Einsatzstaffeln Jagdfliegerschulen 1, 2, 4	

Jagdfliegerführer 2 (*Oberst* Huth)

Stab JG 26: I., II., III.	Fw 190
I./JG 1	Fw 190
II./NJG 2 (attached)	Bf 110, Do 215, Do 217

Jagdfliegerführer 3 (*Oberst* Ibel)

Stab JG 2: I., II., III.	Fw 190
IV./JG 1	Fw 190
II./NJG 3 (attached) Bf 110, Do 217	
Einsatzstaffel Jagdfliegerschule 5	

Fliegerkorps IX (*General der Flieger* Coeler)

Stab KG 2: I., II., III.	Do 217
KGr 106	Ju 88
9./KG 40	Fw 200

Luftflotte 3 (*Generalfeldmarschall* Sperrle)

1./FAGr 123	Ju 88, Bf 110, Fw 190
3./FAGr 122	Ju 88, Bf 110
KüFlGr 506	Ju 88
IV.(Erg)/KG 3	Ju 88
IV.(Erg)/KG 4	He 111
IV.(Erg)/KG 30	Ju 88
IV.(Erg)/KG 55	He 111
Ergänzungsstaffel KG 30	Ju 88

APPENDIX 10
AXIS ORDER OF BATTLE,
GAZALA BATTLES, 26 MAY 1942

Fliegerführer Afrika (*Generalmajor* **Waldau**)

III./JG 53		Bf 109F
I./NJG 2		Ju 88C
Gefechtsverband Sigel	*Stab, II., III./StG 3*	Ju 87B
	III./ZG 26	Bf 110D/E
	12./LG 1	Ju 88A
DAK:	*2. (H)/14*	Hs 126
Luftgau zbV Afrika		

Regia Aeronautica

4a Squadra Aerea, Settore Est

1st Fighter Wing	6th, 17th Gps	Macchi MC.202
2nd Fighter Wing	8th, 13th Gps	Macchi MC.200
4th Fighter Wing	9th, 10th Gps	Macchi MC.202
150th Gp/53rd Fighter Sqn		Macchi MC.200
50th Assault Wing	158th, 159th Gps	Fiat CR.42
3rd Assault Gp		Fiat CR.42
131st, 132nd Torpedo Bomber Gps		Savoia S.79
191st Recon Sqn		Cant Z.1007*bis*

APPENDIX 11
LUFTWAFFE ORDER OF BATTLE,
EASTERN FRONT AND NORWAY, 27 JULY 1942

Luftflotte 5 (*Generaloberst* **Stumpff**)

Wekusta 5	Ju 88, He 111
KGrzbV 108	Ju 52
Feldluftgau Norwegen	
XII., XIV. Flakbrigaden	

Fliegerführer Nord (Ost) (*Oberst* Holle)

JG 5	*Stab, II., III.*	Bf 109
13. (Z)/JG 5		Bf 110
KG 30	*Stab, I., II.*	Ju 88
I./StG 5		Ju 87
1. (F)/120		Ju 88
1. (H)/32		Fw 189, Hs 126

1./KüFlGr 906		He 115

Fliegerführer Lofoten (Oberst Roth)

III./KG 30		Ju 88
1./KüFlGr 406		He 115
3./KüFlGr 906		Bv 138

Fliegerführer Nord (West)

JG 5	*I., IV.*	Fw 190
1. (F)/124		Ju 88
2., 3./KüFlGr 406		Bv 138
1./KüFlGr 706		He 111, Ar 196

Luftflotte 1 (*Generaloberst* Keller)

JG 54	*Stab, I., II., III.*	Bf 109
KG 1	*Stab, II., III., IV.*	Ju 88
KG 53	*Stab, I., II., III.*	He 111, Ju 88 (*III.*)
III./StG 1		Ju 87
FAGr 1:	*3./ObdL*	Ju 88, Bf 109
	5. (F)/122	Ju 88
	3. (F)/Nacht	Do 17
	Wekusta 51	Ju 88
NAGr 11:	*1. (H)/13, 1, 2 (H)/31*	Fw 189, Hs 123
Sonderstaffel Buschmann		He 50, He 60
Feldluftgau XXVI/Petersburg		
2., 6. Flakdivisionen		

Luftwaffenkommando Ost (*General der Flieger* von Greim)

FAGr 2:	*1./ObdL*	Ju 88, Bf 109, Bf 110, Ju 86
	2. (F)/Nacht	Do 17
	Wekusta 6	Ju 88, He 111
KGrzbV 105, 500, 700		Ju 52
11th Slovak Fighter Sqn		Bf 109
Feldluftgau XXV Moskau		

II. Flakkorps (General der Flakartillerie Dessloch)
  12., 18. Flakdivisionen

Fliegerdivision 1 (Generalleutnant Schlemm)

I./JG 51		Bf 109
JG 54	*Stab, I., II.*	Bf 109
III./KG 4		Ju 88
NAGr 5:	*1. (H)/11, 2. (H)/12*	Fw 189, Hs 126
NAGr 15:	*1. (H)/12, 2. (H)/13,*	Fw 189, Hs 126
	6. (H)/32	

Fliegerdivision 4 (*Generalmajor* Plocher)

JG 51	*Stab, II., III., IV., 15.*	Bf 109
KG 3	*Stab, I., II., III.*	He 111
NAGr 2:	*3. (H)/21, 2. (H)/23,*	Fw 189, Hs 126
	1. (H) 41	

2nd Hungarian Air Brigade

1st Fighter Gp	Reggiane Re.2000
4th Bomber Gp	Caproni Ca 135
1st Recon Gp	He 111, Do 17, He 46

Luftflotte 4 (Generaloberst von Richthofen)

2./ObdL		Ju 88, Do 215
4. (F)/121		Ju 88
FAGr 4:	*3. (F)/10*	Ju 88
	4. (F)/122	Ju 88
	1. (F)/Nacht	Do 17
	Wekusta 76	Ju 88
NAGr 1:	*5. (H)/11, 3. (H)/31*	Fw 189, Bf 110
NAGr 3:	*3. (H)/11, 3. (H)/14*	Fw 189, Bf 110
NAGr 4:	*6. (H)/13, 2. (H)/41*	Fw 189
NAGr 6:	*7. (H)/13, 2. (H)/33*	Hs 126, Bf 110
NAGr 7:	*1. (H)/10, 4. (H)/10,*	Fw 189
	6. (H)/41	
NAGr 8:	*3. (H)/13, 4. (H)/23,*	Fw 189
	4. (H)/31	
NAGr 9:	*1. (H)/21, 7. (H)/32,*	Fw 189
	4. (H)/41	
NAGr 10:	*2. (H)/10, 2. (H)/31,*	Fw 189, Hs 126
	5. (H)/32	
NAGr 12:	*7. (H)/13, 2. (H)/32,*	Fw 189, Bf 110
	3. (H)/41, 6. (H)/41	
NAGr 13:	*2. (H)/21, 4. (H)/33,*	Hs 126, Bf 110
	3. (H)/41	
NAGr 14:	*2. (H)/32, 5. (H)/41*	Fw 189, Bf 110
NAGr 16:	*3. (H)/12, 5. (H)/12*	Fw 189
II./KGzbV 1, KGrzbV 4,		Ju 52
5, 9, 50, 102, 900		
Feldluftgau XXVII/Rostow		

I. Flakkorps (*Generalmajor* Reimann)
9., 10., 15, 17. Flakdivisionen

Fliegerführer Süd (*Oberst* von Wild)

SAGr 125	*Stab, 1.,3.*	Bv 138, He 114 , Ar 196
		(*Stab*)
6./KG 26		He 111
20th Romanian Observation Sqn		IAR 39

Fliegerkorps IV (*General der Flieger* Pflugbeil)

JG 3	*Stab, I., II.*	Bf 109
JG 52	*Stab, II., III., 15.*	Bf 109
I./JG 53		Bf 109
III./ZG 1		Bf 110
Attached:	*7./ZG 2*	Bf 110
KG 27	*Stab, I., II., III.*	He 111
KG 55	*Stab I., II., III.*	He 111
II./KG 51		Ju 88
II./KG 76		Ju 88
SchG 1	*Stab, I., II.*	Bf 109 (*I.*), Hs 123, Hs 129 (*II.*)
2. (F)/22		Ju 88

Fliegerkorps VIII (*Generalleutnant* Fiebig)		
JG 77	*Stab, 1., II., III.*	Bf 109
Attached:	*III./JG 3*	Bf 109
KG 51	*Stab, I., III.*	Ju 88
KG 76	*Stab, I., III.*	Ju 88
III./LG 1		Ju 88
KG 100	*Stab, I.*	He 111
StG 2	*Stab, I., II., III.*	Ju 87
StG 77	*Stab, I., II., III.*	Ju 87
II./StG 1		Ju 87
2. (F)/11		Do 17

Romanian Air Corps		
1st Recon Sqn		Bristol Blenheim
2nd Recon Sqn		Do 17
3rd Recon Sqn		Potez 63
2nd Fighter Flotilla:	6th Fighter Gp	IAR 81
	7th Fighter Gp	Bf 109
	8th Fighter Gp	IAR 80
2nd Bomber Flotilla:	1st Bomber Gp	JRS 79
	3rd Bomber Gp	PZL 23, Potez 63, IAR 37
	5th Bomber Gp	He 111
3rd Romanian Army		
11th, 12th, 13th Observation Sqns		IAR 39
4th Romanian Army		
15th, 16th, 17th Observation Sqns		IAR 39

APPENDIX 12
LUFTFLOTTE 3, 10 JULY 1942

ErgJGr Süd		Bf 109
ErgJGr West		Bf 109/Fw 190
AufKlGr 123:	*3. (F)/122*	Ju 88, Bf 109
	1. (F)/123	Ju 88, Bf 109, Bf 110

311

3. (F)/123		Ju 88, Bf 109, Bf 110
1. (H)/13		Hs 126
Wekusta 51		Ju 88

Feldluftgaue Holland, Belgien-Nordfrankreich,Westfrankreich
11., 13., 16. Flakdivisionen
I.,V,VI., XI. Flakbrigaden

Jagdfliegerführer Holland-Ruhrgebiet (*Oberst* Grabmann)

JG 1	*Stab I., II.*	Fw 190

Höherer JagdfliegerführerWest

Jagdfliegerführer 2 (*Oberst* Huth)

JG 26	*Stab, I., II., III., 10.*	Fw 190

Jagdfliegerführer 3 (*Oberst* Ibel)

JG 2	*Stab, I., II., III., 10.*	Fw 190

Fliegerkorps IX (*General der Flieger* Coeler)

KG 2	*Stab, I., II., III.*	Do 217
1. (F)/33		Ju 88, Bf 109, Fw 190
3. (F)/33		Ju 88

Fliegerführer Atlantik (*Generalleutnant* Kessler)

KG 40	*Stab, I., II., III.*	Fw 200, Do 217 (*II.*)
KGr 106		Ju 88
5./BordFlGr 196		Ar 196

APPENDIX 13
LUFTFLOTTE 2, 19 APRIL 1943

Fliegerkorps II (*Generalmajor* Harlinghausen)

KG 54	*Stab, I., II., II., IV. (Erg)*	Ju 88
Attached:	*II./KG 1*	Ju 88
KG 76	*Stab, II., III.*	Ju 88
KG 77	*Stab, I., II., III.*	Ju 88
III./KG 26		He 111
II./KG 30		Ju 88
2. (F)/122		Ju 88, Me 210

Jagdfliegerführer Sizilien (*Generalleutnant* Osterkamp)

II./JG 27		Bf 109
3./JG 53		Bf 109
ZG 1	*Stab, II., III.*	Bf 110, Me 210 (*III.*)
II./NJG 2		Ju 88
Luftgau Sizilien		
XXII. Flakbrigade		

312

Fliegerführer Sardinien (*Oberst* von Wild)

KG 26	Stab, I., II.	He 111
9./JG 53		Bf 109
1. (F)/122		Ju 88, Bf 109

Fliegerkorps Tunis (*Generalmajor* Seidemann)

1. (F)/121		Ju 88

Fliegerführer Mitte (*Oberst* Rath)

JG 53	Stab, I., II., III.	Bf 109
III./SKG 10		Fw 190
II./StG 3		Ju 87
8. (Pz)/SchG 2		Hs 129
4./Minensuchgruppe 1		Ju 52
2. (H)/14		Fw 189

Fliegerführer Afrika

JG 77	Stab, I., II., III.	Bf 109
Attached:	II./JG 51	Bf 109
I./SchG 2		Fw 190
4. (H)/10		Fw 189
Luftgau Afrika		
19., 20. Flakdivisionen		

Fliegerkorps X (*General der Flieger* Waldau)

III./JG 27		Bf 109
LG 1	Stab, I., II., IV. (Erg)	Ju 88
II./KG 100		He 111
Stab SAGr 126:	2./SAGr 126	Ar 196
	2. (F)/123	Ju 88

Lufttransportführer II, Mittelmeer (*Generalmajor* Buchholz)

KGzbV Stab Neapel:	II./KGzbV 323	Me 323
	KGrzbV 800	Ju 52
KGzbV Stab Sizilien:	I., III., IV./KGzbV 1	Ju 52
	KGrzbV 106, 600	Ju 52
Ju 52 (See) Staffel		Ju 52
Lufttransportstaffel 290		Ju 90, Ju 290
Savoia Staffel		Savoia S.82

APPENDIX 14
LUFTFLOTTE 3, 10 JUNE 1943

FAGr 123:	3. (F)/122	Ju 88
	3. (F)/123	Ju 88
	4. (F)/123	Bf 109, Fw 190
	5. (F)/123	Bf 109, Fw 190
	Wekusta 51	Ju 88

NAGr 13	*1., 2.*	Fw 190

Höherer Jagdfliegerführer West (*Oberst* Ibel)
I./JG 27		Bf 109

Jagdfliegerführer 2 (*Generalmajor* Huth)
JG 26	*Stab, II., 8.*	Fw 190, Bf 109 (*8.*)
10. (Jabo)/JG 54		Fw 190
12./JG 54		Fw 190

Jagdfliegerführer 3 (*Oberst* Wiek)
JG 2	*Stab, I., II., III.*	Bf 109, Fw 190 (*III.*)

Angriffsführer England/Fliegerkorps IX (*Oberst* Peltz)
SKG 10	*Stab, I., II.*	Fw 190
KG 2	*Stab, I., II.*	Ju 88
KG 6	*Stab, I., III.*	Ju 88
1. (F)/33		Ju 88
3. (F)/33		Ju 88
1. (F)/123		Ju 88

Fliegerführer Atlantik (*Generalleutnant* Kessler)
V. (Z)/KG 40	Ju 88
III./KG 40	Fw 200
1./SAGr 128	Ar 196, Fw 190
AufklStaffel (See) 222	Bv 222

Luftgau Holland
  XIX. Flakbrigade

Luftgau Belgien-Nordfrankreich
  16. Flakdivision

Luftgau Westfrankreich
  11., 13. Flakdivisionen
  I., V., XI., XII., XVIII. Flakbrigaden

APPENDIX 15
LUFTWAFFE ORDER OF BATTLE,
UNTERNEHMEN 'ZITADELLE', 5 JULY 1943

Luftflotte 6 (*Generaloberst* von Greim)

Feldluftgau XXV/Minsk

Fliegerdivision 1 (*Generalmajor* Deichmann)
JG 1	*Stab, I., II.*	Fw 190, Bf 109 (*I.*)
JG 51	*Stab, I., III., IV.*	Fw 190

JG 54	*Stab, I., II.*	Fw 190, Bf 109 (*II.*)
15. (Span)/JG 51		Bf 109
ZG 1	*Stab, I.*	Bf 110
12./NJG 5		Bf 110
KG 1	*Stab, I., III.*	Ju 88
KG 3	*Stab, I., II., III.*	Ju 88
KG 4	*Stab, II., III.*	He 111
II./KG 51		Ju 88
StG 1	*Stab, II., III.*	Ju 87, Bf 110 (*Stab*)
PzJägKdo Weiss		Ju 87, Hs 129
StörKampfGr, Lft 6	*1., 2., 3.*	Ar 66, Fw 58, Go 145, He 46
FAGr 2:	*4. (F)/11*	Ju 88
	4. (F)/14	Ju 88
	4. (F)/121	Ju 88
	1. (F)/100	Ju 88, Ju 86, Do 215
	2. (F)/Nacht	Do 17, Do 217
	Wekusta 6	Ju 88, He 111
NAGr 3:	*3. (H)/11, 4. (H)/14*	Fw 189
	2. (H)/23, 4. (H)/31	
NAGr 4:	*1., 2., 3.*	Bf 109, Bf 110
NAGr 5:	*1. (H)/11, 2. (H)/12,*	Bf 110, Hs 126
	2. (H)/21, 4. (H)/32	
NAGr 10:	*2. (H)/10, 3. (H)/21,*	Fw 189, Hs 126
	2. (H)/31, 5. (H)/32	
NAGr 15:	*2. (H)/13, 6. (H)/32*	Fw 189
12. Flakdivision		
10. Flakbrigade		

Luftflotte 4 (*General der Flakartillerie* Dessloch)

3. (F)/121		Ju 88
4. (H)/23		Hs 126
I./TG 3		Ju 52
Feldluftgau XXVII/Charkow		

Fliegerkorps I (*Generalleutnant* Angerstein)

2. (F)/22		Ju 88
2. (F)/100		Ju 88, Do 215
Attached: 1st Romanian Air Corps		
2nd Recon Sqn		Ju 88
105th Transport Sqn		Ju 52
1st Fighter Flotilla:	7th Fighter Gp	Bf 109
	8th Attack Gp	Hs 129
	9th Fighter Gp	IAR 80
3rd Bomber Flotilla:	3rd Dive-Bomber Gp	Ju 87
	5th Bomber Gp	Ju 88
	6th Bomber Gp	Ju 88

Fliegerkorps VIII (*Generalmajor* Seidemann)

JG 3	*II., III.*	Bf 109

JG 52	*Stab, I., II., III., 15.*	Bf 109
10./NJG 5		Bf 110
Nachtjagdschwarm, Lft 4		Bf 110
KG 27	*Stab, I., III., 14.*	He 111
KG 55	*Stab, I., II., III.*	He 111
III./KG 51		Ju 88
I./KG 100		He 111
StG 2	*Stab, I., II., III.*	Ju 87, Ju 88 (*Stab*)
StG 77	*Stab, I., II., III.*	Ju 87, Ju 88 (*Stab*)
SchG 1	*Stab, I., II.*	Fw 190, Hs 129, Hs 123 (*III.*)
SchG 2	*Stab, I.*	Fw 190, Hs 129 (*I.*)
PzJägStaffel/JG 51		Hs 129
Störkampfgruppe, Lft 6	*1.– 6.*	Ar 66, Do 17, Fw 58, Fw 189, Go 145, He 46, Hs 126, W.34
FAGr 3:	*4. (F)/122*	Ju 88
	4. (F)/Nacht	Do 17, He 111, Do 217
	Wekusta 76	Ju 88
NAGr 1:	*3. (H)/31, 2. (H)/31*	Fw 189
NAGr 6:	*3. (H)/32, 5. (H)/32, 7. (H)/32, 2. (H)/33*	Fw 189, Hs 126, Bf 110
NAGr 9:	*1. (H)/21, 7. (H)/32*	Fw 189
NAGr 14:	*5. (H)/11, 5. (H)/41*	Fw 189, Bf 110

I. Flakkorps (*Generalleutnant* Reimann)
　10., 17. Flakdivisionen

2nd Hungarian Air Brigade

5/I Fighter Gp	Bf 109
102/1 Bomber Sqn	Ju 88
102/2 Dive-Bomber Sqn	Ju 87
1st Reconnaissance Sqn	Ju 88
3/1 Tactical Recon Sqn	Fw 189
4/I Bomber Sqn	

APPENDIX 16
LUFTFLOTTE 2 FACING OPERATION 'HUSKY', 10 JULY 1943

Luftflotte 2 (*Generalfeldmarschall* von Richthofen)

III./TG 1	Ju 52
III./TG 2	Ju 52
IV./TG 3	Ju 52
I./TG 5	Me 323

Fliegerkorps II (*Generalleutnant* Bülowius)
Italy

II./JG 27	Bf 109

I./JG 53		Bf 109
II./ZG 1		Bf 110
ZG 26	*Stab, III., 10.*	Bf 110
II., III./SKG 10		Fw 190
KG 1	*Stab, I., II.*	Ju 88
KG 6	*Stab, I., III.*	Ju 88
KG 26	*Stab, I., III.*	He 111
KG 76	*Stab, I., II.*	Ju 88
III./KG 30		Ju 88
III./KG 54		Ju 88
II./KG 77		Ju 88
I./LG 1		Ju 88
1. (F)/123		Ju 88
Feldluftgau XXVIII		
3. Flakbrigade		

Sicily

JG 53	*Stab, II., III.*	Bf 109
JG 77	*Stab, I., II.*	Bf 109
IV./JG 3		Bf 109
II./NJG 2		Ju 88
SKG 10	*Stab, II.*	Fw 190
2. (F)/122		Ju 88, Me 210, Me 410
Feldluftgau Sizilien		
22. Flakbrigade		

Fliegerführer Sardinien (*Oberst* Hitschold)

II./JG 51		Bf 109
III./JG 77		Bf 109
SchG 2	*Stab, I., II.*	Fw 190, Hs 129
3. (F)/33		Ju 88
4. (H)/12		Fw 189

Fliegerdivision 2 (*Generalleutnant* Fink)

KG 100	*Stab, II., III.*	Do 217

APPENDIX 17
LUFTWAFFE ORDER OF BATTLE, AEGEAN, OCTOBER 1943

Fliegerkorps X (*General der Flieger* Fiebig)

III., IV./JG 27	Bf 109
11./ZG 26	Bf 110
II./KG 6	Ju 88
II./KG 51	Ju 88
1./KG 100	Do 217
I./StG 3	Ju 87
4., 5./StG 3	Ju 87
13./StG 151	Ju 87

1., 2. (F)/123		Ju 88
SAGr 126:	*2., 3.*	Ar 196
	2./SAGr 125	Ar 196
1./TG 4		Ju 52

APPENDIX 18
THE *LUFTWAFFE*, 1 JUNE 1944

OKL Command

KG 200	Miscellaneous

Fliegerkorps XIV (*General der Flieger* Joachim Coeler)

TG 1	*Stab, I., III.*	Ju 52
TG 3	*Stab, II., IV.*	Ju 52
TG 4	*Stab, I., III.*	Ju 52
II./TG 5		Me 323
TGr 10		Savoia S.81
TGr 30		He 111
TGr 110		Savoia S.82
TGr Brankow		Fiat G.12
4. Transport Staffel		Ju 90, Ju 252

Luftflotte Reich (*Generaloberst* Hans-Jürgen Stumpff)

KG 1	*Stab, I., II., III.*	He 177
III./KG 3		He 111
II./KG 27		He 111
II./KG 77		Ju 88
II./KG 100		He 177
II.I/SG 3		Fw 190
1. (F)/122		Me 410, Bf 110
4. (F)/122		Ju 188
Wekusta ObdL		Ju 188
NAGr 8:	*1., 2.*	Bf 109
3./NAGr 14		Bf 109
II./TG 1		Ju 52

Luftgau I (Königsberg)
Luftgau III/IV (Berlin)
Luftgau VI (Münster)
Luftgau VII (Munich)
Luftgau VIII (Breslau)
Luftgau XI (Hamburg)
Luftgau XII (Wiesbaden)
Luftgau XVII (Vienna)
1., 3., 4., 7., 8., 14., 21., 22., 24., 26. Flakdivisionen
2., 7., 8., 11., 15., 16., 20., 21. Flakbrigaden

Jagdkorps I (*Generalmajor* Josef Schmid)

Jagddivision 1 (*Oberst* Hans-Joachim Hermann)		
JG 1	Stab, I., II., III.	Fw 190, Bf 109 (*III.*)
I./JG 302		Bf 109
NJG 5	Stab, II., IV.	Bf 110
NJGr 10		Bf 109, Bf 110, Fw 190, Ju 88, He 219
Behelfs Beleuchterstaffel 2		Ju 88
Luftbeobachtungstaffel 1		Ju 88, Bf 110

Jagddivision 2 (*Generalmajor* Max-Josef Ibel)		
JG 11	Stab, I., II., III., 10.	Bf 109, Fw 190 (*I., III.*)
III./JG 54		Fw 190
I./JG 301		Bf 109
ZG 26	Stab, I., II., III.	Me 410, Me 262, Bf 110 (*III.*)
NJG 3	Stab, I., II., III., IV.	Ju 88, Bf 110
Luftbeobachtungstaffel 2		Ju 88, Bf 110

Jagddivision 3 (*Generalmajor* Walter Grabmann)		
I./JG 27		Bf 109
II./JG 53		Bf 109
JG 300	Stab, I., II., III.	Fw 190, Bf 109 (*I., III.*)
NJG 1	Stab, I., II., III., IV.	Bf 110, He 219, Me 410 (*I.*)
NJG 2	Stab, I., II., III.	Ju 88
I. (Bel)/KG 7		Ju 88
Luftbeobachtungstaffel 3		Ju 88, Bf 110

Jagddivision 7 (*Generalleutnant* Joachim-Friedrich Huth)		
ZG 76	Stab, I., II.	Me 410, Bf 110 (*II.*)
NJG 6	Stab, I., II., III., IV.	Bf 110, Do 217 (*I.*)
Behelfs Beleuchterstaffel 1		Ju 88
Luftbeobachtungstaffel 7		Ju 88

Jagdfliegerführer Ostmark		
JG 27	Stab, II., III., IV.	Bf 109
II./ZG 1		Bf 110
13th Slovak Fighter Sqn		Bf 109
101st Hungarian Fighter Gp		Bf 109
5/1st Hungarian Night Fighter Sqn		Me 210

Luftflotte 5 (*General der Flieger* Josef Kammhuber)

Wekusta 5	Ju 88
TrGr 20	Ju 52
Seetransportstaffel 2	Ju 52
Feldluftgau Norwegen	
Feldluftgau Finnland	
13., 14. Flakbrigaden	

Fliegerführer 3
    III./JG 5   Bf 109
    1. (F)/124   Ju 88, Ju 188
    1. (H)/32   Fw 189
    SAGr 130:   *1., 2.*   Bv 138

Fliegerführer 4
    1. (F)/22   Ju 88
    1. (F)/120   Ju 188
    SAGr 131:   *1., 2.*   Bv 138, Ar 196

Fliegerführer 5 (*Generalmajor* Ernst-August Roth)
    3./KG 40   He 177
    1./KüFlGr 406   He 115
    1./BordFlGr 196   Ar 196

Jagdfliegerführer Norwegen
    IV./JG 5   Bf 109
    13. (Z)/JG 5   Bf 110

General der Luftwaffe in Finnland (*General der Flieger* Julius Schulz)
    I./SG 5   Ju 87, Fw 190
    NSGr 8   Ju 87
    Schwarm Lappland   Ju 88

Luftflotte 1 (*General der Flieger* Curt Pflugbeil)

FAGr 1:   *3. (F)/22*   Ju 88, Ju 188
                       5. (F)/122   Ju 188
                       4. (F)/Nacht   Do 217
                       Wekusta 1   Ju 88
SAGr 127:   *1., 2., 3.*   Ar 95, Hs 126
Ostfliegerstaffel 1   Ar 66, Go 145
Feldluftgau XXVI (Riga)
2., 6. Flakdivisionen

Jagdabschnittführer Ostland: *II./NJG 100*   Ju 88

Fliegerdivision 3 (*Generalmajor* Walter Boenicke)
    JG 54   *Stab, I., II.*   Fw 190
    14. (Eis)/KG 55   He 111
    SG 3   *Stab, I., II.*   Ju 87, He 111 (*Stab*)
    NSGr 1   Go 145, He 46
    NSGr 3   Ar 66, Go 145
    NSGr 11 (Est)   He 50, Fokker C-V
    NSGr 12 (Lett)   Ar 66
    NAGr 5:   *1., 2.*   Bf 109

Luftflotte 6 (*Generaloberst* Robert, *Ritter* von Greim)

14. (Eis)/KG 3		Ju 88
NSGr 2		Ar 66, Ju 87
FAGr 2:	4. (F)/11	Ju 88, Ju 188
	4. (F)/14	Ju 88, Ju 188
	2. (F)/Nacht	Do 217
	Wekusta 1	Ju 88
NAGr 4:	1., 2., 3.	Bf 109, Fw 189, Hs 126
NAGr 10:	12. (H)/12, 3. (H)/21	Hs 126, Bf 109, Fw 189
NAGr 15:	1., 2.	Fw 189
NAGr 31:	1., 2.	Fw 189
I./TG 3		Ju 52
Jagdabschnittführer 6:	Stab JG 51	Bf 109, Fw 190
Feldluftgau XXVII (Smolensk)		
Flakkorps II		
10., 12., 17., 18., 23. Flakdivisionen		
10., 11. Flakbrigaden		

Fliegerdivision 1 (*Generalmajor* Robert Fuchs)		
I./JG 51		Bf 109
SG 1	Stab, I., II.	Ju 87, Fw 190 (*II.*)

Fliegerdivision 4 (*Generalmajor* Franz Reuss)		
III./JG 51		Bf 109
I./NJG 100		Ju 88, Do 217
III./SG 1		Fw 190
10. (Pz)/SG 1		Ju 87

Fliegerkorps IV (*Generalleutnant* Rudolf Meister)		
KG 4	Stab, II., III.	He 111
KG 27	Stab, I., III.	He 111
KG 53	Stab, I., II., III.	He 111
KG 55	Stab, I., II., III.	He 111
1. (F)/100		Ju 88

Luftflotte 4 (*General der Flakartillerie* Otto Dessloch)

Jagdfliegerführer Balkan:	III./JG 77	Bf 109
	II./JG 301	Bf 109
	IV./NJG 6	Bf 110
	2./NJG 100	Bf 110
4th Romanian Fighter Gp		IAR 80
5th Romanian Fighter Gp		Bf 109, IAR 81
6th Romanian Fighter Gp		IAR 81
7th Romanian Fighter Gp		Bf 109, IAR 81
44th, 50th Romanian Sqns		IAR 80/81
68th Romanian Night Fighter Sqn		Bf 110
FAGr 4:	2. (F)/22	Ju 88

	2. (F)/100	Ju 88
	3. (F)/121	Ju 188
	1. (F)/Nacht	Do 217, He 111
	Wekusta 76	Ju 88
NAGr 1:	13. (H)/14	Fw 189
NAGr 2:	1., 2., 3.	Bf 109
NAGr 6:	1.	Fw 189
NAGr 14:	1., 2., 3.	Bf 109

Aufklärungsführer Schwarzes Meer:
SAGr 125:	1., 3.	Bv 138
II.I/TG 2, III./TG 3		Ju 52

Feldluftgau XXV (Lemberg/Lvov)
Feldluftgau Rumänien (Bucharest)
5., 15. Flakdivisionen

Fliegerkorps I (*Generalmajor* Paul Deichmann)
JG 52	Stab, I., II., III.	Bf 109
SG 10	Stab, I., II., III., 10.	Fw 190, Ju 87 (*10.*)
IV./SG 9		Hs 129
NSGr 5		Ar 66, Go 145

Fliegerkorps VIII (*Generalmajor* Hans Seidemann)
IV./JG 51		Bf 109
I./JG 53		Bf 109
I./KG 4		He 111
14. (Eis)/KG 27		He 111
SG 2	Stab, I., II., III., 10.	Ju 87, Fw 190 (*II.*)
SG 77	Stab, I., II., III., 10.	Fw 190, Ju 87 (*III.*, 10.)
NSGr 4		Go 145

2nd Hungarian Air Brigade
102nd Fighter Gp	Bf 109
102nd Bomber Gp	Me 210
102/1 Dive-Bomber Sqn	Ju 87
1st Recon Sqn	Ju 88

2nd Romanian Air Corps
1st Bomber Flotilla:	4th Bomber Gp	He 111, PZL P.37
	7th Observation Gp	IAR 37
2nd Bomber Flotilla:	1st, 2nd Gps	JRS-79B
3rd Fighter Flotilla:	2nd, 4th Gps	IAR 81

Luftwaffenkommando Südost (*General der Flieger* Martin Fiebig)
3. (F)/2	Bf 110
3. (F)/33	Ju 88, Ju 188
Wekusta 27	Ju 88
IV./TG 1, II./TG 4	Ju 52
I./TG 5	Me 323
1., 3. Seetransportstaffeln (See)	Ju 52
Feldluftgau XXIX (Athens)	

322

Feldluftgau XXX (Belgrade)
19., 20. Flakdivisionen
17. Flakbrigade

Jagdfliegerführer Balkan

II./JG 51	Bf 109
II./JG 301	Bf 109
11./ZG 26	Ju 88
6./NJG 100	Do 217
6th Bulgarian Fighter Regiment	Bf 109
4th Croatian Fighter Gp	Bf 109, Macchi MC.200/202/205
11th Croatian Fighter Gp	Fiat G.50, Morane MS.406

Fliegerführer Kroatien (*Oberst* Walter Hagen)

13./SG 151		Ju 87
NSGr 7		Caproni Ca.314, Fiat CR.42, He 46, Ju 87
NAGr 12:	*1., 2., 3.*	Bf 109
Nahaufklärungsstaffel Kroatien		Hs 126, Do 17, Do 215
1st Croatian Bomber Gp		Do 17, Ca.314

Kommandierender General der Deutschen Luftwaffe in Greichenland (*General der Flieger* Johannes Fink)

2. (F)/123		Ju 86, Ju 88, Bf 109
SAGr 126:	*1.–4.*	Ar 196

Luftflotte 2 (*Generalfeldmarschall* Wolfram von Richthofen)

LG 1	*Stab, I., II.*	Ju 88
Attached:	part *II./KG 76*	Ju 88
Italian Torpedo Bomber Gp		Savoia S.79
FAGr 122:	*2. (F)/122*	Me 410, Ju 88
	1. (F)/123	Ju 88
	Wekusta 26	Ju 88
2./BordFlGr 196		Ar 196
II./TG 1		Savoia S.82
Italian Transport Gp	*I./TG 10*	Savoia S.81
Feldluftgau XXVIII (Milan)		
25. Flakdivision		
3. Flakbrigade		

Jagdführer Oberitalien

Stab JG 77	Bf 109
I./JG 4	Bf 109
III./JG 53	Bf 109
part *II./NJG 6*	Bf 110
1st Italian Fighter Gp	Fiat G.55, Macchi MC.205

| 2nd Italian Fighter Gp | | Bf 109, Fiat G.55 |
| Montefusco Sqn | | Fiat G.55, Macchi MC.205 |

Fliegerführer 2
I., II./JG 77		Bf 109
SG 4	*Stab, I., II.*	Fw 190
NSGr 9		Ju 87, Fiat CR.42, Caproni Ca.314
NAGr 11:	*1.,2.,3.*	Bf 109

Luftflotte 3 (*Generalfeldmarschall* Hugo Sperrle)

FAGr 123:	*1. (F)/121*	Me 410
	4. (F)/123	Bf 109
	5. (F)/123	Bf 109, Fw 190, He 111
Jagdfliegerführer		
Südfrankreich:	*JGr Süd*	Bf 109, Fw 190
IV./TG 4		LeO 451
Feldluftgau Belgien-Nordfrankreich (Brussels)		
Feldluftgau Westfrankreich (Paris)		
Flakkorps III		
13., 16. Flakdivisionen		
1., 5., 12., 18., 19. Flakbrigaden		

Fliegerkorps II (*Generalleutnant* Alfred Bülowius)
| *III./SG 4* | | Fw 190 |
| *NAGr 13:* | *1., 2., 3.* | Bf 109 |

Fliegerkorps IX (*Generalmajor* Dietrich Peltz)
KG 2	*Stab, I., II., III., IV.*	Ju 188 (*I., II.*), Do 217 (*III., IV.*), Ju 188 (*IV.*)
KG 6	*Stab, I., II., III., IV.*	Ju 188, Ju 88 (*II., IV.*)
KG 54	*Stab, I., III.*	Ju 88
I./KG 30		Ju 88
II./KG 51		Me 410
I./KG 66		Ju 188
I./SKG 10		Fw 190
3. (F)/122		Ju 88, Ju 188
6. (F)/123		Ju 88, Ju 188, Do 217

Fliegerkorps X (*Generalleutnant* Alexander Holle)
KG 40	*Stab, I., II., III., IV.*	He 177, Fw 200 (*II., III.*)
FAGr 5		Ju 290
3. (F)/123		Ju 88
1./SAGr 129		Bv 222

Fliegerdivision 2 (*Generalmajor* Hans Korte)
KG 26	*Stab, II., III.*	Ju 88
KG 77	*Stab, I., II.*	Ju 88
III./KG 100		Do 217

6./KG 76		Ju 88
1.(F)/33		Ju 88, Ju 188
2./SAGr 128		Ar 196

Jagdkorps II (Generalmajor Werner Junck)

Jagddivision 4 (Oberst Karl Wiek)

| JG 26 | Stab, I., II., III. | Fw 190, Bf 109 (III.) |
| NJG 4 | Stab, I., II., III. | Bf 109 (Stab), Ju 88 (I., II.), Bf 110 (II., III.), Do 217 (II., III.) |

Jagddivision 5 (Oberst von Bulow)

JG 2	Stab, I., II., III.	Fw 190, Bf 109 (II.)
NJG 5	Stab, I., III.	Bf 110
II./NJG 6		Bf 110

APPENDIX 19
GERMAN AIRCRAFT PRODUCTION

Type	1940	1941	1942	1943	1944
Single-engine fighter	1,870	2,852	4,542	9,626	25,860
Twin-engine fighter	1,840	1,880	2,422	4,100	5,025
Twin-engine bomber	2,744	2,816	3,620	4,266	3,063
Four-engine bomber	38	58	251	491	518
Stuka/Schlacht	611	476	917	1,844	909
Transport	763	969	1,265	2,033	1,002
Trainer	1,328	889	1,170	2,076	3,063
Other (inc. gliders)	1,632	1,836	1,369	1,091	348

APPENDIX 20
EQUIVALENT RANKS

Luftwaffe	RAF	USAAF
Generalfeldmarschall	Marshal of the RAF	General (five star)
Generaloberst	Air Chief Marshal	General (four star)
General der Flieger	Air Marshal	Lieutenant-General
Generalleutnant	Air Vice-Marshal	Major-General
Generalmajor	Air Commodore	Brigadier-General
Oberst	Group Captain	Colonel
Oberstleutnant	Wing Commander	Lieutenant-Colonel
Major	Squadron Leader	Major
Hauptmann	Flight Lieutenant	Captain

325

Oberleutnant	Flying Officer	First Lieutenant
Leutnant	Pilot Officer	Second Lieutenant
Oberfeldwebel	Flight Sergeant	Master Sergeant
Feldwebel	Sergeant	Sergeant
Unteroffizier	Corporal	Corporal
Obergefreiter	Leading Aircraftsman	Private 1st Class
Gefreiter	Aircraftsman 2nd Class	Private
Flieger	Aircraftsman 2nd Class	Private

APPENDIX 21
THE *LUFTWAFFE* PILOT'S ALPHABET

A	Anton	G	Gustav	N	Nordpol	U	Ulrich
B	Berta (or Bertha)	H	Heinrich	O	Otto	V	Viktor
		I	Ida	P	Paula	W	Wilhelm
C	Cäsar	J	Julius	Q	Quelle	X	Xavier (or Xenophon)
D	Dora	K	Kurfürst	R	Richard		
E	Emil	L	Ludwig	S	Siegfried	Y	Ypsilon
F	Friedrich	M	Martha	T	Toni	Z	Zeppelin

Bibliography

BOOKS

Air Ministry, *The Rise and Fall of the German Air Force* (Air Ministry Pamphlet 248), London, 1948/49 (all references from reproduction by WE Inc., Old Greenwich, Conn., 1969)

Absalon, Rudolf (ed.), *Rangliste der generale der deutschen Luftwaffe dem Stand von 20. April 1945*, Podzun Verlag (Freiburg, 1984)

Aders, Gebhard, *History of the German Night-Fighter Force 1917–1945*, Arms & Armour Press (London, 1979)

Aders, Gebhard, and Held, Werner, *Jagdgeschwader 51 'Mölders'*, Motorbuch Verlag (Stuttgart, 1993)

Andersson, Lennart, *Soviet Aircraft and Aviation 1917–1941*, Putnam (London, 1994)

Axworthy, Mark, (with Scafes, Cornel, and Craciunoiu, Cristian), *Third Axis, Fourth Ally: Romanian Armed Forces in the European War 1941–1945*, Arms & Armour Press (London, 1995)

Baker, David, *Adolf Galland: The Authorised Biography*, Windrow & Greene (London, 1996)

Balke, Ulf, *Der Luftkrieg in Europa: Der operativen Einsätze des Kampfgeschwadwer 2 im Zweiten Weltkrieg*, 2 vols, Bernard & Graefe Verlag (Coblenz, 1989)

———, *Kampfgeschwader 100 'Wiking'*, Motorbuch Verlag (Stuttgart, 1981)

Bateson, Richard, *Junkers Ju 87D Variants*, Profile Publications, (Windsor, n.d.)

Baumbach, Werner, *Broken Swastika*, Robert Hale (London, 1986)

Bekker, Cajus, *The Luftwaffe War Diaries (Angriffshöhe 4000)*, Macdonald & Co (London, 1967) and Gerhard Stalling Verlag (Hamburg, 1964)

Beevor, Antony, *Crete: The Battle and Resistance*, John Murray (London, 1991)

Bennett, Ralph, *Ultra and Mediterranean Strategy 1941–1945*, Hamish Hamilton (London, 1989)

Bernard, Dénes; Mujzer, Péter; and Hangya, János, *Horrido: Légicsták a Keleti Fronton*, OMIKK (Budapest, 1993)

Bickers, Richard Townsend, *The Desert Air War 1939–1945*, Leo Cooper (London, 1991)

Bloemertz, Gunther, *Heaven Next Stop*, William Kimber (1953)

Boog, Horst, (ed.), *The Conduct of the Air War in the Second World War: An International Comparison*, Berg Publishers (Oxford, 1992)

Boog, Horst, *Die deutsche Luftwaffenfuhrung 1935–1945*, Deutsches Verlags-Anstalt (Stuttgart, 1982)

Bowyer, Michael J. F., *2 Group RAF*, Crécy Books (London, 1992)

Brookes, Andrew, *Bomber Squadron at War*, Ian Allan (Shepperton, 1983)

Brütting, Georg, *Das waren die deutschen Kampfflieger-Asse 1939–1945*, Motorbuch Verlag (Stuttgart, 1981)

———, *Das waren die deutschen Stuka-Asse 1939–1945*, Motorbuch Verlag (Stuttgart, 1995)

Buffetaut, Yves, *La Bataille Aérienne de Normandie*, Éditions Lela Presse (Boulogne sur Mer, 1994)

Caldwell, Donald L., *JG 26: Top Guns of the Luftwaffe*, Orion Books (New York, 1991)

Campbell, John, *Naval Weapons of World War Two*, Conway Maritime Press (London, 1985)

Chorley, W. R., *Bomber Command Losses*, Midland Counties Publications (1992/1993)

Clayton, A., *The Enemy is Listening: The Story of the Y Service*, Hutchinson (1980) and Crécy Books (1993)

Collier, Basil, *The Defence of the United Kingdom*, HMSO (London, 1957)

Cooke, R. C., and Nesbit, R. C., *Target: Hitler's Oil*, William Kimber (London, 1985)

Cooksley, Peter G., *1940: The Story of No 11 Group, Fighter Command*, Robert Hale (London, 1983)

Cooper, Alan W., *Bombers Over Berlin*, Patrick Stephens (1989)

Cooper, Matthew, *The German Air Force 1933–1945*, Jane's Publishing Co. (London, 1981)

Craven, W. F., and Cate, J. L., *The Army Air Forces in World War II*, 7 vols, Chicago University Press (Chicago 1948–78)

Davies, R. E. G., *Lufthansa*, Paladwr Press (Rockville, 1991)

Delve, Ken, *Nightfighter: The Battle for the Night Skies*, Arms & Armour Press (London, 1995)

Bernád, Dénes; Mujzer, Péter; and Hangya, János, *Horrido: Légicsaták a Keleti Fronton*, OMIKK (Budapest, 1993)

Dickfeld, Adolf, *Footsteps of the Hunter*, J. J. Fedorowicz Publishing (Winnipeg, 1993)

Dierich, Wolfgang, *Kampfgeschwader 51 'Edelweiss'*, Motorbuch Verlag (Stuttgart, 1973). Also published as *Kampfgeschwader Edelweiss*, Purnell Book Services (London, 1975)

———, *Kampfgeschwader 55 'Greif'*, Motorbuch Verlag (Stuttgart, 1975)

Dierich, Wolfgang, (ed.), *Die Verbände der Luftwaffe*, Motorbuch Verlag (Stuttgart, 1976)

Doolittle, Gen. James H., (with Glines, Carroll V.), *I Could Never Be So Lucky Again*, Bantam Books (New York, 1991)

Ellis, John, *Brute Force: Allied Strategy and Tactics in the Second World War*, André Deutsch (London, 1990)

Erickson, John, *The Road to Stalingrad*, Weidenfeld & Nicolson (London, 1977)

———, *The Road to Berlin*, Weidenfeld & Nicolson (London, 1983)

Ethell, Jeffrey, and Price, Alfred, *Target Berlin: Mission 250–March 6 1944*, Book Club Associates (London, 1981)

Faber, Harold, (ed.), *The Luftwaffe: A History*, New York Times Book Co (1977)

Feist, Uwe, *The Fighting Me 109*, Arms & Armour Press (London, 1988)

Foreman, John, *Battle of Britain: The Forgotten Months, November and December 1940*, Air Research Publications (New Malden, 1988)

———, *1941. Part 1: The Battle of Britain to the Blitz*, Air Research Publications (Walton-on-Thames, 1994)

———, *1941. Part 2: The Turning Point*, Air Research Publications (Walton-on-Thames, 1994)

Franks, Norman, *Conflict Over the Bay*, William Kimber (London, 1986)

———, *The Battle of the Airfields*, William Kimber (London, 1982)

———, *The Greatest Air Battle*, Grub Street (London, 1992)

Freeman, Roger, *The US Strategic Bomber*, Macdonald & Jane's (London, 1975)

Freeman, Roger, (with Crouchman, Alan, and Maslen, Vic), *The Mighty Eighth War Diary*, Arms & Armour Press (London, 1990)

Friedman, Norman, *Naval Radar*, Conway Maritime Press (London, 1981)

Galland, Adolf, *The First and the Last*, Methuen (London, 1970)

Gander, Terry, and Chamberlain, Peter, *Small Arms, Artillery and Special Weapons of the Third Reich*, Macdonald & Jane's (London, 1978)

Girbig, Werner, *Jagdgeschwader 5 'Eismeer'*, Motorbuch Verlag (Stuttgart, 1975)

———, *Six Months to Oblivion*, Ian Allan (Shepperton, 1975)

Geust, Carl-Fredrik, *Under the Red Star*, Airlife Publications (Shrewsbury, 1993)

Glantz, David M., and House, Jonathan, *When Titans Clashed: How the Red Army Stopped Hitler*, Unversity of Kansas Press (Lawrence, 1995)

Goulding, James, and Moyes, Philip, *RAF Bomber Command and Its Aircraft 1936–1940*, Ian Allan (Shepperton, 1975)

———, *RAF Bomber Command and Its Aircraft 1941–1945*, Ian Allan (Shepperton, 1978)

Goulter, Christina J. M., *A Forgotten Offensive: RAF Anti-Shipping Operations*, Frank Cass (London, 1995)

Green, William, *Warplanes of the Third Reich*, Galahad Books (New York, 1990)

Griehl, Manfred, *Do 217-317-417: An Operational History*, Airlife (Shrewsbury, 1991)

———, *Junkers Ju 88: Star of the Luftwaffe*, Arms & Armour Press (London, 1990)

Gundelach, Karl, *Die deutsche Luftwaffe im Mittelmeer 1940–1945. Band 1: 1940–1942. Band 2: 1943–1945*, Verlag Peter D. Lang (Frankfurt aM, 1981)

———, *Kampfgeschwader 'General Wever' 4*, Motorbuch Verlag (Stuttgart, 1978)

Halder, Franz, (ed. Burdick, Charles, and Jacobsen, Hans-Adolf), *The Halder War Diary 1939–1942*, Presidio Press (Novato, 1988)

Hardesty, Von, *Red Phoenix: The Rise of Soviet Air Power 1941–1945*, Smithsonian Institution Press (Washington, 1995)

Hastings, Max, *Bomber Command*, Michael Joseph (1979)

Harvey, Maurice, *The Allied Bomber War 1939–1945*, Spellmount (Tunbridge Wells, 1992)

Haupt, Werner, *Die deutschen Luftwaffenfelddivisionen 1941–1945*, Podzun-Pallasverlag (Bad Nauheim, 1994)

Hecks, Karl, *Bombing 1939–1945*, Robert Hale (London, 1990)

Held, Werner, and Obermaier, Ernst, *The Luftwaffe in the North African Campaign 1941–1943*, Schiffer Military History (West Chester, 1992)

Hildebrand, Karl-Friedrich, *Die Generäle der deutschen Luftwaffe 1935–1945*, 3 vols, Biblio Verlag (Osnabrück, 1990–93)

Hinchliffe, Peter, *The Other Battle: Luftwaffe Night Aces versus Bomber Command*, Airlife Publishing (Shrewsbury, 1996)

Hinsley, F. H., *British Intelligence in the Second World War*, HMSO (London, 1974)

HMSO, *Statistical Digest of the War*, HMSO (London, 1951)

Hoeffding, Oleg, *German Air Attacks Against Industry and Railroads in Russia 1941–1945*, Rand Corporation (Santa Monica, 1970)

Hoffmann, Karl Otto, *Geschichte der Luftnachrichtentruppe*, 3 vols, Kurt Vowinckel Verlag (Neckargemünd, 1965–73)

Holland, Jeffrey, *The Aegean Mission: Allied Operations in the Dodecanese 1943*, Greenwood Press (London, 1988)

Hooton, E. R., *Phoenix Triumphant*, Arms & Armour Press (London, 1994)

Hough, Richard, and Richards, Dennis, *The Battle of Britain: The Jubilee History*, Hodder & Stoughton (London, 1989)

Howard-Williams, Jeremy, *Night Intruder*, David & Charles (London, 1976)

Howarth, Stephen, and Laws, Derek, (eds), *The Battle of the Atlantic 1939–1945*, Greenhill Books (London, 1994)

Hümmelchen, Gerhard, *Die deutschen Seeflieger 1935–1945*, J. F. Lehmanns Verlag (Munich, 1976)

Irving, David, *Göring*, Macmillan (London, 1989)

————, *The Destruction of Convoy PQ. 17*, Transworld Publishers (London, 1970)

Ishoven, Armand van, *Messerschmitt Bf 109 at War*, Ian Allan (Shepperton, 1977)

————, *The Luftwaffe in the Battle of Britain*, Ian Allan (Shepperton, 1980)

————, *Ernst Udet: Biographie eines grossen Fliegers*, Manfred Pawlak Verlagsgesellschaft (Herrsching, 1977)

Jackson, Robert, *Fighter: The Story of Air Combat 1936–1945*, Arthur Barker (London, 1979)

Kameradschaft ehemaliger Transportflieger, *Geschichte einer Transportflieger-Gruppe im II. Weltkrieg*, privately published (Ronnenberg, 1989)

Ketley, Barry, and Rolfe, Mark, *Luftwaffe Fledglings 1935–1945*, Hikoki Publications (Aldershot, 1996)

Kiehl, Heinz, *Kampfgeschwader 'Legion Condor' 53*, Motorbuch Verlag (Stuttgart, 1983)

Klink, Ernst, *Das Gesetz des Handelns: Die Operation 'Zitadelle' 1943*, Deutsches Verlags-Anstalt (Stuttgart, 1966)

Knocke, Heinz, *I Flew for the Führer*, Evans Bros (London, 1954)

Koch, Horst-Adalbert, *Flak: Die Geschichte der deutschen Flakartillerie und der Einsatz der Luftwaffenhelfer*, Podzun Verlag (Bad Nauheim, 1965)

Kozhevnikov, M. N., *The Command and Staff of the Soviet Army Air Force in the Greater Patriotic War 1941–1945*, US Government Printing Office (Washington, 1977)

Kucera, Pavel; Bernád, Dénes; and Androvic, Stefan, *Focke-Wulf Fw 189*, MBI (Prague, 1996)

Kühn, Volkmar, *Der Seenotdienst der deutschen Luftwaffe*, Motorbuch Verlag (Stuttgart, 1978)

Kurowski, Frank, (trans. Johnston, David), *Luftwaffe Aces*, J. J. Fedorowicz Publishing (Winnipeg, 1996)

Lacey-Johnson, Lionel, *Point Blank and Beyond*, Airlife Publishing (Shrewsbury, 1991)

Leach, Barry A., *German Strategy Against Russia 1939–1941*, Clarendon Press (Oxford, 1973)

Longmate, Norman, *Air Raid: The Bombing of Coventry 1940*, Hutchinson (London, 1976)

————, *The Bombers: The RAF Offensive Against Germany 1939–1945*, Hutchinson (London, 1983)

MacDonald, Callum, *The Lost Battle*, Macmillan (London, 1993)

McFarland, Stephen L., and Newton, Wesley Philips, *To Command the Sky: The Battle for Air Superiority over Germany 1942–1944*, Smithsonian Institution (Washington, 1991)

Macksey, Kenneth, *Kesselring*, Greenhill Books (London, 1996)

Mark, Eduard, *Aerial Interdiction in Three Wars*, Center for Air Force History (Washington, 1994)

Mason, Francis K., *Battle Over Britain*, 2nd Edn, Aston Publications (Bourne End, 1990)

Middlebrook, Martin, *The Battle of Hamburg*, Allen Lane (London, 1980)

————, *Berlin Raids*, Viking (London, 1988)

————, *The Nuremberg Raid*, Allen Lane (London, 1973)

————, *The Schweinfurt-Regensburg Mission*, Allen Lane (London, 1983)

Mitcham, Samuel W., *Men of the Luftwaffe*, Presidio Press (California, 1988)

Molony, Brig. C. J. C., *The Mediterranean and Middle East*, Vol. V, HMSO (London, 1973)

Mombeek, Erik, (trans. Vasco, John J.), *Defending the Reich: The History of Jagdgeschwader 1 'Oesau'*, JAC Publications (Norwich, 1992)

Mortensen, Daniel R., *A Pattern for Joint Operations: World War II Close Air Support, North Africa*, Office of Air Force History and US Army Center of Military History (Washington, 1987)

Morzik, Fritz, and Hümmelchen, Gerhard, *Die deutschen Transportflieger im Zweiten Weltkrieg*, Bernard & Graefe Verlag (Framkfurt aM, 1966)

Muller, Richard, *The German Air War in Russia*, The Nautical & Aviation Publishing Company of America (Baltimore, 1992)

Murray, Williamson, *Luftwaffe: Strategy for Defeat 1933–1945*, Allen & Unwin (1985)

Neitzel, Sönke, *Der Einsatz der deutschen Luftwaffe über dem Atlantik und der Nordsee 1939–1945*, Bernard & Graefe Verlag (Bonn, 1995)

Nesbitt, Roy C., *The Armed Rovers: Beauforts and Beaufighters over the Mediterranean*, Airlife Publishing (Shrewsbury, 1995)

Niehaus, Werner, *Die Nachrichtentruppe: 1914 bis heute*, Motorbuch Verlag (Stuttgart, 1980)

Nielsen, Andreas, *The German Air Force General Staff (USAF Historical Study 173)*, Arno Press (New York, 1968)

Nissen, Jack, (with Cockerill, A. W.), *Winning the Radar War*, Robert Hale (London, 1987)

Nowarra, Heinz, *Nahaufklärer 1910–1945*, Motorbuch Verlag (Stuttgart, 1981)

———, *Fernaufklärer 1915-1945*, Motorbuch Verlag (Stuttgart, 1982)

Orensteins, Harold S., (trans.), *Soviet Documents on the Use of War Experience*, Vol. 1, Frank Cass & Co (London, 1991)

Osterkamp, Theo, *Durch Höhen und Tiefen jagt ein Herz*, Vowinckel Verlag (Heidelberg, 1952)

Overy, R. J., *The Air War 1939–1945*, Europa Publications (London)

———, *War and Economy in the Third Reich*, Clarendon Press (Oxford, 1994)

Parry, Simon W., *Intruders over Britain: The Luftwaffe Night Offensive 1940–1945*, Air Research Publications/Kristall Publications (Surbiton, 1987)

Perret, Geoffrey, *Winged Victory: The Army Air Forces in World War II*, Random House (New York, 1993)

Playfair, Maj.-Gen. I. S. O., *The Mediterranean and the Middle East. Vol. III (September 1941 to September 1942)*, HMSO (London)

Poolman, Kenneth, *Focke-Wulf Condor: Scourge of the Atlantic*, Macdonald & Jane's (London, 1978)

Postan, M. M., *British War Production*, HMSO (London, 1952)

Price, Alfred, *Aircraft versus Submarines*, Jane's Publishing Co. (London, 1980)

———, *Battle of Britain Day: 15 September 1940*, Sidgwick & Jackson (London, 1990)

———, *Battle Over the Reich*, Ian Allan (Shepperton, 1974)

———, *Blitz on Britain*, Ian Allan (Shepperton, 1976)

———, *The Bomber in World War II*, Macdonald & Jane's (London, 1976)

———, *Heinkel He 177*, Profile Publications (Windsor, 1972)

———, *Instruments of Darkness*, Macdonald & Jane's (London, 1977)

———, *The Last Year of the Luftwaffe: May 1944–May 1945*, Arms & Armour Press (London, 1991)

———, *The Luftwaffe Data Book*, Greenhill Books, London, 1997

———, *The Luftwaffe Handbook*, 2nd Edn, Ian Allan (Shepperton, 1986)

———, *Messerschmitt Bf 110 Night Fighters*, Profile Publications (Windsor, n.d.)

———, *World War II Fighter Conflict*, Macdonald & Jane's (London, 1975)

Prien, Jochen, *Geschichte des Jagdgeschwaders 77*, 3 vols, privately printed (Hamburg, 1991–96)

Pritchard, David, *The Radar War: Germany's Pioneering Achievement 1904–1945*, Patrick Stephens (Wellingborough, 1989)

Probert, Air Commodore Henry, and Cox, Sebastian, *The Battle Re-Thought: A Symposium on the Battle of Britain*, Airlife Publishing (Shrewsbury, 1991)

331

Quarrie, Bruce, *Airborne Assault*, Patrick Stephens (Sparkford, 1991)

Radtke, Siegfried, *Kampfgeschwader 54*, SchildVerlag (Munich, 1990)

Ramsey, Winston, (ed.), *The Blitz Then and Now. Vol. 1: September 3 1939–September 6 1940* and *Vol. 2: September 1940–May 1941*, Battle of Britain Prints International (London, 1987–88)

Ray, John, *The Night Blitz 1940–1941*, Arms & Armour Press (London, 1996)

Reinhardt, Klaus, *Moscow: The Turning Point*, Berg Publishers (Oxford, 1992)

Ries, Karl, *Deutsche Flugzeugführerschulen und ihre Maschinen 1919–1945*, Motorbuch Verlag (Stuttgart, 1988)

Ring, Hans, and Gerbig, Werner, *Jagdgeschwader 27*, Motorbuch Verlag (Stuttgart, 1971)

Roell, Werner P., *Laurels for Prinz Wittgenstein*, Independent Books (Bromley, 1994)

Rosch, Barry C., *Luftwaffe Codes, Markings and Units 1939–1945*, Schiffer Publishing (Atglen, 1995)

Roskill, Capt. S. W., *The War at Sea*, Vol. II, HMSO (London, 1956)

——, *The War at Sea*, Vol. III, Pt 1 (June 1943–May 1944), HMSO (London, 1960)

Rothnie, Niall, *The Baedecker Blitz*, Ian Allan (Shepperton, 1972)

Rohwer, Jürgen, and Hümmelchen, Gerhard, *Chronology of the War at Sea*, Greenhill Books (London, 1992)

Rudel, Hans-Ulrich, (trans. Hudson, Lynton), *Stuka Pilot*, Transworld Publishers (London, 1957)

Ruffner, Kevin Conley, *Luftwaffe Field Divisions 1941–1945*, Osprey Publishing (London, 1994)

Rumpf, Hans, *The Bombing of Germany*, Frederick Muller (London, 1961)

Sárhidai, Gyula; Punka, György; and Kozlik, Viktor, *Hungarian Eagles: A Magyar Királyi Honvéd Légierö 1920–1945*, Hikoki Publications (Aldershot, 1996)

Saward, Dudley, *'Bomber' Harris: The Authorised Biography*, Cassell (London, 1984)

Schmidt, Rudi, *Achtung-Torpedos los!: Der strategische und operative Einsatz des Kampfgeschwaders 26*, Bernard & Graefe Verlag (Coblenz, 1991)

Scutts, Jerry, *Bf 109 Aces of North Africa and the Mediterranean*, Osprey Publishing (London, 1995)

——, *JG 54: Aces of the Eastern Front*, Airlife Publishing (Shrewsbury, 1992)

Searby, Air Commodore John, *The Bomber Battle for Berlin*, Airlife (Shrewsbury, 1991)

Seaton, Albert, *The Russo-German War*, Arthur Barker (London, 1971)

Shores, Christopher F., *Pictorial History of the Mediterranean Air War*, 3 vols, Ian Allan (Shepperton, 1972–74)

——, *2nd Tactical Air Force*, Osprey Publishing (London, 1970)

Shores, Christopher, and Cull, Brian, (with Malizia, Nicola), *Malta: The Hurricane Years, 1940–1941*, Grub Street (London, 1987)

——, *Malta: The Spitfire Year, 1942*, Grub Street (London, 1991)

Shores, Christopher, et al., *Air War for Yugoslavia, Greece and Crete*, Grub Street (London, 1987)

Shores, Christopher, and Ring, Hans, *Fighters Over the Desert*, Neville Spearman (London, 1969)

Shores, Christopher; Ring, Hans; and Hess, William, *Fighters over Tunisia*, Neville Spearman (London, 1975)

Shukman, Harold, (ed.), *Stalin's Generals*, Weidenfeld & Nicolson (London, 1993)

Smith, J. R., and Kay, Antony, *German Aircraft of the Second World War*, Putnam & Co. (London, 1972)

Smith, J. Richard, *The Focke-Wulf Fw 200*, Profile Publications (Leatherhead, 1966)

Smith, Peter C., *Stuka at War*, Ian Allan (Shepperton, 1980)

————, *Stuka Squadron: Stukagruppe 77—The Luftwaffe's Fire Brigade*, Patrick Stephens (Cambridge, 1990)

Soviet Defence Ministry, (trans. Fetzer, Leland), *The Soviet Air Force in World War II: The Official History*, David & Charles (Newton Abbot/London, 1974)

Späte, *Oberstleutnant* Wolfgang, and Bateson, Richard P., *Messerschmitt Me 163 Komet*, Profile Publications (Windsor, 1971)

Spick, Mike, *Luftwaffe Fighter Aces*, Greenhill Books (London, 1996)

Stahl, Peter, *The Diving Eagle: A Ju 88 Pilot's Diary (1940–1941)*, William Kimber (London, 1984)

Steinhoff, Johannes, *The Straits of Messina*, André Deutsch (London, 1971)

Streetly, Martin, *Confound and Destroy: 100 Group and the Bomber Support Campaign*, Jane's Publishing Co. (London, 1985)

Tarrant, V. E., *Stalingrad*, Leo Cooper (London, 1992)

Taylor, Telford, *The Breaking Wave: The German Defeat in the Summer of 1940*, Weidenfeld & Nicolson (London, 1967)

Terraine, John, *The Right of the Line: The Royal Air Force in the European War 1939–1945*, Hodder & Stoughton (London, 1985)

Tessin, Georg, *Verbände und Truppen der deutschen Wehrmacht und Waffen SS 1939–1945. Band 14 (Die Luftstreitkräfte)*, Biblio Verlag (Osnabrück, 1980)

Thomas, Lowell, and Jablonski, Edward, *Bomber Commander*, Sidgwick & Jackson (London, 1977)

Tieke, Wilhelm, *The Caucasus and the Oil*, J. J. Fedorowicz Publishing (Winnipeg, 1995)

Toliver, Raymond F., and Constable, Trevor J., *Das waren die deutschen Jagdflieger-Asse 1939–1945*, Motorbuch Verlag (Stuttgart, 1986)

Tuider, Dr Othmar, *Die Luftwaffe in Österreich 1938–1945*, Österreichischen Bundesverlag (Vienna, 1985)

Tyushkevich, S. A., *The Soviet Armed Forces: A History of Their Organizational Development*, US Government Printing Office (Washington, 1978)

Villa, Brian Loring, *Mountbatten and the Dieppe Raid*, Oxford University Press (1989)

Vogt, Harold, *Schlachtsfeld Luftfahrzeug: Der Einsatz der Schwarzen Männer im II. Weltkrieg*, Flugzeug-Publikations (1994)

Volkogonov, Dmitri, *Stalin: Triumph and Tragedy*, Prima Publishing (Rocklin, 1992)

Wakefield, Kenneth, *The First Pathfinders*, Crécy Books (London, 1992)

Wakefield, Kenneth, (ed.), *The Blitz Then and Now. Vol. 3: May 1941–May 1945*, Battle of Britain Prints International (London, 1990)

Weal, John, *Focke-Wulf Fw 190 Aces of the Russian Front*, Osprey Publishing (London, 1996)

————, *Focke-Wulf Fw 190 Aces of the Western Front*, Osprey Publishing (London, 1996)

Whiting, Charles, *The Three Star Blitz: The Baedecker Raids and the Start of Total War*, Leo Cooper (London, 1987)

Williamson, Gordon, *Aces of the Reich*, Arms & Armour Press (London, 1989)

Wood, Derek, and Dempster, Derek, *The Narrow Margin*, Arrow Books (London, 1967)

Woodman, Richard, *Arctic Convoys*, John Murray (London, 1995)

Wynn, Humphrey, and Young, Susan, *Prelude to Overlord*, Airlife Publishing (Shrewsbury, 1983)

Ziemke, Earl F., *Stalingrad to Berlin: The German Defeat in the East*, Office of the Chief of Military History, US Army (Washington, 1968)

Ziemke, Earl F., and Bauer, Magna E., *Moscow to Stalingrad: Decision in the East*, Military Heritage Press (New York, 1988)

ARTICLES AND ESSAYS

Argyle, Christopher J., 'The Liverpool Blitz', *Air Pictorial*, October 1975

Axworthy, Mark, 'Flank Guard: Romania's Aerial Advance on Stalingrad', *Air Enthusiast*, Nos 64 (July–August 1996) and 65 (September–October 1996)

D'Amico, F., and Valentini, G., 'La Legione Croata in Guerra', *JP4*, April 1993

Bateson, Richard P., 'Bulgaria at War', *Air Pictorial*, March 1972 (Pt 1) and April 1972 (Pt 2)

——, 'Georg Sattler—Mediterranean Bomber Pilot', *Aircraft Illustrated*, August 1970

Boelcke, Willi A., 'Stimulation and Attitude of the German Aircraft Industry during Rearmament and War', in Boog, *The Conduct of the Air War in the Second World War*

Boog, Horst, 'Luftwaffe Support of the German Navy', in Howard and Law, *The Battle of the Atlantic 1939–1945*

Bowyer, Michael, 'High-Flying Raiders', *Aviation News*, 18–31 October 1974

Boyne, Walt, 'Missiles Against the Roma', *Flying Review*, February 1968

Brooks, Robin J., 'When the Luftwaffe Landed in Britain', *The Blitz Then and Now*, Vol. 3

Brown, Pete, 'KG 200: Fact and Fiction', *Aeroplane Monthly*, November 1994

Chamberlain, Peter, 'Bombs and Other Missiles Dropped on the United Kingdom', *The Blitz Then and Now*, Vol. 1

Collis, Bob, 'Jabos Over Suffolk', *The Blitz Then and Now*, Vol. 3

——, 'The First of the Ks', *The Blitz Then and Now*, Vol. 3

——, 'Mosquito versus Hornet', *The Blitz Then and Now*, Vol. 3

——, 'The First Junkers 188 Down on British Soil', *The Blitz Then and Now*, Vol. 3

——, 'Escape to Britain', *The Blitz Then and Now*, Vol. 3

Ehrhardt, P., and Benoit, M., 'La Guerre de Condor', *La Fanta de l'Aviation*, Nos 256–9 (March–June 1991)

Cockburn, Sir Robert, 'The Radio War', *IEE Proceedings*, Vol. 132, Part A, No 6 (October 1985)

Fatutta, Francesco, 'Operazione Rösselsprung', *Reviista Italiana Difesa*, November 1989

Frka, Daniel, 'Croatian Air Force in WW 2', *Scale Models International*, June 1993

Giessler, Capt. Helmuth Giessler, 'The Breakthrough of the "Scharnhorst": Some Radio-Technical Details', *IRE Transactions on Military Electronics*, January 1961

Green, William, 'Finland's Modest Air Arm', *Flying Review*, January 1969

——, 'Magyar Air Cover', *Flying Review*, September and October 1969

Green, William, and Swanborough, Gordon, 'Balkan Interlude', *Air Enthusiast*, No 39 (May–August 1989).

Hartmann, Ernst, 'Eine Fluzeugrführerausbildung im 2. Weltkrieg', *Luftwaffen-Revue*, 4/94 (December 1994)

——, 'Einsatz Kubangebiet: Weitere Einsätze der KGrzbV 23/TGr 30', *Luftwaffen-Revue*, 3/93 (September 1993)

Huan, Claud, 'La bataille aéronavale de l'artique', *La Fanatique de l'Avion*, Nos 198–201 (May–August 1986)

Lutz, Fritz, 'Mein griechisches Abenteuer', *Luftwaffen-Revue*, 2/94 (June 1994)

Marchand, Alain, and Huan, Claude, 'Achtung Minen!', Pt III, *La Fanatique de l'Avion*, No 211 (June 1987)

Morrow Jr, John H., 'The German Aircraft Industry in the First and Second World Wars: A Comparison', in Boog, *The Conduct of the Air War in the Second World War*

Munday, Eric, 'Chain Home Radar and the Blitz', *The Blitz Then and Now*, Vol. 1

Philpott, Brian, 'The Luftwaffe's Night-Fighter Force', *Aviation News*, 18–31 March 1988

Price, Alfred, and Smith, Richard, 'The Heinkel He 177', *Archiv*, Vol. 3 No 9

Saunders, Andy, 'Jabo Attack', *The Blitz Then and Now*, Vol. 3

———, 'Josef Markl's Escapade', *The Blitz Then and Now*, Vol. 1

Schlaug, Georg, 'Luftversorgung eingekesselter Verbände der 2. Armee durch Lasten-segler Go 242 des Luftwaffenkommandos Don (Januar/Februar 1943)', *Luftwaffen-Revue*, 1/94 (March 1994)

Schreiber, *Generalmajor Dr* Jürgen, 'Fliegerische Grundausbildung und Jagdflieger-schulung 1935–1945', *Luftwaffen-Revue*, 4/92 (December 1992)

———, 'Luftwaffen- und Marinehelfer (Flak)', *Luftwaffen-Revue*, 3/93 (September 1992)

Schuh, *Prof.* Horst, 'Bomber und Jäger—Ein Kampftag im Jahre 1944', *Luftwaffen-Revue*, 3/96 (September 1996)

Schumann, Ralf, 'Ritterkreuzträger der Kampfflieger: General der Flieger Ulrich O.-E. Kessler', *Luftwaffen-Revue*, 2/97 (June 1997)

Soumille, Albert, 'L'Aviation Slovaque', *Fanatique*, July 1970

Spencer, Flt Lt Michael, 'Lessons Learned from the First Operational Air-Launched Anti-Ship Missiles', *Maritime Patrol Aviation*, September 1991

Stenman, Kari, 'The Short Saga of Battle Unit Kuhlmey', *Air Enthusiast*, No 34 (September–December 1987)

Toll, Karl, 'Storm Bird', *Airpower*, Vol. 23, No 2 (March 1993)

Verton, Hendrik C., 'Erstes Fluglebnis für Grenadiere 1941', *Luftwaffen-Revue*, 2/95 (June 1995)

Wakefield, Kenneth, 'The Baedeker Raids', *The Blitz Then and Now*, Vol. 3

———, 'The Danger by Day: Fighter-Bomber and High Altitude Attacks', *The Blitz Then and Now*, Vol. 3

———, 'The Fiasco of 1943', *The Blitz Then and Now*, Vol. 3

———, 'The Knickebein Effect', *Aviation News*, 4–17 March 1988

———, 'The Steinbock Raids', *The Blitz Then and Now*, Vol. 3

Watson-Watt, Sir Robert, 'Battle Scars of Military Electronics—The Scharnhorst Break-Through', *IRE Transactions on Military Electronics*, March 1957

Weal, John, 'A Nocturnal Miscellany', *Air International*, Vol. 48 No 3 (March 1995)

Widfeldt, Bo, 'German Aircraft Landed/Crashed in Sweden, WW II', *Archiv*, Vol. 3, Nos 10–12

Wixey, Ken, 'Incidental Combatant', *Air Enthusiast*, No 67 (January/February 1997)

List of Abbreviations

ADD	*Aviatsiya Dal'nego Deystviya*	OG	Great Britain to Gibraltar
Aircraft (German):		ON	Great Britain to North America
Ar	Arado	OS	Great Britain to Sierra Leone
Bf	Bayerische Flugzeugwerke		
Bv	Blohm und Voss	PQ	Iceland to North Russia
DFS	Deutsches Forschungs-institut für Segelflug	SL	Sierra Leone to Great Britain
Do	Dornier	UG	USA to North Africa
Fi`	Fieseler	WN	Northern coastal, westbound
Fw	Focke-Wulf		
Go	Gotha	XK	Gibraltar to Great Britain
He	Heinkel	Note:	Suffix 'F' = Fast, 'S' = Slow
Hs	Henschel	ECM	Electronic counter-measures
Ju	Junkers	*EK*	*Lehr- und Erprobungskommando*
Me	Messerschmitt		
Si	Siebel	*EprGr*	*Erprobungsgruppe*
AI	Airborne Interception	ESM	Electronic support measures
ASV	Air-to-Surface Vessel		
ASW	Anti-submarine warfare	*EVA*	*Elleniki Vassiliki Aeroporia*
BA MA	Bundes Archiv, Militär Archiv	*FAAR*	*Fortele Aeriene Regale ale Romaniei*
BAM	British Air Ministry		
BdFlGr	*Bordfliegergruppe*	*FAGr*	*Fernaufklärungsgruppe*
CAI	*Corpo Aereo Italiano*	*FdL*	*Führer der (See) Luftstreitkräfte*
CAM	Catapult Aircraft Merchant		
COMINT	Communications Intelligence	*FFS*	*Fliegerführerschule*
		FJR	*Fallschirmregiment*
Convoy designations:		*Flak*	*Fliegerabwehrkanon*
CW	Coastal, Westbound	*FlakR*	*Flak Regiment*
KM	Great Britain to North Africa	*FlFü*	*Fliegerführer*
M	Mediterranean (pre-1942)	*Flivo*	*Fliegerverbindungsoffizier*
OA	Thames Outbound	IWM	Imperial War Museum
OB	Liverpool Outbound	*Jabo*	*Jagdbomber*
ON	Great Britain to North America	*JaFü*	*Jagdfliegerführer*
		JG	*Jagdgeschwader*
HG	Gibraltar to Great Britain	*JGr*	*Jagdgruppe*
KM	Great Britain to North Africa	*JKRV*	*Jugoslovensko Kraljevsko Ratno Vazduhplovstvo*
MK	North Africa to Great Britain	*KG*	*Kampfgeschwader*
		KG zbV	*Kampfgeschwader zur besonderen Verwendung*

KGr	*Kampfgruppe*	*RLM*	*Reichsluftministerium*
KGr zbV	*Kampfgruppe zur besonderen*	*SAGr*	*See Aufklärungsgruppe*
	Verwendung	SC	High-explosive bomb
KüFlGr	*Küstfliegrgruppe*	*SchG*	*Schlacht Geschwader* (before
KSG	*Kampfschulgeschwader*		October 1943)
LG	*Lehrgeschwader*	SD	Armour-piercing bomb
LMB	*Luftmine B*	*SG*	*Schlacht Geschwader* (after
LnR	*Luftnachrichten-Regiment*		October 1943)
Lotfe	*Lotfernrohr*	*SHAA*	*Service Historique de l'Armée*
LT	*Lufttorpedo*		*de l'Air*
LwSwR	*Luftwaffe Scheinwerfer-*	SIGINT	Signal Intelligence
	Regiment	*SKL*	*Seekriegsleitung*
NAGr	*Nahaufklärungsgruppe*	*StG*	*Sturzkampf Geschwader*
NJG	*Nachtjagdgeschwader*	*Stuka*	*Sturzkampfflugzeug*
NJRF	*Nachtjagdraumführer*	*TG*	*Transport Geschwader*
NSGr	*Nacht Schlachtgruppe*	*TGr*	*Transportgruppe*
OB	*Oberbefehlshaber*	USAAF	US Army Air Forces
ObdL	*Oberbefehlshaber der Luftwaffe*	USNA	United States National
OKH	*Oberkommando des Heeres*		Archives
OKW	*Oberkommando des*	*VVS-RKKA*	*Voyenno-Vozdushnyye Sily*
	Wehrmacht		*Raboche-Krestyanskaya*
OKL	*Oberkommando der Luftwaffe*		*Krasanaya Armiya*
PRO	Public Record Office	*Wekusta*	*Wetterkundungsstaffel*
PVO	*Protivovoydushaya oborona*	*ZG*	*Zerstörer Geschwader*
RAF	Royal Air Force		

Glossary

A/B Schule	Elementary/Basic Flying Training Schools
Angriffsführer	Attack Director
Armee	Army
Aviatsiya Dal'nego Deystviya	(Russian) Long Range Aviation
Befehlshaber	Commander
Behelfsbeleuchterstaffeln	Illuminator Squadron
Bundes Archiv, Militär Archiv	Military Archive of the Federal German Archives
Blindflug	Instrument Training
Blitzmädchen	Slang term for *Luftwaffehelferinnen*
Bundesluftwaffe	Federal German Air Force
Bordfliegergruppe	Embarked Air Group
Bordfunker	Radio Operator, Aircrew
C Schule	Advanced Flying School
Chef des Ausbildungswesens	Head of Training
Corpo Aereo Italiano	Italian Air Corps
Dunkelnachtjagd	Night-fighting method (literally, 'Dark Night-Fighting')
Düppel	*Luftwaffe* term for chaff
Einsatz	Operational (as in detachment)
Erprobungsgruppe	Development Group
Elleniki Vassiliki Aeroporia	Greek Air Force
Experte	Ace
Fall	Contingency (alternative name for Operation up to 1940)
Fallschirmregiment	Paratroop Regiment
Fortele Aeriene Regale ale Romaniei	Romanian Air Force
Fernaufklärungsgruppe	Long Range Reconnaissance Group
Führer der (See) Luftstreitkräfte	Commander, Naval Air Corps
Flak Regiment	Anti-Aircraft Regiment
Fliegerführerschule	Air Training School
Fliegerabwehrkanon	Anti-Aircraft Gun
Fliegerdivision	Air Division
Fliegerführer	Air Commander
Fliegerkorps	Air Corps
Fliegerverbindungsoffizier	Air Force Liaison Officer
Flugmeldedienst	Reporting Service (Observer Corps)
Fühlungshälter	Contact Keeper
Funkhorchdienst	Signals Intelligence Organisation
Gefechtsverband	Combat Formation

General der Jagd/Kampf/Schlachtflieger	Inspector of Fighters/Bombers/Close Support Aviation (Note: The Inspector was not necessarily a general)
Generalluftzeugmeister	General Officer Commanding Procurement and Supply
Heeresgruppe	Army Group
Hellenachtjagd	Night fighting method (literally, 'bright night fighting')
Himmelbett	Night fighting system (literally, 'Four-Poster Bed')
Höherer Nachrichtenführer	Director of Signals
Horch und Störstaffel	Electronic Warfare Squadron
Jabostaffeln	Fighter-Bomber Squadron
Jägerleitoffizier	Fighter Controller
Jägerschreck	Fighter Fear
Jagdbomber	Fighter-bomber
Jagddivision	Fighter Division
Jagdfliegerführer	Fighter Commander
Jagdgeschwader	Fighter Wing
Jagdgruppe	Fighter Group
Jagdkorps	Fighter Corps
Jugoslovensko Kraljevsko Ratno Vazduhplovstvo	Yugoslav Air Force
Kampfgeschwader	Bomber Wing
Kampfgeschwader zbV	Transport Wing, pre-May 1943
Kampfgruppe	Bomber Group
Kampfgruppe zbV	Transport Group, pre-May 1943
Kampfflieger	Bomber Aircrew
Kette	Formation of three aircraft
Küstfliegergruppe	Coastal Aviation Group
Kampfschulgeschwader	Bomber Training Wing
Kapitän	*Staffel* Commander
Kindermord	Massacre of the Innocents
Kommandeur	*Gruppe* Commander
Kommodore	*Geschwader* Commander
Lehrgeschwader	Demonstration Wing
Lehr- und Erprobungskommando	Demonstration and Development Detachment
Lotfernrohr	Telescopic Bomb Sight
Luftbeobachtungstaffel	Air Observation Squadron
Luftflotte	Operational Air Force (literally, 'Air Fleet')
Luftgau	Air Force District
Luftnachrichten-Regiment	*Luftwaffe* Signals Regiment
Luftnachrichtentruppe	Air Force Signallers
Luftwaffe Scheinwerfer-Regiment	Searchlight Regiment
Luftwaffenhelfer	*Luftwaffe*'s Air Training Corps
Luftwaffenhelferinin	Equivalent to WAAF
Nahaufklärungsgruppe	Short Range Reconnaissance Group
Nachtjagdgeschwader	Night Fighter Wing
Nachtjagdraumführer	Night Fighter Sector Controller
Nachtjagdversuchskommando	Night Fighter Experimental Detachment

Nachtjagdwaffe	Night Fighter Force
Nacht Schlachtgruppe	Night Attack Group
Oberbefehlshaber	Commander-in-Chief
Oberbefehlshaber der Luftwaffe	Commander-in-Chief, *Luftwaffe*
Oberkommando des Heeres	Army Supreme Command
Oberkommando des Wehrmacht	*Wehrmacht* Supreme Command
Oberkommando der Luftwaffe	Air Force Supreme Command
Pirätangriff	Daylight surprise attack
Protivovoydushaya oborona	Russian Air Defence
'Pulk'	*Luftwaffe* slang for a formation (from the Russian word for 'Regiment')
Raum/Räume	Sector/Sectors
Regia Aeronautica	Italian Air Force
Reichsheer	German Army, 1920–1933
Reichsjägerwelle	National Fighter Wavelength
Reichsluftfahrtministerium	German Air Ministry
Ritterkreuz	Knight's Cross (awarded for distinguished service rather than bravery; also with Diamonds and Oak Leaves)
Rotte	Formation of two aircraft
See Aufklärungsgruppe	Naval Reconnaissance Group
Schlacht Geschwader	Ground Attack Wing
Schlacht	Ground attack
Schwarm	Formation of two *Rotten*
Seenotdienst	Air–Sea Rescue Organisation
Service Historique de l'Armée de l'Air	French Air Force Historical Service
Seekriegsleitung	Naval Operations Staff
Sonder	Special
Staatsekretär der Luftfahrt	Secretary of State for Air Transport
Staffel	Squadron
Störangriff	Harassing attack
Sturzkampf Geschwader	Dive-Bomber Wing
Sturzkampfflugzeug	Dive-bomber
Transport Geschwader	Transport Wing, post May 1943
Transportgruppe	Transport Group, post May 1943
Unternehmen	Operation
Voyenno-Vozdushnyye Sily Raboche-Krestyanskaya Krasanaya Armiya	Red Army Military Aviation
Waffenschule	Operational Training Schools
Wehrmacht	Armed Forces
Wetterkundungsstaffel	Meteorological Squadron
'Wilde Sau'	Night fighting system (literally, 'Wild Boar')
X-Verfahren	Bomber support system (literally, 'X Procedure')
Y-Verfahren	Navigation and bomber support system (literally, 'Y Procedure')
'Zähme Sau'	Night fighting system (literally 'Tame Boar')
Zerstörer Geschwader	Heavy Fighter Wing
Zur besonderen Verwendung	For Special Employment

Index

General Index

343

Index of Personalities